Strategic Management Model

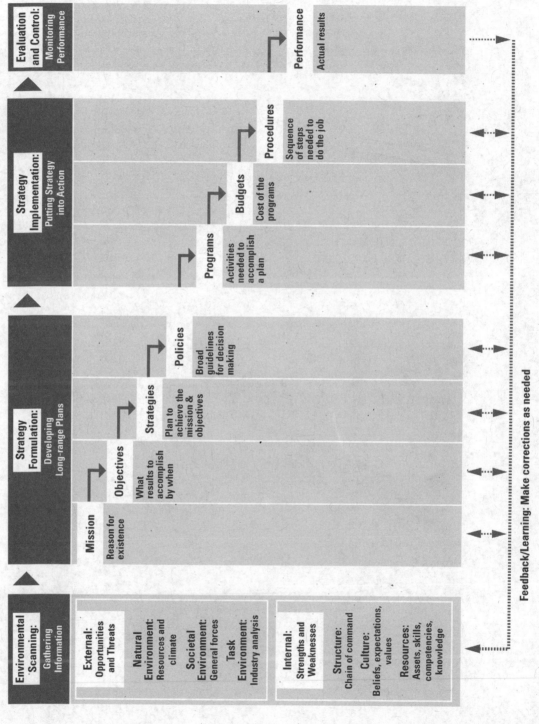

Strategy Formulation: Developing Long-range Plans

Mission
Reason for existence

Objectives
What results to accomplish by when

Strategies
Plan to achieve the mission & objectives

Policies
Broad guidelines for decision making

Strategy Implementation: Putting Strategy into Action

Programs
Activities needed to accomplish a plan

Budgets
Cost of the programs

Procedures
Sequence of steps needed to do the job

Evaluation and Control: Monitoring Performance

Performance
Actual results

Environmental Scanning: Gathering Information

External: Opportunities and Threats

Natural Environment: Resources and climate

Societal Environment: General forces

Task Environment: Industry analysis

Internal: Strengths and Weaknesses

Structure: Chain of command

Culture: Beliefs, expectations, values

Resources: Assets, skills, competencies, knowledge

Feedback/Learning: Make corrections as needed

Dedicated to

KATHY, RICHARD, AND TOM

BETTY, KARI AND JEFF, MADDIE AND MEGAN, SUZI AND NICK, SUMMER AND KACEY, LORI, MERRY AND DYLAN, AND WOOFIE (ARF!).

This book is also dedicated to the following Prentice Hall/Pearson sales representatives who work so hard to promote this book:

NOLA AKALA

DAVID ALEVY

TARA ALGEO

DAVID ARMSTRONG

MIKE ASKEW

LAURA BAILEY

NICK BAKER

ALICIA BARNES

ASHLEY BARNES

ALICE BARR

SHERRY BARTEL

KENDRA BASSI

JAY BECKENSTEIN

JOSH BECKENSTEIN

NICOLE BELL

CATHY BENNETT

KATIE BOLLIN

SCOTT BORDEN

JENNIFER BOYLE

AUNDREA BRIDGES

SUZANNE BROWN

ALEXANDRA BUEHLER

KYLE BURDETTE

WHITNEY CAMERON

RUTH CARDIFF

AMY CAREY

MEGAN CARRICO

MARTI CARTER

ANDREA CATULLO-LINN

MEREDITH CHANDLER

LUKE CLAEYS

KAYLEE CLAYMORE

BRIAN COBB

JENNIFER COLE

TARYLL CONNOLLY

THAYNE CONRAD

DONNA CONROY

CAITLIN COUTHEN

MEGAN JOY COWART

CYNDI CRIMMINS

KASEY CROCKETT

DAN CURRIER

KELLY DAN

MICHLENE DAOUD HEALY

STACY DAVIS

FRANK DEL CASTILLO

MEREDITH DELA ROSA

CHRIS DELANEY

GEORGE DEVENNEY

DANA DODGE (Frick)

KATE DOLDER

BARBARA DONLON

HEIDI DRESSLER

TRACY DYBALSKI

BRIAN DYK

KIM ECK

TRISH EICHHOLD

KRISTIN ELBER

KELSEY ELLIOTT

KATIE EYNON

GENEVA FARROW

MARIA FELIBERTY

MIKE FINER

MICHELLE FINNERTY

CANDAS FLETCHER

ROBERT FLORY

MARCIA FLYNN

BRAD FORRESTER

MARGARET FRENCH

STEPHANIE FRITSON

MARK GAFFNEY

MICHELLE GARCIA-JUCHTER

SYBIL GERAUD

AMBER GOECKE

CAROLYN GOGOLIN

ADAM GOLDSTEIN

BETH GRUNFELD

MICAELA HAIDLE

GREG HAITH

DEMETRIUS HALL

BRIDGET HANNENBERG

BRYAN HARRELL

TARA HARTLEY

KENNY HARVEY

ALISON HASKINS

CAROL HAWKS

JENNIFER HEILBRUNN

CHRISTINE HENRY

LYNN HICKS

JULIE HILDEBRAND

DAUNNE HINGLE

WENDI HOLLAND

CHRISTY HUMENIUK

GENE HUMENIUK

ANDREA IORIO

SUSAN JACKSON

PAM JEFFRIES

BRITTANY JUCHNOWSKI

ANJALI JUSTUS

CHERYL KABB

LAURA KAPPES

GIA KAUL

JULIE KESTENBAUM

KARTAPURKH KHALSA

KIM KIEHLER

AMANDA KILLEEN

WALT KIRBY

MARY-JO KOVACH

ROBYN KOVAR

GREG KRAMP

DANIEL KRAUSS

MICHAEL KRISANDA

GINA LaMANTIA

CHAFIKA LANDERS

DOROTHY LANDRY

DUSTIN LANGE

ALIX LaSCOLA

JOE LEE

APRIL LEMONS

KIMBERLY LENAGHAN

TRICIA LISCIO	COLLEEN O'DELL	MARY SHAPIRO
BETH LUDWIG	DEBBIE OGILIVE	BARBARA SHERRY
CARY LUNA	SARI ORLANSKY	KEN SHIPBAUGH
JEMINA MACHARRY	DAVE OSTROW	DAVE SHULER
KATIE MAHAN	DARCEY PALMER	JESSICA SIEMINSKI
LAURA MANN	KRISTINA PARKER	LEA SILVERMAN
PATRICIA MARTINEZ	TONI PAYNE	AUTUMN SLAUGHTER
CHRISTINA MASTROGIOVANNI	JULIANNE PETERSON	KRISTA SLAVICEK
SONNY MATHARU	MELISSA PFISTNER	SCOTT SMITH
TONY MATHIAS	CANDACE PINATARO	ADRIENNE SNOW
BROOK MATTHEWS	BELEN POLTORAK	LEE SOLOMONIDES
GEORGIA MAY	ELIZABETH POPIELARZ	BEN STEPHEN
ALICIA MCAULIFFE	MEGAN PRENDERGAST	DAN SULLIVAN
MASON McCARTNEY	NICOLE PRICE	JOHN SULLIVAN
KAREN McFADYEN	JILL PROMESSO	LORI SULLIVAN
BRIAN McGARRY	LENNY ANN RAPER	STEPHANIE SURFUS
MICHELLE McGOVERN	JOSH RASMUSSEN	AMANDA SVEC
IRENE McGUINNESS	AMANDA RAY	CHRISTINA TATE
RYAN McHENRY	SONYA REED	SARAH THOMAS
CRISTIN McMICHAEL	RICHARD RESCH	ABBY THORNBLADH
KEVIN MEASELLE	MARY RHODES	KATY TOWNLEY
RAY MEDINA	BRAD RITTER	ELIZABETH TREPKOWSKI
KELLY MEIERHOFER	DAN ROBERTSON	TARA TRIPP
MOLLY MEINERS	MATT ROBINSON	CAROLYN TWIST
MATT MESAROS	JENNIFER ROSEN	JOE VIRZI
SHALON MILLER	DOROTHY ROSENE	AMANDA VOLZ
JAMI MINARD	KELLEEN ROWE	BRITNEY WALKER
WILLIAM MINERICH	RICH ROWE	MADELEINE WATSON
EMILY MITCHELL	PEYTON ROYTEK	BEN WEBER
JILINE MIX	SENG SAECHAO	DANIEL WELLS
JULIE MOREL	STEVE SARTORI	MARK WHEELER
RAFAEL MORENO	LYNDA SAX	LIZ WILDES
TRACY MORSE	BOB SCANLON	MICHELLE WILES
OLIVIA MOUG	MARCUS SCHERER	BRIAN WILLIAMS
DOLLY MUNIZ	KIMBERLY SCHEYVING	ERIN WILLIAMS
TRICIA MURPHY	HEIDI SCHICK (Miller)	CINDY WILLIAMSON
LAUREN MURROW	BRAD SCHICK	RACHEL WILLIS
AMBER MYLLION (Parks)	CHRIS SCHMIDT	SIMON WONG
LINDA NELSON	DEBORAH SCHMIDT	KIMBERLY WOODS
LYNNE NICLAIR	MOLLY SCHMIDT	JACKIE WRIGHT
BOB NISBET	CORRINA SCHULTZ	HEATHER WRUBLESKY
BETSY NIXON	WHITNEY SEAGO	GEORGE YOUNG
TOM NIXON	CHRISTIANA SERLE	MARY ZIMMERMANN
LAURA NOAH	MARTHA SERNAS	KACIE ZIN

Brief Contents

Contents

Preface

Welcome to the 13th edition of *Concepts in Strategic Management and Business Policy: Toward Global Sustainability*. We have examined the latest books, academic journals, and business publications to find the most relevant research, concepts, and techniques in the growing field of strategic management for inclusion. In addition, there are special issue chapters (dealing with technology, entrepreneurship, and not-for-profit strategic issues) on the Web site (www. pearsonhighered.com/wheelen). We continue to be the most comprehensive strategy book on the market, with chapter topics ranging from corporate governance and social responsibility to competitive strategy, functional strategy, and strategic alliances.

This edition continues the theme that runs throughout all 12 chapters: *global environmental sustainability*. This theme complements the existing Global Issues theme carried forward from past editions. Environmental sustainability has become a strategic issue that will become even more important in the years ahead, as all of us struggle to deal with the consequences of climate change, global warming, and energy availability.

FEATURES FOCUSED ON ENVIRONMENTAL SUSTAINABILITY

- Each chapter contains a boxed insert dealing with an issue in environmental sustainability.
- Each chapter ends with *Eco Bits*, interesting tidbits of ecological information, such as the number of plastic bags added to landfills each year.
- Special sections on sustainability are found in Chapters 1 and 3.
- A section on the natural environment is included in the societal and task environments in Chapter 4.

HOW THIS BOOK IS DIFFERENT FROM OTHER STRATEGY TEXTBOOKS

This book contains a **Strategic Management Model** that runs through the first 11 chapters and is made operational through the **Strategic Audit**, a complete case analysis methodology. The Strategic Audit provides a professional framework for case analysis in terms of external and internal factors and takes the student through the generation of strategic alternatives and implementation programs.

To help the student synthesize the many factors in a complex strategy case, we developed three useful techniques:

- **External Factor Analysis (EFAS) Table in Chapter 4**
  This reduces the external Opportunities and Threats to the 8 to 10 most important external factors facing management.
- **Internal Factor Analysis (IFAS) Table in Chapter 5**
  This reduces the internal Strengths and Weaknesses to the 8 to 10 most important internal factors facing management.
- **Strategic Factor Analysis Summary (SFAS) Matrix in Chapter 6**
  This condenses the 16 to 20 factors generated in the EFAS and IFAS Tables into the 8 to 10 most important (strategic) factors facing the company. These strategic factors become the basis for generating alternatives and a recommendation for the company's future direction.

Suggestions for Case Analysis are provided in **Appendix 15.B (end of Chapter 15)** and contain step-by-step procedures for how to use the Strategic Audit in analyzing a case. This appendix includes an example of a student-written Strategic Audit. Thousands of students around the world have applied this methodology to case analysis with great success.

TIME-TESTED FEATURES

This edition contains many of the same features and content that helped make previous editions successful. Some of the features are the following:

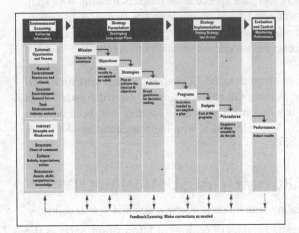

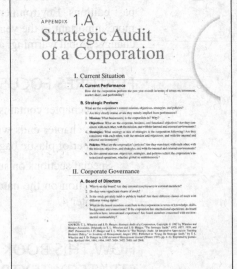

- A **Strategic Management Model** runs throughout the first 11 chapters as a unifying concept. (Explained in *Chapter 1*)

- The **Strategic Audit**, a way to operationalize the strategic decision-making process, serves as a checklist in case analysis. (*Chapter 1*)

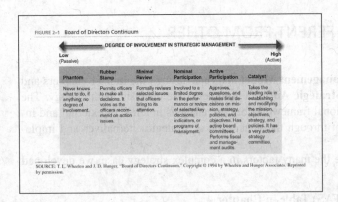

FIGURE 2–1 Board of Directors Continuum

SOURCE: T. L. Wheelen and J. D. Hunger, "Board of Directors Continuum." Copyright © 1994 by Wheelen and Hunger Associates. Reprinted by permission.

- **Corporate governance** is examined in terms of the roles, responsibilities, and interactions of top management and the board of directors and includes the impact of the Sarbanes-Oxley Act. (*Chapter 2*)

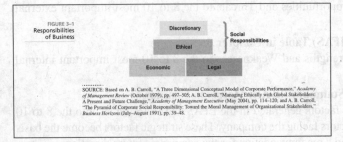

FIGURE 3–1 Responsibilities of Business

SOURCE: Based on A. B. Carroll, "A Three Dimensional Conceptual Model of Corporate Performance," *Academy of Management Review* (October 1979), pp. 497–505; A. B. Carroll, "Managing Ethically with Global Stakeholders: A Present and Future Challenge," *Academy of Management Executive* (May 2004), pp. 114–120; and A. B. Carroll, "The Pyramid of Corporate Social Responsibility: Toward the Moral Management of Organizational Stakeholders," *Business Horizons* (July–August 1991), pp. 39–48.

- **Social responsibility and managerial ethics** are examined in detail in terms of how they affect strategic decision making. They include the process of stakeholder analysis and the concept of social capital. (*Chapter 3*)

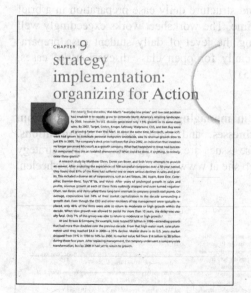

4.1 Environmental Scanning

Before an organization can begin strategy formulation, it must scan the external environment to identify possible opportunities and threats and its internal environment for strengths and weaknesses. **Environmental scanning** is the monitoring, evaluation, and dissemination of information from the external and internal environments to key people within the corporation. A corporation uses this tool to avoid strategic surprise and to ensure its long-term health. Research has found a positive relationship between environmental scanning and profits.[2] Approximately 70%-of executives around the world state that global social, environmental, and business trends are increasingly important to corporate strategy, according to a 2008 survey by McKinsey & Company.[3]

IDENTIFYING EXTERNAL ENVIRONMENTAL VARIABLES

In undertaking environmental scanning, strategic managers must first be aware of the many variables within a corporation's natural, societal, and task environments (see **Figure 1–3**). The

■ Equal emphasis is placed on **environmental scanning** of the societal environment as well as on the task environment. Topics include forecasting and Miles and Snow's typology in addition to competitive intelligence techniques and Porter's industry analysis. (**Chapter 4**)

■ **Core and distinctive competencies** are examined within the framework of the resource-based view of the firm. (**Chapter 5**)

■ **Organizational analysis** includes material on business models, supply chain management, and corporate reputation. (**Chapter 5**)

■ Internal and external strategic factors are emphasized through the use of specially designed **EFAS, IFAS**, and **SFAS tables**. (**Chapters 4, 5, and 6**)

■ **Functional strategies** are examined in light of **outsourcing.** (**Chapter 8**)

■ Two chapters deal with issues in **strategy implementation**, such as organizational and job design plus strategy-manager fit, action planning, corporate culture, and international strategic alliances. (**Chapters 9 and 10**)

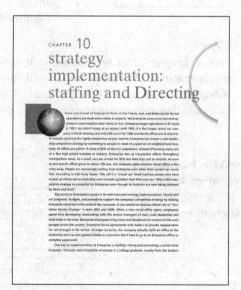

■ A separate chapter on **evaluation and control** explains the importance of measurement and incentives to organizational performance. (**Chapter 11**)

■ **Suggestions for in-depth case analysis** provide a complete listing of financial ratios, recommendations for oral and written analysis, and ideas for further research. (*Chapter 15*)

■ The **Strategic Audit Worksheet** is based on the time-tested Strategic Audit and is designed to help students organize and structure daily case preparation in a brief period of time. The worksheet works exceedingly well for checking the level of daily student case preparation—especially for open class discussions of cases. (*Chapter 15*)

■ Special chapters deal with strategic issues in **managing technology and innovation**, **entrepreneurial ventures and small businesses**, and **not-for-profit organizations**. (*Chapters 12, 13, and 14*, respectively) These issues are often ignored by other strategy textbooks, but are available on this book's Web site at www.pearsonhighered.com/wheelen.

■ An **experiential exercise** focusing on the material covered in each chapter helps the reader to apply strategic concepts to an actual situation.

STRATEGIC PRACTICE EXERCISE

Each year, *Fortune* magazine publishes an article entitled, "America's Most Admired Companies." It lists the 10 most admired companies in the United States and in the world. *Fortune*'s rankings are based on scoring publicly held companies on what it calls "eight key attributes of reputation": innovation, people management, use of corporate assets, social responsibility, quality of management, financial soundness, long-term investment value, and quality of products/services. In 2008, *Fortune* asked Hay Group to survey more than 3,700 people from multiple industries. Respondents were asked to choose the companies they admired most, regardless of industry. *Fortune* has been publishing this list since 1982. The *2008 Fortune* list of the top 10 most admired U.S. companies were (starting with #1): Apple, Berkshire Hathaway, General Electric, Google, Toyota Motor, Starbucks, FedEx, Procter & Gamble, Johnson & Johnson, and Goldman Sachs Group. The next 10 most admired were (from 11 to 20): Target, Southwest Airlines, American Express, BMW, Costco Wholesale, Microsoft, United Parcel Service, Cisco Systems, 3M, and Nordstrom.[114]

Four years earlier in 2004, the list of 10 most admired U.S. companies was: Wal-Mart, Berkshire Hathaway, South-west Airlines, General Electric, Dell Computer, Microsoft, Johnson & Johnson, Starbucks, FedEx, and IBM.[115]

■ Why did the most admired U.S. firm in 2004 (Wal-Mart) drop off the 10 ten listing in 2008?

■ Why did Apple go from not even being on the 10 ten U.S. listing in 2004 to No. 1 in 2008?

■ Which firms appeared on both top 10 lists? Why?

■ Why did some firms drop off the list from 2004 to 2008 and why did others get included?

■ What companies should be on the most admired list this year? Why?

Try One of These Exercises

1. Go to the library and find a "Most Admired Companies" *Fortune* article from the 1980s or early 1990s and compare that list to the latest one. (See www.fortune.com for the latest list.) Which companies have fallen out of the top 10? Pick one of the companies and investigate why it is no longer on the list.

■ A list of **key terms** and the pages in which they are discussed enable the reader to keep track of important concepts as they are introduced in each chapter.

- **Learning objectives** begin each chapter.
- **Each Part ends with a short case that acts to integrate the material discussed within the previous chapters.**

The text has been class-tested in strategy courses and revised based on feedback from students and instructors. The first 11 chapters are organized around a Strategic Management Model that begins each chapter and provides a structure for both content and case analysis. We emphasize those concepts that have proven to be most useful in understanding strategic decision making and in conducting case analysis. Our goal was to make the text as comprehensive as possible without getting bogged down in any one area. Endnote references are provided for those who wish to learn more about any particular topic.

The following support materials have been developed to accompany the 13th edition:

PowerPoint Slides

PowerPoint slides, provided in a comprehensive package of text outlines and figures corresponding to the text, are designed to aid the educator and supplement in-class lectures.

CourseSmart

CourseSmart eTextbooks were developed for students looking to save on required or recommended textbooks. Students simply select their eText by title or author and purchase immediate access to the content for the duration of the course using any major credit card. With a CourseSmart eText, students can search for specific keywords or page numbers, take notes online, print out reading assignments that incorporate lecture notes, and bookmark important passages for later review. For more information or to purchase a CourseSmart eTextbook, visit www.coursesmart.com.

T. L. W.
Saint Petersburg, Florida

J. D. H.
St. Joseph, Minnesota

New to This Edition

This Indian edition of *Strategic Management and Business Policy* is a balanced attempt to retain the strengths of the original edition while attempting to make it more acceptable to the Indian students and instructors. This objective has been accomplished by adapting the text to fit the Indian environment. At multiple places throughout the book, the text has been adapted to fit the Indian industries. Major changes were done in this respect to Chapter 2 which is on corporate governance.

Secondly, to make the text more acceptable and understandable, Western examples and managerial practices have been complimented or substituted with Indian examples and case studies. Success stories/cases of Apollo, ITC Bingo, Dabur, ICICI, Zapak, Satyam, ITC e-Choupal, Haldiram, Wipro, Nirma, Big Bazaar, Pantaloon, Mahindra & Mahindra, Bharti, etc. give this edition its Indian twist. These replacements/additions are targeted at increasing the relevance of the text in the Indian context, thereby, enhancing the understanding and achieving a synergistic learning.

Unique to the 13th Indian edition are the mind maps at the end of every chapter. Mind maps are the ultimate organisational thinking tools. They are the easiest ways to put information into your brain and to take information out of your brain as they literally 'map out' your thoughts. The mind maps help students organize and picture the concepts in a compact and complete way,

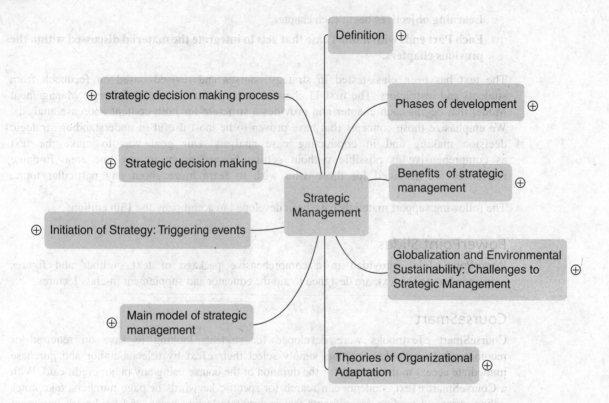

Strategic Management

- Definition
- Phases of development
- Benefits of strategic management
- Globalization and Environmental Sustainability: Challenges to Strategic Management
- Theories of Organizational Adaptation
- Main model of strategic management
- Initiation of Strategy: Triggering events
- Strategic decision making
- strategic decision making process

thereby increasing their attention and recalling abilities. The mind maps do not substitute the text but compliment it by helping the students revise and recall the concepts at a glance.

This edition also contains more comprehensive end-of-chapter questions. Keeping in mind the Indian examination system, a more exhaustive list of practice questions has been added at the end of each chapter.

P. K.
Panjab University

Acknowledgments

We thank the many people at Prentice Hall/Pearson who helped to make this edition possible. We thank our editor, Kim Norbuta. We are especially grateful to Kim's project manager, Claudia Fernandes, who managed to keep everything on an even keel. We also thank Becca Groves and Emily Bush, who took the book through the production process.

In addition, we express our appreciation to Wendy Klepetar, Management Department Chair of Saint John's University and the College of Saint Benedict, for her support and provision of the resources so helpful to revise a textbook. Both of us acknowledge our debt to Dr. William Shenkir and Dr. Frank S. Kaulback, former Deans of the McIntire School of Commerce of the University of Virginia, for the provision of a work climate most supportive to the original development of this book.

Lastly, to the many strategy instructors and students who have moaned to us about their problems with the strategy course: We have tried to respond to your problems and concerns as best we could by providing a comprehensive yet usable text coupled with recent and complex cases. To you, the people who work hard in the strategy trenches, we acknowledge our debt. This book is yours.

T. L. W.
Saint Petersburg, Florida

J. D. H.
St. Joseph, Minnesota

Contributor's Acknowledgments

I would like to thank the companies — Apollo, ITC Bingo, Dabur, ICICI, Zapak, Satyam, ITC e-choupal, Haldiram, Wipro, Nirma, Big Bazaar, Pantaloon, Mahindra & Mahindra and Bharti — who not only shared their experiences with me but also gave me permission to use them in this 13th edition.

I express my deep appreciation for all the faculty members and students who sent their feedback and gave me the idea of using mind maps. It is due to their cooperation that this Indian edition has been made possible.

P. K.
Panjab University

PART 1

Introduction to Strategic Management and Business Policy

CHAPTER 1

basic concepts of Strategic Management

ITC is one of India's foremost private sector companies with a market capitalization of over U.S. $33 billion and a turnover of U.S. $7 billion (*as on Oct 2011). ITC is rated among the World's Best Big Companies, Asia's "Fab 50" and the World's Most Reputable Companies by Forbes magazine, among India's Most Respected Companies by Businessworld and India's Most Valuable Companies by Business Today. ITC ranks among India's "10 Most Valuable (Company) Brands", in a study conducted by Brand Finance and published by the Economic Times. ITC also ranks among Asia's 50 best performing companies compiled by Business Week.[1]

ITC has a diversified presence in cigarettes, hotels, paperboards and specialty papers, packaging, agri-business, packaged foods and confectionery, information technology, branded apparel, personal care, stationery, safety matches, and other FMCG products[2]. ITC is also gaining market share even in its nascent businesses of packaged foods and confectionery, branded apparel, personal care, and stationery.

As one of India's most valuable and respected corporations, it is widely perceived to be nation oriented.

How does a company becomes successful and stays successful? Certainly not by playing safe and following traditional ways of doing business.

ITC's diversified status originates from its corporate strategy aimed at creating multiple drivers of growth across its value chain which has linkages with the company's core competencies. ITCs core competencies are extensive distribution channel, superior brand-building capabilities, supply chain management.[3]

Keeping in line with its corporate strategy, in mid-March 2007, ITC announced its foray into fast growing, ready to eat snack market through Bingo.

In India, the category of snacks is characterized by organized players and unorganized sector. The organized sector is one of the fastest growing FMCG categories. The organized snacks category is sub-divided into the traditional segment (bhujia, chanachur, etc.), western segment (potato chips, cheese balls, etc.), and the finger snacks segment, which is, in India, an adaptation of traditional offerings to the western format.[4]

In mid-March of 2007, ITC announced its foray into the Rs 2,000-crore fast-moving branded snack market, dominated by Frito-Lay.[5] The launch of Bingo was ITC Foods' fifth major line of foods business after the highly successful Staples, biscuits, ready-to-eat, and confectionery businesses.[6] Business Standard's Annual Brand Derby cited Bingo as the most successful launch of 2007. Ten months after it entered the category with its wafer snack brand, Bingo, ITC's foray into the Rs 2,000-crore branded snack market fetched the company a 16% market share across the country.[7]

It has never been easy for any new entrant to grab a quarter of the market, especially when pitted against a cash-rich multinational like Frito Lay, owned by PepsiCo. The game becomes

Learning Objectives

After reading this chapter, you should be able to:

- Understand the benefits of strategic management
- Explain how globalization and environmental sustainability influence strategic management
- Understand the basic model of strategic management and its components
- Identify some common triggering events that act as stimuli for strategic change
- Understand strategic decision-making modes
- Use the strategic audit as a method of analyzing corporate functions and activities

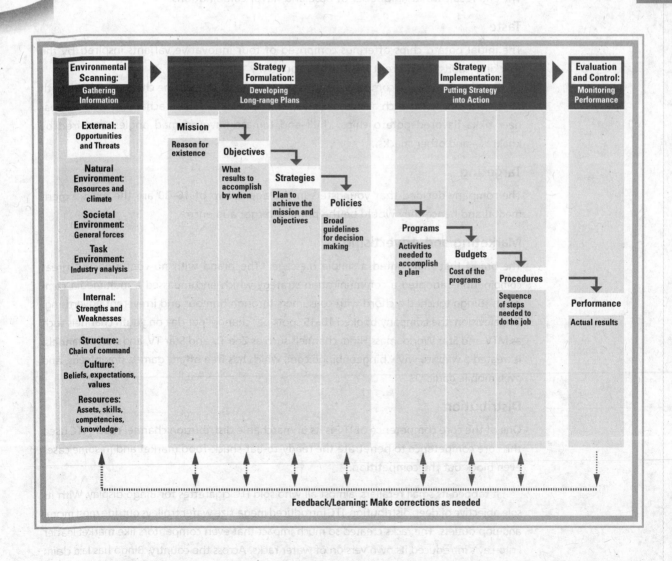

Environmental Scanning: Gathering Information	Strategy Formulation: Developing Long-range Plans	Strategy Implementation: Putting Strategy into Action	Evaluation and Control: Monitoring Performance

External: Opportunities and Threats

Natural Environment: Resources and climate

Societal Environment: General forces

Task Environment: Industry analysis

Internal: Strengths and Weaknesses

Structure: Chain of command

Culture: Beliefs, expectations, values

Resources: Assets, skills, competencies, knowledge

Mission — Reason for existence

Objectives — What results to accomplish by when

Strategies — Plan to achieve the mission and objectives

Policies — Broad guidelines for decision making

Programs — Activities needed to accomplish a plan

Budgets — Cost of the programs

Procedures — Sequence of steps needed to do the job

Performance — Actual results

Feedback/Learning: Make corrections as needed

tougher when it is a product that belongs to a pure impulse purchase category. What made the brand tick? What makes it stand out of the clutter?

Research

ITC concluded that to seize the market opportunity and compete successfully against the branded incumbent, Frito-Lay, they needed to leverage market research to ensure a good understanding of consumer habits, identify, and develop a differentiated product, and create excitement in an otherwise mundane category. After making the decision to launch Bingo, ITC embarked on an intensive two year program to create a variety of salty snacks, exploring flavor, texture, and shapes. ITC started the process by sending a cross-functional team of eight individuals across the country to research the snacking habits of the Indian consumer.[8] After travelling to 14 cities and speaking to more than 1,000 people, the team came back with an insight on Indian consumers' snacking habits. Based on the insights, different base foods were tested including corn, rice and even pasta, and dried mango. The end result was a unique set of base and flavor combinations.[9]

Taste

The initial potato chips offerings comprised of four innovative variants inspired by the snacking habits of different parts of the country.[10]

For the recipes, the company went to the chefs in its hotels. The chefs came back with 16 flavors with twists such as bindaas masti chaas, chatkila nimbu achar and tandoori paneer tikka-flavored potato chips, chilli–and tomato-flavored mad angles—inspired by khakras—and other snacks.[11]

Targeting

The company decided that youngsters in the age group of 16–30 are the most experimental and hence they would be the primary target audience.

Marketing and Advertising

The brand that highlighted a simple message "The brand with no confusion but great combination" adopted a communication strategy which encompassed a multimedia campaign. Bingo touched a chord with consumers through humour and irreverent advertising. On television, the company booked 10–15 spots per channel per day on youth channels such as MTV and Star World, mass Hindi channels such as Zee TV and Star TV, and news channels. It created a website www.bingeonbingo.com, which has free offers, games, downloads, and even mobile games.[12]

Distribution

One of the core competence of ITC is its unmatchable distribution channel reach. ITC used this core competence to penetrate the ready-to-eat-snack-food market and in some cases even block out the competition.[13]

It tapped its small retailers, almost all who sold ITC cigarettes for Bingo display. With its sole objective of deep distribution, ITC introduced mega-size wafer trolleys outside most mom-and-pop outlets. The racks created so much impact that even competitors like market leader Frito-Lay's introduced its own version of wafer racks. Across the country, Bingo has laid claim to the large format outlets by tying-up with big retailers like Future Group's Food Bazaar.

This incredible leveraging of distribution system contributed to the success of Bingo. An added source of advantage for Bingo was the strong farm linkages that ITC has for sourcing the selected grades of potatoes that go into the making of the chips.[14]

The launch of Bingo was symbolic of ITC Foods' distinct approach of introducing innovative and differentiated products in a largely undifferentiated market place. The Bingo range of potato chips saw sales growing by 48% during the December 2010 quarter.[15]

1.1   The Study of Strategic Management

Strategic management is a set of managerial decisions and actions that determines the long-run performance of a corporation. It includes environmental scanning (both external and internal), strategy formulation (strategic or long-range planning), strategy implementation, and evaluation and control. The study of strategic management, therefore, emphasizes the monitoring and evaluating of external opportunities and threats in light of a corporation's strengths and weaknesses. Originally called *business policy*, strategic management incorporates such topics as strategic planning, environmental scanning, and industry analysis.

PHASES OF STRATEGIC MANAGEMENT

Many of the concepts and techniques that deal with strategic management have been developed and used successfully by business corporations such as General Electric and the Boston Consulting Group. Over time, business practitioners and academic researchers have expanded and refined these concepts. Initially, strategic management was of most use to large corporations operating in multiple industries. Increasing risks of error, costly mistakes, and even economic ruin are causing today's professional managers in all organizations to take strategic management seriously in order to keep their companies competitive in an increasingly volatile environment.

As managers attempt to better deal with their changing world, a firm generally evolves through the following four **phases of strategic management**:[16]

Phase 1—Basic financial planning: Managers initiate serious planning when they are requested to propose the following year's budget. Projects are proposed on the basis of very little analysis, with most information coming from within the firm. The sales force usually provides the small amount of environmental information. Such simplistic operational planning only pretends to be strategic management, yet it is quite time consuming. Normal company activities are often suspended for weeks while managers try to cram ideas into the proposed budget. The time horizon is usually one year.

Phase 2—Forecast-based planning: As annual budgets become less useful at stimulating long-term planning, managers attempt to propose five-year plans. At this point they consider projects that may take more than one year. In addition to internal information, managers gather any available environmental data—usually on an ad hoc basis—and extrapolate current trends five years into the future. This phase is also time consuming, often involving a full month of managerial activity to make sure all the proposed budgets fit together. The process gets very political as managers compete for larger shares of funds. Endless meetings take place to evaluate proposals and justify assumptions. The time horizon is usually three to five years.

Phase 3—Externally oriented (strategic) planning: Frustrated with highly political yet ineffectual five-year plans, top management takes control of the planning process by initiating strategic planning. The company seeks to increase its responsiveness to changing markets and competition by thinking strategically. Planning is taken out of the hands of lower-level managers and concentrated in a planning staff whose task is to develop strategic plans for the corporation. Consultants often provide the sophisticated and innovative techniques that the planning staff uses to gather information and forecast future trends. Ex-military experts develop competitive intelligence units. Upper-level managers meet once a year at a resort "retreat" led by key members of the planning staff to evaluate and update the current strategic plan. Such top-down planning emphasizes formal strategy formulation and leaves the implementation issues to lower management levels. Top management typically develops five-year plans with help from consultants but minimal input from lower levels.

Phase 4—Strategic management: Realizing that even the best strategic plans are worthless without the input and commitment of lower-level managers, top management forms planning groups of managers and key employees at many levels, from various departments and workgroups. They develop and integrate a series of strategic plans aimed at achieving the company's primary objectives. Strategic plans at this point detail the implementation, evaluation, and control issues. Rather than attempting to perfectly forecast the future, the plans emphasize probable scenarios and contingency strategies. The sophisticated annual five-year strategic plan is replaced with strategic thinking at all levels of the organization throughout the year. Strategic information, previously available only centrally to top management, is available via local area networks and intranets to people throughout the organization. Instead of a large centralized planning staff, internal and external planning consultants are available to help guide group strategy discussions. Although top management may still initiate the strategic planning process, the resulting strategies may come from anywhere in the organization. Planning is typically interactive across levels and is no longer top down. People at all levels are now involved.

General Electric, one of the pioneers of strategic planning, led the transition from strategic planning to strategic management during the 1980s.[17] By the 1990s, most other corporations around the world had also begun the conversion to strategic management.

BENEFITS OF STRATEGIC MANAGEMENT

Strategic management emphasizes long-term performance. Many companies can manage short-term bursts of high performance, but only a few can sustain it over a longer period of time. For example, of the original *Forbes 100* companies listed in 1917, only 13 have survived to the present day. To be successful in the long-run, companies must not only be able to *execute* current activities to satisfy an existing market, but they must also *adapt* those activities to satisfy new and changing markets.[18]

Research reveals that organizations that engage in strategic management generally outperform those that do not.[19] The attainment of an appropriate match, or "fit," between an organization's environment and its strategy, structure, and processes has positive effects on the organization's performance.[20] Strategic planning becomes increasingly important as the environment becomes more unstable.[21] Traditionally Indian banking sector has been dominated by public sector banks that have focused on serving masses rather than service quality.[22,23,24] Till the beginning of the 1990s, this strategy was working for the public sector banks in India. However, global changes coupled with India's financial reforms and internal competition brought some major changes in Indian banking sector. Due to these changes, Indian banking sector saw influx of private and foreign banks. These banks entered the Indian markets with their own portfolio and standard of services, thereby, pushing the industry into the choppy waters of intense competition. As a result, the share of private and foreign banks in total assets increased to 27.6% at March-end 2006 from 24.7% at March-end 2005—it was less than 10% at the inception of economic reforms in 1993.[25]

To succeed, the public sector banks needed new models of leadership and management. The success of these banks depended upon their degree of flexibility in terms of their strategies and structures. To help these banks, in early 2005, Indian finance minister introduced certain changes to increase the transactional efficiency of the public sector banks by giving them greater operational flexibility and some autonomy.[26]

These changes have led to public sector banks giving, not only private but also foreign banks, a run for their money. For example, SBI, transitioned from a manual ledger system to computerized back office operations and branches in 1990s. It realized that business process reorganization was needed along with technology transformation and therefore it embarked on a path of transforming its processes. By 2006, 52% of SBI's branches were on Centralized Online Real Time Environment Banking Solution (CBS)[27]. It was the result of such initiatives by public sector banks that the mean efficiency score of private sector commercial banks as a group, in 2003, was paradoxically lower than that of public sector banks and foreign banks in India[28].

A survey of nearly 50 corporations in a variety of countries and industries found three most highly rated benefits of strategic management to be:

- Clearer sense of strategic vision for the firm.
- Sharper focus on what is strategically important.
- Improved understanding of a rapidly changing environment.[29]

A recent survey by McKinsey & Company of 800 executives found that formal strategic planning processes improve overall satisfaction with strategy development.[30] To be effective, however, strategic management need not always be a formal process. It can begin with a few simple questions:

1. Where is the organization now? (Not where do we hope it is!)
2. If no changes are made, where will the organization be in one year? two years? five years? 10 years? Are the answers acceptable?
3. If the answers are not acceptable, what specific actions should management undertake? What are the risks and payoffs involved?

Bain & Company's *2007 Management Tools and Trends* survey of 1,221 global executives revealed strategic planning to be the most used management tool—used by 88% of respondents. Strategic planning is particularly effective at identifying new opportunities for growth and in ensuring that all managers have the same goals.[31] Other highly-ranked strategic management tools were mission and vision statements (used by 79% of respondents), core competencies (79%), scenario and contingency planning (69%), knowledge management (69%), strategic alliances (68%), and growth strategy tools (65%).[32] A study by Joyce, Nohria, and Roberson of 200 firms in 50 subindustries found that devising and maintaining an engaged, focused strategy was the first of four essential management practices that best differentiated between successful and unsuccessful companies.[33] Based on these and other studies, it can be concluded that strategic management is crucial for long-term organizational success.

Research into the planning practices of companies in the oil industry concludes that the real value of modern strategic planning is more in the *strategic thinking* and *organizational learning* that is part of a future-oriented planning process than in any resulting written strategic plan.[34] Small companies, in particular, may plan informally and irregularly. Nevertheless, studies of small- and medium-sized businesses reveal that the greater the level of planning intensity, as measured by the presence of a formal strategic plan, the greater the level of financial performance, especially when measured in terms of sales increases.[35]

Planning the strategy of large, multidivisional corporations can be complex and time consuming. It often takes slightly more than a year for a large company to move from situation assessment to a final decision agreement. For example, strategic plans in the global oil industry tend to cover four to five years. The planning horizon for oil exploration is even longer—up to 15 years.[36] Because of the relatively large number of people affected by a strategic decision in a large firm, a formalized, more sophisticated system is needed to ensure that strategic planning leads to successful performance. Otherwise, top management becomes isolated from developments in the business units, and lower-level managers lose sight of the corporate mission and objectives.

1.2 Globalization and Environmental Sustainability: Challenges to Strategic Management

Not too long ago, a business corporation could be successful by focusing only on making and selling goods and services within its national boundaries. International considerations were minimal. Profits earned from exporting products to foreign lands were considered as a frosting on the cake, but not really essential to corporate success. During the 1960s, for example, most U.S. companies organized themselves around a number of product divisions that made and sold goods only in the United States. All manufacturing and sales outside the United States were typically managed through one international division. An international assignment was usually considered a message that the person was no longer promotable and should be looking for another job. Before the 1990s, India was a regime of self-reliance and very high-trade barriers in form of import duties and restrictions on imports. When it started, Tata International, then called Commercial and Industrial Exports Limited, was fashioned on the Japanese trading houses.[37] Following the merchantilism philosophy, Government of India supported trading houses because of the foreign exchange earnigs that they could bring in.

Similarly, until the later part of the 20th century, a business firm could be very successful without being environmentally sensitive. Companies dumped their waste products in nearby streams or lakes and freely polluted the air with smoke containing noxious gases. Responding to complaints, governments eventually passed laws restricting the freedom to pollute the environment. Lawsuits forced companies to stop old practices. Nevertheless, until the dawn of the 21st century, most executives considered pollution abatement measures to be a cost of business that should be either minimized or avoided. Rather than clean up a polluting manufacturing site, they often closed the plant and moved manufacturing offshore to a developing nation with fewer environmental restrictions. In India too sustainability, is used to describe competitive advantage and profits and not environment. See **Strategy Highlight 1.1** to know more about environment cost of industry in India.

IMPACT OF GLOBALIZATION

Today, everything has changed. **Globalization**, the integrated internationalization of markets and corporations, has changed the way modern corporations do business. As Thomas Friedman points out in *The World Is Flat*, jobs, knowledge, and capital are now able to move across borders with far greater speed and far less friction than was possible only a few years ago.[38] For example, the inter-connected nature of the global financial community meant that the mortgage lending problems of US banks led to a global financial crisis in 2008. The worldwide availability of the Internet and supply-chain logistical improvements, such as containerized shipping, mean that companies can now locate anywhere and work with multiple partners to serve any market. To reach the economies of scale necessary to achieve the low costs, and thus the low prices, needed to be competitive, companies are now thinking of a global market instead of national markets. Nike and Reebok, for example, manufacture their athletic shoes in various countries throughout Asia for sale on every continent. Many other companies in North America and Western Europe are outsourcing their manufacturing, software development, or customer service to companies in China, Eastern Europe, or India. Large pools of talented software programmers, English language proficiency, and lower wages in India enables IBM to employ 75,000 people in its global delivery centers in Bangalore, Delhi, or Kolkata to serve the needs of clients in Atlanta, Munich, or Melbourne.[39] Instead of using one international division to manage everything outside the home country, large corporations are now using matrix structures in which product units are interwoven with country or regional units. International assignments are now considered as a key for anyone interested in reaching top management.

STRATEGY highlight 1.1

ENVIRONMENT COST OF INDUSTRY IN INDIA: BHOPAL TRAGEDY

India has achieved astonishing growth rates in the past decade but with severe environmental damages such as deforestation and deterioration of air quality. In India it is estimated that the damage and degradation of natural resources is equivalent to about 10% of the country's GDP.[1]

India's industrial sector is expanding rapidly and has become a major source of pollution. This is particularly so in more industrialized states such as Gujarat, Maharashtra, Tamil Nadu, and Andhra Pradesh.[2] The main polluting factors are iron and steel, pulp and paper, petrochemical, mining, oil refinery, and coal-based power generation units.

In India, one of the major reasons for environmental pollution is lack of implementation of laws and not absence of it. Classic case study of this is Bhopal gas leak.

The Bhopal facility was part of India's green revolution aimed to increase the productivity of crops. The plant was setup to manufacture and sell pesticides to Indian market. On the night of December 23, 1984, a large amount of water got into one of the tables storing methyl isocyanate (MIC), which reacts with water resulting in a dangerous chemical reaction.[3] The reaction created gas which in turn created a dense cloud over a resident population of more than half a million people. Thousands of people were killed (estimates ranging from 3,800[4] to as high as 20,000[5]) in their sleep or as they fled in terror, and hundreds of thousands remain injured or affected (estimates range as high as 400,000) to this day.

In retrospect, experts believe that Carbide dropped the safety standards at the Bhopal plant well below those maintained at a nearly identical facility in West Virginia.[6] Furthermore, Carbide was able to operate its deteriorating plant because industrial safety and environmental laws and regulations were not strictly enforced by the state of Madhya Pradesh.

Lessons were learnt but the Indian economy is growing at a tremendous rate and at significant cost in environmental, health and public safety, as large and small companies throughout the subcontinent continue to pollute.

1. R. K. Pachauri, "The Future of India's Economic Growth: The Natural Resources and Energy Dimension," *Futures,* Vol. 36 (2004), 703–713.

2. *India: State of the Environment 2001*, Ministry of Environment & Forests, Government of India, accessed on http://envfor.nic.in/mef/mef.html

3. S. M. Enzler, "Top 10 of Anthropogenic and Natural Environmental Disasters," posted on September 2006, accessed on 11 Oct 2011, from http://www.lenntech.com/environmental-disasters.htm#1._Bhopal:_the_Union_Carbide_gas_leak

4. Union Carbide Corporation, The Incident, Response, and Settlement, accessed on 11 Oct 2011, from http://www.bhopal.com/incident-response-and-settlement

5. Greenpeace, The Bhopal Disaster, accessed on 11 Oct 2011, from http://www.greenpeace.org/usa/en/campaigns/toxics/justice-for-bhopal/

6. TED Case Studies, Bhopal Disaster, Case number 233, accessed on 11 Oct 2011, from http://www1.american.edu/ted/bhopal.htm

As more industries become global, strategic management is becoming an increasingly important way to keep track of international developments and position a company for long-term competitive advantage. For example, General Electric moved a major research and development lab for its medical systems division from Japan to China in order to learn more about developing new products for developing economies. Microsoft's largest research center outside Redmond, Washington, is in Beijing. Similarly, Motorola has R&D facilities in India, which developed a sub-$40 cellular phone for emerging markets. Microsoft in January 2005 launched its third international research center in India. Intel has many India-based engineers working for its communication and semiconductor product lines.[40] Hyundai Motor Company has set up the R&D centre in Hyderabad called Hyundai Motor India Engineering (HMIE). HMIE is a centre with one of the most advanced research and development facilities that focuses on state-of-the-art product and design engineering and rigorous quality enhancement.[41] Other international companies are outsourcing design activity for their products that range from auto parts to consumer electronics.

Recently, pharmaceutical companies have also started eying India as a means for gaining long-term competitive advantage. Indian companies can reap huge cost savings and as a result help pharma companies to relieve some pressure of developing new drugs to replace older ones that are going off patent. India has the highest number of FDA-approved drug manufacturing plants outside the United States.[42] According to Wilbur Chung, a Wharton professor, "Whatever China develops is rolled out to the rest of the world. China may have a lower GDPper-capita than developed countries, but the Chinese have a strong sense of how productsshould be designed for their market."[43]

GLOBAL issue

REGIONAL TRADE ASSOCIATIONS REPLACE NATIONAL TRADE BARRIERS

Formed as the European Economic Community in 1957, the **European Union (EU)** is the most significant trade association in the world. The goal of the EU is the complete economic integration of its 27 member countries so that goods made in one part of Europe can move freely without ever stopping for a customs inspection. The EU includes Austria, Belgium, Bulgaria, Cyprus, Czech Republic, Denmark, Estonia, Finland, France, Germany, Greece, Hungary, Ireland, Italy, Latvia, Lithuania, Luxembourg, Malta, Netherlands, Poland, Portugal, Romania, Slovakia, Slovenia, Spain, Sweden, and the United Kingdom. Others, including Croatia, Macedonia, and Turkey, have either recently applied or are in the process of applying. The EU is less than half the size of the United States of America, but has 50% more population. One currency, the euro, is being used throughout the region as members integrate their monetary systems. The steady elimination of barriers to free trade is providing the impetus for a series of mergers, acquisitions, and joint ventures among business corporations. The requirement of at least 60% local content to avoid tariffs has forced many U.S. and Asian companies to abandon exporting in favor of having a strong local presence in Europe.

Canada, the United States, and Mexico are affiliated economically under the **North American Free Trade Agreement (NAFTA)**. The goal of NAFTA is improved trade among the three member countries rather than complete economic integration. Launched in 1994, the agreement required all three members to remove all tariffs among themselves over 15 years, but they were allowed to have their own tariff arrangements with nonmember countries. Cars and trucks must have 62.5% North American content to qualify for duty-free status. Transportation restrictions and other regulations have been being significantly reduced. A number of Asian and European corporations, such as Sweden's Electrolux, have built manufacturing facilities in Mexico to take advantage of the country's lower wages and easy access to the entire North American region.

South American countries are also working to harmonize their trading relationships with each other and to form trade associations. The establishment of the **Mercosur (Mercosul** in Portuguese) free-trade area among Argentina, Brazil, Uruguay, and Paraguay means that a manufacturing presence within these countries is becoming essential to avoid tariffs for nonmember countries. Venezuela has applied for admission to Mercosur. The **Andean Community** (Comunidad Andina de Naciones) is a free-trade alliance composed of Columbia, Ecuador, Peru, Bolivia, and Chile. On May 23, 2008, the **Union of South American Nations** was formed to unite the two existing free-trade areas with a secretariat in Ecuador and a parliament in Bolivia.

In 2004, the five Central American countries of El Salvador, Guatemala, Honduras, Nicaragua, and Costa Rica plus the United States signed the **Central American Free Trade Agreement (CAFTA)**. The Dominican Republic joined soon thereafter. Previously, Central American textile manufacturers had to pay import duties of 18%–28% to sell their clothes in the United States unless they bought their raw material from U.S. companies. Under CAFTA, members can buy raw material from anywhere and their exports are duty free. In addition, CAFTA eliminated import duties on 80% of U.S. goods exported to the region, with the remaining tariffs being phased out over 10 years.

The **Association of Southeast Asian Nations (ASEAN)**—composed of Brunei Darussalam, Cambodia, Indonesia, Laos, Malaysia, Myanmar, Philippines, Singapore, Thailand, and Vietnam—is in the process of linking its members into a borderless economic zone by 2020. Tariffs had been significantly reduced among member countries by 2008. Increasingly referred to as ASEAN+3, ASEAN now includes China, Japan, and South Korea in its annual summit meetings. The ASEAN nations negotiated linkage of the ASEAN Free Trade Area (AFTA) with the existing free-trade area of Australia and New Zealand. With the EU extending eastward and NAFTA extending southward to someday connect with CAFTA and the Union of South American Nations, pressure is building on the independent Asian nations to join ASEAN.

The formation of regional trade associations and agreements, such as the European Union, NAFTA, Mercosur, Andean Community, CAFTA, and ASEAN, is changing how international business is being conducted. See the **Global Issue** feature to learn how regional trade associations are forcing corporations to establish a manufacturing presence wherever they wish to market goods or else face significant tariffs. These associations have led to the increasing harmonization of standards so that products can more easily be sold and moved across national boundaries. International considerations have led to the strategic alliance between British Airways and American Airlines and to the acquisition of the Miller Brewing Company by South African Breweries (SAB), among others.

IMPACT OF ENVIRONMENTAL SUSTAINABILITY

Environmental sustainability refers to the use of business practices to reduce a company's impact upon the natural, physical environment. For example, to meet its environmental responsibilities, Johnson and Johnson Ltd's has invested in technology in its plant in Mumbai, where biodegradable waste is recycled.

However, India's first ever eco-friendly building is the Resource Efficient TERI Retreat for Environmental Awareness and Training (RETREAT) located in Gurgaon district. A complex of Tata Energy Research Institute (TERI), it is powered by renewable energy system, which uses waste biomass and solar radiation as sources of energy. It also boasts of having the first solar-roof in India. Air conditioning is provided by an earth air tunnel[44]. In short, the complex emits no waste.

Aditya Birla Group's (India) company, Grasim industries, is one of the few companies in India to experiment with alternate fuel for manufacturing cement. Effort of this group is commendable. Grasim has tried the following wastes as fuel in its kilns, resulting in partial substitution:

- Sludge from effluent treatment plants
- Tyre chips
- Agricultural waste
- Refinery sludge
- Paint sludge

Grasim (an Aditya Birla Group company) has taken the initiative to burn waste as fuel in its kilns. Moreover, as a prelude to its eco-friendly social responsibility and economic success, the company has established waste handling facilities at two units—Grasim South Cement and Vikram Cement. The company has installed a municipal solid waste processing plant near Jaipur. It is one of the first of its kind in India.[45] **Strategy Highlight 1.2** discusses some more of these initiatives in detail. Climate change is playing a growing role in business decisions. More than half of the global executives surveyed by McKinsey & Company in 2007 selected "environmental issues, including climate change," as the most important issue facing them over the next five years.[46] According to Eileen Claussen, President of the Pew Center on Global Climate Change:

> *There is a growing consensus among corporate leaders that taking action on climate change is a responsible business decision. From market shifts to regulatory constraints, climate change poses real risks and opportunities that companies must begin planning for today, or risk losing ground to their more forward-thinking competitors. Prudent steps taken now to address climate change can improve a company's competitive position relative to its peers and earn it a seat at the table to influence climate policy. With more and more action at the state level and increasing scientific clarity, it is time for businesses to craft corporate strategies that address climate change.*[47]

Porter and Reinhardt warn that "in addition to understanding its emissions costs, every firm needs to evaluate its vulnerability to climate-related effects such as regional shifts in the availability of energy and water, the reliability of infrastructures and supply chains, and the prevalence of infectious diseases."[48] Swiss Re, the world's second-largest reinsurer, estimated that the overall economic costs of climate catastrophes related to climate change threatens to double to $150 billion per year by 2014. The insurance industry's share of this loss would be $30–$40 billion annually.[49]

The effects of climate change on industries and companies throughout the world can be grouped into six categories of risks: regulatory, supply chain, product and technology, litigation, reputational, and physical.[50]

1. **Regulatory Risk:** Companies in much of the world are already subject to the Kyoto Protocol, which requires the developed countries (and thus the companies operating within them) to reduce carbon dioxide and other greenhouse gases by an average of 6% from 1990 levels by 2012. The European Union has an emissions trading program that allows companies that emit

STRATEGY highlight 1.2

ENVIRONMENTAL SUSTAINABILITY NEXT GREAT CHALLENGE IN INDIA'S DEVELOPMENT PATH

India makes up 2.4% of the world's land, while supporting 16% of the world's population. The compounding result is a severely unsustainable use of natural resources for several generations. Currently, India is experiencing rapid and widespread environmental degradation at alarming rates.[1] The biggest challenge for India's development path is environmental sustainability.

Strengthening Institutions for Sustainable Growth:

Country Environmental Analysis for India, a report by World Bank published in 2007, said that the country-wise average compliance ratio of industries monitored is only at 50% and that the country needed to improve its monitoring standards.[2]

Many companies are pitching into this concept and adopting a strategy of creating enduring value through its businesses. In this approach, companies focus on creating sustainable businesses and livelihood opportunities. This is referred to as triple bottom-line. In the triple bottom-line approach the social and environmental factors have to be incorporated, not as an add-on to a company's economic activities but as an essential and integral part of the strategic intent of the company linking the business success with society.[3] In this approach, therefore, the performance is measured in economic, environmental, and social terms.

In India many companies have adopted triple bottom-line approach successfully. ITC, on the environmental front, claimed to be the only company in India to have achieved carbon-positive and water-positive status. Also, its operations released close to zero solid waste. On the social front, the company took its "e-Choupal" initiative to farmers giving them crop-specific information in local languages.[4]

A company highlights its contributions to tripple bottom line by submitting sustainability report in compliance with the latest G3 Guidelines of the Netherlands-based global reporting initiative (GRI). ITC was among the first top 10 companies to submit its sustainability report.[5]

In India other companies that develop their sustainability reports are Bhilai Steel Plant, Tata Steel, Reliance Industries, Ford India, Indian Oil, Dr Reddy's Laboratories Ltd., Jubilant Organosys, etc. CII ITC Centre of Excellence for Sustainable Development focuses on promoting the uptake of this tool among small and medium companies of India.[6]

These initiatives on carbon sequestration, waste recycling, creating rainwater harvesting potential, and creating sustainable livelihoods demonstrate the Indian corporate sectors' commitment to environmental sustainability issues.

1. FSD, Foundation for Sustainable Development, Environmental Sustainability Issues in India, accessed on 11 Oct 2011, from http://www.fsdinternational.org/country/india/envissues

2. D. Aarti, "Environmental Sustainability a Big Challenge," posted on 04 Nov 2007, accessed on 11 Oct 2011, from http://www.hindu.com/2007/04/11/stories/2007041100491300.htm

3. M. Mehra, "Triple Bottomline Approaches for Building Corporations that Last," accessed on 11 Oct 2011, from World Council for Corporate Governance website http://www.wcfcg.net/triplebottom.htm

4. ITC Portal, ITC Units to Adopt Triple Bottomline, posted on December 2004 in Business Standard, accessed on 11 Oct 2011, from http://itcportal.com/about-itc/newsroom/press-reports/PressReport.aspx?id=512&type=C&news=ITC-units-adopt-triple-bottomline

5. The Hindu Bureau, Sustainability Report: ITC Among First 10 in the World, posted on 09 Mar 2007, in the Business Line, accessed on 11 Oct 2011, from http://www.thehindubusinessline.in/bline/2007/03/09/stories/2007030901530200.htm

6. CII, Sustainability Report, recovered from CII- ITC Centre of Excellence for Sustainable Development, accessed on 11 Oct 2011, from http://www.sustainabledevelopment.in/services/corporate_substainability_management/activities/sustainability_reporting.htm

greenhouse gases beyond a certain point to buy additional allowances from other companies whose emissions are lower than that allowed. Companies can also earn credits toward their emissions by investing in emissions abatement projects outside their own firms. Although the United States withdrew from the Kyoto Protocol, various regional, state, and local government policies affect company activities in the U.S. For example, seven Northeastern states, six Western states, and four Canadian provinces have adopted proposals to cap carbon emissions and establish carbon-trading programs. India signed and ratified the protocol in August, 2002. As a signatory, of the protocol, India is obliged to frame rules for reducing emission of GHGs. For achieving target of reducing the emissions, India needed to frame tougher laws related to fuel efficiency.

As per some statistics, India is the second-largest car market in the world. India imports 78% of the fuel it consumes and these figures are to touch 94% by 2030, which according to environmentalists is alarming as it interprets that the level of emission of GHGs especially CO_2 would go up radically over this period of time. As a proactive action, Supreme Court of India has laid down certain guidelines. For example, all the buses and auto rickshaws in Delhi are now compressed natural gas (CNG) driven.[51]

2. **Supply Chain Risk:** Suppliers will be increasingly vulnerable to government regulations—leading to higher component and energy costs as they pass along increasing carbon-related costs to their customers. Global supply chains will be at risk from an increasing intensity of major storms and flooding. Higher sea levels resulting from the melting of polar ice will create problems for seaports. China, where much of the world's manufacturing is currently being outsourced, is becoming concerned with environmental degradation. In 2006, 12 Chinese ministries produced a report on global warming foreseeing a 5%–10% reduction in agricultural output by 2030; more droughts, floods, typhoons, and sandstorms; and a 40% increase in population threatened by plague.[52]

   The increasing scarcity of fossil-based fuel is already boosting transportation costs significantly. For example, Tesla Motors, the maker of an electric-powered sports car, transferred assembly of battery packs from Thailand to California because Thailand's low wages were more than offset by the costs of shipping thousand-pound battery packs across the Pacific Ocean.[53] Although the world production of oil had leveled off at 85 million barrels a day by 2008, the International Energy Agency predicted global demand to increase to 116 million barrels by 2030. Given that output from existing fields was falling 8% annually, oil companies must develop up to seven million barrels a day in additional capacity to meet projected demand. Nevertheless, James Mulva, CEO of ConocoPhilips, estimated in late 2007 that the output of oil will realistically stall at around 100 million barrels a day.[54]

3. **Product and Technology Risk:** Environmental sustainability can be a prerequisite to profitable growth. For example, worldwide investments in sustainable energy (including wind, solar, and water power) more than doubled to $70.9 billion from 2004 to 2006.[55] According to Nielsen's 2011 Global Online Environment and Sustainability Survey of more than 25,000 Internet respondents in 51 countries, it was found that among the environmental and sustainability efforts that matter to Indian consumers, 86% of Indian consumers surveyed place faith in energy efficient products and appliances, followed by recyclable packaging (79%). Least impact was given to products not tested on animals (41%), and fair trade products (44%).[56] Therefore, Indian consumers were not only aware of environmental issues but also stated that to some extent a company's mindfulness of its impact on environment and society influences their purchase decision. Carbon-friendly products using new technologies are becoming increasingly popular with consumers. Those automobile companies, for example, that were quick to introduce hybrid or alternative energy cars gained a competitive advantage.

4. **Litigation Risk:** Companies that generate significant carbon emissions face the threat of lawsuits similar to those in the tobacco, pharmaceutical, and building supplies (e.g., asbestos) industries. In India, it is estimated that the damage and degradation of natural resources is equivalent to about 10% of the country's GDP.[57] The Ministry of Environment and Forests (MoEF) recognizes the need to strike a balance between development and protecting the environment. It believes that there needs to be a balance in administering and enforcing the laws and policies. As a result, government passed Environment Protection Act, 1986 to increase the powers of the Ministry. The Act is built on the 42nd amendment to India's constitution.[58] The Act was an attempt to give powers to ministry to protect public health, forests, and wildlife.

   Agreeing with the government's attitude of environmental responsibility, the Supreme Court of India in December 2008 noted that courts cannot afford to deal lightly with cases involving public health. These observations were made in a case related to a Rae Bareli-based company, Modi Carpets, which was reportedly found discharging its polluted trade effluent into river Sai without any treatment.[59] This strict stand of the government led to many manufacturing outfits, in 98 industries, adding to pollution in the capital, to either close down their operations or upgrade themselves to knowledge-based industries.[60]

5. **Reputational Risk:** A company's impact on the environment can heavily affect its overall reputation. The Carbon Trust, a consulting group, found that in some sectors the value of a company's brand could be at risk because of negative perceptions related to climate change. In contrast, a company with a good record of environmental sustainability may create a competitive advantage in terms of attracting and keeping loyal consumers, employees, and investors. The Tata, over the years has developed a very respectable reputation in the minds of everday Indian consumers. The group has achieved this by aggressively pursuing several CSR initiatives as an integral part of its overall strategy. It makes it mandatory for group companies to have a vision and mission, explicitly stating its environmental corporate policy and communicate it to all employees to set up environmental management systems and annual budget for environmental improvement. Furthermore, each unit is required to train its workforce on environmental issues, scrutinize resource consumption and the quality of air, water, and land, set quantitative objectives, and review performance for continuous improvement (preferably beyond legal compliance). Each unit is required to publish its annual environmental performance in annual reports and is encouraged to adopt eco-labels and accreditations such as ISO 14000/01.[61] Tools have recently been developed to measure sustainability on a variety of factors. For example, the Sustainable Asset Management (SAM) Group of Zurich, Switzerland, has been assessing and documenting the sustainability performance of over 1,000 corporations annually since 1999. SAM lists the top 15% of firms in its *Sus-tainability Yearbook* and classifies them into gold, silver, and bronze categories.[62] *Business Week* published its first list of the world's 100 most sustainable corporations January 29, 2007. The *Dow Jones Sustainability Indexes* and the *KLD Broad Market Social Index*, which evaluate companies on a range of environmental, social, and governance criteria are used for investment decisions.[63] Financial services firms, such as Goldman Sachs, Bank of America, JPMorgan Chase, and Citigroup have adopted guidelines for lending and asset management aimed at promoting clean-energy alternatives.[64]

6. **Physical Risk:** The direct risk posed by climate change includes the physical effects of droughts, floods, storms, and rising sea levels. Average Arctic temperatures have risen four to five degrees Fahrenheit (two to three degrees Celsius) in the past 50 years, leading to melting glaciers and sea levels rising one inch per decade.[65] Industries most likely to be affected are insurance, agriculture, fishing, forestry, real estate, and tourism. Physical risk can also affect other industries, such as oil and gas, through higher insurance premiums paid on facilities in vulnerable areas. Coca-Cola, for example, studies the linkages between climate change and water availability in terms of how this will affect the location of its new bottling plants. The warming of the Tibetan plateau has led to a thawing of the permafrost—thereby threatening the newly-completed railway line between China and Tibet.[66] (See the **Environmental Sustainability Issue** feature for a more complete list of projected effects of climate change.)

Although global warming remains a controversial topic, the best argument in favor of working toward environmental sustainability is a variation of Pascal's Wager on the existence of God:

> *The same goes for global warming. If you accept it as reality, adapting your strategy and practices, your plants will use less energy and emit fewer effluents. Your packaging will be more biodegradable, and your new products will be able to capture any markets created by severe weather effects. Yes, global warming might not be as damaging as some predict, and you might have invested more than you needed, but it's just as Pascal said: Given all the possible outcomes, the upside of being ready and prepared for a "fearsome event" surely beats the alternative.[67]*

ENVIRONMENTAL sustainability issue

PROJECTED EFFECTS OF CLIMATE CHANGE

According to the Intergovernmental Panel on Climate Change (IPCC), the global climate system is projected to include a number of changes during the 21st century:

TEMPERATURE INCREASE

- Global average warming of approximately 0.2 degrees Celsius each decade.
- Long-term warming associated with doubled carbon dioxide concentrations in the range of 2 to 4.5 degrees Celsius.
- Fewer cold days and nights; warmer and more frequent hot days and nights.
- Increased frequency, intensity, and duration of heat waves in central Europe, western U.S., East Asia, and Korea.

SEA LEVEL RISE

- Sea level will continue to rise due to thermal expansion of seawater and loss of land ice at greater rates.
- Sea level rise of 18 to 59 centimeters by the end of the 21st century.
- Warming will continue contributing to sea level rise for many centuries even if greenhouse gas concentrations are stabilized.

PRECIPITATION AND HUMIDITY

- Increasing numbers of wet days in high latitudes; increasing numbers of dry spells in subtropical areas.

- Annual precipitation increases in most of northern Europe, Canada, northeastern U.S., and the Arctic.
- Winter precipitation increases in northern Asia and the Tibetan Plateau.
- Dry spells increase in length and frequency in the Mediterranean, Australia, and New Zealand; seasonal droughts increase in many mid-latitude continent interiors.

EXTREME WEATHER-RELATED EVENTS

- Increasing intense tropical cyclone activity.
- Increasing frequency of flash floods and large-area floods in many regions.
- Increasing risk of drought in Australia, eastern New Zealand, and the Mediterranean, with seasonal droughts in central Europe and Central America.
- Increasing wildfires in arid and semi-arid areas such as Australia and the western U.S.

OTHER RELATED EFFECTS

- Decreasing snow season length and depth in Europe and North America.
- Fewer cold days and nights leading to decreasing frosts.
- Accelerated glacier loss.
- Reduction in and warming of permafrost.

SOURCE: F. G. Sussman and J. R. Freed, "Adapting to Climate Change: A Business Approach," Paper prepared for the Pew Center on Global Climate Change (April 2008), pp. 5–6.

1.3 Theories of Organizational Adaptation

Globalization and environmental sustainability present real challenges to the strategic management of business corporations. How can any one company keep track of all the changing technological, economic, political–legal, and sociocultural trends around the world and make the necessary adjustments? This is not an easy task. Various theories have been proposed to account for how organizations obtain fit with their environment. The theory of **population ecology,** for example, proposes that once an organization is successfully established in a particular environmental niche, it is unable to adapt to changing conditions. Inertia prevents the organization from changing. The company is thus replaced (is bought out or goes bankrupt) by other organizations more suited to the new environment. Although it is a popular theory in sociology, research fails to support the arguments of population ecology.[68] **Institution theory,** in contrast, proposes that organizations can and do adapt to changing conditions by imitating

STRATEGY highlight 1.3

HIGH-TECH OPERATIONS HELP RECYCLE HIGH-TECH EQUIPMENT AT WIPRO

The discarded electronic devices that enter the waste stream are called e-waste. This contains many harmful chemicals like lead that pose significant environmental and health hazards. Computers contribute a significant portion of the population of electronic devices. Computer e-waste management has become an important issue in environment sustainability arena.

In India, people and companies tend to give it to the store they purchased it from or merely slip it into household trash. This disregard has prompted Wipro Infotech to take environmentally conscious proactive steps for controlling e-waste.

Wipro Infotech provides technology and software services and consulting services in the Middle East and ASEAN. Wipro has been actively working on electronic waste (e-waste) management since August 2005. It not only endeavors to have 100% e-waste recycling for its e-waste but also endeavors to have a similar kind of awareness among its business associates.

The e-waste could enter the value chain from two sources. If a computer or its spare part is under Wipro's active service, it is sent to Bangalore for repairs. At Bangalore, the part is tested. If categorized as scrap, the parts are collected and a consolidated shipment is sent to the e-waste processors periodically. Alternatively, a corporate or individual customer can discard the old computer as scrap and bring it to the nearest Wipro collection centre. In this case it can be directly sent to the processors for processing. The disposal of e-waste through this system involves logistic and handling costs of around US $4 for a typical computer system consisting of base CPU, monitor, and keyboard. Though these small costs have to be borne by the customer, yet the benefits outweigh the costs. Wipro helps its customers in efficient management of valuable resources by helping them with identification of suitable and certified e-waste disposal partners. These e-waste processors include names such as Trishiraya Recycling and Ash Recyclers. Moreover, Wipro also monitors the disposal of e-waste by these agencies to assure customers' of its processing under environmentally clean processes and ensure compliance with pollution control norms. If desired, for large consignments, the company also provides documentary evidence to customers.

These endeavors are helping Wipro in meeting its mission of being an environmentally conscious company.

....
Adapted from L. Krajewski, L. Ritzman, M. Malhotra, *Operations Management*, 8th Edition (New Delhi: Dorling Kindersley India Pvt. Ltd, India), p. 18.
Courtesy : Wipro Infotech, India.
For more details visit www.wipro.in/products/ew.htm

other successful organizations. To its credit, many examples can be found of companies that have adapted to changing circumstances by imitating an admired firm's strategies and management techniques.[69] The theory does not, however, explain how or by whom successful new strategies are developed in the first place. The **strategic choice perspective** goes one step further by proposing that not only do organizations adapt to a changing environment, but they also have the opportunity and power to reshape their environment. This perspective is supported by research indicating that the decisions of a firm's management have at least as great an impact on firm performance as overall industry factors.[70] Because of its emphasis on managers making rational strategic decisions, the strategic choice perspective is the dominant one taken in strategic management. Its argument that adaptation is a dynamic process fits with the view of **organizational learning theory,** which says that an organization adjusts defensively to a changing environment and uses knowledge offensively to improve the fit between itself and its environment. This perspective expands the strategic choice perspective to include people at all levels becoming involved in providing input into strategic decisions.[71]

In agreement with the concepts of organizational learning theory, an increasing number of companies are realizing that they must shift from a vertically organized, top-down type of organization to a more horizontally managed, interactive organization. They are attempting to adapt more quickly to changing conditions by becoming "learning organizations." See **Strategy Highlight 1.3**.

1.4 Creating a Learning Organization

Strategic management has now evolved to the point that its primary value is in helping an organization operate successfully in a dynamic, complex environment. To be competitive in dynamic environments, corporations are becoming less bureaucratic and more flexible. In stable environments such as those that existed in years past, a competitive strategy simply involved defining a competitive position and then defending it. As it takes less and less time for one product or technology to replace another, companies are finding that there is no such thing as a permanent competitive advantage. Many agree with Richard D'Aveni, who says in his book *Hypercompetition* that any sustainable competitive advantage lies not in doggedly following a centrally managed five-year plan but in stringing together a series of strategic short-term thrusts (as Intel does by cutting into the sales of its own offerings with periodic introductions of new products).[72] This means that corporations must develop *strategic flexibility*—the ability to shift from one dominant strategy to another.[73]

Strategic flexibility demands a long-term commitment to the development and nurturing of critical resources. It also demands that the company become a **learning organization**—an organization skilled at creating, acquiring, and transferring knowledge and at modifying its behavior to reflect new knowledge and insights. Organizational learning is a critical component of competitiveness in a dynamic environment. It is particularly important to innovation and new product development.[74] For example, both Hewlett-Packard and British Petroleum (BP) use an extensive network of informal committees to transfer knowledge among their cross-functional teams and to help spread new sources of knowledge quickly.[75] Siemens, a major electronics company, created a global knowledge-sharing network, called ShareNet, in order to quickly spread information technology throughout the firm. Based on its experience with ShareNet, Siemens established PeopleShareNet, a system that serves as a virtual expert marketplace for facilitating the creation of cross-cultural teams composed of members with specific knowledge and competencies.[76]

Learning organizations are skilled at four main activities:

- Solving problems systematically
- Experimenting with new approaches
- Learning from their own experiences and past history as well as from the experiences of others
- Transferring knowledge quickly and efficiently throughout the organization[77]

Business historian Alfred Chandler proposes that high-technology industries are defined by "paths of learning" in which organizational strengths derive from learned capabilities.[78] According to Chandler, companies spring from an individual entrepreneur's knowledge, which then evolves into organizational knowledge. This organizational knowledge is composed of three basic strengths: technical skills, mainly in research; functional knowledge, such as production and marketing; and managerial expertise. This knowledge leads to new businesses where the company can succeed and creates an entry barrier to new competitors. Chandler points out that once a corporation has built its learning base to the point where it has become a core company in its industry, entrepreneurial startups are rarely able to successfully enter. Thus, organizational knowledge becomes a competitive advantage.

Strategic management is essential for learning organizations to avoid stagnation through continuous self-examination and experimentation. People at all levels, not just top management, participate in strategic management—helping to scan the environment for critical information, suggesting changes to strategies and programs to take advantage of environmental shifts, and working with others to continuously improve work methods, procedures, and evaluation techniques. For example, Motorola developed an action learning format in which people from marketing, product development, and manufacturing meet to argue and reach agreement about the needs of the market, the best new product, and the schedules of each group producing it. This action learning approach overcame the problems that arose previously when the three departments met and formally agreed on plans but continued with their work as if nothing had happened.[79] Research indicates that involving more people in the strategy process results in people not only viewing the process more positively, but also acting in ways that make the process more effective.[80]

Organizations that are willing to experiment and are able to learn from their experiences are more successful than those that are not.[81]

1.5 Basic Model of Strategic Management

Strategic management consists of four basic elements:

- **Environmental scanning**
- **Strategy formulation**
- **Strategy implementation**
- **Evaluation and control**

ENVIRONMENTAL SCANNING

Environmental scanning is the monitoring, evaluating, and disseminating of information from the external and internal environments to key people within the corporation. Its purpose is to identify **strategic factors**—those external and internal elements that will determine the future of the corporation. The simplest way to conduct environmental scanning is through **SWOT analysis**. SWOT is an acronym used to describe the particular **S**trengths, **W**eaknesses, **O**pportunities, and **T**hreats that are strategic factors for a specific company. The **external environment** consists of variables (**O**pportunities and **T**hreats) that are outside the organization and not typically within the short-run control of top management. These variables form the context within which the corporation exists. **Figure 1–3** depicts key environmental variables. They may be general forces and trends within the natural or societal environments or specific factors that operate within an organization's specific task environment—often called its *industry*. (These external variables are defined and discussed in more detail in **Chapter 4**.)

The **internal environment** of a corporation consists of variables (**S**trengths and **W**eaknesses) that are within the organization itself and are not usually within the short-run control of top management. These variables form the context in which work is done. They include the corporation's structure, culture, and resources. Key strengths form a set of core competencies that the corporation can use to gain competitive advantage. (These internal variables and core competencies are defined and discussed in more detail in **Chapter 5**.)

STRATEGY FORMULATION

Strategy formulation is the development of long-range plans for the effective management of environmental opportunities and threats, in light of corporate strengths and weaknesses (SWOT). It includes defining the corporate mission, specifying achievable objectives, developing strategies, and setting policy guidelines.

FIGURE 1–1
Basic Elements of
the Strategic
Management
Process

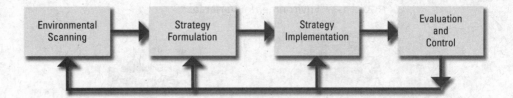

Figure 1–1 illustrates how these four elements interact; **Figure 1–2** expands each of these elements and serves as the model for this book. This model is both rational and prescriptive. It is a planning model that presents what a corporation *should* do in terms of the strategic management process, not what any particular firm may actually do. The rational planning model predicts that as environmental uncertainty increases, corporations that work more diligently to analyze and predict more accurately the changing situation in which they operate will outperform those that do not. Empirical research studies support this model.[82] The terms used in Figure 1–2 are explained in the following pages.

FIGURE 1–2   Strategic Management Model

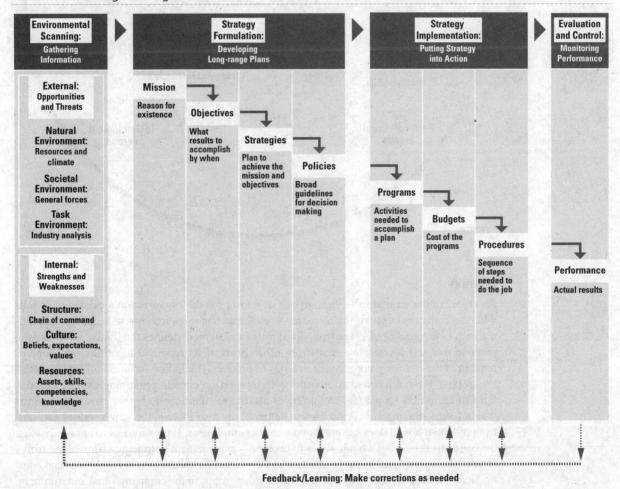

SOURCE: T. L. Wheelen, "Strategic Management Model," adapted from "Concepts of Management," presented to Society for Advancement of Management (SAM), International Meeting, Richmond, VA, 1981. T.L. Wheelen and SAM. Copyright © 1982, 1985, 1988, and 2005 by T.L. Wheelen and J.D. Hunger. Revised 1989, 1995, 1998, 2000 and 2005. Reprinted with permission.

FIGURE 1–3   Environmental Variables

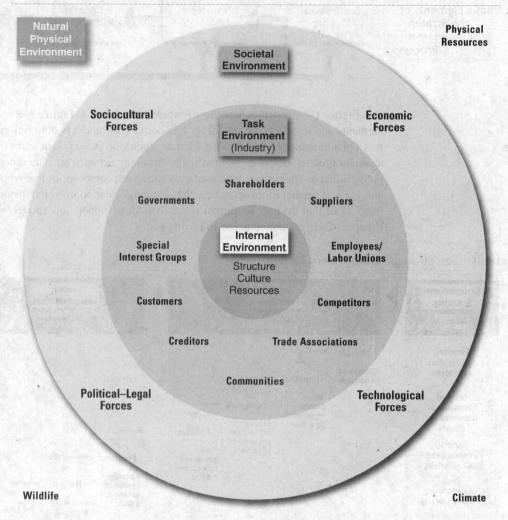

Mission

An organization's **mission** is the purpose or reason for the organization's existence. It tells what the company is providing to society—either a service such as housecleaning or a product such as automobiles. A well-conceived mission statement defines the fundamental, unique purpose that sets a company apart from other firms of its type and identifies the scope or domain of the company's operations in terms of products (including services) offered and markets served. Research reveals that firms with mission statements containing explicit descriptions of customers served and technologies used have significantly higher growth than firms without such statements.[83] A mission statement may also include the firm's values and philosophy about how it does business and treats its employees. It puts into words not only what the company is now but what it wants to become—management's strategic vision of the firm's future. The mission statement promotes a sense of shared expectations in employees and communicates a public image to important stakeholder groups in the company's task environment. Some people like to consider vision and mission as two different concepts: Mission describes what the organization is now; **vision** describes what the organization would like to become. We prefer to combine these ideas into a single mission statement.[84] Some companies prefer to list their values and philosophy of doing business in a separate publication called a *values* *statement.* For a listing of the many things that could go into a mission statement, see **Strategy Highlight 1.4**.

One example of a mission statement is that of Google:

To organize the world's information and make it universally accessible and useful.[85]

Another classic example is that etched in bronze at Newport News Shipbuilding, unchanged since its founding in 1886:

We shall build goods ships here—at a profit if we can—at a loss if we must—but always good ships.[86]

Some examples of Indian companies mission statements are:

Bharatgas has dominated the LP gas market in India. Its mission statements states,[87] "To make Bharatgas a dominant brand in the segments we market, by becoming trendsetters in customer service, safety, and quality."

Bank of Baroda, is a saga of vision, enterprise, financial prudence, and corporate governance. Its mission statement states, "To be a top ranking National Bank of International Standards committed to augmenting stake holders' value through concern, care, and competence."[88]

Nirma is a classic example of the success of Indian entrepreneurship, in FMCG sector, in the face of stiff competition. Its mission statement reads, "Nirma is a customer-focused company committed to consistently offer better quality products and services that maximize value to the customer."[89]

This customer centric philosophy is evident in all the policies, procedures and decision taken at Nirma. At Nirma, the human resource endeavors to develop new products and processes, maintain effective quality, comply with safety, environment, and social obligations to meet its strategic emphasis of cost effectiveness. For this, Nirma prioritizes its employee training and development programs and developing an environment of belongingness toward organization.

A mission may be defined narrowly or broadly in scope. An example of a *broad* mission statement is that used by many corporations: "Serve the best interests of shareowners, customers, and employees." A broadly defined mission statement such as this keeps the company from restricting itself to one field or product line, but it fails to clearly identify either what it makes or which products/markets it plans to emphasize. Because this broad statement is so general, a *narrow* mission statement, such as the preceding examples by Google and Newport News Shipbuilding, is generally more useful. A narrow mission very clearly states the organization's primary business, but it may limit the scope of the firm's activities in terms of the product or service offered, the technology used, and the market served. Research indicates that a narrow mission statement may be best in a turbulent industry because it keeps the firm focused on what it does best; whereas, a broad mission statement may be best in a stable environment that lacks growth opportunities.[90]

Objectives

Objectives are the end results of planned activity. They should be stated as *action verbs* and tell what is to be accomplished by when and quantified if possible. The achievement of corporate objectives should result in the fulfillment of a corporation's mission. In effect, this is what society gives back to the corporation when the corporation does a good job of fulfilling its mission. For example, by providing society with gums, candy, iced tea, and carbonated drinks, Cadbury Schweppes, has become the world's largest confectioner by sales. One of its prime objectives is to increase sales 4%–6% each year. Even though its profit margins were lower than those of Nestlé, Kraft, and Wrigley, its rivals in confectionary, or those of Coca-Cola or Pepsi, its rivals in soft drinks, Cadbury Schweppes' management established the objective of increasing profit margins from around 10% in 2007 to the mid-teens by 2011.[91]

STRATEGY highlight 1.4

DO YOU HAVE A GOOD MISSION STATEMENT?

Andrew Campbell, a director of Ashridge Strategic Management Centre and a long-time contributor to *Long Range Planning*, proposes a means for evaluating a mission statement. Arguing that mission statements can be more than just an expression of a company's purpose and ambition, he suggests that they can also be a company flag to rally around, a signpost for all stakeholders, a guide to behavior, and a celebration of a company's culture. For a company trying to achieve all of the above, evaluate its mission statement using the following 10-question test. Score each question 0 for no, 1 for somewhat, or 2 for yes. According to Campbell, a score of over 15 is exceptional, and a score of less than 10 suggests that more work needs to be done.

1. Does the statement describe an inspiring purpose that avoids playing to the selfish interests of the stakeholders?

2. Does the statement describe the company's responsibility to its stakeholders?

3. Does the statement define a business domain and explain why it is attractive?

4. Does the statement describe the strategic positioning that the company prefers in a way that helps to identify the sort of competitive advantage it will look for?

5. Does the statement identify values that link with the organization's purpose and act as beliefs with which employees can feel proud?

6. Do the values resonate with and reinforce the organization's strategy?

7. Does the statement describe important behavior standards that serve as beacons of the strategy and the values?

8. Are the behavior standards described in a way that enables individual employees to judge whether they are behaving correctly?

9. Does the statement give a portrait of the company, capturing the culture of the organization?

10. Is the statement easy to read?

SOURCE: Reprinted from *Long Range Planning*, Vol. 30, No. 6, 1997, Campbell "Mission Statements," pp. 931–932, Copyright © 1997 with permission of Elsevier.

The term *goal* is often used interchangeably with the term objective. In this book, we prefer to differentiate the two terms. In contrast to an objective, we consider a *goal* as an open-ended statement of what one wants to accomplish, with no quantification of what is to be achieved and no time criteria for completion. For example, a simple statement of "increased profitability" is thus a goal, not an objective, because it does not state how much profit the firm wants to make the next year. A good objective should be action-oriented and begin with the word *to*. An example of an objective is "to increase the firm's profitability in 2010 by 10% over 2009."

Some of the areas in which a corporation might establish its goals and objectives are:

- Profitability (net profits)
- Efficiency (low costs, etc.)
- Growth (increase in total assets, sales, etc.)
- Shareholder wealth (dividends plus stock price appreciation)
- Utilization of resources (ROE or ROI)
- Reputation (being considered a "top" firm)
- Contributions to employees (employment security, wages, diversity)
- Contributions to society (taxes paid, participation in charities, providing a needed product or service)
- Market leadership (market share)
- Technological leadership (innovations, creativity)

- Survival (avoiding bankruptcy)
- Personal needs of top management (using the firm for personal purposes, such as providing jobs for relatives)

Strategies

A **strategy** of a corporation forms a comprehensive master plan that states how the corporation will achieve its mission and objectives. It maximizes competitive advantage and minimizes competitive disadvantage. For example, even though Cadbury Schweppes was a major competitor in confectionary and soft drinks, it was not likely to achieve its challenging objective of significantly increasing its profit margin within four years without making a major change in strategy. Management therefore decided to cut costs by closing 33 factories and reducing staff by 10%. It also made the strategic decision to concentrate on the confectionary business by divesting its less-profitable Dr Pepper/Snapple soft drinks unit. Management was also considering acquisitions as a means of building on its existing strengths in confectionary by purchasing either Kraft's confectionary unit or the Hershey Company.

The typical business firm usually considers three types of strategy: corporate, business, and functional.

1. **Corporate strategy** describes a company's overall direction in terms of its general attitude toward growth and the management of its various businesses and product lines. Corporate strategies typically fit within the three main categories of stability, growth, and retrenchment. Cadbury Schweppes, for example, was following a corporate strategy of retrenchment by selling its marginally profitable soft drink business and concentrating on its very successful confectionary business.

2. **Business strategy** usually occurs at the business unit or product level, and it emphasizes improvement of the competitive position of a corporation's products or services in the specific industry or market segment served by that business unit. Business strategies may fit within the two overall categories, *competitive* and *cooperative* strategies. For example, Intel, a manufacturer of computer microprocessors, uses its alliance (cooperative strategy) with Microsoft to differentiate itself (competitive strategy) from AMD, its primary competitor.

   In India, Pantaloons and Big Bazaar, have used similar competitive strategy to differentiate its hypermarkets from its competitors. Big Bazaar sells a wide range and line of products. Its product lines range from apparels and accessories for the whole family besides dress material, suitings and shirtings, saris, home textile and furnishing, home needs, plastic ware and thermo ware, kitchen needs, food and grocery, utensils and steel, gages, gifts and stationary, medicines, and optical among others. The business strategy at Big Bazaar is one of minimal pricing targeted at the middle end of the market.[92] It offers distinct services to customers such as a car park, a trolley system, and convenience store. Therefore, the mantra of the organization is to ensure value for money, by providing variety of stuff under single roof, at everyday low prices.[93]

   Similarly, Kingfisher Airlines followed a cooperative strategy in 2007. It introduced Indians to a new way to book flight tickets: FlyBuySmsTM. For this the company entered into strategic alliance with PayMate, India's leading wireless transactions company. As a result of this out of the box strategy, Kingfisher Airlines became the first Indian airline to introduce SMS-based service. This service allowed its prospective customers to "search, book, and pay" from tickets' start-to finish on the mobile itself without any manual intervention.[94]

3. **Functional strategy** is the approach taken by a functional area to achieve corporate and business unit objectives and strategies by maximizing resource productivity. It is

concerned with developing and nurturing a distinctive competence to provide a company or business unit with a competitive advantage. Examples of research and development (R&D) functional strategies are technological followership (imitation of the products of other companies) and technological leadership (pioneering an innovation). For years, Magic Chef had been a successful appliance maker by spending little on R&D but by quickly imitating the innovations of other competitors. This helped the company to keep its costs lower than those of its competitors and consequently to compete with lower prices. In terms of marketing functional strategies, Procter & Gamble (P&G) is a master of marketing "pull"—the process of spending huge amounts on advertising in order to create customer demand. This supports P&G's competitive strategy of differentiating its products from those of its competitors.

Business firms use all three types of strategy simultaneously. A **hierarchy of strategy** is a grouping of strategy types by level in the organization. Hierarchy of strategy is a nesting of one strategy within another so that they complement and support one another. (See **Figure 1–4**.) Functional strategies support business strategies, which, in turn, support the corporate strategy(ies).

Just as many firms often have no formally stated objectives, many firms have unstated, incremental, or intuitive strategies that have never been articulated or analyzed. Often the only way to spot a corporation's implicit strategies is to look not at what management says but at what it does. Implicit strategies can be derived from corporate policies, programs approved (and disapproved), and authorized budgets. Programs and divisions favored by budget increases and staffed by managers who are considered to be on the fast promotion track reveal where the corporation is putting its money and its energy.

Policies

A **policy** is a broad guideline for decision making that links the formulation of a strategy with its implementation. Companies use policies to make sure that employees throughout the firm make decisions and take actions that support the corporation's mission, objectives, and

FIGURE 1–4
Hierarchy of Strategy

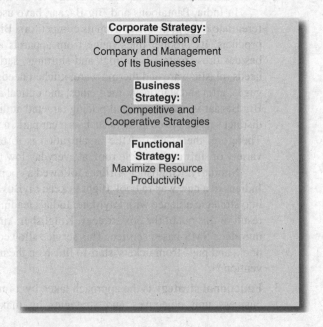

Corporate Strategy:
Overall Direction of
Company and Management
of Its Businesses

Business Strategy:
Competitive and
Cooperative Strategies

Functional Strategy:
Maximize Resource
Productivity

strategies. For example, when Cisco decided on a strategy of growth through acquisitions, it established a policy to consider only companies with no more than 75 employees, 75% of whom were engineers.[95] Consider the following company policies:

- **3M:** 3M says researchers should spend 15% of their time working on something other than their primary project. (This supports 3M's strong product development strategy.)
- **Intel:** Intel cannibalizes its own product line (undercuts the sales of its current products) with better products before a competitor does so. (This supports Intel's objective of market leadership.)
- **General Electric:** GE must be number one or two wherever it competes. (This supports GE's objective to be number one in market capitalization.)
- **Southwest Airlines:** Southwest offers no meals or reserved seating on airplanes. (This supports Southwest's competitive strategy of having the lowest costs in the industry.)
- **Exxon:** Exxon pursues only projects that will be profitable even when the price of oil drops to a low level. (This supports Exxon's profitability objective.)

Policies such as these provide clear guidance to managers throughout the organization. (Strategy formulation is discussed in greater detail in **Chapters 6, 7,** and **8.**)

STRATEGY IMPLEMENTATION

Strategy implementation is a process by which strategies and policies are put into action through the development of programs, budgets, and procedures. This process might involve changes within the overall culture, structure, and/or management system of the entire organization. Except when such drastic corporatewide changes are needed, however, the implementation of strategy is typically conducted by middle- and lower-level managers, with review by top management. Sometimes referred to as *operational planning*, strategy implementation often involves day-to-day decisions in resource allocation.

Programs

A **program** is a statement of the activities or steps needed to accomplish a single-use plan. It makes a strategy action oriented. It may involve restructuring the corporation, changing the company's internal culture, or beginning a new research effort. For example, Boeing's strategy to regain industry leadership with its proposed 787 Dreamliner meant that the company had to increase its manufacturing efficiency in order to keep the price low. To significantly cut costs, management decided to implement a series of programs:

- Outsource approximately 70% of manufacturing.
- Reduce final assembly time to three days (compared to 20 for its 737 plane) by having suppliers build completed plane sections.
- Use new, lightweight composite materials in place of aluminum to reduce inspection time.
- Resolve poor relations with labor unions caused by downsizing and outsourcing.

Another example is a set of programs used by automaker BMW to achieve its objective of increasing production efficiency by 5% each year: (a) shorten new model development time from 60 to 30 months, (b) reduce preproduction time from a year to no more than five months, and (c) build at least two vehicles in each plant so that production can shift among models depending upon demand.

Budgets

A **budget** is a statement of a corporation's programs in terms of dollars. Used in planning and control, a budget lists the detailed cost of each program. Many corporations demand a certain percentage return on investment, often called a "hurdle rate," before management will approve a new program. This ensures that the new program will significantly add to the corporation's profit performance and thus build shareholder value. The budget thus not only serves as a detailed plan of the new strategy in action, it also specifies through pro forma financial statements the expected impact on the firm's financial future.

For example, General Motors budgeted $4.3 billion to update and expand its Cadillac line of automobiles. With this money, the company was able to increase the number of models from five to nine and to offer more powerful engines, sportier handling, and edgier styling. The company reversed its declining market share by appealing to a younger market. (The average Cadillac buyer in 2000 was 67 years old.)[96] Another example is the $8 billion budget that General Electric established to invest in new jet engine technology for regional-jet airplanes. Management decided that an anticipated growth in regional jets should be the company's target market. The program paid off when GE won a $3 billion contract to provide jet engines for China's new fleet of 500 regional jets in time for the 2008 Beijing Olympics.[97]

Procedures

Procedures, sometimes termed Standard Operating Procedures (SOP), are a system of sequential steps or techniques that describe in detail how a particular task or job is to be done. They typically detail the various activities that must be carried out in order to complete the corporation's program. For example, when the home improvement retailer Home Depot noted that sales were lagging because its stores were full of clogged aisles, long checkout times, and too few salespeople, management changed its procedures for restocking shelves and pricing the products. Instead of requiring its employees to do these activities at the same time they were working with customers, management moved these activities to when the stores were closed at night. Employees were then able to focus on increasing customer sales during the day. Similarly, Taj Group of Hotels, over the years, has won international acclaim for its quality hotels and its excellence in dining, business facilities, interiors, and world-class personalized service. A key element of their business approach is quick hit teams of people from various functional areas and managers who come up with ways to improve operations in different sections of the hotel.

Multiple small changes have added up to creation of a vibrant self-correcting organization, which responds intelligently to changing business conditions. For example, when the hotel witnessed a peculiar problem of high breakages in the main kitchen and high incorrect flow of cutlery and crockery during washing, it setup a research team. The team studied the problem and set about to rectify it. The system of "one piece at a time" into the dishwasher was implemented. The layout of the dishwashing area was changed to facilitate a single-piece flow. As a result, the breakage of crockery came down by 28%.[98] Both UPS and FedEx put such an emphasis on consistent, quality service that both companies have strict rules for employee behavior, ranging from how a driver dresses to how keys are held when approaching a customer's door. (Strategy implementation is discussed in more detail in **Chapters 9** and **10**.)

EVALUATION AND CONTROL

Evaluation and control is a process in which corporate activities and performance results are monitored so that actual performance can be compared with desired performance. Managers at all levels use the resulting information to take corrective action and resolve problems. Although evaluation and control is the final major element of strategic management, it can also pinpoint weaknesses in previously implemented strategic plans and thus stimulate the entire process to begin again.

Performance is the end result of activities.[99] It includes the actual outcomes of the strategic management process. The practice of strategic management is justified in terms of its ability to improve an organization's performance, typically measured in terms of profits and return on investment. For evaluation and control to be effective, managers must obtain clear, prompt, and unbiased information from the people below them in the corporation's hierarchy. Using this information, managers compare what is actually happening with what was originally planned in the formulation stage.

For example, when market share (followed by profits) declined at Dell in 2007, Michael Dell, founder, returned to the CEO position and reevaluated his company's strategy and operations. Planning for continued growth, the company's expansion of its computer product line into new types of hardware, such as storage, printers, and televisions, had not worked as planned. In some areas, like televisions and printers, Dell's customization ability did not add much value. In other areas, like services, lower-cost competitors were already established. Michael Dell concluded, "I think you're going to see a more streamlined organization, with a much clearer strategy."[100]

The evaluation and control of performance completes the strategic management model. Based on performance results, management may need to make adjustments in its strategy formulation, in implementation, or in both. (Evaluation and control is discussed in more detail in **Chapter 11**.)

FEEDBACK/LEARNING PROCESS

Note that the strategic management model depicted in **Figure 1–2** includes a feedback/learning process. Arrows are drawn coming out of each part of the model and taking information to each of the previous parts of the model. As a firm or business unit develops strategies, programs, and the like, it often must go back to revise or correct decisions made earlier in the process. For example, poor performance (as measured in evaluation and control) usually indicates that something has gone wrong with either strategy formulation or implementation. It could also mean that a key variable, such as a new competitor, was ignored during environmental scanning and assessment. In the case of Dell, the personal computer market had matured and by 2007 there were fewer growth opportunities available within the industry. Even Jim Cramer, host of the popular television program, *Mad Money*, was referring to computers in 2008 as "old technology" having few growth prospects. Dell's management needed to re-assess the company's environment and find better opportunities to profitably apply its core competencies. For example, the case of Nirma. It today is a success story, which is discussed in almost all the B-schools in India. It started as a one-man operation in 1969. However, at the time when Nirma was introduced in the Indian market, Hindustan Lever Limited (HLL, the Indian subsidiary of Unilever) and its products were the market leaders.[101]

Nirma started its production in December 1969, in a small shed. Dr Patel, did not believe that better quality always demanded higher price.[102]

He concentrated on operational aspects like production, packaging and a low profile marketing strategy. Result was an innovative quality product. As a result of its indigenous operational strategies, Nirma catered to the consumers at a fraction of the price of HLLs then leading brand. This product managed to change the habits of Indian housewives for washing clothes. However, when Nirma washing powder was introduced in the low income market, HLLs senior executives were dismissive of the new product and ignored it saying that it did not cater to the same market segment.

Result was that by 1992, Nirma had sales of 333,000 tons p.a. and a market share of 55% and HLL was forced to take a closer look at the new segment created by Nirma.[103]

1.6 Initiation of Strategy: Triggering Events

After much research, Henry Mintzberg discovered that strategy formulation is typically not a regular, continuous process: "It is most often an irregular, discontinuous process, proceeding in fits and starts. There are periods of stability in strategy development, but also there are periods of flux, of groping, of piecemeal change, and of global change."[104] This view of strategy formulation as an irregular process can be explained by the very human tendency to continue on a particular course of action until something goes wrong or a person is forced to question his or her actions. This period of strategic drift may result from inertia on the part of the organization, or it may reflect management's belief that the current strategy is still appropriate and needs only some fine-tuning.

Most large organizations tend to follow a particular strategic orientation for about 15 to 20 years before making a significant change in direction.[105] This phenomenon, called *punctuated equilibrium,* describes corporations as evolving through relatively long periods of stability (equilibrium periods) punctuated by relatively short bursts of fundamental change (revolutionary periods).[106] After this rather long period of fine-tuning an existing strategy, some sort of shock to the system is needed to motivate management to seriously reassess the corporation's situation.

A **triggering event** is something that acts as a stimulus for a change in strategy. Some possible triggering events are:[107]

- **New CEO:** By asking a series of embarrassing questions, a new CEO cuts through the veil of complacency and forces people to question the very reason for the corporation's existence.
- **External intervention:** A firm's bank suddenly refuses to approve a new loan or suddenly demands payment in full on an old one. A key customer complains about a serious product defect.
- **Threat of a change in ownership:** Another firm may initiate a takeover by buying a company's common stock.
- **Performance gap:** A *performance gap* exists when performance does not meet expectations. Sales and profits either are no longer increasing or may even be falling.
- **Strategic inflection point:** Coined by Andy Grove, past-CEO of Intel Corporation, a *strategic inflection point* is what happens to a business when a major change takes place due to the introduction of new technologies, a different regulatory environment, a change in customers' values, or a change in what customers prefer.[108]

Unilever is an example of one company in which a triggering event forced management to radically rethink what it was doing. See **Strategy Highlight 1.5** to learn how a slumping stock price stimulated a change in strategy at Unilever.

1.7 Strategic Decision Making

The distinguishing characteristic of strategic management is its emphasis on strategic decision making. As organizations grow larger and more complex, with more uncertain environments, decisions become increasingly complicated and difficult to make. In agreement with the strategic choice perspective mentioned earlier, this book proposes a strategic decision-making framework that can help people make these decisions regardless of their level and function in the corporation.

STRATEGY highlight 1.5

TRIGGERING EVENT AT UNILEVER

Unilever, the world's second-largest consumer goods company, received a jolt in 2004 when its stock price fell sharply after management had warned investors that profits would be lower than anticipated. Even though the company had been the first consumer goods company to enter the world's emerging economies in Africa, China, India, and Latin America with a formidable range of products and local knowledge, its sales faltered when rivals began to attack its entrenched position in these markets. Procter & Gamble's (P&G) acquisition of Gillette had greatly bolstered P&G's growing portfolio of global brands and allowed it to undermine Unilever's global market share. For example, when P&G targeted India for a sales initiative in 2003–04, profit margins fell at Unilever's Indian subsidiary from 20% to 13%.

An in-depth review of Unilever's brands revealed that its brands were doing as well as were those of its rivals. Something else was wrong. According to Richard Rivers, Unilever's head of corporate strategy, "We were just not executing as well as we should have."

Unilever's management realized that it had no choice but to make-over the company from top to bottom. Over decades of operating in almost every country in the world, the company had become fat with unnecessary bureaucracy and complexity. Unilever's traditional emphasis on the autonomy of its country managers had led to a lack of synergy and a duplication of corporate structures. Country managers had been making strategic decisions without regard for their effect on other regions or on the corporation as a whole. Starting at the top, two joint chairmen were replaced by one sole chief executive. In China, three companies with three chief executives were replaced by one company with one person in charge. Overall staff was cut from 223,000 in 2004 to 179,000 in 2008. By 2010, management planned close to 50 of its 300 factories and to eliminate 75 of 100 regional centers. Twenty thousand more jobs were selected to be eliminated over a four-year period. Ralph Kugler, manager of Unilever's home and personal care division, exhibited confidence that after these changes, the company was better prepared to face competition. "We are much better organized now to defend ourselves," he stated.

SOURCE: Summarized from "The Legacy that Got Left on the Shelf," *The Economist* (February 2, 2008), pp. 77–79.

WHAT MAKES A DECISION STRATEGIC

Unlike many other decisions, **strategic decisions** deal with the long-run future of an entire organization and have three characteristics:

1. **Rare:** Strategic decisions are unusual and typically have no precedent to follow.
2. **Consequential:** Strategic decisions commit substantial resources and demand a great deal of commitment from people at all levels.
3. **Directive:** Strategic decisions set precedents for lesser decisions and future actions throughout an organization.[109]

One example of a strategic decision with all of these characteristics was that made by Genentech, a biotechnology company that had been founded in 1976 to produce protein-based drugs from cloned genes. After building sales to $9 billion and profits to $2 billion in 2006, the company's sales growth slowed and its stock price dropped in 2007. The company's products were reaching maturity with few new ones in the pipeline. To regain revenue growth, management decided to target autoimmune diseases, such as multiple sclerosis, rheumatoid arthritis, lupus, and 80 other ailments for which there was no known lasting treatment. This was an enormous opportunity, but also a very large risk for the company. Existing drugs in this area either weren't effective for many patients or caused side effects that were worse than the disease. Competition from companies like Amgen and Novartis were already vying for leadership in this area. A number of Genentech's first attempts in the area had failed to do well against the competition.

The strategic decision to commit resources to this new area was based on a report from a British physician that the Genentech's cancer drug Rituxan eased the agony of rheumatoid arthritis in five of his patients. CEO Arthur Levinson was so impressed with this report that he immediately informed Genentech's board of directors. He urged them to support a full research program for Rituxan in autoimmune disease. With the board's blessing, Levinson launched a program to study the drug as a treatment for rheumatoid arthritis, MS, and lupus. The company deployed a third of its 1,000 researchers to pursue new drugs to fight autoimmune diseases. In 2006, Rituxan was approved to treat rheumatoid arthritis and captured 10% of the market. The company was working on some completely new approaches to autoimmune disease. The research mandate was to consider ideas others might overlook. "There's this tremendous herd instinct out there," said Levinson. "That's a great opportunity, because often the crowd is wrong."[110]

MINTZBERG'S MODES OF STRATEGIC DECISION MAKING

Some strategic decisions are made in a flash by one person (often an entrepreneur or a powerful chief executive officer) who has a brilliant insight and is quickly able to convince others to adopt his or her idea. Other strategic decisions seem to develop out of a series of small incremental choices that over time push an organization more in one direction than another. According to Henry Mintzberg, the three most typical approaches, or modes, of strategic decision making are entrepreneurial, adaptive, and planning (a fourth mode, logical incrementalism, was added later by Quinn):[111]

- **Entrepreneurial mode:** Strategy is made by one powerful individual. The focus is on opportunities; problems are secondary. Strategy is guided by the founder's own vision of direction and is exemplified by large, bold decisions. The dominant goal is growth of the corporation. Amazon.com, founded by Jeff Bezos, is an example of this mode of strategic decision making. The company reflected Bezos' vision of using the Internet to market books and more. Although Amazon's clear growth strategy was certainly an advantage of the entrepreneurial mode, Bezos' eccentric management style made it difficult to retain senior executives.[112]

- **Adaptive mode:** Sometimes referred to as "muddling through," this decision-making mode is characterized by reactive solutions to existing problems, rather than a proactive search for new opportunities. Much bargaining goes on concerning priorities of objectives. Strategy is fragmented and is developed to move a corporation forward incrementally. This mode is typical of most universities, many large hospitals, a large number of governmental agencies, and a surprising number of large corporations. Encyclopaedia Britannica Inc. operated successfully for many years in this mode, but it continued to rely on the door-to-door selling of its prestigious books long after dual-career couples made that marketing approach obsolete. Only after it was acquired in 1996 did the company change its door-to-door sales to television advertising and Internet marketing. The company now charges libraries and individual subscribers for complete access to Brittanica.com and offers CD-ROMs in addition to a small number of its 32-volume print set.[113]

- **Planning mode:** This decision-making mode involves the systematic gathering of appropriate information for situation analysis, the generation of feasible alternative strategies, and the rational selection of the most appropriate strategy. It includes both the proactive search for new opportunities and the reactive solution of existing problems. IBM under CEO Louis Gerstner is an example of the planning mode. When Gerstner accepted the position of CEO in 1993, he realized that IBM was in serious difficulty. Mainframe computers, the company's primary product line, were suffering a rapid decline both in sales and market share. One of Gerstner's first actions was to convene a two-day meeting on corporate strategy with senior executives. An in-depth analysis of IBM's product lines revealed that the only part of the company that was growing was services, but it was a relatively small segment and not very profitable. Rather than focusing on making and selling its own computer hardware, IBM made the strategic decision to invest in services that integrated information technology. IBM thus decided to provide a complete set of services from building systems to defining architecture to actually running and managing the computers for the customer—regardless of who made the products. Because it was no longer important that the company be completely vertically integrated, it sold off its DRAM, disk-drive, and laptop computer businesses and exited software application development. Since making this strategic decision in 1993, 80% of IBM's revenue growth has come from services.[114]

■ **Logical incrementalism:** A fourth decision-making mode can be viewed as a synthesis of the planning, adaptive, and, to a lesser extent, the entrepreneurial modes. In this mode, top management has a reasonably clear idea of the corporation's mission and objectives, but, in its development of strategies, it chooses to use "an interactive process in which the organization probes the future, experiments and learns from a series of partial (incremental) commitments rather than through global formulations of total strategies."[115] Thus, although the mission and objectives are set, the strategy is allowed to emerge out of debate, discussion, and experimentation. This approach appears to be useful when the environment is changing rapidly and when it is important to build consensus and develop needed resources before committing an entire corporation to a specific strategy. In his analysis of the petroleum industry, Grant described strategic planning in this industry as "planned emergence." Corporate headquarters established the mission and objectives but allowed the business units to propose strategies to achieve them.[116]

STRATEGIC DECISION-MAKING PROCESS: AID TO BETTER DECISIONS

Good arguments can be made for using either the entrepreneurial or adaptive modes (or logical incrementalism) in certain situations.[117] This book proposes, however, that in most situations the planning mode, which includes the basic elements of the strategic management process, is a more rational and thus better way of making strategic decisions. Research indicates that the planning mode is not only more analytical and less political than are the other modes, but it is also more appropriate for dealing with complex, changing environments.[118] We therefore propose the following eight-step **strategic decision-making process** to improve the making of strategic decisions (see **Figure 1–5**):

1. **Evaluate current performance results** in terms of (a) return on investment, profitability, and so forth, and (b) the current mission, objectives, strategies, and policies.

2. **Review corporate governance**—that is, the performance of the firm's board of directors and top management.

3. **Scan and assess the external environment** to determine the strategic factors that pose **O**pportunities and **T**hreats.

4. **Scan and assess the internal corporate environment** to determine the strategic factors that are Strengths (especially core competencies) and Weaknesses.

5. **Analyze strategic (SWOT) factors** to (a) pinpoint problem areas and (b) review and revise the corporate mission and objectives, as necessary.

6. **Generate, evaluate, and select the best alternative strategy** in light of the analysis conducted in step 5.

7. **Implement selected strategies** via programs, budgets, and procedures.

8. **Evaluate implemented strategies** via feedback systems, and the control of activities to ensure their minimum deviation from plans.

This rational approach to strategic decision making has been used successfully by corporations such as Warner-Lambert, Target, General Electric, IBM, Avon Products, Bechtel Group Inc., and Taisei Corporation. See **Strategy Highlight 1.6** to learn more about how strategic decision are rare consequential and directive.

1.8 The Strategic Audit: Aid to Strategic Decision-Making

The strategic decision-making process is put into action through a technique known as the strategic audit. A **strategic audit** provides a checklist of questions, by area or issue, that enables a systematic analysis to be made of various corporate functions and activities. (See **Appendix 1.A** at the end of this chapter.) Note that the numbered primary headings in the audit are the same as the numbered blocks in the strategic decision-making process in **Figure 1–5**. Beginning with an evaluation of current performance, the audit continues with environmental scanning, strategy formulation, and strategy implementation, and it concludes with evaluation and control. A strategic audit is a type of management audit and is extremely useful as a diagnostic tool to pinpoint corporatewide problem areas and to highlight organizational strengths and weaknesses.[119] A strategic audit can help determine why a certain area is creating problems for a corporation and help generate solutions to the problem.

A strategic audit is not an all-inclusive list, but it presents many of the critical questions needed for a detailed strategic analysis of any business corporation. Some questions or even some areas might be inappropriate for a particular company; in other cases, the questions may be insufficient for a complete analysis. However, each question in a particular area of a strategic audit can be broken down into an additional series of sub-questions. An analyst can develop these sub-questions when they are needed for a complete strategic analysis of a company.

STRATEGY highlight 1.6

STRATEGIC DECISIONS AT ZAPAK.COM

One example of strategic decision with all of these characteristics was the launch of Zapak.com, an online gaming portal. Zapak's success story is one of its belief in the potential of opportunity, and doing everything to turn that opportunity to a sustainable and profitable business.

The company's decision to enter into Indian online gaming industry was contrary to the belief held by major international players. However, the company decided to commit substantial resources to its decision. It went against the herd instinct, evaluated the environment, predicted the trend, and as a result proved the crowd wrong.

India has a gaming mindset, which is waiting to explode.[1] With 54% of the Indian population below the age group of 25years and having the world's largest youth population, India's only getting younger.[2] Internet usage has seen an upward swing in the last few years. The size of the Indian gaming industry was estimated at around INR 7.9 billion in 2009, compared to INR 6.5 billion in 2008, implying a growth of 22% during the period. The industry is expected to grow at a CAGR of 32% between 2009 and 2014 to reach INR 31.9 billion by 2014.[3]

Despite these statistics and the success of social networking giants such as Orkut and Facebook, U.S. online gaming majors like Miniclip and Bigfish did not visualize much market for gaming in India for better part of 2000's. Existing gaming habits of Indian users were inclined towards video games, plus the low numbers of PC and Internet penetration in India did not excite these international players.

Furthermore, none in Zapak's core team except for COO Rohit Sharma (who was heading the casual games channel of India Times in 2000) had an experience in game development. They only had experience in the dotcom industry.

However, that did not deter Zapak from seeing the vision. The team built each and every entity of Zapak from the scratch, be it the technology, the environment, or the content. After an intensive market research, i.e., observing the gaming patterns across the world and analyzing the psyche of the Indian gaming audience, the team cracked down the content strategy. It positioned itself as a brand that caters to consumer needs to

1. have fun.
2. be recognized.
3. feel a sense of achievement and
4. have a sense of belonging.

Brand ZAPAK meets the need of today's youth for world class digital entertainment content. Zapak is a way of life that empowers the youth of today to control/expand their entertainment options.

The success of Zapak has opened up the market for online gaming in the country, drawing multiple players like bees to the nectar. In order to retain its steady foothold in this competitive market, the company has believed in building a strong value chain by providing end-to-end gaming experience for the users.

As a result of its strategic decisions today, Zapak Digital Entertainment Ltd, an Anil Dhirubhai Ambani Group (ADAG) company, is India's largest online gaming company. Zapak, has over 750 games, about six million registered users, over 100 million page views a month, and nearly 250 advertisers[4] and is India's largest online casual gaming portal. Its success has led to the company expanding its value chain into gaming cafes, cd games distribution, events, and MMOG (massive multiplayer online game) products. From content to technology to distribution to merchandise, it has set up a value chain providing end-to-end gaming, a feat none of the gaming portals in the world have managed to achieve till date.

With this value chain as the backbone, Zapak has become a trend, which has revolutionized the Indian gaming market. Zapak was listed by Google India as one of the top 10 most searched phrases in India.

Courtesy: ZAPAK.com

1. Indian Express Newspapers (Mumbai) Limited (Mumbai, India), Online Gaming in India worth 21 crores, posted on 23 Apr 2007, accessed on 11 Oct 2011, from Express computer online website http://www.expresscomputeronline.com/20070423/market05.shtml

2. ITNation India Pvt. Ltd, Reliance ADAG Launches Zapak.com, posted by Techtree News Staff, 27 Nov 2006 17:26 hrs IST, accessed on 11 Oct 2011, from http://www.techtree.com/India/News/Reliance_ADAG_Launches_Zapakcom/551-77456-585.html

3. Gaming Xpress Team, FICCI report 2010: Indian Gaming Industry estimates, posted on 03 Mar 2010 16:22 hrs IST, accessed on 11 Oct 2011, from http://www.gamingxpress.com/newsitem/items/ficci-report-2010-indian-gaming-industry-estimates.html

4. S. Vimali, "Zapak: Taking Casual Games Seriously!" *SiliconIndia Magazine*, posted on December 2008, accessed on 11 Oct 2011, from http://www.siliconindia.com/magazine/articledesc.php?articleid=HETS614158728

Note: * TRAI Figure from RNCO Industry research Solutions, India—Broadband and IPTV to Lead Telecom Sector, posted on 10 Apr 2009, accessed on 11 Oct 2011, from http://www.rncos.com/Blog/2009/04/India-Broadband-and-IPTV-to-Lead-Telecom-Sector.html

FIGURE 1–5
Strategic Decision-
Making Process

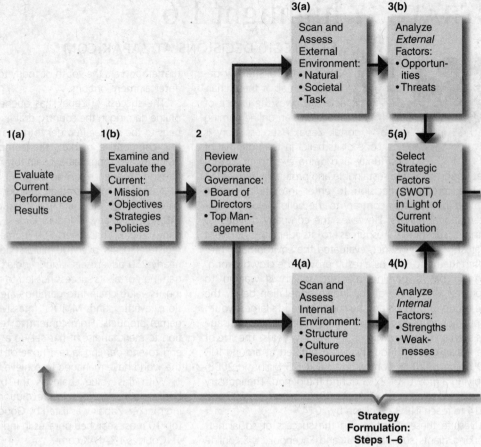

SOURCE: T. L. Wheelen and J. D. Hunger, *Strategic Decision-Making Process*. Copyright © 1994 and 1997 by Wheelen & Hunger Associates. Reprinted by permission.

ECO-BITS

- The world's primary energy consumption by fuel in 2004 was 35% oil, 25% coal, 21% natural gas, 10% biomass and waste, 6% nuclear, 2% hydroelectric, and 1% other renewable.[120]

- The price per watt of photovoltaic modules used in solar power dropped from $18 in 1980 to $4 in 2007.[121]

- Since 1869 world crude oil prices, adjusted for inflation, have averaged $21.66 per barrel in 2006 dollars. By 2008, the price per barrel reached $140 for the first time in history.[122]

DISCUSSION QUESTIONS

1. Why has strategic management become so important to today's corporations?

2. How does strategic management typically evolve in a corporation?

3. What is a learning organization? Is this approach to strategic management better than the more traditional top-down approach in which strategic planning is primarily done by top management?

4. Why are strategic decisions different from other kinds of decisions?

5. When is the planning mode of strategic decision making superior to the entrepreneurial and adaptive modes?

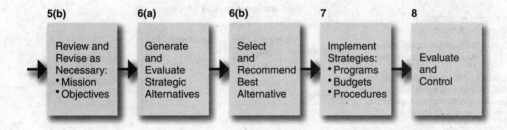

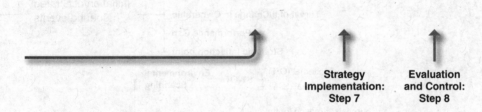

6. What is strategic management? How is it different from business environment? Discuss the phases of strategic management.

7. What are the common triggering events that act as stimuli for strategic change?

8. Climate change in an industry can put a company through different types of risks. Discuss these six categories of risks.

9. Discuss the various theories of organizational adaptation.

10. Discuss the basic model of strategic management.

11. Discuss the role of strategic audit in strategic decision making process.

STRATEGIC PRACTICE EXERCISES

Mission statements vary widely from one company to another. Why is one mission statement better than another?
Collect mission statements for 10 public and private sector organization in India. Use Campbell's questions in **Strategy**

Highlight 1.4 as a starting point to evaluate the mission statements. Who defines mission statements better in India, public sector or private sector companies?

Let's Summarize the Chapter with a Mind Map

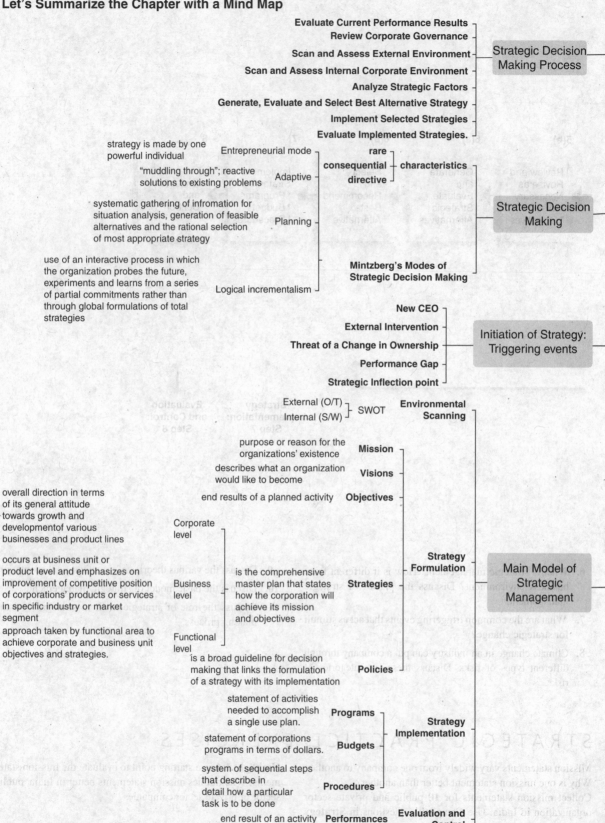

Strategic Decision Making Process
- Evaluate Current Performance Results
- Review Corporate Governance
- Scan and Assess External Environment
- Scan and Assess Internal Corporate Environment
- Analyze Strategic Factors
- Generate, Evaluate and Select Best Alternative Strategy
- Implement Selected Strategies
- Evaluate Implemented Strategies.

Strategic Decision Making

Mintzberg's Modes of Strategic Decision Making
- Entrepreneurial mode — strategy is made by one powerful individual
- Adaptive — "muddling through"; reactive solutions to existing problems
- Planning — systematic gathering of infromation for situation analysis, generation of feasible alternatives and the rational selection of most appropriate strategy
- Logical incrementalism — use of an interactive process in which the organization probes the future, experiments and learns from a series of partial commitments rather than through global formulations of total strategies

characteristics
- rare
- consequential
- directive

Initiation of Strategy: Triggering events
- New CEO
- External Intervention
- Threat of a Change in Ownership
- Performance Gap
- Strategic Inflection point

Main Model of Strategic Management

Environmental Scanning
- SWOT — External (O/T), Internal (S/W)

Strategy Formulation
- Mission — purpose or reason for the organizations' existence
- Visions — describes what an organization would like to become
- Objectives — end results of a planned activity
- Strategies — is the comprehensive master plan that states how the corporation will achieve its mission and objectives
  - Corporate level — overall direction in terms of its general attitude towards growth and developmentof various businesses and product lines
  - Business level — occurs at business unit or product level and emphasizes on improvement of competitive position of corporations' products or services in specific industry or market segment
  - Functional level — approach taken by functional area to achieve corporate and business unit objectives and strategies.
- Policies — is a broad guideline for decision making that links the formulation of a strategy with its implementation

Strategy Implementation
- Programs — statement of activities needed to accomplish a single use plan.
- Budgets — statement of corporations programs in terms of dollars.
- Procedures — system of sequential steps that describe in detail how a particular task is to be done

Evaluation and Control
- Performances — end result of an activity
- Feedback/ Learning process

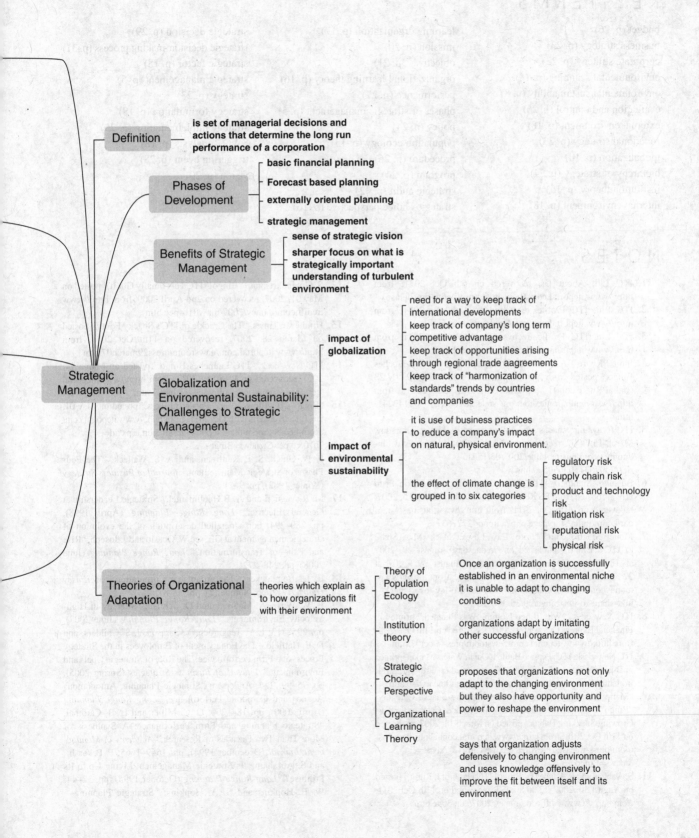

Strategic Management

Definition — is set of managerial decisions and actions that determine the long run performance of a corporation

Phases of Development
- basic financial planning
- Forecast based planning
- externally oriented planning
- strategic management

Benefits of Strategic Management
- sense of strategic vision
- sharper focus on what is strategically important understanding of turbulent environment

Globalization and Environmental Sustainability: Challenges to Strategic Management

impact of globalization
- need for a way to keep track of international developments
- keep track of company's long term competitive advantage
- keep track of opportunities arising through regional trade aagreements
- keep track of "harmonization of standards" trends by countries and companies

impact of environmental sustainability
- it is use of business practices to reduce a company's impact on natural, physical environment.
- the effect of climate change is grouped in to six categories
  - regulatory risk
  - supply chain risk
  - product and technology risk
  - litigation risk
  - reputational risk
  - physical risk

Theories of Organizational Adaptation — theories which explain as to how organizations fit with their environment

- **Theory of Population Ecology** — Once an organization is successfully established in an environmental niche it is unable to adapt to changing conditions
- **Institution theory** — organizations adapt by imitating other successful organizations
- **Strategic Choice Perspective** — proposes that organizations not only adapt to the changing environment but they also have opportunity and power to reshape the environment
- **Organizational Learning Theory** — says that organization adjusts defensively to changing environment and uses knowledge offensively to improve the fit between itself and its environment

KEY TERMS

budget (p. 26)
business strategy (p. 23)
corporate strategy (p. 23)
environmental scanning (p. 18)
environmental sustainability (p. 8)
evaluation and control (p. 26)
external environment (p. 18)
functional strategy (p. 23)
globalization (p. 10)
hierarchy of strategy (p. 24)
institution theory (p. 15)
internal environment (p. 18)

learning organization (p. 17)
mission (p. 20)
objectives (p. 21)
organizational learning theory (p. 16)
performance (p. 27)
phases of strategic management (p. 5)
policy (p. 24)
population ecology (p. 15)
procedure (p. 26)
program (p. 24)
strategic audit (p. 32)
strategic choice perspective (p. 16)

strategic decision (p. 29)
strategic decision-making process (p. 31)
strategic factor (p. 18)
strategic management (p. 5)
strategy (p. 23)
strategy formulation (p. 18)
strategy implementation (p. 25)
SWOT analysis (p. 18)
triggering event (p. 28)
vision (p. 20)

NOTES

1. ITC Ltd, About Us, recovered on 6th Oct 2011, from http://www.itcportal.com/about-itc/itc-profile/itc-profile.aspx
2. ITC Ltd, ITC Profile, recovered on 11th Oct 2011, from http://www.itcportal.com/sets/itc_frameset.htm
3. ITC Ltd, ITC Profile, recovered on 11th Oct 2011, from http://www.itcportal.com/sets/itc_frameset.htm
4. India PRwire—A Dark Blue Company, "ITC Foods Launches Bingo," posted from New Delhi, India, 2007-03-14 21:07:28 (IndiaPRwire.com), recovered on 11th Oct 2011, from http://www.indiaprwire.com/pressrelease/food/200703142241.htm
5. ITC forays into snacks segment; to invest Rs 150 cr, Thursday, March 15, 2007, recovered on 11th Oct 2011, http://www.hinduonnet.com/businessline/2007/03/15/stories/2007031503650500.htm
6. Business Standard, "ITC Rolls Out Bingo to Take on Frito Lay's," posted from BS Reporter / New Delhi, March 15, 2007, recovered on 11th Oct 2011, from http://www.business-standard.com/india/storypage.php?autono=277763
7. Money control.com, "Frito Lay Loses Snack Mkt Share to ITC's Bingo," published on Wednesday, August 29, 2007 at 18:56 hrs, Updated at Wednesday, August 29, 2007 at 22:32 hrs, recovered on 11th Oct 2011, from http://www.moneycontrol.com/india/news/business/frito-lay-loses-snack-mkt-share-to-itcs-bingo/20/35/300325
8. ITC Newsdesk, "With Bingo Nothing Was Planned," printed in Financial Express October 09, 2007, recovered on 11th Oct 2011, from http://www.itcportal.com/newsroom/press09oct07.htm
9. ITC Newsdesk, ITC, Pepsico Battle It Out in Wafers Market, printed in Business Standard, June 6, 2007, recovered on 11th Oct 2011, from http://www.itcportal.com/newsroom/press06june07-b.htm
10. "Marks Company's Foray into the Evolving Snacks Category: "Bingo" Set to Tickle Indian Snacking Palate & Cater to the Fast Growing Snacking Habits," posted on March 14, 2007, recovered on 11th Oct 2011, from http://www.itcportal.com/about-itc/newsroom/press-releases/PressRelease.aspx?id=127&type=C&news=Bingo
11. S. Aabhas and R. Pandeya, "Bingo! ITC Has Got It Right," posted on August 30, 2007 12:06 hrs IST, recovered on 11th Oct 2011, from http://www.rediff.com/money/2007/aug/30itc.htm
12. S. Govindkrishna, "'Bingo!' ITC Has Finally Got It," posted on May 01, 2007, recovered on 2nd April 2009, from http://www.rediff.com/money/2007/may/01bspec.htm
13. Hindustan Times, "The Crackle of ITC's Snacky Foray," posted on March 28, 2007, recovered on 11th Oct 2011, from http://www.itcportal.com/newsroom/press29march07.htm
14. ITC Newsdesk, "ITC Launches Bingo," posted on March 14, 2007, recovered on 11th Oct 2011, from http://www.itcportal.com/newsroom/press_releases_14mar07.htm
15. "Bingo! ITC Turns Around Foods Business," posted on May 01, 2011, recovered on 11th Oct 2011, from http://www.itcportal.com/about-itc/newsroom/press-reports/PressReport.aspx?id=1070&type=C&news=Bingo-
16. F. W. Gluck, S. P. Kaufman, and A. S. Walleck, "The Four Phases of Strategic Management," *Journal of Business Strategy* (Winter 1982), pp. 9–21.
17. M. R. Vaghefi and A. B Huellmantel, "Strategic Leadership at General Electric," *Long Range Planning* (April 1998), pp. 280–294. For a detailed description of the evolution of strategic management at GE, see W. Ocasio and J. Joseph, "Rise and Fall—or Transformation?" *Long Range Planning* (June 2008), pp. 248–272.
18. E. D. Beinhocker, "The Adaptable Corporation," *McKinsey Quarterly* (2006, Number 2), pp. 77–87.
19. B. W. Wirtz, A. Mathieu, and O. Schilke, "Strategy in High-Velocity Environments," *Long Range Planning* (June 2007), pp. 295–313; L. F. Teagarden, Y. Sarason, J. S. Childers, and D. E. Hatfield, "The Engagement of Employees in the Strategy Process and Firm Performance: The Role of Strategic Goals and Environment," *Journal of Business Strategies* (Spring 2005), pp. 75–99; T. J. Andersen, "Strategic Planning, Autonomous Actions and Corporate Performance," *Long Range Planning* (April 2000), pp. 184–200; C. C. Miller and L. B. Cardinal, "Strategic Planning and Firm Performance: A Synthesis of More Than Two Decades of Research," *Academy of Management Journal* (December 1994), pp. 1649–1665; P. Pekar Jr., and S. Abraham, "Is Strategic Management Living Up to Its Promise?" *Long Range Planning* (October 1995), pp. 32–44; W. E. Hopkins and S. A. Hopkins, "Strategic Planning—

Financial Performance Relationship in Banks: A Causal Examination," *Strategic Management Journal* (September 1997), pp. 635–652.

20. E. J. Zajac, M. S. Kraatz, and R. F. Bresser, "Modeling the Dynamics of Strategic Fit: A Normative Approach to Strategic Change," *Strategic Management Journal* (April 2000), pp. 429–453; M. Peteraf and R. Reed, "Managerial Discretion and Internal Alignment Under Regulatory Constraints and Change," *Strategic Management Journal* (November 2007), pp. 1089–1112; C. S. Katsikeas, S. Samiee, and M. Theodosiou, "Strategy Fit and Performance Consequences of International Marketing Standardization," *Strategic Management Journal* (September 2006), pp. 867–890.

21. P. Brews and D. Purohit, "Strategic Planning in Unstable Environments," *Long Range Planning* (February 2007), pp. 64–83.

22. S. S. Debasish, "Service Quality in Commercial Banks: A Comparative Analysis of Selected Banks in India," *Indian Journal of Marketing*, Vol. 1, No. 1 (2002), pp. 3–10.

23. M. Minakshi and S. Arora, "Customer Satisfaction—A Comparative Analysis of Public and Private Sector Banks," *Abhigyan*, Vol. XVII, No. 3 (1999), pp. 19–30.

24. S. Arora, "Bank Selection Criteria—A Comparative Analysis of Public, Private and Foreign Sector Bank Customers," *Abhigyan*, Vol. XVIII, No. 4 (2000), pp. 29–33.

25. S. Swain (2007), "Money & Banking: The Financial Express," *Thriving on Innovation*, recovered from Financial Express website http://www.financialexpress.com/fe_full_story.php?content_id=167407, recovered on 23 June 2008, posted on June 18, 2007.

26. Media Release Febuary 23, 2005, Indian Public Sector Banks Now Can Complete Freely with Foreign and Private Banks—Chidambaram, recovered from http://www.indiadaily.com/editorial/1688.asp, recovered on 10th June 2007.

27. Lal, Rajiv and Rachna Tahilyani, State Bank of India: Transforming a State Owned Giant, Harvard Business School, 38 pages. Publication date: Mar 28, 2011. Prod. #: 511114-PDF-ENG

28. Milind Sathye (2003), " Efficiency of banks in a developing economy: The case of India," European Journal of Operational Research, Volume 148, Issue 3, 1 August 2003, Pages 662-671

29. I. Wilson, "Strategic Planning Isn't Dead—It Changed," *Long Range Planning* (August 1994), p. 20.

30. R. Dye and O. Sibony, "How to Improve Strategic Planning," *McKinsey Quarterly* (2007, Number 3), pp. 40–48.

31. W. M. Becker and V. M. Freeman, "Going from Global Trends to Corporate Strategy," *McKinsey Quarterly* (2006, Number 2), pp. 17–27.

32. D. Rigby and B. Bilodeau, *Management Tools and Trends 2007*, Bain & Company (2007).

33. W. Joyce, "What Really Works: Building the 4+2 Organization," *Organizational Dynamics* (Vol. 34, Issue 2, 2005), pp. 118–129. See also W. Joyce, N. Nohria, and B. Roberson, *What Really Works: The 4+2 Formula for Sustained Business Success* (HarperBusiness), 2003.

34. R. M. Grant, "Strategic Planning in a Turbulent Environment: Evidence from the Oil Majors," *Strategic Management Journal* (June 2003), pp. 491–517.

35. M. J. Peel and J. Bridge, "How Planning and Capital Budgeting Improve SME Performance," *Long Range Planning* (December 1998), pp. 848–856; L. W. Rue and N. A. Ibrahim, "The Relationship Between Planning Sophistication and Performance in Small Businesses," *Journal of Small Business Management* (October 1998), pp. 24–32; J. C. Carland and J. W. Carland, "A Model of Entrepreneurial Planning and Its Effect on Performance," paper presented to Association for Small Business and Entrepreneurship (Houston, TX, 2003).

36. R. M. Grant, "Strategic Planning in a Turbulent Environment: Evidence from the Oil Majors," *Strategic Management Journal* (June 2003), pp. 491–517.

37. A. Sujata, "Tata International Has Emerged as the Global Face of the Tata Group," posted on March 2004, recovered on 11th Oct 2011, from http://www.tata.in/article.aspx?artid=uma9RJD0EHA=

38. T. L. Friedman, *The World Is Flat* (NY: Farrar, Strauss & Giroux), 2005.

39. A. K. Gupta, V. Govindarajan, and H. Wang, *The Quest for Global Dominance*, 2nd ed. (San Francisco: Jossey-Bass, 2008).

40. Wharton School of the University of Pennsylvania (2005), Knowledge@Wharton, R&D in India: The Curtain Rises, The Play Has Begun... , posted on November 21, 2005, recovered on 11th Oct 2011, from http://knowledge.wharton.upenn.edu/article.cfm?articleid=1278&specialid=40

41. Hyundai Motor India Ltd Profile: R & D Centre, recovered on 11th Oct 2011, from http://www.hyundai.com/in/en/Company-Infomation/HMI/RDCenter/RND.htm

42. Computer Patent Annuities Limited 2009, Legal Outsourcing, Study: India Outsourcing Potential in Pharma R&D, posted on August 22, 2008, recovered on 11th Oct 2011, from http://www.cpaglobal.com/ip-review-online/3090/study_india_outsourcing_potential_in_pharma_rd

43. Quoted in "Companies that Expand Abroad: 'Knowledge Seekers' vs. Conquerors," *Knowledge @ Wharton.com* (March 24, 2004), p. 1.

44. Indian Institute of Materials Management, "Corporate India Gets ECO Friendly," recovered on 11th Oct 2011, from http://www.iimm.org/knowledge_bank/8_corporate-india-gets-eco-friendly.htm

45. S. K. Maheshwari, Alternative Fuel Solutions, Grasim Industries Limited, August 2007, recovered on 11th Oct 2011, from http://www.grasim.com/media/press_reports/alternative_fuel_solutions.htm

46. S. M. J. Bonini, G. Hintz, and L. T. Mendonca, "Addressing Consumer Concerns about Climate Change," *McKinsey Quarterly* (March 2008), pp. 1–9.

47. A. J. Hoffman, *Getting Ahead of the Curve: Corporate Strategies that Address Climate Change* (Ann Arbor: University of Michigan, 2006), p. iii.

48. M. E. Porter and F. L. Reinhardt, "A Strategic Approach to Climate," *Harvard Business Review* (October 2007), p. 22.

49. "The Rising Costs of Global Warming," *Futurist* (November–December 2005), p. 13.

50. J. Lash and F. Wellington, "Competitive Advantage on a Warming Planet," *Harvard Business Review* (March 2007), pp. 95–102.

51. Igoverment, Obama plays tough on global warming, Copyright Blue Slate Media, posted on January 22, 2009, 4:54:40 PM, recovered on 11th Oct 2011 from http://www.igovernment.in/PrintStory.aspx?Id=6741

52. "Melting Asia," *The Economist* (June 7, 2008), pp. 29–32.

53. P. Engardio, "Can the U.S. Bring Jobs Back from China?" *Business Week* (June 30, 2008), pp. 39–43.

54. P. Roberts, "Tapped Out," *National Geographic* (June 2008), pp. 87–91.

55. T. Rooselt IV and J. Llewelyn, "Investors Hunger for Clean Energy," *Harvard Business Review* (October 2007), p. 38.

56. Nielsen, "Indian Consumers Conscious of Environmental Benefits of Sustainable Practices," posted on August 28, 2011, Mumbai, India, recovered on 11th Oct 2011, form http://in.nielsen.com/news/20110828.shtml

57. R. K. Pachauri, "The Future of India's Economic Growth: The Natural Resources and Energy Dimension," *Futures,* Vol. 36 (2004), 703–713.

58. Ganapati Information Technology Services, Environmental Pollution in India, recovered on 11th Oct 2011, from http://www.gits4u.com/envo/envo4.htm#Pollution%20due%20to%20Mining

59. Zee News Limited, "Courts Can't Afford to Deal with Pollution Cases Causally: SC," recovered on 11th Oct 2011, from http://www.zeenews.com/Nation/2008-12-12/490556news.html#

60. Zee News Limited, "Delhi's Polluting Industries to Be Made Hitech," posted on Sunday, January 10, 2010, 19:43 hrs, recovered on 11th Oct 2011, from http://zeenews.india.com/news/business/delhi-s-polluting-industries-to-be-made-hi-ech_594584.html

61. Collage Article 13, Executive summary and recommendations: CSR in India—perspectives for business May 2007, posted on May 1, 2007, prepared by Article 13 Group, UK, prepared for Collage Article 13, India, recovered on 11th Oct 2011, from http://www.article13.com/OurPublications/CSR%20in%20India_May%202007.pdf

62. R. Ringger and S. A. DiPiazza, *Sustainability Yearbook 2008* (PricewaterhouseCoopers, 2008).

63. L. T. Mendonca and J. Oppenheim, "Investing in Sustainability: An Interview with Al Gore and David Blood," *McKinsey Quarterly* (May 2007).

64. A. J. Hoffman, *Getting Ahead of the Curve: Corporate Strategies that Address Climate Change* (Ann Arbor: University of Michigan, 2006), p. 2.

65. J. K. Bourne, Jr., "Signs of Change," *National Geographic* (Special Report on Changing Climate, 2008), pp. 7–21.

66. "Melting Asia," *The Economist* (June 7, 2008), pp. 29–32.

67. J. Welch and S. Welch, "The Global Warming Wager," *Business Week* (February 26, 2007), p. 130.

68. J. A. C. Baum, "Organizational Ecology," in *Handbook of Organization Studies*, edited by S. R. Clegg, C. Handy, and W. Nord (London: Sage, 1996), pp. 77–114.

69. B. M. Staw and L. D. Epstein, "What Bandwagons Bring: Effects of Popular Management Techniques on Corporate Performance, Reputation, and CEO Pay," *Administrative Science Quarterly* (September 2000), pp. 523–556; M. B. Lieberman and S. Asaba, "Why Do Firms Imitate Each Other?" *Academy of Management Review* (April 2006), pp. 366–385.

70. T. W. Ruefli and R. R. Wiggins, "Industry, Corporate, and Segment Effects and Business Performance: A Non-Parametric Approach," *Strategic Management Journal* (September 2003), pp. 861–879; Y. E. Spanos, G. Zaralis, and S. Lioukas, "Strategy and Industry Effects on Profitability: Evidence from Greece," *Strategic Management Journal* (February 2004), pp. 139–165; E. H. Bowman and C. E. Helfat, "Does Corporate Strategy Matter?" *Strategic Management Journal* (January 2001), pp. 1–23; T. H. Brush, P. Bromiley, and M. Hendrickx, "The Relative Influence of Industry and Corporation on Business Segment Performance: An Alternative Estimate," *Strategic Management Journal* (June 1999), pp. 519–547; K. M. Gilley, B. A. Walters, and

B. J. Olson, "Top Management Team Risk Taking Propensities and Firm Performance: Direct and Moderating Effects," *Journal of Business Strategies* (Fall 2002), pp. 95–114.

71. For more information on these theories, see A. Y. Lewin and H. W. Voloberda, "Prolegomena on Coevolution: A Framework for Research on Strategy and New Organizational Forms," *Organization Science* (October 1999), pp. 519–534, and H. Aldrich, *Organizations Evolving* (London: Sage, 1999), pp. 43–74.

72. R. A. D'Aveni, *Hypercompetition* (New York: The Free Press, 1994). Hypercompetition is discussed in more detail in Chapter 4.

73. R. S. M. Lau, "Strategic Flexibility: A New Reality for World-Class Manufacturing," *SAM Advanced Management Journal* (Spring 1996), pp. 11–15.

74. M. A. Hitt, B. W. Keats, and S. M. DeMarie, "Navigating in the New Competitive Landscape: Building Strategic Flexibility and Competitive Advantage in the 21st Century," *Academy of Management Executive* (November 1998), pp. 22–42.

75. D. Lei, J. W. Slocum, and R. A. Pitts, "Designing Organizations for Competitive Advantage: The Power of Unlearning and Learning," *Organizational Dynamics* (Winter 1999), pp. 24–38; M. Goold, "Making Peer Groups Effective: Lessons from BP's Experience," *Long Range Planning* (October 2005), pp. 429–443.

76. S. C. Voelpel, M. Dous, and T. H. Davenport, "Five Steps to Creating a Global Knowledge-Sharing System: Siemens' ShareNet," *Academy of Management Executive* (May 2005), pp. 9–23.

77. D. A. Garvin, "Building a Learning Organization," *Harvard Business Review* (July/August 1993), p. 80. See also P. M. Senge, *The Fifth Discipline: The Art and Practice of the Learning Organization* (New York: Doubleday, 1990).

78. A. D. Chandler, *Inventing the Electronic Century* (New York: The Free Press, 2001).

79. T. T. Baldwin, C. Danielson, and W. Wiggenhorn, "The Evolution of Learning Strategies in Organizations: From Employee Development to Business Redefinition," *Academy of Management Executive* (November 1997), pp. 47–58.

80. N. Collier, F. Fishwick, and S. W. Floyd, "Managerial Involvement and Perceptions of Strategy Process," *Long Range Planning* (February 2004), pp. 67–83; J. A. Parnell, S. Carraher, and K. Holt, "Participative Management's Influence on Effective Strategic Planning," *Journal of Business Strategies* (Fall 2002), pp. 161–179; M. Ketokivi and X. Castaner, "Strategic Planning as an Integrative Device," *Administrative Science Quarterly* (September 2004), pp. 337–365.

81. E. W. K. Tsang, "Internationalization as a Learning Process: Singapore MNCs in China," *Academy of Management Executive* (February 1999), pp. 91–101; J. M. Shaver, W. Mitchell, and B. Yeung, "The Effect of Own-Firm and Other Firm Experience on Foreign Direct Investment Survival in the U.S., 1987–92," *Strategic Management Journal* (November 1997), pp. 811–824; P. Kale and H. Singh, "Building Firm Capabilities through Learning: The Role of the Alliance Learning Process in Alliance Capability and Firm-Level Alliance Success," *Strategic Management Journal* (October 2007), pp. 981–1000; H. Barkema and M. Schijven, "How Do Firms Learn to Make Acquisitions? A Review of Past Research and an Agenda for the Future," *Journal of Management* (June 2008), pp. 594–634; D. D. Bergh and E. N-K Lim, "Learning How to Restructure: Absorptive Capacity and Improvisational Views of Restructuring Actions and Performance," *Strategic Management Journal* (June 2008), pp. 593–616.

82. R. Wiltbank, N. Dew, S. Read, and S. D. Sarasvathy, "What To Do Next? The Case for Non-Predictive Strategy," *Strategic Management Journal* (October 2006), pp. 981–998; J. A. Smith, "Strategies for Start-Ups," *Long Range Planning* (December 1998), pp. 857–872.

83. J. S. Sidhu, "Business-Domain Definition and Performance: An Empirical Study," *SAM Advanced Management Journal* (Autumn 2004), pp. 40–45.

84. See A. Campbell and S. Yeung, "Brief Case: Mission, Vision, and Strategic Intent," *Long Range Planning* (August 1991), pp. 145–147; S. Cummings and J. Davies, "Mission, Vision, Fusion," *Long Range Planning* (December 1994), pp. 147–150.

85. S. Baker, "Google and the Wisdom of Clouds," *Business Week* (December 24, 2007), pp. 49–55. Courtesy of Google Inc. GOOGLE is a trademark of Google Inc.

86. J. Cosco, "Down to the Sea in Ships," *Journal of Business Strategy* (November/December 1995), p. 48.

87. Ebharatgas, recovered on 11th Oct 2011, from http://www.ebharatgas.com/ebgas/pages/general/gen_menu2.jsp

88. Bank of Baroda, recovered on 11th Oct 2011, from http://www.bankofbaroda.co.in/aboutus.asp

89. Nirma, recovered on 11th Oct 2011, from http://www.nirma.co.in/vision_mission.htm

90. J. S. Sidhu, E. J. Nijssen, and H. R. Commandeur, "Business Domain Definition Practice: Does It Affect Organizational Performance?" *Long Range Planning* (June 2000), pp. 376–401.

91. "Time to Break Off a Chunk," *The Economist* (December 15, 2007), pp. 75–76.

92. Pantaloon Retail (India) Ltd, Big Bazaar, recovered on 11th Oct 2011, from http://www.pantaloon.com/fashion-bigbazaar.asp

93. Financial Express, Pantaloon expands reach of Big Bazaar, posted on Jan 30, 2002 at 0000 hrs IST, recovered on 11th Oct 2011, from http://www.financialexpress.com/news/pantaloon-expands-reach-of-big-bazaar/36157/0

94. India PRwire—A Dark Blue Company, Kingfisher Airlines partners with PayMate to launch FlyBuySmsTM, the first of its kind sms based mobile flight ticketing service, posted from Mumbai, Maharashtra, India, 2007-10-11 14:30:00, recovered on 11th Oct 2011, from http://www.indiaprwire.com/pressrelease/telecommunications/200710115010.htm

95. K. M. Eisenhardt and D. N. Sull, "Strategy as Simple Rules," *Harvard Business Review* (January 2001), p. 110.

96. D. Welch, "Cadillac Hits the Gas," *Business Week* (September 4, 2000), p. 50.

97. S. Holmes, "GE: Little Engines That Could," *Business Week* (January 20, 2003), pp. 62–63.

98. L. J. Karjewski, L. P. Ritzman, and M. K. Malhotra, *Operations Management: Processes and Value Chains* (New Delhi: Dorling Kindersley (India) Pvt. Ltd, 2008), p. 635.

99. H. A. Simon, *Administrative Behavior*, 2nd edition (New York: The Free Press, 1957), p. 231.

100. L. Lee and P. Burrows, "Is Dell Too Big for Michael Dell?" *Business Week* (February 12, 2007), p. 33.

101. I Love India.com, Nirma Ltd, recovered on 11th Oct 2011, from http://www.iloveindia.com/economy-of-india/top-50-companies/nirma.html

102. A. Sushant, "Success Story of Nirma," recovered on 11th Oct 2011, from http://toostep.com/insight/success-story-of-nirma

103. L. J. Karjewski, L. P. Ritzman, and M. K. Malhotra, *Operations Management: Processes and Value Chains* (New Delhi: Dorling Kindersley (India) Pvt. Ltd, 2008), p. 54.

104. H. Mintzberg, "Planning on the Left Side and Managing on the Right," *Harvard Business Review* (July–August 1976), p. 56.

105. R. A. Burgelman and A. S. Grove, "Let Chaos Reign, Then Reign In Chaos—Repeatedly: Managing Strategic Dynamics for Corporate Longevity," *Strategic Management Journal* (October 2007), pp. 965–979.

106. See E. Romanelli and M. L. Tushman, "Organizational Transformation as Punctuated Equilibrium: An Empirical Test," *Academy of Management Journal* (October 1994), pp. 1141–1166.

107. S. S. Gordon, W. H. Stewart, Jr., R. Sweo, and W. A. Luker, "Convergence versus Strategic Reorientation: The Antecedents of Fast-Paced Organizational Change," *Journal of Management*, Vol. 26, No. 5 (2000), pp. 911–945.

108. Speech to the 1998 Academy of Management, reported by S. M. Puffer, "Global Executive: Intel's Andrew Grove on Competitiveness," *Academy of Management Executive* (February 1999), pp. 15–24.

109. D. J. Hickson, R. J. Butler, D. Cray, G. R. Mallory, and D. C. Wilson, *Top Decisions: Strategic Decision Making in Organizations* (San Francisco: Jossey-Bass, 1986), pp. 26–42.

110. A. Weintraub, "Genentech's Gamble," *Business Week* (December 17, 2007), pp. 44–48.

111. H. Mintzberg, "Strategy-Making in Three Modes," *California Management Review* (Winter 1973), pp. 44–53.

112. F. Vogelstein, "Mighty Amazon," *Fortune* (May 26, 2003), pp. 60–74.

113. M. Wong, "Once-Prized Encyclopedias Fall into Disuse," *Des Moines Register* (March 9, 2004), p. 3D.

114. L. V. Gerstner, *Who Says Elephants Can't Dance?* (New York: HarperCollins, 2002).

115. J. B. Quinn, *Strategies for Change: Logical Incrementalism* (Homewood, IL.: Irwin, 1980), p. 58.

116. R. M. Grant, "Strategic Planning in a Turbulent Environment: Evidence from the Oil Majors," *Strategic Management Journal* (June 2003), pp. 491–517.

117. G. Gavetti and J. W. Rivkin, "Seek Strategy the Right Way at the Right Time," *Harvard Business Review* (January 2008), pp. 22–23.

118. P. J. Brews and M. R. Hunt, "Learning to Plan and Planning to Learn: Resolving the Planning School/Learning School Debate," *Strategic Management Journal* (October 1999), pp. 889–913; I. Gold and A. M. A. Rasheed, "Rational Decision-Making and Firm Performance: The Moderating Role of the Environment," *Strategic Management Journal* (August 1997), pp. 583–591; R. L. Priem, A. M. A. Rasheed, and A. G. Kotulic, "Rationality in Strategic Decision Processes, Environmental Dynamism and Firm Performance," *Journal of Management*, Vol. 21, No. 5 (1995), pp. 913–929; J. W. Dean, Jr., and M. P. Sharfman, "Does Decision Process Matter? A Study of Strategic Decision-Making Effectiveness," *Academy of Management Journal* (April 1996), pp. 368–396.

119. T. L. Wheelen and J. D. Hunger, "Using the Strategic Audit," *SAM Advanced Management Journal* (Winter 1987), pp. 4–12; G. Donaldson, "A New Tool for Boards: The Strategic Audit," *Harvard Business Review* (July–August 1995), pp. 99–107.

120. "The Power and the Glory," *The Economist*, Special Report on Energy (June 21, 2008), pp. 3–6.

121. "Another Silicon Valley?" *The Economist*, Special Report on Energy (June 21, 2008), pp. 14–15.

122. J. L. Williams, "Oil Price History and Analysis," *WTRG Economics* (http://www.wtrg.com/prices.htm, accessed June 27, 2008).

Strategic Audit of a Corporation

I. Current Situation

A. Current Performance

How did the corporation perform the past year overall in terms of return on investment, market share, and profitability?

B. Strategic Posture

What are the corporation's current mission, objectives, strategies, and policies?

1. Are they clearly stated, or are they merely implied from performance?

2. **Mission:** What business(es) is the corporation in? Why?

3. **Objectives:** What are the corporate, business, and functional objectives? Are they consistent with each other, with the mission, and with the internal and external environments?

4. **Strategies:** What strategy or mix of strategies is the corporation following? Are they consistent with each other, with the mission and objectives, and with the internal and external environments?

5. **Policies:** What are the corporation's policies? Are they consistent with each other, with the mission, objectives, and strategies, and with the internal and external environments?

6. Do the current mission, objectives, strategies, and policies reflect the corporation's international operations, whether global or multidomestic?

II. Corporate Governance

A. Board of Directors

1. Who is on the board? Are they internal (employees) or external members?

2. Do they own significant shares of stock?

3. Is the stock privately held or publicly traded? Are there different classes of stock with different voting rights?

4. What do the board members contribute to the corporation in terms of knowledge, skills, background, and connections? If the corporation has international operations, do board members have international experience? Are board members concerned with environmental sustainability?

SOURCE: T.L. Wheelen, J.D. Hunger, Strategic Audit of a Corporation, Copyright © 1982 by Wheelen & Hunger Associates. Reprinted by permission. Revised 1988, 1991, 1994, 1997, 2000, 2002, 2005, and 2008.

5. How long have the board members served on the board?

6. What is their level of involvement in strategic management? Do they merely rubber-stamp top management's proposals or do they actively participate and suggest future directions? Do they evaluate management's proposals in terms of environmental sustainability?

B. Top Management

1. What person or group constitutes top management?

2. What are top management's chief characteristics in terms of knowledge, skills, background, and style? If the corporation has international operations, does top management have international experience? Are executives from acquired companies considered part of the top management team?

3. Has top management been responsible for the corporation's performance over the past few years? How many managers have been in their current position for less than three years? Were they promoted internally or externally hired?

4. Has top management established a systematic approach to strategic management?

5. What is top management's level of involvement in the strategic management process?

6. How well does top management interact with lower-level managers and with the board of directors?

7. Are strategic decisions made ethically in a socially responsible manner?

8. Are strategic decisions made in an environmentally sustainable manner?

9. Do top executives own significant amounts of stock in the corporation?

10. Is top management sufficiently skilled to cope with likely future challenges?

III. External Environment: Opportunities and Threats (SW**OT**)

A. Natural Physical Environment: Sustainability Issues

1. What forces from the natural physical environmental are currently affecting the corporation and the industries in which it competes? Which present current or future threats? Opportunities?
   a. Climate, including global temperature, sea level, and fresh water availability
   b. Weather-related events, such as severe storms, floods, and droughts
   c. Solar phenomena, such as sun spots and solar wind

2. Do these forces have different effects in other regions of the world?

B. Societal Environment

1. What general environmental forces are currently affecting both the corporation and the industries in which it competes? Which present current or future threats? Opportunities?
   a. Economic
   b. Technological
   c. Political–legal
   d. Sociocultural

2. Are these forces different in other regions of the world?

C. Task Environment

1. What forces drive industry competition? Are these forces the same globally or do they vary from country to country? Rate each force as **high, medium,** or **low.**
   a. Threat of new entrants
   b. Bargaining power of buyers
   c. Threat of substitute products or services
   d. Bargaining power of suppliers
   e. Rivalry among competing firms
   f. Relative power of unions, governments, special interest groups, etc.

2. What key factors in the immediate environment (that is, customers, competitors, suppliers, creditors, labor unions, governments, trade associations, interest groups, local communities, and shareholders) are currently affecting the corporation? Which are current or future Threats? Opportunities?

D. Summary of External Factors
(List in the EFAS Table 4–5, p. 152)

Which of these forces and factors are the most important to the corporation and to the industries in which it competes at the present time? Which will be important in the future?

IV. Internal Environment:
Strengths and Weaknesses (<u>SW</u>OT)

A. Corporate Structure

1. How is the corporation structured at present?
   a. Is the decision-making authority centralized around one group or decentralized to many units?
   b. Is the corporation organized on the basis of functions, projects, geography, or some combination of these?

2. Is the structure clearly understood by everyone in the corporation?

3. Is the present structure consistent with current corporate objectives, strategies, policies, and programs, as well as with the firm's international operations?

4. In what ways does this structure compare with those of similar corporations?

B. Corporate Culture

1. Is there a well-defined or emerging culture composed of shared beliefs, expectations, and values?

2. Is the culture consistent with the current objectives, strategies, policies, and programs?

3. What is the culture's position on environmental sustainability?

4. What is the culture's position on other important issues facing the corporation (that is, on productivity, quality of performance, adaptability to changing conditions, and internationalization)?

5. Is the culture compatible with the employees' diversity of backgrounds?

6. Does the company take into consideration the values of the culture of each nation in which the firm operates?

C. Corporate Resources

1. **Marketing**
   a. What are the corporation's current marketing objectives, strategies, policies, and programs?
      i. Are they clearly stated or merely implied from performance and/or budgets?
      ii. Are they consistent with the corporation's mission, objectives, strategies, and policies and with internal and external environments?
   b. How well is the corporation performing in terms of analysis of market position and marketing mix (that is, product, price, place, and promotion) in both domestic and international markets? How dependent is the corporation on a few customers? How big is its market? Where is it gaining or losing market share? What percentage of sales comes from developed versus developing regions? Where are current products in the product life cycle?
      i. What trends emerge from this analysis?
      ii. What impact have these trends had on past performance and how might these trends affect future performance?
      iii. Does this analysis support the corporation's past and pending strategic decisions?
      iv. Does marketing provide the company with a competitive advantage?
   c. How well does the corporation's marketing performance compare with that of similar corporations?
   d. Are marketing managers using accepted marketing concepts and techniques to evaluate and improve product performance? (Consider product life cycle, market segmentation, market research, and product portfolios.)
   e. Does marketing adjust to the conditions in each country in which it operates?
   f. Does marketing consider environmental sustainability when making decisions?
   g. What is the role of the marketing manager in the strategic management process?

2. **Finance**
   a. What are the corporation's current financial objectives, strategies, and policies and programs?
      i. Are they clearly stated or merely implied from performance and/or budgets?
      ii. Are they consistent with the corporation's mission, objectives, strategies, and policies and with internal and external environments?
   b. How well is the corporation performing in terms of financial analysis? (Consider ratio analysis, common size statements, and capitalization structure.) How balanced, in terms of cash flow, is the company's portfolio of products and businesses? What are investor expectations in terms of share price?
      i. What trends emerge from this analysis?
      ii. Are there any significant differences when statements are calculated in constant versus reported dollars?
      iii. What impact have these trends had on past performance and how might these trends affect future performance?
      iv. Does this analysis support the corporation's past and pending strategic decisions?
      v. Does finance provide the company with a competitive advantage?
   c. How well does the corporation's financial performance compare with that of similar corporations?
   d. Are financial managers using accepted financial concepts and techniques to evaluate and improve current corporate and divisional performance? (Consider financial leverage, capital budgeting, ratio analysis, and managing foreign currencies.)
   e. Does finance adjust to the conditions in each country in which the company operates?
   f. Does finance cope with global financial issues?
   g. What is the role of the financial manager in the strategic management process?

3. **Research and Development (R&D)**
   a. What are the corporation's current R&D objectives, strategies, policies, and programs?
      i. Are they clearly stated or merely implied from performance or budgets?
      ii. Are they consistent with the corporation's mission, objectives, strategies and policies and with internal and external environments?
      iii. What is the role of technology in corporate performance?
      iv. Is the mix of basic, applied, and engineering research appropriate given the corporate mission and strategies?
      v. Does R&D provide the company with a competitive advantage?
   b. What return is the corporation receiving from its investment in R&D?
   c. Is the corporation competent in technology transfer? Does it use concurrent engineering and cross-functional work teams in product and process design?
   d. What role does technological discontinuity play in the company's products?
   e. How well does the corporation's investment in R&D compare with the investments of similar corporations? How much R&D is being outsourced? Is the corporation using value-chain alliances appropriately for innovation and competitive advantage?
   f. Does R&D adjust to the conditions in each country in which the company operates?
   g. Does R&D consider environmental sustainability in product development and packaging?
   h. What is the role of the R&D manager in the strategic management process?

4. **Operations and Logistics**
   a. What are the corporation's current manufacturing/service objectives, strategies, policies, and programs?
      i. Are they clearly stated or merely implied from performance or budgets?
      ii. Are they consistent with the corporation's mission, objectives, strategies, and policies and with internal and external environments?
   b. What are the type and extent of operations capabilities of the corporation? How much is done domestically versus internationally? Is the amount of outsourcing appropriate to be competitive? Is purchasing being handled appropriately? Are suppliers and distributors operating in an environmentally sustainable manner? Which products have the highest and lowest profit margins?
      i. If the corporation is product oriented, consider plant facilities, type of manufacturing system (continuous mass production, intermittent job shop, or flexible manufacturing), age and type of equipment, degree and role of automation and/or robots, plant capacities and utilization, productivity ratings, and availability and type of transportation.
      ii. If the corporation is service oriented, consider service facilities (hospital, theater, or school buildings), type of operations systems (continuous service over time to same clientele or intermittent service over time to varied clientele), age and type of supporting equipment, degree and role of automation and use of mass communication devices (diagnostic machinery, video machines), facility capacities and utilization rates, efficiency ratings of professional and service personnel, and availability and type of transportation to bring service staff and clientele together.
   c. Are manufacturing or service facilities vulnerable to natural disasters, local or national strikes, reduction or limitation of resources from suppliers, substantial cost increases of materials, or nationalization by governments?
   d. Is there an appropriate mix of people and machines (in manufacturing firms) or of support staff to professionals (in service firms)?
   e. How well does the corporation perform relative to the competition? Is it balancing inventory costs (warehousing) with logistical costs (just-in-time)? Consider costs per unit of labor, material, and overhead; downtime; inventory control management and scheduling of service staff; production ratings; facility utilization percentages; and number of clients successfully treated by category (if service firm) or percentage of orders shipped on time (if product firm).

      i. What trends emerge from this analysis?

      ii. What impact have these trends had on past performance and how might these trends affect future performance?

      iii. Does this analysis support the corporation's past and pending strategic decisions?

      iv. Does operations provide the company with a competitive advantage?

  f. Are operations managers using appropriate concepts and techniques to evaluate and improve current performance? Consider cost systems, quality control and reliability systems, inventory control management, personnel scheduling, TQM, learning curves, safety programs, and engineering programs that can improve efficiency of manufacturing or of service.

  g. Do operations adjust to the conditions in each country in which it has facilities?

  h. Do operations consider environmental sustainability when making decisions?

  i. What is the role of the operations manager in the strategic management process?

5. **Human Resources Management (HRM)**

  a. What are the corporation's current HRM objectives, strategies, policies, and programs?

      i. Are they clearly stated or merely implied from performance and/or budgets?

      ii. Are they consistent with the corporation's mission, objectives, strategies, and policies and with internal and external environments?

  b. How well is the corporation's HRM performing in terms of improving the fit between the individual employee and the job? Consider turnover, grievances, strikes, layoffs, employee training, and quality of work life.

      i. What trends emerge from this analysis?

      ii. What impact have these trends had on past performance and how might these trends affect future performance?

      iii. Does this analysis support the corporation's past and pending strategic decisions?

      iv. Does HRM provide the company with a competitive advantage?

  c. How does this corporation's HRM performance compare with that of similar corporations?

  d. Are HRM managers using appropriate concepts and techniques to evaluate and improve corporate performance? Consider the job analysis program, performance appraisal system, up-to-date job descriptions, training and development programs, attitude surveys, job design programs, quality of relationships with unions, and use of autonomous work teams.

  e. How well is the company managing the diversity of its workforce? What is the company's record on human rights? Does the company monitor the human rights record of key suppliers and distributors?

  f. Does HRM adjust to the conditions in each country in which the company operates? Does the company have a code of conduct for HRM for itself and key suppliers in developing nations? Are employees receiving international assignments to prepare them for managerial positions?

  g. What is the role of outsourcing in HRM planning?

  h. What is the role of the HRM manager in the strategic management process?

6. **Information Technology (IT)**

  a. What are the corporation's current IT objectives, strategies, policies, and programs?

      i. Are they clearly stated or merely implied from performance and/or budgets?

      ii. Are they consistent with the corporation's mission, objectives, strategies, and policies and with internal and external environments?

  b. How well is the corporation's IT performing in terms of providing a useful database, automating routine clerical operations, assisting managers in making routine decisions, and providing information necessary for strategic decisions?

      i. What trends emerge from this analysis?

      ii. What impact have these trends had on past performance and how might these trends affect future performance?

       iii. Does this analysis support the corporation's past and pending strategic decisions?

       iv. Does IT provide the company with a competitive advantage?

  c. How does this corporation's IT performance and stage of development compare with that of similar corporations? Is it appropriately using the Internet, intranet, and extranets?

  d. Are IT managers using appropriate concepts and techniques to evaluate and improve corporate performance? Do they know how to build and manage a complex database, establish Web sites with firewalls and virus protection, conduct system analyses, and implement interactive decision-support systems?

  e. Does the company have a global IT and Internet presence? Does it have difficulty with getting data across national boundaries?

  f. What is the role of the IT manager in the strategic management process?

D. Summary of Internal Factors (List in the IFAS Table 5–2, p.193)

Which of these factors are core competencies? Which, if any, are distinctive competencies? Which of these factors are the most important to the corporation and to the industries in which it competes at the present time? Which might be important in the future? Which functions or activities are candidates for outsourcing?

V. Analysis of Strategic Factors (SWOT)

A. Situational Analysis (List in SFAS Matrix, Figure 6–1, p. 210)

Of the external (EFAS) and internal (IFAS) factors listed in III.D and IV.D, which are the strategic (most important) factors that strongly affect the corporation's present and future performance?

B. Review of Mission and Objectives

1. Are the current mission and objectives appropriate in light of the key strategic factors and problems?

2. Should the mission and objectives be changed? If so, how?

3. If they are changed, what will be the effects on the firm?

VI. Strategic Alternatives and Recommended Strategy

A. Strategic Alternatives (See the TOWS Matrix, Figure 6–3, p. 212)

1. Can the current or revised objectives be met through more careful implementation of those strategies presently in use (for example, fine-tuning the strategies)?

2. What are the major feasible alternative strategies available to the corporation? What are the pros and cons of each? Can corporate scenarios be developed and agreed on? (Alternatives must fit the natural physical environment, societal environment, industry, and corporation for the next three to five years.)

  a. Consider *stability*, *growth*, and *retrenchment* as corporate strategies.

  b. Consider *cost leadership* and *differentiation* as business strategies.

    c. Consider any functional strategic alternatives that might be needed for reinforcement of an important corporate or business strategic alternative.

B. Recommended Strategy

1. Specify which of the strategic alternatives you are recommending for the corporate, business, and functional levels of the corporation. Do you recommend different business or functional strategies for different units of the corporation?

2. Justify your recommendation in terms of its ability to resolve both long- and short-term problems and effectively deal with the strategic factors.

3. What policies should be developed or revised to guide effective implementation?

4. What is the impact of your recommended strategy on the company's core and distinctive competencies?

VII. Implementation

A. What Kinds of Programs (for Example, Restructuring the Corporation or Instituting TQM) Should Be Developed to Implement the Recommended Strategy?

1. Who should develop these programs?
2. Who should be in charge of these programs?

B. Are the Programs Financially Feasible? Can Pro Forma Budgets Be Developed and Agreed On? Are Priorities and Timetables Appropriate to Individual Programs?

C. Will New Standard Operating Procedures Need to Be Developed?

VIII. Evaluation and Control

A. Is the Current Information System Capable of Providing Sufficient Feedback on Implementation Activities and Performance? Can It Measure Strategic Factors?

1. Can performance results be pinpointed by area, unit, project, or function?
2. Is the information timely?
3. Is the corporation using benchmarking to evaluate its functions and activities?

B. Are Adequate Control Measures in Place to Ensure Conformance with the Recommended Strategic Plan?

1. Are appropriate standards and measures being used?
2. Are reward systems capable of recognizing and rewarding good performance?

CHAPTER **2**

corporate
Governance

There was a saying that Hyderabad had two major attractions: the Charminar and Ramalinga Raju, who created the company, Satyam Computer Services.[1] In 2002, Mr. Raju was awarded the "Corporate Citizen of the Year" award during the Asian Business Leadership Summit held in Hong Kong. He was also named as the "IT Man of the Year" by *Dataquest* in 2001 and was conferred the "Entrepreneur of the Year Award" by Ernst & Young, India in 2007.[2]

On paper Ramalinga Raju, seemed to be doing everything right. On 24th June 1987, satyam was incorporated as a Private Limited Co. for providing software development and consultancy services to large corporations. The company was promoted by B. Rama Raju and B. Ramalinga Raju.[3] The company set up two Software Technology Parks, one at Mayfair Centre, Secunderabad and other at Qutuballapur of Ranga Reddy Dist. of A.P.[4] Since 1991, when the company announced its offshore software project with John Deere & Co.—Satyam's first Fortune 500 customer— and its IPO was oversubscribed by 17 times, to 2008, when its revenue crossed U.S. $2-billion mark, the company had achieved some great heights. In 2008, Satyam a leading global business and information technology company, delivering consulting, systems integration, and outsourcing solutions to clients in over 20 industries and more than 65 countries (Figures as of September 30, 2008),[5] became the first company to be invited by the National Stock Exchange (NSE) to ring the opening bell (op-cit 3).

The company's journey had been eventful, designed for growth, and marked by numerous pioneering achievements and global awards.

The story took a turn on 7 January 2009, when Chairman B. Ramalinga Raju sent a letter to board tendering his resignation and admitting to fraud and fabrication of accounting books. In his letter, he confessed that as of 30 September 2008, Satyam's balance sheet carried inflated (nonexistent) cash and bank balances of Rs. 5,040 crore (as against Rs. 5,361 crore reflected in the books); and a nonexistent accrued interest of Rs. 376 crore. There were understated liability and overstated debtors' position. The gap between actual operating profit and the one reflected in the books of accounts had arisen purely on account of inflated profits over several years (limited only to Satyam standalone, books of subsidiaries reflecting true performance).[6] According to Raju's disclosure, the fraud was to the tune of Rs. 7,800 crore.[7] The news got the stock crashing down by 66.5% to Rs. 60 from a high of Rs. 188.70.[8]

Learning Objectives

After reading this chapter, you should be able to:

- Describe the role and responsibilities of the board of directors in corporate governance
- Understand how the composition of a board can affect its operation
- Describe the impact of the Sarbanes-Oxley Act on corporate governance in the United States
- Discuss trends in corporate governance
- Explain how executive leadership is an important part of strategic management

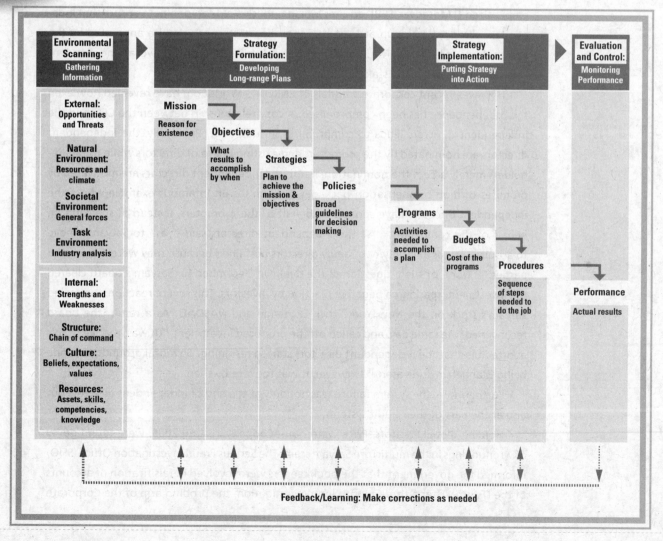

Environmental Scanning: Gathering Information

External: Opportunities and Threats

Natural Environment: Resources and climate

Societal Environment: General forces

Task Environment: Industry analysis

Internal: Strengths and Weaknesses

Structure: Chain of command

Culture: Beliefs, expectations, values

Resources: Assets, skills, competencies, knowledge

Strategy Formulation: Developing Long-range Plans

Mission
Reason for existence

Objectives
What results to accomplish by when

Strategies
Plan to achieve the mission & objectives

Policies
Broad guidelines for decision making

Strategy Implementation: Putting Strategy into Action

Programs
Activities needed to accomplish a plan

Budgets
Cost of the programs

Procedures
Sequence of steps needed to do the job

Evaluation and Control: Monitoring Performance

Performance
Actual results

Feedback/Learning: Make corrections as needed

In an attempt to save the company, Mr. Raju announced $1.6-billion acquisition of Maytas Properties and Maytas Infra Ltd. Credit Lyonnais Securities Asia (CLSA) considers it as one of the worst corporate governance events in India.[9]

This scam turned both national and international attention to the Indian business. It brought the corporate governance practices, role of independent directors in board of directors, and auditing practices in India under microscopic scrutiny.

Satyam's board, at the time of this fiasco consisted of big names such as management professors, Professor Rao, Dean, ISB; Professor Krishna Palepu, HBS; Professor V.S. Raju, a former Director of two IITs; Mr. T.R. Prasad, a former Union Cabinet Secretary, and Mr. Vinod Dham, the father of Pentium chip, and others.[10]

OECD Principles of Corporate Governance defines "Board independence usually requires sufficient number of members to be independent of management." This requires that such members should not be employed by the company or its affiliates and not be closely related to the company or its management through significant economic, family or other ties. Independence from controlling shareholders or other controlling body is emphasized.[11] Moreover, SEBI requires Indian publicly held companies to ensure that independent directors make up at least half their board strength and be appointed by the shareholders (op-cit 12). The motivation behind this rule was to have an independent voice which spoke for the stakeholders.

However, recent corporate scandals of ENRON & WorldCom have revealed how even this independence has been compromised. A cozy relationship between the CEO and the independent directors leads to compromises in judgment. Practically, the independent directors are nominated by the promoters and existing board of directors while the shareholders merely accept the nomination. If not, the independent directors are motivated by promises of high compensation packages. Satyam's is an infamous example where the independent directors have spoken on behalf of the promoters, instead of speaking on behalf of the companies.[12] All the independent directors said "yes" to Satyam's move to acquire Maytas and only two family directors abstained because they were "interested parties."[13] None of them questioned the deal. On December 16, Satyam's board cleared the investment, sparking a negative reaction by investors. This severe reaction pummeled Satyam's stock on the New York Stock Exchange and NASDAQ. As a result, the board reconvened, the same day, and called off the proposed investment.[14] It was in wake of this aborted bid that the independent directors started resigning, on moral grounds, first one being Mangalam Srinivasan.[15] However, it was too late by then.

Furthermore, the system failure was not only at the end of independent directors but also at the part of their audit systems.

Holding global auditors, Price waterhouseCoopers, in April 2009, were found guilty of wrongdoings in the multicrore Satyam scam. The Serious Fraud Investigation Office (SFIO) informed the government that the bookkeepers were involved in falsification of accounts of the IT firm. After a three-month long investigation, the probing arm of the Corporate

Affairs Ministry concluded that the auditors kept silent despite knowing about the failure of the IT firm's audit system in 2007.[16]

The Satyam fiasco has left a big question mark on corporate governance and auditing practices in India while sending a negative signal to the foreign institutional investors. India's corporate governance codes are on par with the best in the world. However, the Satyam scam has highlighted the need to assess the enforcement of these practices. Lessons learnt from this scam have highlighted the need for the government to fix obligations of independent directors and role they plan in a company.

2.1 Role of the Board of Directors

A *corporation* is a mechanism established to allow different parties to contribute capital, expertise, and labor for their mutual benefit. The investor/shareholder participates in the profits of the enterprise without taking responsibility for the operations. Management runs the company without being responsible for personally providing the funds. To make this possible, laws have been passed that give shareholders limited liability and, correspondingly, limited involvement in a corporation's activities. That involvement does include, however, the right to elect directors who have a legal duty to represent the shareholders and protect their interests. As representatives of the shareholders, directors have both the authority and the responsibility to establish basic corporate policies and to ensure that they are followed.[17]

The board of directors, therefore, has an obligation to approve all decisions that might affect the long-run performance of the corporation. This means that the corporation is fundamentally governed by the *board of directors* overseeing *top management*, with the concurrence of the *shareholder*. The term corporate governance refers to the relationship among these three groups in determining the direction and performance of the corporation.[18] The board of directors is the highest governing authority within the management structure of a company. In India, operations of a company are managed under the directions of the board within the framework set by the Companies Act, 1956.

It is the duty of the board to select, evaluate, and approve appropriate compensation for the company's chief executive officer (CEO), to evaluate the attractiveness of and pay dividends, recommend stock splits, oversee share repurchase programs, approve the company's financial statements, and recommend or strongly discourage acquisitions and mergers. They are responsible for providing stewardship of not only management functions but also operations of the institution.

Over the past decade, shareholders and various interest groups have seriously questioned the role of the board of directors in corporations. They are concerned that inside board members may use their position to feather their own nests and that outside board members often lack sufficient knowledge, involvement, and enthusiasm to do an adequate job of monitoring and providing guidance to top management. Instances of widespread corruption and questionable accounting practices at Enron, Satyam, Reliance Communications among others seem to justify their concerns. Satyam debacle highlighted as to how independent directors on the board of the organization can be kept completely in the dark.

The general public has not only become more aware and more critical of many boards' apparent lack of responsibility for corporate activities, it has begun to push government to demand accountability. As a result, the board as a rubber stamp of the CEO or as a bastion of the "old-boy" selection system is being replaced by more active, more professional boards. See **Strategy Highlight 2.1** for comparison of Indian and US laws.

RESPONSIBILITIES OF THE BOARD

In India, like in other countries, the principal role of the board—as representatives of the shareholders—is to monitor the working of the organization and to protect the interests of all stakeholders. With increase in complexity in the structure of organizations, the expectations from the board of directors have increased. Indian boards in today's competitive global era must move away from the so-called rubber stamp board to being a strategic asset for the company. The laws and standards defining the responsibilities of the board vary from country to country. However, there is a developing worldwide consensus concerning the major responsibilities of the board. Interviews with 200 directors from eight countries (Canada,

STRATEGY highlight 2.1

COMPARISON OF SOME CORPORATE GOVERNANCE HIGHLIGHTS UNDER INDIAN AND US LAW

Laws and standards defining the responsibilities of board of directors· vary from country to country. The following table highlights some of these changes. It lists down the corporate governance practices that are required under Indian Companies Act, 1956. The specific table deals with the regulations and guidelines of the Securities and Exchange Board of India and the requirements of the listing agreements entered into with the Indian stock exchange vis-à-vis New York Stock Exchange rules.

Indian law	NYSE rule applicable to U.S. listed companies
Under Indian law, if the chairman of board of directors is a non executive director, at least one-third of the board must be comprised of independent directors and if he is an executive director, at least half the board must be comprised of independent directors. However, if the non executive chairman is a promoter of the company or is related to any promoter or person occupying management positions at the board level or at one level below the board, at least one-half of the board of the company must be comprised of independent directors. The chairman of our board is neither an executive of the company, nor is he a promoter of the company or related to any promoter or person occupying management positions at the board level or at one level below the board and four out of twelve members of our board are independent, which satisfies the requirement under Indian law.	Companies must have a majority of independent directors (NYSE Corporate Governance Standard 303A.01).
Under Indian law, there is no such requirement.	Non management directors must meet at regular scheduled executive sessions without management (NYSE Corporate Governance Standard 303A.03).
Under Indian law, a nominating/corporate governance committee is not required.	Companies must have a nominating/corporate governance committee composed entirely of independent directors (NYSE Corporate Governance Standard 303A.04).
Indian law does not require the adoption and disclosure of corporate governance guidelines.	Companies must adopt and disclose corporate governance guidelines (NYSE Corporate Governance Standard 303A.09).
Under Indian law, a company's board of directors set the compensation for non executive directors. Non mandatory Indian law recommends that companies establish a remuneration committee composed of non executive directors and an independent chairman to determine the compensation of executive directors.	Companies must have a compensation committee composed entirely of independent directors (NYSE Corporate Governance Standard 303A.05).

Source: Excerpts covered from a document "ITEM 16 G. CORPORATE GOVERNANCE" accessed on 11 Oct 2011, from http://www.tatacommunications.com/downloads/investors/CorpGovComplianceNYSE.pdf

STRATEGY highlight 2.2

SOME KEY RESPONSIBILITIES OF THE BOARD IN INDIA

■ Strategy formulation, budgets, business plans, etc.

■ Monitoring the effectiveness of the company's governance practices.

■ Selecting, compensating, monitoring key executives, and overseeing succession planning.

■ Executive and board remuneration.

■ Ensuring a formal and transparent board nomination and election process.

■ Monitoring and managing potential conflicts of interest of management, board members, and shareholders, including misuse of corporate assets, and abuse in related party transactions.

■ Ensuring the integrity of the corporation's accounting and financial reporting systems, including independent audit, ensuring control systems for risk management, financial and operational controls, and compliance.

■ Overseeing the process of disclosure and communications.

France, Germany, Finland, Switzerland, the Netherlands, the United Kingdom, and Venezuela) revealed strong agreement on the following five **board of director responsibilities**, listed in order of importance:

1. Setting corporate strategy, overall direction, mission, or vision

2. Hiring and firing the CEO and top management

3. Controlling, monitoring, or supervising top management

4. Reviewing and approving the use of resources

5. Caring for shareholder interests[19]

These results are in agreement with a survey by the National Association of Corporate Directors, in which U.S. CEOs reported that the four most important issues boards should address are corporate performance, CEO succession, strategic planning, and corporate governance.[20] Directors in the United States must make certain, in addition to the duties just listed, that the corporation is managed in accordance with the laws of the state in which it is incorporated. Because more than half of all publicly traded companies in the United States are incorporated in the state of Delaware, this state's laws and rulings have more impact than do those of any other state.[21] Directors must also ensure management's adherence to lawsand regulations,such as those dealing with the issuance of securities,insider trading,andother conflict-of-interest situations. They must also be aware of the needs and demands ofconstituent groups so that they can achieve a judicious balance among the interests of thesediverse groups while ensuring the continued functioning of the corporation. In India, in law, the board owes a strict judiciary duty to ensure that the company is run in the long-term interest of owners. Its key responsibilities include[22]:

1. Determination of board functions, i.e., premises within which the board is to work annually.

2. Setting values, mission, and vision statements for the organization.

3. Responsibility to prepare strategic plan, next years operating plan, and budget. The board should provide objectives against which performance shall be measured, activities involved, accountable persons, resources required, and time frame.

4. Responsibility to ensure that the company has adequate resources to meet its objectives.

5. Responsibility to monitor progress towards achieving the agreed objectives.

6. Responsibility to prepare work plan for the year with monthly benchmarks and time-lines.

7. Responsibility to mentor, monitor, and evaluate the chief executive office.

8. Responsibility to ensure compliance and disclosure to various acts such as the Companies Act, the SEBI Act, The Income Tax, Sales Tax, and other tax and labor laws.

9. Responsibility to communicate with the stakeholders.

10. Other responsibilities include setting performance objectives, monitoring corporate performance, overseeing mergers and acquisitions, and other capital expenditures.

In a legal sense, the board is required to direct the affairs of the corporation but not to manage them. It is charged by law to act with **due care**. If a director or the board as a whole fails to act with due care and, as a result, the corporation is in some way harmed, the careless director or directors can be held personally liable for the harm done. This is no small concern given that one survey of outside directors revealed that more than 40% had been named as part of lawsuits against corporations.[23] For example, board members of Equitable Life in Britain were sued for up to $5.4 billion for failure to question the CEO's reckless policies.[24] For this reason, corporations have found that they need directors and officers' liability insurance in order to attract people to become members of boards of directors.

A 2008 global survey of directors by McKinsey & Company revealed the average amount of time boards spend on a given issue during their meetings:[25]

- Strategy (development and analysis of strategies)—24%
- Execution (prioritizing programs and approving mergers and acquisitions)—24%
- Performance management (development of incentives and measuring performance)—20%
- Governance and compliance (nominations, compensation, audits)—17%
- Talent management—11%

Role of the Board in Strategic Management

How does a board of directors fulfill these many responsibilities? The *role of the board of directors in strategic management* is to carry out three basic tasks:

- **Monitor:** By acting through its committees, a board can keep abreast of developments inside and outside the corporation, bringing to management's attention developments it might have overlooked. A board should at the minimum carry out this task.

- **Evaluate and influence:** A board can examine management's proposals, decisions, and actions; agree or disagree with them; give advice and offer suggestions; and outline alternatives. More active boards perform this task in addition to monitoring.

- **Initiate and determine:** A board can delineate a corporation's mission and specify strateg options to its management. Only the most active boards take on this task in addition to the two previous ones. See **Strategy Highlight 2.2** to know about the key responsibilities of board of directors in India.

Board of Directors' Continuum

A board of directors is involved in strategic management to the extent that it carries out the three tasks of monitoring, evaluating and influencing, and initiating and determining. The **board of directors' continuum** shown in **Figure 2–1** shows the possible degree of involvement (from low to high) in the strategic management process. Boards can range from phantom boards with no real involvement to catalyst boards with a very high degree of involvement.[26]

FIGURE 2–1   Board of Directors' Continuum

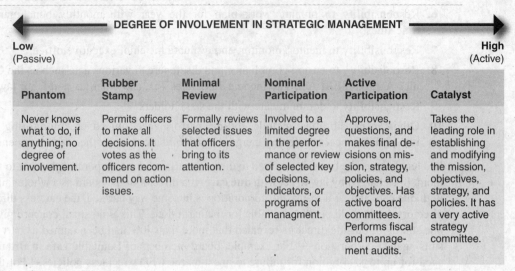

Phantom	**Rubber Stamp**	**Minimal Review**	**Nominal Participation**	**Active Participation**	**Catalyst**
Never knows what to do, if anything; no degree of involvement.	Permits officers to make all decisions. It votes as the officers recommend on action issues.	Formally reviews selected issues that officers bring to its attention.	Involved to a limited degree in the performance or review of selected key decisions, indicators, or programs of managment.	Approves, questions, and makes final decisions on mission, strategy, policies, and objectives. Has active board committees. Performs fiscal and management audits.	Takes the leading role in establishing and modifying the mission, objectives, strategy, and policies. It has a very active strategy committee.

DEGREE OF INVOLVEMENT IN STRATEGIC MANAGEMENT

Low (Passive) — High (Active)

SOURCE: T. L. Wheelen and J. D. Hunger, "Board of Directors' Continuum," Copyright © 1994 by Wheelen and Hunger Associates. Reprinted by permission.

Research suggests that active board involvement in strategic management is positively related to a corporation's financial performance and its credit rating.[27]

Highly involved boards tend to be very active. They take their tasks of monitoring, evaluating and influencing, and initiating and determining very seriously; they provide advice when necessary and keep management alert. As depicted in **Figure 2–1**, their heavy involvement in the strategic management process places them in the active participation or even catalyst positions. Although 74% of public corporations have periodic board meetings devoted primarily to the review of overall company strategy, the boards may not have had much influence in generating the plan itself.[28] A 2008 global survey of directors by McKinsey & Company found that 43% of respondents had high to very high influence in creating corporate value. About 38% stated that they had moderate influence and 18% reported that they had little to very little influence. Those boards reporting high influence typically shared a common plan for creating value and had healthy debate about what actions the company should take to create value. Together with top management, these high-influence boards considered global trends and future scenarios and developed plans. In contrast, those boards with low influence tended not to do any of these things.[29] These results are supported by a 2006 survey by Korn/Ferry International revealing that 30% of directors felt that their CEO was not utilizing them to their full capacity. In the same study, 73% of the directors indicated that were not content with an oversight role mandated by regulation and wanted to be more involved in setting strategic plans.[30] Nevertheless, studies indicate that boards are becoming increasingly active. For example, in a global survey of directors conducted by McKinsey & Company in 2005, 64% of the respondents indicated that they were more actively involved in the core areas of company performance and value creation than they had been five years earlier. This percentage was higher in large companies (77%) and in publicly held companies (75%).[31]

These and other studies suggest that most large publicly owned corporations have boards that operate at some point between nominal and active participation. Some corporations with actively participating boards are Target, Medtronic, Best Western, Service Corporation International, Bank of Montreal, Mead Corporation, Rolm and Haas, Whirlpool, 3M, Apria Healthcare, General Electric, Pfizer, and Texas Instruments.[32] Target, a corporate governance leader, has a board that each year sets three top priorities, such as strategic direction, capital allocation, and succession planning. Each of these priority topics is placed at the top of the agenda for at least one meeting. Target's board also devotes one meeting a year to setting the strategic direction for each major operating division.[33]

As a board becomes less involved in the affairs of the corporation, it moves farther to the left on the continuum (see **Figure 2–1**). On the far left are passive phantom or rubber-stamp boards that typically never initiate or determine strategy unless a crisis occurs. In these situations, the CEO also serves as Chairman of the Board, personally nominates all directors, and works to keep board members under his or her control by giving them the "mushroom treatment"—throw manure on them and keep them in the dark!

Generally, the smaller the corporation, the less active is its board of directors in strategic management.[34] In an entrepreneurial venture, for example, the privately held corporation may be 100% owned by the founders—who also manage the company. In this case, there is no need for an active board to protect the interests of the owner-manager shareholders—the interests of the owners and the managers are identical. In this instance, a board is really unnecessary and only meets to satisfy legal requirements. If stock is sold to outsiders to finance growth, however, the board becomes more active. Key investors want seats on the board so they can oversee their investment. To the extent that they still control most of the stock, however, the founders dominate the board. Friends, family members, and key shareholders usually become members, but the board acts primarily as a rubber stamp for any proposals put forward by the owner-managers. In this type of company, the founder tends to be both CEO and Chairman of the Board and the board includes few people who are not affiliated with the firm or family.[35] This cozy relationship between the board and management should change, however, when the corporation goes public and stock is more widely dispersed. The founders, who are still acting as management, may sometimes make decisions that conflict with the needs of the other shareholders (especially if the founders own less than 50% of the common stock). In this instance, problems could occur if the board fails to become more active in terms of its roles and responsibilities. In India, the move towards making boards more active in terms of their responsibilities and roles has been relatively slow and has more than often, met with resistance, from directors set in their old ways. However, in India many companies have voluntarily developed the board appraisal system. In 2004, a family business like Dabur India Ltd implemented a process of performance evaluation for its board of directors. Under this system, an evaluation committee comprising of 10 board members assesses the performance of each board member, including the chairman and vice chairman, in three areas of strategy: monitoring management performance and development/compensation, statutory compliance, and corporate governance.[36] It is one of the leading Indian companies that has consciously worked at reducing the Burman family influence on the business and has made transition towards a professionally managed business.[37] Other companies that have made similar endeavors in India include Colgate Palmolive (India) Pvt Ltd, which adopted a self-evaluation procedure in 1997, Cognizant Technologies, Infosys Technologies, and Wipro Ltd.

MEMBERS OF A BOARD OF DIRECTORS

The boards of most publicly owned corporations are composed of both inside and outside directors. **Inside directors** (sometimes called management directors) are typically officers or executives employed by the corporation. **Outside directors** (sometimes called nonmanagement directors) may be executives of other firms but are not employees of the board's corporation. Although there is yet no clear evidence indicating that a high proportion of outsiders on a board results in improved financial performance,[38] there is a trend in the United States to increase the number of outsiders on boards and to reduce the total size of the board.[39] The board of directors of a typical large U.S. corporation has an average of 10 directors, 2 of whom are insiders.[40] Outsiders thus account for 80% of the board members in large U.S. corporations (approximately the same as in Canada). Boards in the UK typically have 5 inside and 5 out side directors, whereas France boards usually consist of 3 insiders and 8 outsiders. Japanese boards, in contrast, contain 2 outsiders and 12 insiders.[41] The board of directors in a typical small U. S. corporation has four out of five members, of who mainly one or two are outsiders.[42] In India, according to the existing policy of Department of Public Enterprises, O.M. No. 18(6)/91-GM dated March 16, 1992, the Board of Directors of Public Sector Undertakings should consist of (i) full-time functional directors whose number should not exceed 50% of the actual strength of the board; (ii) government directors whose number should not exceed one-sixth of the actual strength of the board subject to the condition that in no case the number should exceed two; and (iii) nonofficial part-time directors whose number should be at least one-third of the actual strength of the board.[43] Research from large and small corporations reveals a negative relationship between board size and firm profitability.[44]

People who favor a high proportion of outsiders state that outside directors are less biased and more likely to evaluate management's performance objectively than are inside directors. This is the main reason why the U.S. Securities and Exchange Commission (SEC) in 2003 required that a majority of directors on the board be independent outsiders. The SEC also required that all listed companies staff their audit, compensation, and nominating/corporate governance committees entirely with independent, outside members. This view is in agreement with **agency theory**, which states that problems arise in corporations because the agents (top management) are not willing to bear responsibility for their decisions unless they own a substantial amount of stock in the corporation. The theory suggests that a majority of a board needs to be from outside the firm so that top management is prevented from acting selfishly to the detriment of the shareholders. For example, proponents of agency theory argue that managers in management-controlled firms (contrasted with owner-controlled firms in which the founder or family still own a significant amount of stock) select less risky strategies with quick payoffs in order to keep their jobs.[45] This view is supported by research revealing that manager-controlled firms (with weak boards) are more likely to go into debt to diversify into unrelated markets (thus quickly boosting sales and assets to justify higher salaries for themselves), thus resulting in poorer long-term performance than owner-controlled firms.[46] Boards with a larger proportion of outside directors tend to favor growth through international expansion and innovative venturing activities than do boards with a smaller proportion of outsiders.[47] Outsiders tend to be more objective and critical of corporate activities. For example, research reveals that the likelihood of a firm engaging in illegal behavior or being sued declines with the addition of outsiders on the board.[48] Research on family businesses has found that boards with a larger number of outsiders on the board tended to have better corporate governance and better performance than did boards with fewer outsiders.[49]

In contrast, those who prefer inside over outside directors contend that outside directors are less effective than are insiders because the outsiders are less likely to have the necessary interest, availability, or competency. **Stewardship theory** proposes that, because of their long tenure with the corporation, insiders (senior executives) tend to identify with the corporation and its success. Rather than use the firm for their own ends, these executives are thus most interested in guaranteeing the continued life and success of the corporation. (See **Strategy Highlight 2.3** for a discussion of Agency Theory contrasted with Stewardship Theory.) Excluding all insiders but the CEO reduces the opportunity for outside directors to see potential successors in action or to obtain alternate points of view of management decisions. Outside directors may sometimes serve on so many boards that they spread their time and interest too thin to actively fulfill their responsibilities. The average board member of a U.S. Fortune 500 firm serves on three boards. Research indicates that firm performance decreases as the number of directorships held by the average board member increases.[50] Although only 40% of surveyed U.S. boards currently limit the number of directorships a board member may hold in other cor-porations,60% limit the number of boards on which their CEO may be a member.[51] In India, the Companies Act, 1956

STRATEGY highlight 2.3

AGENCY THEORY VERSUS STEWARDSHIP THEORY IN CORPORATE GOVERNANCE

Managers of large, modern publicly held corporations are typically not the owners. In fact, most of today's top managers own only nominal amounts of stock in the corporation they manage. The real owners (shareholders) elect boards of directors who hire managers as their agents to run the firm's day-to-day activities. Once hired, how trustworthy are these executives? Do they put themselves or the firm first?

Agency Theory. As suggested in the classic study by Berle and Means, top managers are, in effect, "hired hands" who may very likely be more interested in their personal welfare than that of the shareholders. For example, management might emphasize strategies, such as acquisitions, that increase the size of the firm (to become more powerful and to demand increased pay and benefits) or that diversify the firm into unrelated businesses (to reduce short-term risk and to allow them to put less effort into a core product line that may be facing difficulty) but that result in a reduction of dividends and/or stock price.

Agency theory is concerned with analyzing and resolving two problems that occur in relationships between principals (owners/shareholders) and their agents (top management):

1. The agency problem that arises when (a) the desires or objectives of the owners and the agents conflict or (b) it is difficult or expensive for the owners to verify what the agent is actually doing. One example is when top management is more interested in raising its own salary than in increasing stock dividends.

2. The risk-sharing problem that arises when the owners and agents have different attitudes toward risk. Executives may not select risky strategies because they fear losing their jobs if the strategy fails.

According to agency theory, the likelihood that these problems will occur increases when stock is widely held (that is, when no one shareholder owns more than a small percentage of the total common stock), when the board of directors is composed of people who know little of the company or who are personal friends of top management, and when a high percentage of board members are inside (management) directors.

To better align the interests of the agents with those of the owners and to increase the corporation's overall performance, agency theory suggests that top management have a significant degree of ownership in the firm and/or have a strong financial stake in its long-term performance. In support of this argument, research indicates a positive relationship between corporate performance and the amount of stock owned by directors.

Stewardship Theory. In contrast, stewardship theory suggests that executives tend to be more motivated to act in the best interests of the corporation than in their own self-interests. Whereas agency theory focuses on extrinsic rewards that serve the lower-level needs, such as pay and security, stewardship theory focuses on the higher-order needs, such as achievement and self-actualization. Stewardship theory argues that senior executives over time tend to view the corporation as an extension of themselves. Rather than use the firm for their own ends, these executives are most interested in guaranteeing the continued life and success of the corporation. The relationship between the board and top management is thus one of principal and steward, not principal and agent ("hired hand"). Stewardship theory notes that in a widely held corporation, the shareholder is free to sell his or her stock at any time. In fact, the average share of stock is held less than 10 months. A diversified investor or speculator may care little about risk at the company level—preferring management to assume extraordinary risk so long as the return is adequate. Because executives in a firm cannot easily leave their jobs when in difficulty, they are more interested in a merely satisfactory return and put heavy emphasis on the firm's continued survival. Thus, stewardship theory argues that in many instances top management may care more about a company's long-term success than do more short-term oriented shareholders.

For more information about agency and stewardship theory, see A. A. Berle and G. C. Means, *The Modern Corporation and Private Property* (NY: Macmillan, 1936). Also see J. H. Davis, F. D. Schoorman, and L. Donaldson, "Toward a Stewardship Theory of Management," *Academy of Management Review* (January 1997), pp. 20–47; P. J. Lane, A. A. Cannella, Jr. & M. H. Lubatkin, "Agency Problems as Antecedents to Unrelated Mergers and Diversification: Amihud and Lev Reconsidered," *Strategic Management Journal* (June 1998), pp. 555–578; M. L. Hayward and D. C. Hambrick, "Explaining the Premiums Paid for Large Acquisitions: Evidence of CEO Hubris," *Administrative Science Quarterly* (March 1997), pp. 103–127; and C. M. Christensen and S. D. Anthony, "Put Investors in their Place," *Business Week* (May 28, 2007), p. 108.

prescribes in Section 277 that a person cannot hold more than 15 directorships and Section 278 provides that in considering the limit, directorship as an alternate director should be excluded, whereas the clause restricts committee memberships to 10.[52]

Those who question the value of having more outside board members point out that the term *outsider* is too simplistic because some outsiders are not truly objective and should be considered more as insiders than as outsiders.

The board may comprise of different kinds of directors. The Company Law in India does not distinguish between styles and titles of directors. The various types of directors may be:

1. Executive director is also called as inside director. Executive members are full-time employees of the company, i.e., executives of the company, who act as members of the board. Their status and power is derived from their position in the hierarchy of the company. The drawbacks usually are more than the advantages and as a result their number in a board is limited. The number of functional directors therefore should be restricted to necessary minimum. Clause 49 of SEBI's Listing Agreement requires every listed entity to reserve half the board for independent directors if the chairman is an executive director.

2. Non executive director [53] refers to those directors who do not hold any management position in the company. These are people who have been chosen to sit exclusively on the board of the company. They are outside directors for whom directorship is a part-time assignment. As per Clause 49, the expression "independent director" means non executive director of the company who[54]:

   a. apart from receiving director's remuneration, does not have any material relationships or transactions with the company, its promoters, its senior management or its holding company, its subsidiaries, and/or associated companies;

   b. is not related to promoters or management at the board level or at one level below the board;

   c. has not been an executive of the company in the immediately preceding three financial years;

   d. is not a partner or an executive of the statutory audit firm or the internal audit firm that is associated with the company, and has not been a partner or an executive of any such firm for the last three years. This will also apply to legal firm(s) and consulting firm(s) that have material association with the entity.

   e. is not a supplier, service provider, or customer of the company. This should include lessor–lessee type relationships also; and

   f. is not a substantial shareholder of the company, i.e., owning 2% or more of the block of voting shares.

Difference Between Executive and Non executive Director		
	Executive Director	**Non executive Director**
1.	Executive directors do get involved in the day-to-day running of the business.	Non executive directors do not get involved in the day-to-day running of the business.
2.	Executive directors perform operational and strategic business functions such as: • managing people • looking after assets • hiring and firing • entering into contracts	Non executive directors use their experience and expertise to provide independent advice and objectivity, and they usually have a role in monitoring executive management.

3.	Executive directors work full time.	They usually work part time, attending board meetings and spending time on specific projects.
4.		Non executive directors are expected to monitor and challenge the performance of the executive directors and the management, and to take a determined stand in the interests of the firm and its stakeholders.
5.	Executive directors receive a salary. A company may decide to include shares, share options, pension provision, company cars, or incentive schemes in directors' remuneration packages.	Non executive directors may receive a salary if employed or receive fees if self-employed.
6.	They are generally held equally liable under certain statutory requirements such as tax laws.	

3. **Nominee Director:** There are certain scenarios where a third party, in order to ensure safety of their interest, appoint someone on the board of directors. These third parties refer to stakeholders such as government, foreign collaborators, holding companies and financial institutions or other lenders, etc. The phenomenon of nominee directors has become an important feature of the modern Indian corporate scenario.

4. **Representative director** is a director appointed on the board to represent the interest of a stakeholder group such as consumer, employees, suppliers, etc. The representative director is exected to act in two capacities. First as an enabler where they are expected to help in enriching the business by bringing in valuable experience, expertise, and specialization. Second as a "conscience" of the board by reflecting the interests of stakeholders, they are representing.[55]

5. **Shadow director** is also called a deemed director. Deemed director is a person who is not named or appointed as director but gives instructions (not professional advice). Other directors are expected to act according to the instructions issued. Shadow directors are deemed to be directors, and for certain statutory provisions stand in the same shoes as a director, who though normally not a member of the board, remains in the background and exercises powers over the board decisions.[56]

6. **Associate director** is a title given to senior managers even though they are not on the board. Sometimes this designation is given as a sign of appreciation and recognition for work done. Though not a director, if he represents himself as a director in dealings with other parties, he will be liable as a director.

Companies usually try and balance the types of directors in order to develop a ideal mix. For example, Hero Honda's board of directors consists of executive, technical, and non executive independent directors.[57] Similarly IFCI consists of its CEO, chairman, and 10 independent members.[58] In addition to the board of directors, many external agencies also act as watchdogs for a company's corporate governance practices. For example, TIAA-CREF's Corporate Governance team monitors governance practices of the 4,000 companies in which it invests its pension funds through its Corporate Assessment Program. If its analysis of a company reveals problems, TIAA-CREF first sends letters stating its concerns, followed up by visits, and it finally sponsors a shareholder resolution in opposition to management's actions.[59] Institutional investors are also powerful in many other countries. In Germany, bankers are represented on almost every board—primarily because they own large blocks of stock in German corporations. In Denmark, Sweden, Belgium, and Italy, however, investment companies assume this role. For example, the investment company Investor casts 42.5% of the Electrolux shareholder votes, thus guaranteeing itself positions on the Electrolux board.

Boards of directors have been working to increase the number of women and minorities serving on boards. Korn/Ferry International reports that of the Fortune 1000 largest U.S. firms, 85% had at least one woman director in 2006 (compared to 69% in 1995), comprising 15% of total directors. Approximately one-half of the boards in Europe included a female director, comprising 9% of total directors. (The percentage of female directors in Europe in 2006 ranged from less than 1% in Portugal to almost 40% in Norway.)[60] Korn/Ferry's survey also revealed that 76% of the U.S. boards had at least one ethnic minority in 2006 (African-American, 47%; Latino, 19%; Asian, 10%) as director compared to only 47% in 1995, comprising around 14% of total directors.[61] Among the top 200 S&P companies in the U.S., however, 84% have at least one African-American director.[62] The globalization of business is having an impact on board membership. According to the Spencer Stuart executive recruiting firm, 33% of U.S. boards had an international director.[63] Europe was the most "globalized" region of the world, with most companies reporting one or more non-national directors.[64] Although Asian and Latin American boards are still predominantly staffed by nationals, they are working to add more international directors.[65]

Outside directors serving on the boards of large Fortune 1000 U.S. corporations annually earned on average $58,217 in cash plus an average of $75,499 in stock options. Most of the companies (63%) paid their outside directors an annual retainer plus a fee for every meeting attended.[66] Directors serving on the boards of small companies usually received much less compensation (around $10,000). One study found directors of a sample of large U.S. firms to hold on an average 3% of their corporations' outstanding stock.[67] In India, the payment of remuneration to directors is regulated by various provisions under the Companies Act, 1956.[68] The Companies Act, 1956 is the central legislation in India that empowers the Central Government to regulate the formation, financing, functioning, and winding up of companies.[69] It provides for the powers and responsibilities of the directors and managers, raising of the capital, holding of company meetings, maintenance and audit of company accounts, powers of inspection, etc.

The Companies Act was extensively amended in 1988 on the recommendations of the Sachar Committee. One of the areas of amendment was in respect of appointment of managing/whole-time directors and payment of remuneration to them. Section 198 specifies the overall limit of remuneration payable to directors, whereas Section 269 specifies that the remuneration payable to a managing or whole-time director is paid in accordance with the provisions of Schedule XIII or else necessary approval is obtained by the concerned company from the Central Government. Section 309, inter alia, specifies the mode of payment of remuneration to ordinary directors.[70]

As a result of the amendment, it became obligatory for every public company or private company which is a subsidiary of a public company, having the prescribed amount of paid up share capital, to appoint a managing director or a whole-time director. Today, the prescribed amount for this purpose is Rs 5 crores.[71] The power of the appointment and payment of remuneration to directors was also delegated to the shareholders of the respective companies, subject to certain conditions as specified in the Act.

The Act has prescribed the overall limit of the remuneration payable to all the directors at 11% of the net profits of the company for that particular financial year. The net profit is required to be computed in the manner specified by the Act. A company can pay a maximum of 5% of its net profits for a particular year to a managing/whole-time director and a maximum of 10% to all the managing/whole-time directors put together.[71, 72]

Codetermination: Should Employees Serve on Boards?

Codetermination, the inclusion of a corporation's workers on its board, began only recently in the United States. Corporations such as Chrysler, Northwest Airlines, United Airlines (UAL), and Wheeling-Pittsburgh Steel added representatives from employee associations to their boards as part of union agreements or Employee Stock Ownership Plans (ESOPs). For example, United Airlines workers traded 15% in pay cuts for 55% of the company (through an ESOP) and 3 of the firm's 12 board seats. In this instance, workers represent themselves on the board not so much as employees but primarily as owners. At Chrysler, however, the United Auto Workers union obtained a temporary seat on the board as part of a union contract agreement in exchange for changes in work rules and reductions in benefits. This was at a time when Chrysler was facing bankruptcy in the late 1970s. In situations like this when a director represents an internal stakeholder, critics raise the issue of conflict of interest. Can a member of the board, who is privy to confidential managerial information, function, for example, as a union leader whose primary duty is to fight for the best benefits for his or her members? Although the movement to place employees on the boards of directors of U.S. companies shows little likelihood of increasing (except through employee stock ownership), the European experience reveals an increasing acceptance of worker participation (without ownership) on corporate boards.

Germany pioneered codetermination during the 1950s with a two-tiered system: (1) a supervisory board elected by shareholders and employees to approve or decide corporate strategy and policy and (2) a management board (composed primarily of top management) appointed by the supervisory board to manage the company's activities. Most other WesternEuropean countries have either passed similar codetermination legislation (as in Sweden, Denmark, Norway, and Austria) or use worker councils to work closely with management (asin Belgium, Luxembourg, France, Italy, Ireland, and the Netherlands). In past decade, India adopted various programs and strategies to encourage worker participation in the decision-making process. Though these programs were viewed as highway to greater worker participation in the economy, by the Indian Government, yet in India, there have been very few examples of codetermination and if it has been adopted, the percentage representation has been negligible. Certain guidelines have been framed by the Securities and Exchange Board of India (SEBI). These guidelines apply only to listed companies in respect of ESOP issued on or after June 19, 1999. For example, a listed company needs to obtain specific shareholder approval in case of grant of stock options to employees of subsidiary/holding company. If grant of stock options to specific employees, during any one year, is equal to or exceeding 1% of the issued capital (excluding outstanding warrants and conversions) of the company at the time of grant, then it shall be subjected to approval by the shareholders by way of separate resolution.[73]

Interlocking Directorates

CEOs often nominate chief executives (as well as board members) from other firms to membership on their own boards in order to create an interlocking directorate. A *direct* **interlocking directorate** occurs when two firms share a director or when an executive of one firm sits on the board of a second firm. An *indirect* interlock occurs when two corporations have directors who also serve on the board of a third firm, such as a bank.

Although the Clayton Act and the Banking Act of 1933 prohibit interlocking directorates by U.S. companies competing in the same industry, interlocking continues to occur in almost all corporations, especially large ones. Interlocking occurs because large firms have a large impact on other corporations and these other corporations, in turn, have some control over the firm's inputs and marketplace. For example, most large corporations in the United States, Japan, and Germany are interlocked either directly or indirectly with financial institutions.[74] Eleven of the 15 largest U.S. corporations have at least two board members who sit together on another board. About 20% of the 1,000 largest U.S. firms share at least one board member.[75]

STRATEGY highlight 2.4

ESOP OPTIONS IN INDIA

The statutory guidelines on ESOP, in context of accounting treatment of compensation cost, are pronounced by Securities and Exchange Board of India (SEBI) called Securities and Exchange Board of India (Employee Stock Option Scheme and Employee Stock Purchase Scheme) Guidelines, 1999. These guidelines apply only to listed companies and ESOPs issues after June 19, 1999. Some of the ESOP schemes in India are as follows:

HLL Limited (as per figures upto 2006) has issued four stock options. The exercise price of options in all cases was linked to the market price on/near the date of grant. The options issued in 2001 and 2002 were rendered unattractive as the stock price of HLL fell significantly from the market price relevant then.[1] Hindustan Unilever (earlier Hindustan Lever) rolled out its performance share scheme in 2006 to replace its standard stock option plan in place since 2001.[2] In October 2011, Hindustan Unilever Limited informed the exchange that the committee of the board in its meeting held on September 23, 2011, had further allotted 87,230 equity shares of Re.1/- each under ESOP, which as per the shareholder's resolution dated May 29, 2006 is known as "2006 HLL Performance Share Scheme."[3]

ITC has also issued multiple ESOP options. The company decided to issue ordinary shares up to 5% of the issued and subscribed capital of the company as on March 31, 2000, that is, 5% of 1,22,70,745 ordinary shares of Rs 10 each. The scheme would come into effect after the necessary approvals. The company decided to convene an extraordinary general meeting (EGM) of shareholders on January 17, 2001 to seek their approval on the ESOP scheme. The scheme is as per the SEBI (Employee Stock Option Scheme and Employee Stock Purchase Scheme) Guidelines 1999.[4] As on March 2010, ITC issued and allotted 15,09,900 ordinary shares of Re. 1 each, upon exercise of 1,50,990 options by optionees under the company's Employee Stock Option Schemes. Consequently, the issued and subscribed share capital of the company stand increased to Rs 381.04 crore divided into 381,04,58,780 ordinary shares of Re 1 each.[5]

Infosys Limited (as per figures upto 2003) issued three plans, i.e., 1994 Plan, 1998 Plan (Plan I and II), and 1999 Plan. Infosys temporarily suspended grant of options under 1998 and 1999 plans for seeking regulatory and accounting clarity, whereas 1994 lapsed in 2000. Under the 1994 plan—the most lucrative—2,575 employees were given stock options.[6]

Other companies that have adopted ESOP schemes include names such as Polaris Limited, Rolta Limited, Glenmark Pharmaceuticals Limited, Aurobindo Pharma Limited, Matrix Limited, and Nicholas Piramal (NPIL).

1. S. Banka, "ESOP Schemes—An Insight," Capital Market, The Chartered Accountant, posted on April 2006, accessed on 11 Oct 2011, from http://220.227.161.86/102661504-1511.pdf

2. S. S. Dagar, "Carrots with Strings," Business Today, posted on 4 Nov 2007, accessed on 11 Oct 2011, from http://businesstoday.intoday.in/story/carrots-with-strings/1/783.html

3. Corporate Information & Corporate Announcements, accessed on 11 Oct 2011, from http://www.nseindia.com/marketinfo/companyinfo/eod/announcements.jsp?symbol=HINDUNILVR

4. Bureau, ITC board clears ESOP, The Business Line, Financial Daily, from The Hindu Group of Publications, posted on Thursday 30 Nov 2000, accessed on 11 Oct 2011, from http://www.thehindubusinessline.in/2000/11/30/stories/14301803.htm

5. NirmalBang Research, ITC allots shares under ESOP, posted on 16 Mar 2010 at 09:48 hrs IST, accessed on 11 Oct 2011, from http://www.nirmalbang.com/nb-research/show-news-details.aspx?newsid=312

6. R. Menon, "Infy's ESOP Fable Ends, For Now," DataQuest, posted on Wednesday 07 April 2004, accessed on 11 Oct 2011, from http://dqindia.ciol.com/content/industrymarket/newsanalysis/2004/104040703.asp

Interlocking directorates are useful for gaining both inside information about an uncertain environment and objective expertise about potential strategies and tactics.[76] For example, Kleiner Perkins, a high-tech venture capital firm, not only has seats on the boards of the companies in which it invests, but it also has executives (which Kleiner Perkins hired) from one entrepreneurial venture who serve as directors on others. Kleiner Perkins refers to its network of interlocked firms as its *keiretsu*, a Japanese term for a set of companies with interlocking business relationships and share-holdings.[77] Family-owned corporations, however, are less likely to have interlocking directorates than are corporations with highly dispersed stock ownership, probably because family-owned corporations do not like to dilute their corporate control by adding outsiders to boardroom discussions.

There is some concern, however, when the chairs of separate corporations serve on each other's boards. Twenty-two such pairs of corporate chairs (who typically also served as their firm's CEO) existed in 2003. In one instance, the three chairmen of Anheuser-Busch, SBC Communications, and Emerson Electric served on all three of the boards. Typically a CEO sits on only one board in addition to his or her own—down from two additional boards in previous years. Although such interlocks may provide valuable information, they are increasingly frowned upon because of the possibility of collusion.[78] Nevertheless, evidence indicates that well-interlocked corporations are better able to survive in a highly competitive environment.[79] See **Strategy Highlight 2.4** to learn about the ESOP options in India.

NOMINATION AND ELECTION OF BOARD MEMBERS

Traditionally the CEO of a corporation decided whom to invite to board membership and merely asked the shareholders for approval in the annual proxy statement. All nominees were usually elected. There are some dangers, however, in allowing the CEO free rein in nominating directors. The CEO might select only board members who, in the CEO's opinion, will not disturb the company's policies and functioning. Given that the average length of service of a U.S. board member is for three three-year terms (but can range up to 20 years for some boards), CEO-friendly, passive boards are likely to result. This is especially likely given that only 7% of surveyed directors indicated that their company had term limits for board members. Nevertheless, 60% of U.S. boards and 58% of European boards have a mandatory retirement age—typically around 70.[80] Research reveals that boards rated as least effective by the Corporate Library, a corporate governance research firm, tend to have members serving longer (an average of 9.7 years) than boards rated as most effective (7.5 years).[81] Directors selected by the CEO often feel that they should go along with any proposal the CEO makes. Thus board members find themselves accountable to the very management they are charged to oversee. Because this is likely to happen, more boards are using a nominating committee to nominate new outside board members for the shareholders to elect. About 97% of large U.S. corporations now use nominating committees to identify potential directors. This practice is less common in Europe where 60% of boards use nominating committees.[82]

Many corporations whose directors serve terms of more than one year divides the board into classes and staggers elections so that only a portion of the board stands for election each year. This is called a *staggered board*. About 63% of U.S. boards currently have staggered boards.[83] Arguments in favor of this practice are that it provides continuity by reducing the chance of an abrupt turnover in its membership and that it reduces the likelihood of electing people unfriendly to management (who might be interested in a hostile takeover) through cumulative voting. An argument against staggered boards is that they make it more difficult for concerned shareholders to curb a CEO's power—especially when that CEO is also Chairman of the Board. An increasing number of shareholder resolutions to replace staggered boards with annual elections of all board members are currently being passed at annual meetings.

When nominating people for election to a board of directors, it is important that nominees have previous experience dealing with corporate issues. For example, research reveals that a firm makes better acquisition decisions when the firm's outside director's have had experience with such decisions.[84] In India, directors are elected by the shareholders in their general meeting. In certain situations, the board may also appoint a director. However, to ensure impartiality, Clause 49 suggests that the task of nomination be done by the nomination committee.

Under Clause 49, companies are required to have various committees such as a "nomination committee," "compensation committee," "governance committee," and other committees to adhere to corporate governance. The "nomination committee" of the board is to be composed entirely of independent directors. These directors are responsible for the evaluation and nomination of board members. A substantial portion of the board should be elected by the shareholders. A nomination committee is required to recommend to the board, corporate governance guidelines applicable to the company; identify, review, and evaluate individuals qualified to become members of the board; to set the compensation of the chief executive officer and perform other compensation oversight; review and recommend the nomination of board members; and assist the board with other related tasks, as assigned from time to time.[85]

A survey of directors of U.S. corporations revealed the following criteria in a good director:

- Willing to challenge management when necessary—95%
- Special expertise important to the company—67%
- Available outside meetings to advise management—57%
- Expertise on global business issues—41%
- Understands the firm's key technologies and processes—39%
- Brings external contacts that are potentially valuable to the firm—33%
- Has detailed knowledge of the firm's industry—31%
- Has high visibility in his or her field—31%
- Is accomplished at representing the firm to stakeholders—18%[86]

ORGANIZATION OF THE BOARD

The size of a board in the United States is determined by the corporation's charter and its bylaws, in compliance with state laws. Although some states require a minimum number of board members, most corporations have quite a bit of discretion in determining board size. The average large, publicly held U.S. firm has 10 directors on its board. The average small, privately-held company has four to five members. The average size of boards elsewhere is Japan, 14; Non-Japan Asia, 9; Germany, 16; UK, 10; and France, 11.[87] In Indian context, traditionally boards had a number of institutional nominees, government nominees (in the case of public sector undertakings, or PSUs), and nominees of the promoter group (in the case of companies belonging to large Indian business houses).[88] Moreover, following the tightening of corporate governance norms, fresh directors had to be inducted to cater to the statutory need of having a mandated proportion of independent directors thus increasing the size of boards. Thus, in the sample studied in the ICRA survey, the average board size was 11.6 members, and the median was 12. The average size of a company's board is 12, and a large majority had boards with 9–12 members.[89]

Approximately 70% of the top executives of U.S. publicly held corporations hold the dual designation of Chairman and CEO (Only 5% of the firms in the UK have a combined Chair/CEO).[90] The combined Chair/CEO position is being increasingly criticized because of the potential for conflict of interest. The CEO is supposed to concentrate on strategy, planning, external relations, and responsibility to the board. The Chairman's responsibility is to ensure that the board and its committees perform their functions as stated in the board's charter. Further, the Chairman schedules board meetings and presides over the annual shareholders' meeting. Critics of having one person in the two offices ask how the board can properly oversee top management if the Chairman is also a part of top management. For this reason, the Chairman and CEO roles are separated by law in Germany, the Netherlands, South Africa, and Finland. A similar law has been considered in the United Kingdom and Australia. Although research is mixed regarding the impact of the combined Chair/CEO position on overall corporate financial performance, firm stock price and credit ratings both respond negatively to announcements of CEOs also assuming the Chairman position.[91] Research also shows that corporations with a combined Chair/CEO have a greater likelihood of fraudulent financial reporting when CEO stock options are not present.[92]

Many of those who prefer that the Chairman and CEO positions be combined agree that the outside directors should elect a **lead director**. This person is consulted by the Chair/CEO regarding board affairs and coordinates the annual evaluation of the CEO.[93] The lead director position is very popular in the United Kingdom, where it originated. Of those U.S. companies combining the Chairman and CEO positions, 96% had a lead director.[94] This is one way to give the board more power without undermining the power of the Chair/CEO. The lead director becomes increasingly important because 94% of U.S. boards in 2006 (compared to only 41% in 2002) held regular executive sessions without the CEO being present.[95] Nevertheless, there are many ways in which an unscrupulous Chair/CEO can guarantee a director's loyalty. Research indicates that an increase in board independence often results in higher levels of CEO ingratiation behavior aimed at persuading directors to support CEO proposals. Long-tenured directors who support the CEO may use social pressure to persuade a new board member to conform to the group. Directors are more likely to be recommended for membership on other boards if they "don't rock the boat" and engage in low levels of monitoring and control behavior.[96] Even in those situations when the board has a nominating committee composed only of outsiders, the committee often obtains the CEO's approval for each new board candidate.[97]

The most effective boards accomplish much of their work through committees. Although they do not usually have legal duties, most committees are granted full power to act with the authority of the board between board meetings. Typical standing committees (in order of prevalence) are the audit (100%), compensation (99%), nominating (97%), corporate governance (94%), stock options (84%), director compensation (52%), and executive (43%) committees.[98]

According to the ICRA survey, in India, some 50% of the surveyed companies have separate CEO and Chairman, but in a majority of such companies the Chairman was either a former chief executive of the same company or a nominee of the dominant promoter group (opcit. 86).

In India, under Clause 49, companies are required to have various committees such as a "nomination committee," "compensation committee," "governance committee," and other committees like to adhere to corporate governance (opcit. 82). The ICRA survey revealed that the average number of board meetings held in a year, in India, was 7.69, whereas the median was seven meetings with four board meetings required for the adoption of quarterly accounts and one meeting typically coinciding with the annual general meeting. The practice matched the expectations, i.e., minimum of five board meetings a year. The outlier in this respect was provided by the PSU giants such as ONGC and MTNL, each of which had more than 15 board meetings in a year (opcit. 85).

Average director attendance, as worked out from the survey, stood at a high of 83% with a median of 84%, minimum of 66%, and maximum of 92%.[99] The survey further stated that though director absenteeism was a negative from governance perspective; mere attendance alone was not a measure of a director's involvement. Far more important was the level of participation in, and commitment to, board proceedings, which the survey was not in a position to comment on (opcit. 84 and 85).

IMPACT OF THE SARBANES-OXLEY ACT CORPORATE GOVERNANCE

In response to the many corporate scandals uncovered since 2000, the U.S. Congress passed the **Sarbanes-Oxley Act (SOX)** in June 2002. This act was designed to protect shareholders from the excesses and failed oversight that characterized failures at Enron, Tyco, WorldCom, Adelphia Communications, Qwest, and Global Crossing, among other prominent firms. Several key elements of Sarbanes-Oxley were designed to formalize greater board independence and oversight. For example, the act requires that all directors serving on the audit committee be independent of the firm and receive no fees other than for services of the director. In addition, boards may no longer grant loans to corporate officers. The act has also established formal procedures for individuals (known as "whistleblowers") to report incidents of questionable accounting or auditing. Firms are prohibited from retaliating against anyone reporting wrongdoing. Both the CEO and CFO must certify the corporation's financial information. The act bans auditors from providing both external and internal audit services to the same company. It also requires that a firm identify whether it has a "financial expert" serving on the audit committee who is independent from management.

Although the cost to a large corporation of implementing the provisions of the law was $8.5 million in 2004, the first year of compliance, the costs to a large firm fell to $1–$5 million annually during the following years as accounting and information processes were refined and made more efficient.[100] Pitney Bowes, for example, saved more than $500,000 in 2005 simply by consolidating four accounts receivable offices into one. Similar savings were realized at Cisco and Genentech.[101] An additional benefit of the increased disclosure requirements is more reliable corporate financial statements. Companies are now reporting numbers with fewer adjustments for unusual charges and write-offs, which in the past have been used to boost reported earnings.[102] The new rules have also made it more difficult for firms to post-date executive stock options. "This is an unintended consequence of disclosure," remarked Gregory Taxin, CEO of Glass, Lewis & Company, a stock research firm[103]. See the **Global Issue** feature to learn how corporate governance is being improved in other parts of the world. As for India, SOX does not apply directly. The regulators in India have amended Clause 49 to make company managements more responsive. In Clause 49, stress has been laid on disclosures by companies by making periodic disclosures from time to time.[104]

However, indirectly due to globalization of financial markets, the requirements of SOX is increasingly becoming relevant to growing number of Indian companies, in particular, the companies who want to become global players or attract capital from abroad. An investor is likely to put a better valuation on a company whose management is more transparent.

The principles embodied within SOX have universal support from shareholders around the globe. SOX could act as a learning note for changes to protect shareholders. Learning from SOX, Indian companies need to voluntarily establish processes to improve controls, transparency, and accountability. These when incorporated in the structure of an organization would help ensure safety of interests of stakeholders.[105]

Improving Governance

In implementing the Sarbanes-Oxley Act, the U.S. Securities and Exchange Commission (SEC) required in 2003 that a company disclose whether it has adopted a code of ethics that applies to the CEO and to the company's principal financial officer. Among other things, the SEC requires that the audit, nominating, and compensation committees be staffed entirely by outside directors. The New York Stock Exchange reinforced the mandates of Sarbanes-Oxley by requiring that companies have a nominating/governance committee composed entirely of independent outside directors. Similarly, NASDAQ rules require that nominations for new directors be made by either a nominating committee of independent outsiders or by a majority of independent outside directors.[106]

GLOBAL issue

CORPORATE GOVERNANCE IMPROVEMENTS THROUGHOUT THE WORLD

Countries throughout the world are working to improve corporate governance. Provisions that are roughly equivalent to Sarbanes-Oxley are in place in France and Japan, while both China and Canada are implementing similar rules. In the UK, the Cadbury Report has led to revisions to the Combined Code of Conduct that have placed additional responsibilities on nonmanagement directors, altered board and committee composition, and modified the roles of the CEO and Chairman. The adoption of recommendations from the government-sponsored Cromme Commission has reduced the power of management directors and increased the transparency of Germany's two-tier system of governance. Italy has implemented the Draghi Law of 1998 and the Preda Code of Conduct. Since many corporations in non-Japan Asia are family-controlled or have stock that is at least partially owned by the state, the Anglo-American system of corporate governance does not quite fit. Nevertheless, many of the changes in other parts of the world, such as CEO performance reviews and executive succession planning, are taking place in Asian corporations.

In an attempt to make Korean businesses more attractive to foreign investors, for example, the South Korean government recommended that companies listed on the stock exchange introduce a two-tiered structure. One structure was to consist entirely of non executive (outside) directors. One of the few companies to immediately adopt this new system of governance was Pohang Iron & Steel Company Ltd (POSCO), the world's largest steelmaker. POSCO was listed on the New York Stock Exchange and had significant operations in the United States, plus a joint venture with U.S. Steel. According to Youn-Gil Ro, Corporate Information Team Manager, "We needed professional advice on international business practices as well as American practices."

....

SOURCES: A. L. Nazareth, "Keeping SarbOx Is Crucial," *Business Week* (November 13, 2006), p. 134; *33rd Annual Board of Directors Study* (New York: Korn/Ferry International, 2007); C. A. Mallin, editor, *Handbook on International Corporate Governance* (Northampton, MA: Edward Elgar Publishing, 2006). *Globalizing the Board of Directors: Trends and Strategies* (New York: Conference Board, 1999), p. 16.

Partially in response to Sarbanes-Oxley, a survey of directors of Fortune 1000 U.S. companies by Mercer Delta Consulting and the University of Southern California revealed that 60% of directors were spending more time on board matters than before Sarbanes-Oxley, with 85% spending more time on their company's accounts, 83% more on governance practices, and 52% on monitoring financial performance.[107] Newly elected outside directors with financial management experience increased to 10% of all outside directors in 2003 from only 1% of outsiders in 1998.[108] About 78% of Fortune 1000 U.S. boards in 2006 required that directors own stock in the corporation, compared to just 36% in Europe, and 26% in Asia.[109]

Evaluating Governance

To help investors evaluate a firm's corporate governance, a number of independent rating services, such as Standard & Poor's (S&P), Moody's, Morningstar, The Corporate Library, Institutional Shareholder Services (ISS), and Governance Metrics International (GMI), have established criteria for good governance. *Business Week* annually publishes a list of the best and worst boards of U.S. corporations. Whereas rating service firms like S&P, Moody's, and The Corporate Library use a wide mix of research data and criteria to evaluate companies, ISS and GMI have been criticized because they primarily use public records to score firms, using simple checklists.[110] In contrast, the S&P Corporate Governance Scoring System researches four major issues:

■ Ownership Structure and Influence

■ Financial Stakeholder Rights and Relations

■ Financial Transparency and Information Disclosure

■ Board Structure and Processes

Although the S&P scoring system is proprietary and confidential, independent research using generally accepted measures of S&P's four issues revealed that moving from the poorest- to the best-governed categories nearly doubled a firm's likelihood of receiving an investment-grade credit rating.[111]

Avoiding Governance Improvements

A number of corporations are concerned that various requirements to improve corporate governance will constrain top management's ability to effectively manage the company. For example, more U.S. public corporations have gone private in the years since the passage of Sarbanes-Oxley than before its passage. Other companies use multiple classes of stock to keep outsiders from having sufficient voting power to change the company. Insiders, usually the company's founders, get stock with extra votes, while others get second-class stock with fewer votes. For example, Brian Roberts, CEO of Comcast, owns "superstock" that represents only 0.4% of outstanding common stock but guarantees him one-third of the voting stock. The Investor Responsibility Research Center reports that 11.3% of the companies it monitored in 2004 had multiple classes, up from 7.5% in 1990.[112]

Another approach to sidestepping new governance requirements is being used by corporations such as Google, Infrasource Services, Orbitz, and W&T Offshore. If a corporation in which an individual group or another company controls more than 50% of the voting shares decides to become a "controlled company," the firm is then exempt from requirements by the New York Stock Exchange and NASDAQ that a majority of the board and all members of key board committees be independent outsiders. According to governance authority Jay Lorsch, this will result in a situation in which "the majority shareholders can walk all over the minority."[113]

TRENDS IN CORPORATE GOVERNANCE

The role of the board of directors in the strategic management of a corporation is likely to be more active in the future. Although neither the composition of boards nor the board leadership structure has been consistently linked to firm financial performance, better governance does lead to higher credit ratings and stock prices. A McKinsey survey reveals that investors are willing to pay 16% more for a corporation's stock if it is known to have good corporate governance. The investors explained that they would pay more because, in their opinion (1) good governance leads to better performance over time, (2) good governance reduces the risk of the company getting into trouble, and (3) governance is a major strategic issue.[114]

Some of today's trends in governance (particularly prevalent in the United States and the United Kingdom) that are likely to continue include the following:

- Boards are getting more involved not only in reviewing and evaluating company strategy but also in shaping it.
- Institutional investors, such as pension funds, mutual funds, and insurance companies, are becoming active on boards and are putting increasing pressure on top management to improve corporate performance. This trend is supported by a U.S. SEC requirement that a mutual fund must publicly disclose the proxy votes cast at company board meetings in its portfolio. This reduces the tendency for mutual funds to rubber-stamp management proposals.[115]
- Shareholders are demanding that directors and top managers own more than token amounts of stock in the corporation. Research indicates that boards with equity ownership use quantifiable, verifiable criteria (instead of vague, qualitative criteria) to evaluate the CEO.[116] When compensation committee members are significant shareholders, they tend to offer the CEO less salary but with a higher incentive component than do compensation committee members who own little to no stock.[117]

- Nonaffiliated outside (nonmanagement) directors are increasing their numbers and power in publicly held corporations as CEOs loosen their grip on boards. Outside members are taking charge of annual CEO evaluations.

- Women and minorities are being increasingly represented on boards.

- Boards are establishing mandatory retirement ages for board members—typically around age 70.

- Boards are evaluating not only their own overall performance, but also that of individual directors.

- Boards are getting smaller—partially because of the reduction in the number of insiders but also because boards desire new directors to have specialized knowledge and expertise instead of general experience.

- Boards continue to take more control of board functions by either splitting the combined Chair/CEO into two separate positions or establishing a lead outside director position.

- Boards are eliminating 1970s anti-takeover defenses that served to entrench current management. In just one year, for example, 66 boards repealed their staggered boards and 25 eliminated poison pills.[118]

- As corporations become more global, they are increasingly looking for board members with international experience.

- Instead of merely being able to vote for or against directors nominated by the board's nominating committee, shareholders may eventually be allowed to nominate board members. This was originally proposed by the U.S. Securities and Exchange Commission in 2004, but was not implemented. Supported by the AFL-CIO, a more open nominating process would enable shareholders to vote out directors who ignore shareholder interests.[119]

- Society, in the form of special interest groups, increasingly expects boards of directors to balance the economic goal of profitability with the social needs of society. Issues dealing with workforce diversity and environmental sustainability are now reaching the board level. (See the **Environmental Sustainability Issue** feature for an example of a conflict between a CEO and the board of directors over environmental issues.)

2.2 The Role of Top Management

The top management function is usually conducted by the CEO of the corporation in coordination with the COO (Chief Operating Officer) or president, executive vice president, and vice presidents of divisions and functional areas.[120] Even though strategic management involves everyone in the organization, the board of directors holds top management primarily responsible for the strategic management of a firm.[121]

RESPONSIBILITIES OF TOP MANAGEMENT

Top management responsibilities, especially those of the CEO, involve getting things accomplished through and with others in order to meet the corporate objectives. Top management's job is thus multidimensional and is oriented toward the welfare of the total organization. Specific top management tasks vary from firm to firm and are developed from an analysis of the mission, objectives, strategies, and key activities of the corporation. Tasks are typically divided among the

ENVIRONMENTAL sustainability issue

CONFLICT AT THE BODY SHOP

When Anita Roddick opened the first Body Shop in 1976, she probably had no idea that she would become one of the first "green" business executives. She simply liked the idea of selling cosmetics in small sizes that were made from natural ingredients. By 1998, her entrepreneurial venture grew through franchising into a global business with 1,594 shops in 47 countries. Roddick's personal philosophy in favor of human rights, endangered wildlife, and the environment, while being strongly against the use of animals in testing cosmetics, became an inherent part of the company's philosophy of business. Reflecting an environmental awareness far in advance of other firms, the company's publication, *This Is the Body Shop,* stated: "We aim to avoid excessive packaging, to refill our bottles, and to recycle our packaging and use raw materials from renewable sources when technologically and economically feasible." The company drafted the European Union's *Eco-Management and Audit Regulation* in 1991 and the company's first environmental statement, *The Green Book,* in 1992.

The Body Shop became a publicly traded corporation in 1984 when it was listed on London's Unlisted Securities Market for just 95 pence per stock. By 1986, the stock price had increased ten-fold in value and was listed on the London Stock Exchange. The company grew quickly to be worth 700 million British pounds in 1991. Although the influx of money from the sale of stock enabled the company to expand throughout the world, there were disadvantages to having shareholders and a board of directors. Some shareholders began to complain that the company was diverting money into social projects instead of maximizing profits. Roddick had used her position as CEO to join the Body Shop with Greenpeace's "Save the Whales" campaign and to form alliances with Amnesty International and Friends of the Earth. Although the company continued to grow in size, its market value was declining by 1998. Tiring

of Roddick's social and environmental "radicalism," the board forced her to resign as CEO. Roddick and her husband (with just 18% of the stock) remained on the board as co-chairmen until 2002, when they were replaced. Roddick continued to carry out public relations functions for the company and traveled the world in search of new product ideas, but no longer had any control over the strategic direction of the firm she had founded.

On March 17, 2006, the Body Shop's board agreed to the company's sale to L'Oreal for a premium of 34.2% over the company's stock price. The sale was perceived by observers as quite ironic, given that for years Anita Roddick had criticized L'Oreal for its animal testing practices and for its exploitation of women in the workplace. On its Web site, Naturewatch said: "We feel that the Body Shop has 'sold out' and is not standing on its principles." Animal rights activists and some consumers vowed to boycott Body Shop stores. Within three weeks of the announcement, the Body Shop's "satisfaction" rating compiled by BrandIndex fell 11 points, to 14, its "buzz" rating fell by 10 points, to −4, and its "general impression" fell by 3 points, to 19. One Body Shop customer reflected the widespread dissatisfaction: "The Body Shop used to be my high street "safe house," a place where I could walk into and know that what I bought was okay, that people were actually benefiting from my purchase. . . . By buying from the Body Shop, you are now no longer supporting ethical consumerism. If I want legitimate fair-trade, nonanimal tested products, I can find them easily, at the same price, elsewhere."

SOURCES: E. A. Fogarty, J. P. Vincelette, and T. L. Wheelen, "The Body Shop International PLC: Anita Roddick, OBE," in T. L. Wheelen and J. D. Hunger, *Strategic Management and Business Policy,* 8th Edition (Upper Saddle River, NJ: Prentice Hall, 2002), pp. 7.1–7.26; D. Purkayastha and R. Fernando, *The Body Shop: Social Responsibility or Sustained Greenwashing?* (Hyderabad, India: ICFAI Center for Management Research, 2006).

members of the top management team. A diversity of skills can thus be very important. Research indicates that top management teams with a diversity of functional backgrounds, experiences, and length of time with the company tend to be significantly related to improvements in corporate market share and profitability.[122] In addition, highly diverse teams with some international experience tend to emphasize international growth strategies and strategic innovation, especially in uncertain environments, to boost financial performance.[123] The CEO, with the support of the rest of the top management team, must successfully handle two primary responsibilities that are crucial to the effective strategic management of the corporation: (1) provide executive leadership and a strategic vision and (2) manage the strategic planning process.

Executive Leadership and Strategic Vision

Executive leadership is the directing of activities toward the accomplishment of corporate objectives. Executive leadership is important because it sets the tone for the entire corporation. A **strategic vision** is a description of what the company is capable of becoming. It is often communicated in the company's mission and vision statements (as described in **Chapter 1**). People in an organization want to have a sense of mission, but only top management is in the position to specify and communicate this strategic vision to the general workforce. Top management's enthusiasm (or lack of it) about the corporation tends to be contagious. The importance of executive leadership is illustrated by Steve Reinemund, past-CEO of PepsiCo: "A leader's job is to define overall direction and motivate others to get there."[124]

Successful CEOs are noted for having a clear strategic vision, a strong passion for their company, and an ability to communicate with others. They are often perceived to be dynamic and charismatic leaders—which is especially important for high firm performance and investor confidence in uncertain environments.[125] They have many of the characteristics of **transformational leaders**—that is, leaders who provide change and movement in an organization by providing a vision for that change.[126] For instance, the positive attitude characterizing many well-known industrial leaders—such as Bill Gates at Microsoft, Anita Roddick at the Body Shop, Richard Branson at Virgin, Steve Jobs at Apple Computer, Phil Knight at Nike, Bob Lutz at General Motors, and Louis Gerstner at IBM—has energized their respective corporations. These transformational leaders have been able to command respect and to influence strategy formulation and implementation because they tend to have three key characteristics:[127]

1. **The CEO articulates a strategic vision for the corporation:** The CEO envisions the company not as it currently is but as it can become. The new perspective that the CEO's vision brings to activities and conflicts gives renewed meaning to everyone's work and enables employees to see beyond the details of their own jobs to the functioning of the total corporation.[128] Louis Gerstner proposed a new vision for IBM when he proposed that the company change its business model from computer hardware to services: "If customers were going to look to an integrator to help them envision, design, and build end-to-end solutions, then the companies playing that role would exert tremendous influence over the full range of technology decisions—from architecture and applications to hardware and software choices."[129] In a survey of 1,500 senior executives from 20 different countries, when asked the most important behavioral trait a CEO must have, 98% responded that the CEO must convey "a strong sense of vision."[130]

2. **The CEO presents a role for others to identify with and to follow:** The leader empathizes with followers and sets an example in terms of behavior, dress, and actions. The CEO's attitudes and values concerning the corporation's purpose and activities are clear-cut and constantly communicated in words and deeds. For example, when design engineers at General Motors had problems with monitor resolution using the Windows operating system, Steve Ballmer, CEO of Microsoft, personally crawled under conference room tables to plug in PC monitors and diagnose the problem.[131] People know what to expect and have trust in their CEO. Research indicates that businesses in which the general manager has the trust of the employees have higher sales and profits with lower turnover than do businesses in which there is a lesser amount of trust.[132]

3. **The CEO communicates high performance standards and also shows confidence in the followers' abilities to meet these standards:** The leader empowers followers by raising their beliefs in their own capabilities. No leader ever improved performance by setting easily attainable goals that provided no challenge. Communicating high expectations to others can often lead to high performance.[133] The CEO must be willing to follow through by coaching people. As a result, employees view their work as very important and thus motivating.[134] Ivan Seidenberg, chief executive of Verizon Communications, was closely involved in deciding Verizon's strategic direction, and he showed his faith in his people by

letting his key managers handle important projects and represent the company in public forums. "All of these people could be CEOs in their own right. They are warriors and they are on a mission," explained Seidenberg. Grateful for his faith in them, his managers were fiercely loyal both to him and the company.[135]

The negative side of confident executive leaders is that their very confidence may lead to *hubris*, in which their confidence blinds them to information that is contrary to a decided course of action. For example, overconfident CEOs tend to charge ahead with mergers and acquisitions even though they are aware that most acquisitions destroy shareholder value. Research by Tate and Malmendier found that "overconfident CEOs are more likely to conduct mergers than rational CEOs at any point in time. Overconfident CEOs view their company as undervalued by outside investors who are less optimistic about the prospects of the firm." Overconfident CEOs were most likely to make acquisitions when they could avoid selling new stock to finance them, and they were more likely to do deals that diversified their firm's lines of businesses.[136]

Managing the Strategic Planning Process

As business corporations adopt more of the characteristics of the learning organization, strategic planning initiatives can come from any part of an organization. A survey of 156 large corporations throughout the world revealed that, in two-thirds of the firms, strategies were first proposed in the business units and sent to headquarters for approval.[137] However, unless top management encourages and supports the planning process, strategic management is not likely to result. In most corporations, top management must initiate and manage the strategic planning process. It may do so by first asking business units and functional areas to propose strategic plans for themselves, or it may begin by drafting an overall corporate plan within which the units can then build their own plans. Research suggests that bottom-up strategic planing may be most appropriate in multidivisional corporations operating in relatively stable environments but that top-down strategic planning may be most appropriate for firms operating in turbulent environments.[138] Other organizations engage in concurrent strategic planning in which all the organization's units draft plans for themselves after they have been provided with the organization's overall mission and objectives.

Regardless of the approach taken, the typical board of directors expects top management to manage the overall strategic planning process so that the plans of all the units and functional areas fit together into an overall corporate plan. Top management's job therefore includes the tasks of evaluating unit plans and providing feedback. To do this, it may require each unit to justify its proposed objectives, strategies, and programs in terms of how well they satisfy the organization's overall objectives in light of available resources. If a company is not organized into business units, top managers may work together as a team to do strategic planning. CEO Jeff Bezos tells how this is done at Amazon.com:

> *We have a group called the S Team—S meaning "senior" [management]—that stays abreast of what the company is working on and delves into strategy issues. It meets for about four hours every Tuesday. Once or twice a year the S Team also gets together in a two-day meeting where different ideas are explored. Homework is assigned ahead of time. . . . Eventually we have to choose just a couple of things, if they're big, and make bets.[139]*

In contrast to the seemingly continuous strategic planning being done at Amazon.com, most large corporations conduct the strategic planning process just once a year—often at off-site strategy workshops attended by senior executives.[140]

Many large organizations have a *strategic planning staff* charged with supporting both top management and the business units in the strategic planning process. This staff may prepare the background materials used in senior management's off-site strategy workshop. This planning staff typically consists of fewer than ten people, headed by a senior executive with the title of Director of Corporate Development or Chief Strategy Officer. The staff's major responsibilities are to:

1. Identify and analyze companywide strategic issues, and suggest corporate strategic alternatives to top management.
2. Work as facilitators with business units to guide them through the strategic planning process.[141]

ECO-BITS

- DuPont, originally founded in 1802 to make gunpowder and explosives, was a major producer in 1990 of nitrous oxides and fluorocarbons—gases with a global warming potential 310 and 11,700 times that of carbon dioxide, respectively.

- DuPont was the first company to phase-out CFCs and the first to develop and commercialize CFC alternatives for refrigeration and air conditioning.

- DuPont's reputation changed from "Top U.S. Polluter of 1995" to *Business Week*'s list of "Top Green Companies" in 2005; meanwhile, its earnings per share increased from $1 in 2003 to $3.25 in 2007.[142]

DISCUSSION QUESTIONS

1. When does a corporation need a board of directors?
2. Who should and should not serve on a board of directors? What about environmentalists or union leaders?
3. Should a CEO be allowed to serve on another company's board of directors?
4. What would be the result if the only insider on a corporation's board were the CEO?
5. Should all CEOs be transformational leaders? Would you like to work for a transformational leader?
6. Pick up a recent corporate governance scam in India. Analyze the causes and also discuss the ways it could have been prevented.
7. Outline the roles and responsibilites of the board of directors.

8. What are the requirements outlined for the board of directors of Public Sector Undertakings by the Department of Public Enterprises?
9. What are the different types of directors in India?
10. Write short notes on the following:
    a. Remuneration of directors
    b. Clause 49
    c. Interlocking directorates
    d. Nomination and election of board of directors.
11. Outline the impact of Sarbanes-Oxley Act on India.
12. Discuss the recent trends in corporate governance.

STRATEGIC PRACTICE EXERCISE

A. Think of the **best manager** for whom you have ever worked. What was it about this person that made him or her such a good manager? Consider the following statements as they pertain to that person. Fill in the blank *in front of each statement* with one of the following values:

STRONGLY AGREE = 5; AGREE = 4; NEUTRAL = 3;
DISAGREE = 2; STRONGLY DISAGREE = 1.

1. ___ I respect him/her personally, and want to act in a way that merits his/her respect and admiration. ___
2. ___ I respect her/his competence about things she/he is more experienced about than I. ___
3. ___ He/she can give special help to those who cooperate with him/her. ___

4. ___ He/she can apply pressure on those who cooperate with him/her. ___
5. ___ He/she has a legitimate right, considering his/her position, to expect that his/her suggestions will be carried out. ___

Let's Summarize the Chapter with a Mind Map

Articulate strategic
vision of the corporation

Presents role for others to identify
with and to follow

Communicates high performance
standards and also shows
confidence in the followers abilities
to meet these standards.

Role of Top Management

Boards are getting
more involved

Increased pressures form
institutional investors is motivating
companies to improve their
corporate governance practices

Directors and top managements are
being asked to own more stock
options in the companies.

Nonaffiliated directors
are increasing

Guidelines for who can become
members are being set

Boards are expected to balance
economic goals with societal needs

Trends in Corporate Goverance

Act was designed to protect
shareholders from the excesses
and failed oversight that
characterizes failures at companies
like enron.

As for India, The Sarbanes Oxley
ACT (SOX) does not apply directly.
The regulators in India have
amended Clause 49 to make
company managements more
responsive. In Clause 49, stress
has been laid on disclosures by
companies by making periodic
disclosures from time to time

Sarbanes Oxley Act

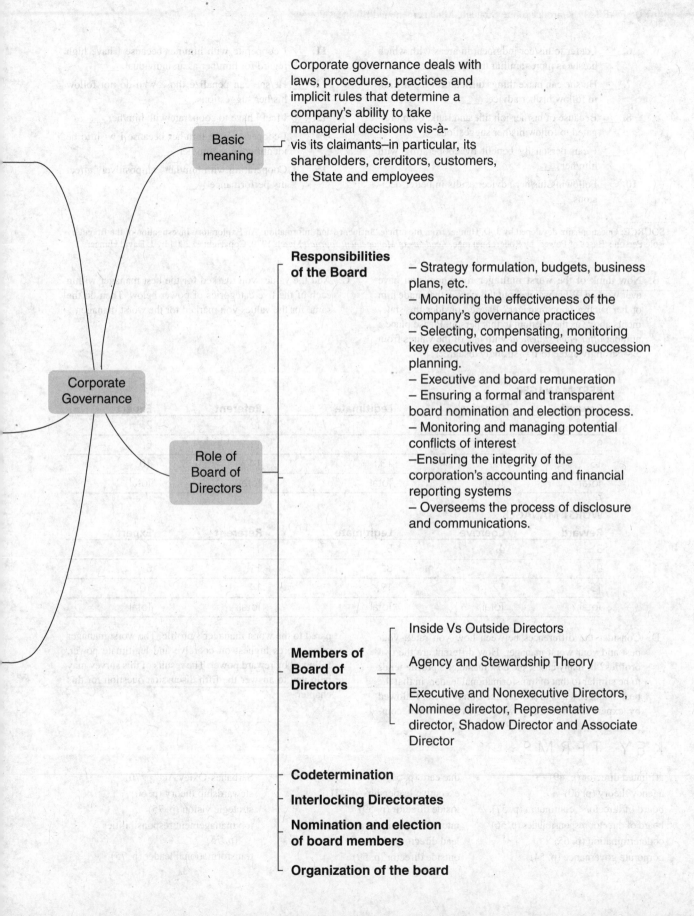

Corporate Governance

Basic meaning

Corporate governance deals with laws, procedures, practices and implicit rules that determine a company's ability to take managerial decisions vis-à-vis its claimants–in particular, its shareholders, crerditors, customers, the State and employees

Role of Board of Directors

Responsibilities of the Board

– Strategy formulation, budgets, business plans, etc.
– Monitoring the effectiveness of the company's governance practices
– Selecting, compensating, monitoring key executives and overseeing succession planning.
– Executive and board remuneration
– Ensuring a formal and transparent board nomination and election process.
– Monitoring and managing potential conflicts of interest
–Ensuring the integrity of the corporation's accounting and financial reporting systems
– Overseems the process of disclosure and communications.

Members of Board of Directors

Inside Vs Outside Directors

Agency and Stewardship Theory

Executive and Nonexecutive Directors, Nominee director, Representative director, Shadow Director and Associate Director

Codetermination

Interlocking Directorates

Nomination and election of board members

Organization of the board

6. ___ I defer to his/her judgment in areas with which he/she is more familiar than I. ___

7. ___ He/she can make things difficult for me if I fail to follow his/her advice. ___

8. ___ Because of his/her job title and rank, I am obligated to follow his/her suggestions. ___

9. ___ I can personally benefit by cooperating with him/her. ___

10. ___ Following his/her advice results in better decisions. ___

11. ___ I cooperate with him/her because I have high regard for him/her as an individual. ___

12. ___ He/she can penalize those who do not follow his/her suggestions. ___

13. ___ I feel I have to cooperate with him/her. ___

14. ___ I cooperate with him/her because I wish to be identified with him/her. ___

15. ___ Cooperating with him/her can positively affect my performance. ___

SOURCE: Questionnaire developed by J. D. Hunger from the article "Influence and Information: An Exploratory Investigation of the Boundary Role Person's Bases of Power" by Robert Spekman, *Academy of Management Journal*, March 1979. Copyright © 2004 by J. David Hunger.

B. Now think of the **worst manager** for whom you have ever worked. What was it about this person that made him or her such a poor manager? Please consider the statements above as they pertain to that person. Please place a number *after each statement* with one of the values from 5 = strongly agree to 1 = strongly disagree.

C. Add the values you marked for the best manager within each of the five categories of power below. Then do the same for the values you marked for the worst manager.

BEST MANAGER

Reward	Coercive	Legitimate	Referent	Expert
3.	4.	5.	1.	2.
9.	7.	8.	11.	6.
15.	12.	13.	14.	10.
Total	Total	Total	Total	Total

WORST MANAGER

Reward	Coercive	Legitimate	Referent	Expert
3.	4.	5.	1.	2.
9.	7.	8.	11.	6.
15.	12.	13.	14.	10.
Total	Total	Total	Total	Total

D. Consider the differences between how you rated your best and your worst manager. How different are the two profiles? In many cases, the best manager's profile tends to be similar to that of transformational leaders in that the best manager tends to score highest on referent, followed by expert and reward, power—especially when compared to the worst manager's profile. The worst manager often scores highest on coercive and legitimate power, followed by reward power. The results of this survey may help you to answer the fifth discussion question for this chapter.

KEY TERMS

affiliated director (p. 49)

agency theory (p. 60)

board of directors' continuum (p. 57)

board of director responsibilities (p. 56)

codetermination (p. 65)

corporate governance (p. 54)

due care (p. 57)

executive leadership (p. 75)

inside director (p. 59)

interlocking directorate (p. 65)

lead director (p. 69)

outside director (p. 59)

Sarbanes-Oxley Act (p. 70)

stewardship theory (p. 60)

strategic vision (p. 75)

top management responsibilities (p. 73)

transformational leader (p. 75)

NOTES

1. Babu Venkatesha, Truth about Satyam: Rise and fall of Rama-linga Raju, Posted on Thu, Jan 8 2009. 4:00 AM IST, recovered on 20th April 2009, from Hindustan Times Media website, http://www.livemint.com/2009/01/07213322/Truth-about-Satyam-Rise-and-f.html?atype=tp

2. Forbes.com LLC™, B. Ramalinga Raju, recovered on 20th April 2009, from http://people.forbes.com/profile/b-ramalinga-raju/70160

3. Satyam Computer Services Limited, recovered on 20th April 2009 from http://www.satyam.com/about/milestones.asp

4. e-Eighteen.com Ltd, Satyam Computer Services, recovered on 20th April 2009, from http://www.moneycontrol.com/stocks/company_info/company_history.php?sc_did=SCS

5. Satyam Computer Services Limited, recovered on 20th Apr 2009, from http://www.satyam.com/about/about_us.asp

6. The Financial Express, Satyam fraud: Full text of Raju's letter to board, posted on 2009-01-07 17:05:27+05:30 IST, Updated: January 07, 2009 at 17:05 hrs IST, recovered on 20th Apr 2009, from http://www.financialexpress.com/news/satyam-fraud-full-text-of-rajus-letter-to-board/407799/.

7. Indian Express, Tough to guess size of Satyam scam: SEBI, posted on Wednesday, January 21, 2009 at 16:26 hrs IST, recovered on 20th Apr 2009, from http://www.indianexpress.com/news/tough-to-guess-size-of-satyam-scam-sebi/413545/

8. Economic Times, Satyam fraud clouds corporate governance of India Inc., posted on 7 Jan 2009, 1234 hrs IST , recovered on 20th April 2009 from the Bennett Coleman & Co. Ltd site, http://economictimes.indiatimes.com/articleshow/3946405.cms

9. CNBC tv 18, Satyam-Maytas deal: ADRs hit; Templeton, CLSA unhappy, posted Tue, Dec 16, 2008 at 18:57, Updated at Tue, Dec 16, 2008 at 21:41, recovered on 20th April 2009, from http://www.moneycontrol.com/india/news/fii-view/satyam-maytas-deal-adrs-hit-templeton-clsa-unhappy-/371134

10. The Hindu Business Line, "Satyam's Independent Directors Had Raised Concerns Over the deal," posted on Friday, December 19, 2008, recovered on 20th April 2009, from http://www.thehindubusinessline.com/bline/2008/12/19/stries/2008121951600400.htm

11. S. Gopalakrishnan, Role & Responsibilities of Independent Directors, The Chartered Accountant, January 2005, pp. 861–866, recovered on 20th Apr 2009, from http://www.icai.org/resource_file/10500jan05p861-866.pdf

12. Editorial, International Business Times, Satyam: Corporate governance revisited, posted on 20 January 2009 @ 02:40 am IST, recovered on 20th April 2009, from http://www.ibtimes.co.in/articles/20090119/editorial-satyam-corporate-governance-norms-revisited_all.htm

13. Economic Times, Satyam board of directors' role comes under spotlight, posted on 18 Dec 2008, 0719 hrs IST, TNN, recovered on 20th April 2009 from the Bennett Coleman & Co. Ltd site, http://economictimes.indiatimes.com/Infotech/Software/Satyam_board_of_directors_role_comes_under_spotlight_/articleshow/3855141.cms

14. India Knowledge@Wharton, Scandal at Satyam: Truth, Lies and Corporate Governance, posted on January 09, 2009 on Wharton School of the University of Pennsylvania website, recovered on 20th April 2009, from http://knowledge.wharton.upenn.edu/india/article.cfm?articleid=4344

15. Thai Indian News, Satyam director went by 'conscience' to quit board, posted on December 26th, 2008 - 8:26 pm ICT by IANS, recovered from 20th April 2009, from http://www.thaindian.com/newsportal/business/satyam-director-went-by-conscience-to-quit-board_100135361.html

16. Zee News Limited, Auditor PW party to falsification of Satyam accounts: SFIO, posted on New Delhi, 17th April 2009, recovered on 20th April 2009, from http://www.zeenews.com/business/companies-commodities/2009-04-17/524351news.html

17. A. G. Monks and N. Minow, *Corporate Governance* (Cambridge, MA: Blackwell Business, 1995), pp. 8–32.

18. Ibid., p. 1.

19. A. Demb, and F. F. Neubauer, "The Corporate Board: Confronting the Paradoxes," *Long Range Planning* (June 1992), p. 13. These results are supported by a 1995 Korn/Ferry International survey in which chairs and directors agreed that strategy and management succession, in that order, are the most important issues the board expects to face.

20. Reported by E. L. Biggs in "CEO Succession Planning: An Emerging Challenge for Boards of Directors," *Academy of Management Executive* (February 2004), pp. 105–107.

21. A. Borrus, "Less Laissez-Faire in Delaware?" *Business Week* (March 22, 2004), pp. 80–82.

22. S. Gopalakrishnan, Role and Responsibilities of Independent Directors, The Chartered Accountant, JANUARY 2005, pg 866-861.

23. L. Light, "Why Outside Directors Have Nightmares," *Business Week* (October 23, 1996), p. 6.

24. "Where's All the Fun Gone?" *Economist* (March 20, 2004), p. 76.

25. A. Chen, J. Osofsky, and E. Stephenson, "Making the Board More Strategic: A McKinsey Global Survey," *McKinsey Quarterly* (March 2008), pp. 1–10.

26. Nadler proposes a similar five-step continuum for board involvement ranging from the least involved "passive board" to the most involved "operating board," plus a form for measuring board involvement in D. A. Nadler, "Building Better Boards," *Harvard Business Review* (May 2004), pp. 102–111.

27. H. Ashbaugh, D. W. Collins, and R. LaFond, "The Effects of Corporate Governance on Firms' Credit Ratings," unpublished paper (March, 2004); W. Q. Judge Jr., and C. P. Zeithaml, "Institutional and Strategic Choice Perspectives on Board Involvement in the Strategic Choice Process," *Academy of Management Journal* (October 1992), pp. 766–794; J. A. Pearce II, and S. A. Zahra, "Effective Power-Sharing Between the Board of Directors and the CEO," *Handbook of Business Strategy*, 1992/93 Yearbook (Boston: Warren, Gorham, and Lamont, 1992), pp. 1.1–1.16.

28. *Current Board Practices,* American Society of Corporate Secretaries, 2002 as reported by B. Atkins in "Directors Don't Deserve such a Punitive Policy,"*Directors & Boards* (Summer 2002), p. 23.

29. A. Chen, J. Osofsky, and E. Stephenson, "Making the Board More Strategic: A McKinsey Global Survey," *McKinsey Quarterly* (March 2008), pp. 1–10.

30. *33rd Annual Board of Directors Study* (New York: Korn/Ferry International, 2007).

31. "What Directors Know About their Companies: A McKinsey-Survey,"*McKinsey Quarterly Web Exclusive* (March 2006).

32. D. A. Nadler, "Building Better Boards," *Harvard Business Review* (May 2004), pp. 102–111; L. Lavelle, "The Best and Worst Boards," *Business Week* (October 7, 2002), pp. 104–114.

33. Nadler, p. 109.

34. M. K. Fiegener, "Determinants of Board Participation in the Strategic Decisions of Small Corporations,"*Entrepreneurship Theory and Practice* (September 2005), pp. 627–650.

35. Fiegener; A. L. Ranft and H. M. O'Neill, "Board Composition and High-Flying Founders: Hints of Trouble to Come?" *Academy of Management Executive* (February 2001), pp. 126–138.

36. Financial Express, Dabur India To Evaluate Board Of Directors, Posted: 2004-01-19 00:00:00+05:30 IST, Updated: Jan 19, 2004 at 0000 hrs IS, Recovered on 11th Oct 2011, from The Indian Express Limited website, http://www.financialexpress.com/news/dabur-india-to-evaluate-board-of-directors/97569/

37. Jaffe Dennis T., Joseph Rosenthat and Anish Gupta, Dabur India Ltd, Families in Business, February 2002, pg 37-41, Recovered on 11th Oct 2011from http://www.dennisjaffe.com/articles/DaburFamily.pdf

38. D. R. Dalton, M. A. Hitt, S. Trevis Certo, and C. M. Dalton, "The Fundamental Agency Problem and Its Mitigation," Chapter One in *Academy of Management Annals*, edited by J. F. Westfall and A. F. Brief (London: Rutledge, 2007); Y. Deutsch, "The Impact of Board Composition on Firms' Critical Decisions: A Meta-Analytic Review," *Journal of Management* (June 2005), pp. 424–444; D. F. Larcher, S. A. Richardson, and I. Tuna, "Does Corporate Governance Really Matter?" *Knowledge @ Wharton* (September 8–21, 2004); J. Merritt and L. Lavelle, "A Different Kind of Governance Guru," *Business Week* (August 9, 2004), pp. 46–47; A. Dehaene, V. DeVuyst, and H. Ooghe, "Corporate Performance and Board Structure in Belgian Companies," *Long Range Planning* (June 2001), pp. 383–398; M. W. Peng, "Outside Directors and Firm Performance During Institutional Transitions," *Strategic Management Journal* (May 2004), pp. 453–471.

39. D. R. Dalton, M. A. Hitt, S. Trevis Certo, and C. M. Dalton, "The Fundamental Agency Problem and Its Mitigation," Chapter One in *Academy of Management Annals*, edited by J. F. Westfall and A. F. Brief (London: Rutledge, 2007).

40. *33rd Annual Board of Directors Study* (New York: Korn/Ferry International, 2007), p. 11.

41. *30th Annual Board of Directors Study* (New York: Korn/Ferry International, 2003).

42. M. K. Fiegerer, "Determinants of Board Participation in the Strategic Decisions of Small Corporations," *Entrepreneurship Theory and Practice* (September 2005), pp. 627–650; S. K. Lee and G. Filbeck, "Board Size and Firm Performance: Case of Small Firms," *Proceedings of the Academy of Accounting and Financial Studies* (2006), pp. 43–46; W. S. Schulze, M. H. Lubatkin, R. N. Dino, and A. K. Buchholtz, "Agency Relationships in Family Firms: Theory and Evidence," *Organization Science* (March–April, 2001), pp. 99–116.

43. Department of Public Enterprises Composition of Board of Directors of Public Sector Undertakings, DPE OM No. 18(6)/2000-GM dated November 26, 2001, recovered on 11th Oct 2011, from http://dpe.nic.in/v29a.htm

44. S. K. Lee and G. Filbeck, "Board Size and Firm Performance: The Case of Small Firms," *Proceedings of the Academy of Accounting and Financial Studies* (2006), pp. 43–46.

45. J. J. Reur and R. Ragozzino, "Agency Hazards and Alliance Portfolios," *Strategic Management Journal* (January 2006), pp. 27–43.

46. M. Goranova, T. M. Alessandri, P. Brades, and R. Dharwadkar, "Managerial Ownership and Corporate Diversification: A Longitudinal View," *Strategic Management Journal* (March 2007), pp. 211–225; B. K. Boyd, S. Gove, and M. A. Hitt, "Consequences of Measurement Problems in Strategic Management Research: The Case of Amihud and Lev," *Strategic Management Journal* (April 2005), pp. 367–375; J. P. Katz and B. P. Niehoff, "How Owners Influence Strategy—A Comparison of Owner-Controlled and Manager-Controlled Firms," *Long Range Planning* (October 1998), pp. 755–761; M. Kroll, P. Wright, L. Toombs, and H. Leavell, "Form of Control: A Critical Determinant of Acquisition Performance and CEO Rewards," *Strategic Management Journal* (February 1997), pp. 85–96.

47. L. Tihanyi, R. A. Johnson, R. E. Hoskisson, and M. A. Hitt, "Institutional Ownership Differences and International Diversification: The Effects of Boards of Directors and Technological Opportunity," *Academy of Management Journal* (April 2003), pp. 195–211; A. E. Ellstrand, L. Tihanyi, and J. L. Johnson, "Board Structure and International Political Risk," *Academy of Management Journal* (August 2002), pp. 769–777; S. A. Zahra, D. O. Neubaum, and M. Huse, "Entrepreneurship in Medium-Size Companies: Exploring the Effects of Ownership and Governance Systems," *Journal of Management*, Vol. 26, No. 5 (2000), pp. 947–976.

48. G. Kassinis and N. Vafeas, "Corporate Boards and Outside Stakeholders as Determinants of Environmental Litigation," *Strategic Management Journal* (May 2002), pp. 399–415; P. Dunn, "The Impact of Insider Power on Fraudulent Financial Reporting," *Journal of Management*, Vol. 30, No. 3 (2004), pp. 397–412.

49. R. C. Anderson and D. M. Reeb, "Board Composition: Balancing Family Influence in S&P 500 Firms," *Administrative Science Quarterly* (June 2004), pp. 209–237; W. S. Schulze, M. H. Lubatkin, R. N. Dino, and A. K. Buckholtz, "Agency Relationships in Family Firms: Theory and Evidence," *Organization Science* (March–April, 2001), pp. 99–116.

50. M. N. Young, A. K. Bushholtz, and D. Ahlstrom, "How Can Board Members Be Empowered If They Are Spread Too Thin?" *SAM Advanced Management Journal* (Autumn 2003), pp. 4–11.

51. *33rd Annual Board of Directors Study* (New York: Korn/Ferry International, 2007), p. 21.

52. Securities and Exchange Board of India, Issues under Clause 49 and proposed amendments, recovered on 11th Oct 2011, from http://www.sebi.gov.in/commreport/clause49.html

53. International Finance Corporation, Types of Directors, Powered by Legal pundits International Services Pvt. Ltd, recovered on 11th Oct 2011, from http://india.smetoolkit.org/india/en/content/en/37041/Types-of-Directors

54. Securities and Exchange Board of India, Issues under Clause 49 and proposed amendments, recovered on 11th Oct 2011, from http://www.sebi.gov.in/commreport/clause49.html

55. M. Y. Khan, "Role of Public Representative Director in Corporate Governance," *The Business Line*, posted on Tuesday, September 18, 2007, recovered on 11th Oct 2011, from The Hindu Group of Publications website http://www.thehindubusinessline.com/2007/09/18/stories/2007091851300900.htm

56. Batgach network approved by Institute of Chartered Accountants of India, Newsletter, recovered on 11th Oct 2011, from http://www.batgach.com/pdf/1.pdf

57. Hero Honda, recovered on 11th Oct 2011, from http://www.herohonda.com/co_board_directors.htm

58. IFCI Ltd, recovered on 11th Oct 2011 from http://www.ifciltd.com/AboutUs/BoardofDirectors/tabid/83/Default.aspx

59. "TIAA-CREF's Role in Corporate Governance," *Investment Forum* (June 2003), p. 13.

60. "Jobs for the Girls," *The Economist* (May 3, 2008), p. 73; "Girl Power," *The Economist* (January 5, 2008), p. 54.

61. *33rd Annual Board of Directors Study* (New York: Korn/Ferry International, 2007), p. 11; T. Neff and J. H. Daum, "The Empty Boardroom," *Strategy + Business* (Summer 2007), pp. 57–61.

62. R. O. Crockett, "The Rising Stock of Black Directors," *Business Week* (February 27, 2006), p. 34.

63. J. Daum, "Portrait of Boards on the Cusp of Historic Change," *Directors & Boards* (Winter 2003), p. 56; J. Daum, "SSBI: Audit Committees Are Leading the Change," *Directors & Boards* (Winter 2004), p. 59.

64. *30th Annual Board of Directors Study* (New York: Korn/Ferry International, 2003) p. 38.

65. *Globalizing the Board of Directors: Trends and Strategies* (New York: The Conference Board, 1999).

66. *33rd Annual Board of Directors Study* (New York: Korn/Ferry International, 2007), p. 15.

67. R. W. Pouder and R. S. Cantrell, "Corporate Governance Reform: Influence on Shareholder Wealth," *Journal of Business Strategies* (Spring 1999), pp. 48–66.

68. The Financial Express, Is there any control on directors' remuneration? Posted: 2005-11-20 00:00:00+05:30 IST Updated: November 20, 2005 at 00:00 hrs IST, recovered on 11th Oct 2011, from The Indian Express Limited website, http://www.financialexpress.com/news/is-there-any-control-on-directors-remuneration/82881/0

69. Net Lawman Ltd., Companies Act, 1956: Remuneration of Directors, recovered on 11th Oct 2011, from http://www.netlawman.co.in/acts/companies-act-1956.php?pageContentID=1086

70. Business.gov.in, Companies Laws: Corporate Governance, recovered on 11th Oct 2011, from Government of India website http://business.gov.in/corporate_governance/companies_laws.php

71. Business Line, Corporate Law Forum: Mr L. V. V. Iyer replies to Readers Queries, posted Monday, February 07, 2000, recoveres on 11th Oct 2011, from The Hindu Group website, http://www.thehindubusinessline.com/2000/02/07/stories/020718ka.htm

72. P. P. Krishna, Corporate Governance and Directors Remuneration, The Chartered Accountant, May 2005, pp. 1483–1489, recovered on 11th Oct 2011, from www.icai.org/resource_file/10641may05p1483-89.pdf

73. Draft Guidelines on Employee Stock Option Plans/Employee Stock Purchase Plans (ESOP/ ESPP), recovered on 11th Oct 2011, from http://www.iimahd.ernet.in/~jrvarma/reports/esop/GuidLine.pdf

74. M. L. Gerlach, "The Japanese Corporate Network: A Blockmodel Analysis," *Administrative Science Quarterly* (March 1992), pp. 105–139.

75. W. E. Stead and J. G. Stead, *Sustainable Strategic Management* (Armonk, NY: M. E. Sharp, 2004), p. 47.

76. J. D. Westphal, M. L. Seidel, and K. J. Stewart, "Second-Order Imitation: Uncovering Latent Effects of Board Network Ties," *Administrative Science Quarterly* (December 2001), pp. 717–747; M. A. Geletkanycz, B. K. Boyd, and S. Finkelstein, "The Strategic Value of CEO External Directorate Networks: Implications for CEO Compensation," *Strategic Management Journal* (September 2001), pp. 889–898; M. A. Carpenter and J. D. Westphal, "The Strategic Context of External Network Ties: Examining the Impact of Director Appointments on Board Involvement in Strategic Decision Making," *Academy of Management Journal* (August 2001), pp. 639–660.

77. M. Warner, "Inside the Silicon Valley Money Machine," *Fortune* (October 26, 1998), pp. 128–140.

78. D. Jones and B. Hansen, "Chairmen Still Doing Do-Si-Do," *USA Today* (November 5, 2003), p. 3B; J. H. Daum and T. J. Neff, "SSBI: Audit Committees Are Leading the Charge," *Directors & Boards* (Winter 2003), p. 59.

79. J. A. C. Baum and C. Oliver, "Institutional Linkages and Organizational Mortality," *Administrative Science Quarterly* (June 1991) pp. 187–218; J. P. Sheppard, "Strategy and Bankruptcy: An Exploration into Organizational Death," *Journal of Management* (Winter 1994), pp. 795–833.

80. *33rd Annual Board of Directors Study* (New York: Korn/Ferry International, 2007), p. 44 and *Directors' Compensation and Board Practices in 2003*, Research Report R-1339-03-RR (New York: Conference Board, 2003) Table 49, p. 38.

81. J. Canavan, B. Jones, and M. J. Potter, "Board Tenure: How Long Is Too Long?" *Boards & Directors* (Winter 2004), pp. 39–42.

82. *33rd Annual Board of Directors Study* (New York: Korn/Ferry International, 2007), p. 17 and *30th Annual Board of Directors Study Supplement: Governance Trends of the Fortune 1000* (New York: Korn/Ferry International, 2004), p. 5.

83. D. F. Larcker and S. A. Richardson, "Does Governance Really Matter?" *Knowledge @ Wharton* (September 8–21, 2004).

84. M. L. McDonald, J. D. Westphal, and M. E. Graebner, "What Do they Know? The Effects of Outside Director Acquisition Experience on Firm Acquisition Experience," *Strategic Management Journal* (November 2008), pp. 1155–1177.

85. The Financial Express, Sebi Clause 49 to make corporate governance more effective, Posted: 2005-10-24 02:09:32+05:30 IST, Updated: October 24, 2005 at 02:09 hrs IST, recovered on 11th Oct 2011, from The Indian Express Limited website http://www.financialexpress.com/news/sebi-clause-49-to-make-corporate-governance-more-effective/154340/

86. *26th Annual Board of Directors Study* (New York: Korn/Ferry International, 1999), p. 30.

87. *30th Annual Board of Directors Study* (New York: Korn/Ferry International, 2003), pp. 8, 31, 44.

88. The Hindu Business Line, "India Inc. needs to do more on corporate governance front," posted on Feb. 17 2005 from New Delhi , Recovered on 11th Oct 2011from The Hindu Business Line website http://www.thehindubusinessline.com/2005/02/18/stories/2005021801701000.htm

89. ICRA, Emerging Board Practices—A Survey, ICRA Rating Feature February 2005, recovered on 11th Oct 2011, from http://www.icra.in/Files/PDF/ArticleFiles/2005-February-EmergingboardCGR.pdf

90. D. R. Dalton, M. A. Hitt, S. Trevis Certo, and C. M. Dalton, "The Fundamental Agency Problem and Its Mitigation," Chapter One in *Academy of Management Annals*, edited by J. F. Westfall and A. F. Brief (London: Rutledge, 2007); P. Coombes and S. C-Y Wong, "Chairman and CEO—One Job or Two?" *McKinsey Quarterly* (2004, No. 2), pp. 43–47.

91. A. Desai, M. Kroll, and P. Wright, "CEO Duality, Board Monitoring, and Acquisition Performance," *Journal of Business*

Strategies (Fall 2003), pp. 147–156; D. Harris and C. E. Helfat, "CEO Duality, Succession, Capabilities and Agency Theory: Commentary and Research Agenda," *Strategic Management Journal* (September 1998), pp. 901–904; C. M. Daily and D. R. Dalton, "CEO and Board Chair Roles Held Jointly or Separately: Much Ado About Nothing," *Academy of Management Executive* (August 1997), pp. 11–20; D. L. Worrell, C. Nemec, and W. N. Davidson III, "One Hat Too Many: Key Executive Plurality and Shareholder Wealth," *Strategic Management Journal* (June 1997), pp. 499–507; J. W. Coles and W. S. Hesterly, "Independence of the Chairman and Board Composition: Firm Choices and Shareholder Value," *Journal of Management*, Vol. 26, No. 2 (2000), pp. 195–214; H. Ashbaugh, D. W. Collins, and R. LaFond, "The Effects of Corporate Governance on Firms' Credit Ratings," unpublished paper, March 2004.

92. J. P. O'Connor, R. I. Priem, J. E. Coombs, and K. M. Gilley, "Do CEO Stock Options Prevent or Promote Fraudulent Financial Reporting?" *Academy of Management Journal* (June 2006), pp. 483–500.

93. N. R. Augustine, "How Leading a Role for the Lead Director?" *Directors & Boards* (Winter 2004), pp. 20–23.

94. D. R. Dalton, M. A. Hitt, S. Trevis Certo, and C. M. Dalton, "The Fundamental Agency Problem and Its Mitigation," Chapter One in *Academy of Management Annals*, edited by J. F. Westfall and A. F. Brief (London: Rutledge, 2007).

95. *33rd Annual Board of Directors Study* (New York: Korn/Ferry International, 2007), p. 21.

96. J. D. Westphal and I. Stern, "Flattery Will Get You Everywhere (Especially If You Are a Male Caucasian): How Ingratiation, Boardroom Behavior, and Demographic Minority Status Affect Additional Board Appointments at U.S. Companies," *Academy of Management Journal* (April 2007), pp. 267–288; J. D. Westphal, "Board Games: How CEOs Adapt to Increases in Structural Board Independence from Management," *Administrative Science Quarterly* (September 1998), pp. 511–537; J. D. Westphal and P. Khanna, "Keeping Directors in Line: Social Distancing as a Control Mechanism in the Corporate Elite," *Administrative Science Quarterly* (September 2003), pp. 361–398.

97. H. L. Tosi, W. Shen, and R. J. Gentry, "Why Outsiders on Boards Can't Solve the Corporate Governance Problem," *Organizational Dynamics*, Vol. 32, No. 2 (2003), pp. 180–192.

98. *33rd Annual Board of Directors Study* (New York: Korn/Ferry International, 2007), p. 12. Other committees are succession planning (39%), finance (30%), corporate responsibility (17%), and investment (15%).

99. Business Standard, Boards Score well in ICRA study, posted on February 17, 2005 from New Delhi, recovered on 11th Oct 2011, from http://www.business-standard.com/india/news/boards-score-well-in-icra-study/203282/

100. "The Trial of Sarbanes-Oxley," *The Economist* (April 22, 2006), pp. 59–60; *33rd Annual Board of Directors Study* (New York: Korn/Ferry International, 2007), p. 14; S. Wagner and L. Dittmar, "The Unexpected Benefits of Sarbanes-Oxley," *Harvard Business Review* (April 2006), pp. 133–140.

101. A. Borrus, "Learning to Love Sarbanes-Oxley," *Business Week* (November 21, 2005), pp. 126–128.

102. D. Henry, "Not Everyone Hates SarbOx," *Business Week* (January 29, 2007), p. 37.

103. D. Henry, "A SarbOx Surprise," *Business Week* (January 12, 2006), p. 38.

104. The Indian Express Limited, Will India have "real" corporate governance? Posted on January 30, 2005 at 00:00 hrs IST, recovered on 11th Oct 2011, from http://www.screenindia.com/news/will-india-have-real-corporate-governance/47564/

105. KRChoksey Research, Sarabanes-Oxley Act(SOX): Is India Inc. listening, posted on May 7, 2005, recovered on 11th Oct 2011, from http://www.valuenotes.com/krc/krc_weekender_07may05.pdf?ArtCd=35050&Cat=&Id=

106. *30th Annual Board of Directors Study Supplement: Governance Trends of the Fortune 1000* (New York: Korn/Ferry International, 2004), p. 5.

107. "Where's All the Fun Gone?" *Economist* (March 20, 2004), pp. 75–77.

108. Daum and Neff (2004), p. 58.

109. *33rd Annual Board of Directors Study* (New York: Korn/Ferry International, 2007), p. 7.

110. J. Sonnenfeld, "Good Governance and the Misleading Myths of Bad Metrics." *Academy of Management Executive* (February 2004), pp. 108–113.

111. H. Ashbaugh, D. W. Collins, and R. LaFond, "The Effects of Corporate Governance on Firms' Credit Ratings," unpublished paper (March 2002).

112. I. Sager, "Access Denied: A Private Matter," *Business Week* (January 26, 2004), p. 13; J. Weber, "One Share, Many Votes," *Business Week* (March 29, 2004), pp. 94–95.

113. E. Thorton, "Corporate Control Freaks," *Business Week* (May 31, 2004), p. 86.

114. D. R. Dalton, C. M. Daily, A. E. Ellstrand, and J. L. Johnson, "Meta-Analytic Reviews of Board Composition, Leadership Structure, and Financial Performance," *Strategic Management Journal* (March 1998), pp. 269–290; G. Beaver, "Competitive Advantage and Corporate Governance—Shop Soiled and Needing Attention!" *Strategic Change* (September–October 1999), p. 330.

115. A. Borrus and L. Young, "Nothing Like a Little Exposure," *Business Week* (September 13, 2004), p. 92.

116. P. Silva, "Do Motivation and Equity Ownership Matter in Board of Directors' Evaluation of CEO Performance?" *Journal of Management Issues* (Fall 2005), pp. 346–362.

117. L. He and M. J. Conyon, "The Role of Compensation Committees in CEO and Committee Compensation Decisions," paper presented to *Academy of Management* (Seattle, WA, 2003).

118. P. Coy, E. Thornton, M. Arndt, B. Grow, and A. Park, "Shake, Rattle, and Merge," *Business Week* (January 10, 2005), pp. 32–35.

119. L. Lavelle, "A Fighting Chance for Boardroom Democracy," *Business Week* (June 9, 2003), p. 50; L. Lavelle, "So That's Why Boards Are Waking Up," *Business Week* (January 19, 2004), pp. 72–73.

120. For a detailed description of the COO's role, see N. Bennett and S. A. Miles, "Second in Command," *Harvard Business Review* (May 2006), pp. 71–78.

121. S. Finkelstein and D. C. Hambrick, *Strategic Leadership: Top Executives and Their Impact on Organizations* (St. Louis: West, 1996).

122. H. G. Barkema and O. Shvyrkov, "Does Top Management Team Diversity Promote or Hamper Foreign Expansion?" *Strategic Management Journal* (July 2007), pp. 663–680; D. C. Hambrick, T. S. Cho, and M-J Chen, "The Influence of Top Management Team Heterogeneity on Firms' Competitive Moves," *Administrative Science Quarterly* (December 1996), pp. 659–684.

123. P. Pitcher and A. D. Smith, "Top Management Heterogeneity: Personality, Power, and Proxies," *Organization Science*

(January–February 2001), pp. 1–18; M. A. Carpenter and J. W. Fredrickson, "Top Management Teams, Global Strategic Posture, and the Moderating Role of Uncertainty," *Academy of Management Journal* (June 2001), pp. 533–545; M. A. Carpenter, "The Implications of Strategy and Social Context for the Relationship Between Top Management Team Heterogeneity and Firm Performance," *Strategic Management Journal* (March 2002), pp. 275–284; L. Tihanyi, A. E. Ellstrand, C. M. Daily, and D. R. Dalton, "Composition of the Top Management Team and Firm International Expansion," *Journal of Management*, Vol. 26, No. 6 (2000), pp. 1157–1177.

124. "One on One with Steve Reinemund," *Business Week* (December 17, 2001), Special advertising insert on leadership by Heidrick & Struggles, executive search firm.

125. D. A. Waldman, G. G. Ramirez, R. J. House, and P. Puranam, "Does Leadership Matter? CEO Leadership Attributes and Profitability Under Conditions of Perceived Environmental Uncertainty," *Academy of Management Journal* (February 2001), pp. 134–143; F. J. Flynn and B. M. Staw, "Lend Me Your Wallets: The Effect of Charismatic Leadership on External Support for an Organization," *Strategic Management Journal* (April 2004), pp. 309–330.

126. J. Burns, *Leadership* (New York: HarperCollins, 1978); B. Bass, "From Transactional to Transformational Leadership: Learning to Share the Vision," *Organizational Dynamics*, Vol. 18 (1990), pp. 19–31; W. Bennis and B. Nanus, *Leaders: Strategies for Taking Charge* (New York: HarperCollins, 1997).

127. Based on R. J. House, "A 1976 Theory of Charismatic Leadership," in J. G. Hunt and L. L. Larson (Eds.), *Leadership: The Cutting Edge* (Carbondale, IL: Southern Illinois University Press, 1976), pp. 189–207. Also see J. Choi, "A Motivational Theory of Charismatic Leadership: Envisioning, Empathy, and Empowerment," *Journal of Leadership and Organizational Studies* (2006), Vol. 13, No. 1, pp. 24–43.

128. I. D. Colville and A. J. Murphy, "Leadership as the Enabler of Strategizing and Organizing," *Long Range Planning* (December 2006), pp. 663–677.

129. L. V. Gerstner Jr., *Who Says Elephants Can't Dance?* (New York: HarperCollins, 2002), p. 124.

130. M. Lipton, "Demystifying the Development of an Organizational Vision," *Sloan Management Review* (Summer 1996), p. 84.

131. S. Hahn, "Why High Tech Has to Stay Humble," *Business Week* (January 19, 2004), pp. 76–77.

132. J. H. David, F. D. Schoorman, R. Mayer, and H. H. Tan, "The Trusted General Manager and Business Unit Performance:

Empirical Evidence of a Competitive Advantage," *Strategic Management Journal* (May 2000), pp. 563–576.

133. D. B. McNatt and T. A. Judge, "Boundary Conditions of the Galatea Effect: A Field Experiment and Constructive Replication," *Academy of Management Journal* (August 2004), pp. 550–565.

134. R. F. Piccolo and J. A. Colquitt, "Transformational Leadership and Job Behaviors: The Mediating Role of Core Job Characteristics," *Academy of Management Journal* (April 2006), pp. 327–340; J. E. Bono and T. A. Judge, "Self-Concordance at Work: Toward Understanding the Motivational Effects of Transformational Leaders," *Academy of Management Journal* (October 2003), pp. 554–571.

135. T. Lowry, R. O. Crockett, and I. M. Kunii, "Verizon's Gutsy Bet," *Business Week* (August 4, 2003), pp. 52–62.

136. G. Tate and U. Malmendier, "Who Makes Acquisitions? CEO Overconfidence and the Market's Reaction," summarized by *Knowledge @ Wharton* (February 25, 2004).

137. M. C. Mankins and R. Steele, "Stop Making Plans, Start Making Decisions," *Harvard Business Review* (January 2006), pp. 76–84.

138. T. R. Eisenmann and J. L. Bower, "The Entrepreneurial M Form: Strategic Integration in Global Media Firms," *Organization Science* (May–June 2000), pp. 348–355.

139. J. Kirby and T. A. Stewart, "The Institutional Yes," *Harvard Business Review* (October 2007), p. 76.

140. M. C. Mankins and R. Steele, "Stop Making Plans, Start Making Decisions," *Harvard Business Review* (January 2006), pp. 76–84; G. P. Hodgkinson, R. Whittington, G. Johnson, and M. Schwarz, "The Role of Strategy Workshops in Strategy Development Processes: Formality, Communication, Co-ordination and Inclusion," *Long Range Planning* (October 2006), pp. 479–496; B. Frisch and L. Chandler, "Off-Sites That Work," *Harvard Business Review* (June 2006), pp. 117–126.

141. For a description of the Chief Strategy Officer, see R. T. S. Breene, P. F. Nunes, and W. E. Shill, "The Chief Strategy Officer," *Harvard Business Review* (October 2007), pp. 84–93; R. Dye, "How Chief Strategy Officers Think about their Role: A Roundtable," *McKinsey Quarterly* (May 2008), pp. 1–8.

142. C. Laszlo, *Sustainable Value: How the World's Leading Companies Are Doing Well by Doing Good* (Stanford, CA: Stanford University Press, 2008), pp. 81–88.

social responsibility and ethics in Strategic Management

ITC e-Choupals: A Case Study

ITC is one of India's most valuable companies. One of the key objectives of the company is to strive for a 'Citizen First' kind of corporate image. ITC has always attached critical importance to its responsibility to contribute to preserving and enriching the environment.[1] ITC's contribution to sustainable development extends beyond environment, health, and safety considerations. Through its philosophy of "Transforming Lives and Landscapes," ITC works at empowering farmers, greening wastelands, irrigating dry lands, creating women entrepreneurs, and educating rural children. Through these initiatives, ITC has touched the lives of over two million villagers across the country.[2]

One of its most recognized efforts has been ITCs e-Choupal project.

In 1996–1997, ITCs International Business Division (IBD) was an agri-business which primarily procured and exported agricultural commodities in raw or processed form. It was India's largest overall agricultural exporter.

Indian agricultural markets were opened up in 1996–1997 under the World Trade Organization's rules. With the opening of the Indian economy, IBD faced increasing competition from large, low-cost suppliers of agricultural products in the United States, Brazil, and other countries. These competitors competed on basis of quality, value and price. IBD, in order to find a position for itself in a $1 billion market, needed to match quality and quantity specifications of international markets.

Traditionally, Indian agricultural business value chain was one where Indian farmer was trapped in a vicious cycle of low risk taking ability, low investment, low productivity, weak market orientation, low value addition, low margin and low risk taking ability. Moreover, due to fragmented farms, weak infrastructure commodities market, the market system in India was based on the village *mandi* system. The *mandi* system does not monitor the quality of the product and furthermore, in *mandi* system the trend was to aggregate the produce and thus the quality information was lost.

Due to these market constraints, IBDs procurement costs were much higher. A report on the state of Indian agriculture released in 1997 by McKinsey and Company (FAIDA

- Conduct a stakeholder analysis
- Explain why people may act unethically
- Describe different views of ethics according to the utilitarian, individual rights, and justice approaches

nsibility
een
e

ility

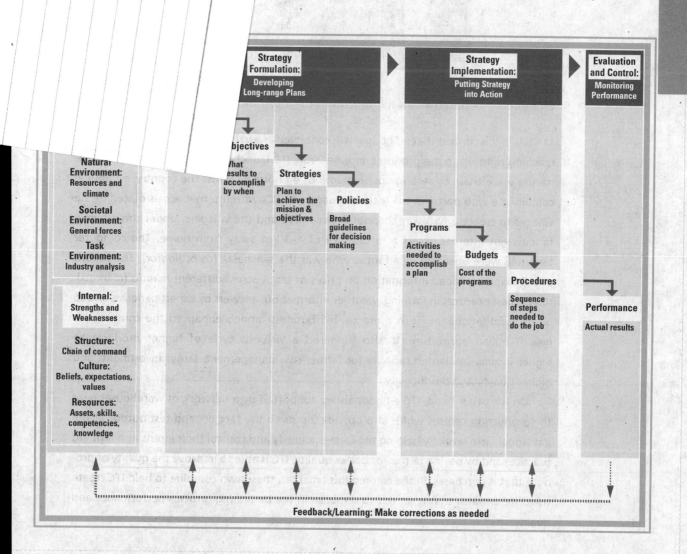

| | **Strategy Formulation:** Developing Long-range Plans | | | **Strategy Implementation:** Putting Strategy into Action | | | **Evaluation and Control:** Monitoring Performance |

Natural Environment: Resources and climate

Societal Environment: General forces

Task Environment: Industry analysis

Internal: Strengths and Weaknesses

Structure: Chain of command

Culture: Beliefs, expectations, values

Resources: Assets, skills, competencies, knowledge

bjectives
What results to accomplish by when

Strategies
Plan to achieve the mission & objectives

Policies
Broad guidelines for decision making

Programs
Activities needed to accomplish a plan

Budgets
Cost of the programs

Procedures
Sequence of steps needed to do the job

Performance
Actual results

Feedback/Learning: Make corrections as needed

report; Confederation of Indian Industry and McKinsey and Company, 1997) lamented India's low productivity and wastage in production and distribution, particularly arising from the small size of landholdings in the country, as a source of higher costs to processors. In order to overcome these market limitations, IBD needed to go in for operational innovation through better control over supply chain, right up to the producer.[3]

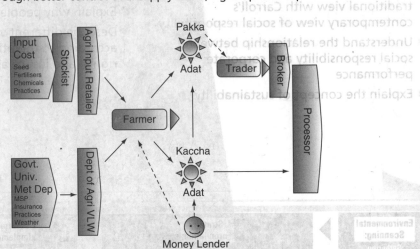

e-Choupals: IT based vertical Integration for International Value chains.

It is in this context that e-Choupal was conceived as a value chain management system, reaching right up to the producer. In June 2000, ITC launched an endeavour to reorganize the value chain by setting up a network of e-Choupals across the country. e-Choupal combined a web portal in the local language and PCs with Internet access placed in the villages to create a two-way channel between ITC and the villagers. Under this scheme, farmers got internet access at a distance of 1–3 km away from home. The computer terminals were operated by a farmer who was the *sanchalak* (co-ordinator). The portals at e-Choupal provided information on prices of crops across different *mandis* (markets), tips on best practices in farming, weather information, answers by expert panelists and so on, in local languages. Such a market-led business model, enhanced the competitiveness of Indian agriculture. It also triggered a virtuous cycle of higher productivity, higher incomes, enlarged capacity for farmer risk management, larger investments and higher quality and productivity.

On the other hand, ITC e-Choupals are supported by a network of warehouses near the production centres which also provide inputs to the farmers and test output at the individual farm level. By helping the farmer identify and control their inputs and farming practices and by paying better for better quality, ITC is able to improve the quality of produce that it purchases. In the commodities market, these two combine to help ITC create the differentiator that it set out to establish in the beginning (process performance and quality).

The effort has paid rich dividends in the domestic markets as well. It is able to customize its products to local tastes as it is able to identify sources of inputs currently. For example, the Aashirvaad brand of *atta* that is sold in the Delhi markets has a different combination, compared to the one sold in the South. The e-Choupal network is now being used to sell ITC as well as third-party products to the villages.

"e-Choupal" services today reach out to more than 3.5 million farmers growing a range of crops – soybean, coffee, wheat, rice, pulses, and shrimp—in over 33,000 villages through 5300 kiosks across six states (Madhya Pradesh, Karnataka, Andhra Pradesh, Uttar Pradesh, Maharashtra, and Rajasthan) (process performance).[4]

Today the major services provided by e-Choupals to the farmers include relevant and real-time information (commodity prices, local weather, and news), customized knowledge (farm management, risk management), supply chain for farm inputs (screened for quality, demand aggregation for competitive prices, and efficient logistics) and direct marketing channel for farm produce (lower transaction costs, better value through traceability). This has, therefore, changed the bottomline for the farmers and interprets into higher incomes through increased yields, improved quality, reduced transaction costs, power of scale to the small farmer, customized knowledge despite heterogeneity and real-time information despite distances.

e-Choupal linked the Indian farmer with consumers in local and global markets, by leveraging ITC's time-tested and proven competencies in marketing and distribution. e-Choupal empowers the farmer's decision making with information (because the price is known in the village itself). Therefore, e-Choupal delivers real-time information and customized knowledge to farmer's decision making ability, securing better quality, and price. In the process many overheads like multiple transportation and handling, bagging, etc. are erased.[5]

Therefore, ITC has managed to use operations as a competitive weapon and capture a major part of market for itself and benefit rural India. Their actual value proposition is a provision of future's price information and the creation of an alternative buying infrastructure, which is supported by computers and connectivity. Financial sustainability of the e-Choupals depends on the ability to recover the investment of the ITC infrastructure but the returns to this project are not from transactions related to computer only but rather from larger re-engineering of the agricultural supply chain.[6]

For its e-Choupal project, ITC has won multiple national and international awards over the years. The list includes the "Corporate Social Responsibility Award 2004,"[7] the UNIDO award as a part of "Innovative Agribusiness Solutions 2008,"[4] the "Ashoka – Changemakers Health For All" Award 2006, the "Stockholm Challenge 2006" and "Golden Peacock Global Award for Corporate Social Responsibility (CSR) in Emerging Economies for 2005" among others.[8] ITC Chairman Y. C. Deveshwar said, "ITC has demonstrated that it is possible, and, most crucial to combine the need for creating shareholder value with the super ordinate goal of creating national value.[6]"

Conclusions and Lessons Learnt

Availability of relevant and right information at right time can and will help Indian agriculture to improve productivity and at the same time tap the international markets. Information helps channel members integrate their efforts and take timely action, prepare strategies for next season, speculate the market changes, and also avoid unfavorable circumstances. In liberalised and globalised India, the productivity of agriculture will depend on information flow across an integrated value chain. However, due to the market forces and infrastructural limitations, the efforts of Indian Government to implement information based vertical integration i.e. duplication of e-Choupal success, will not reap similar results as that of ITC model. Duplication of ITC e-Choupal model will have to be ownership of private conglomerates with an agenda of social responsibility.

3.1 Social Responsibilities of Strategic Decision Makers

Should strategic decision makers be responsible only to shareholders, or do they have broader responsibilities? The concept of **social responsibility** proposes that a private corporation has responsibilities to society that extend beyond making a profit. Strategic decisions often affect more than just the corporation. A decision to retrench by closing some plants and discontinuing product lines, for example, affects not only the firm's workforce but also the communities where the plants are located and the customers with no other source for the discontinued product. Such situations raise questions of the appropriateness of certain missions, objectives, and strategies of business corporations. Managers must be able to deal with these conflicting interests in an ethical manner to formulate a viable strategic plan.

RESPONSIBILITIES OF A BUSINESS FIRM

What are the responsibilities of a business firm and how many of them must be fulfilled? Milton Friedman and Archie Carroll offer two contrasting views of the responsibilities of business firms to society.

Friedman's Traditional View of Business Responsibility

Urging a return to a laissez-faire worldwide economy with a minimum of government regulation, Milton Friedman argues against the concept of social responsibility. A business person who acts "responsibly" by cutting the price of the firm's product to prevent inflation, or by making expenditures to reduce pollution, or by hiring the hard-core unemployed, according to Friedman, is spending the shareholder's money for a general social interest. Even if the businessperson has shareholder permission or encouragement to do so, he or she is still acting from motives other than economic and may, in the long run, harm the very society the firm is trying to help. By taking on the burden of these social costs, the business becomes less efficient—either prices go up to pay for the increased costs or investment in new activities and research is postponed. These results negatively affect—perhaps fatally—the long-term efficiency of a business. Friedman thus referred to the social responsibility of business as a "fundamentally subversive doctrine" and stated that:

> There is one and only one social responsibility of business—to use its resources and engage in activities designed to increase its profits so long as it stays within the rules of the game, which is to say, engages in open and free competition without deception or fraud.[9]

Carroll's Four Responsibilities of Business

Friedman's contention that the primary goal of business is profit maximization is only one side of an ongoing debate regarding corporate social responsibility (CSR). According to William J. Byron, distinguished professor of ethics at Georgetown University and past-president of Catholic University of America, profits are merely a means to an end, not an end in itself. Just as a person needs food to survive and grow, so does a business corporation need profits to survive and grow. "Maximizing profits is like maximizing food." Thus, contends Byron, maximization of profits cannot be the primary obligation of business.[10]

As shown in **Figure 3–1**, Archie Carroll proposes that the managers of business organizations have four responsibilities: economic, legal, ethical, and discretionary.[11]

1. **Economic** responsibilities of a business organization's management are to produce goods and services of value to society so that the firm may repay its creditors and shareholders.

FIGURE 3–1
Responsibilities
of Business

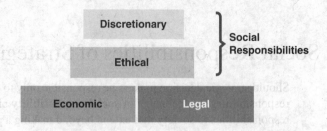

SOURCE: Based on A. B. Carroll, "A Three Dimensional Conceptual Model of Corporate Performance," *Academy of Management Review* (October 1979), pp. 497–505; A. B. Carroll, "Managing Ethically with Global Stakeholders: A Present and Future Challenge," *Academy of Management Executive* (May 2004), pp. 114–120; and A. B. Carroll, "The Pyramid of Corporate Social Responsibility: Toward the Moral Management of Organizational Stakeholders," *Business Horizons* (July–August 1991), pp. 39–48.

2. **Legal** responsibilities are defined by governments in laws that management is expected to obey. For example, Indian Public sector units are required to hire and promote people based on their credentials rather than to discriminate on non-job-related characteristics such as race, gender, or religion.

3. **Ethical** responsibilities of an organization's management are to follow the generally held beliefs about behavior in a society. For example, society generally expects firms to work with the employees and the community in planning for layoffs, even though no law may require this. The affected people can get very upset if an organization's management fails to act according to generally prevailing ethical values.

4. **Discretionary** responsibilities are the purely voluntary obligations a corporation assumes. Examples are philanthropic contributions, training the hard-core unemployed, and providing day-care centers. The difference between ethical and discretionary responsibilities is that few people expect an organization to fulfill discretionary responsibilities, whereas many expect an organization to fulfill ethical ones.[12]

Carroll lists these four responsibilities *in order of priority*. A business firm must first make a profit to satisfy its economic responsibilities. To continue in existence, the firm must follow the laws, thus fulfilling its legal responsibilities. There is evidence that companies found guilty of violating laws have lower profits and sales growth after conviction.[13] To this point Carroll and Friedman are in agreement. Carroll, however, goes further by arguing that business managers have responsibilities beyond economic and legal ones.

Having satisfied the two basic responsibilities, according to Carroll, a firm should look to fulfilling its social responsibilities. Social responsibility, therefore, includes both ethical and discretionary, but not economic and legal, responsibilities. A firm can fulfill its ethical responsibilities by taking actions that society tends to value but has not yet put into law. When ethical responsibilities are satisfied, a firm can focus on discretionary responsibilities—purely voluntary actions that society has not yet decided are important. For example, when Cisco Systems decided to dismiss 6,000 full-time employees, it provided a novel severance package. Those employees who agreed to work for a local nonprofit organization for a year would receive one-third of their salaries plus benefits and stock options and be the first to be rehired. Nonprofits were delighted to hire such highly qualified people and Cisco was able to maintain its talent pool for when it could hire once again.[14]

As societal values evolve, the discretionary responsibilities of today may become the ethical responsibilities of tomorrow. For example, Aravind Eye Care System was started in 1976 in Madurai by Dr G. Venkataswamy with a mission to create an alternative, affordable, and sustainable eye care system. His mission was motivated by his drive to eradicate needless blindness. With the help of his family, which shared his ideals of compassion, dignity, equity, eye care to all, transparency, and sharing, he created a remarkable eye care facility. Thirty-five percent of patients pay for the hospital's services, whereas 65% of the patients are operated on for free.[15] Today, Aravind, a family-led, trust-owned, and professionally run organization, has evolved into one of the finest eye care facilities in the world. Besides the hospitals, they have a center for manufacturing intraocular lenses, an eye bank, a training institute for ophthalmologists, a medical research foundation, and a college of ophthalmology.[16] The hospitals are totally self-sustaining. Through a unique fee system and effective management, Aravind is able to provide free eye care to almost two-thirds of its patients.[17]

Carroll suggests that to the extent that business corporations fail to acknowledge discretionary or ethical responsibilities, society, through government, will act, making them legal responsibilities. Moreover, government may do this without regard to an organization's economic responsibilities. As a result, the organization may have greater difficulty in earning a profit than it would have if it had voluntarily assumed some ethical and discretionary responsibilities.

Both Friedman and Carroll argue their positions based on the impact of socially responsible actions on a firm's profits. Friedman says that socially responsible actions hurt a firm's efficiency. Carroll proposes that lack of social responsibility results in increased government regulations, which reduces a firm's efficiency.

Friedman's position on social responsibility appears to be losing traction with business executives. For example, a 2006 survey of business executives across the world by McKinsey & Company revealed that only 16% felt that business should focus solely on providing the highest possible returns to investors while obeying all laws and regulations, contrasted with 84% who stated that business should generate high returns to investors but balance it with contributions to the broader public good.[18] A 2007 survey of global executives by the Economist Intelligence Unit found that the percentage of companies giving either high or very high priority to corporate social responsibility had risen from less than 40% in 2004 to over 50% in 2007 and was expected to increase to almost 70% by 2010.[19]

According to a study undertaken by an industry body in June 2009, which studied the CSR activities of 300 corporate houses, indicated that corporate India has spread its CSR activities across 20 states and union territories, with Maharashtra gaining the most from them. About 36% of the CSR activities are concentrated in the state, followed by about 12% in Gujarat, 10% in Delhi, and 9% in Tamil Nadu. The study further highlighted that companies had identified 26 different themes for their CSR initiatives. Of these, community welfare tops the list, followed by education, environment, healthcare, as well as rural development.[20]

Empirical research now indicates that socially responsible actions may have a positive effect on a firm's financial performance. Although a number of studies in the past have found no significant relationship,[21] an increasing number are finding a small, but positive relationship.[22] A recent in-depth analysis by Margolis and Walsh of 127 studies found that "there is a positive association and very little evidence of a negative association between a company's social performance and its financial performance."[23] Another meta-analysis of 52 studies on social responsibility and performance reached this same conclusion.[24]

According to Porter and Kramer, "social and economic goals are not inherently conflicting, but integrally connected."[25] Being known as a socially responsible firm may provide a company with *social capital*, the goodwill of key stakeholders, that can be used for competitive advantage.[26] Target, for example, tries to attract socially concerned younger consumers by offering brands from companies that can boost ethical track records and community involvement.[27] In a 2004 study conducted by the strategic marketing firm Cone, Inc., eight in ten Americans said that corporate support of social causes helps earn their loyalty. This was a 21% increase since 1997.[28]

Being socially responsible does provide a firm more positive overall reputation.[29] A survey of more than 700 global companies by the Conference Board reported that 60% of the managers state that citizenship activities led to (1) goodwill that opened doors in local communities and (2) an enhanced reputation with consumers.[30] Another survey of 140 U.S. firms revealed that being more socially responsible regarding environmental sustainability resulted not only in competitive advantages but also in cost savings.[31] For example, companies that take the lead in being environmentally friendly, such as by using recycled materials, preempt attacks from environmental groups and enhance their corporate image. Programs to reduce pollution, for example, can actually reduce waste and maximize resource productivity. One study that examined 70 ecological initiatives taken by 43 companies found the average payback period to be 18 months.[32] Other examples of benefits received from being socially responsible are[33]:

- Their environmental concerns may enable them to charge premium prices and gain brand loyalty (e.g., Ben & Jerry's Ice Cream).

- Their trustworthiness may help them generate enduring relationships with suppliers and distributors without requiring them to spend a lot of time and money policing contracts.

- They can attract outstanding employees who prefer working for a responsible firm (e.g., Procter & Gamble and Starbucks).

- They are more likely to be welcomed into a foreign country (e.g., Levi Strauss).

- They can utilize the goodwill of public officials for support in difficult times.

- They are more likely to attract capital infusions from investors who view reputable companies as desirable for long-term investments. For example, mutual funds investing in socially responsible companies more than doubled in size from 1995 to 2007 and outperformed the S&P 500 list of stocks.[34]

SUSTAINABILITY: MORE THAN ENVIRONMENTAL?

As a term, sustainability may include more than just ecological concerns and the natural environment. Crane and Matten point out that the concept of sustainability can be broadened to include economic and social as well as environmental concerns. They argue that it is sometimes impossible to address the sustainability of the natural environment without considering the social and economic aspects of relevant communities and their activities. For example, even though environmentalists may oppose road-building programs because of their effect on wildlife and conservation efforts, others point to the benefits to local communities of less traffic congestion and more jobs.[35] Dow Jones & Company, a leading provider of global business news and information, developed a sustainability index that considers not only environmental, but also economic and social factors. See the **Environmental Sustainability Issue** feature to learn the criteria Dow Jones uses in its index.

The broader concept of sustainability has much in common with Carroll's list of business responsibilities presented earlier. In order for a business corporation to be sustainable, that is, to be successful over a long period of time, it must satisfy all of its economic, legal, ethical, and discretionary responsibilities. Sustainability thus involves many issues, concerns, and tradeoffs—leading us to an examination of corporate stakeholders.

CORPORATE STAKEHOLDERS

The concept that business must be socially responsible sounds appealing until we ask, "Responsible to whom?" A corporation's task environment includes a large number of groups with interest in a business organization's activities. These groups are referred to as **stakeholders** because they affect or are affected by the achievement of the firm's objectives.[36] Should a corporation be responsible only to some of these groups, or does business have an equal responsibility to all of them?

ENVIRONMENTAL sustainability issue

INDIAN STATES WITH BEST ENVIRONMENTAL SUSTAINABILITY INDEX

In India, most recent effort to measure environmental sustainability includes the effort to rate the Indian states. In 2008, the Centre for Development Finance (CDF) at the Institute for Financial Management and Research (IFMR) developed a comprehensive environmental sustainability index (ESI) for Indian states. The ESI tracks environment performance of 28 states and projects their ability to protect the environment in future.[1] The rankings are relative and measured on a scale of 0–100 which allows one to compare the performance of a state vis-à-vis another. In constructing the ESI, the building blocks of the index were taken in reference with the driving force-pressure-state-impact response (DPSIR) framework. Driving forces are the basic need, human activities, and production-consumption processes that affect the environment.[2] ESI is an equally weighted average of 15 indicators which has 44 variables.[3] The resulting index comprises ESI in five components, i.e., population pressure, pressure on environment, environmental quality, impact on human health and ecosystem vitality, and policy response.[2] The ESI names Himachal Pradesh, Manipur, Mizoram, Kerala, Sikkim, West Bengal, and Meghalaya as best states in India, with ESI rating from 61 to 100,[4] with Arunachal Pradesh, Uttranchal, and Mizoram toping the indicator list. This indicates that among all the other states in India, these states have higher initial factors of endowments, less population, slower rate of extraction, and also have more responsive society and policy.

1. Announcement, Business Standard, IFMR-CDF launches Environmental Sustainability Index (ESI) in India, posted on Announcement/Economy, 29 Dec 2008, 18:39 hrs IST, accessed on 11 Oct 2011, from http://www.business-standard.com/india/news/ifmr-cdf-launches-environmental-sustainability-index-esi-in-india/344645/
2. IFMR Web site, ESI Framework, accessed on 11 Oct 2011, from http://www.greenindiastandards.com/esi-framework.php?src=fwork
3. IFMR, ESI Methodology, accessed on 11 Oct 2011, from http://www.greenindiastandards.com/methodology.php
4. IFMR, accessed on 11 Oct 2011, from http://www.greenindiastandards.com/

A survey of the U.S. general public by Harris Poll revealed that 95% of the respondents felt that U.S. corporations owe something to their workers and the communities in which they operate and that they should sometimes sacrifice some profit for the sake of making things better for their workers and communities. People were concerned that business executives seemed to be more interested in making profits and boosting their own pay than they were in the safety and quality of the products made by their companies.[37] The percentage of the U.S. general public that agreed that business leaders could be trusted to do what is right "most of the time or almost always" fell from 36% in 2002 to 28% in 2006.[38] These negative feelings receive some support from a study that revealed that the CEOs at the 50 U.S. companies that outsourced the greatest number of jobs received a greater increase in pay than did the CEOs of 365 U.S. firms overall.[39]

In any one strategic decision, the interests of one stakeholder group can conflict with those of another. For example, a business firm's decision to use only recycled materials in its manufacturing process may have a positive effect on environmental groups but a negative effect on shareholder dividends. In another example, Maytag Corporation's top management decided to move refrigerator production from Galesburg, Illinois, to a lower-wage location in Mexico. On the one hand, shareholders were generally pleased with the decision because it would lower costs. On the other hand, officials and local union people were very unhappy at the loss of jobs when the Galesburg plant closed. Which group's interests should have priority?

In order to answer this question, the corporation may need to craft an *enterprise strategy*—an overarching strategy that explicitly articulates the firm's ethical relationship with its stakeholders. This requires not only that management clearly state the firm's key ethical values, but also that it understands the firm's societal context, and undertakes stakeholder analysis to identify the concerns and abilities of each stakeholder.[40]

ENVIRONMENTAL sustainability issue

THE DOW JONES SUSTAINABILITY INDEX

Dow Jones & Company, a leading provider of global business news and information, pioneered in 1999 the first index of common stocks that rates corporations according to their performance on sustainability. This index has grown to include multiple sustainability indexes, such as a World Index, North America Index, and United States Index, among others. The Dow Jones Sustainability Index (DJSI) follows a "best in class" approach that identifies sustainability leaders in each industry. Companies are evaluated against general and industry-specific criteria and ranked with their peers. Data come from questionnaires, submitted documentation, corporate policies, reports, and available public information. Since its inception, the Dow Jones Sustainability Index has slightly outperformed its well-known Dow Jones Industrial Index. Based on SAM (Sustainable Asset Management AG) Research's corporate sustainability assessment, Dow Jones includes not only environmental, but also economic and social criteria in its sustainability index.

■ **Environmental sustainability.** This includes environmental reporting, eco-design and efficiency, environmental management systems, and executive commitment to environmental issues.

■ **Economic sustainability.** This includes codes of conduct and compliance, anti-corruption policies, corporate governance, risk and crisis management, strategic planning, quality and knowledge management, and supply chain management.

■ **Social sustainability.** This includes corporate citizenship, philanthropy, labor practices, human capital development, social reporting, talent attraction and retention, and stakeholder dialog.

....

NOTE: For more information on SAM Sustainable Asset Management, see *Sustainability Yearbook 2008*, available from PriceWaterHouseCoopers (www.pwc.com).

SOURCES: Dow Jones Indexes Web site (www.djindexes.com/) as of July 15, 2008 and A. Crane and D. Matten, *Business Ethics: A European Perspective* (Oxford: Oxford University Press, 2004), pp. 214–215.

Stakeholder Analysis

Stakeholder analysis is the identification and evaluation of corporate stakeholders. This can be done in a three-step process.

The *first step* in stakeholder analysis is to identify primary stakeholders, those who have a *direct connection* with the corporation and who have sufficient bargaining power to *directly* affect corporate activities. Primary stakeholders are directly affected by the corporation and usually include customers, employees, suppliers, shareholders, and creditors.

But who exactly are a firm's customers or employees and what do they want? This is not always a simple exercise. For example, Intel's customers were clearly computer manufacturers because that's to whom Intel sold its electronic chips. When a math professor found a small flaw in Intel's Pentium microprocessor in 1994, computer users demanded that Intel replace the defective chips. At first Intel refused to do so because it hadn't sold to these individuals. According to then-CEO Andy Grove, "I got irritated and angry because of user demands that we take back a device we didn't sell." Intel wanted the PC users to follow the supply chain and complain to the firms from whom they had bought the computers. Gradually Grove was persuaded that Intel had a direct duty to these consumers. "Although we didn't sell to these individuals directly, we marketed to them... It took me a while to understand this," explained Grove. In the end, Intel paid $450 million to replace the defective parts.[41]

Aside from the Intel example, business corporations usually know their primary stakeholders and what they want. The corporation systematically monitors these stakeholders because they are important to a firm's meeting its economic and legal responsibilities. Employees want a fair day's pay and fringe benefits. Customers want safe products and value for price paid. Shareholders want dividends and stock price appreciation. Suppliers want predictable orders and bills paid. Creditors want commitments to be met on time. In the normal course of affairs, the relationship between a firm and each of its primary stakeholders is regulated by written or verbal agreements and laws. Once a problem is identified, negotiation takes place based on costs and benefits to each party. (Government is not usually considered a primary stakeholder because laws apply to all in a category and usually cannot be negotiated.)

The *second step* in stakeholder analysis is to identify the *secondary stakeholders*—those who have only an *indirect* stake in the corporation but who are also affected by corporate activities. These usually include nongovernmental organizations (NGOs, such as Greenpeace), activists, local communities, trade associations, competitors, and governments. Because the corporation's relationship with each of these stakeholders is usually not covered by any written or verbal agreement, there is room for misunderstanding. As in the case of NGOs and activists, there actually may be no relationship until a problem develops—usually brought up by the stakeholder. In the normal course of events, these stakeholders do not affect the corporation's ability to meet its economic or legal responsibilities. Aside from competitors, these secondary stakeholders are not usually monitored by the corporation in any systematic fashion. As a result, relationships are usually based on a set of questionable assumptions about each other's needs and wants. Although these stakeholders may not directly affect a firm's short-term profitability, their actions could determine a corporation's reputation and thus its long-term performance.

The *third step* in stakeholder analysis is to estimate the effect on each stakeholder group from any particular strategic decision. Because the primary decision criteria are typically economic, this is the point where secondary stakeholders may be ignored or discounted as unimportant. For a firm to fulfill its ethical or discretionary responsibilities, it must seriously consider the needs and wants of its secondary stakeholders in any strategic decision. For example, how much will specific stakeholder groups lose or gain? What other alternatives do they have to replace what may be lost?

Stakeholder Input

Once stakeholder impacts have been identified, managers should decide whether stakeholder input should be invited into the discussion of the strategic alternatives. A group is more likely to accept or even help implement a decision if it has some input into which alternative is chosen and how it is to be implemented. In the case of Maytag's decision to close its Galesburg, Illinois, refrigeration plant, the community was not a part of the decision. Nevertheless, management decided to inform the local community of its decision three years in advance of the closing instead of the 60 days required by law. Although the announcement created negative attention, it gave the Galesburg employees and townspeople more time to adjust to the eventual closing.

Given the wide range of interests and concerns present in any organization's task environment, one or more groups, at any one time, probably will be dissatisfied with an organization's activities—even if management is trying to be socially responsible. A company may have some stakeholders of which it is only marginally aware. For example, when Ford Motor Company extended its advertising to magazines read by gay and lesbian readers in 2005, management had no idea that the American Family Association (AFA) would argue that this was tantamount to promoting a homosexual agenda and call for a boycott of all Ford products. In response, Ford pulled its ads. Gay and lesbian groups then protested Ford's backpedaling. Ford then placed corporate ads in many of the same publications, which gays saw as clumsy and the AFA saw as backsliding.[42]

Therefore, before making a strategic decision, strategic managers should consider how each alternative will affect various stakeholder groups. What seems at first to be the best decision because it appears to be the most profitable may actually result in the worst set of consequences to the corporation. One example of a company that does its best to consider its responsibilities to its primary and secondary stakeholders when making strategic decisions is Dabur. See **Strategy Highlight 3.1**

STRATEGY highlight 3.1

GOOD GOVERNANCE, ETHICAL CONDUCT AND SOCIAL RESPONSIBILITY; VALUES IN EVERY STRATEGY DECISION

Dabur India Limited is the fourth largest FMCG company in India with interests in healthcare, personal care, and food products. The company's vision statement says that Dabur is dedicated to the health and well being of every household.

THE COMPANY'S CORE VALUES STATEMENT

Dabur's first responsibility is to the society; the mothers, fathers, and all others who use its products and services. In meeting their needs, the company continuously works towards ensuring high quality for all its products. It also constantly strives to understand its consumer needs and develop products to fulfill those needs in an innovative manner. Dabur also offers its suppliers and distributors an opportunity to make a fair profit and accepts personal responsibility and accountability to meet the business needs. It is committed to the achievement of business success with integrity. "We are honest with consumers, with business partners and with each other," the company says:

"We are responsible to our employees... the men and women who work with us. People are our most important asset. We respect their dignity and recognize their merit. We believe they are the key facets of the company and it is their contribution that has enabled Dabur to achieve its current status. We take special care of our employees, and recognize and reward a good performance. There are special training and skill upgradation programs to keep our employees constantly abreast with current business demands. Dabur nurtures a familial bond with its people, creating a harmonious and value-based work environment that encourages team spirit, as also rewarding individual initiative. Each of our employees is an important component in building a cohesive force, which ultimately helps us to achieve our vision of health and well being for every household.

At Dabur, the commitment to good governance, ethical conduct, and social responsibility is core to its way of doing business and is strongly aligned with its drive to create and increase value for all stakeholders. We are responsible to the communities where we live and work and to the world community as well. We must be good citizens—support good works and charities and bear our fair share of taxes. We define corporate social responsibility as conducting business in ways that provide social, environmental, and economic benefits to the communities and geographies where we operate. Our CSR initiatives are driven through Sustainable Development Society or SUNDESH, which was set up in 1993. The society—a nonprofit organization—promotes research and welfare activities in rural areas. It provides healthcare facilities to women and children, gives nonformal education to children and adults and train people in vocations such as bee keeping, mushroom farming, tailoring, etc. to provide them additional source of income.

Dabur is also committed to maintain ecological balance, as a responsibility toward nature, which provides raw material for most of the products Dabur manufacture.[8] We have been working on developing sustainable cultivated source for herbal ingredients, so as to reduce the strain on natural habitat of these herbs. We have also set up the most modern tissue culture facility for micro propagation of medicinal herbs. We are also involved in reforestation in the Himalayan range, which would help in maintaining the green cover there.

Our final responsibility is to our stakeholders. Business must make sound profit. We must experiment with new ideas. We must experiment and innovate to develop new products and processes. Reserves must be created for adverse times. We all are leaders in our area of responsibility with a deep commitment to deliver results. We are determined to be the best at doing what matters most. We work together on the principle of mutual trust and transparency in a boundary-less organization. We are intellectually honest in advocating proposals, including recognizing risks. When we operate according to these principles, the stockholders should realize a fair return."

....
Source: Dabur India Ltd.

3.2 Ethical Decision Making

Some people joke that there is no such thing as "business ethics." They call it an oxymoron—a concept that combines opposite or contradictory ideas. Unfortunately, there is some truth to this sarcastic comment. For example, a survey by the Ethics Resource Center of 1,324 employees of 747 U.S.

companies found that 48% of employees surveyed said that they had engaged in one or more unethical and/or illegal actions during the past year. The most common questionable behaviors involved cutting corners on quality (16%), covering up incidents (14%), abusing or lying about sick days (11%), and lying to or deceiving customers (9%).[43] Some 52% of workers reported observing at least one type of misconduct in the workplace, but only 55% reported it.[44] From 1996 to 2005, top managers at 2,270 firms (29.2% of the firms analyzed) had backdated or otherwise manipulated stock option grants to take advantage of favorable share-price movements.[45] In a survey, 53% of employees in corporations of all sizes admitted that they would be willing to misrepresent corporate financial statements if asked to do so by a superior.[46] A survey of 141 chief financial executives (CFOs) revealed that 17% had been pressured by their CEOs over a five-year period to misrepresent the company's financial results. Five percent admitted that they had succumbed to the request.[47]

The results of a survey conducted by Economist Intelligence Unit (EIU) for Kroll Inc. in 2007 indicated that globally four out of five companies suffered from fraud in the last three years. Popularly referred to as Kroll Global Fraud Report, it was the first of its kind in an attempt that surveyed around 900 top corporate officials. It noted that while 60% of Indian and Chinese corporates feel vulnerable to bribery and corruption, threat to intellectual property (IP) was much more in China (at 38%) than in India (14%).[48]

The same survey in 2010 reported that Asia-Pacific had the highest number of companies reportedly hit by at least one fraud in last year of any region (92%), and has an above average incidence for nine of the eleven frauds.[49] This increased fraud had been attributed to increased technology in this region. Moreover, in India the top three frauds to which companies in India feel most vulnerable are information theft, loss, or attack (39% call their companies highly or moderately vulnerable); regulatory or compliance breach (29%); and intellectual property (IP) theft and counterfeiting (27%).[50] An alarming 29% of fraud in India has as its key perpetrator vendors, suppliers, agents, and partners combined. Therefore, given the lack of ethical behavior, the researching agency suggests companies to invest in exhaustive whistleblower systems and adopt due diligence while choosing channel partners.

A study, called "Early Warning Signals of Corporate Frauds," conducted by the Pune-based India Forensic Consultancy Services, from January 2008 to August 2008 has come out with shocking revelations. The study has revealed that at least 1,200 companies out of 4,867 companies listed on the Bombay Stock Exchange and 1,288 companies listed on the National Stock Exchange as on March 31, 2007, including 25–30 companies in the benchmark Sensex and Nifty indices have messaged their financial statements.[51]

Another annual study by KPMG, titled India Fraud Survey Report, has effectively castigated Indian companies over the years. In 2008, the report has castigated Indian Inc. both at the employee and the management levels. It suggested a lack of morality at both levels. The results of 2008 survey highlighted that more than 80% of the respondents recognize fraud as a problem and 70% believe it to be a trend, which is likely to increase over the next two years.[52] The results had not changed over the years. The 2010 survey results were not much different. The survey highlighted that majority of the respondents indicated that the incidence of fraud, overall and within their industry and company, were rising. The results agreed with the results of Global Fraud report and indicated that supply chain fraud (procurement, distribution, and revenue leakage) is the single most exposed area. Weak internal control systems, eroding ethical values, and a reluctance on the part of the line managers to take decisive action against the perpetrators are cited as the most vital underlying reasons for frauds being on the rise.

A study of more than 5,000 graduate students at 32 colleges and universities in the United States and Canada revealed that 56% of business students and 47% of nonbusiness students admitted to cheating at least once during the past year. Cheating was more likely when a student's peers also cheated.[53] In another example, 6,000 people paid $30 to enter a VIP section on ScoreTop.com's Web site to obtain access to actual test questions posted by those who had recently taken the Graduate Management Admission Test (GMAT). In response, the Graduate

Management Admission Council promised to cancel the scores of anyone who posted "live" questions to the site or knowingly read them.[54] Given this lack of ethical behavior among students, it is easy to understand why some could run into trouble if they obtained a job at a corporation having an unethical culture, such as Enron, WorldCom, or Tyco. (See **Strategy Highlight 3.2** for examples of unethical practices at Enron and Worldcom.)

SOME REASONS FOR UNETHICAL BEHAVIOR

Why are many business people perceived to be acting unethically? It may be that the involved people are not even aware that they are doing something questionable. There is no worldwide standard of conduct for business people. This is especially important given the global nature of business activities. Cultural norms and values vary between countries and even between different geographic regions and ethnic groups within a country. For example, what is considered in one country to be a bribe to expedite service is sometimes considered in another country to be normal business practice. Some of these differences may derive from whether a country's governance system is *rule-based* or *relationship-based*. Relationship-based countries tend to be less transparent and have a higher degree of corruption than do rule-based countries.[55] See the **Global Issue** feature for an explanation of country governance systems and how they may affect business practices.

STRATEGY highlight 3.2

UNETHICAL PRACTICES AT ENRON AND WORLDCOM EXPOSED BY "WHISTLE-BLOWERS"

Corporate scandals at Enron, WorldCom, and Tyco, among other international companies, have caused people around the world to seriously question the ethics of business executives. Enron, in particular, has become infamous for the questionable actions of its top executives in the form of (1) off-balance sheet partnerships used to hide the company's deteriorating finances, (2) revenue from long-term contracts being recorded in the first year instead of being spread over multiple years, (3) financial reports being falsified to inflate executive bonuses, and (4) manipulation of the electricity market—leading to a California energy crisis. Only Sherron Watkins, an Enron accountant, was willing to speak out regarding the questionable nature of these practices. In a now-famous memo to then-CEO Kenneth Lay, Watkins warned:

I realize that we have had a lot of smart people looking at this and a lot of accountants including AA & Co. [Arthur Andersen] have blessed the accounting

treatment. None of that will protect Enron if these transactions are ever disclosed in the bright light of day.

At WorldCom, Cynthia Cooper, an internal auditor, noted that some of the company's capital expenditures should have been listed on the second-quarter financial statements as expenses. When she mentioned this to both WorldCom's controller and its chief financial officer, she was told to stop what she was doing and to delay the audit until the third quarter (when expensing the transactions would not be noticed). Instead, Cooper informed the board of directors' audit committee. Two weeks later, WorldCom announced that it was reducing earnings by $3.9 billion, the largest restatement in history.

SOURCE: G. Colvin, "Wonder Women of Whistleblowers," *Fortune* (August 12, 2002), p. 56; W. Zellner, "The Deadly Sins of Enron," *Business Week* (October 14, 2002), pp. 26–28; M. J. Mandel, "And the Enron Award Goes to . . . Enron," *Business Week* (May 20, 2002), p. 46.

Another possible reason for what is often perceived to be unethical behavior lies in differences in values between business people and key stakeholders. Some businesspeople may believe profit maximization is the key goal of their firm, whereas concerned interest groups may have other priorities, such as the hiring of minorities and women or the safety of their neighborhoods. Of the six values measured by the Allport-Vernon-Lindzey Study of Values test (aesthetic, economic, political, religious, social, and theoretical), both U.S. and UK executives consistently score highest on economic and political values and lowest on social and religious ones. This is similar to the value profile of managers from Japan, Korea, India, and Australia, as well as those of U.S. business school students. U.S. Protestant ministers, in contrast, score highest on religious and social values and very low on economic values.[56]

GLOBAL issue

HOW RULE-BASED AND RELATIONSHIP-BASED GOVERNANCE SYSTEMS AFFECT ETHICAL BEHAVIOR

The developed nations of the world operate under governance systems quite different from those used by developing nations. The developed nations and the business firms within them follow well-recognized rules in their dealings and financial reporting. To the extent that a country's rules force business corporations to publicly disclose in-depth information about the company to potential shareholders and others, that country's financial and legal system is said to be *transparent*. Transparency is said to simplify transactions and reduce the temptation to behave illegally or unethically. Finland, the United Kingdom, Hong Kong, the United States, and Australia have very transparent business climates. The Kurtzman Group, a consulting firm, developed an *opacity index* that measures the risks associated with unclear legal systems, regulations, economic policies, corporate governance standards, and corruption in 48 countries. The countries with the most opaque/least transparent ratings are Indonesia, Venezuela, China, Nigeria, India, Egypt, and Russia.

Developing nations tend to have *relationship-based governance*. Transactions are based on personal and implicit agreements, not on formal contracts enforceable by a court. Information about a business is largely local and private—thus cannot be easily verified by a third party. In contrast, *rule-based governance* relies on publicly verifiable information—the type of information that is typically not available in a developing country. The rule-based system has an infrastructure, based on accounting, auditing, ratings systems, legal cases, and codes, to provide and monitor this information. If present in a developing nation, the infrastructure is not very sophisticated. This is why investing in a developing country is very risky. The relationship-based system in a developing nation is inherently nontransparent due to the local and nonverifiable nature of its information. A business person needs to develop and nurture a wide network of personal relationships. *What* you know is less important than *who* you know.

The investment in time and money needed to build the necessary relationships to conduct business in a developing nation creates a high entry barrier for any newcomers to an industry. Thus, key industries in developing nations tend to be controlled by a small number of companies, usually privately owned, family-controlled conglomerates. Because public information is unreliable and insufficient for decisions, strategic decisions may depend more on a CEO playing golf with the prime minister than with questionable market share data. In a relationship-based system, the culture of the country (and the founder's family) strongly affects corporate culture and business ethics. What is "fair" depends on whether one is a family member, a close friend, a neighbor, or a stranger. Because behavior tends to be less controlled by laws and agreed-upon standards than by tradition, businesspeople from a rule-based developed nation perceive the relationship-based system in a developing nation to be less ethical and more corrupt. According to Larry Smeltzer, ethics professor at Arizona State University: "The lack of openness and predictable business standards drives companies away. Why would you want to do business in, say, Libya, where you don't know the rules?"

SOURCE: S. Li, S. H. Park, and S. Li, "The Great Leap Forward: The Transition from Relation-Based Governance to Rule-Based Governance," *Organizational Dynamics*, Vol. 33, No. 1 (2003), pp. 63–78; M. Davids, "Global Standards, Local Problems," *Journal of Business Strategy* (January/February 1999), pp. 38–43; "The Opacity Index," *Economist* (September 18, 2004), p. 106.

This difference in values can make it difficult for one group of people to understand another's actions. For example, even though some people feel that the advertising of cigarettes and alcoholic drinks (especially to youth) is unethical, the people managing these companies can respond that they are simply offering a product; "*Let the buyer beware*" is a traditional saying in free-market capitalism. They argue that customers in a free market democracy have the right to choose how they spend their money and live their lives. Social progressives may contend that business people working in tobacco, alcoholic beverages, and gambling industries are acting unethically by making and advertising products with potentially dangerous and expensive side effects, such as cancer, alcoholism, and addiction. People working in these industries could respond by asking whether it is ethical for people who don't smoke, drink, or gamble to reject another person's right to do so.

Seventy percent of executives representing 111 diverse national and multinational corporations reported that they bend the rules to attain their objectives.[57] The three most common reasons given were:

- Organizational performance required it—74%
- Rules were ambiguous or out of date—70%
- Pressure from others and everyone does it—47%

The financial community's emphasis on short-term earnings performance is a significant pressure for executives to "manage" quarterly earnings. For example, a company achieving its forecasted quarterly earnings figure signals the investment community that its strategy and operations are proceeding as planned. Failing to meet its targeted objective signals that the company is in trouble—thus causing the stock price to fall and shareholders to become worried. Research by Degeorge and Patel involving more than 100,000 quarterly earnings reports revealed that a preponderance (82%) of reported earnings *exactly* matched analysts' expectations or exceeded them by 1%. The disparity between the number of earnings reports that missed estimates by a penny and the number that exceeded them by a penny suggests that executives who risked falling short of forecasts "borrowed" earnings from future quarters.[58]

In explaining why executives and accountants at Enron engaged in unethical and illegal actions, former Enron vice president Sherron Watkins used the "*frogs in boiling water*" analogy. If, for example, one were to toss a frog into a pan of boiling water, according to the folk tale, the frog would quickly jump out. It might be burned, but the frog would survive. However, if one put a frog in a pan of cold water and turned up the heat very slowly, the frog would not sense the increasing heat until it was too lethargic to jump out and would be boiled. According to Watkins:

> *Enron's accounting moved from creative to aggressive, to fraudulent, like the pot of water moving from cool to lukewarm to boiling; those involved with the creative transactions soon found themselves working on the aggressive transactions and were finally in the uncomfortable situation of working on fraudulent deals.*[59]

Moral Relativism

Some people justify their seemingly unethical positions by arguing that there is no one absolute code of ethics and that morality is relative. Simply put, **moral relativism** claims that morality is relative to some personal, social, or cultural standard and that there is no method for deciding whether one decision is better than another.

At one time or another, most managers have probably used one of the four types of moral relativism—naïve, role, social group, or cultural—to justify questionable behavior.[60]

Naïve relativism: Based on the belief that all moral decisions are deeply personal and that individuals have the right to run their own lives, adherents of moral relativism argue that each person should be allowed to interpret situations and act on his or her own moral values. This is not so much a belief as it is an excuse for not having a belief or is a common excuse for not taking action when observing others lying or cheating.

Role relativism: Based on the belief that social roles carry with them certain obligations to that role, adherents of role relativism argue that a manager in charge of a work unit must put aside his or her personal beliefs and do instead what the role requires, that is, act in the best interests of the unit. Blindly following orders was a common excuse provided by Nazi war criminals after World War II.

Social group relativism: Based on a belief that morality is simply a matter of following the norms of an individual's peer group, social group relativism argues that a decision is considered legitimate if it is common practice, regardless of other considerations ("everyone's doing it"). A real danger in embracing this view is that the person may incorrectly believe that a certain action is commonly accepted practice in an industry when it is not.

Cultural relativism: Based on the belief that morality is relative to a particular culture, society, or community, adherents of cultural relativism argue that people should understand the practices of other societies, but not judge them. This view not only suggests that one should not criticize another culture's norms and customs, but also that it is acceptable to personally follow these norms and customs ("When in Rome, do as the Romans do.").

Although these arguments make some sense, moral relativism could enable a person to justify almost any sort of decision or action, so long as it is not declared illegal.

Kohlberg's Levels of Moral Development

Another reason why some business people might be seen as unethical is that they may have no well-developed personal sense of ethics. A person's ethical behavior is affected by his or her level of moral development, certain personality variables, and such situational factors as the job itself, the supervisor, and the organizational culture.[61] Kohlberg proposes that a person progresses through three **levels of moral development**.[62] Similar in some ways to Maslow's hierarchy of needs, in Kohlberg's system, the individual moves from total self-centeredness to a concern for universal values. Kohlberg's three levels are as follows:

1. **The preconventional level:** This level is characterized by a concern for self. Small children and others who have not progressed beyond this stage evaluate behaviors on the basis of personal interest—avoiding punishment or quid pro quo.

2. **The conventional level:** This level is characterized by considerations of society's laws and norms. Actions are justified by an external code of conduct.

3. **The principled level:** This level is characterized by a person's adherence to an internal moral code. An individual at this level looks beyond norms or laws to find universal values or principles.

Research appears to support Kohlberg's concept. For example, one study found that individuals higher in cognitive moral development, lower in Machiavellianism, with a more internal locus of control, a less-relativistic moral philosophy, and higher job satisfaction are less likely to plan and enact unethical choices.[63]

ENCOURAGING ETHICAL BEHAVIOR

Following Carroll's work, if business people do not act ethically, government will be forced to pass laws regulating their actions—and usually increasing their costs. For self-interest, if for no other reason, managers should be more ethical in their decision making. One way to do that is by developing codes of ethics. Another is by providing guidelines for ethical behavior.

Codes of Ethics

A **code of ethics** specifies how an organization expects its employees to behave while on the job. Developing codes of ethics can be a useful way to promote ethical behavior, especially for people who are operating at Kohlberg's conventional level of moral development. Such codes are currently being used by more than half of business corporations. A code of ethics (1) clarifies company expectations of employee conduct in various situations and (2) makes clear that the company expects its people to recognize the ethical dimensions in decisions and actions.[64]

Various studies indicate that an increasing number of companies are developing codes of ethics and implementing ethics training workshops and seminars. However, research also indicates that when faced with a question of ethics, managers tend to ignore codes of ethics and try to solve dilemmas on their own.[65] To combat this tendency, the management of a company that wants to improve its employees' ethical behavior should not only develop a comprehensive code of ethics but also communicate the code in its training programs, in its performance appraisal system, policies and procedures, and through its own actions.[66] It may even include key values in its values and mission statements. According to a 2004 survey of CEOs by the Business Roundtable Institute for Corporate Ethics, 74% of CEOs confirmed that their companies had made changes within the previous two years in how they handled or reported ethics issues. Specific changes reported were:

- Enhanced internal reporting and communications—33%
- Ethics hotlines—17%
- Improved compliance procedures—12%
- Greater oversight by the board of directors—10%[67]

In India, corporations such as Tata Motors[68] and IndusInd Bank[69] have made extensive efforts to support whistle blowers. In India, as in other countires, disclosure of information in the public interest by the employees of an organization is increasingly gaining acceptance. Public bodies take proactive steps to ensure better governance standards and probity/transparency in the conduct of affairs of public institutions. An increase in the corporate frauds across the corporate world has necessitated various legislative measures for safeguarding the public interest. This has seen the enactment of certain acts such as Whistleblower Protection Act in the U.S., Public Interest Disclosure Act in the UK, and similar acts in a few other countries.[70] Moreover, in India, various agencies are lobbying for such an act. An attempt was made through a bill presented in Rajya Sabha in 2006.

The Whistle Blowers (Protection in Public Interest Disclosures) Bill, 2006.

It is a bill to provide for protection from criminal or civil liability, departmental inquiry, demotion, harassment, and discrimination of whistle blowers, i.e., the persons who bring to light specific instances of illegality, criminality, corruption, miscarriage of justice, any danger to public health and safety in any government, public, or private enterprises to an authority designated for the purposes and matters connected therewith, and incidental thereto.[71]

Though India has a long way to go, yet the Government of India (2007) has authorized the Central Vigilance Commission (CVC) as the "designated agency" to receive written complaints for disclosure on any allegation of corruption or misuse of office and recommend appropriate action. In this regard, the Commission, which will accept such complaints, has the responsibility of keeping the identity of the complainant secret.[72]

Corporations appear to benefit from well-conceived and implemented ethics programs. For example, companies with strong ethical cultures and enforced codes of conduct have fewer unethical choices available to employees—thus fewer temptations.[73] A study by the Open Compliance and Ethics Group found that no company with an ethics program in place for 10 years or more experienced "reputational damage" in the last five years.[74] Some of the companies identified in surveys as having strong moral cultures are Canon, Hewlett-Packard, Johnson & Johnson, Levi Strauss, Medtronic, Motorola, Newman's Own, Patagonia, S. C. Johnson, Shorebank, Smucker, and Sony.[75]

A corporation's management should consider establishing and enforcing a code of ethical behavior for those companies with which it does business—especially if it outsources its manufacturing to a company in another country. For example, Gap International, one of American's largest fashion retailers, developed one of the most rigorous codes of conduct for its suppliers. Its suppliers must comply with all child-labor laws on hiring, working hours, overtime, and working conditions. Workers must be at least 14 years of age. Rather than simply canceling business with suppliers using child labor, Gap requires suppliers to stop using child workers and to provide them with schooling instead, while continuing to pay them regularly and guaranteeing them a job once they reach legal age. In one year, Gap canceled contracts with 23 factories that did not meet its standards.[76]

Gap's experience, however, may be unusual. Recent surveys of over one hundred companies in the Global 2000 uncovered that 64% have some code of conduct that regulates supplier conduct, but only 40% require suppliers to actually take any action with respect to the code, such as disseminating it to employees, offering training, certifying compliance, or even reading or acknowledging receipt of the code.[77]

It is important to note that having a code of ethics for suppliers does not prevent harm to a corporation's reputation if one of its offshore suppliers is able to conceal abuses. Numerous Chinese factories, for example, keep double sets of books to fool auditors and distribute scripts for employees to recite if they are questioned. Consultants have found new business helping Chinese companies evade audits.[78]

Guidelines for Ethical Behavior

Ethics is defined as the consensually accepted standards of behavior for an occupation, a trade, or a profession. *Morality,* in contrast, is the precepts of personal behavior based on religious or philosophical grounds. *Law* refers to formal codes that permit or forbid certain behaviors and may or may not enforce ethics or morality.[79] Given these definitions, how do we arrive at a comprehensive statement of ethics to use in making decisions in a specific occupation, trade, or profession? A starting point for such a code of ethics is to consider the three basic approaches to ethical behavior[80]:

1. **Utilitarian approach:** The **utilitarian approach** proposes that actions and plans should be judged by their consequences. People should therefore behave in a way that will produce the greatest benefit to society and produce the least harm or the lowest cost. A problem with this approach is the difficulty in recognizing all the benefits and the costs of any particular decision. Research reveals that only the stakeholders who have the most *power* (ability to affect the company), *legitimacy* (legal or moral claim on company resources), and *urgency* (demand for immediate attention) are given priority by CEOs.[81] It is therefore likely that only the most obvious stakeholders will be considered, while others are ignored.

2. **Individual rights approach:** The **individual rights approach** proposes that human beings have certain fundamental rights that should be respected in all decisions. A particular decision or behavior should be avoided if it interferes with the rights of others. A problem with this approach is in defining "fundamental rights."

3. **Justice approach:** The **justice approach** proposes that decision makers be equitable, fair, and impartial in the distribution of costs and benefits to individuals and groups. It follows the principles of *distributive justice* (people who are similar on relevant dimensions such as job seniority should be treated in the same way) and *fairness* (liberty should be equal for all persons). The justice approach can also include the concepts of *retributive justice*

Let's Summarize the Chapter with a Mind Map

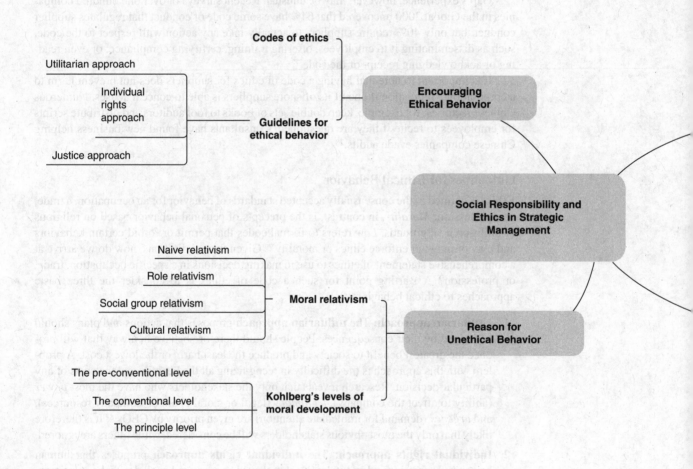

Codes of ethics

Utilitarian approach

Individual rights approach

Justice approach

Guidelines for ethical behavior

Encouraging Ethical Behavior

Social Responsibility and Ethics in Strategic Management

Naive relativism

Role relativism

Social group relativism

Cultural relativism

Moral relativism

Reason for Unethical Behavior

The pre-conventional level

The conventional level

The principle level

Kohlberg's levels of moral development

Responsibilities of a business firm

Friedman's traditional view of business responsibility

- Argues against concept of social responsibility

- Spending shareholder money for social responsibility even with shareholder permission, still may harm the company in long run

- Maximization of profits cannot be the primary obligation of the business

Carroll's four responsibilities of business

- Managers in business have four responsibilities; economic, ethical, legal and discretionary

Sustainability

- Common with Carroll's view of business responsibilities

- Dow Jones sustaiaility index

- Environmental sustainability index (ESI) for Indian states (punishment should be proportional to the offense) and *compensatory justice* (wrongs should be compensated in proportion to the offense). Affirmative action issues such as reverse discrimination are examples of conflicts between distributive and compensatory justice.

Cavanagh proposes that we solve ethical problems by asking the following three questions regarding an act or a decision:

1. **Utility:** Does it optimize the satisfactions of all stakeholders?
2. **Rights:** Does it respect the rights of the individuals involved?
3. **Justice:** Is it consistent with the canons of justice?

For example, is padding an expense account ethical? Using the utility criterion, this action increases the company's costs and thus does not optimize benefits for shareholders or customers. Using the rights approach, a person has no right to the money (otherwise, we wouldn't call it "padding"). Using the justice criterion, salary and commissions constitute ordinary compensation, but expense accounts compensate a person only for expenses incurred in doing his or her job—expenses that the person would not normally incur except in doing the job.[82]

Another approach to resolving ethical dilemmas is by applying the logic of the philosopher Immanuel Kant. Kant presents two principles (called **categorical imperatives**) to guide our actions:

1. A person's action is ethical only if that person is willing for that same action to be taken by everyone who is in a similar situation. This is the same as the Golden Rule: Treat others as you would like them to treat you. For example, padding an expense account would be considered ethical if the person were also willing for everyone else to do the same if they were the boss. Because it is very doubtful that any manager would be pleased with expense account padding, the action must be considered unethical.
2. A person should never treat another human being simply as a means but always as an end. This means that an action is morally wrong for a person if that person uses others merely as means for advancing his or her own interests. To be moral, the act should not restrict other people's actions so that they are disadvantaged in some way.[83]

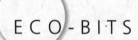

ECO-BITS

- An Australian nut orchard converts the shells of old Macintosh computers into houses for pest-eating birds.
- Nike gathers old athletic shoes and turns them into raw material for "sports surfaces" like tennis courts and running tracks.
- The British company Ecopods sells stylish coffins made from hardened recycled paper.
- It takes three months for a recycled aluminum can to return to the supermarket shelf in reincarnated form.[84]

DISCUSSION QUESTIONS

1. What is the relationship between corporate governance and social responsibility?
2. What is your opinion of Gap International's having a code of conduct for its suppliers? What would Milton Friedman say? Contrast his view with Archie Carroll's view.
3. Does a company have to act selflessly to be considered socially responsible? For example, when building a new plant, a corporation voluntarily invested in additional equipment that enabled it to reduce its pollution emissions beyond any current laws. Knowing that it would be

very expensive for its competitors to do the same, the firm lobbied the government to make pollution regulations more restrictive on the entire industry. Is this company socially responsible? Were its managers acting ethically?

4. Are people living in a relationship-based governance system likely to be unethical in business dealings?

5. Given that people rarely use a company's code of ethics to guide their decision making, what good are the codes?

STRATEGIC PRACTICE EXERCISE

It is 1982. Zombie Savings and Loan is in trouble. This is a time when many savings and loans (S&Ls) are in financial difficulty. Zombie holds many 30-year mortgages at low fixed-interest rates in its loan portfolio. Interest rates have risen significantly, and the Deregulation Act of 1980 has given Zombie and other S&Ls the right to make business loans and hold up to 20% of its assets as such. Because interest rates in general have risen, but the rate that Zombie receives on its old mortgages has not, Zombie must now pay out higher interest rates to its deposit customers or see them leave, and it has negative cash flow until rates fall below the rates in its mortgage portfolio or Zombie itself fails.

In present value terms, Zombie is insolvent, but the accounting rules of the time do not require marking assets to market, so Zombie is allowed to continue to operate and is faced with two choices: It can wait and hope interest rates fall before it is declared insolvent and is closed down, or it can raise fresh (insured) deposits and make risky loans that have high interest rates. Risky loans promise high payoffs (if they are repaid), but the probability of loss to Zombie and being closed later with greater loss to the Federal Savings & Loan Insurance Corporation (FSLIC) is high. Zombie stays in business if its gamble pays off, and it loses no more than it has already lost if the gamble does not pay off. Indeed, if not closed, Zombie will raise increasingly greater new deposits and make more risky loans until it either wins or is shut down by the regulators.

Waiting for lower interest rates and accepting early closure if lower rates do not arrive is certainly in the best interest of the FSLIC and of the taxpayers, but the manager of Zombie has more immediate responsibilities, such as employees' jobs, mortgage customers, depositors, the local neighborhood, and his or her job. As a typical S&L, Zombie's depositors are its shareholders and vote according to how much money they have in savings accounts with Zombie. If Zombie closes, depositors may lose some, but not all, of their money, because their deposits are insured by the FSLIC. There is no other provider of home mortgages in the immediate area. What should the manager do?

SOURCE: Adapted from D. W. Swanton, "Teaching Students the Nature of Moral Hazard: An Ethical Component for Finance Classes," paper presented to the annual meeting of the *Academy of Finance*, Chicago (March 13, 2003). Reprinted with permission.

KEY TERMS

categorical imperatives (p. 108)

code of ethics (p. 104)

ethics (p. 105)

individual rights approach (p. 105)

justice approach (p. 105)

law (p. 105)

levels of moral development (p. 103)

morality (p. 105)

moral relativism (p. 102)

social responsibility (p. 91)

stakeholder analysis (p. 96)

stakeholders (p. 95)

utilitarian approach (p. 105)

whistle-blowers (p. 84)

NOTES

1. TheBusinessLine. (2008). Bet on corporate social responsibility portfolio: ITC, posted on http://www.thehindu businessline.com/2006/08/10/stories/2006081002300300.htm. Retrieved from http://www.thehindubusinessline.com/2006/08/10/stories/2006081002300300.htm

2. ECF, I. Corporate Social Responsibility. Retrieved 28/04/11, 2011, from http://www.itcecf.com/about_us/corporate_social_responsibility.html

3. ITC. (2009). The ITC Profile Retrieved June 2nd 2009, from http://www.itcportal.com/sets/itc_frameset.htm

4. ITCportal. (2008). ITC wins Top UNIDO Award for e-Choupal. Retrieved May 15th, 2009, from http://www.itcportal.com/newsroom/itc-wins-top-unido-award.htm

5. Bapna Mukti, posted on 02 July 2007, recovered on 2nd May 2009, from, website http://www.expresscomputeronline.com/20070702/management02.shtml. (July 2007). ITC's

e-Choupal: reshaping the lives of farmers. Retrieved 20/04/11, 2011

6. Kumar, R. (2004). e-Choupals: A Study on the Financial Sustainability of Village Internet Centers in Rural Madhya Pradesh. Information Technologies & International Development, 2(1), 45-73.

7. I4D. (2005). ITC's e-Choupal wins 'Corporate Social Responsibility Award 2004'. i4D, June

8. Upton, D. F. and Virginia A. (Oct2003). ITC e-Choupal Initiative. Harvard Business School Cases, 20p.

9. M. Friedman, "The Social Responsibility of Business Is to Increase Its Profits," *New York Times Magazine* (September 13, 1970), pp. 30, 126–127; M. Friedman *Capitalism and Freedom* (Chicago: University of Chicago Press, 1963), p. 133.

10. W. J. Byron, *Old Ethical Principles for the New Corporate Culture*, presentation to the College of Business, Iowa State University, Ames, Iowa (March 31, 2003).

11. A. B. Carroll, "A Three-Dimensional Conceptual Model of Corporate Performance," *Academy of Management Review* (October 1979), pp. 497–505. This model of business responsibilities was reaffirmed in A. B. Carroll, "Managing Ethically with Global Stakeholders: A Present and Future Challenge," *Academy of Management Executive* (May 2004), pp. 114–120.

12. Carroll refers to discretionary responsibilities as philanthropic responsibilities in A. B. Carroll, "The Pyramid of Corporate Social Responsibility: Toward the Moral Management of Organizational Stakeholders," *Business Horizons* (July–August 1991), pp. 39–48.

13. M. S. Baucus and D. A. Baucus, "Paying the Piper: An Empirical Examination of Longer-Term Financial Consequences of Illegal Corporate Behavior," *Academy of Management Journal* (February 1997), pp. 129–151.

14. J. Oleck, "Pink Slips with a Silver Lining," *Business Week* (June 4, 2001), p. 14.

15. About US, Recovered on 11th Oct 2011, from http://www.aravind.org/aboutus/genesis.aspx

16. Ramachandran K , Thomas Schmidheiny and Rachna Jha, Family and Corporate Philanthropy: Emerging Trends In India, ISB INSIGHT, 5 Autumn 09, recovered on 11th Cot 2011, from http://www.isb.edu/familybusiness/File/FamilyCorporatePhilanthrophy.pdf

17. Rangan V. Kasturi, Aravind Eye Hospital, Madurai, India: In Service for Sight, Harvard Business Case study, 20Pg, Aprl 01, 1993, Prod. #: 593098-PDF-ENG

18. "The McKinsey Global Survey of Business Executives: Business and Society," *McKinsey Quarterly*, Web edition (March 31, 2006).

19. "Just Good Business," *The Economist*, Special Report on Social Responsibility (January 19, 2008), p. 4.

20. S. Sikta, "Corporate Philanthropy: Gaining popularity in India? DQ Channels," posted on Tuesday, August 02, 2011, recovered on 11th Oct 2011, from http://dqchannels.ciol.com/content/reselleralert/111080205.asp

21. A. McWilliams and D. Siegel, "Corporate Social Responsibility and Financial Performance: Correlation or Misspecification?" *Strategic Management Journal* (May 2000), pp. 603–609; P. Rechner and K. Roth, "Social Responsibility and Financial Performance: A Structural Equation Methodology," *International Journal of Management* (December 1990), pp. 382–391; K. E. Aupperle, A. B. Carroll, and J. D. Hatfield, "An Empirical Examination of the Relationship Between Corporate Social Responsibility and Profitability," *Academy of Management Journal* (June 1985), p. 459.

22. M. M. Arthur, "Share Price Reactions to Work-Family Initiatives: An Institutional Perspective," *Academy of Management Journal* (April 2003), pp. 497–505; S. A. Waddock and S. B. Graves, "The Corporate Social Performance—Financial Performance Link," *Strategic Management Journal* (April 1997), pp. 303–319; M. V. Russo and P. A. Fouts, "Resource Based Perspective on Corporate Environmental Performance and Profitability" *Academy of Management Journal* (July 1997), pp. 534–559; H. Meyer, "The Greening of Corporate America," *Journal of Business Strategy* (January/February 2000), pp. 38–43.

23. J. D. Margolis and J. P. Walsh, "Misery Loves Companies: Rethinking Social Initiatives by Business," *Administrative Science Quarterly* (June 2003), pp. 268–305.

24. M. F. L. Orlitzky, F. L. Schmidt, and S. L. Rynes, "Corporate Social and Financial Performance: A Meta Analysis," *Organization Studies*, Vol. 24 (2003), pp. 403–441.

25. M. Porter and M. R. Kramer, "The Competitive Advantage of Corporate Philanthropy," *Harvard Business Review* (December 2002), p. 59.

26. P. S. Adler and S. W. Kwon, "Social Capital: Prospects for a New Concept," *Academy of Management Journal* (January 2002), pp. 17–40. Also called "moral capital" in P. C. Godfrey, "The Relationship Between Corporate Philanthropy and Shareholder Wealth: A Risk Management Perspective," *Academy of Management Review* (October 2005), pp. 777–799.

27. L. Gard, "We're Good Guys, Buy from Us," *Business Week* (November 22, 2004), pp. 72–74.

28. C. J. Prince, "Give and Receive," *Entrepreneur* (November 2005), pp. 76–78.

29. C. J. Fombrun, "Corporate Reputation as an Economic Asset," in M. A. Hitt, E. R. Freeman, and J. S. Harrison (Eds.), *The Blackwell Handbook of Strategic Management* (Oxford: Blackwell Publishers, 2001), pp. 289–310.

30. S. A. Muirhead, C. J. Bennett, R. E. Berenbeim, A. Kao, and D. J. Vidal, *Corporate Citizenship in the New Century* (New York: The Conference Board, 2002), p. 6.

31. *2002 Sustainability Survey Report*, PriceWaterhouseCoopers, reported in "Corporate America's Social Conscience," Special Advertising Section, *Fortune* (May 26, 2003), pp. 149–157.

32. C. L. Harman and E. R. Stafford, "Green Alliances: Building New Business with Environmental Groups" *Long Range Planning* (April 1997), pp. 184–196.

33. D. B. Turner and D. W. Greening, "Corporate Social Performance and Organizational Attractiveness to Prospective Employees," *Academy of Management Journal* (July 1997), pp. 658–672; S. Preece, C. Fleisher, and J. Toccacelli, "Building a Reputation Along the Value Chain at Levi Strauss," *Long Range Planning* (December 1995), pp. 88–98; J. B. Barney and M. H. Hansen, "Trustworthiness as a Source of Competitive Advantage," *Strategic Management Journal* (Special Winter Issue, 1994), pp. 175–190: R. V. Aguilera, D. E. Rupp, C. A. Williams, and J. Ganapathi, "Putting the S Back in Corporate Social Responsibility: A Multilevel Theory of Social Change in Organizations," *Academy of Management Review* (July 2007), pp. 836–863; S. Bonini and S. Chenevert, "The State of Corporate Philanthropy: A McKinsey Global Survey," *McKinsey Quarterly*, Web edition (March 1, 2008); P. Kotler and N. Lee, eds., *Corporate Social Responsibility: Doing the Most Good for Your Company and Your Cause* (Hoboken, NJ: Wiley, 2005).

34. "Numbers: Do-Good Investments Are Holding Up Better," *Business Week* (July 14 & 21, 2008), p. 15.

35. A. Crane and D. Matten, *Business Ethics: A European Perspective* (Oxford: Oxford University Press, 2004), p. 22.

36. R. E. Freeman and D. R. Gilbert, *Corporate Strategy and the Search for Ethics* (Upper Saddle River, NJ: Prentice Hall, 1988), p. 6.

37. M. Arndt, W. Zellner, and P. Coy, "Too Much Corporate Power?" *Business Week* (September 11, 2000), pp. 144–158.

38. L. T. Mendonca and M. Miller, "Exploring Business's Social Contract: An Interview with Daniel Yankellvich," *McKinsey Quarterly* (2007, Number 2).

39. "Report: CEOs of Companies with Greatest Outsourcing Got Biggest Pay," *Des Moines Register* (August 31, 2004), p. B5.

40. W. E. Stead and J. G. Stead, *Sustainable Strategic Management* (Armonk, NY: M. E. Sharpe, 2004), p. 41.

41. "Andy Grove to Corporate Boards: It's Time to Take Charge," *Knowledge @ Wharton* (September 9–October 5, 2004).

42. "Ford Flip-Flop Annoys both Gays and Fundamentalists," *Roundel* (February 2006), p. 23.

43. "Nearly Half of Workers Take Unethical Actions—Survey," *Des Moines Register* (April 7, 1997), p. 18B.

44. M. Hendricks, "Well, Honestly!" *Entrepreneur* (December 2006), pp. 103–104.

45. "Dates from Hell," *The Economist* (July 22, 2006), pp. 59–60.

46. J. Kurlantzick, "Liar, Liar," *Entrepreneur* (October 2003), p. 70.

47. M. Roman, "True Confessions from CFOs," *Business Week* (August 12, 2002), p. 40.

48. The Times of India, "Corporate Fraud Thrives on Higher Attrition," says report, posted on September 26, 2007, 01:02 hrs IST, TNN, recovered on 11th Oct 2011, from Bennett Coleman & Co. Ltd website http://timesofindia.indiatimes.com/article show/2424859.cms

49. Kroll Consulting, Global Fraud Report 2010, recovered on 11th Oct 2011, form http://www.krollconsulting.com/media/pdfs/FraudReport_English-US_Oct10.pdf

50. M. R. Mayya, "Corporate Frauds: A Shocking Revelation," Rediff News, posted on April 13, 2009, recovered on 11th Oct 2011, from http://business.rediff.com/column/2009/apr/13/bcrisis-corporate-frauds-a-shocking-revelation.htm

51. M. R. Venkatesh, "Fraud Survey: Will India Inc Respond?" posted on March 26, 2008, recovered on 11th Oct 2011, from http://www.rediff.com/money/2008/mar/26mrv.htm

52. KPMG, India Fraud Report 2010, recovered on 11th Oct 2011, from https://www.in.kpmg.com/SecureData/aci/Files/KPMG_Fraud_Survey_2010.pdf

53. D. L. McCabe, K. D. Butterfield, and L. K. Trevino, "Academic Dishonesty in Graduate Business Programs: Prevalence, Causes, and Proposed Action," *Academy of Management Learning & Education* (September 2006), pp. 294–305.

54. L. Lavelle, "The GMAT Cheat Sheet," *Business Week* (July 14 & 21, 2008), p. 34.

55. S. Li, S. H. Park, and S. Li, "The Great Leap Forward: The Transition from Relation-Based Governance to Rule-Based Governance," *Organizational Dynamics*, Vol. 33, No. 1 (2004), pp. 63–78; M. Davids, "Global Standards, Local Problems," *Journal of Business Strategy* (January/February 1999), pp. 38–43; "The Opacity Index," *Economist* (September 18, 2004), p. 106.

56. K. Kumar, "Ethical Orientation of Future American Executives: What the Value Profiles of Business School Students Portend," *SAM Advanced Management Journal* (Autumn 1995), pp. 32–36,

47; M. Gable and P. Arlow, "A Comparative Examination of the Value Orientations of British and American Executives," *International Journal of Management* (September 1986), pp. 97–106; W. D. Guth and R. Tagiuri, "Personal Values and Corporate Strategy," *Harvard Business Review* (September–October 1965), pp. 126–127; G. W. England, "Managers and Their Value Systems: A Five Country Comparative Study," *Columbia Journal of World Business* (Summer 1978), p. 35.

57. J. F. Veiga, T. D. Golden, and K. Dechant, "Why Managers Bend Company Rules," *Academy of Management Executive* (May 2004), pp. 84–91.

58. H. Collingwood, "The Earnings Game," *Harvard Business Review* (June 2001), pp. 65–74; J. Fox, "Can We Trust Them Now?" *Fortune* (March 3, 2003), pp. 97–99.

59. S. Watkins, "Former Enron Vice President Sherron Watkins on the Enron Collapse," *Academy of Management Executive* (November 2003), p. 122.

60. R. E. Freeman and D. R. Gilbert, Jr., *Corporate Strategy and the Search for Ethics* (Englewood Cliffs, NJ: Prentice Hall, 1988), pp. 24–41.

61. L. K. Trevino, "Ethical Decision Making in Organizations: A Person-Situation Interactionist Model," *Academy of Management Review* (July 1986), pp. 601–617.

62. L. Kohlberg, "Moral Stage and Moralization: The Cognitive-Development Approach," in *Moral Development and Behavior*, edited by T. Lickona (New York: Holt, Rinehart & Winston, 1976).

63. J. K. Gephart, D. A. Harrison, and L. K. Trevino, "The Who, When, and Where of Unethical Choices: Meta-Analytic Answers to Fundamental Ethics Questions." Paper presented to the *Academy of Management* annual meeting, Philadelphia, PA (2007).

64. J. Keogh, ed., *Corporate Ethics: A Prime Business Asset* (New York: The Business Roundtable, 1988), p. 5.

65. G. F. Kohut, and S. E. Corriher, "The Relationship of Age, Gender, Experience and Awareness of Written Ethics Policies to Business Decision Making," *SAM Advanced Management Journal* (Winter 1994), pp. 32–39; J. C. Lere and B. R. Gaumitz, "The Impact of Codes of Ethics on Decision Making: Some Insights from Information Economics," *Journal of Business Ethics*, Vol. 48 (2003), pp. 365–379.

66. W. I. Sauser, "Business Ethics: Back to Basics," *Management in Practice* (2005, No. 2), pp. 2–3; J. M. Stevens, H. K. Steensma, D. A. Harrison, and P. L. Cochran, "Symbolic or Substantive Document? The Influence of Ethics Codes on Financial Executives' Decisions," *Strategic Management Journal* (February 2005), pp. 181–195.

67. *Business Roundtable Institute for Corporate Ethics Announces Key Findings from "Mapping the Terrain" Survey of CEOs*, press release (Charlottesville, VA: Business Roundtable Institute for Corporate Ethics, June 10, 2004).

68. Tata Motors, recovered on 11th Oct 2011, from http://ir.tatamotors.com/pdf/whistle-blower-policy.pdf

69. Indusind Bank, recovered on 11th Oct 2011, from http://www.indusind.com/downloads/wbp_final_draft.pdf

70. RBI, Policy Developments in Commercial Banking (Part 1 of 2), recovered on 11th Oct 2011, from http://rbi.org.in/scripts/PublicationsView.aspx?id=8849

71. THE WHISTLE BLOWERS (PROTECTION IN PUBLIC INTEREST DISCLOSURES) BILL, 2006, recovered on 11th

Oct 2011, from http://www.karmayog.org/anticorruption/upload/4729/ Whistle%20Blowers%20Bill_XI_2006.pdf

72. Central Vigilance Commission, GOI Resolution on Public Interest Disclosure and Protection of Informer, Published Date: March 30, 2007, 4:21 PM, recovered on 11th Oct 2011, from http://www.publicnotice.in/show_notice_details.php?id=2088

73. J. K. Gephart, D. A. Harrison, and L. K. Trevino, "The Who, When, and Where of Unethical Choices: Meta-Analytic Answers to Fundamental Ethics Questions." Paper presented to the *Academy of Management* annual meeting, Philadelphia, PA (2007).

74. "A 'How Am I Doing?' Guide for Ethics Czars," *Business Ethics* (Fall 2005), p. 11.

75. S. P. Feldman, "Moral Business Cultures: The Keys to Creating and Maintaining Them," *Organizational Dynamics* (2007, Vol. 36, No. 2), pp. 156–170. Also see the "World's Most Ethical Companies," published annually by Ethisphere at http://ethisphere.com.

76. "Clean, Wholesome and American?" *The Economist* (November 3, 2007), pp. 78–79.

77. M. Levin, "Building an Ethical Supply Chain," *Sarbanes-Oxley Compliance Journal* (April 3, 2008).

78. A. Bernstein, S. Holmes, and X. Ji, "Secrets, Lies, and Sweatshops," *Business Week* (November 27, 2006), pp. 50–58.

79. T. J. Von der Embse, and R. A. Wagley, "Managerial Ethics: Hard Decisions on Soft Criteria," *SAM Advanced Management Journal* (Winter 1988), p. 6.

80. G. F. Cavanagh, *American Business Values*, 3rd ed. (Upper Saddle River, NJ: Prentice Hall, 1990), pp. 186–199.

81. B. R. Agle, R. K. Mitchell, and J. A. Sonnenfeld, "Who Matters Most to CEOs? An Investigation of Stakeholder Attributes and Salience, Corporate Performance, and CEO Values," *Academy of Management Journal* (October 1999), pp. 507–525.

82. G. F. Cavanagh, *American Business Values*, 3rd ed. (Upper Saddle River, NJ: Prentice Hall, 1990, pp. 195–196.

83. I. Kant, "The Foundations of the Metaphysic of Morals," in *Ethical Theory: Classical and Contemporary Readings*, 2nd ed., by L. P. Pojman (Belmont, CA: Wadsworth Publishing, 1995), pp. 255–279.

84. J. Rice and A. Fields, "20 Things You Didn't Know About Recycling." *Discover* (May 2008), p. 80.

Ending Case for Part One

BLOOD BANANAS

Every company hates to be blackmailed, but that was exactly what was happening to one of America's largest fruit growing and processing companies, Chiquita Brands. Carlos Castaño, leader of the United Self Defense Forces of Columbia (AUC), a Colombian paramilitary organization, had just proposed that it would be in the best interests of Chiquita Brands and its subsidiary in Colombia, Banadex, to pay the AUC a few thousand dollars per month for "security" services. The security services were little more than protection from the AUC itself. Unfortunately, the local law enforcement agencies as well as the U.S. government were in no position to offer legitimate protection from paramilitary groups like the AUC. Chiquita was forced to decide whether to pay the AUC for protection or risk the lives of Chiquita employees in Colombia.

Chiquita Brands International Inc., headquartered in Cincinnati, Ohio, was a leading international marketer and distributor of high-quality fresh produce that was sold under the Chiquita® premium brand and related trademarks. The company was one of the largest banana producers in the world and a major supplier of bananas in Europe and North America. The company had revenues of approximately $4.5 billion and employed about 25,000 people in 70 countries in 2006.

Chiquita Brands, formerly United Brands and United Fruit, had been operating fruit plantations in Colombia for nearly 100 years. Chiquita's Banadex was responsible for 4,400 direct and an additional 8,000 indirect jobs in Colombia, jobs that were almost entirely performed by local (Colombian) workers. The company "contributed almost $70 million annually to the Colombian economy in the form of capital expenditures, payroll, taxes, social security, pensions, and local purchases of goods and services." Banadex was responsible for managing Chiquita's extensive plantation holding and was Chiquita's most profitable international operation.

This case was written by Steven M. Cox, Bradley W. Brooks, and S. Catherine Anderson of the Queens University of Charlotte and appeared in the *Journal of Critical Incidents*, Volume 1 (2008). Copyright © 2008 by Steven M. Cox, Bradley W. Brooks, and S. Catherine Anderson. Edited for publication in *Strategic Management and Business Policy*, 12th edition and *Concepts in Strategic Management and Business Policy*, 12th edition. Reprinted by permission of the authors and the Society for Case Research.

By the 1990s, Colombia had become a very violent country. Kidnappings and murders of wealthy Colombians and foreigners had become commonplace. The U.S. State Department had issued several advisories warning U.S. citizens about the dangers of travel to the country. In 1997, Carlos Castaño, leader of the AUC, met with senior officials of Banadex and offered to provide security services to the Banadex workers and property in Colombia. The AUC, often described as a "death squad," was one of the most violent, paramilitary organizations that existed in Colombia. Estimated by the U.S. State Department to number between 8,000 and 11,000 members, their activities included assassinations, guerrilla warfare, and drug trafficking. So far the AUC had not been designated a Foreign Terrorist Organization by the U.S. State Department, so it was not illegal to do business with the AUC. The implication of the offer for Banadex employees was obvious. Extortion or not, the implication of nonparticipation by Banadex would put employees at serious risk.

The options for Chiquita were straightforward: agree to pay, refuse to pay, or exit the country. The ramifications of any of the actions, however, were not pleasant.

Agree to Pay: If Chiquita agreed to pay for "protection" they might forestall killings and kidnappings; however, they would be financing a group of terrorists. The money it paid would be used to further the activities of AUC.

Refuse to Pay: If Chiquita chose to reject the offer of "protection" from Castaño, then there was the real likelihood that Banadex employees would be kidnapped and/or executed. There was ample evidence of the brutality of the AUC and similar organizations currently operating in Colombia. While a legitimate security company might be found to protect the plantations and employees, the cost to hire sufficient men to withstand a force of 8,000–11,000 paramilitary fighters would be inordinately expensive. Only governments had the strength to mount such a protective service and neither the U.S. nor Colombian governments were willing to support such an effort. Furthermore, it was unlikely that the Colombian government would welcome a mercenary force hired by Chiquita into the country.

Exit the Country: If the decision was made to abandon the plantations in Colombia what would happen to the 12,000 individuals whose livelihoods depended upon the work or workers on the plantation? Contributing $70 million annually to the economy, a rapid exit would represent a significant loss to the Colombian people. Further, Banadex exports represented a

significant portion of the bananas sold by Chiquita brands. The loss of this supply would not only affect Chiquita Brands' profitability and shareholder value but also the profitability of numerous Chiquita distributors around the world.

Study Question

1. What should Chiquita do?

PART 2

Scanning the
Environment

environmental scanning and Industry Analysis

The Arctic is undergoing an extraordinary transformation—a transformation that will have global impact not only on wildlife, but upon many countries and a number of industries. Some of the most significant environmental changes are retreating sea ice, melting glaciers, thawing permafrost, increasing coastal erosion, and shifting vegetation zones. The average temperature of the Arctic has risen at twice the rate of the rest of the planet. According to *Impacts of a Warming Arctic: Arctic Climate Impact Assessment*, a 2004 report by the eight-nation Arctic Council, the melting of the area's highly reflective snow and sea ice is uncovering darker land and ocean surfaces, further increasing the absorption of the sun's heat. Reductions in Arctic sea ice will drastically shrink marine habitats for polar bears, ice seals, and some seabirds. The warming of the tundra will likely boost greenhouse gases by releasing long-stored quantities of methane and carbon dioxide.

In addition to containing a large percentage of the world's water as ice, the Arctic is a large storehouse of natural resources. Given that the Arctic Ocean could be ice-free in the summer by 2040, countries bordering the Arctic are already positioning themselves for exploitation of these resources. Lawson Brigham, Alaska Office Director of the U.S. Arctic Research Commission and a former chief of strategic planning for the U.S. Coast Guard, examined how regional warming will affect transportation systems, resource development, indigenous Arctic peoples, regional environmental degradation and protection schemes, and overall geopolitical issues. From this, he proposes four possible scenarios for the Arctic in 2040:

1. **Globalized frontier:** In this scenario, the Arctic by 2040 has become an integral component of the global economic system, but is itself a semi-lawless frontier with participants jockeying for control. The summer sea ice has completely disappeared for a two-week period, allowing greater marine access and commercial shipping throughout the area. The famous "Northwest Passage" dreamed by 16th century navigators is now a reality. Rising prices for oil, natural gas, nickel, copper, zinc, and freshwater in conjunction with an easily accessible and less-harsh climate have made Arctic natural resource exploitation economically viable. Even though overfishing has reduced fish stocks, Arctic tourism is flourishing. By now, well-worn oil and gas pipelines in western Siberia and Alaska are experiencing recurring serious

Learning Objectives

After reading this chapter, you should be able to:

- Recognize aspects of an organization's environment that can influence its long-term decisions
- Identify the aspects of an organization's environment that are most strategically important
- Conduct an industry analysis to understand the competitive forces that influence the intensity of rivalry within an industry
- Understand how industry maturity affects industry competitive forces

- Categorize international industries based on their pressures for coordination and local responsiveness
- Construct strategic group maps to assess the competitive positions of firms in an industry
- Identify key success factors and develop an industry matrix
- Use publicly available information to conduct competitive intelligence
- Know how to develop an industry scenario
- Be able to construct an EFAS table that summarizes external environmental factors

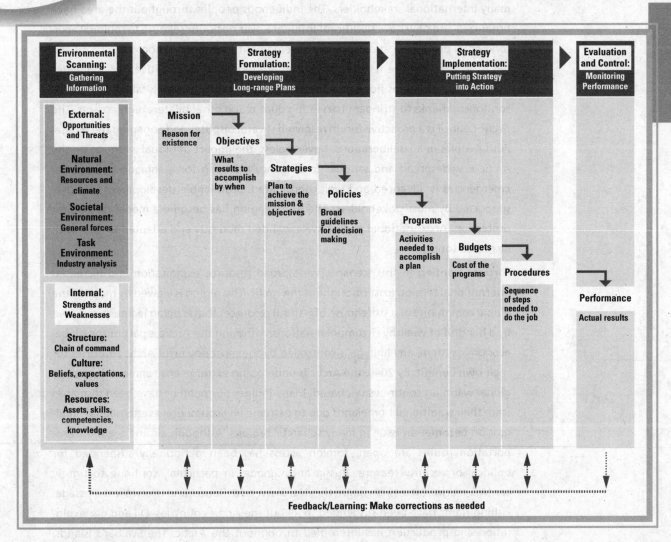

Environmental Scanning: Gathering Information

External: Opportunities and Threats

Natural Environment: Resources and climate

Societal Environment: General forces

Task Environment: Industry analysis

Internal: Strengths and Weaknesses

Structure: Chain of command

Culture: Beliefs, expectations, values

Resources: Assets, skills, competencies, knowledge

Strategy Formulation: Developing Long-range Plans

Mission — Reason for existence

Objectives — What results to accomplish by when

Strategies — Plan to achieve the mission & objectives

Policies — Broad guidelines for decision making

Strategy Implementation: Putting Strategy into Action

Programs — Activities needed to accomplish a plan

Budgets — Cost of the programs

Procedures — Sequence of steps needed to do the job

Evaluation and Control: Monitoring Performance

Performance — Actual results

Feedback/Learning: Make corrections as needed

spills. By 2020, Canada, Denmark (Greenland), Norway, Russia, and the United States had asserted their sovereignty over sea bed resources beyond 200 nautical miles—leaving only two small regions in the central Arctic Ocean under international jurisdiction. Environmental concerns that once fostered polar cooperation have been replaced by economic and political interests. The protection, development, and governance of the Svalbard Islands became a problem when Russia refused to recognize Norway's 200-nautical mile exclusive economic zone around the islands. Issues regarding freedom of navigation and commercial access rights are highly contentious. The eight permanent members of the Arctic Council have increasingly excluded outside participation in the Council's deliberations.

2. **Adaptive frontier:** In this scenario, the Arctic in 2040 is being drawn much more slowly into the global economy. The area is viewed as an international resource. Competition among the Arctic countries for control of the region's resources never grew beyond a low level and the region is the scene of international cooperation among many international stakeholders. The indigenous peoples throughout the area have organized and now have significant influence over decisions relating to regional environmental protection and economic development. The exploitation of Arctic oil and gas is restricted to the few key areas that are most cost-competitive. Air and water transportation systems flourish throughout the area. Commercially viable fishing has continued, thanks to stringent harvesting quotas and other bilateral agreements. The Arctic Council is a proactive forum resolving several disputes and engaging the indigenous peoples in all deliberations. Nevertheless, the impact of global warming on the Arctic is widespread and serious. Contingency planning for manmade and natural emergencies is advanced and well coordinated. Sustainable development is widely supported by most stakeholders. The Arctic region has become a model for habitat protection. Arctic national parks have expanded modestly and adapted to deal with increased tourism.

3. **Fortress frontier:** In this scenario, widespread resource exploitation and increased international tension exist throughout the Arctic. The region is viewed by much of the global community as a storehouse of natural resources that is being jealously guarded by a handful of wealthy circumpolar nations. Although the Arctic is part of the global economic system, any linkage is controlled by the most powerful Arctic countries for their own benefit. By 2040, the Arctic is undergoing extreme environmental stress, as global warming continues unabated. Many indigenous peoples have been displaced from their traditional homelands due to extreme environmental events. Illegal immigration becomes an issue in many subarctic regions. Although air and marine transportation routes are open, foreign access has been periodically suspended for political or security reasons. Russia and Canada, in particular, continue to tightly control marine access through the Northern Sea Route and Northwest Passage. Fishing rights have been suspended to all but the Arctic countries. Oil and gas exploration and production has intensified throughout the Arctic. The Svalbard Islands, claimed by Norway, have been a source of potential conflict over access to living and

nonliving resources. Norway, Russia, and the United States have increased military forces in the region. Rather than dealing with sustainable development, the Arctic Council focuses on economic and security concerns, such as illegal immigrants and controlling the flow of exports from the Arctic consortium. Early in the 21st century, the five countries bordering the Arctic declared their sovereignty over resources beyond 200 nautical miles to the edge of the continental shelf extensions. By 2030, the Arctic Council unilaterally took jurisdiction over the two small regions that remained within international jurisdiction. Arctic tourism thrives, since many other traditional destinations are experiencing turmoil and a shortage of necessities.

4. **Equitable frontier:** In this scenario, the Arctic is integrated with the global economic system by 2040, but international concern for sustainable development has slowed the region's economic development. Mutual respect and cooperation among the circumpolar nations allows for the development of a respected Arctic governance system. Even though the world is working hard to reduce greenhouse gas emissions, the Arctic continues to warm. Transport user fees and other eco-taxes are used to support endangered wildlife and impacted indigenous communities. The growth of the Northern Sea Route and Northwest Passage has enabled significant efficiencies in commercial shipping. Canada and Russia have maintained stringent marine regulations that emphasize environmental protection. Despite differences over freedom of navigation, the United States, Canada, and Russia have negotiated an agreement that allows a seamless voyage around Alaska and through the routes under a uniform set of operational procedures. The Arctic Council has created regional disaster teams to respond to maritime and other emergencies. Boundary disputes have been resolved and fishing rights have been allocated to various nations. The University of the Arctic has brought quality online education to easy reach of all northern citizens. The Arctic Council has brokered an agreement to allow 30,000 environmental refugees to settle in subarctic territories. Oil exploration and production in the Arctic has slowed considerably. Arctic tourism continues its steady growth, prompting national and regional parliaments to establish additional wilderness lands funded by tourist fees. There is low military presence in the region, thanks to the diplomatic efforts of the Arctic Council.

The Arctic is a complex, but relatively small region. These four scenarios suggest how climate change combined with a growing need for natural resources might impact this region and the world.[1]

■ Which of the four preceding scenarios is most likely?

■ Which industries are likely to be affected (either positively or negatively) by the warming of the Arctic?

■ If in an affected industry, how could a business corporation prepare for each of these scenarios?

A changing environment can help as well as hurt a company. Many pioneering companies have gone out of business because of their failure to adapt to environmental change or, even worse, because of their failure to create change. For example, Baldwin Locomotive, the major manufacturer of steam locomotives, was very slow in making the switch to diesel locomotives. General Electric and General Motors soon dominated the diesel locomotive business and Baldwin went out of business. The dominant manufacturers of vacuum tubes failed to make the change to transistors and consequently lost this market. Eastman Kodak, the pioneer and market leader of chemical-based film photography, continues to struggle with its transition to the newer digital technology. Failure to adapt is, however, only one side of the coin. The aforementioned Arctic warming example shows how a changing environment can create new opportunities at the same time it destroys old ones. The lesson is simple: To be successful over time, an organization needs to be in tune with its external environment. There must be a strategic fit between what the environment wants and what the corporation has to offer, as well as between what the corporation needs and what the environment can provide.

Current predictions are that the environment for all organizations will become even more uncertain with every passing year. What is **environmental uncertainty**? It is the *degree of complexity* plus the *degree of change* that exists in an organization's external environment. As more and more markets become global, the number of factors a company must consider in any decision becomes huge and much more complex. With new technologies being discovered every year, markets change and products must change with them.

On the one hand, environmental uncertainty is a threat to strategic managers because it hampers their ability to develop long-range plans and to make strategic decisions to keep the corporation in equilibrium with its external environment. On the other hand, environmental uncertainty is an opportunity because it creates a new playing field in which creativity and innovation can play a major part in strategic decisions.

4.1 Environmental Scanning

Before an organization can begin strategy formulation, it must scan the external environment to identify possible opportunities and threats and its internal environment for strengths and weaknesses. **Environmental scanning** is the monitoring, evaluation, and dissemination of information from the external and internal environments to key people within the corporation. A corporation uses this tool to avoid strategic surprise and to ensure its long-term health. Research has found a positive relationship between environmental scanning and profits.[2] Approximately 70% of executives around the world state that global social, environmental, and business trends are increasingly important to corporate strategy, according to a 2008 survey by McKinsey & Company.[3] A similar report called the CDP India Report is the output of a Carbon Disclosure Project. The CDP 2010 report focuses on the level of companies' understanding of risks and opportunities, carbon footprint, actions taken to reduce their carbon footprint, policy engagement, and finding strategic advantages in India. CDP 2010 responses from Indian companies suggest that there has been a shift in emphasis and in climate regulation, from an approach dominated by risk to one that now embraces opportunity. Nearly 97% of the respondents identify opportunities arising from addressing climate change, in comparison to 80% identifying risks, as a result of regulatory, physical, or commercial drivers.[4]

STRATEGY highlight 4.1

COSTS INCURRED WITH SPENDING ON REDUCING CARBON EMISSIONS IN INDIA

Countries and companies, especially in developing countries, are reluctant to adopt additional measures that help them to reduce carbon footprint. This attitude stems from additional costs that are involved in adopting these carbon emission-reducing technologies. There are significant costs associated with technologies that reduce carbon emissions. These are as follows:

1. Spending on newer energy resources: The government/management has to spend on new alternate and greener energy resources rather than relying on traditional fossil fuel-based energy resources and technologies. In order to reduce carbon emission, these stakeholders have to invest in alternate and recycling energy-based technologies and buildings. For example, Technopolis, Kolkata, has invested in carbon-reducing technologies and building plan measures on demand management side only. The net result has been an average annual GHG reduction by 9,000 tonnes of CO_2, translating into corresponding CERs.[1] Initiatives like LEED INDIA endorses a complete-building approach to sustainability by focusing on sustainable site development, water savings, energy efficiency, materials selection and indoor environmental quality.

2. Spending on building more energy-efficient products: The government/management has to invest in R&D to develop technologies to build more energy-efficient products. R&D costs would increase the cost of product and services. For example, there is a call for telecom companies in India to invest in this category and reduce their carbon footprint. For any telecom company, the major energy consumer is its network equipment, i.e., telecom towers and the base transceiver station (BTS). These consume up to 86% of energy—of which the tower site uses 65% while the core network uses 21%. In India, most of these towers are in rural areas, with irregular power supply; therefore, they rely on fossil fuel energy. Hence, with over 3,10,000 towers, this consumption works out to be over two billion liters of diesel annually.[2] Therefore, there is a need for these companies to invest into newer and more energy-efficient technologies.

3. There would be costs incurred due to reduced economic development: This would result in factors such as unemployment, industries spending on equipments, technologies for reducing carbon emissions, policies, administrative and legislative costs, and so on. For example, McKinsey estimates (not conservative and pessimistic compared to the estimate of Greenpeace and UCS), that it would cost 2.3% of GDP in India to halve the carbon emissions growth by 2030.[3]

These additional costs demotivate the government/management investing into reducing carbon emissions. However, many companies are investing into these measures and as highlighted by CDP 2010, there has been a shift in emphasis and in climate regulation, from an approach dominated by risk to one that now embraces opportunity.[4]

1. Agneya, Buildings to reduce carbon footprint and earn carbon credits, posted on 18 Feb 2011, accessed on 19 Oct 2011, from http://agneyablog.wordpress.com/2011/02/18/green-buildings-to-reduce-carbon-footprint-and-earn-carbon-credits/

2. Gupta, Katyayan, Indian Telecom Regulator Seeks to Reduce Carbon Footprint and Operational Expenditure of Operators by Moving Towards 'Green Telecom', posted on 7 Feb 2010, accessed on 19 Oct 2011, from https://telecomjunction.wordpress.com/2011/02/07/indian-telecom-regulator-seeks-to-reduce-carbon-footprint-and-operational-expenditure-of-operators-by-moving-towards-green-telecom/

3. Cashmo.net, India on Reducing Carbon Emissions – An Economic Development Perspective, posted on 7 Feb 2010, accessed on 19 Oct 2011, from http://www.cashmo.net/economic/india-on-reducing-carbon-emissions-%E2%80%93-an-economic-development-perspective.html

4. WWF, CII and CII-ITC Center For Excellence For Sustainable Development, Carbon Disclosure Project 2010; India 200 Report, accessed on 19 Oct 2011, from http://assets.wwfindia.org/downloads/cdp_report_2010.pdf

IDENTIFYING EXTERNAL ENVIRONMENTAL VARIABLES

In undertaking environmental scanning, strategic managers must first be aware of the many variables within a corporation's natural, societal, and task environments (see **Figure 1–3**). The **natural environment** includes physical resources, wildlife, and climate that are an inherent part of existence on Earth. These factors form an ecological system of interrelated life.

The **societal environment** is mankind's social system that includes general forces that do not directly touch on the short-run activities of the organization that can, and often do, influence its long-run decisions. These factors affect multiple industries and are as follows:

- **Economic forces** that regulate the exchange of materials, money, energy, and information.
- **Technological forces** that generate problem-solving inventions.
- **Political–legal forces** that allocate power and provide constraining and protecting laws and regulations.
- **Sociocultural forces** that regulate the values, mores, and customs of society.

The **task environment** includes those elements or groups that directly affect a corporation and, in turn, are affected by it. These are governments, local communities, suppliers, competitors, customers, creditors, employees/labor unions, special-interest groups, and trade associations. A corporation's task environment is typically the industry within which the firm operates. **Industry analysis** (popularized by Michael Porter) refers to an in-depth examination of key factors within a corporation's task environment. The natural, societal, and task environments must be monitored to detect the strategic factors that are likely in the future to have a strong impact on corporate success or failure. Changes in the natural environment usually affect a business corporation first through its impact on the societal environment in terms of resource availability and costs and then upon the task environment in terms of the growth or decline of particular industries. See **Strategy Highligh 4.1** to learn how cost is incurred while trying to reduce carbon emission.

Scanning the Natural Environment

The natural environment includes physical resources, wildlife, and climate that are an inherent part of existence on Earth. Until the 20th century, the natural environment was generally perceived by business people to be a given—something to exploit, not conserve. It was viewed as a free resource, something to be taken or fought over, like arable land, diamond mines, deep water harbors, or fresh water. Once they were controlled by a person or entity, these resources were considered assets and thus valued as part of the general economic system—a resource to be bought, sold, or sometimes shared. Side effects, such as pollution, were considered to be *externalities*, costs not included in a business firm's accounting system, but felt by others. Eventually these externalities were identified by governments, which passed regulations to force business corporations to deal with the side effects of their activities.

The concept of sustainability argues that a firm's ability to continuously renew itself for long-term success and survival is dependent not only upon the greater economic and social system of which it is a part, but also upon the natural ecosystem in which the firm is embedded.[5] A business corporation must thus scan the natural environment for factors that might previously have been taken for granted, such as the availability of fresh water and clean air. Global warming means that aspects of the natural environment, such as sea level, weather, and climate, are becoming increasingly uncertain and difficult to predict. Management must therefore scan not only the natural environment for possible strategic factors, but also include in its strategic decision-making processes the impact of its activities upon the natural environment. In a world concerned with global warming, a company should measure its carbon emmissions and invest into alternatives to reduce its *carbon footprint*—the amount of greenhouse gases it is emitting into the air (for costs associated with reducing carbon footprint see **Strategy Highlight 4.1**). Research reveals that scanning the market for environmental issues is positively related to firm performance because it helps management identify opportunities to fulfill future market demand based upon environmentally friendly products or processes.[6] See the **Environmental Sustainability Issue** feature to learn how individuals can also measure and shrink their personal carbon footprints.

ENVIRONMENTAL sustainability issue

MEASURING AND SHRINKING YOUR PERSONAL CARBON FOOTPRINT

As people become more "green," that is more conscious of environmental sustainability, they wonder what they can do as individuals to reduce the emission of greenhouse gases. This is an important issue given that a typical American produces more than 20 tons of carbon dioxide annually—a very large carbon footprint. Even a homeless American has a carbon footprint of 8.5 tons, more than twice the global average! The first problem for concerned individuals is finding a way to measure the size of their own carbon footprint. The second problem is developing feasible programs to reduce that footprint in some meaningful way.

The Web site *carbonrally.com* solves these problems by presenting competitive environmental challenges and keeping score by translating green actions into pounds of carbon dioxide averted. For instance, cutting the time of a daily shower by two minutes for a month reduces CO_2 emissions by 15.3 pounds. According to Kelsey Schroeder, who has logged savings of more than 1,000 pounds of emissions, "This has been a great motivational technique. We just want to keep going and see if we can do better."

How does Carbonrally calculate someone's carbon shoe size? Since everything a person does that is powered by fossil fuels has a carbon dioxide cost, many activities have the potential of being counted. Commuting in a gasoline powered car has obvious carbon costs, but so does eating a hamburger. Since livestock are responsible for an esti-

mated 18% of global carbon emissions, eating a hamburger results in carbon emissions by the consumer. Something as small as an iPod adds to a person's carbon footprint due not only to the energy used to produce and transport the product, but also to the energy used to charge it over its lifetime—approximately 68 pounds of CO_2. Both the Nature Conservancy and the U.S. Environmental Protection Agency provide ways to measure an individual carbon footprint. The EPA even offers a carbon calculator on its Web site, epa.gov.

Carbonrally offers concrete ways to start cutting carbon emissions. One 2008 contest challenged people to avoid bottled soda, tea, and sports drinks for a month for an average individual savings of 25.7 pounds of CO_2.

Other challenges were using a clothesline to dry one laundry load a week, unplugging computers every night for one month, and using a personal cup for coffee instead of using a disposable cup. By the end of 2008, nearly 15,000 individuals had completed a challenge, effectively reducing over 1,622.57 tons of CO_2.

Given that global carbon dioxide emissions total more than 28 billion tons annually, one person's reductions can seem very small. Why bother? Carbonrally might respond that the best way to change the world is one person at a time.

SOURCE: B. Walsh and T. Sharples, "Sizing Up Carbon Footprints," *Time* (May 26, 2008), pp. 53–55 and www.carbonrally.com.

Scanning the Societal Environment: STEEP Analysis

The number of possible strategic factors in the societal environment is very high. The number becomes enormous when we realize that, generally speaking, each country in the world can be represented by its own unique set of societal forces—some of which are very similar to those of neighboring countries and some of which are very different.

For example, even though Korea and China share Asia's Pacific Rim area with Thailand, Taiwan, and Hong Kong (sharing many similar cultural values), they have very different views about the role of business in society. It is generally believed in Korea and China (and to a lesser extent in Japan) that the role of business is primarily to contribute to national development; however in Hong Kong, Taiwan, and Thailand (and to a lesser extent in the Philippines, Indonesia, Singapore, and Malaysia), the role of business is primarily to make profits for the shareholders.[7] Such differences may translate into different trade regulations and varying difficulty in the *repatriation of profits* (the transfer of profits from a foreign subsidiary to a corporation's headquarters) from one group of Pacific Rim countries to another.

STEEP Analysis: Monitoring Trends in the Societal and Natural Environments. As shown in **Table 4–1**, large corporations categorize the societal environment in any one geographic region into four areas and focus their scanning in each area on trends that have corporatewide relevance. By including trends from the natural environment, this scanning can be called **STEEP Analysis**, the scanning of Sociocultural, Technological, Economic, Ecological, and Political-legal environmental forces.[8] (It may also be called *PESTEL Analysis* for Political, Economic, Sociocultural, Technological, Ecological, and Legal forces.) Obviously, trends in any one area may be very important to firms in one industry but of lesser importance to firms in other industries.

Trends in the *economic* part of the societal environment can have an obvious impact on business activity. For example, an increase in interest rates means fewer sales of major home appliances. Why? A rising interest rate tends to be reflected in higher mortgage rates. Because higher mortgage rates increase the cost of buying a house, the demand for new and used houses tends to fall. Because most major home appliances are sold when people change houses, a reduction in house sales soon translates into a decline in sales of refrigerators, stoves, and dishwashers and reduced profits for everyone in the appliance industry. Changes in the price of oil have a similar impact upon multiple industries, from packaging and automobiles to hospitality and shipping.

The rapid economic development of Brazil, Russia, India, and China (often called the *BRIC* countries) is having a major impact on the rest of the world. By 2007, China had become the world's second-largest economy according to the World Bank. With India graduating more English-speaking scientists, engineers, and technicians than all other nations combined, it has become the primary location for the outsourcing of services, computer software, and telecommunications.[9] Eastern Europe has become a major manufacturing supplier to the European Union countries. According to the International Monetary Fund, emerging markets make up less than one-third of total world gross domestic product (GDP), but account for more than half of GDP growth.[10]

TABLE 4–1	Some Important Variables in the Societal Environment		
Economic	**Technological**	**Political–Legal**	**Sociocultural**
GDP trends	Total government spending for R&D	Antitrust regulations	Lifestyle changes
Interest rates	Total industry spending for R&D	Environmental protection laws	Career expectations
Money supply		Global warming legislation	Consumer activism
Inflation rates	Focus of technological efforts	Immigration laws	Rate of family formation
Unemployment levels	Patent protection	Tax laws	Growth rate of population
Wage/price controls	New products	Special incentives	Age distribution of population
Devaluation/revaluation	New developments in technology transfer from lab to marketplace	Foreign trade regulations	Regional shifts in population
Energy alternatives		Attitudes toward foreign companies	Life expectancies
Energy availability and cost	Productivity improvements through automation	Laws on hiring and promotion	Birthrates
Disposable and discretionary income	Internet availability	Stability of government	Pension plans
Currency markets	Telecommunication infrastructure	Outsourcing regulation	Health care
Global financial system	Computer hacking activity	Foreign "sweat shops"	Level of education
			Living wage
			Unionization

Changes in the *technological* part of the societal environment can also have a great impact on multiple industries. Improvements in computer microprocessors have not only led to the widespread use of personal computers but also to better automobile engine performance in terms of power and fuel economy through the use of microprocessors to monitor fuel injection. Digital technology allows movies and music to be available instantly over the Internet or through cable service, but it also means falling fortunes for video rental shops such as the Movie Gallery and CD stores such as Tower Records. Advances in nanotechnology are enabling companies to manufacture extremely small devices that are very energy efficient. Developing biotechnology, including gene manipulation techniques, is already providing new approaches to dealing with disease and agriculture. Researchers at George Washington University have identified a number of technological breakthroughs that are already having a significant impact on many industries:

- **Portable information devices and electronic networking:** Combining the computing power of the personal computer, the networking of the Internet, the images of the television, and the convenience of the telephone, these appliances will soon be used by a majority of the population of industrialized nations to make phone calls, send e-mail, and transmit documents and other data. Even now, homes, autos, and offices are being connected (via wires and wirelessly) into intelligent networks that interact with one another. This trend is being supported by the development of *cloud computing*, in which a person can tap into computing power elsewhere through a Web connection.[11] The traditional stand-alone desktop computer may soon join the manual typewriter as a historical curiosity.

- **Alternative energy sources:** The use of wind, geothermal, hydroelectric, solar, biomass, and other alternative energy sources should increase considerably. Over the past two decades, the cost of manufacturing and installing a photovoltaic solar-power system has decreased by 20% with every doubling of installed capacity. The cost of generating electricity from conventional sources, in contrast, has been rising along with the price of petroleum and natural gas.[12]

- **Precision farming:** The computerized management of crops to suit variations in land characteristics will make farming more efficient and sustainable. Farm equipment dealers such as Case and John Deere add this equipment to tractors for an additional $6,000 or so. It enables farmers to reduce costs, increase yields, and decrease environmental impact. The old system of small, low-tech farming is becoming less viable as large corporate farms increase crop yields on limited farmland for a growing population. The concept of precision farming is appropriate to solve many problems inherent to the Indian farming system; it has some practical difficulties for Indian conditions, but it is not impossible to adopt. Research efforts are needed to find out its applicability in the Indian agricultural scenario. In 2000, the M. S. Swaminathan Research Foundation, Chennai, India joined hands with Israel to initiate PF on an experimental basis, including conducting training programs.[13] One such experiment was first started in 2004–2005 in Dharmapuri district, Tamil Nadu. In the first year, farmers were not ready to accept this project because of their frustration due to continuous drought since 2002. However, after seeing the success of the first 100 farmers and high market rate of the produce from this scheme, farmers started registering in large numbers for the second (90% subsidy) and third years (80% subsidy).[14]

- **Virtual personal assistants:** Very smart computer programs that monitor e-mail, faxes, and phone calls will be able to take over routine tasks, such as writing a letter, retrieving a file, making a phone call, or screening requests. Acting like a secretary, a person's virtual assistant could substitute for a person at meetings or in dealing with routine actions.

- **Genetically altered organisms:** A convergence of biotechnology and agriculture is creating a new field of life sciences. Plant seeds can be genetically modified to produce more needed vitamins or to be less attractive to pests and more able to survive.

Animals (including people) could be similarly modified for desirable characteristics and to eliminate genetic disabilities and diseases.

■ **Smart, mobile robots:** Robot development has been limited by a lack of sensory devices and sophisticated artificial intelligence systems. Improvements in these areas mean that robots will be created to perform more sophisticated factory work, run errands, do household chores, and assist the disabled.[15]

Trends in the *political–legal* part of the societal environment have a significant impact not only on the level of competition within an industry but also on which strategies might be successful.[16] For example, Competition Act, 2002 has replaced the Monopolies and Restrictive Trade Practices (MRTP) Act, 1969, in India. The law has been put forth to prohibit and penalize anti-competitive practices by enterprises and regulate potentially anti-competitive mergers.[17] The Act prohibits anti-competitive agreements (including cartels), which determine prices or control or limit or share markets among players or result in bid rigging. It prohibits abuse of dominant position through unfair and discriminatory prices or conditions (including predatory pricing), limiting or restricting production, denying market access, etc. Moreover, it entrusts the Competition Commission the responsibility of undertaking competition advocacy, awareness, and training about competition issues.[18]

As large companies find it more difficult to acquire another firm in the same or a related industry, they are typically driven to diversify into unrelated industries.[19] High levels of taxation and constraining labor laws in Western European countries stimulate companies to alter their competitive strategies or find better locations elsewhere. It is because Germany has some of the highest labor and tax costs in Europe that German companies have been forced to compete at the top end of the market with high-quality products or else move their manufacturing to lower-cost countries.[20] Government bureaucracy can create multiple regulations and make it almost impossible for a business firm to operate profitably in some countries. For example, the number of days needed to obtain the government approvals necessary to start a new business vary from only one day in Singapore to 14 in Mexico, 59 in Saudi Arabia, 87 in Indonesia, to 481 in the Congo.[21]

The $66 trillion global economy operates through a set of rules established by the World Trade Organization (WTO). Composed of 153 member nations and 30 observer nations, the WTO is a forum for governments to negotiate trade agreements and settle trade disputes. Originally founded in 1947 as the General Agreement on Tariffs and Trade (GATT), the WTO was created in 1995 to extend the ground rules for international commerce. The system's purpose is to encourage free trade among nations with the least undesirable side effects. Among its principles is trade without discrimination. This is exemplified by its *most-favored nation* clause, which states that a country cannot grant a trading partner lower customs duties without granting them to all other WTO member nations. Another principle is that of lowering trade barriers gradually though negotiation. It implements this principle through a series of rounds of trade negotiations. As a result of these negotiations, industrial countries' tariff rates on industrial goods had fallen steadily to less than 4% by the mid-1990s. The WTO is currently negotiating its ninth round of negotiations, called the Doha Round. The WTO is also in favor of fair competition, predictability of member markets, and the encouragement of economic development and reform. As a result of many negotiations, developed nations have started to allow duty-free and quota-free imports from almost all products from the least-developed countries.[22]

Demographic trends are part of the *sociocultural* aspect of the societal environment. Even though the world's population is growing from 3.71 billion people in 1970 to 6.82 billion in 2010 to 8.72 billion by 2040, not all regions will grow equally. Most of the growth will be in the developing nations. The population of the developed nations will fall from 14% of the total world population in 2000 to only 10% in 2050.[23] Around 75% of the world will live in a city by 2050 compared to little more than half in 2008.[24] Developing nations will continue to have more young than old people, but it will be the reverse in the industrialized nations.

TABLE 4–2	Generation	Born	Age in 2005	Number
Current U.S. Generations	WWII/Silent Generation	1932–1945	60–73	32 million
	Baby Boomers	1946–1964	41–59	77 million
	Generation X	1965–1977	28–40	45 million
	Generation Y	1978–1994	11–27	70 million

SOURCE: Developed from data listed in D. Parkinson, *Voices of Experience: Mature Workers in the Future Workforce* (New York: The Conference Board, 2002), p. 19.

For example, the demographic bulge in the U.S. population caused by the baby boom in the 1950s continues to affect market demand in many industries. This group of 77 million people now in their 50s and 60s is the largest age group in all developed countries, especially in Europe. **(See Table 4–2.)** Although the median age in the United States will rise from 35 in 2000 to 40 by 2050, it will increase from 40 to 47 during the same time period in Germany, and it will increase up to 50 in Italy as soon as 2025.[25] By 2050, one in three Italians will be over 65, nearly double the number in 2005.[26] With its low birthrate, Japan's population is expected to fall from 127.6 million in 2004 to around 100 million by 2050.[27] China's stringent birth control policy is causing the ratio of workers to retirees to fall from 20 to 1 during the early 1980s to 2.5 to one by 2020.[28] Companies with an eye on the future can find many opportunities to offer products and services to the growing number of "woofies" (well-off old folks—defined as people over 50 with money to spend).[29] These people are very likely to purchase recreational vehicles (RVs), take ocean cruises, and enjoy leisure sports, such as boating, fishing, and bowling, in addition to needing financial services and health care. Anticipating the needs of seniors for prescription drugs is one reason the Walgreen Company has been opening a new corner pharmacy every 19 hours![30]

To attract older customers, retailers will need to place seats in their larger stores so aging shoppers can rest. Washrooms need to be more accessible. Signs need to be larger. Restaurants need to raise the level of lighting so people can read their menus. Home appliances need simpler and larger controls. Automobiles need larger door openings and more comfortable seats. Zimmer Holdings, an innovative manufacturer of artificial joints, is looking forward to its market growing rapidly over the next 20 years. According to J. Raymond Elliot, chair and CEO of Zimmer, "It's simple math. Our best years are still in front of us."[31]

Eight current sociocultural trends are transforming North America and the rest of the world:

1. **Increasing environmental awareness:** Recycling and conservation are becoming more than slogans. Busch Gardens, for example, has eliminated the use of disposable styrofoam trays in favor of washing and reusing plastic trays.

2. **Growing health consciousness:** Concerns about personal health fuel the trend toward physical fitness and healthier living. As a result, sales growth is slowing at fast-food "burgers and fries" retailers such as McDonald's. Changing public tastes away from sugar-laden processed foods forced Interstate Bakeries, the maker of Twinkies and Wonder Bread, to declare bankruptcy in 2004. In 2008, the French government was considering increasing sales taxes on extra-fatty, salty, or sugary products.[32] The European Union forbade the importation of genetically altered grain ("Frankenfood") because of possible side effects. The spread of AIDS to more than 40 million people worldwide adds even further impetus to the health movement.

3. **Expanding seniors market:** As their numbers increase, people over age 55 will become an even more important market. Already some companies are segmenting the senior

population into Young Matures, Older Matures, and the Elderly—each having a different set of attitudes and interests. Both mature segments, for example, are good markets for the health care and tourism industries; whereas, the elderly are the key market for long-term care facilities. The desire for companionship by people whose children are grown is causing the pet care industry to grow 4.5% annually in the United States. In 2007, for example, 71.1 million households in the U.S. spent $41 billion on their pets—more than the gross domestic product of all but 16 countries in the world.[33]

4. **Impact of Generation Y Boomlet:** Born between 1978 and 1994 to the baby boom and X generations, this cohort is almost as large as the baby boom generation. In 1957, the peak year of the postwar boom, 4.3 million babies were born. In 1990, there were 4.2 million births in Generation Y's peak year. By 2000, they were overcrowding elementary and high schools and entering college in numbers not seen since the baby boomers. Now in its teens and 20s, this cohort is expected to have a strong impact on future products and services.

5. **Declining mass market:** Niche markets are defining the marketers' environment. People want products and services that are adapted more to their personal needs. For example, Estée Lauder's "All Skin" and Maybelline's "Shades of You" lines of cosmetic products are specifically made for African-American women. "Mass customization"—the making and marketing of products tailored to a person's requirements (Dell for example, and Gateway computers)—is replacing the mass production and marketing of the same product in some markets. Only 10% of the 6,200 magazines sold in the United States in 2004 were aimed at the mass market, down from 30% in the 1970s.[34]

6. **Changing pace and location of life:** Instant communication via e-mail, cell phones, and overnight mail enhances efficiency, but it also puts more pressure on people. Merging the personal computer with the communication and entertainment industries through telephone lines, satellite dishes, and cable television increases consumers' choices and allows workers to leave overcrowded urban areas for small towns and telecommute via personal computers and modems.

7. **Changing household composition:** The joint family is an ancient Indian institution, but it has undergone some change in the late 20th century. Although several generations living together is the ideal, actual living, arrangements vary widely depending on region, social status, and economic circumstances. The family as a unit is in its transition stage and many Indians now are leaving joint families and opting for nuclear families—a couple with their unmarried children—is the most common pattern in the West. This transition has led to rise in the number of dual-earner couples in India that has not only increased the standard of living but has also given rise to issues such as how to balance home and work and how to devote enough time to children.

8. **Increasing diversity of workforce and markets:** India is known as "politically one country but socio-culturally many countries in one." In India, comparing people in terms of language, style of dress, cultural dances, etc. even from two neighboring states is like comparing Karnataka to Italy. As per studies in India, the language and culture changes ever 100 km. From a media planning perspective, there are 5,600 daily newspapers, 15,000 weekly newspapers, and 20,000 magazines in 21 languages across the country. This diversity is just the tip of the iceberg that planners must negotiate through when planning their media buys. An organization in order to succeed in Indian diversity needs to have a broad spectrum of thought to manage at the marketplace while maintaining the universality of the product and brand. It is like a twin-edged sword. An optimal environment should be that which seeks to optimize the contributions of diverse workforce, suppliers, and the communities where they work. It should reflect both the marketplace and the customers.[35] Organizations such as IBM go out of their way to ensure

that they extend diversity beyond the traditional realms of race, gender, religion, disability, or sexual orientation. These organizations have aligned diversity with globalization, so that it becomes a natural extension of their organizations' strategy. Tata Group has a Second Career Internship Program for women professionals. It provides opportunity and explores the expertise of talented women professionals who have opted to take a career break after some initial years of work.[36]

Heavy immigration from the developing to the developed nations is increasing the number of minorities in all developed countries and forcing an acceptance of the value of diversity in races, religions, and life style. For example, 24% of the Swiss population was born elsewhere.[37] Traditional minority groups are increasing their numbers in the workforce and are being identified as desirable target markets. For example, Sears, Roebuck transformed 97 of its stores in October 2004 into "multicultural stores" containing fashions for Hispanic, African-American, and Asian shoppers.[38]

International Societal Considerations. Each country or group of countries in which a company operates presents a unique societal environment with a different set of economic, technological, political–legal, and sociocultural variables for the company to face. International societal environments vary so widely that a corporation's internal environment and strategic management process must be very flexible. Cultural trends in Germany, for example, have resulted in the inclusion of worker representatives in corporate strategic planning. Because Islamic law (*sharia*) forbids interest (*riba*), loans of capital in Islamic countries must be arranged on the basis of profit-sharing instead of interest rates.[39]

Differences in societal environments strongly affect the ways in which a **multinational corporation (MNC)**, a company with significant assets and activities in multiple countries, conducts its marketing, financial, manufacturing, and other functional activities. For example, Europe's lower labor productivity, due to a shorter work week and restrictions on the ability to lay off unproductive workers, forces European-based MNCs to expand operations in countries where labor is cheaper and productivity is higher.[40] Moving manufacturing to a lower-cost location, such as China, was a successful strategy during the 1990s, but a country's labor costs rise as it develops economically. For example, China required all firms in January 2008 to consult employees on material work-related issues, enabling the country to achieve its stated objective of having trade unions in all of China's non-state-owned enterprises. By September 2008, the All-China Federation of Trade Unions had signed with 80% of the largest foreign companies.[41]

To account for the many differences among societal environments from one country to another, consider **Table 4–3**. It includes a list of economic, technological, political–legal, and sociocultural variables for any particular country or region. For example, an important economic variable for any firm investing in a foreign country is currency convertibility. Without convertibility, a company operating in Russia cannot convert its profits from rubles to dollars or euros. In terms of sociocultural variables, many Asian cultures (especially China) are less concerned with the values of human rights than are European and North American cultures. Some Asians actually contend that U.S. companies are trying to impose Western human rights requirements on them in an attempt to make Asian products less competitive by raising their costs.[42]

Before planning its strategy for a particular international location, a company must scan the particular country environment(s) in question for opportunities and threats, and it must compare those with its own organizational strengths and weaknesses. Focusing only on the developed nations may cause a corporation to miss important market opportunities in the developing nations of the world. Although those nations may not have developed to the point that they have significant demand for a broad spectrum of products, they may very likely be on the threshold of rapid growth in the demand for specific products like cell phones.

TABLE 4–3	Some Important Variables in *International* Societal Environments		
Economic	**Technological**	**Political–Legal**	**Sociocultural**
Economic development	Regulations on technology transfer	Form of government	Customs, norms, values
Per capita income	Energy availability/cost	Political ideology	Language
Climate	Natural resource availability	Tax laws	Demographics
GDP trends	Transportation network	Stability of government	Life expectancies
Monetary and fiscal policies	Skill level of workforce	Government attitude toward foreign companies	Social institutions
Unemployment levels	Patent-trademark protection	Regulations on foreign ownership of assets	Status symbols
Currency convertibility	Internet availability	Strength of opposition groups	Lifestyle
Wage levels	Telecommunication infrastructure	Trade regulations	Religious beliefs
Nature of competition	Computer hacking technology	Protectionist sentiment	Attitudes toward foreigners
Membership in regional economic associations, e.g., EU, NAFTA, ASEAN	New energy sources	Foreign policies	Literacy level
		Terrorist activity	Human rights
Membership in World Trade Organization (WTO)		Legal system	Environmentalism
		Global warming laws	"Sweat shops"
		Immigration laws	Pension plans
Outsourcing capability			Health care
Global financial system			Slavery

This would be the ideal time for a company to enter this market—before competition is established. The key is to be able to identify the *trigger point* when demand for a particular product or service is ready to boom. See the **Global Issue** boxed highlight for an in-depth explanation of a technique to identify the optimum time to enter a particular market in a developing nation.

Creating a Scanning System. How can anyone monitor and keep track of all the trends and factors in the worldwide societal environment? With the existence of the Internet, it is now possible to scan the entire world. Nevertheless, the vast amount of raw data makes scanning for information similar to drinking from a fire hose. It is a daunting task for even a large corporation with many resources. To deal with this problem, in 2002 IBM created a tool called *WebFountain* to help the company analyze the vast amounts of environmental data available on the Internet. WebFountain is an advanced information discovery system designed to help extract trends, detect patterns, and find relationships within vast amounts of raw data. For example, IBM sought to learn whether there was a trend toward more positive discussions about e-business. Within a week, the company had data that experts within the company used to replace their hunches with valid conclusions. The company uses WebFountain to:

- Locate negative publicity or investor discontent
- Track general trends
- Learn competitive information
- Identify emerging competitive threats
- Unravel consumer attitudes[43]

GLOBAL issue

IDENTIFYING POTENTIAL MARKETS IN DEVELOPING NATIONS

Research by the Deloitte & Touche Consulting Group reveals that the demand for a specific product increases exponentially at certain points in a country's development. Identifying this trigger point of demand is thus critical to entering emerging markets at the best time. A *trigger point* is the time when enough people have enough money to buy what a company has to sell but before competition is established. This can be determined by using the concept of *purchasing power parity (PPP)*, which measures the cost in dollars of the U.S.–produced equivalent volume of goods that an economy produces.

PPP offers an estimate of the material wealth a nation can purchase, rather than the financial wealth it creates as typically measured by Gross Domestic Product (GDP). As a result, restating a nation's GDP in PPP terms reveals much greater spending power than market exchange rates would suggest. For example, a shoe shine costing $5 to $10 in New York City can be purchased for 50¢ in Mexico City. Consequently the people of Mexico City can enjoy the same standard of living (with respect to shoe shines) as people in New York City with only 5% to 10% of the money. Correcting for PPP restates all Mexican shoe shines at their U.S. purchase value of $5. If one million shoe shines

were purchased in Mexico last year, using the PPP model would effectively increase the Mexican GDP by $5 million to $10 million. Using PPP, China becomes the world's second-largest economy after the United States, followed by Japan, India, and Germany.

A trigger point identifies when demand for a particular product is about to rapidly increase in a country. Identifying a trigger point can be a very useful technique for determining when to enter a new market in a developing nation. Trigger points vary for different products. For example, an apparent trigger point for long-distance telephone services is at $7,500 in GDP per capita—a point when demand for telecommunications services increases rapidly. Once national wealth surpasses $15,000 per capita, demand increases at a much slower rate with further increases in wealth. The trigger point for life insurance is around $8,000 in GDP per capita. At this point, the demand for life insurance increases between 200% and 300% above those countries with GDP per capita below the trigger point.

SOURCE: D. Fraser and M. Raynor, "The Power of Parity," *Forecast* (May/June, 1996), pp. 8–12; "A Survey of the World Economy: The Dragon and the Eagle," Special Insert, *Economist* (October 2, 2004), p. 8; "The Big Mac Index: Food for Thought," *Economist* (May 29, 2004), pp. 71–72.

Scanning the Task Environment

As shown in **Figure 4–1**, a corporation's scanning of the environment includes analyses of all the relevant elements in the task environment. These analyses take the form of individual reports written by various people in different parts of the firm. At Procter & Gamble (P&G), for example, people from each of the brand management teams work with key people from the sales and market research departments to research and write a "competitive activity report" each quarter on each of the product categories in which P&G competes. People in purchasing also write similar reports concerning new developments in the industries that supply P&G. These and other reports are then summarized and transmitted up the corporate hierarchy for top management to use in strategic decision making. If a new development is reported regarding a particular product category, top management may then send memos asking people throughout the organization to watch for and report on developments in related product areas. The many reports resulting from these scanning efforts, when boiled down to their essentials, act as a detailed list of external strategic factors.

FIGURE 4–1
Scanning External
Environment

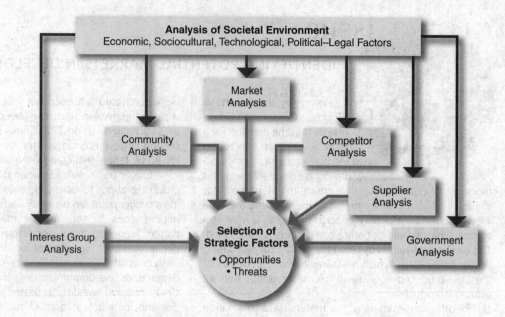

FIGURE 4–1
Scanning External Environment

IDENTIFYING EXTERNAL STRATEGIC FACTORS

The origin of competitive advantage lies in the ability to identify and respond to environmental change well in advance of competition.[44] Although this seems obvious, why are some companies better able to adapt than others? One reason is because of differences in the ability of managers to recognize and understand external strategic issues and factors. For example, in a global survey conducted by the Fuld-Gilad-Herring Academy of Competitive Intelligence, two-thirds of 140 corporate strategists admitted that their firms had been surprised by as many as three high-impact events in the past five years. Moreover, as recently as 2003, 97% stated that their companies had no early warning system in place.[45]

No firm can successfully monitor all external factors. Choices must be made regarding which factors are important and which are not. Even though managers agree that strategic importance determines what variables are consistently tracked, they sometimes miss or choose to ignore crucial new developments.[46] Personal values and functional experiences of a corporation's managers as well as the success of current strategies are likely to bias both their perception of what is important to monitor in the external environment and their interpretations of what they perceive.[47]

This willingness to reject unfamiliar as well as negative information is called *strategic myopia*.[48] If a firm needs to change its strategy, it might not be gathering the appropriate external information to change strategies successfully. For example, when Daniel Hesse became CEO of Sprint Nextel in December 2007, he assumed that improving customer service would be one of his biggest challenges. He quickly discovered that none of the current Sprint Nextel executives were even thinking about the topic. "We weren't talking about the customer when I first joined," said Hesse. "Now this is the No. 1 priority of the company."[49]

One way to identify and analyze developments in the external environment is to use the **issues priority matrix** (see **Figure 4–2**) as follows:

1. Identify a number of likely trends emerging in the natural, societal, and task environments. These are strategic environmental issues—those important trends that, if they occur, determine what the industry or the world will look like in the near future.

2. Assess the probability of these trends actually occurring, from low to medium to high.

FIGURE 4–2
Issues Priority
Matrix

Probable Impact on Corporation

FIGURE 4–2
Issues Priority
Matrix

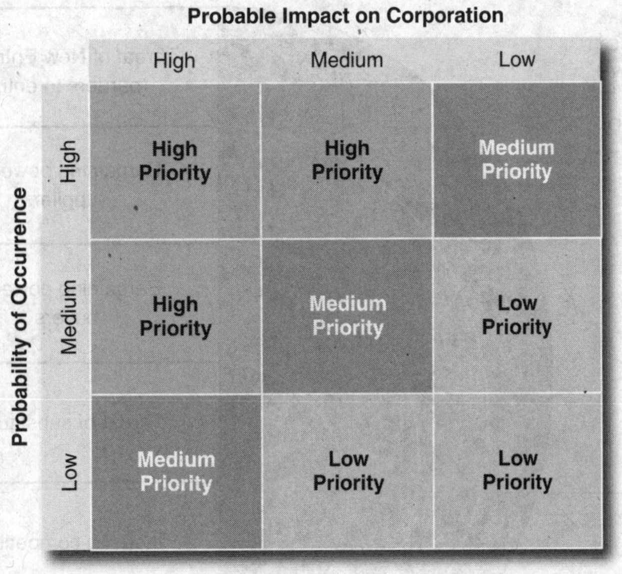

SOURCE: *Reprinted from* Long-Range Planning, *Vol. 17, No. 3, 1984, Campbell, "Foresight Activities in the U.S.A.: Time for a Re-Assessment?" p. 46. Copyright © 1984 with permission from Elsevier.*

3. Attempt to ascertain the likely impact (from low to high) of each of these trends on the corporation being examined.

A corporation's *external strategic factors* are the key environmental trends that are judged to have both a medium to high probability of occurrence and a medium to high probability of impact on the corporation. The issues priority matrix can then be used to help managers decide which environmental trends should be merely scanned (low priority) and which should be monitored as strategic factors (high priority). Those environmental trends judged to be a corporation's strategic factors are then categorized as opportunities and threats and are included in strategy formulation.

4.2 Industry Analysis: Analyzing the Task Environment

An **industry** is a group of firms that produces a similar product or service, such as soft drinks or financial services. An examination of the important stakeholder groups, such as suppliers and customers, in a particular corporation's task environment is a part of industry analysis.

PORTER'S APPROACH TO INDUSTRY ANALYSIS

Michael Porter, an authority on competitive strategy, contends that a corporation is most concerned with the intensity of competition within its industry. The level of this intensity is determined by basic competitive forces, as depicted in **Figure 4–3.** "The collective strength of these forces," he contends, "determines the ultimate profit potential in the industry, where profit potential is measured in terms of long-run return on invested capital."[50] In carefully scanning its industry, a corporation must assess the importance to its success of each of six forces: threat of new entrants, rivalry among existing firms, threat of substitute products or services, bargaining power of buyers is medium but increasing (prices are falling as the low-priced shoe

FIGURE 4–3
Elements of Porter's Five Forces Model in an Industry.

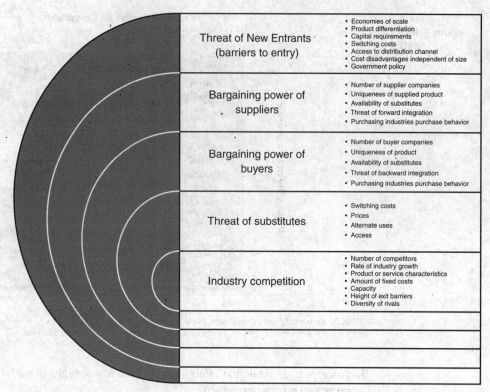

Threat of New Entrants (barriers to entry)	• Economies of scale • Product differentiation • Capital requirements • Switching costs • Access to distribution channel • Cost disadvantages independent of size • Government policy
Bargaining power of suppliers	• Number of supplier companies • Uniqueness of supplied product • Availability of substitutes • Threat of forward integration • Purchasing industries purchase behavior
Bargaining power of buyers	• Number of buyer companies • Uniqueness of product • Availability of substitutes • Threat of backward integration • Purchasing industries purchase behavior
Threat of substitutes	• Switching costs • Prices • Alternate uses • Access
Industry competition	• Number of competitors • Rate of industry growth • Product or service characteristics • Amount of fixed costs • Capacity • Height of exit barriers • Diversity of rivals

market has grown to be half of the U.S. branded athletic shoe market), and threat of other stakeholders is medium to high (government regulations and human rights concerns are growing). Based on current trends in each of these competitive forces, the industry's level of competitive intensity will continue to be high—meaning that sales increases and profit margins should continue to be modest for the industry as a whole.[51]

Threat of New Entrants

New entrants to an industry typically bring to it new capacity, a desire to gain market share, and substantial resources. They are, therefore, threats to an established corporation. The threat of entry depends on the presence of entry barriers and the reaction that can be expected from existing competitors. An **entry barrier** is an obstruction that makes it difficult for a company to enter an industry. Some of the possible barriers to entry are:

- **Economies of scale:** Scale economies in the production and sale of microprocessors, for example, gave Intel a significant cost advantage over any new rival.

- **Product differentiation:** Corporations such as Procter & Gamble and General Mills, which manufacture products such as Tide and Cheerios, create high entry barriers through their high levels of advertising and promotion.

- **Capital requirements:** The need to invest huge financial resources in manufacturing facilities in order to produce large commercial airplanes creates a significant barrier to entry to any competitor for Boeing and Airbus.

STRATEGY highlight 4.2

INDIAN RETAIL INDUSTRY ANALYSIS

The Indian retail industry has grown at a compounded annual growth rate (CAGR) of 13.3% for the financial year 2006–2010.[1] India has been ranked as the fourth most attractive nation for retail investment among 30 emerging markets by the US-based global management consulting firm, A. T. Kearney, in its Global Retail Development Index (GRDI) 2011.[2] A transition is taking place from the traditional retail sector to organized retail. Retailing in India has emerged from the neighborhood 'Kirana' stores catering to relationship and familiarity to the consumers to shopping centers catering to convenience of the consumers.

The PEST analysis of the industry shows that politically the environment is in favor of the retailing industry. Politically, India has a stable environment for business. Despite having multiparty system, it possesses certain characteristics, i.e., socialistic, democratic, and secular republic with a parliamentary system of government; apart from the democratically elected legislatures, the existence of an independent judiciary, a free and vibrant press, a single legal and accounting system adds to the political stability of India and its competitiveness as compared to other developing nations. Economic and social indicators show positive trend. Driven by changing consumption patterns, favorable demographics, expanding middle class and greater government support, the Indian retail sector is showing great potential for the retail industry. As Indian retail industry is complex, in order to achieve operational efficiency and cost-effectiveness, retailers are adopting the latest technologies. PEST analysis highlights that India is a country with tremendous opportunities for the retailing sector. However, main challenges for the industry in India are in areas of skilled human resource, infrastructure, regulatory framework, FDI policy, privatization, and logistics and supply chain management.

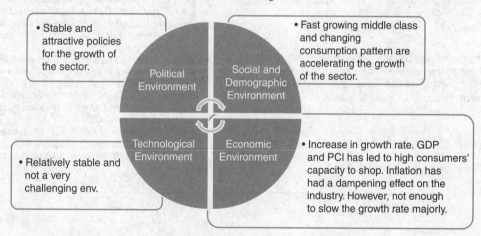

- Stable and attractive policies for the growth of the sector.

Political Environment

Social and Demographic Environment

- Fast growing middle class and changing consumption pattern are accelerating the growth of the sector.

Technological Environment

Economic Environment

- Relatively stable and not a very challenging env.

- Increase in growth rate. GDP and PCI has led to high consumers' capacity to shop. Inflation has had a dampening effect on the industry. However, not enough to slow the growth rate majorly.

Porter's five forces model for Indian retail industry highlights that this sector is an highly unorganized sector. A study in 2007 showed organized retail sector at 3% of total Indian retail business in India,[3] implying that 97% of the sector is unorganized and, therefore, dominated by commoditized products. The industry competition is also high because of the increased ratio of fixed cost to variable cost in the industry. Since this industry is dominated by commoditized products, awareness and availability of substitute products is a real threat for this industry. Furthermore, buyers have low switching costs and as information at their disposal increases, their bargaining power also increases. Suppliers to this industry compete on the basis of costs, especially in the unorganized sector and, therefore, the bargaining power is in the hands of the suppliers, especially the one who can control their prices and opt for alternate distribution channels. Unorganized sector of the retail industry in India has relatively moderate entry barriers. Small stores that can reduce the cost of entry and cater to a niche can enter the unorganized sector. However, the dynamics have changed with the entry of large retail outlets in this industry and the bargaining power of buyers and suppliers; substitutes have all worked in favor of the big retail giants. The very factor that the industry was commoditized has worked in favor of these big giants who have been able to compete on basis of price and earn profits.

The industry is a fragmented industry in growth stage of its life cycle. The size of retail operations are limited by

(Continued)

the nature of the industry. However, the key strategy to exploiting this growth would be consolidation of operations. Any company that can find a way to standardize its operations and consolidate them over the value chain to increase the economies of scale would be able to take advantage of this growth. This trend can be seen in operations of players such as Big Bazaar, Pantaloon, and Reliance Fresh who have been able to dominate the Indian scene by adopting this strategy. These players are changing the competitive landscape of the Indian retail industry by finding new ways of consolidating and standardizing their operations and reaping economies of scale.

Bargaining Power of Buyers	Bargaining Power of Suppliers	Industry Competitors	Substitutes	New entrants Medium to High
• Low switching costs • Increased buyer information	• Cost competitiveness • Ability to integrate and customize value chain due to the retailer	• High fixed costs • Commoditized products • Increased number of competitors both in organized and unorganized sectors	• Increased availability and awareness • Price competition	• Medium to high from unorganized and organized sectors

1. CARE Research, Indian Retail Industry, posted on March 2011, accessed on 19 Oct 2011, from http://www.bizreportshop.com/product/care/Indian-Retail-Industry-March-2011_175253.html

2. India Brand Equity Foundation, Retail, posted on September 2011, accessed on 19 Oct 2011, from http://www.ibef.org/industry/retail.aspx

3. Vyas Preeta, Ankush Sharma, Indian Organised Apparel Retail Sector and DSS, workind paper no 2007-07-01, July 2007, IIM Ahemdabad, accessed on 19 Oct 2011, from www.iimahd.ernet.in/publications/data/2007-07-01preeta.pdf

OTHER REFERENCES.

• Global Competitiveness Report 2006-07

• Tripathi Vibhuti , Indian Organized Retail Industry: A Value-addition on Private Labels, accessed on 2 Apr 2009, from Indian Institute Of Information Technology website http://bcognizance.iiita.ac.in/jan-mar08/perspective/2.html
• Bhat P.N. Mari, Indian Demographic Scenario, 2025, posted on June 2001, a paper prepared at the request of Centre for Policy Research, New Delhi, accessed on 2 Apr 2009, from http://www.iegindia.org/dispap/dis27.pdf
• Kumar. S (2007). Retail Industry -Where does India Stand? accessed on 2 Apr 2009, from http://www.coolavenues.com/know/mktg/sanjeev_retail_1.php3
• Federation of Indian Chambers of Commerce and Industry, Indian retail: on the fast track: Bridging the capability gaps, Published on 1 Sep 2008.
• in-house magazine of Group TCI, "Indian retail industry: Looking ahead", cover story, posted on July 2006, accessed on 19 Oct 2011, from www.grouptci.com/cover-story-July06.pdf

■ **Switching costs:** Once a software program such as Excel or Word becomes established in an office, office managers are very reluctant to switch to a new program because of the high training costs.

■ **Access to distribution channels:** Small entrepreneurs often have difficulty obtaining supermarket shelf space for their goods because large retailers charge for space on their shelves and give priority to the established firms who can pay for the advertising needed to generate high customer demand.

■ **Cost disadvantages independent of size:** Once a new product earns sufficient market share to be accepted as the *standard* for that type of product, the maker has a key advantage. Microsoft's development of the first widely adopted operating system (MS-DOS) for the IBM-type personal computer gave it a significant competitive advantage over potential competitors. Its introduction of Windows helped to cement that advantage so that the Microsoft operating system is now on more than 90% of personal computers worldwide.

■ **Government policy:** Governments can limit entry into an industry through licensing requirements by restricting access to raw materials, such as oil-drilling sites in protected areas.

Rivalry among Existing Firms

In most industries, corporations are mutually dependent. A competitive move by one firm can be expected to have a noticeable effect on its competitors and thus may cause retaliation. For example, the entry by mail order companies such as Dell and Gateway into a PC industry previously dominated by IBM, Apple, and Compaq increased the level of competitive activity to such an extent that any price reduction or new product introduction was quickly followed by similar moves from other PC makers. The same is true of prices in airline industry. According to Porter, intense rivalry is related to the presence of several factors, including:

■ **Number of competitors:** When competitors are few and roughly equal in size, such as in the auto and major home appliance industries, they watch each other carefully to make sure that they match any move by another firm with an equal countermove.

■ **Rate of industry growth:** Any slowing in passenger traffic tends to set off price wars in the airline industry because the only path to growth is to take sales away from a competitor.

■ **Product or service characteristics:** A product can be very unique, with many qualities differentiating it from others of its kind or it may be a *commodity*, a product whose characteristics are the same, regardless of who sells it. For example, most people choose a gas station based on location and pricing because they view gasoline as a commodity.

■ **Amount of fixed costs:** Because airlines must fly their planes on a schedule, regardless of the number of paying passengers for any one flight, they offer cheap standby fares whenever a plane has empty seats.

■ **Capacity:** If the only way a manufacturer can increase capacity is in a large increment by building a new plant (as in the paper industry), it will run that new plant at full capacity to keep its unit costs as low as possible—thus producing so much that the selling price falls throughout the industry.

■ **Height of exit barriers: Exit barriers** keep a company from leaving an industry. The brewing industry, for example, has a low percentage of companies that voluntarily leave the industry because breweries are specialized assets with few uses except for making beer.

■ **Diversity of rivals:** Rivals that have very different ideas of how to compete are likely to cross paths often and unknowingly challenge each other's position. This happens often in the retail clothing industry when a number of retailers open outlets in the same location—thus taking sales away from each other. This is also likely to happen in some countries or regions when multinational corporations compete in an increasingly global economy. See **Strategy Highlight 4.2** to know more about the Indian retail industry analysis.

Threat of Substitute Products or Services

A **substitute product** is a product that appears to be different but can satisfy the same need as another product. For example, e-mail is a substitute for the fax, Nutrasweet is a substitute for sugar, the Internet is a substitute for video stores, and bottled water is a substitute for a cola. According to Porter, "Substitutes limit the potential returns of an industry by placing a ceiling on the prices firms in the industry can profitably charge."[52] To the extent that switching costs are low, substitutes may have a strong effect on an industry. Tea can be considered a substitute for coffee. If the price of coffee goes up high enough, coffee drinkers will slowly begin switching to tea. The price of tea thus puts a price ceiling on the price of coffee. Sometimes a difficult task, the identification of possible substitute products or services means searching for products or services that can perform the same function, even though they have a different appearance and may not appear to be easily substitutable.

Bargaining Power of Buyers

Buyers affect an industry through their ability to force down prices, bargain for higher quality or more services, and play competitors against each other. A buyer or a group of buyers is powerful if some of the following factors hold true:

- A buyer purchases a large proportion of the seller's product or service (for example, oil filters purchased by a major auto maker).
- A buyer has the potential to integrate backward by producing the product itself (for example, a newspaper chain could make its own paper).
- Alternative suppliers are plentiful because the product is standard or undifferentiated (for example, motorists can choose among many gas stations).
- Changing suppliers costs very little (for example, office supplies are easy to find).
- The purchased product represents a high percentage of a buyer's costs, thus providing an incentive to shop around for a lower price (for example, gasoline purchased for resale by convenience stores makes up half their total costs).
- A buyer earns low profits and is thus very sensitive to costs and service differences (for example, grocery stores have very small margins).
- The purchased product is unimportant to the final quality or price of a buyer's products or services and thus can be easily substituted without affecting the final product adversely (for example, electric wire bought for use in lamps).

Bargaining Power of Suppliers

Suppliers can affect an industry through their ability to raise prices or reduce the quality of purchased goods and services. A supplier or supplier group is powerful if some of the following factors apply:

- The supplier industry is dominated by a few companies, but it sells to many (for example, the petroleum industry).
- Its product or service is unique and/or it has built up switching costs (for example, word processing software).
- Substitutes are not readily available (for example, electricity).
- Suppliers are able to integrate forward and compete directly with their present customers (for example, a microprocessor producer such as Intel can make PCs).
- A purchasing industry buys only a small portion of the supplier group's goods and services and is thus unimportant to the supplier (for example, sales of lawn mower tires are less important to the tire industry than are sales of auto tires).

Relative Power of Other Stakeholders

A sixth force should be added to Porter's list to include a variety of stakeholder groups from the task environment. Some of these groups are governments (if not explicitly included elsewhere), local communities, creditors (if not included with suppliers), trade associations, special-interest groups, unions (if not included with suppliers), shareholders, and complementors. According to Andy Grove, Chairman and past CEO of Intel, a **complementor** is a company (e.g., Microsoft) or an industry whose product works well with a firm's (e.g., Intel's) product and without which the product would lose much of its value.[53] An example of complementary industries is the tire and automobile industries. Key international stakeholders who determine many of the international trade regulations and standards are the World Trade Organization, the European Union, NAFTA, ASEAN, and Mercosur.

The importance of these stakeholders varies by industry. For example, environmental groups in Maine, Michigan, Oregon, and Iowa successfully fought to pass bills outlawing disposable bottles and cans, and thus deposits for most drink containers are now required. This effectively raised costs across the board, with the most impact on the marginal producers who could not internally absorb all these costs. The traditionally strong power of national unions in the United States' auto and railroad industries has effectively raised costs throughout these industries but is of little importance in computer software.

INDUSTRY EVOLUTION

Over time, most industries evolve through a series of stages from growth through maturity to eventual decline. The strength of each of the six forces mentioned earlier varies according to the stage of industry evolution. The industry life cycle is useful for explaining and predicting trends among the six forces that drive industry competition. For example, when an industry is new, people often buy the product, regardless of price, because it fulfills a unique need. This usually occurs in a **fragmented industry**—where no firm has large market share, and each firm serves only a small piece of the total market in competition with others (for example, cleaning services).[54] As new competitors enter the industry, prices drop as a result of competition. Companies use the experience curve (discussed in **Chapter 5**) and economies of scale to reduce costs faster than the competition. Companies integrate to reduce costs even further by acquiring their suppliers and distributors. Competitors try to differentiate their products from one another's in order to avoid the fierce price competition common to a maturing industry.

By the time an industry enters maturity, products tend to become more like commodities. This is now a **consolidated industry**—dominated by a few large firms, each of which struggles to differentiate its products from those of the competition. As buyers become more sophisticated over time, purchasing decisions are based on better information. Price becomes a dominant concern, given a minimum level of quality and features, and profit margins decline. The automobile, petroleum, and major home appliance industries are examples of mature, consolidated industries each controlled by a few large competitors. In the case of the United States major home appliance industry, the industry changed from being a fragmented industry (pure competition) composed of hundreds of appliance manufacturers in the industry's early years to a consolidated industry (mature oligopoly) composed of three companies controlling over 90% of United States appliance sales. A similar consolidation is occurring now in European major home appliances.

As an industry moves through maturity toward possible decline, its products' growth rate of sales slows and may even begin to decrease. To the extent that exit barriers are low, firms begin converting their facilities to alternate uses or sell them to other firms. The industry tends to consolidate around fewer but larger competitors. The tobacco industry is an example of an industry currently in decline.

CATEGORIZING INTERNATIONAL INDUSTRIES

According to Porter, world industries vary on a continuum from multidomestic to global (see **Figure 4–4**).[55] **Multidomestic industries** are specific to each country or group of countries. This type of international industry is a collection of essentially domestic industries, such as retailing and insurance. The activities in a subsidiary of a multinational corporation (MNC) in this type of industry are essentially independent of the activities of the MNC's subsidiaries in other

FIGURE 4–4
Continuum
of International
Industries

Multidomestic ←————————————————————————→ **Global**

Industry in which companies tailor
their products to the specific needs
of consumers in a particular country.
• Retailing
• Insurance
• Banking

Industry in which companies manufacture
and sell the same products, with only minor
adjustments made for individual countries
around the world.
• Automobiles
• Tires
• Television sets

countries. Within each country, it has a manufacturing facility to produce goods for sale within that country. The MNC is thus able to tailor its products or services to the very specific needs of consumers in a particular country or group of countries having similar societal environments.

Global industries, in contrast, operate worldwide, with MNCs making only small adjustments for country-specific circumstances. In a global industry an MNC's activities in one country are significantly affected by its activities in other countries. MNCs in global industries produce products or services in various locations throughout the world and sell them, making only minor adjustments for specific country requirements. Examples of global industries are commercial aircraft, television sets, semiconductors, copiers, automobiles, watches, and tires. The largest industrial corporations in the world in terms of sales revenue are, for the most part, MNCs operating in global industries.

The factors that tend to determine whether an industry will be primarily multidomestic or primarily global are:

1. *Pressure for coordination* within the MNCs operating in that industry
2. *Pressure for local responsiveness* on the part of individual country markets

To the extent that the pressure for coordination is strong and the pressure for local responsiveness is weak for MNCs within a particular industry, that industry will tend to become global. In contrast, when the pressure for local responsiveness is strong and the pressure for coordination is weak for multinational corporations in an industry, that industry will tend to be multidomestic. Between these two extremes lie a number of industries with varying characteristics of both multidomestic and global industries. These are **regional industries**, in which MNCs primarily coordinate their activities within regions, such as the Americas or Asia.[56] The major home appliance industry is a current example of a regional industry becoming a global industry. Japanese appliance makers, for example, are major competitors in Asia, but only minor players in Europe or America. The dynamic tension between the pressure for coordination and the pressure for local responsiveness is contained in the phrase, *"Think globally but act locally."*

INTERNATIONAL RISK ASSESSMENT

Some firms develop elaborate information networks and computerized systems to evaluate and rank investment risks. Small companies may hire outside consultants, such as Boston's Arthur D. Little Inc., to provide political-risk assessments. Among the many systems that exist to assess political and economic risks are the Business Environment Risk Index, the Economist Intelligence Unit, and Frost and Sullivan's World Political Risk Forecasts. The Economist Intelligence Unit, for example, provides a constant flow of analysis and forecasts on more than 200 countries and eight key industries. Regardless of the source of data, a firm must develop its own method of assessing risk. It must decide on its most important risk factors and then assign weights to each.

STRATEGIC GROUPS

A **strategic group** is a set of business units or firms that "pursue similar strategies with similar resources."[57] Categorizing firms in any one industry into a set of strategic groups is very useful as a way of better understanding the competitive environment.[58] Research shows that some strategic groups in the same industry are more profitable than others.[59] Because a corporation's structure and culture tend to reflect the kinds of strategies it follows, companies or business units belonging to a particular strategic group within the same industry tend to be strong rivals and tend to be more similar to each other than to competitors in other strategic groups within the same industry.[60]

For example, although McDonald's and Olive Garden are a part of the same industry, the restaurant industry, they have different missions, objectives, and strategies, and thus they belong to different strategic groups. They generally have very little in common and pay little attention to each other when planning competitive actions. Burger King and Hardee's, however, have a great deal in common with McDonald's in terms of their similar strategy of producing a high volume of low-priced meals targeted for sale to the average family. Consequently, they are strong rivals and are organized to operate similarly.

Strategic groups in a particular industry can be mapped by plotting the market positions of industry competitors on a two-dimensional graph, using two strategic variables as the vertical and horizontal axes (See **Figure 4–5**):

1. Select two broad characteristics, such as price and menu, that differentiate the companies in an industry from one another.

2. Plot the firms, using these two characteristics as the dimensions.

3. Draw a circle around those companies that are closest to one another as one strategic group, varying the size of the circle in proportion to the group's share of total industry sales. (You could also name each strategic group in the restaurant industry with an identifying title, such as quick fast food or buffet-style service.)

FIGURE 4–5
Mapping Strategic Groups in the U.S. Restaurant Chain Industry

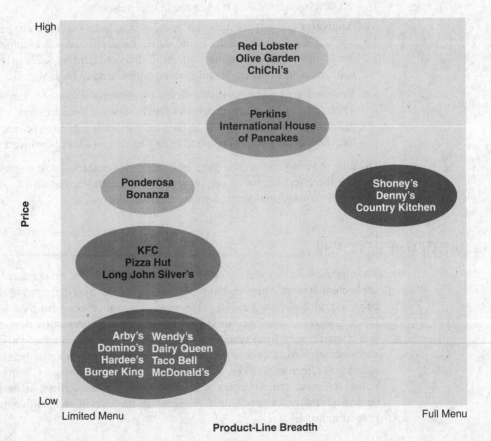

Other dimensions, such as quality, service, location, or degree of vertical integration, could also be used in additional graphs of the restaurant industry to gain a better understanding of how the various firms in the industry compete. Keep in mind, however, that the two dimensions should not be highly correlated; otherwise, the circles on the map will simply lie along the diagonal, providing very little new information other than the obvious.

STRATEGIC TYPES

In analyzing the level of competitive intensity within a particular industry or strategic group, it is useful to characterize the various competitors for predictive purposes. A **strategic type** is a category of firms based on a common strategic orientation and a combination of structure, culture, and processes consistent with that strategy. According to Miles and Snow, competing firms within a single industry can be categorized into one of four basic types on the basis of their general strategic orientation.[61] This distinction helps explain why companies facing similar situations behave differently and why they continue to do so over long periods of time.[62] These general types have the following characteristics:

- **Defenders** are companies with a limited product line that *focus on improving the efficiency of their existing operations*. This cost orientation makes them unlikely to innovate in new areas. With its emphasis on efficiency, Lincoln Electric is an example of a defender.

- **Prospectors** are companies with fairly broad product lines that *focus on product innovation and market opportunities*. This sales orientation makes them somewhat inefficient. They tend to emphasize creativity over efficiency. Rubbermaid's emphasis on new product development makes it an example of a prospector.

- **Analyzers** are corporations that *operate in at least two different product-market areas*, one stable and one variable. In the stable areas, efficiency is emphasized. In the variable areas, innovation is emphasized. Multidivisional firms, such as IBM and Procter & Gamble, which operate in multiple industries, tend to be analyzers.

- **Reactors** are corporations that *lack a consistent strategy-structure-culture relationship*. Their (often ineffective) responses to environmental pressures tend to be piecemeal strategic changes. Most major U.S. airlines have recently tended to be reactors—given the way they have been forced to respond to new entrants such as Southwest and JetBlue.

Dividing the competition into these four categories enables the strategic manager not only to monitor the effectiveness of certain strategic orientations, but also to develop scenarios of future industry developments (discussed later in this chapter).

HYPERCOMPETITION

Most industries today are facing an ever-increasing level of environmental uncertainty. They are becoming more complex and more dynamic. Industries that used to be multidomestic are becoming global. New flexible, aggressive, innovative competitors are moving into established markets to rapidly erode the advantages of large previously dominant firms. Distribution channels vary from country to country and are being altered daily through the use of sophisticated information systems. Closer relationships with suppliers are being forged to reduce costs, increase quality, and gain access to new technology. Companies learn to quickly imitate the successful strategies of market leaders, and it becomes harder to sustain any competitive advantage for very long. Consequently, the level of competitive intensity is increasing in most industries.

Richard D'Aveni contends that as this type of environmental turbulence reaches more industries, competition becomes **hypercompetition**. According to D'Aveni:

In hypercompetition the frequency, boldness, and aggressiveness of dynamic movement by the players accelerates to create a condition of constant disequilibrium and change. Market stability is threatened by short product life cycles, short product design cycles, new technologies, frequent entry by unexpected outsiders, repositioning by incumbents, and tactical redefinitions of market boundaries as diverse industries merge. In other words, environments escalate toward higher and higher levels of uncertainty, dynamism, heterogeneity of the players and hostility.[63]

In hypercompetitive industries such as computers, competitive advantage comes from an up-to-date knowledge of environmental trends and competitive activity coupled with a willingness to risk a current advantage for a possible new advantage. Companies must be willing to *cannibalize* their own products (that is, replace popular products before competitors do so) in order to sustain their competitive advantage. See **Strategy Highlight 4.3** to learn how Microsoft is operating in the hypercompetitive industry of computer software. (Hypercompetition is discussed in more detail in **Chapter 6**.)

USING KEY SUCCESS FACTORS TO CREATE AN INDUSTRY MATRIX

Within any industry there are usually certain variables—key success factors—that a company's management must understand in order to be successful. **Key success factors** are variables that can significantly affect the overall competitive positions of companies within any particular industry. They typically vary from industry to industry and are crucial to determining a company's ability to succeed within that industry. They are usually determined by the

STRATEGY highlight 4.3

MICROSOFT IN A HYPERCOMPETITIVE INDUSTRY

Microsoft is a hypercompetitive firm operating in a hypercompetitive industry. It has used its dominance in operating systems (DOS and Windows) to move into a very strong position in application programs such as word processing and spreadsheets (Word and Excel). Even though Microsoft held 90% of the market for personal computer operating systems in 1992, it still invested millions in developing the next generation—Windows 95 and Windows NT. These were soon followed by Windows Me, XP, and Vista. Instead of trying to protect its advantage in the profitable DOS operating system, Microsoft actively sought to replace DOS with various versions of Windows. Before hypercompetition, most experts argued against *cannibalization* of a company's own product line because it destroys a very profitable product instead of harvesting it like a "cash cow." According to this line of thought, a company would be better off defending its older products. New products would be introduced only

if it could be proven that they would not take sales away from current products. Microsoft was one of the first companies to disprove this argument against cannibalization.

Bill Gates, Microsoft's co-founder, chair, and CEO, realized that if his company did not replace its own DOS product line with a better product, someone else would (such as Linux or IBM's OS/2 Warp). He knew that success in the software industry depends not so much on company size as on moving aggressively to the next competitive advantage before a competitor does. "This is a hypercompetitive market," explained Gates. "Scale is not all positive in this business. Cleverness is the position in this business." By 2008, Microsoft still controlled over 90% of operating systems software and had achieved a dominant position in applications software as well.

SOURCE: Richard A. D'Aveni, "Hypercompetition: Managing the Dynamics of Strategic Maneuvering." Copyright © 1994 by Richard A. D'Aveni. All rights reserved.

| | | **Company A** | **Company A** | **Company B** | **Company B** |
Key Success Factors	**Weight**	**Rating**	**Weighted Score**	**Rating**	**Weighted Score**
	1	2	3	4	5	6
Total	1.00		══		══

TABLE 4–4   Industry Matrix

SOURCE: T. L. Wheelen and J. D. Hunger, *Industry Matrix*. Copyright © 1997, 2001, and 2005 by Wheelen & Hunger Associates. Reprinted with permission.

economic and technological characteristics of the industry and by the competitive weapons on which the firms in the industry have built their strategies.[64] For example, in the major home appliances industry, a firm must achieve low costs typically by building large manufacturing facilities dedicated to making multiple versions of one type of appliance such as washing machines because the incumbent firms such as Samsung, LG, Videocon, etc. have a strong presence as a mass merchandiser. They have extensive and exclusive distribution channels catering to a varied product line and range. Therefore, a new entrant must offer a full line of appliances and provide some innovative means of keeping store ordering costs minimum (to overcome dealer switching costs). Because the consumer expects reliability and durability in an appliance, a firm must have excellent R&D. Any appliance manufacturer that is unable to deal successfully with these key success factors will not survive in the long run in the Indian market.

An **industry matrix** summarizes the key success factors within a particular industry. As shown in **Table 4–4**, the matrix gives a weight for each factor based on how important that factor is for success within the industry. The matrix also specifies how well various competitors in the industry are responding to each factor. To generate an industry matrix using two industry competitors (called A and B), complete the following steps for the industry being analyzed:

1. In **Column 1** (*Key Success Factors*), list the 8 to 10 factors that appear to determine success in the industry.

2. In **Column 2** (*Weight*), assign a weight to each factor, from **1.0** (*Most Important*) to **0.0** (*Not Important*) based on that factor's probable impact on the overall industry's current and future success. **(All weights must sum to 1.0 regardless of the number of strategic factors.)**

3. In **Column 3** (*Company A Rating*), examine a particular company within the industry—for example, Company A. Assign a rating to each factor from **5** (*Outstanding*) to **1** (*Poor*) based on Company A's current response to that particular factor. Each rating is a judgment regarding how well that company is specifically dealing with each key success factor.

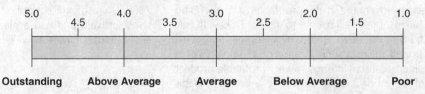

4. In **Column 4** (*Company A Weighted Score*), multiply the weight in **Column 2** for each factor by its rating in **Column 3** to obtain that factor's weighted score for Company A.

5. In **Column 5** (*Company B Rating*), examine a second company within the industry - in this case, Company B. Assign a rating to each key success factor from **5.0** (Outstanding) to **1.0** (Poor), based on Company B's current response to each particular factor.

6. In **Column 6** (*Company B Weighted Score*), multiply the weight in **Column 2** for each factor times its rating in **Column 5** to obtain that factor's weighted score for Company B.

7. Finally, add the weighted scores for all the factors in **Columns 4** and **6** to determine the total weighted scores for companies A and B. **The total weighted score indicates how well each company is responding to current and expected key success factors in the industry's environment.** Check to ensure that the total weighted score truly reflects the company's current performance in terms of profitability and market share. (An average company should have a total weighted score of 3.)

The industry matrix can be expanded to include all the major competitors within an industry through the addition of two additional columns for each additional competitor.

4.3 Competitive Intelligence

Much external environmental scanning is done on an informal and individual basis. Information is obtained from a variety of sources—suppliers, customers, industry publications, employees, industry experts, industry conferences, and the Internet.[65] For example, scientists and engineers working in a firm's R&D lab can learn about new products and competitors' ideas at professional meetings; someone from the purchasing department, speaking with supplier-representatives' personnel, may also uncover valuable bits of information about a competitor. A study of product innovation found that 77% of all product innovations in scientific instruments and 67% in semiconductors and printed circuit boards were initiated by the customer in the form of inquiries and complaints.[66] In these industries, the sales force and service departments must be especially vigilant.

A recent survey of global executives by McKinsey & Company found that the single factor contributing most to the increasing competitive intensity in their industries was the improved capabilities of competitors.[67] Yet, without competitive intelligence, companies run the risk of flying blind in the marketplace. In a 2008 survey of global executives, the majority revealed that their companies typically learned about a competitor's price change or significant innovation too late to respond before it was introduced into the market.[68] According to work by Ryall, firms can have competitive advantages simply because their rivals have erroneous beliefs about them.[69] This is why competitive intelligence has become an important part of environmental scanning in most companies.

Competitive intelligence is a formal program of gathering information on a company's competitors. Often called *business intelligence*, it is one of the fastest growing fields within strategic management. Research indicates that there is a strong association between corporate performance and competitive intelligence activities.[70] According to a survey of competitive intelligence professionals, the primary reasons for practicing competitive intelligence are to build industry awareness (90.6%), support the strategic planning process (79.2%), develop new products (73.6%), and create new marketing strategies and tactics.[71] As early as the 1990s, 78% of large U.S. corporations conducted competitive intelligence activities.[72] In about a third of the firms, the competitive/business intelligence function is housed in its own unit, with the remainder being housed within marketing, strategic planning, information services, business development (merger and acquisitions), product development, or other units.[73] According to a 2007 survey of 141 large American corporations, spending on competitive intelligence activities was rising from $1 billion in 2007 to $10 billion by 2012.[74] At General Mills, for example, all employees have been trained to recognize and tap sources of competitive information. Janitors no longer simply place orders with suppliers of cleaning materials; they also ask about relevant practices at competing firms! In India, competitive intelligence or business intelligence (BI)'s overall impact on business is poorly understood and is still considered as "nice to have." Many enterprises and entrepreneurs rely on gut feelings while making decisions.

The overall BI market in India is at a nascent stage, with a huge uptapped opportunity for vendors to capture. According to Gartner, a global IT research and advisory firm, India is the fastest growing BI platform market in Asia (including Japan). The BI market in India is predicted to reach revenues of $65.4 million (about Rs 290+ crore) in 2011, an increase of 16% over 2010.[75] These companies are motivated by success stories like the one of Goodlass Nerolac. The company is a leading player in the organized Indian paints market and introduced All Scapes. A premium quality product was targeted at the decorative paint segment. In its initial months of launch, the product was a disappointment for the company. It did not meet the expectations of its planners. The company needed to take corrective action to salvage costs and demonstrate their RoI. However, to be able to do that, it needed to know what was wrong. In an attempt to single out the cause of failure within the marketing mix, Goodlass Nerolac undertook a BI venture. After analyzing the sales of the product, the problem was identified in the distribution channel. The company, having identified the problem area developed and implemented strategies such as stocking paint to strengthen the dealer network. As a result, the sales volume that the company had achieved earlier in one year was attained in only six months.[76]

SOURCES OF COMPETITIVE INTELLIGENCE

Most corporations use outside organizations to provide them with environmental data. Firms such as A. C. Nielsen Co. provide subscribers with bimonthly data on brand share, retail prices, percentages of stores stocking an item, and percentages of stock-out stores. Strategists can use this data to spot regional and national trends as well as to assess market share. Information on market conditions, government regulations, industry competitors, and new products can be bought from "information brokers" such as Market Research.com (Findex), LexisNexis (company and country analyses), and Finsbury Data Services. Company and industry profiles are generally available from the Hoover's Web site, at www.hoovers.com. Many business corporations have established their own in-house libraries and computerized information systems to deal with the growing mass of available information.

The Internet has changed the way strategists engage in environmental scanning. It provides the quickest means to obtain data on almost any subject. Although the scope and quality of Internet information is increasing geometrically, it is also littered with "noise," misinformation, and utter nonsense. For example, a number of corporate Web sites are sending unwanted guests to specially constructed bogus Web sites.[77] Unlike the library, the Internet lacks the tight bibliographic control standards that exist in the print world. There is no ISBN or Dewey Decimal System to identify, search, and retrieve a document. Many Web documents lack the name of the author and the date of publication. A Web page providing useful information may be accessible on the Web one day and gone the next. Unhappy ex-employees, far-out environmentalists, and prank-prone hackers create "blog" Web sites to attack and discredit an otherwise reputable corporation. Rumors with no basis in fact are spread via chat rooms and personal Web sites. This creates a serious problem for researchers. How can one evaluate the information found on the Internet? For a way to evaluate intelligence information, see **Strategy Highlight 4.4.**

Some companies choose to use industrial espionage or other intelligence-gathering techniques to get their information straight from their competitors. According to a survey by the American Society for Industrial Security, PricewaterhouseCoopers, and the United States

STRATEGY highlight 4.4

EVALUATING COMPETITIVE INTELLIGENCE

A basic rule in intelligence gathering is that before a piece of information can be used in any report or briefing, it must first be evaluated in two ways. *First*, the source of the information should be judged in terms of its truthfulness and reliability. How trustworthy is the source? How well can a researcher rely upon it for truthful and correct information? One approach is to rank the reliability of the source on a scale from A (extremely reliable), B (reliable), C (unknown reliability), D (probably unreliable), to E (very questionable reliability). The reliability of a source can be judged on the basis of the author's credentials, the organization sponsoring the information, and past performance, among other factors. *Second*, the information or data should be judged in terms of its likelihood of being correct. The correctness of the data may be ranked on a scale from 1 (correct), 2 (probably correct), 3 (unknown), 4 (doubtful), to 5 (extremely doubtful). The correctness of a piece of data or information can be judged on the basis of its agreement with other bits of separately-obtained information or with a general trend supported by previous data. For every piece of information found on the Internet, for example, list not only the URL of the Web page, but also the evaluation of the information from A1 (good stuff) to E5 (bad doodoo).

Information found through library research in sources such as Moody's Industrials, Standard & Poor's, or Value Line can generally be evaluated as having a reliability of A. The correctness of the data can still range anywhere from 1 to 5, but in most instances is likely to be either 1 or 2, but probably no worse than 3 or 4. Web sites are quite different.

Web sites, such as those sponsored by the U.S. Securities and Exchange Commission (www.sec.gov), the Economist (www.economist.com), or Hoovers Online (www.hoovers.com) are extremely reliable. Company-sponsored Web sites are generally reliable, but are not the place to go for trade secrets, strategic plans, or proprietary information. For one thing, many firms think of their Web sites primarily in terms of marketing and provide little data aside from product descriptions and distributors. Other companies provide their latest financial statements and links to other useful Web sites. Nevertheless, some companies in very competitive industries may install software on their Web site to ascertain a visitor's web address. Visitors from a competitor's domain name are thus screened before they are allowed to access certain Web sites. They may not be allowed beyond the product information page or they may be sent to a bogus Web site containing misinformation. Cisco Systems, for example, uses its Web site to send visitors from other high-tech firms to a special Web page asking if they would like to apply for a job at Cisco!

Chamber of Commerce, Fortune 1000 companies lost an estimated $59 billion in one year alone due to the theft of trade secrets.[78] By using current or former competitors' employees and private contractors, some firms attempt to steal trade secrets, technology, business plans, and pricing strategies. For example, Avon Products hired private investigators to retrieve from a public dumpster documents (some of them shredded) that Mary Kay Corporation had thrown away. Oracle Corporation also hired detectives to obtain the trash of a think tank that had defended the pricing practices of its rival Microsoft. Studies reveal that 32% of the trash typically found next to copy machines contains confidential company data, in addition to personal data (29%) and gossip (39%).[79] Even P&G, which defends itself like a fortress from information leaks, is vulnerable. A competitor was able to learn the precise launch date of a concentrated laundry detergent in Europe when one of its people visited the factory where machinery was being made. Simply asking a few questions about what a certain machine did, whom it was for, and when it would be delivered was all that was necessary.

Some of the firms providing investigatory services are Kroll Inc. with 4,000 employees in 25 countries, Fairfax, Security Outsourcing Solutions, Trident Group, and Diligence Inc.[80] Trident, for example, specializes in helping American companies enter the Russian market and is a U.S.-based corporate intelligence firm founded and managed by former veterans of Russian intelligence services, like the KGB.[81]

To combat the increasing theft of company secrets, the United States government passed the Economic Espionage Act in 1996. The law makes it illegal (with fines up to $5 million and

10 years in jail) to steal any material that a business has taken "reasonable efforts" to keep secret and that derives its value from not being known.[82] The Society of Competitive Intelligence Professionals (www.scip.org) urges strategists to stay within the law and to act ethically when searching for information. The society states that illegal activities are foolish because the vast majority of worthwhile competitive intelligence is available publicly via annual reports, Web sites, and libraries. Unfortunately, a number of firms hire "kites," consultants with questionable reputations, who do what is necessary to get information when the selected methods do not meet SPIC ethical standards or are illegal. This allows the company that initiated the action to deny that it did anything wrong.[83]

MONITORING COMPETITORS FOR STRATEGIC PLANNING

The primary activity of a competitive intelligence unit is to monitor **competitors**—organizations that offer same, similar, or substitutable products or services in the business area in which a particular company operates. To understand a competitor, it is important to answer the following 10 questions:

1. Why do your competitors exist? Do they exist to make profits or just to support another unit?

2. Where do they add customer value—higher quality, lower price, excellent credit terms, or better service?

3. Which of your customers are the competitors most interested in? Are they cherry-picking your best customers, picking the ones you do not want, or going after all of them?

4. What is their cost base and liquidity? How much cash do they have? How do they get their supplies?

5. Are they less exposed with their suppliers than your firm? Are their suppliers better than yours?

6. What do they intend to do in the future? Do they have a strategic plan to target your market segments? How committed are they to growth? Are there any succession issues?

7. How will their activity affect your strategies? Should you adjust your plans and operations?

8. How much better than your competitor do you need to be in order to win customers? Do either of you have a competitive advantage in the marketplace?

9. Will new competitors or new ways of doing things appear over the next few years? Who is a potential new entrant?

10. If you were a customer, would you choose your product over those offered by your competitors? What irritates your current customers? What competitors solve these particular customer complaints?[84]

To answer these and other questions, competitive intelligence professionals utilize a number of analytical techniques. In addition to the previously discussed SWOT analysis, Michael Porter's industry forces analysis, and strategic group analysis, some of these techniques are Porter's four-corner exercise, Treacy and Wiersema's value disciplines, Gilad's blind spot analysis, and war gaming.[85] See **Appendix 4.A** for more information about these competitive analysis techniques.

Done right, competitive intelligence is a key input to strategic planning. Avnet Inc., one of the world's largest distributors of electronic components, uses competitive intelligence in its growth by acquisition strategy. According to John Hovis, Avnet's senior vice president of corporate planning and investor relations:

> *Our competitive intelligence team has a significant responsibility in tracking all of the varied competitors, not just our direct competitors, but all the peripheral competitors that have a potential to impact our ability to create value. . . . One of the things we are about is finding new acquisition candidates, and our competitive intelligence unit is very much involved with our acquisition team, in helping to profile potential acquisition candidates.*[86]

4.4 Forecasting

Environmental scanning provides reasonably hard data on the present situation and current trends, but intuition and luck are needed to accurately predict whether these trends will continue. The resulting forecasts are, however, usually based on a set of assumptions that may or may not be valid.

DANGER OF ASSUMPTIONS

Faulty underlying assumptions are the most frequent cause of forecasting errors. Nevertheless, many managers who formulate and implement strategic plans rarely consider that their success is based on a series of basic assumptions. Many strategic plans are simply based on projections of the current situation. For example, few people in 2007 expected the price of oil (light, sweet crude, also called West Texas intermediate) to rise above $80 per barrel and were extremely surprised to see the price approach $150 by July 2008, especially since the price had been around $20 per barrel in 2002. U.S. auto companies, in particular, had continued to design and manufacture large cars, pick-up trucks, and SUVs under the assumption of gasoline being available for around $2.00 a gallon. Market demand for these types of cars collapsed when the price of gasoline passed $3.00 to reach $4.00 a gallon in July 2008. In another example, many banks made a number of questionable mortgages based on the assumption that housing prices would continue to rise as they had in the past. When housing prices fell in 2007, these "sub-prime" mortgages were almost worthless—causing a number of banks to sell out or fail in 2008. Assumptions like these can be dangerous to your health!

USEFUL FORECASTING TECHNIQUES

Various techniques are used to forecast future situations. They do not tell the future; they merely state what can be, not what will be. As such, they can be used to form a set of reasonable assumptions about the future. Each technique has its proponents and its critics. A study of nearly 500 of the world's largest corporations revealed trend extrapolation to be the most widely practiced form of forecasting—over 70% use this technique either occasionally or frequently.[87] Simply stated, *extrapolation* is the extension of present trends into the future. It rests on the assumption that the world is reasonably consistent and changes slowly in the short run. Time-series methods are approaches of this type; they attempt to carry a series of historical events forward into the future. The basic problem with extrapolation is that a historical trend is based on a series of patterns or relationships among so many different variables that a change in any one can drastically alter the future direction of the trend. As a rule of thumb, the further back into the past you can find relevant data supporting the trend, the more confidence you can have in the prediction.

Brainstorming, expert opinion, and statistical modeling are also very popular forecasting techniques. *Brainstorming* is a non-quantitative approach that requires simply the presence of people with some knowledge of the situation to be predicted. The basic ground rule is to propose ideas without first mentally screening them. No criticism is allowed. "Wild" ideas are encouraged. Ideas should build on previous ideas until a consensus is reached.[88] This is a good technique to use with operating managers who have more faith in "gut feel" than in more quantitative number-crunching techniques. *Expert opinion* is a nonquantitative technique in which experts in a particular area attempt to forecast likely developments. This type of forecast is based on the ability of a knowledgeable person(s) to construct probable future developments based on the interaction of key variables. One application, developed by the RAND Corporation, is the *Delphi technique,* in which separated experts independently assess the likelihoods of specified events. These assessments are combined and sent back to each expert for fine-tuning until agreement is reached. These assessments are most useful if they are shaped into several possible scenarios that allow decision makers to more fully understand their implication.[89] *Statistical modeling* is a quantitative technique that attempts to discover causal or at least explanatory factors that link two or more time series together. Examples of statistical modeling are regression analysis and other econometric methods. Although very useful in the grasping of historic trends, statistical modeling, such as trend extrapolation, is based on historical data. As the patterns of relationships change, the accuracy of the forecast deteriorates.

Prediction markets is a recent forecasting technique enabled by easy access to the Internet. As emphasized by James Surowiecki in *The Wisdom of Crowds*, the conclusions of large groups can often be better than those of experts because such groups can aggregate a large amount of dispersed wisdom.[90] Prediction markets are small-scale electronic markets, frequently open to any employee, that tie payoffs to measurable future events, such as sales data for a computer workstation, the number of bugs in an application, or a product usage patterns. These markets yield prices on prediction contracts—prices that can be interpreted as market-aggregated forecasts.[91] Companies including Microsoft, Google, and Eli Lilly have asked their employees to participate in prediction markets by betting on whether products will sell, when new offices will open, and whether profits will be high in the next quarter. Early predictions have been exceedingly accurate.[92] Intrade.com offers a free Web site in which people can buy or sell various predictions in a manner similar to buying or selling common stock. On May 26, 2008, for example, Intrade.com listed the buying price for democratic presidential candidate Barack Obama as $91.50 compared to $8.00 for Hillary Clinton, and $37.70 for John McCain. Thus far, prediction markets have not been documented for long-term forecasting, so its value in strategic planning has not yet been established. Other forecasting techniques, such as *cross-impact analysis (CIA)* and *trend-impact analysis (TIA)*, have not established themselves successfully as regularly employed tools.[93]

Scenario writing is the most widely used forecasting technique after trend extrapolation. Originated by Royal Dutch Shell, *scenarios* are focused descriptions of different likely futures presented in a narrative fashion. A scenario thus may be merely a written description of some future state, in terms of key variables and issues, or it may be generated in combination with other forecasting techniques. Often called scenario planning, this technique has been successfully used by 3M, Levi-Strauss, General Electric, United Distillers, Electrolux, British Airways, and Pacific Gas and Electricity, among others.[94] According to Mike Eskew, Chairman and CEO of United Parcel Service, UPS uses scenario writing to envision what its customers might need five to ten years in the future.[95] The four Arctic scenarios that began this chapter are an example of scenario writing that should be an input to a transportation company's strategic planning.

An **industry scenario** is a forecasted description of a particular industry's likely future. Such a scenario is developed by analyzing the probable impact of future societal forces on key groups in a particular industry. The process may operate as follows:[96]

1. Examine possible shifts in the natural environment and in societal variables globally.

2. Identify uncertainties in each of the six forces of the task environment (that is, potential entrants, competitors, likely substitutes, buyers, suppliers, and other key stakeholders).

3. Make a range of plausible assumptions about future trends.

4. Combine assumptions about individual trends into internally consistent scenarios.

5. Analyze the industry situation that would prevail under each scenario.

6. Determine the sources of competitive advantage under each scenario.

7. Predict competitors' behavior under each scenario.

8. Select the scenarios that are either most likely to occur or most likely to have a strong impact on the future of the company. Use these scenarios as assumptions in strategy formulation.

4.5 The Strategic Audit: A Checklist for Environmental Scanning

One way of scanning the environment to identify opportunities and threats is by using the Strategic Audit found in **Appendix 1.A** at the end of **Chapter 1**. The audit provides a checklist of questions by area of concern. For example, Part III of the audit examines the natural, societal, and task environments. It looks at the societal environment in terms of economic, technological, political-legal, and sociocultural forces. It also considers the task environment (industry) in terms of threat of new entrants, bargaining power of buyers and suppliers, threat of substitute products, rivalry among existing firms, and the relative power of other stakeholders.

4.6 Synthesis of External Factors—EFAS

After strategic managers have scanned the societal and task environments and identified a number of likely external factors for their particular corporation, they may want to refine their analysis of these factors by using a form such as that given in **Table 4–5**. Using an **EFAS (External Factors Analysis Summary) Table** is one way to organize the external factors into the generally accepted categories of opportunities and threats as well as to analyze how well a particular company's management (rating) is responding to these specific factors in light of the perceived importance (weight) of these factors to the company. To generate an EFAS Table for the company being analyzed, complete the following steps:

1. In **Column 1 (*External Factors*)**, list the eight to ten most important opportunities and threats facing the company.

2. In **Column 2 (*Weight*)**, assign a weight to each factor from **1.0** (*Most Important*) to **0.0** (*Not Important*) based on that factor's probable impact on a particular company's current strategic position. The higher the weight, the more important is this factor to the current and future success of the company. (**All weights must sum to 1.0 regardless of the number of factors.**)

3. In **Column 3 (*Rating*)**, assign a rating to each factor from **5.0** (*Outstanding*) to **1.0** (*Poor*) based on that particular company's specific response to that particular factor. Each rating is a judgment regarding how well the company is currently dealing with each specific external factor.

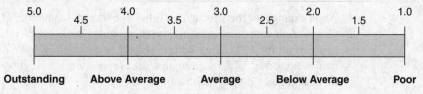

5.0	4.0	3.0	2.0	1.0
4.5	3.5	2.5	1.5	
Outstanding	Above Average	Average	Below Average	Poor

TABLE 4-5   External Factor Analysis Summary (EFAS Table): Maytag as Example

External Factors	Weight	Rating	Weighted Score	Comments
	1	2	3	4	5
Opportunities				
■ Economic integration of European Community	.20	4.1	.82	Acquisition of Hoover
■ Demographics favor quality appliances	.10	5.0	.50	Maytag quality
■ Economic development of Asia	.05	1.0	.05	Low Maytag presence
■ Opening of Eastern Europe	.05	2.0	.10	Will take time
■ Trend to "Super Stores"	.10	1.8	.18	Maytag weak in this channel
Threats				
■ Increasing government regulations	.10	4.3	.43	Well positioned
■ Strong U.S. competition	.10	4.0	.40	Well positioned
■ Whirlpool and Electrolux strong globally	.15	3.0	.45	Hoover weak globally
■ New product advances	.05	1.2	.06	Questionable
■ Japanese appliance companies	.10	1.6	.16	Only Asian presence in Australia
Total Scores	1.00		3.15	

NOTES:

1. List opportunities and threats (8–10) in Column 1.
2. Weight each factor from 1.0 (Most Important) to 0.0 (Not Important) in Column 2 based on that factor's probable impact on the company's strategic position. **The total weights must sum to 1.00**.
3. Rate each factor from 5.0 (Outstanding) to 1.0 (Poor) in Column 3 based on the company's response to that factor.
4. Multiply each factor's weight times its rating to obtain each factor's weighted score in Column 4.
5. Use Column 5 (comments) for rationale used for each factor.
6. Add the individual weighted scores to obtain the total weighted score for the company in Column 4. This tells how well the company is responding to the factors in its external environment.

SOURCE: T.L. Wheelen, J.D. Hunger, "External Factors Analysis Summary (EFAS)". Copyright © 1987, 1988, 1989, 1990, and 2005 by T. L Wheelen. Copyright © 1991, 2003, and 2005 by Wheelen & Hunger Associates. Reprinted by permission.

4. In **Column 4** (*Weighted Score*), multiply the weight in **Column 2** for each factor times its rating in **Column 3** to obtain that factor's weighted score.

5. In **Column 5** (*Comments*), note why a particular factor was selected and how its weight and rating were estimated.

6. Finally, add the weighted scores for all the external factors in **Column 4** to determine the total weighted score for that particular company. The **total weighted** score indicates how well a particular company is responding to current and expected factors in its external environment. The score can be used to compare that firm to other firms in the industry. Check to ensure that the total weighted score truly reflects the company's current performance in terms of profitability and market share. **The total weighted score for an average firm in an industry is always 3.0.**

As an example of this procedure, **Table 4–5** includes a number of external factors for Maytag Corporation with corresponding weights, ratings, and weighted scores provided. This table is appropriate for 1995, long before Maytag was acquired by Whirlpool. Note that Maytag's total weight was 3.15, meaning that the corporation was slightly above average in the major home appliance industry at that time.

ECO-BITS

- The International Panel on Climate Change reports that carbon dioxide emissions are rising faster than its worst-case scenario and that without new government action greenhouse gases will rise 25% to 90% over 2000 levels by 2030.

- China surpassed the United States in carbon emissions in 2006 by producing 6.6 billion tons of carbon dioxide, 24% of the world's annual production of CO_2.

- The total number of people affected by natural disasters has tripled over the past decade to two billion people.

- By 2025, 1.8 billion people could be living in water-scarce areas with the likely result being mass migrations out of these areas.[97]

DISCUSSION QUESTIONS

1. Discuss how a development in a corporation's natural and societal environments can affect the corporation through its task environment.

2. According to Porter, what determines the level of competitive intensity in an industry?

3. According to Porter's discussion of industry analysis, is Pepsi Cola a substitute for Coca-Cola?

4. How can a decision maker identify strategic factors in a corporation's external international environment?

5. Compare and contrast trend extrapolation with the writing of scenarios as forecasting techniques.

6. Discuss the structure of IFAS and EFAS.

7. Write short notes on the following:
   a. Competitive intelligence industry in India
   b. Source of competitive intelligence
   c. Industry evolution

8. Pick an industry in India and evaluate using Porter's five forces model? What strategies can you suggest to convert the unattractive forces in to attractive ones?

STRATEGIC PRACTICE EXERCISE

How far should people in a business firm go in gathering competitive intelligence? Where do you draw the line?

Evaluate each of the following approaches that a person could use to gather information about competitors. For each approach, mark your feeling about its appropriateness:

1 (DEFINITELY NOT APPROPRIATE), 2 (PROBABLY NOT APPROPRIATE), 3 (UNDECIDED), 4 (PROBABLY APPROPRIATE), OR 5 (DEFINITELY APPROPRIATE).

The business firm should try to get useful information about competitors by:

_____ Carefully studying trade journals

_____ Wiretapping the telephones of competitors

_____ Posing as a potential customer to competitors

_____ Getting loyal customers to put out a phony "request for proposal" soliciting competitors' bids

_____ Buying competitors' products and taking them apart

_____ Hiring management consultants who have worked for competitors

_____ Rewarding competitors' employees for useful "tips"

_____ Questioning competitors' customers and/or suppliers

_____ Buying and analyzing competitors' garbage

_____ Advertising and interviewing for nonexistent jobs

Let's Summarize the Chapter with a Mind Map

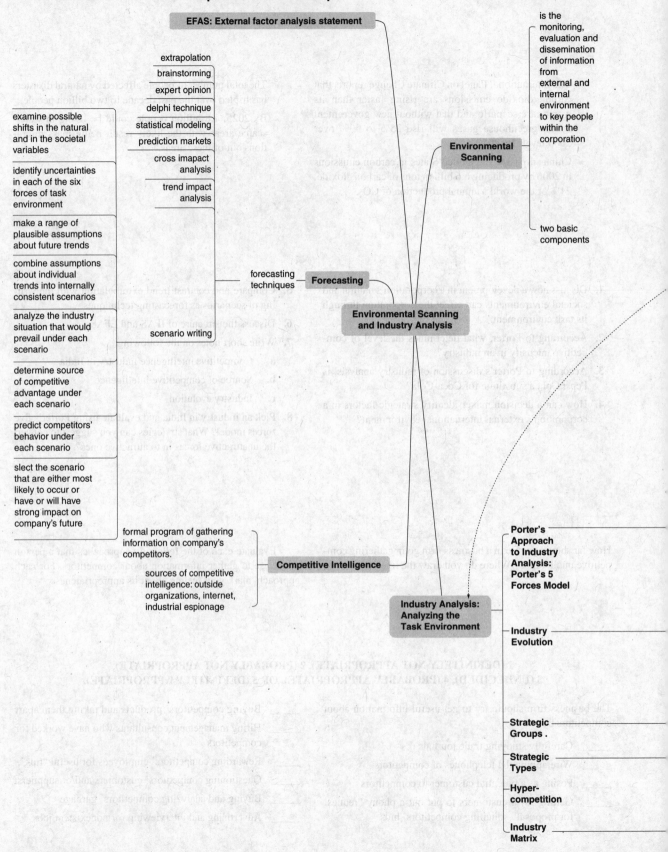

EFAS: External factor analysis statement

extrapolation

brainstorming

expert opinion

delphi technique

statistical modeling

prediction markets

cross imapct analysis

trend impact analysis

examine possible shifts in the natural and in the societal variables

identify uncertainties in each of the six forces of task environment

make a range of plausible assumptions about future trends

combine assumptions about individual trends into internally consistent scenarios

analyze the industry situation that would prevail under each scenario

determine source of competitive advantage under each scenario

predict competitors' behavior under each scenario

slect the scenario that are either most likely to occur or have or will have strong impact on company's future

forecasting techniques

Forecasting

scenario writing

Environmental Scanning and Industry Analysis

Environmental Scanning

is the monitoring, evaluation and dissemination of information from external and internal environment to key people within the corporation

two basic components

formal program of gathering information on company's competitors.

sources of competitive intelligence: outside organizations, internet, industrial espionage

Competitive Intelligence

Industry Analysis: Analyzing the Task Environment

Porter's Approach to Industry Analysis: Porter's 5 Forces Model

Industry Evolution

Strategic Groups .

Strategic Types

Hyper-competition

Industry Matrix

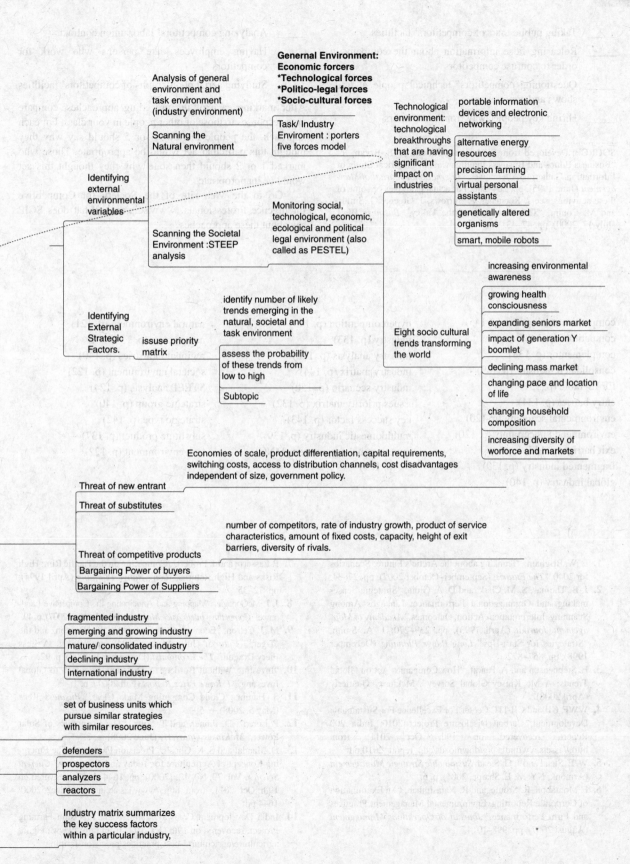

General Environment:
Economic forcers
***Technological forces**
***Politico-legal forces**
***Socio-cultural forces**

Analysis of general
environment and
task environment
(industry environment)

Scanning the
Natural environment

Task/ Industry
Enviroment : porters
five forces model

Technological
environment:
technological
breakthroughs
that are having
significant
impact on
industries

portable information
devices and electronic
networking

alternative energy
resources

precision farming

virtual personal
assistants

genetically altered
organisms

smart, mobile robots

Identifying
external
environmental
variables

Scanning the Societal
Environment :STEEP
analysis

Monitoring social,
technological, economic,
ecological and political
legal environment (also
called as PESTEL)

increasing environmental
awareness

growing health
consciousness

expanding seniors market

impact of generation Y
boomlet

declining mass market

changing pace and location
of life

changing household
composition

increasing diversity of
worforce and markets

Identifying
External
Strategic
Factors.

issue priority
matrix

identify number of likely
trends emerging in the
natural, societal and
task environment

assess the probability
of these trends from
low to high

Subtopic

Eight socio cultural
trends transforming
the world

Economies of scale, product differentiation, capital requirements,
switching costs, access to distribution channels, cost disadvantages
independent of size, government policy.

Threat of new entrant

Threat of substitutes

number of competitors, rate of industry growth, product of service
characteristics, amount of fixed costs, capacity, height of exit
barriers, diversity of rivals.

Threat of competitive products

Bargaining Power of buyers

Bargaining Power of Suppliers

fragmented industry

emerging and growing industry

mature/ consolidated industry

declining industry

international industry

set of business units which
pursue similar strategies
with similar resources.

defenders

prospectors

analyzers

reactors

Industry matrix summarizes
the key success factors
within a particular industry,

_____ Taking public tours of competitors' facilities

_____ Releasing false information about the company in order to confuse competitors

_____ Questioning competitors' technical people at trade shows and conferences

_____ Hiring key people away from competitors

_____ Analyzing competitors' labor union contracts

_____ Having employees date persons who work for competitors

_____ Studying aerial photographs of competitors' facilities

....

SOURCE: Developed from W. A. Jones, Jr., and N. B. Bryan, Jr., "Business Ethics and Business Intelligence: An Empirical Study of Information-Gathering Alternatives," *International Journal of Management* (June 1995), pp. 204–208. For actual examples of some of these activities, see J. Kerstetter, P. Burrows, J. Greene, G. Smith, and M. Conlin, "The Dark Side of the Valley," *Business Week* (July 17, 2000), pp. 42–43.

After marking each of the preceding approaches, compare your responses to those of other people in your class. For each approach, the people marking 4 or 5 should say why they thought this particular act would be appropriate. Those who marked 1 or 2 should then state why they thought this act would be inappropriate.

Go to the Web site of the Society for Competitive Intelligence Professionals (www.scip.org). What does SCIP say about these approaches?

KEY TERMS

competitive intelligence (p. 145)

competitors (p. 148)

complementor (p. 138)

consolidated industry (p. 139)

EFAS Table (p. 151)

entry barrier (p. 134)

environmental scanning (p. 120)

environmental uncertainty (p. 120)

exit barrier (p. 137)

fragmented industry (p. 139)

global industry (p. 140)

hypercompetition (p. 143)

industry (p. 133)

industry analysis (p. 122)

industry matrix (p. 144)

industry scenario (p. 150)

issues priority matrix (p. 132)

key success factor (p. 143)

multidomestic industry (p. 139)

multinational corporation (MNC) (p. 129)

natural environment (p. 121)

new entrant (p. 134)

regional industries (p. 140)

societal environment (p. 122)

STEEP analysis (p. 124)

strategic group (p. 140)

strategic type (p. 142)

substitute product (p. 137)

task environment (p. 122)

NOTES

1. L. W. Brigham, "Thinking about the Arctic's Future: Scenarios for 2040," *The Futurist* (September–October 2007), pp. 27–34.

2. J. B. Thomas, S. M. Clark, and D. A. Gioia, "Strategic Sensemaking and Organizational Performance: Linkages Among Scanning, Interpretation, Action, Outcomes," *Academy of Management Journal* (April 1993), pp. 239–270; J. A. Smith, "Strategies for Start-Ups," *Long Range Planning* (December 1998), pp. 857–872.

3. E. Stephenson and A. Pandit, "How Companies Act on Global Trends: A Mc Kinsey Global Survey", Mckinsey Quarterly (April 2008).

4. WWF, CII and CII-ITC Center For Excellence For Sustainable Development, Carbon Disclosure Project 2010; India 200 Report, recovered on 19th Oct 2011, from http://assets.wwfindia.org/downloads/cdp_report_2010.pdf

5. W. E. Stead and J. G. Stead, *Sustainable Strategic Management* (Armonk, NY: M. E. Sharpe, 2004), p. 6.

6. F. Montabon, R. Sroufe, and R. Narasimhan, "An Examination of Corporate Reporting, Environmental Management Practices and Firm Performance," *Journal of Operations Management* (August 2007), pp. 998–1014.

7. P. Lasserre and J. Probert, "Competing on the Pacific Rim: High Risks and High Returns," *Long Range Planning* (April 1994), pp. 12–35.

8. J. J. McGonagle, "Mapping and Anticipating the Competitive Landscape," *Competitive Intelligence Magazine* (March–April 2007), p. 49.

9. M. J. Cetron, "Economics: Prospects for the 'Dragon' and the 'Tiger,'" *Futurist* (July–August 2004), pp. 10–11; "A Less Fiery Dragon," *The Economist* (December 1, 2007), p. 92.

10. "Investing Without Borders: A Different Approach to Global Investing," *T. Rowe Price Report* (Fall 2007), p. 1.

11. S. Hamm, "Cloud Computing Made Clear," *Business Week* (May 5, 2008), p. 59.

12. P. Lorenz, D. Pinner, and T. Seitz, "The Economics of Solar Power," *McKinsey Quarterly* (June 2008), p. 2.

13. D. Mandal and S. K. Ghosh, "Precision Farming—The Emerging Concept of Agriculture for Today and Tomorrow," *Current Science*, Vol. 79, No. 12, (2000), pp. 1644–1647, recovered on 19th Oct 2011, from http://www.ias.ac.in/currsci/dec252000/1644.pdf

14. India Development Gateway, Tamil Nadu Precision Farming Project, recovered on 19th Oct 2011, from http://www.indg.in/agriculture/agricultural-best-practices/precision-farming

15. W. E. Halal, "The Top 10 Emerging Technologies," *Special Report* (World Future Society, 2000).

16. F. Dobbin and T. J. Dowd, "How Policy Shapes Competition: Early Railroad Foundings in Massachusetts," *Administrative Science Quarterly* (September 1997), pp. 501–529.

17. Competition Act of 2002, No. 12 of 2003, recovered on 19th Oct 2011, from http://www.cci.gov.in/images/media/competition_act/act2002.pdf

18. Girish Pai K, Competition Act of 2002 – An Overview, recovered on 19th Oct 2011, from http://markandgirish.com/download/Indian%20Competition%20Law.pdf

19. A. Shleifer and R. W. Viskny, "Takeovers in the 1960s and the 1980s: Evidence and Implications," in *Fundamental Issues in Strategy: A Research Agenda*, edited by R. P. Rumelt, D. E. Schendel, and D. J. Teece (Boston: Harvard Business School Press, 1994), pp. 403–418.

20. "The Problem with Solid Engineering," *The Economist* (May 20, 2006), pp. 71–73.

21. "Doing Business," *The Economist* (September 9, 2006), p. 98.

22. Web site, *World Trade Organization*, www.wto.org (accessed July 31, 2008).

23. M. J. Cetron and O. Davies, "Trends Now Shaping the Future," *The Futurist* (March–April 2005), pp. 28–29; M. Cetron and O. Davies, "Trends Shaping Tomorrow's World," *The Futurist* (March–April 2008), pp. 35–52.

24. "Trend: Urbane Urban Portraits," *Business Week* (April 28, 2008), p. 57.

25. "Old Europe," *Economist* (October 2, 2004), pp. 49–50.

26. M. J. Cetron and O. Davies, "Trends Now Shaping the Future," *The Futurist* (March–April 2005), p. 30.

27. "The Incredible Shrinking Country," *Economist* (November 13, 2004), pp. 45–46.

28. D. Levin, "Tradition Under Stress," *AARP Bulletin* (July–August 2008), pp. 16–18.

29. J. Wyatt, "Playing the Woofie Card," *Fortune* (February 6, 1995), pp. 130–132.

30. D. Carpenter, "Walgreen Pursues 12,000 Corners of Market," *Des Moines Register* (May 9, 2004), pp. 1D, 5D.

31. M. Arndt, "Zimmer: Growing Older Gracefully," *Business Week* (June 9, 2003), pp. 82–84.

32. "France Considering Raising Tax on Fatty, Sugary Foods," *(Minneapolis) Star Tribune* (August 7, 2008), p. A7.

33. H. Yen, "Empty Nesters Push Growth of Pet Health Care Businesses," *The (Ames, IA) Tribune* (September 27, 2003), p. C8; D. Brady and C. Palmeri, "The Pet Economy," *Business Week* (August 6, 2007), pp. 45–54; "Pampering Your Pet," *St. Cloud (MN) Times* (September 8, 2007), p. 3A.

34. A. Bianco, "The Vanishing Mass Market," *Business Week* (July 12, 2004), pp. 61–68.

35. B. Ramesh, S. Cherian, and V. Agarwal, Managing Diversity, sponsored by Larsen & Toubro Limited, EmSyS, recovered on 2nd May 2009, from http://www.lntemsys.com/Diversity%20Management.pdf

36. N. Rajesh, Multi-cultural Workforcean Imperative, Data Quest, posted on Thursday, 19th June 2008, recovered on 2nd May 2009, from http://dqindia.ciol.com/content/strategy/management/2008/108061901.asp

37. "The Trouble with Migrants," *The Economist* (November 24, 2007), pp. 56–57.

38. "Multicultural Retailing," *Arizona Republic* (October 10, 2004), p. D4.

39. "Islamic Finance: West Meets East," *Economist* (October 25, 2003), p. 69.

40. "Giants Forced to Dance," *The Economist* (May 26, 2007), pp. 67–68.

41. "Membership Required," *The Economist* (August 2, 2008), p. 66.

42. J. Naisbitt, *Megatrends Asia* (New York: Simon & Schuster, 1996), p. 79.

43. A. Menon and A. Tomkins, "Learning About the Market's Periphery: IBM's WebFountain," *Long Range Planning* (April 2004), pp. 153–162.

44. I. M. Cockburn, R. M. Henderson, and S. Stern, "Untangling the Origins of Competitive Advantage," *Strategic Management Journal* (October–November, 2000), Special Issue, pp. 1123–1145.

45. L. Fuld, "Be Prepared," *Harvard Business Review* (November 2003), pp. 20–21.

46. H. Wissema, "Driving through Red Lights," *Long Range Planning* (October 2002), pp. 521–539; B. K. Boyd and J. Fulk, "Executive Scanning and Perceived Uncertainty: A Multidimensional Model," *Journal of Management*, Vol. 22, No. 1 (1996), pp. 1–21.

47. P. G. Audia, E. A. Locke, and K. G. Smith, "The Paradox of Success: An Archival and a Laboratory Study of Strategic Persistence Following Radical Environmental Change," *Academy of Management Journal* (October 2000), pp. 837–853; M. L. McDonald and J. D. Westphal, "Getting By with the Advice of Their Friends" CEOs Advice Networks and Firms' Strategic Responses to Poor Performance," *Administrative Science Quarterly* (March 2003), pp. 1–32; R. A. Bettis and C. K. Prahalad, "The Dominant Logic: Retrospective and Extension," *Strategic Management Journal* (January 1995), pp. 5–14; J. M. Stofford and C. W. F. Baden-Fuller, "Creating Corporate Entrepreneurship," *Strategic Management Journal* (September 1994), pp. 521–536; J. M. Beyer, P. Chattopadhyay, E. George, W. H. Glick, and D. Pugliese, "The Selective Perception of Managers Revisited," *Academy of Management Journal* (June 1997), pp. 716–737.

48. H. I. Ansoff, "Strategic Management in a Historical Perspective," in *International Review of Strategic Management*, Vol. 2, No. 1 (1991), edited by D. E. Hussey (Chichester, England: Wiley, 1991), p. 61.

49. S. E. Ante, "Sprint's Wake-Up Call," *Business Week* (March 3, 2008), p. 54.

50. M. E. Porter, *Competitive Strategy* (New York: The Free Press, 1980), p. 3.

51. M. McCarthy, "Rivals Scramble to Topple Nike's Sneaker Supremacy," *USA Today* (April 3, 2003), pp. B1–B2; S. Holmes, "Changing the Game on Nike," *Business Week* (January 22, 2007), p. 80.

52. Porter, *Competitive Strategy*, (New York: The Free Press, 1980), p. 23.

53. A. S. Grove, "Surviving a 10x Force," *Strategy & Leadership* (January/February 1997), pp. 35–37.

54. A fragmented industry is defined as one whose market share for the leading four firms is equal to or less than 40% of total industry sales. See M. J. Dollinger, "The Evolution of Collective Strategies in Fragmented Industries," *Academy of Management Review* (April 1990), pp. 266–285.

55. M. E. Porter, "Changing Patterns of International Competition," *California Management Review* (Winter 1986), pp. 9–40.

56. A. M. Rugman, *The Regional Multinationals: MNEs and Global Strategic Management* (Cambridge: Cambridge University Press, 2005).

57. K. J. Hatten and M. L. Hatten, "Strategic Groups, Asymmetrical Mobility Barriers, and Contestability," *Strategic Management Journal* (July–August 1987), p. 329.

58. J. C. Short, D. J. Ketchen Jr., T. B. Palmer, and G. T. M. Hult, "Firm, Strategic Group, and Industry Influences on Performance," *Strategic Management Journal* (February 2007), pp. 147–167; J. D. Osborne, C. I. Stubbart, and A. Ramaprasad, "Strategic Groups and Competitive Enactment: A Study of Dynamic Relationships Between Mental Models and Performance," *Strategic Management Journal* (May 2001), pp. 435–454; A. Fiegenbaum and H. Thomas, "Strategic Groups as Reference Groups: Theory, Modeling and Empirical Examination of Industry and Competitive Strategy," *Strategic Management Journal* (September 1995), pp. 461–476; H. R. Greve, "Managerial Cognition and the Mimities Adoption of Market Positions: What You See Is What You Do," *Strategic Management Journal* (October 1998), pp. 967–988.

59. G. Leask and D. Parker, "Strategic Groups, Competitive Groups and Performance Within the U.K. Pharmaceutical Industry: Improving Our Understanding of the Competitive Process," *Strategic Management Journal* (July 2007), pp. 723–745.

60. C. C. Pegels, Y. I. Song, and B. Yang, "Management Heterogeneity, Competitive Interaction Groups, and Firm Performance," *Strategic Management Journal* (September 2000), pp. 911–923; W. S. Desarbo and R. Grewal, "Hybrid Strategic Groups," *Strategic Management Journal* (March 2008), pp. 293–317.

61. R. E. Miles and C. C. Snow, *Organizational Strategy, Structure, and Process* (New York: McGraw-Hill, 1978). See also D. J. Ketchen, Jr., "An Interview with Raymond E. Miles and Charles C. Snow," *Academy of Management Executive* (November 2003), pp. 97–104.

62. B. Kabanoff and S. Brown, "Knowledge Structures of Prospectors, Analyzers, and Defenders: Content, Structure, Stability, and Performance," *Strategic Management Journal* (February 2008), pp. 149–171.

63. R. A. D'Aveni, *Hypercompetition* (New York: The Free Press, 1994), pp. xiii–xiv.

64. C. W. Hofer and D. Schendel, *Strategy Formulation: Analytical Concepts* (St. Paul: West Publishing Co., 1978), p. 77.

65. "Information Overload," *Journal of Business Strategy* (January–February 1998), p. 4.

66. E. Von Hipple, *Sources of Innovation* (New York: Oxford University Press, 1988), p. 4.

67. "An Executive Takes on the Top Business Trends: A McKinsey Global Survey," *McKinsey Quarterly* (April 2006).

68. K. Coyne and J. Horn, "How Companies Respond to Competitors: A McKinsey Global Survey," *McKinsey Quarterly* (August 2008).

69. M. D. Ryall, "Subjective Rationality, Self-Confirming Equilibrium, and Corporate Strategy", *Management Science* (Vol. 49, 2003), pp. 936–949.

70. C. H. Wee and M. L. Leow, "Competitive Business Intelligence in Singapore," *Journal of Strategic Marketing* (Vol. 2, 1994), pp. 112–139.

71. A. Badr, E. Madden, and S. Wright, "The Contributions of CI to the Strategic Decision Making Process: Empirical Study of the European Pharmaceutical Industry," *Journal of Competitive Intelligence and Management* (Vol. 3, No. 4, 2006), pp. 15–35.

72. R. G. Vedder, "CEO and CIO Attitudes about Competitive Intelligence," *Competitive Intelligence Magazine* (October–December 1999), pp. 39–41.

73. D. Fehringer, B. Hohhof, and T. Johnson, "State of the Art: Competitive Intelligence," Research Report of the *Competitive Intelligence Foundation* (2006), p. 6.

74. "Competitive Intelligence Spending 'to Rise Tenfold' in 5 Years," *Daily Research News* (June 19, 2007).

75. Silicon India, Y our "Intelligence Tool" to Better BI, posted on Wednesday, 21st September 2011, 13:35 IST, recovered on 19th Oct 2011, from http://www.siliconindia.com/shownews/Your_Intelligence_Tool_to_Better_BI_-nid-92146-cid-3.html

76. Expresscomputers, Business Intelligence market poised for take-off, recovered on 19th Oct 2011, from Indian Express Group (Mumbai, India) website http://www.expresscomput-eronline.com/20030113/indtrend1.shtml

77. S. H. Miller, "Beware Rival's Web Site Subterfuge," *Competitive Intelligence Magazine* (January–March 2000), p. 8.

78. E. Iwata, "More U.S. Trade Secrets Walk Out Door with Foreign Spies," *USA Today* (February 13, 2003), pp. B1, B2.

79. Twenty-nine Percent Spy on Co-Workers," *USA Today* (August 19, 2003), p. B1.

80. M. Orey, "Corporate Snoops," *Business Week* (October 9, 2006), pp. 46–49; E. Javers, "Spies, Lies, & KPMG," *Business Week* (February 26, 2007), pp. 86–88.

81. E. Javers, "I Spy—For Capitalism," *Business Week* (August 13, 2007), pp. 54–56.

82. B. Flora, "Ethical Business Intelligence in NOT Mission Impossible," *Strategy & Leadership* (January/February 1998), pp. 40–41.

83. A. L. Penenberg and M. Berry, *Spooked: Espionage in Corporate America* (Cambridge, MA: Perseus Publishing, 2000).

84. T. Kendrick and J. Blackmore, "Ten Things You Really Need to Know About Competitors," *Competitive Intelligence Magazine* (September–October 2001), pp. 12–15.

85. For the percentage of CI professionals using each analytical technique, see A. Badr, E. Madden, and S. Wright, "The Contributions of CI to the Strategic Decision Making Process: Empirical Study of the European Pharmaceutical Industry," *Journal of Competitive Intelligence and Management* (Vol. 3, No. 4, 2006), pp. 15–35; and D. Fehringer, B. Hohhof, and T. Johnson, "State of the Art: Competitive Intelligence," Research Report of the *Competitive Intelligence Foundation* (2006).

86. "CI at Avnet: A Bottom-Line Impact," *Competitive Intelligence Magazine* (July–September 2000), p. 5. For further information on competitive intelligence, see C. S. Fleisher and D. L. Blenkhorn, *Controversies in Competitive Intelligence: The Enduring Issues* (Westport, CT: Praeger Publishers, 2003); C. Vibert, *Competitive Intelligence: A Framework for Web-Based Analysis and Decision Making* (Mason, OH: Thomson/Southwestern, 2004); and C. S. Fleisher and B. E. Bensoussan, *Strategic and Competitive Analysis* (Upper Saddle River, NJ: Prentice Hall, 2003).

87. H. E. Klein and R. E. Linneman, "Environmental Assessment: An International Study of Corporate Practices," *Journal of Business Strategy* (Summer 1984), p. 72.

88. A. F. Osborn, *Applied Imagination* (NY: Scribner, 1957); R. C. Litchfield, "Brainstorming Reconsidered: A Goal-Based View," *Academy of Management Review* (July 2008), pp. 649–668; R. I. Sutton, "The Truth About Brainstorming," *Inside Innovation*, insert to *Business Week* (September 26, 2006), pp. 17–21.

89. R. S. Duboff, "The Wisdom of Expert Crowds," *Harvard Business Review* (September 2007), p. 28.

90. J. Surowiecki, *The Wisdom of Crowds* (NY: Doubleday, 2004).

91. R. Dye, "The Promise of Prediction Markets: A Roundtable," *McKinsey Quarterly* (April 2008), pp. 83–93.

92. C. R. Sunstein, "When Crowds Aren't Wise," *Harvard Business Review* (September 2006), pp. 20–21.

93. See L. E. Schlange and U. Juttner, "Helping Managers to Identify the Key Strategic Issues," *Long Range Planning* (October 1997), pp. 777–786, for an explanation and application of the cross-impact matrix.

94. G. Ringland, *Scenario Planning: Managing for the Future* (Chichester, England: Wiley, 1998); N. C. Georgantzas and W. Acar, *Scenario-Driven Planning: Learning to Manage Strategic Uncertainty* (Westport, CN: Quorum Books, 1995); L. Fahey and R. M. Randall (eds), *Learning from the Future: Competitive Foresight Scenarios* (New York: John Wiley & Sons, 1998).

95. M. Eskew, "Stick with Your Vision," *Harvard Business Review* (July–August 2007), pp. 56–57.

96. This process of scenario development is adapted from M. E. Porter, *Competitive Advantage* (New York: The Free Press, 1985), pp. 448–470.

97. J. C. Glenn, "Scanning the Global Situation and Prospects for the Future," *The Futurist* (January–February 2008), pp. 41–46.

98. M. E. Porter, *Competitive Strategy: Techniques for Analyzing Industries and Competitors* (New York: The Free Press, 1980), pp. 47–75.

99. M. Treacy and F. Wiersema, *The Discipline of Market Leaders* (Reading, MA: Addison-Wesley, 1995).

100. Presentation by W. A. Rosenkrans, Jr., to the Iowa Chapter of the Society of Competitive Intelligence Professionals, Des Moines, IA (August 5, 2004).

101. B. Gilad, *Early Warning* (New York: AMACOM, 2004), pp. 97–103. Also see C. S. Fleisher and B. E. Bensoussan, *Strategic and Competitive Analysis* (Upper Saddle River, NJ: Prentice Hall, 2003), pp. 122–143.

102. Presentation by W. A. Rosenkrans, Jr., to the Iowa Chapter of the Society of Competitive Intelligence Professionals, Des Moines, IA (August 5, 2004). See also S. M. Shaker and M. P. Gembicki, *War Room Guide to Competitive Intelligence* (New York: McGraw-Hill, 1999).

103. L. Fahey, "Invented Competitors: A New Competitor Analysis Methodology," *Strategy & Leadership*, Vol. 30, No. 6 (2002), pp. 5–12.

104. A. Beurschgens, "Using Business War Gaming to Generate Actionable Intelligence," *Competitive Intelligence Magazine* (January–February 2008), pp. 43–45.

Competitive Analysis Techniques

Analytical techniques commonly used in competitive intelligence are *SWOT analysis, Porter's industry forces, ratio analysis*, and *strategic group analysis* (also called *competitive cluster analysis*). In addition to these are Porter's *four-corner exercise*, Treacy and Wiersema's *value disciplines*, and Gilad's *blind spot analysis*. These can be used in a *war game simulation* in which people role-play different competitors and their possible future strategies.

Porter's four-corner exercise involves analyzing a specific competitor's future goals, assumptions, current strategies, and capabilities in order to compile a competitor's response profile. See **Figure 4–6.** Having knowledge of a competitor's goals allows predictions about how likely the competitor is to change strategy and respond to changing conditions. Identifying a competitor's assumptions about itself and the industry can reveal blind spots about how management perceives its environment. Considering a competitor's current strategy and how long it has been in place may indicate whether the company is likely to continue in its current direction. If a strategy is not stated explicitly, one should consider its actions and policies in order to note its implicit strategy. The last step is to objectively evaluate a competitor's capabilities in terms of strengths and weaknesses. The competitor's goals, assumptions, and current strategy influence the likelihood, timing, nature, and intensity of a competitor's reactions. Its strengths and weaknesses determine its ability to initiate or react to strategic moves and to deal with environmental changes.[98]

Treacy and Wiersema's value disciplines involves the evaluation of a competitor in terms of three dimensions: product leadership, operational excellence, and customer intimacy. (See **Figure 4–7.**) After analyzing 80 market-leading companies, Treacy and Wiersema noted that each of these firms developed a compelling and unmatched value proposition on one dimension but was able to maintain acceptable standards on the other two dimensions. *Operationally excellent* companies deliver a combination of quality, price, and ease of purchase that no other can match in their market. An example is Dell Computer, a master of operational excellence. A *product leader* consistently strives to provide its market with leading-edge products or new applications of existing products or services. Johnson & Johnson is an example of a product leader that finds new ideas, develops them quickly, and then looks for ways to improve them. A company that delivers value through *customer intimacy* bonds with its customers and develops high customer loyalty. IBM is an example of a company that pursues excellence in customer intimacy. IBM's current strategy is to provide a total information technology service to its customers so that customers can totally rely on IBM to take care of any Information Technology (IT) problems.[99] According to Wayne Rosenkrans, past president of SCIP, it is possible to mark a spot on each of the three value dimensions shown in **Figure 4–7** for each competitor being analyzed. Then one can draw lines connecting each of the marks, resulting in a triangle that reveals that competitor's overall value proposition.

Gilad's blind spot analysis is based on the premise that the assumptions held by decision makers regarding their own company and their industry may act as perceptual biases or blind spots. As a result, (1) the firm may not be aware of strategically important developments, (2) the firm may inaccurately perceive strategically important developments, or (3) even if the firm is aware of important developments, it may learn too slowly to allow for a timely response. It is important to gather sufficient information about a competitor and its executives to be able to list top management's assumptions about buyers' preferences, the nature of the supply chain, the industry's key success factors, barriers to entry, and the threat

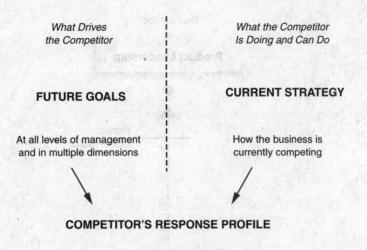

FIGURE 4–6
Four-Corner
Exercise: Porter's
Components
of Competitor
Analysis

FUTURE GOALS

At all levels of management
and in multiple dimensions

*What Drives
the Competitor*

CURRENT STRATEGY

How the business is
currently competing

*What the Competitor
Is Doing and Can Do*

COMPETITOR'S RESPONSE PROFILE

Is the competitor satisfied with current position?

What likely moves or strategy shifts will the competitor make?

Where is the competitor vulnerable?

What will provoke the greatest and most effective retaliation by the competitor?

ASSUMPTIONS

Held about itself
and the industry

CAPABILITIES

Both strengths
and weaknesses

appeal of substitutes to customers. One should analyze the industry objectively without regard to these assumptions. Any gap between an objective industry analysis and a competitor's top management assumptions is a potential blind spot. One should include these blind spots when considering how this competitor might respond to environmental change.[100]

Rosenkrans suggests that an analyst should first use Porter's industry forces technique to develop the four-corner analysis. Then the analyst should use the four-corner analysis to generate a strategic group (cluster) analysis. Finally, the analyst should include the three value dimensions to develop a blind spot analysis.

These techniques can be used to conduct a war game simulating the various competitors in the industry. Gather people from various functional areas in your own corporation and put them into teams identified as industry competitors. Each company team should perform a complete analysis of the competitor it is role-playing. Each company team first creates starting strategies for its company and presents it to the entire group. Each company team then creates counter-strategies and presents them to the

FIGURE 4–7 Value Discipline Triad

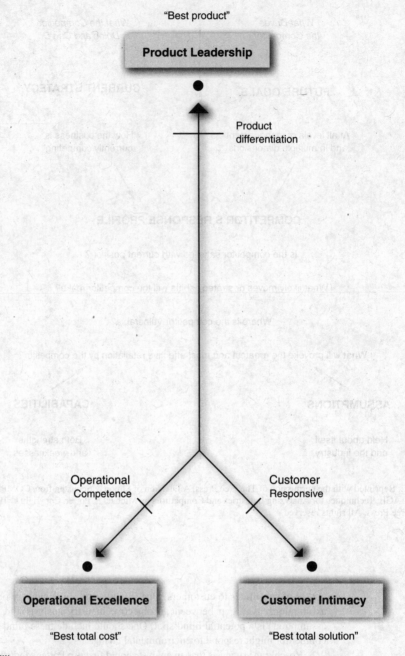

"Best product"

Product Leadership

Product
differentiation

Operational
Competence

Customer
Responsive

Operational Excellence

Customer Intimacy

"Best total cost"

"Best total solution"

SOURCE: From DISCIPLINE OF MARKET LEADERS by Michael Treacy. Copyright © 1997 Michael Treacy. Reprinted by permission of Perseus Books Group.

entire group. After all the presentations are complete, the full group creates new strategic considerations to be included as items to monitor in future environmental scanning.[101] Some of the companies that have used war gaming successfully are Kimberly Clark, Baxter Healthcare, Lockheed Martin, Hewlett-Packard, and Dow Corning. If a corporation does not have the expertise needed to run a war game, it can utilize management consultants, like KappaWest, who prepare and facilitate a complete war game simulation.

Some competitive intelligence analysts take the war game approach one step further by creating an "invented" company that could appear in the future but does not exist today. A team brainstorms what type of strategy the invented competitor might employ. The strategy is often based on a new breakthrough product that is radically different from current offerings. Its goals, strategies, and competitive posture should be different from any currently being used in the industry. According to Liam Fahey, an authority on competitive intelligence, "the invented competitor is proving to be a spur to bold and innovative thinking."[102] War games are especially useful when (externally) the market is shifting, competitive rules are changing, new competitors are entering the industry, a significant competitor is changing its strategy, a firm's competitive position is weakening, the "uncontrollables" are getting stronger, and/or when (internally) the company is "flying blind," its current strategy is stale or confused, managers are over-confident or arrogant, and/or the firm suffers from a "silo" mentality.[103]

internal scanning: Organizational Analysis

On January 10, 2008, a new automobile from Tata Motors was introduced to the world at the Indian Auto Show in New Delhi. Called the *People's Car*, the new auto was planned to sell for $2,500 in India. Even though many manufacturers were hoping to introduce cheap small cars into India and other developing nations, Tata Motors seemed to have significant advantages that other companies lacked. India's low labor costs meant that Tata could engineer a new model for 20% of the $350 million it would cost in developed nations. A factory worker in Mumbai earned just $1.20 per hour, less than auto workers earned in China. The car was kept very simple. The company would save about $900 per car by skipping equipment that the U.S., Europe, and Japan required for emissions control. The People's Car did not have features like antilock brakes, air bags, or support beams to protect passengers in case of a crash. The dashboard contained just a speedometer, fuel gauge, and oil light. It lacked a radio, reclining seats, or power steering. It came with a small 650 cc engine that generated only 70 horsepower, but obtained 50 to 60 miles per gallon. The car's suspension system used old technology that was cheap, but resulted in a rougher ride than in more expensive cars. More importantly, Tata Motors would save money by using an innovative distribution strategy. Instead of selling completed cars to dealers, Tata planned to supply kits that would then be assembled by the dealers. By eliminating large, centralized assembly plants, Tata could cut the car's retail price by 20%.

Although Tata Motors intended to initially sell the people's car in India and then offer it in other developing markets, management felt that they could build a car that would meet U.S. or European specifications for around $6,000—still a low price for an automobile. Given that Tata Motors was able to acquire Jaguar and Land Rover from Ford later in the year, other auto companies had to admit that Tata was on its way to becoming a major competitor in the industry.[1]

Learning Objectives

After reading this chapter, you should be able to:

- Apply the resource view of the firm to determine core and distinctive competencies
- Use the VRIO framework and the value chain to assess an organization's competitive advantage and how it can be sustained
- Understand a company's business model and how it could be imitated

- Assess a company's corporate culture and how it might affect a proposed strategy
- Scan functional resources to determine their fit with a firm's strategy
- Construct an IFAS Table that summarizes internal factors

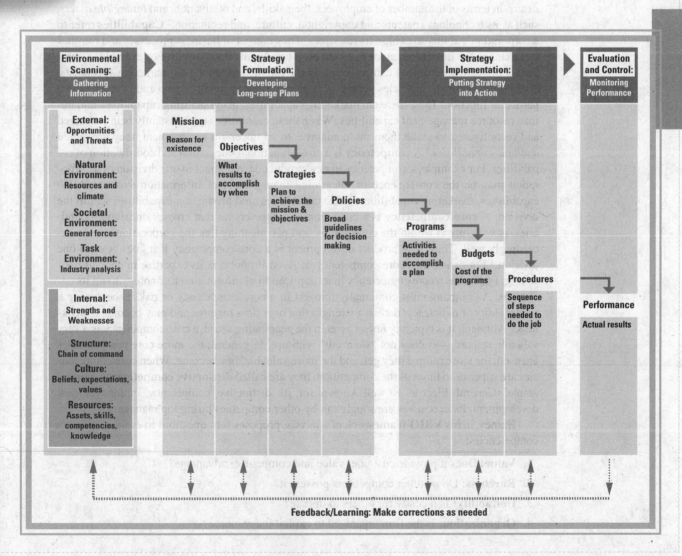

Environmental Scanning: Gathering Information		Strategy Formulation: Developing Long-range Plans				Strategy Implementation: Putting Strategy into Action				Evaluation and Control: Monitoring Performance

External: Opportunities and Threats

Natural Environment: Resources and climate

Societal Environment: General forces

Task Environment: Industry analysis

Internal: Strengths and Weaknesses

Structure: Chain of command

Culture: Beliefs, expectations, values

Resources: Assets, skills, competencies, knowledge

Mission
Reason for existence

Objectives
What results to accomplish by when

Strategies
Plan to achieve the mission & objectives

Policies
Broad guidelines for decision making

Programs
Activities needed to accomplish a plan

Budgets
Cost of the programs

Procedures
Sequence of steps needed to do the job

Performance
Actual results

Feedback/Learning: Make corrections as needed

165

5.1 A Resource-Based Approach to Organizational Analysis

Scanning and analyzing the external environment for opportunities and threats is not enough to provide an organization a competitive advantage. Analysts must also look within the corporation itself to identify *internal strategic factors*—critical *strengths and weaknesses* that are likely to determine whether a firm will be able to take advantage of opportunities while avoiding threats. This internal scanning, often referred to as **organizational analysis**, is concerned with identifying and developing an organization's resources and competencies.

CORE AND DISTINCTIVE COMPETENCIES

Resources are an organization's assets and are thus the basic building blocks of the organization. They include *tangible assets*, such as its plant, equipment, finances, and location, *human assets*, in terms of the number of employees, their skills, and motivation, and *intangible assets*, such as its technology (patents and copyrights), culture, and reputation.[2] **Capabilities** refer to a corporation's ability to exploit its resources. They consist of business processes and routines that manage the interaction among resources to turn inputs into outputs. For example, a company's marketing capability can be based on the interaction among its marketing specialists, distribution channels, and sales people. A capability is functionally based and is resident in a particular function. Thus, there are marketing capabilities, manufacturing capabilities, and human resource management capabilities. When these capabilities are constantly being changed and reconfigured to make them more adaptive to an uncertain environment, they are called *dynamic capabilities*.[3] A **competency** is a cross-functional integration and coordination of capabilities. For example, a competency in new product development in one division of a corporation may be the consequence of integrating management of information systems (MIS) capabilities, marketing capabilities, R&D capabilities, and production capabilities within the division. A **core competency** is a collection of competencies that crosses divisional boundaries, is widespread within the corporation, and is something that the corporation can do exceedingly well. Thus, new product development is a core competency if it goes beyond one division.[4] For example, a core competency of Avon Products is its expertise in door-to-door selling. FedEx has a core competency in its application of information technology to all its operations. A company must continually reinvest in a core competency or risk its becoming a *core rigidity* or *deficiency,* that is, a strength that over time matures and may become a weakness.[5] Although it is typically not an asset in the accounting sense, a core competency is a very valuable resource—it does not "wear out" with use. In general, the more core competencies are used, the more refined they get, and the more valuable they become. When core competencies are superior to those of the competition, they are called **distinctive competencies**. For example, General Electric is well known for its distinctive competency in management development. Its executives are sought out by other companies hiring top managers.[6]

Barney, in his **VRIO framework** of analysis, proposes four questions to evaluate a firm's competencies:

1. **Value:** Does it provide customer value and competitive advantage?
2. **Rareness:** Do no other competitors possess it?
3. **Imitability:** Is it costly for others to imitate?
4. **Organization:** Is the firm organized to exploit the resource?

If the answer to each of these questions is *yes* for a particular competency, it is considered to be a strength and thus a distinctive competence.[7] This should give the company a competitive advantage and lead to higher performance.[8]

It is important to evaluate the importance of a company's resources, capabilities, and competencies to ascertain whether they are internal strategic factors—that is, particular strengths and weaknesses that will help determine the future of the company. This can be done by comparing measures of these factors with measures of (1) the company's past performance, (2) the company's key competitors, and (3) the industry as a whole. To the extent that a resource (such as a firm's cash situation), capability, or competency is significantly different from the firm's own past, its key competitors, or the industry average, that resource is likely to be a strategic factor and should be considered in strategic decisions.

Even though a distinctive competency is certainly considered to be a corporation's key strength, a key strength may not always be a distinctive competency. As competitors attempt to imitate another company's competency (especially during hypercompetition), what was once a distinctive competency becomes a minimum requirement to compete in the industry.[9] Even though the competency may still be a core competency and thus a strength, it is no longer unique. For example, when Nirma entered into the market of detergents, its ability to manufacture at low cost was a distinctive competency. This distinctive competence helped Nirma penetrate the market dominated by a MNC, i.e., Hindustan Lever Ltd. In 1992, Nirma had sales of 333,000 tons per annum and a market share of 55%.[10] However, as HLL and others imitated Nirma's processes and introduced their versions of "value-for-money" products, the cost-leadership strategy, continued to be Nimra's strength but was less and less distinctive competency.

USING RESOURCES TO GAIN COMPETITIVE ADVANTAGE

Proposing that a company's sustained competitive advantage is primarily determined by its resource endowments, Grant proposes a five-step, resource-based approach to strategy analysis.

1. Identify and classify the firm's resources in terms of strengths and weaknesses.
2. Combine the firm's strengths into specific capabilities and core competencies.
3. Appraise the profit potential of these capabilities and competencies in terms of their potential for sustainable competitive advantage and the ability to harvest the profits resulting from their use. Are there any distinctive competencies?
4. Select the strategy that best exploits the firm's capabilities and competencies relative to external opportunities.
5. Identify resource gaps and invest in upgrading weaknesses.[11]

Where do these competencies come from? A corporation can gain access to a distinctive competency in four ways:

- It may be an asset endowment, such as a key patent, coming from the founding of the company. For example, Xerox grew on the basis of its original copying patent.
- It may be acquired from someone else. For example, Whirlpool bought a worldwide distribution system when it purchased Philips's appliance division.
- It may be shared with another business unit or alliance partner. For example, Apple Computer worked with a design firm to create the special appeal of its personal computers and iPods.
- It may be carefully built and accumulated over time within the company. For example, Honda carefully extended its expertise in small motor manufacturing from motorcycles to autos and lawnmowers.[12]

There is some evidence that the best corporations prefer organic internal growth over acquisitions. One study of large global companies identified firms that outperformed their peers on both revenue growth and profitability over a decade. These excellent performers generated value from knowledge-intensive intangibles, such as copyrights, trade secrets, or strong brands, not from acquisitions.[13]

The desire to build or upgrade a core competency is one reason entrepreneurial and other fast-growing firms often tend to locate close to their competitors. They form *clusters*— geographic concentrations of interconnected companies and industries. For example, in India, there are seven large IT clusters. The country's seven clusters exist in seven tier I cities, i.e., Bangalore, Delhi, Chennai, Hyderabad, Pune, Mumbai, and Kolkata. Though clusters have developed in many other cities such as Vadodara, Bhubaneswar, Ahmedabad, Goa, Chandigarh, and Trivandrum,[14] yet dominant cluster is the one at Bangalore. Bangalore cluster was one of the original clusters in India which developed in response to foreign markets and as such has come to be known worldwide for its achievements in the high-technology domain. Today, almost all technology MNCs have located some of their global activities in one of the technology parks in the city thereby integrating Bangalore into their global value chains.[15] An ode to the cluster is that Bangalore/Bengaluru has been named as "Silicon Valley of India."[16]

Similarly, Gujarat is home to the world's largest diamond cluster. It is a processing hub between the miners and sorters of diamonds (in Russia, South Africa, Botswana, and elsewhere) and the customers of finished diamonds. About 85% of the world's diamonds (57% by value) are cut and polished in Gujarat.[17] In Gujarat, two towns, i.e., Navsari and Surat are known for their diamond processing capabilities. At present there are more than 6,000 diamond-cutting units in Surat. Training, exposure, and technology are the three major reasons for Surat's success story. Today, India is the world leader in cutting, polishing, and re-cutting of diamonds.[18]

Similarly, woollen and cotton hosiery clusters exist in Tripura, Ludhiana, Kolkata, and Delhi. Auto and auto ancillary clusters are in Jamshedpur, Pune, and Chennai; leather clusters in Agra and Chennai; and pharmaceutical clusters in Ahmedabad and Hyderabad. In India, understanding the merit of clustering of companies, Government of India promotes cluster formation. To promote clusters, GOI has set up support and entrepreneurship programs and improved the infrastructure. Approximately, 350 small-scale industry clusters, and 2,000 rural and artisan-based clusters exist in India, according to a study conducted by UNIDO in 1996.[19]

DETERMINING THE SUSTAINABILITY OF AN ADVANTAGE

Just because a firm is able to use its resources, capabilities, and competencies to develop a competitive advantage does not mean it will be able to sustain it. Two characteristics determine the sustainability of a firm's distinctive competency(ies): durability and imitability.

Durability is the rate at which a firm's underlying resources, capabilities, or core competencies depreciate or become obsolete. New technology can make a company's core competency obsolete or irrelevant. For example, Intel's skills in using basic technology developed by others to manufacture and market quality microprocessors was a crucial capability until management realized that the firm had taken current technology as far as possible with the Pentium chip. Without basic R&D of its own, it would slowly lose its competitive advantage to others. It thus formed a strategic alliance with HP to gain access to a needed technology.

Imitability is the rate at which a firm's underlying resources, capabilities, or core competencies can be duplicated by others. To the extent that a firm's distinctive competency gives it competitive advantage in the marketplace, competitors will do what they can to learn and imitate that set of skills and capabilities. Competitors' efforts may range from *reverse engineering* (which involves taking apart a competitor's product in order to find out how it works), to hiring employees from the competitor, to outright patent infringement. A core competency can be easily imitated to the extent that it is transparent, transferable, and replicable.

■ **Transparency** is the speed with which other firms can understand the relationship of resources and capabilities supporting a successful firm's strategy. For example, Gillette has always supported its dominance in the marketing of razors with excellent R&D. A competitor could never understand how the Sensor or Mach 3 razor was produced simply by taking one apart. Gillette's razor design was very difficult to copy, partially because the manufacturing equipment needed to produce it was so expensive and complicated.

■ **Transferability** is the ability of competitors to gather the resources and capabilities necessary to support a competitive challenge. For example, it may be very difficult for a wine maker to duplicate a French winery's key resources of land and climate, especially if the imitator is located in Iowa.

■ **Replicability** is the ability of competitors to use duplicated resources and capabilities to imitate the other firm's success. For example, even though many companies have tried to imitate Procter & Gamble's success with brand management by hiring brand managers away from P&G, they have often failed to duplicate P&G's success. The competitors failed to identify less visible P&G coordination mechanisms or to realize that P&G's brand management style conflicted with the competitor's own corporate culture.

It is relatively easy to learn and imitate another company's core competency or capability if it comes from **explicit knowledge**, that is, knowledge that can be easily articulated and communicated. This is the type of knowledge that competitive intelligence activities can quickly identify and communicate. **Tacit knowledge**, in contrast, is knowledge that is *not* easily communicated because it is deeply rooted in employee experience or in a corporation's culture.[20] Tacit knowledge is more valuable and more likely to lead to a sustainable competitive advantage than is explicit knowledge because it is much harder for competitors to imitate.[21] As explained by Michael Dell, founder of the Dell computer company, "others can understand what they do, but they can't do it."[22] The knowledge may be complex and combined with other types of knowledge in an unclear fashion in such a way that even management cannot clearly explain the competency.[23] Tacit knowledge is thus subject to a paradox. For a corporation to be successful and grow, its tacit knowledge must be clearly identified and codified if the knowledge is to be spread throughout the firm. Once tacit knowledge is identified and written down, however, it is easily imitable by competitors.[24] This forces companies to establish complex security systems to safeguard their key knowledge.

An organization's resources and capabilities can be placed on a continuum to the extent they are durable and can't be imitated (that is, aren't transparent, transferable, or replicable) by another firm. This **continuum of sustainability** is depicted in **Figure 5–1**. At one extreme are slow-cycle resources, which are sustainable because they are shielded by patents, geography, strong brand names, or tacit knowledge. These resources and capabilities are distinctive competencies because they provide a sustainable competitive advantage. Gillette's razor technology is a good example of a product built around slow-cycle resources. The other

FIGURE 5–1
Continuum of
Resource
Sustainability

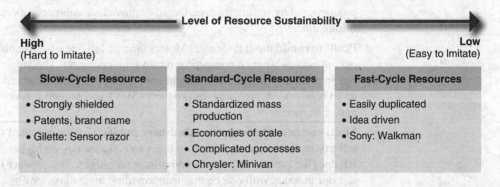

Level of Resource Sustainability

High
(Hard to Imitate)

Low
(Easy to Imitate)

Slow-Cycle Resource	Standard-Cycle Resources	Fast-Cycle Resources
• Strongly shielded • Patents, brand name • Gilette: Sensor razor	• Standardized mass production • Economies of scale • Complicated processes • Chrysler: Minivan	• Easily duplicated • Idea driven • Sony: Walkman

extreme includes fast-cycle resources, which face the highest imitation pressures because they are based on a concept or technology that can be easily duplicated, such as Sony's walkman. To the extent that a company has fast-cycle resources, the primary way it can compete successfully is through increased speed from lab to marketplace. Otherwise, it has no real sustainable competitive advantage.

With its low-cost position and innovative marketing strategy, Tata Motors appeared to have a competitive advantage in making and selling its new People's Car at the lowest price in the industry. Would this low-cost competitive advantage be sustainable? In terms of durability, the car's lack of safety or emissions equipment could be a disadvantage when India and other developing nations begin to require such technology. Given that most developing nations also have low labor costs, Tata's low wages could be easily imitated—probably fairly quickly. For example, the Renault—Nissan auto firm had already formed an alliance in 2008 with Indian motorcycle maker Bajal Auto to launch a $3,000 car in India in 2009.[25] Tata Motor's strategy of selling its new car in kit form was highly imitable, assuming that a competitor's car could be kept simple enough for dealers to assemble easily. Overall, the sustainability of Tata Motors' competitive advantage seemed fairly low, given the fast-cycle nature of its resources.

5.2 Business Models

When analyzing a company, it is helpful to learn what sort of business model it is following. This is especially important when analyzing Internet-based companies. A **business model** is a company's method for making money in the current business environment. It includes the key structural and operational characteristics of a firm—how it earns revenue and makes a profit. A business model is usually composed of five elements:

- Who it serves?
- What it provides?
- How it makes money?
- How it differentiates and sustains competitive advantage?
- How it provides its product/service?[26]

The simplest business model is to provide a good or service that can be sold so that revenues exceed costs and expenses. Other models can be much more complicated. Some of the many possible business models are:

- **Customer solutions model:** IBM uses this model to make money not by selling IBM products, but by selling its expertise to improve its customers' operations. This is a consulting model.

- **Profit pyramid model:** General Motors offers a full line of automobiles in order to close out any niches where a competitor might find a position. The key is to get customers to buy in at the low-priced, low-margin entry point (Saturn's basic sedans) and move them up to high-priced, high-margin products (SUVs and pickup trucks) where the company makes its money.

- **Multi-component system/installed base model:** Gillette invented this classic model to sell razors at break-even pricing in order to make money on higher-margin razor blades. HP does the same with printers and printer cartridges. The product is thus a system, not just one product, with one component providing most of the profits.

- **Advertising model:** Similar to the multi-component system/installed base model, this model offers its basic product free in order to make money on advertising. Originating in the newspaper industry, this model is used heavily in commercial radio and television. Internet-based firms, such as Google, offer free services to users in order to expose them to the advertising that pays the bills. This model is analogous to Mary Poppins' "spoonful of sugar (content) helps the medicine (advertising) go down."

- ■ **Switchboard model:** In this model a firm acts as an intermediary to connect multiple sellers to multiple buyers. Financial planners juggle a wide range of products for sale to multiple customers with different needs. This model has been successfully used by eBay and Amazon.com.

- ■ **Time model:** Product R&D and speed are the keys to success in the time model. Being the first to market with a new innovation allows a pioneer like Sony to earn high margins. Once others enter the market with process R&D and lower margins, it's time to move on.

- ■ **Efficiency model:** In this model a company waits until a product becomes standardized and then enters the market with a low-priced, low-margin product that appeals to the mass market. This model is used by Wal-Mart, Dell, and Southwest Airlines.

- ■ **Blockbuster model:** In some industries, such as pharmaceuticals and motion picture studios, profitability is driven by a few key products. The focus is on high investment in a few products with high potential payoffs—especially if they can be protected by patents.

- ■ **Profit multiplier model:** The idea of this model is to develop a concept that may or may not make money on its own but, through synergy, can spin off many profitable products. Walt Disney invented this concept by using cartoon characters to develop high-margin theme parks, merchandise, and licensing opportunities.

- ■ **Entrepreneurial model:** In this model, a company offers specialized products/services to market niches that are too small to be worthwhile to large competitors but have the potential to grow quickly. Small, local brew pubs have been very successful in a mature industry dominated by Anheuser-Busch. This model has often been used by small high-tech firms that develop innovative prototypes in order to sell off the companies (without ever selling a product) to Microsoft or DuPont.

- ■ **De Facto industry standard model:** In this model, a company offers products free or at a very low price in order to saturate the market and become the industry standard. Once users are locked in, the company offers higher-margin products using this standard. For example, Microsoft packaged Internet Explorer free with its Windows software in order to take market share from Netscape's Web browser.[27]

In order to understand how some of these business models work, it is important to learn where on the value chain the company makes its money. Although a company might offer a large number of products and services, one product line might contribute most of the profits. For example, ink and toner supplies for Hewlett-Packard's printers make up more than half of the company's profits while accounting for less than 25% of its sales.[28] For an example of a new business model in India, see **Strategy Highlight 5.1**.

5.3 Value-Chain Analysis

A **value chain** is a linked set of value-creating activities that begin with basic raw materials coming from suppliers, moving on to a series of value-added activities involved in producing and marketing a product or service, and ending with distributors getting the final goods into the hands of the ultimate consumer. See **Figure 5–2** for an example of a typical value chain for a manufactured product. The focus of value-chain analysis is to examine the corporation in the context of the overall chain of value-creating activities, of which the firm may be only a small part.

STRATEGY highlight 5.1

BUSINESS MODELS IN INDIA

The rural regions in India comprise of maximum percentage of consumers. The rural population in India accounts for around 627 million, i.e., approximately 74% of the total population.[1] Therefore, targeting rural market will bring in bigger revenues. The rural market in Indian economy generates almost more than half of the country's income. However, rural markets come with their own set of problems like though vastly scattered, social status in rural regions is very precariou and income levels and literary rate is extremly low. Lastly, traditional values and superstitions play a very important role in everyday life in rural India. These set of unique marketing challenges warrant a unique and adaptive business model. Eveready is one the companies which has been able to adapt its business model to make a mark in rural india.

Eveready Industries India Ltd. (Eveready) is one of India's leading FMCG companies. possessing expertise in manufacturing, marketing, and distributing a diverse range of products to the entire length and breadth of the country. Its portfolio comprises of dry cell batteries, rechargeable batteries, flashlights, packet tea, mosquito repellents, and lighting.[2]

Eveready has positioned itself as an integrated cost leadership and product differentiation business strategy. However, the business model was not innovative in terms of integrated business line strategy but the ability of the company to add customer convenience to the equation. It further added a supply chain advantage to its business model, i.e., of better customer reach. In line with its business model Eveready has introduced various innovations in distribution to reach the maximum number of customers. Eveready's extensive distribution network includes 1,000 vans, more than 4,000 distributors, and 44 warehouses. These vans reach 60,000 retail outlets directly, each van making 50–60 calls per day.[3] The salesman loads up these vans from the nearest stock point and works the surrounding markets, while moving on to the next stock point.[4]

Similarly, Tata Motors sensing the problem in last-mile connectivity in India, launched its Ace series of mini-trucks in 2005 which has, since then, been a thumping success. Other companies that have embraced rural marketing challenges have been ITC's e-choupal, Unilever, Godrej, etc. These companies have introduced new products and adapted business models to embrace rural market opportunities and challenges.

1. Rural Marketing in India Economy, last updated 25/05/2011, accessed on 25 Oct 2011, from http://business.mapsofindia.com/rural-economy/state-development/marketing.html
2. Eveready Industries India Ltd., Information Update, Financial Results for the quarter ended 30 Jun 2009, accessed on 25 Oct 2011, from http://www.evereadyindustries.com/investors/pdf/EIIL-Update-Q10910.pdf
3. Anderson Jamie & Costas Markides, Strategic Innovation at the Base of the Economic Pyramid, accessed on 25 Oct 2011, from http://www.jamieandersononline.com/uploads/ANDERSON_MARKIDES_SI_at_Base_of_Economic_Pyramid_FINAL.pdf
4. Kashyap Pardeep & Rahul Raut, The Rural Marketing Book, Biztantra Publishers, pg 180, accessed 25 Oct 2011, from http://books.google.co.in/books?id=fTGBFrny6rsC&pg=PA180&lpg=PA180&dq=eveready+and+rural+marketing&source=bl&ots=d-WMbhFE3D&sig=NRCyitz_6QVxHDQFvyIQsbuiZOs&hl=en&ei=jSSqTtiPFY-nrAeg8IW8DA&sa=X&oi=book_result&ct=result&resnum=5&ved=0CEAQ6AEwBA#v=onepage&q=eveready%20and%20rural%20marketing&f=false

Very few corporations include a product's entire value chain. Ford Motor Company did when it was managed by its founder, Henry Ford I. During the 1920s and 1930s, the company owned its own iron mines, ore-carrying ships, and a small rail line to bring ore to its mile-long River Rouge plant in Detroit. Visitors to the plant would walk along an elevated walkway, where they could watch iron ore being dumped from the rail cars into huge furnaces. The resulting steel was poured and rolled out onto a moving belt to be fabricated into auto frames and parts while the visitors watched in awe. As visitors walked along the walkway, they observed an automobile being built piece by piece. Reaching the end of the moving line, the finished automobile was driven out of the plant into a vast adjoining parking lot. Ford trucks would then load the cars for delivery to dealers. Although the Ford dealers were not employees of the company, they had almost no power in the arrangement. Dealerships were awarded by the company and taken away if a dealer was at all disloyal. Ford Motor Company at that time was completely vertically integrated, that is, it controlled (usually by ownership) every stage of the value chain, from the iron mines to the retailers.

FIGURE 5–2
Typical Value
Chain for a
Manufactured
Product

INDUSTRY VALUE-CHAIN ANALYSIS

The value chains of most industries can be split into two segments, *upstream* and *downstream* segments. In the petroleum industry, for example, *upstream* refers to oil exploration, drilling, and moving of the crude oil to the refinery, and *downstream* refers to refining the oil plus transporting and marketing gasoline and refined oil to distributors and gas station retailers. Even though most large oil companies are completely integrated, they often vary in the amount of expertise they have at each part of the value chain. Amoco, for example, had strong expertise downstream in marketing and retailing. British Petroleum, in contrast, was more dominant in upstream activities like exploration. That's one reason the two companies merged to form BP Amoco.

An industry can be analyzed in terms of the profit margin available at any point along the value chain. For example, auto industry's revenues and profits are divided among many value-chain activities, including manufacturing, new and used car sales, gasoline retailing, insurance, after-sales service and parts, and lease financing. From a revenue standpoint, auto manufacturers dominate the industry, accounting for almost 60% of total industry revenues. Profits, however, are a different matter. Auto leasing has been the most profitable activity in the value chain, followed by insurance and auto loans. The core activities of manufacturing and distribution, however, earn significantly smaller shares of the total industry profits than they do of total revenues. For example, because auto sales have become marginally profitable, dealerships are now emphasizing service and repair. As a result of various differences along the industry value chain, manufacturers have moved aggressively into auto financing.[29]

In analyzing the complete value chain of a product, note that even if a firm operates up and down the entire industry chain, it usually has an area of expertise where its primary activities lie. A company's *center of gravity* is the part of the chain that is most important to the company and the point where its greatest expertise and capabilities lie—its core competencies. According to Galbraith, a company's center of gravity is usually the point at which the company started. After a firm successfully establishes itself at this point by obtaining a competitive advantage, one of its first strategic moves is to move forward or backward along the value chain in order to reduce costs, guarantee access to key raw materials, or to guarantee distribution.[30] This process, called *vertical integration,* is discussed in more detail in **Chapter 7**.

In the paper industry, for example, Weyerhauser's center of gravity is in the raw materials and primary manufacturing parts of the value chain as shown in **Figure 5–2**. Weyerhauser's expertise is in lumbering and pulp mills, which is where the company started. It integrated forward by using its wood pulp to make paper and boxes, but its greatest capability still lay in getting the greatest return from its lumbering activities. In contrast, P&G is primarily a consumer products company that also owned timberland and operated pulp mills. Its expertise is in the fabrication and distribution parts of the **Figure 5–2** value chain. P&G purchased these assets to guarantee access to the large quantities of wood pulp it needed to expand its disposable diaper, toilet tissue, and napkin products. P&G's strongest capabilities have always been in the downstream activities of product development, marketing, and brand management. It has never been as efficient in upstream paper activities as Weyerhauser. It had no real distinctive competency on that part of the value chain. When paper supplies became more plentiful (and competition got rougher), P&G gladly sold its land and mills to focus more on the part of the value chain where it could provide the greatest value at the lowest cost—creating and marketing innovative consumer products. As was the case with P&G's experience in the paper industry, it makes sense for a company to outsource any weak areas it may control internally on the industry value chain.

CORPORATE VALUE-CHAIN ANALYSIS

Each corporation has its own internal value chain of activities. See **Figure 5–3** for an example of a corporate value chain. Porter proposes that a manufacturing firm's *primary activities* usually begin with inbound logistics (raw materials handling and warehousing), go through an operations process in which a product is manufactured, and continue on to outbound logistics (warehousing and distribution), to marketing and sales, and finally to service (installation, repair, and sale of parts). Several *support activities*, such as procurement (purchasing), technology development (R&D), human resource management, and firm infrastructure (accounting, finance, strategic planning), ensure that the primary value chain activities operate effectively and efficiently. Each of a company's product lines has its own distinctive value chain. Because most corporations make several different products or services, an internal analysis of the firm involves analyzing a series of different value chains.

The systematic examination of individual value activities can lead to a better understanding of a corporation's strengths and weaknesses. According to Porter, "Differences among competitor value chains are a key source of competitive advantage."[31]. Corporate value chain analysis involves the following three steps:

1. **Examine each product line's value chain in terms of the various activities involved in producing that product or service:** Which activities can be considered strengths (core competencies) or weaknesses (core deficiencies)? Do any of the strengths provide competitive advantage and can they thus be labeled distinctive competencies?

2. **Examine the "linkages" within each product line's value chain:** *Linkages* are the connections between the way one value activity (for example, marketing) is performed and the cost of performance of another activity (for example, quality control). In seeking ways for a corporation to gain competitive advantage in the marketplace, the same function can be performed in different ways with different results. For example, quality inspection of 100% of output by the workers themselves instead of the usual 10% by quality control

FIGURE 5–3
A Corporation's Value Chain

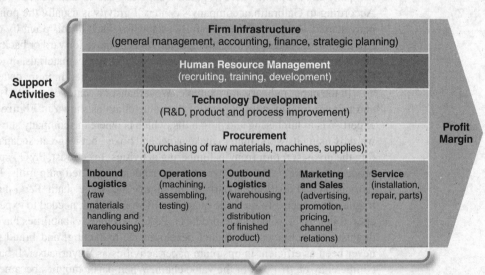

SOURCE: *Reprinted with the permission of The Free Press, a Division of Simon & Schuster, from* COMPETITIVE ADVANTAGE: Creating and Sustaining Superior Performance *by Michael E. Porter. Copyright © 1985, 1998 by The Free Press. All rights reserved.*

inspectors might increase production costs, but that increase could be more than offset by the savings obtained from reducing the number of repair people needed to fix defective products and increasing the amount of salespeople's time devoted to selling instead of exchanging already-sold but defective products.

3. **Examine the potential synergies among the value chains of different product lines or business units:** Each value element, such as advertising or manufacturing, has an inherent economy of scale in which activities are conducted at their lowest possible cost per unit of output. If a particular product is not being produced at a high enough level to reach economies of scale in distribution, another product could be used to share the same distribution channel. This is an example of **economies of scope**, which result when the value chains of two separate products or services share activities, such as the same marketing channels or manufacturing facilities. The cost of joint production of multiple products can be lower than the cost of separate production.

5.4 Scanning Functional Resources and Capabilities

The simplest way to begin an analysis of a corporation's value chain is by carefully examining its traditional functional areas for potential strengths and weaknesses. Functional resources and capabilities include not only the financial, physical, and human assets in each area but also the ability of the people in each area to formulate and implement the necessary functional objectives, strategies, and policies. These resources and capabilities include the knowledge of analytical concepts and procedural techniques common to each area as well as the ability of the people in each area to use them effectively. If used properly, these resources and capabilities serve as strengths to carry out value-added activities and support strategic decisions. In addition to the usual business functions of marketing, finance, R&D, operations, human resources, and information systems/technology, we also discuss structure and culture as key parts of a business corporation's value chain.

BASIC ORGANIZATIONAL STRUCTURES

Although there is an almost infinite variety of structural forms, certain basic types predominate in modern complex organizations. **Figure 5–4** illustrates three basic **organizational structures**. The conglomerate structure is a variant of divisional structure and is thus not depicted as a fourth structure. Generally speaking, each structure tends to support some corporate strategies over others:

- **Simple structure** has no functional or product categories and is appropriate for a small, entrepreneur-dominated company with one or two product lines that operates in a reasonably small, easily identifiable market niche. Employees tend to be generalists and jacks-of-all-trades. In terms of stages of development (to be discussed in **Chapter 9**), this is a Stage I company.

- **Functional structure** is appropriate for a medium-sized firm with several product lines in one industry. Employees tend to be specialists in the business functions that are important to that industry, such as manufacturing, marketing, finance, and human resources. In terms of stages of development (discussed in **Chapter 9**), this is a Stage II company.

- **Divisional structure** is appropriate for a large corporation with many product lines in several related industries. Employees tend to be functional specialists organized according to product/market distinctions. General Motors, for example, groups its various auto lines into the separate divisions of Saturn, Chevrolet, Pontiac, Buick, and Cadillac. Management

FIGURE 5–4
Basic
Organizational
Structures

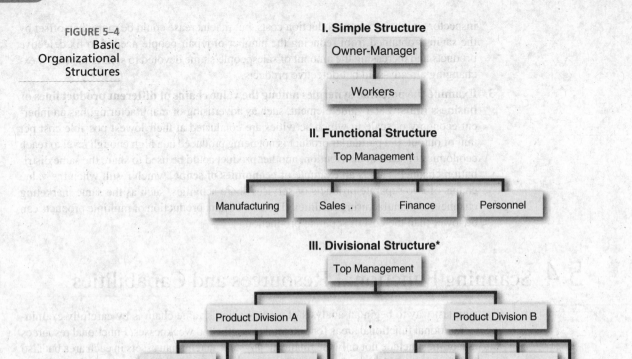

I. Simple Structure

Owner-Manager

Workers

II. Functional Structure

Top Management

Manufacturing   Sales   Finance   Personnel

III. Divisional Structure*

Top Management

Product Division A   Product Division B

Manufacturing   Finance   Manufacturing   Finance

Sales   Personnel   Sales   Personnel

*Strategic Business Units and the conglomerate structure are variants of the divisional structure.

attempts to find some synergy among divisional activities through the use of committees and horizontal linkages. In terms of stages of development (to be discussed in **Chapter 9**), this is a Stage III company.

■ **Strategic business units (SBUs)** are a modification of the divisional structure. Strategic business units are divisions or groups of divisions composed of independent product-market segments that are given primary responsibility and authority for the management of their own functional areas. *An SBU may be of any size or level, but it must have (1) a unique mission, (2) identifiable competitors, (3) an external market focus, and (4) control of its business functions.*[32] The idea is to decentralize on the basis of strategic elements rather than on the basis of size, product characteristics, or span of control and to create horizontal linkages among units previously kept separate. For example, rather than organize products on the basis of packaging technology like frozen foods, canned foods, and bagged foods, General Foods organized its products into SBUs on the basis of consumer-oriented menu segments: breakfast food, beverage, main meal, dessert, and pet foods. In terms of stages of development (to be discussed in **Chapter 9**), this is also a Stage III company.

■ **Conglomerate structure** is appropriate for a large corporation with many product lines in several unrelated industries. A variant of the divisional structure, the conglomerate structure (sometimes called a holding company) is typically an assemblage of legally independent firms (subsidiaries) operating under one corporate umbrella but controlled through the subsidiaries' boards of directors. The unrelated nature of the subsidiaries prevents any attempt at gaining synergy among them. In terms of stages of development (discussed in **Chapter 9**), this is also a Stage III company.

If the current basic structure of a corporation does not easily support a strategy under consideration, top management must decide whether the proposed strategy is feasible or whether the structure should be changed to a more advanced structure such as a matrix or network. (Advanced structural designs such as the matrix and network are discussed in **Chapter 9**.)

CORPORATE CULTURE: THE COMPANY WAY

There is an oft-told story of a person new to a company asking an experienced co-worker what an employee should do when a customer calls. The old-timer responded: "There are three ways to do any job—the right way, the wrong way, and the company way. Around here, we always do things the company way." In most organizations, the "company way" is derived from the corporation's culture. **Corporate culture** is the collection of beliefs, expectations, and values learned and shared by a corporation's members and transmitted from one generation of employees to another. The corporate culture generally reflects the values of the founder(s) and the mission of the firm.[33] It gives a company a sense of identity: "This is who we are. This is what we do. This is what we stand for." The culture includes the dominant orientation of the company, such as R&D at HP, high productivity at Nucor, customer service at Nordstrom, innovation at Google, or product quality at BMW. It often includes a number of informal work rules (forming the "company way") that employees follow without question. These work practices over time become part of a company's unquestioned tradition. The culture, therefore, reflects the company's values.

Corporate culture has two distinct attributes, intensity and integration.[34] *Cultural intensity* is the degree to which members of a unit accept the norms, values, or other culture content associated with the unit. This shows the culture's depth. Organizations with strong norms promoting a particular value, such as quality at BMW, have intensive cultures, whereas new firms (or those in transition) have weaker, less intensive cultures. Employees in an intensive culture tend to exhibit consistent behavior, that is, they tend to act similarly over time. *Cultural integration* is the extent to which units throughout an organization share a common culture. This is the culture's breadth. Organizations with a pervasive dominant culture may be hierarchically controlled and power-oriented, such as a military unit, and have highly integrated cultures. All employees tend to hold the same cultural values and norms. In contrast, a company that is structured into diverse units by functions or divisions usually exhibits some strong subcultures (for example, R&D versus manufacturing) and a less integrated corporate culture.

Corporate culture fulfills several important functions in an organization:

1. Conveys a sense of identity for employees.
2. Helps generate employee commitment to something greater than themselves.
3. Adds to the stability of the organization as a social system.
4. Serves as a frame of reference for employees to use to make sense of organizational activities and to use as a guide for appropriate behavior.[35]

Corporate culture shapes the behavior of people in a corporation, thus affecting corporate performance. For example, corporate cultures that emphasize the socialization of new employees have less employee turnover, leading to lower costs.[36] Because corporate cultures have a powerful influence on the behavior of people at all levels, they can strongly affect a corporation's ability to shift its strategic direction. A strong culture should not only promote survival, but it should also create the basis for a superior competitive position by increasing motivation

GLOBAL issue

MANAGING CORPORATE CULTURE FOR GLOBAL COMPETITIVE ADVANTAGE: ABB VERSUS MATSUSHITA

Zurich-based ABB Asea Brown Boveri AG is a worldwide builder of power plants, electrical equipment, and industrial factories in 140 countries. By establishing one set of multicultural values throughout its global operations, ABB's management believes that the company will gain an advantage over its rivals Siemens AG of Germany, France's Alcatel-Alsthom NV, and the U.S.'s General Electric Company. ABB is a company with no geographic base. Instead, it has many "home" markets that can draw on expertise from around the globe. ABB created a set of 500 global managers who could adapt to local cultures while executing ABB's global strategies. These people are multilingual and move around each of ABB's 5,000 profit centers in 140 countries. Their assignment is to cut costs, improve efficiency, and integrate local businesses with the ABB worldview.

Few multinational corporations are as successful as ABB in getting global strategies to work with local operations. In agreement with the resource-based view of the firm, the past Chairman of ABB, Percy Barnevik, stated, "Our strength comes from pulling together. . . . If you can make this work real well, then you get a competitive edge out of the organization which is very, very difficult to copy."

Contrast ABB's globally-oriented corporate culture with the more Japanese-oriented parochial culture of Matsushita Electric Industrial Corporation (MEI) of Japan. Operating under the brand names of Panasonic and Technic,

MEI is the third-largest electrical company in the world. Konosuke Matsushita founded the company in 1918. His management philosophy led to the company's success but became institutionalized in the corporate culture—a culture that was more focused on Japanese values than on cross-cultural globalization. As a result, MEI's corporate culture does not adapt well to local conditions. Not only is MEI's top management *exclusively* Japanese, its subsidiary managers are *overwhelmingly* Japanese. The company's distrust of non-Japanese managers in the United States and some European countries results in a "rice-paper ceiling" that prevents non-Japanese people from being promoted into MEI subsidiaries' top management. Foreign employees are often confused by the corporate philosophy that has not been adapted to suit local realities. MEI's corporate culture perpetuates a cross-cultural divide that separates the Japanese from the non-Japanese managers, leaving the non-Japanese managers feeling frustrated and undervalued. This divide prevents the flow of knowledge and experience from regional operations to the headquarters and may hinder MEI's ability to compete globally.

....

SOURCES: Summarized from J. Guyon, "ABB Fuses Units with One Set of Values," *Wall Street Journal* (October 2, 1996), p. A15 and N. Holden, "Why Globalizing with a Conservative Corporate Culture Inhibits Localization of Management: The Telling Case of Matsushita Electric," *International Journal of Cross Cultural Management*, Vol. 1, No. 1 (2001), pp. 53–72.

and facilitating coordination and control.[37] For example, a culture emphasizing constant renewal may help a company adapt to a changing, hypercompetitive environment.[38] To the extent that a corporation's distinctive competence is embedded in an organization's culture, it will be a form of tacit knowledge and very difficult for a competitor to imitate. The **Global Issue** feature shows the differences between ABB Asea Brown Boveri AG and Matsushita Electric in terms of how they manage their corporate cultures in a global industry.

A change in mission, objectives, strategies, or policies is not likely to be successful if it is in opposition to the accepted culture of a firm. Foot-dragging and even sabotage may result, as employees fight to resist a radical change in corporate philosophy. As with structure, if an organization's culture is compatible with a new strategy, it is an internal strength. But if the corporate culture is not compatible with the proposed strategy, it is a serious weakness.

Corporate culture is also important when considering an acquisition. The merging of two dissimilar cultures, if not handled wisely, can create some serious internal conflicts. Procter & Gamble's management knew, for example, that their 2005 acquisition of Gillette might create some cultural problems. Even though both companies were strong consumer goods marketers, they each had a fundamental difference that led to many, subtle differences between the cultures: Gillette sold its razors, toothbrushes, and batteries to men; whereas, P&G sold its health and beauty aids to women. Art Lafley, P&G's CEO, admitted a year after the merger that it would take an additional year to 15 months to align the two companies.[39]

STRATEGIC MARKETING ISSUES

The marketing manager is a company's primary link to the customer and the competition. The manager, therefore, must be especially concerned with the market position and marketing mix of the firm as well as with the overall reputation of the company and its brands.

Market Position and Segmentation

Market position deals with the question, "Who are our customers?". It refers to the selection of specific areas for marketing concentration and can be expressed in terms of market, product, and geographic locations. Through market research, corporations are able to practice *market segmentation* with various products or services so that managers can discover what niches to seek, which new types of products to develop, and how to ensure that a company's many products do not directly compete with one another.

Marketing Mix

Marketing mix refers to the particular combination of key variables under a corporation's control that can be used to affect demand and to gain competitive advantage. These variables are product, place, promotion, and price. Within each of these four variables are several subvariables, listed in **Table 5–1**, that should be analyzed in terms of their effects on divisional and corporate performance.

Product Life Cycle

One of the most useful concepts in marketing, insofar as strategic management is concerned, is the **product life cycle**. As depicted in **Figure 5–5**, the product life cycle is a graph showing time plotted against the monetary sales of a product as it moves from introduction through growth and maturity to decline. This concept enables a marketing manager to examine the marketing mix of a particular product or group of products in terms of its position in its life cycle.

TABLE 5–1	Product	Place	Promotion	Price
Marketing Mix Variables	Quality	Channels	Advertising	List price
	Features	Coverage	Personal selling	Discounts
	Options	Locations	Sales promotion	Allowances
	Style	Inventory	Publicity	Payment periods
	Brand name	Transport		Credit items
	Packaging			
	Sizes			
	Services			
	Warranties			
	Returns			

SOURCE: KOTLER, PHILIP, MARKETING MANAGEMENT, 11th edition © 2003, p. 16. Reprinted by Pearson Education, Inc., Upper Saddle River, NJ.

Brand and Corporate Reputation

A **brand** is a name given to a company's product which identifies that item in the mind of the consumer. Over time and with proper advertising, a brand connotes various characteristics in the consumers' minds. For example, Disney stands for family entertainment. Ivory suggests "pure" soap. BMW means high-performance autos. A brand can thus be an important corporate resource. If done well, a brand name is connected to the product to such an extent that a brand may stand for an entire product category, such as Kleenex for facial tissue. The objective is for the customer to ask for the brand name (Coke or Pepsi) instead of the product category (cola). The world's 10 most valuable brands in 2007 were Coca-Cola, Microsoft, IBM, GE, Nokia, Toyota, Intel, McDonald's, Disney, and Mercedes-Benz, in that order. According to *Business Week*, the value of the Coca-Cola brand is worth $65.3 billion.[40] Tata, Reliance Anil Dhirubhai Ambani Group, and Airtel were identified as the top three most valuable brands in India by 4Ps Business and Marketing magazine in its annual ranking 2008.[41] Other brands in the top 10 included Maruti, Reliance Industries, ICICI, Infosys, Hero Honda, Times of India, and Maggi.

A *corporate brand* is a type of brand in which the company's name serves as the brand. Of the world's top 10 world brands listed previously, all are company names. The value of a corporate brand is that it typically stands for consumers' impressions of a company and can thus be extended onto products not currently offered—regardless of the company's actual expertise. For example, Caterpillar, a manufacturer of heavy earth-moving equipment, used consumer associations with the Caterpillar brand (*rugged, masculine, construction-related*) to market work boots. Thus, consumer impressions of a brand can suggest new product categories to enter even though a company may have no competencies in making or marketing that type of product or service.[42]

A **corporate reputation** is a widely held perception of a company by the general public. It consists of two attributes: (1) stakeholders' perceptions of a corporation's ability to produce quality goods and (2) a corporation's prominence in the minds of stakeholders.[43] A good corporate reputation can be a strategic resource. It can serve in marketing as both a signal and an entry barrier. It contributes to its goods having a price premium.[44] Reputation is especially important when the quality of a company's product or service is not directly

FIGURE 5–5
Product Life Cycle

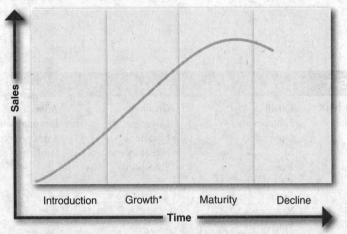

* The right end of the Growth stage is often called Competitive Turbulence because of price and distribution competition that shakes out the weaker competitors. For further information, see C. R. Wasson, *Dynamic Competitive Strategy and Product Life Cycles*. 3rd ed. (Austin, TX: Austin Press, 1978).

observable and can be learned only through experience. For example, retail stores are willing to stock a new product from P&G or Anheuser-Busch because they know that both companies market only good-quality products that are highly advertised. Like tacit knowledge, reputation tends to be long-lasting and hard for others to duplicate—thus providing sustainable competitive advantage.[45] It can have a significant impact on a firm's stock price.[46] Research reveals a positive relationship between corporate reputation and financial performance.[47]

STRATEGIC FINANCIAL ISSUES

A financial manager must ascertain the best sources of funds, uses of funds, and control of funds. All strategic issues have financial implications. Cash must be raised from internal or external (local and global) sources and allocated for different uses. The flow of funds in the operations of an organization must be monitored. To the extent that a corporation is involved in international activities, currency fluctuations must be dealt with to ensure that profits aren't wiped out by the rise or fall of the dollar versus the yen, euro, or other currencies. Benefits in the form of returns, repayments, or products and services must be given to the sources of outside financing. All these tasks must be handled in a way that complements and supports overall corporate strategy. A firm's capital structure (amounts of debt and equity) can influence its strategic choices. For example, increased debt tends to increase risk aversion and decrease the willingness of management to invest in R&D.[48]

Financial Leverage

The mix of externally generated short-term and long-term funds in relation to the amount and timing of internally generated funds should be appropriate to the corporate objectives, strategies, and policies. The concept of **financial leverage** (the ratio of total debt to total assets) is helpful in describing how debt is used to increase the earnings available to common shareholders. When the company finances its activities by sales of bonds or notes instead of through stock, the earnings per share are boosted: the interest paid on the debt reduces taxable income, but fewer shareholders share the profits than if the company had sold more stock to finance its activities. The debt, however, does raise the firm's break-even point above what it would have been if the firm had financed from internally generated funds only. High leverage may therefore be perceived as a corporate strength in times of prosperity and ever-increasing sales, or as a weakness in times of a recession and falling sales. This is because leverage acts to magnify the effect on earnings per share of an increase or decrease in dollar sales. Research indicates that greater leverage has a positive impact on performance for firms in stable environments, but a negative impact for firms in dynamic environments.[49]

Capital Budgeting

Capital budgeting is the analyzing and ranking of possible investments in fixed assets such as land, buildings, and equipment in terms of the additional outlays and additional receipts that will result from each investment. A good finance department will be able to prepare such capital budgets and to rank them on the basis of some accepted criteria or *hurdle rate* (for example, years to pay back investment, rate of return, or time to break-even point) for the purpose of strategic decision making. Most firms have more than one hurdle rate and vary it as a function of the type of project being considered. Projects with high strategic significance, such as entering new markets or defending market share, will often have low hurdle rates.[50]

STRATEGIC RESEARCH AND DEVELOPMENT (R&D) ISSUES

The R&D manager is responsible for suggesting and implementing a company's technological strategy in light of its corporate objectives and policies. The manager's job, therefore, involves (1) choosing among alternative new technologies to use within the corporation, (2) developing methods of embodying the new technology in new products and processes, and (3) deploying resources so that the new technology can be successfully implemented.

R&D Intensity, Technological Competence, and Technology Transfer

The company must make available the resources necessary for effective research and development. A company's **R&D intensity** (its spending on R&D as a percentage of sales revenue) is a principal means of gaining market share in global competition. The amount spent on R&D often varies by industry. In recent years research and development (R&D) is vital to the success, and even the survival, of almost any business technological innovation and is a primary competitive factor across virtually all industries. Statistics show that over past few years the R&D expenditure by Indian companies has increased. Some statistics estimate that R&D expenditure accounts for less than 1% of GDP.[51] Accounting for 2% of global R&D outlays in 2010, Chinese and Indian headquartered companies upped R&D investment by more than 38%, almost identical to the previous year's growth pace.[52] Experts predict that the next big technological innovations could emerge from India, China, or Russia.

This has been attributed to the presence of organizations which are providing state of art technology and on the job training to the population of these countires. More than 150 MNCs have a presence in the Indian research and development industry. For example, Microsoft has built its largest development centre outside the United States in India, GE has an R&D centre in Bangalore, Dell has a facility in Bangalore, the Daimler-Chrysler Research Centre, Royal Shell Group centre in Bangalore, Rolls-Royce has tied up with the Indian Institute of Science (IISc), Bangalore, and the Imperial College of UK to work jointly on developing alloys for developing "greener" aircraft engines.[53] A good rule of thumb for R&D spending is that a corporation should spend at a "normal" rate for that particular industry unless its strategic plan calls for unusual expenditures.

Simply spending money on R&D or new projects does not mean, however, that the money will produce useful results. For example, Pharmacia Upjohn spent more of its revenues on research than any other company in any industry (18%), but it was ranked low in innovation.[54] A company's R&D unit should be evaluated for **technological competence** in both the development and the use of innovative technology. Not only should the corporation make a consistent research effort (as measured by reasonably constant corporate expenditures that result in usable innovations), it should also be proficient in managing research personnel and integrating their innovations into its day-to-day operations. A company should also be proficient in **technology transfer**, the process of taking a new technology from the laboratory to the marketplace. Aerospace parts maker Rockwell Collins, for example, is a master of developing new technology, such as the "heads-up display" (transparent screens in an airplane cockpit that tell pilots speed, altitude, and direction), for the military and then using it in products built for the civilian market.[55]

R&D Mix

Basic R&D is conducted by scientists in well-equipped laboratories where the focus is on theoretical problem areas. The best indicators of a company's capability in this area are its patents and research publications. *Product R&D* concentrates on marketing and is concerned with product or product-packaging improvements. The best measurements of ability in this area are the number of successful new products introduced and the percentage of total sales and profits coming from products introduced within the past five years. *Engineering (or process) R&D*

is concerned with engineering, concentrating on quality control, and the development of design specifications and improved production equipment. A company's capability in this area can be measured by consistent reductions in unit manufacturing costs and by the number of product defects.

Most corporations will have a mix of basic, product, and process R&D, which varies by industry, company, and product line. The balance of these types of research is known as the **R&D mix** and should be appropriate to the strategy being considered and to each product's life cycle. For example, it is generally accepted that product R&D normally dominates the early stages of a product's life cycle (when the product's optimal form and features are still being debated), whereas process R&D becomes especially important in the later stages (when the product's design is solidified and the emphasis is on reducing costs and improving quality).

Impact of Technological Discontinuity on Strategy

The R&D manager must determine when to abandon present technology and when to develop or adopt new technology. Richard Foster of McKinsey and Company states that the displacement of one technology by another (**technological discontinuity**) is a frequent and strategically important phenomenon. Such a discontinuity occurs when a new technology cannot simply be used to enhance the current technology, but actually substitutes for that technology to yield better performance. For each technology within a given field or industry, according to Foster, the plotting of product performance against research effort/expenditures on a graph results in an S-shaped curve. He describes the process depicted in **Figure 5–6**:

> *Early in the development of the technology a knowledge base is being built and progress requires a relatively large amount of effort. Later, progress comes more easily. And then, as the limits of that technology are approached, progress becomes slow and expensive. That is when R&D dollars should be allocated to technology with more potential. That is also—not so incidentally— when a competitor who has bet on a new technology can sweep away your business or topple an entire industry.*[56]

FIGURE 5–6
Technological Discontinuity

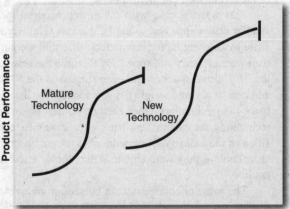

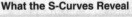

What the S-Curves Reveal

Mature Technology

New Technology

Product Performance

Research Effort/Expenditure

In the corporate planning process, it is generally assumed that incremental progress in technology will occur. But past developments in a given technology cannot be extrapolated into the future because every technology has its limits. The key to competitiveness is to determine when to shift resources to a technology that has more potential.

SOURCE: *From "Are You Investing in the Wrong Technology?" P. Pascarella, Industry Week, July 25, 1983. Reprinted by permission of Penton Media, Inc.*

Computerized information technology is currently on the steep upward slope of its S-curve in which relatively small increments in R&D effort result in significant improvement in performance. This is an example of *Moore's Law*, which states that silicon chips (microprocessors) double in complexity every 18 months.[57] The presence of a technological discontinuity in the world's steel industry during the 1960s explains why the large capital expenditures by U.S. steel companies failed to keep them competitive with the Japanese firms that adopted the new technologies. As Foster points out, "History has shown that as one technology nears the end of its S-curve, competitive leadership in a market generally changes hands."[58]

Christensen explains in *The Innovator's Dilemma* why this transition occurs when a "disruptive technology" enters an industry. In a study of computer disk drive manufacturers, he explains that established market leaders are typically reluctant to move in a timely manner to a new technology. This reluctance to switch technologies (even when the firm is aware of the new technology and may have even invented it!) is because the resource allocation process in most companies gives priority to those projects (typically based on the old technology) with the greatest likelihood of generating a good return on investment—those projects appealing to the firm's current customers (whose products are also based on the characteristics of the old technology). For example, in the 1980s a disk drive manufacturer's customers (PC manufacturers) wanted a better (faster) 5 1/4″ drive with greater capacity. These PC makers were not interested in the new 3 1/2″ drives based on the new technology because (at that time) the smaller drives were slower and had less capacity. Smaller size was irrelevant since these companies primarily made desk top personal computers which were designed to hold large drives.

The new technology is generally riskier and of little appeal to the current customers of established firms. Products derived from the new technology are more expensive and do not meet the customers' requirements—requirements based on the old technology. New entrepreneurial firms are typically more interested in the new technology because it is one way to appeal to a developing market niche in a market currently dominated by established companies. Even though the new technology may be more expensive to develop, it offers performance improvements in areas that are attractive to this small niche, but of no consequence to the customers of the established competitors.

This was the case with the entrepreneurial manufacturers of 3 1/2″ disk drives. These smaller drives appealed to the PC makers who were trying to increase their small PC market share by offering laptop computers. Size and weight were more important to these customers than were capacity and speed. By the time the new technology was developed to the point that the 3 1/2″ drive matched and even surpassed the 5 1/4″ drive in terms of speed and capacity (in addition to size and weight), it was too late for the established 5 1/4″ disk drive firms to switch to the new technology. Once their customers begin demanding smaller products using the new technology, the established firms were unable to respond quickly and lost their leadership position in the industry. They were able to remain in the industry (with a much reduced market share) only if they were able to utilize the new technology to be competitive in the new product line.[59]

The same phenomenon can be seen in many product categories ranging from flat-panel display screens to railroad locomotives to digital photography to musical recordings. For example, George Heilmeier created the first practical liquid-crystal display (LCD) in 1964 at RCA Labs. RCA unveiled the new display in 1968 with much fanfare about LCDs being the future of TV sets, but then refused to fund further development of the new technology. In contrast, Japanese television and computer manufacturers invested in long-term development of LCDs. Today, Japanese, Korean, and Taiwanese companies dominate the $39 billion LCD business and RCA no longer makes televisions. Interestingly, Heilmeier received the Kyoto Prize in 2005 for his LCD invention.[60]

STRATEGIC OPERATIONS ISSUES

The primary task of the operations (manufacturing or service) manager is to develop and operate a system that will produce the required number of products or services, with a certain quality, at a given cost, within an allotted time. Many of the key concepts and techniques popularly used in manufacturing can be applied to service businesses.

In very general terms, manufacturing can be intermittent or continuous. In *intermittent systems* (job shops), the item is normally processed sequentially, but the work and sequence of the process vary. An example is an auto body repair shop. At each location, the tasks determine the details of processing and the time required for them. These job shops can be very labor intensive. For example, a job shop usually has little automated machinery and thus a small amount of fixed costs. It has a fairly low break-even point, but its variable cost line (composed of wages and costs of special parts) has a relatively steep slope. Because most of the costs associated with the product are variable (many employees earn piece-rate wages), a job shop's variable costs are higher than those of automated firms. Its advantage over other firms is that it can operate at low levels and still be profitable. After a job shop's sales reach break-even, however, the huge variable costs as a percentage of total costs keep the profit per unit at a relatively low level. In terms of strategy, this firm should look for a niche in the marketplace for which it can produce and sell a reasonably small quantity of custom-made goods.

In contrast, *continuous systems* are those laid out as lines on which products can be continuously assembled or processed. An example is an automobile assembly line. A firm using continuous systems invests heavily in fixed investments such as automated processes and highly sophisticated machinery. Its labor force, relatively small but highly skilled, earns salaries rather than piece-rate wages. Consequently, this firm has a high amount of fixed costs. It also has a relatively high break-even point, but its variable cost line rises slowly. This is an example of **operating leverage**, the impact of a specific change in sales volume on net operating income. The advantage of high operating leverage is that once the firm reaches break-even, its profits rise faster than do those of less automated firms having lower operating leverage. Continuous systems reap benefits from economies of scale. In terms of strategy, this firm needs to find a high-demand niche in the marketplace for which it can produce and sell a large quantity of goods. However, a firm with high operating leverage is likely to suffer huge losses during a recession. During an economic downturn, the firm with less automation and thus less leverage is more likely to survive comfortably because a drop in sales primarily affects variable costs. It is often easier to lay off labor than to sell off specialized plants and machines.

Experience Curve

A conceptual framework that many large corporations have used successfully is the experience curve (originally called the learning curve). The **experience curve** suggests that unit production costs decline by some fixed percentage (commonly 20%–30%) each time the total accumulated volume of production in units doubles. The actual percentage varies by industry and is based on many variables: the amount of time it takes a person to learn a new task, scale economies, product and process improvements, and lower raw materials cost, among others. For example, in an industry with an 85% experience curve, a corporation might expect a 15% reduction in unit costs for every doubling of volume. The total costs per unit can be expected to drop from $100 when the total production is 10 units, to $85 ($100 x 85%) when production increases to 20 units, and to $72.25 ($85 x 85%) when it reaches 40 units. Achieving these results often means investing in R&D and fixed assets; higher fixed costs and less flexibility thus result. Nevertheless the manufacturing strategy is one of building capacity ahead of demand in order to achieve the lower unit costs that develop from the experience curve. On the basis of some future point on the experience curve, the corporation should price the product or service very low to preempt competition and increase market demand. The resulting high number of units sold and high market share should result in high profits, based on the low unit costs.

Management commonly uses the experience curve in estimating the production costs of (1) a product never before made with the present techniques and processes or (2) current products produced by newly introduced techniques or processes. The concept was first applied in the airframe industry and can be applied in the service industry as well. For example, a cleaning company can reduce its costs per employee by having its workers use the same equipment and techniques to clean many adjacent offices in one office building rather than just cleaning a few offices in multiple buildings. Although many firms have used experience curves extensively, an unquestioning acceptance of the industry norm (such as 80% for the airframe industry or 70% for integrated circuits) is very risky. The experience curve of the industry as a whole might not hold true for a particular company for a variety of reasons.[61]

Flexible Manufacturing for Mass Customization

The use of large, continuous, mass-production facilities to take advantage of experience-curve economies has recently been criticized. The use of Computer-Assisted Design and Computer-Assisted Manufacturing (CAD/CAM) and robot technology means that learning times are shorter and products can be economically manufactured in small, customized batches in a process called *mass customization*—the low-cost production of individually customized goods and services.[62] Economies of scope (in which common parts of the manufacturing activities of various products are combined to gain economies even though small numbers of each product are made) replace **Economies of scale** (in which unit costs are reduced by making large numbers of the same product) in flexible manufacturing. *Flexible manufacturing* permits the low-volume output of custom-tailored products at relatively low unit costs through economies of scope. It is thus possible to have the cost advantages of continuous systems with the customer-oriented advantages of intermittent systems. The auto maker, BMW, for example, uses flexible manufacturing to customize cars to suit each buyer's preference. It replaced its two assembly lines in its Spartanburg, South Carolina, plant with one flexible assembly line in 2006. According to spokesperson Bunny Richardson, "Until now, if we wanted to introduce an additional model, we'd have to construct a new line."[63]

STRATEGIC HUMAN RESOURCE (HRM) ISSUES

The primary task of the manager of human resources is to improve the match between individuals and jobs. Research indicates that companies with good HRM practices have higher profits and a better survival rate than do firms without these practices.[64] A good HRM department should know how to use attitude surveys and other feedback devices to assess employees' satisfaction with their jobs and with the corporation as a whole. HRM managers should also use job analysis to obtain job description information about what each job needs to accomplish in terms of quality and quantity. Up-to-date job descriptions are essential not only for proper employee selection, appraisal, training, and development for wage and salary administration, and for labor negotiations, but also for summarizing the corporate-wide human resources in terms of employee-skill categories. Just as a company must know the number, type, and quality of its manufacturing facilities, it must also know the kinds of people it employs and the skills they possess. The best strategies are meaningless if employees do not have the skills to carry them out or if jobs cannot be designed to accommodate the available workers. IBM, Procter & Gamble, and Hewlett-Packard, for example, use employee profiles to ensure that they have the best mix of talents to implement their planned strategies. Because project managers at IBM are now able to scan the company's databases to identify employee capabilities and availability, the average time needed to assemble a team has declined 20% for a savings of $500 million overall.[65]

Increasing Use of Teams

Management is beginning to realize that it must be more flexible in its utilization of employees in order for human resources to be classified as a strength. Human resource managers, therefore, need to be knowledgeable about work options such as part-time work, job sharing, flex-time, extended leaves, and contract work, and especially about the proper use of teams. Many companies in India are autonomous (self managing work teams), in which group of people work together without a surpervisor to plan, coordinate, and evaluate their own work. For example, in India, Murugappa Group by adopting this strategy at one of its plants found that it increased productivity and quality. Murugappa Group is one of India's leading business conglomerates and market leaders in diverse areas of business including engineering, abrasives, finance, general insurance, cycles, sugar, farm inputs, fertilizers, plantations, bio-products, and nutraceuticals. Its 29 businesses have manufacturing facilities spread across 13 states in India.[66] The strategy was adopted at the Pudukottai plant. This is a greenfield project that was completed in a record time of 270 days. It is India's first fully automated sugar plant, with outsourced maintenance functions. Autonomous work culture is the process of developing a style of work that leads to a lean and responsive work structure. The work culture has facilitated free communication and transparency in dealings, incremented employee morale, and created an environment of trust and openness.[67]

As a way to move a product more quickly through its development stage, companies like Motorola, Chrysler, NCR, Boeing, and General Electric are using *cross-functional work teams*. Instead of developing products in a series of steps—beginning with a request from sales, which leads to design, then to engineering and on to purchasing, and finally to manufacturing (and often resulting in a costly product rejected by the customer)—companies are tearing down the traditional walls separating the departments so that people from each discipline can get involved in projects early on. In a process called *concurrent engineering*, the once-isolated specialists now work side by side and compare notes constantly in an effort to design cost-effective products with features customers want. Taking this approach enabled Chrysler Corporation to reduce its product development cycle from 60 to 36 months.[68] For such cross-functional work teams to be successful, the groups must receive training and coaching. Otherwise, poorly implemented teams may worsen morale, create divisiveness, and raise the level of cynicism among workers.[69]

Virtual teams are groups of geographically and/or organizationally dispersed coworkers that are assembled using a combination of telecommunications and information technologies to accomplish an organizational task.[70] In the U.S. alone, more than half of companies having over 5,000 employees use virtual teams involving around 8.4 million people.[71] According to the Gartner Group, more than 60% of professional employees now work in virtual teams.[72] Internet, intranet, and extranet systems are combining with other new technologies, such as desktop video conferencing and collaborative software, to create a new workplace in which teams of workers are no longer restrained by geography, time, or organizational boundaries. This technology allows about 12% of the U.S. workforce, who have no permanent office at their companies, to do team projects over the Internet and report to a manager thousands of miles away. More than 20 million people in the U.S. are engaged in telecommuting.[73] Charles Grantham of Work Design Collaborative predicts that 40% of the workforce will be working remotely by 2012.[74] In India the BPO industry boom is a resultant of virtual team philosophy. At a generic level, business process outsourcing (BPO) industry is organized around virtual team model in one way or the other. BPO is one of the fastest growing segments of Information Technology Enabled Services (ITES) industry.[75] According to a study, "Roadmap 2012 – capitalising on the expanding BPO landscape", conducted by Nasscom and Everest Group, the revenue of the Indian BPO industry is expected to touch $50 billion. This will add 2.5% to the gross domestic product by 2012. Currently, the sector employs 7 lakh people, and has annual revenue of about $11 billion. Over the next 5 years the BPO industry will give employment opportunities to about 2 million people.[76]

As more companies outsource some of the activities previously conducted internally, the traditional organizational structure is being replaced by a series of virtual teams, which rarely, if ever, meet face-to-face. Such teams may be established as temporary groups to accomplish a specific task or may be more permanent to address continuing issues such as strategic planning. Membership on these teams is often fluid, depending upon the task to be accomplished. They may include not only employees from different functions within a company, but also members of various stakeholder groups, such as suppliers, customers, and law or consulting firms. The use of virtual teams to replace traditional face-to-face work groups is being driven by five trends:

1. Flatter organizational structures with increasing cross-functional coordination need
2. Turbulent environments requiring more inter-organizational cooperation
3. Increasing employee autonomy and participation in decision making
4. Higher knowledge requirements derived from a greater emphasis on service
5. Increasing globalization of trade and corporate activity[77]

5.5 Union Relations and Temporary/Part-Time Workers

If a corporation is unionized, a good human resource manager should be able to work closely with the union. In India, Trade Unions Act 1926 provides recognition to labor unions and union membership is concentrated in the organized sector, and affiliated with regional or national federations such as the Indian National Trade Union Congress, the All-India Trade Union Congress, the Centre of Indian Trade Unions, etc.[78] The Economic Survey 2010–2011 shows that in the year 2010, according to provisional Labour Bureau data, there were 79 strikes in 2010, the calculation of loss of productivity due to industrial disruptions was around 17 lakh days lost in 2010.[79] Changing trends in Indian trade have led to increased acceptance of trade unions to both workers and employers, who find their demands and patterns of negotiations more reasonable and in accordance with the current situation. This has led to affiliated plant level trade unions, which if tapped properly, can help in increasing efficiency across various aspects of organization. For example, quality of work life (QWL) among other factors depends upon organizationally driven factors like policies and procedures such as training and education, grievance handling, career advancement opportunities, monetary benefits, etc. An effective relationship with trade unions can help design and implement policies which contribute to better QWL.[80]

To save jobs and increase the standards of living of workers, Indian unions are increasingly willing to support new strategic initiatives and employee involvement programs. These unions not only support strategic initiatives but are also involved in welfare activities of their own, such as providing housing and organizing cooperative societies to improve the quality of workers' lives. For example, the Textile Labour Association (TLA), Ahmedabad, has ventured to organize self-employed women in the Self Employed Women's Association (SEWA) and has even started banking activities for this purpose.[81]

Outside India, the union role are influenced by culture for example: European unions tend to be militant, politically oriented, and much less interested in working with management to increase efficiency. Nationwide strikes occur quickly. In contrast, Japanese unions are typically tied to individual companies and are usually supportive of management. These differences among countries have significant implications for the management of multinational corporations.

To increase flexibility, avoid layoffs, and reduce labor costs, corporations are using more temporary workers.[82] Retailers, business process outsourcing providers and project-led organisations, and industries were first ones to adopt temporary hiring model. However, motivated by the advantages, off late the temporary model has been adopted by new sectors such as energy, healthcare, and pharmaceuticals sectors in India.[83] Temporary employees are being used for both blue-collared and white-collared functions. In India, almost 80 million people

ENVIRONMENTAL sustainability issue

USING ENERGY EFFICIENCY FOR COMPETITIVE ADVANTAGE AND QUALITY OF WORK LIFE

Amory Lovins, Co-founder and Chairman of the Rocky Mountain Institute, works to educate business executives on how the efficient use of energy can lead not only to lower costs, but also to competitive advantage and increased labor productivity. His Rocky Mountain Institute is a nonprofit organization that develops and implements programs for energy and resource efficiency. According to Lovins:

In my team's latest redesigns for $30 billion worth of facilities in 29 sectors, we consistently found about 30 to 60 percent energy savings that could be captured through retrofits, which paid for themselves in two to three years. In new facilities, 40 to 90 percent savings could be gleaned—and with nearly always lower capital cost.

Lovins' Rocky Mountain Institute promotes the use of *micropower*, on-site or decentralized energy production, such as waste-heat, or gas-fired cogeneration, wind and solar power, geothermal, small hydro, and waste- or biomass-fueled plants. Lovins points out that a sixth of the world's electricity and a third of new electricity now comes from micropower because it's cheaper with lower financial risk.

Lovins points out that energy redesigns often have side effects that may be far more valuable than the direct savings. For example, a typical office pays around 160 times more in payroll than for energy. According to Lovins, his programs routinely get a 6% to 16% increase gain in labor productivity in more efficient buildings having improved thermal, visual, and acoustic comfort. "When people can see what they are doing, hear themselves think, breathe cleaner air, and feel more comfortable, they do more and better work," says Lovins.

SOURCE: Material based on M. Hirschland, J. M. Oppenheim, and A. P. Webb, "Using Energy More Efficiently: An Interview with the Rocky Mountain Institute's Amory Lovins," *McKinsey Quarterly* (July 2008), pp. 1–7.

---

are working on temporary basis, however a meager 0.5% of them are employed in the organized sector. Some estimates put the number of temperory workers at about 120,000 to 130,000 in over 500 companies, including ICICI Lombard, Bharti, Reliance Infocomm, HP, Wipro BPO, Transworks, and so on.[84] These workers though temporary, work more or equal to permanent employees and are still paid at a lower rate than the full-time permanent employees.

Quality of Work Life and Human Diversity

Human resource departments have found that to reduce employee dissatisfaction and unionization efforts (or, conversely, to improve employee satisfaction and existing union relations), they must consider the *quality of work life* in the design of jobs. Partially a reaction to the traditionally heavy emphasis on technical and economic factors in job design, quality of work life emphasizes improving the human dimension of work. The knowledgeable human resource manager, therefore, should be able to improve the corporation's quality of work life by (1) introducing participative problem solving, (2) restructuring work, (3) introducing innovative reward systems, and (4) improving the work environment. It is hoped that these improvements will lead to a more participative corporate culture and thus higher productivity and quality products. Ford Motor Company, for example, rebuilt and modernized its famous River Rouge plant using flexible equipment and new processes. Employees work in teams and use Internet-connected PCs on the shop floor to share their concerns instantly with suppliers or product engineers. Workstations were redesigned to make them more ergonomic and reduce repetitive-strain injuries. "If you feel good while you're working, I think quality and productivity will increase, and Ford thinks that too, otherwise, they wouldn't do this," observed Jerry Sullivan, president of United Auto Workers Local 600.[85]

Companies are also discovering that by redesigning their plants and offices for improved energy efficiency, they can receive a side effect of improving their employees' quality of work life—thus raising labor productivity. See the **Environmental Sustainability Issue** feature to learn how improved energy efficiency can not only cut costs, but also boost employee morale.

Human diversity refers to the mix in the workplace of people from different races, cultures, and backgrounds. Realizing that the demographics are changing toward an increasing percentage of minorities and women in the U.S. workforce, companies are now concerned with hiring and promoting people without regard to ethnic background. Research does indicate that an increase in racial diversity leads to an increase in firm performance.[86] In a survey of 131 leading European companies, 67.2% stated that a diverse work force can provide competitive advantage.[87] A manager from Nestlé stated: "To deliver products that meet the needs of individual consumers, we need people who respect other cultures, embrace diversity, and never discriminate on any basis."[88] Good human resource managers should be working to ensure that people are treated fairly on the job and not harassed by prejudiced co-workers or managers. Otherwise, they may find themselves subject to lawsuits. Coca-Cola Company, for example, agreed to pay $192.5 million because of discrimination against African-American salaried employees in pay, promotions, and evaluations from 1995 and 2000. According to Chairman and CEO Douglas Daft, "Sometimes things happen in an unintentional manner. And I've made it clear that can't happen anymore."[89]

An organization's human resources may be a key to achieving a sustainable competitive advantage. Advances in technology are copied almost immediately by competitors around the world. People, however, are not as willing to move to other companies in other countries. This means that the only long-term resource advantage remaining to corporations operating in the industrialized nations may lie in the area of skilled human resources.[90] Research does reveal that competitive strategies are more successfully executed in those companies with a high level of commitment to their employees than in those firms with less commitment.[91]

STRATEGIC INFORMATION SYSTEMS/TECHNOLOGY ISSUES

The primary task of the manager of information systems/technology is to design and manage the flow of information in an organization in ways that improve productivity and decision making. Information must be collected, stored, and synthesized in such a manner that it will answer important operating and strategic questions. A corporation's information system can be a strength or a weakness in multiple areas of strategic management. It can not only aid in environmental scanning and in controlling a company's many activities, it can also be used as a strategic weapon in gaining competitive advantage.

Impact on Performance

Information systems/technology offers four main contributions to corporate performance. *First,* (beginning in the 1970s with mainframe computers) it is used to automate existing back-office processes, such as payroll, human resource records, accounts payable and receivable, and to establish huge databases. *Second,* (beginning in the 1980s) it is used to automate individual tasks, such as keeping track of clients and expenses, through the use of personal computers with word processing and spreadsheet software. Corporate databases are accessed to provide sufficient data to analyze the data and create what-if scenarios. These first two contributions tend to focus on reducing costs. *Third,* (beginning in the 1990s) it is used to enhance key business functions, such as marketing and operations. This third contribution focuses on productivity improvements. The system provides customer support and help in distribution and logistics. For example, Federal Express found that by allowing customers to directly access its package-tracking database via its Internet Web site instead of their having to ask a human operator, the company saved up to $2 million annually.[92] Business processes are analyzed to increase efficiency and productivity via reengineering. Enterprise resource planning (ERP) application software, such as SAP, PeopleSoft, Oracle, Baan, and J.D. Edwards, is used to integrate worldwide business activities so that employees need to enter information only once and that information is available to all corporate systems (including accounting) around the world. *Fourth*, (beginning in 2000) it is used to develop competitive advantage. For example, American Hospital Supply (AHS), a leading manufacturer and distributor of a broad line of products for doctors, laboratories, and hospitals, developed an order entry distribution system that directly linked the majority of its customers to AHS computers. The system was successful because it simplified ordering processes for customers, reduced costs for both AHS and the customer, and allowed AHS to provide pricing incentives to the customer. As a result, customer loyalty was high and AHS's share of the market became large.

A current trend in corporate information systems/technology is the increasing use of the Internet for marketing, intranets for internal communication, and extranets for logistics and distribution. An *intranet* is an information network within an organization that also has access to the external worldwide Internet. Intranets typically begin as ways to provide employees with company information such as lists of product prices, fringe benefits, and company policies. They are then converted into extranets for supply chain management. An *extranet* is an information network within an organization that is available to key suppliers and customers. The key issue in building an extranet is the creation of "fire walls" to block extranet users from accessing the firm's or other users' confidential data. Once this is accomplished, companies can allow employees, customers, and suppliers to access information and conduct business on the Internet in a completely automated manner. By connecting these groups, companies hope to obtain a competitive advantage by reducing the time needed to design and bring new products to market, slashing inventories, customizing manufacturing, and entering new markets.[93]

A recent development in information systems/technology is Web 2.0. *Web 2.0* refers to the use of wikis, blogs, RSS (Really Simple Syndication), social networks (e.g., MySpace and Facebook), podcasts, and mash-ups through company Web sites to forge tighter links with customers and suppliers and to engage employees more successfully. A 2008 survey by McKinsey revealed the percentage of companies using individual Web 2.0 technologies to be Web services (58%), blogs (34%), RSS (33%), wikis (32%), podcasts (29%), social networking (28%), peer-to-peer (18%), and mash-ups (10%). The most heavily used tool is Web services, software that makes it easier to exchange information and conduct transactions. Wikis and blogs are being increasingly used in companies throughout the world. Satisfied users of these information technologies report that they are using these tools to interact with their customers, suppliers, and outside experts in product development efforts known as *co-creation*. For example, LEGO invited customers to suggest new models interactively and then financially rewarded the people whose ideas proved marketable.[94]

Supply Chain Management

The expansion of the marketing-oriented Internet into intranets and extranets is making significant contributions to organizational performance through supply chain management. **Supply chain management** is the forming of networks for sourcing raw materials, manufacturing products or creating services, storing and distributing the goods, and delivering them to customers and consumers.[95] Research indicates that supplier network resources have a significant impact on firm performance.[96] A survey of global executives revealed that their interest in supply chains was first to reduce costs, and then to improve customer service and get new products to market faster.[97] More than 85% of senior executives stated that improving their firm's supply-chain performance was a top priority. Companies, like Wal-Mart, Dell, and Toyota, who are known to be exemplars in supply-chain management, spend only 4% of their revenues on supply chain costs compared to 10% by the average firm.[98]

Industry leaders are integrating modern information systems into their corporate value chains to harmonize companywide efforts and to achieve competitive advantage. For example, Heineken beer distributors input actual depletion figures and replenishment orders to the

Netherlands brewer through their linked Web pages. This interactive planning system generates time-phased orders based on actual usage rather than on projected demand. Distributors are then able to modify plans based on local conditions or changes in marketing. Heineken uses these modifications to adjust brewing and supply schedules. As a result of this system, lead times have been reduced from the traditional 10–12 weeks to 4–6 weeks. This time savings is especially useful in an industry competing on product freshness. In another example, Procter & Gamble participates in an information network to move the company's line of consumer products through Wal-Mart's many stores. *Radio-frequency identification (RFID)* tags containing product information is used to track goods through inventory and distribution channels. As part of the network with Wal-Mart, P&G knows by cash register and by store what products have passed through the system every hour of each day. The network is linked by satellite communications on a real-time basis. With actual point-of-sale information, products are replenished to meet current demand and minimize stockouts while maintaining exceptionally low inventories.[99]

5.6 The Strategic Audit: A Checklist for Organizational Analysis

One way of conducting an organizational analysis to ascertain a company's strengths and weakness is by using the Strategic Audit found in **Appendix 1.A** at the end of Chapter 1. The audit provides a checklist of questions by area of concern. For example, Part IV of the audit examines corporate structure, culture, and resources. It looks at organizational resources and capabilities in terms of the functional areas of marketing, finance, R&D, operations, human resources, and information systems, among others.

5.7 Synthesis of Internal Factors

After strategists have scanned the internal organizational environment and identified factors for their particular corporation, they may want to summarize their analysis of these factors using a form such as that given in **Table 5–2**. This **IFAS (Internal Factor Analysis Summary) Table** is one way to organize the internal factors into the generally accepted categories of strengths and weaknesses as well as to analyze how well a particular company's management is responding to these specific factors in light of the perceived importance of these factors to the company. Use the VRIO framework (**V**alue, **R**areness, **I**mitability, & **O**rganization) to assess the importance of each of the factors that might be considered strengths. Except for its internal orientation, this IFAS Table is built the same way as the EFAS Table described in **Chapter 4** (in **Table 4–5**). To use the IFAS Table, complete the following steps:

1. In **Column 1** (*Internal Factors*), list the eight to ten most important strengths and weaknesses facing the company.

2. In **Column 2** (*Weight*), assign a weight to each factor from **1.0** (*Most Important*) to **0.0** (*Not Important*) based on that factor's probable impact on a particular company's current strategic position. The higher the weight, the more important is this factor to the current and future success of the company. **All weights must sum to 1.0 regardless of the number of factors.**

| TABLE 5–2 | Internal Factor Analysis Summary (IFAS Table): Maytag as Example |

Internal Factors	Weight	Rating	Weighted Score	Comments
1	2	3	4	5
Strengths				
■ Quality Maytag culture	.15	5.0	.75	Quality key to success
■ Experienced top management	.05	4.2	.21	Know appliances
■ Vertical integration	.10	3.9	.39	Dedicated factories
■ Employer relations	.05	3.0	.15	Good, but deteriorating
■ Hoover's international orientation	.15	2.8	.42	Hoover name in cleaners
Weaknesses				
■ Process-oriented R&D	.05	2.2	.11	Slow on new products
■ Distribution channels	.05	2.0	.10	Superstores replacing small dealers
■ Financial position	.15	2.0	.30	High debt load
■ Global positioning	.20	2.1	.42	Hoover weak outside the United Kingdom and Australia
■ Manufacturing facilities	.05	4.0	.20	Investing now
Total Scores	**1.00**		**3.05**	

NOTES:

1. List strengths and weaknesses (8–10) in Column 1.
2. Weight each factor from **1.0** (Most Important) to **0.0** (Not Important) in Column 2 based on that factor's probable impact on the company's strategic position. **The total weights must sum to 1.00.**
3. Rate each factor from **5.0** (Outstanding) to **1.0** (Poor) in Column 3 based on the company's response to that factor.
4. Multiply each factor's weight times its rating to obtain each factor's weighted score in Column 4.
5. Use Column 5 (comments) for rationale used for each factor.
6. Add the individual weighted scores to obtain the total weighted score for the company in Column 4. This tells how well the company is responding to the factors in its internal environment.

SOURCE: T.L. Wheelen & J.D. Hunger, "Internal Factor Analysis Summary (IFAS)" Copyright © 1987, 1988, 1989, 1990 and 2005 by T.L. Wheelen. Copyright © 1991, 2003, and 2005 by Wheelen and Hunger Associates. Reprinted by permission.

3. In **Column 3** (*Rating*), assign a rating to each factor from **5.0** (*Outstanding*) to **1.0** (*Poor*) based on management's specific response to that particular factor. Each rating is a judgment regarding how well the company's management is currently dealing with each specific internal factor.

4. In **Column 4** (*Weighted Score*), multiply the weight in **Column 2** for each factor times its rating in **Column 3** to obtain that factor's weighted score.

5. In **Column 5** (*Comments*), note why a particular factor was selected and/or how its weight and rating were estimated.

6. Finally, add the weighted scores for all the internal factors in **Column 4** to determine the total weighted score for that particular company. The **total weighted score** indicates how well a particular company is responding to current and expected factors in its internal environment. The score can be used to compare that firm to other firms in its industry. Check to ensure that the total weighted score truly reflects the company's current performance in terms of profitability and market share. **The total weighted score for an average firm in an industry is always 3.0.**

Let's Summarize the Chapter with a Mind Map

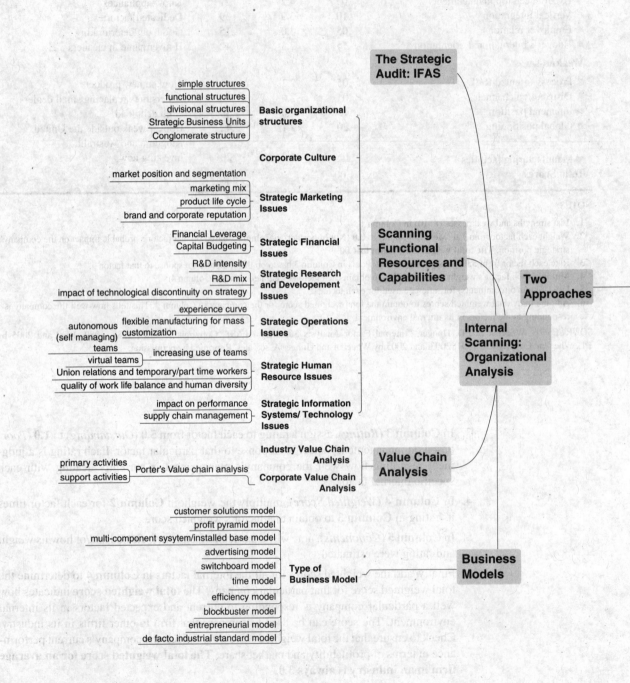

The Strategic Audit: IFAS

- simple structures
- functional structures
- divisional structures
- Strategic Business Units
- Conglomerate structure

Basic organizational structures

Corporate Culture

- market position and segmentation
- marketing mix
- product life cycle
- brand and corporate reputation

Strategic Marketing Issues

- Financial Leverage
- Capital Budgeting

Strategic Financial Issues

- R&D intensity
- R&D mix
- impact of technological discontinuity on strategy

Strategic Research and Developement Issues

- experience curve
- flexible manufacturing for mass customization

Strategic Operations Issues

- autonomous (self managing) teams
- virtual teams
- increasing use of teams
- Union relations and temporary/part time workers
- quality of work life balance and human diversity

Strategic Human Resource Issues

- impact on performance
- supply chain management

Strategic Information Systems/ Technology Issues

Scanning Functional Resources and Capabilities

Industry Value Chain Analysis

- primary activities
- support activities

Porter's Value chain analysis

Corporate Value Chain Analysis

Value Chain Analysis

Internal Scanning: Organizational Analysis

Two Approaches

- customer solutions model
- profit pyramid model
- multi-component sysytem/installed base model
- advertising model
- switchboard model
- time model
- efficiency model
- blockbuster model
- entrepreneurial model
- de facto industrial standard model

Type of Business Model

Business Models

Resource Based View

Competence and Distinctive Competencies

- resources — are an organization's assets and are thus basic building blocks of the organization
- capabilities — refers to a corporation's ability to exploit its resources
- competence — is a cross functional integration and coordination of capabilities
- core competence — is a collection of competencies that crosses divisional boundaries, is widespread within the corporation, and is something that the corporation can do exceedingly well.
  - model to evaluate core competencies (VRIO)
    - value: does it provide customer value and competitive advantage?
    - rareness: Do no other competitors possess it?
    - imitability: is it costly for others to imitate
    - organization — is the firm organized to export?
  - Distinctive competencies: when core competencies are superior to those of the competition

Use resources to gain competitive advantage

- five step research based approach to strategy analysis
  - identify and classify firm's resources into strengths and weaknesses
  - combine strengths into capabilities and core competencies
  - appraise the profit potential of these capabilities and core competencies for sustainable competitive advantage and above average rate of returns
  - select strategy based on core competence and capabilities
  - identify resource gaps and invest in upgrading weaknesses
- where do core competencies come from?
  - asset endowment coming from founding company
  - acquired from someone else
  - shared with another business unit or alliance partner
  - carefully built and accumulated over time by the company

Determining the sustainability of an advantage

- durability — is the rate at which a firm's underlying resources, capabilities or core competencies depreciate or become obsolete
- imitability — is the rate at which a firm's underlying resources, capabilities or core competencies can be duplicated by others
  - transparency — is the speed with which firms can understand the relationship of resources and capabilities supporting a firm strategy
  - transferability — is the ability of competitor to gather the resources and capabilities necessary to support a competitive challenge
  - replicability — is the ability of competitors to use duplicated resources and capabilities to imitate the other firms success.
- knowledge
  - explicit
  - tacit
- sustainability
  - slow cycle resource
  - standard cycle resource
  - fast cycle resource

Industrial Organization View

Opposite to the resource based view. Talks in terms of outside approach to environmental scanning. Assumes 100% mobility of resources and capabilities. Dictates that a company should see what industry requires to be successful and then acquire them.

As an example of this procedure, **Table 5–2** includes a number of internal factors for Maytag Corporation in 1995 (before Maytag was acquired by Whirlpool) with corresponding weights, ratings, and weighted scores provided. Note that Maytag's total weighted score is 3.05, meaning that the corporation is about average compared to the strengths and weaknesses of others in the major home appliance industry.

ECO-BITS

- The average number of plastic bottles used each year in the U.S. per person: 200
- The average number of plastic bottles recycled each year in the U.S. per person: 40

- Revenue produced in 2007 by recycling and ancillary industries: $236 billion
- Share of electronic waste that is hauled overseas, stripped unsafely, and dumped: 80%[101]

DISCUSSION QUESTIONS

1. What is the relevance of the resource-based view of the firm to strategic management in a global environment?

2. How can value-chain analysis help identify a company's strengths and weaknesses?

3. In what ways can a corporation's structure and culture be internal strengths or weaknesses?

4. What are the pros and cons of management's using the experience curve to determine strategy?

5. How might a firm's management decide whether it should continue to invest in current known technology or in new, but untested technology? What factors might encourage or discourage such a shift?

6. What is IFAS? Preapre an IFAS for a company and discuss the analysis.

7. Compare and contrast EFAS and IFAS matrixes.

8. Discuss what is strategic audit and its utility to an organization. Outline the checklist for organizational analysis.

9. What is a business model? Study any one industry and discuss the business models of three companies which have succeeded in innovating the conventional business models.

10. "The concept of core competence does not exist in the industrial organization based approach to strategy" Do you agree or disagree? Please explain.

11. Write short notes on following:
   a. Strategic audit
   b. Supply chain management
   c. Issue of QWL and human diversity in organizations
   d. Technological discontinuity.

STRATEGIC PRACTICE EXERCISES

Can you analyze a corporation using the Internet? Try the following exercise.

1. Form into teams of around three to five people. Select a well-known publicly owned company to research. Inform the instructor of your choice.

2. Assign each person a separate task. One task might be to find the latest financial statements. Another would be to learn as much as possible about its top management and board of directors. Another might be to identify its business model. Another might be to identify its key competitors.

3. Conduct research on the company *using the Internet only*.

4. Meet with your team members to discuss what you have found. What are the company's opportunities, threats, strengths, and weaknesses? Go back to the Internet for more information, if needed.

5. Prepare a 3- to 5 page typed report of the company. The report should include the following:
   a. Does the firm have any core competencies? Are any of these distinctive (better than the competition) competencies? Does the firm have any competitive advantage? Provide a SWOT analysis using EFAS and IFAS Tables.
   b. What is the likely future of this firm if it continues on its current path?
   c. Would you buy stock in this company? Assume that your team has $25,000 to invest. Allocate the money among the four to five primary competitors in this industry. List the companies, the number of shares purchased of each, the cost of each share as of a given date, and the total cost for each purchase assuming a typical commission used by an Internet broker, such as E-Trade or Scottrade.

KEY TERMS

brand (p. 180)

business model (p. 170)

capabilities (p. 166)

capital budgeting (p. 181)

competency (p. 166)

conglomerate structure (p. 176)

continuum of sustainability (p. 169)

core competencies (p. 166)

corporate culture (p. 177)

corporate reputation (p. 180)

distinctive competencies (p. 166)

divisional structure (p. 175)

durability (p. 168)

economies of scale (p. 186)

economies of scope (p. 175)

experience curve (p. 185)

explicit knowledge (p. 169)

financial leverage (p. 181)

functional structure (p. 175)

IFAS Table (p. 192)

imitability (p. 168)

marketing mix (p. 179)

operating leverage (p. 185)

organizational analysis (p. 166)

organizational structures (p. 175)

product life cycle (p. 179)

R&D intensity (p. 182)

R&D mix (p. 183)

replicability (p. 169)

resource (p. 166)

simple structure (p. 175)

strategic business units (SBUs) (p. 176)

supply chain management (p. 191)

tacit knowledge (p. 169)

technological competence (p. 182)

technological discontinuity (p. 183)

technology transfer (p. 182)

transferability (p. 169)

transparency (p. 168)

value chain (p. 171)

virtual teams (p. 187)

VRIO framework (p. 166)

NOTES

1. D. Welch and N. Lakshman, "My Other Car Is a Tata," *Business Week* (January 14, 2008), pp. 33–34.

2. R. M. Grant, *Contemporary Strategy Analysis*, 6th edition (Malden, MA: Blackwell Publishing, 2008), pp. 130–131.

3. G. Schreyogg and M. Kliesch-Eberl, "How Dynamic Can Organizational Capabilities Be? Towards a Dual-Process Model of Capability Dynamization," *Strategic Management Journal* (September 2007), pp. 913–933.

4. M. Javidan, "Core Competence: What Does It Mean in Practice?" *Long Range Planning* (February 1998), pp. 60–71.

5. M. A. Hitt, B. W. Keats, and S. M. DeMarie, "Navigating in the New Competitive Landscape: Building Strategic Flexibility and Competitive Advantage in the 21st Century," *Academy of Management Executive* (November 1998), pp. 22–42; C. E. Helfat and M. A. Peteraf, "The Dynamic Resources-Based View: Capability Life Cycles," *Strategic Management Journal* (October 2003), pp. 997–1010.

6. D. Brady and K. Capell, "GE Breaks the Mold to Spur Innovation," *Business Week* (April 26, 2004), pp. 88–89.

7. J. B. Barney, *Gaining and Sustaining Competitive Advantage*. 2nd ed. (Upper Saddle River, NJ: Prentice Hall, 2002), pp. 159–172. Barney's VRIO questions are very similar to those proposed by G. Hamel and S. K. Prahalad in their book, *Competing for the Future* (Boston: Harvard Business School Press, 1994) on pages 202–207 in which they state that to be distinctive, a competency must (a) provide customer value, (b) be competitor unique, and (c) be extendable to develop new products and/or markets.

8. S. L. Newbert, "Value, Rareness, Competitive Advantage, and Performance: A Conceptual-Level Empirical Investigation of the Resource-Based View of the Firm," *Strategic Management Journal* (July 2008), pp. 745–768.

9. Barney, p. 161.

10. Karjewski Lee j., Ritzman Larry P. and Malhotra Manoj K., Operations Management: Processes and Value Chains, Dorling Kindersley (India) Pvt. Ltd, New Delhi, 2008, pg 54.

11. R. M. Grant, "The Resource-Based Theory of Competitive Advantage: Implications for Strategy Formulation," *California Management Review* (Spring 1991), pp. 114–135.

12. P. J. Verdin, and P. J. Williamson, "Core Competencies, Competitive Advantage and Market Analysis: Forging the Links," in *Competence-Based Competition*, edited by G. Hamel and A. Heene (New York: John Wiley and Sons, 1994), pp. 83–84; S. K. Ethiraj, P. Kale, M. S. Krishnan, and J. V. Singh, "Where Do Capabilities Come From and How Do They Matter? A Study in the Software Services Industry," *Strategic Management Journal* (January 2005), pp. 701–719.

13. J. Devan, M. B. Klusas, and T. W. Ruefli, "The Elusive Goal of Corporate Outperformance," *McKinsey Quarterly Online* (April 2007).

14. Tatiana Khomiakova, Information Technology Clusters in India, Transition Studies Review, Vol 14, Number 2/November, 2007, Springer Wien, 355-378.

15. Taeube Florian & Petra Sonderegger, Cluster Lifecyle And Diaspora Effects: Evidence From The Indian IT Cluster In Bangalore, June 17 - 19, 2009, Paper to be presented at the Summer Conference 2009 CBS - Copenhagen Business School, recovered on 25th Oct 2011, from http://www2.druid.dk/conferences/viewpaper.php?id=5468&cf=32

16. Business Week, India's Silicon Valley, recovered on 25th Oct 2011, from http://www.businessweek.com/adsections/indian/infotech/2001/silicon.html

17. Lee Yue Man, Sarah Pinto, Rupert Simons, Nina Stochniol & Clara Zverina, The Gujarat Diamond Cluster: Is It Forever?, Microeconomics of Competitiveness Spring 2008, May 2nd 2008, recovered on 25th Oct 2011, from http://www.isc. hbs.edu/pdf/Student_Projects/India_(Gujarat)_Diaonds_2008.pdf

18. NMCC Govt. of India, Surat Diamond Cluster, recovered on 25th Oct 2011 from http://nmcc-vikas.gov.in/Cluster/SuratDiamond.aspx

19. NMCC Govt. of India, Surat Diamond Cluster, recovered on 25th Oct 2011 from http://nmcc-vikas.gov.in/clusters.html

20. M. Polanyi, *The Tacit Dimension* (London: Routledge & Kegan Paul, 1966).

21. S. K. McEvily and B. Chakravarthy, "The Persistence of Knowledge-Based Advantage: An Empirical Test for Product Performance and Technological Knowledge," *Strategic Management Journal* (April 2002), pp. 285–305.

22. K. Maney, "Dell Business Model Turns to Muscle as Rivals Struggle," *USA Today* (January 20, 2003), p. 2B.

23. P. E. Bierly III, "Development of a Generic Knowledge Strategy Typology," *Journal of Business Strategies* (Spring 1999), p. 3.

24. R. W. Coff, D. C. Coff, and R. Eastvold, "The Knowledge-Leveraging Paradox: How to Achieve Scale Without Making Knowledge Imitable," *Academy of Management Review* (April 2006), pp. 452–465.

25. D. Welch and N. Lakshman, p. 33.

26. S. Abraham, "Experiencing Strategic Conversations about the Central Forces of our Time," *Strategy & Leadership*, Vol. 31, No. 2 (2003), pp. 61–62.

27. C. A. de Kluyver and J. A. Pearce II, *Strategy: A View from the Top* (Upper Saddle River, NJ: Prentice Hall, 2003), pp. 63–66.

28. P. Burrows, "Ever Wonder Why Ink Costs So Much?" *Business Week* (November 14, 2005), pp. 42–44.

29. O. Gadiesh and J. L. Gilbert, "Profit Pools: A Fresh Look at Strategy," *Harvard Business Review* (May–June, 1998). pp. 139–147.

30. J. R. Galbraith, "Strategy and Organization Planning," in *The Strategy Process: Concepts, Contexts, and Cases*, 2nd ed., edited by H. Mintzberg and J. B. Quinn (Englewood Cliffs, N.J.: Prentice Hall, 1991), pp. 315–324.

31. M. Porter, *Competitive Advantage: Creating and Sustaining Superior Performance* (New York: The Free Press, 1985), p. 36.

32. M. Leontiades, "A Diagnostic Framework for Planning," *Strategic Management Journal* (January–March 1983), p. 14.

33. E. H. Schein, *The Corporate Culture Survival Guide* (San Francisco: Jossey-Bass, 1999), p. 12; L. C. Harris and E. Ogbonna, "The Strategic Legacy of Company Founders," *Long Range Planning* (June 1999), pp. 333–343.

34. D. M. Rousseau, "Assessing Organizational Culture: The Case for Multiple Methods," in *Organizational Climate and Culture*, edited by B. Schneider (San Francisco: Jossey-Bass, 1990), pp. 153–192.

35. L. Smircich, "Concepts of Culture and Organizational Analysis," *Administrative Science Quarterly* (September 1983), pp. 345–346; D. Ravasi and M. Schultz, "Responding to Organizational Identity Threats: Exploring the Role of Organizational Culture," *Academy of Management Journal* (June 2006), pp. 433–458.

36. D. G. Allen, "Do Organizational Socialization Tactics Influence Newcomer Embeddedness and Turnover?" *Journal of Management* (April 2006), pp. 237–256.

37. J. B. Sorensen, "The Strength of Corporate Culture and the Reliability of Firm Performance," *Administrative Science Quarterly* (March 2002), pp. 70–91; R. E. Smerek and D. R. Denison, "Social Capital in Organizations: Understanding the Link to Firm Performance," presentation to the *Academy of Management* (Philadelphia, 2007).

38. K. E. Aupperle, "Spontaneous Organizational Reconfiguration: A Historical Example Based on Xenophon's Anabasis," *Organization Science* (July–August 1996), pp. 445–460.

39. "Face Value: A Post-Modern Proctoid," *The Economist* (April 15, 2006), p. 68.

40. D. Kiley, B. Helm, L. Lee, G. Edmundson, C. Edwards, and M. Scott, "Best Global Brands," *Business Week* (August 6, 2007), pp. 56–64.

41. IBNlive, Brand value: 100 companies which make India proud, posted on Fri, Aug 08, 2008 at 16:33, Updated on Tue, Aug 12, 2008 at 00:06 in Business section, recovered on 25th Oct 2011, from Cable News Network LP, LLLP. A Time Warner Company website http://ibnlive.in.com/news/brand-value-100-companies-which-make-india-proud/70685-7.html

42. R. T. Wilcox, "The Hidden Potential of Powerful Brands," *Batten Briefings* (Summer 2003), pp. 1, 4–5.

43. V. P. Rindova, I. O. Williamson, A. P. Petkova, and J. M. Sever, "Being Good or Being Known: An Empirical Examination of the Dimensions, Antecedents, and Consequences of Organizational Reputation," *Academy of Management Journal* (December 2005), pp. 1033–1049.

44. V. P. Rindova, I. O. Williamson, A. P. Petkova, and J. M. Sever, "Being Good or Being Known: An Empirical Examination of the Dimensions, Antecedents, and Consequences of Organizational Reputation," *Academy of Management Journal* (December 2005), pp. 1033–1049.

45. C. Fombrun and C. Van Riel, "The Reputational Landscape," Corporate Reputation Review, Vol. 1, Nos. 1&2 (1997), pp. 5–13.

46. P. Engardio and M. Arndt, "What Price Reputation?" *Business Week* (July 9 & 16, 2007), pp. 70–79.

47. P. W. Roberts and G. R. Dowling, "Corporate Reputation and Sustained Financial Performance," *Strategic Management Journal* (December 2002), pp. 1077–1093; J. Shamsie, "The Context of Dominance: An Industry-Driven Framework for Exploiting Reputation," *Strategic Management Journal* (March 2003), pp. 199–215; M. D. Michalisin, D. M. Kline, and R. D. Smith, "Intangible Strategic Assets and Firm Performance: A Multi-Industry Study of the Resource-Based View," *Journal of Business Strategies* (Fall 2000), pp. 91–117; S. S. Standifird, "Reputation and E-Commerce: eBay Auctions and the Asymmetrical Impact of Positive and Negative Ratings," *Journal of Management*, Vol. 27, No. 3 (2001), pp. 279–295.

48. R. L. Simerly and M. Li, "Environmental Dynamism, Capital Structure and Performance: A Theoretical Integration and an Empirical Test," *Strategic Management Journal* (January 2000), pp. 31–49.

49. R. L. Simerly and M. Li, "Environmental Dynamism, Capital Structure and Performance: A Theoretical Integration and an Empirical Test," *Strategic Management Journal* (January 2000), pp. 31–49; A. Heisz and S. LaRochelle-Cote, "Corporate Financial Leverage in Canadian Manufacturing: Consequences for Employment and Inventories," *Canadian Journal of Administrative Science* (June 2004), pp. 111–128.

50. J. M. Poterba and L. H. Summers, "A CEO Survey of U.S. Companies' Time Horizons and Hurdle Rates," *Sloan Management Review* (Fall 1995), pp. 43–53.

51. Girish K. R. and Kanchan Dinakar, More tax incentives needed for R&D, The Hindu Business Line, posted on Saturday, Feb 23, 2008, recovered on 25th Oct 2011, from http://www.thehindubusinessline.com/2008/02/23/stories/2008022350460900.htm

52. Booz&Co., Corporate R&D Spending Rebounds In 2010, Finds Booz & Company Global Innovation 1000 Study, posted on New York, NY, October 24, 2011, recovered on 25th Oct 2011, from http://www.booz.com/global/home/press/article/ 49852237

53. IBEF (India Brand Equity Foundation), Research and Development, posted on December 2007 , recovered on 25th Oct 2011, from http://www.ibef.org/industry/research.aspx

54. B. O'Reilly, "The Secrets of America's Most Admired Corporations: New Ideas and New Products," *Fortune* (March 3, 1997), p. 62.

55. C. Palmeri, "Swords to Plowshares—And Back Again," *Business Week* (February 11, 2008), p. 66.

56. P. Pascarella, "Are You Investing in the Wrong Technology?" *Industry Week* (July 25, 1983), p. 37.

57. D. J. Yang, "Leaving Moore's Law in the Dust," *U.S. News & World Report* (July 10, 2000), pp. 37–38; R. Fishburne and M. Malone, "Laying Down the Laws: Gordon Moore and Bob Metcalfe in Conversation," *Forbes ASAP* (February 21, 2000), pp. 97–100.

58. Pascarella, p. 38.

59. C. M. Christensen, *The Innovator's Dilemma* (Boston: Harvard Business School Press, 1997).

60. O. Port, "Flat-Panel Pioneer," *Business Week* (December 12, 2005), p. 22. This phenomenon has also been discussed in terms of paradigm shifts in which a new development makes the old game obsolete—See Joel A. Barker, *Future Edge* (New York: William Morrow and Company, 1992).

61. For examples of experience curves for various products, see M. Gottfredson, S. Schaubert, and H. Saenz, "The New Leader's Guide to Diagnosing the Business," *Harvard Business Review* (February 2008), pp. 63–73.

62. B. J. Pine, *Mass Customization: The New Frontier in Business Competition* (Boston: Harvard Business School Press, 1993).

63. D. Coates, "The Art of Assembly," *Sports Car International* (September 2007), p. 14; "One Line for Two: Spartanburg Revamps Assembly Process," *Roundel* (January 2006), p. 31.

64. S. L Rynes, K. G. Brown, and A. E. Colbert, "Seven Common Misconceptions about Human Resource Practices: Research Findings Versus Practitioner Belief," *Academy of Management Executive* (August 2002), pp. 92–103; R. S. Schuler and S. E. Jackson, "A Quarter-Century Review of Human Resource Management in the U.S.: The Growth in Importance of the International Perspective," in *Strategic Human Resource Management*, 2nd ed., edited by R. S. Schuler and S. E. Jackson (Malden, MA: Blackwell Publishing, 2007), pp. 214–240; M. Guthridge and A. B. Komm, "Why Multinationals Struggle to Manage Talent," *McKinsey Quarterly* (May 2008), pp. 1–5.

65. J. McGregor and S. Hamm, "Managing the Global Workforce," *Business Week* (January 28, 2008), pp. 34–48; D. A. Ready and J. A. Conger, "Make Your Company a Talent Factory," *Harvard Business Review* (June 2007), pp. 68–77.

66. Murugappa Group, Group profile, recovered on 25th Oct 2011, from http://www.murugappa.com/corporate/group_profile.htm

67. Murugappa Group, HR Initiatives And Welfare Programmes, recovered on 25th Oct 2011, from http://www.murugappa.com/companies/eidparry/hr_initiatives.htm

68. R. Sanchez, "Strategic Flexibility in Product Competition," *Strategic Management Journal* (Summer 1995), p. 147.

69. A. R. Jassawalla and H. C. Sashittal, "Building Collaborative Cross-Functional New Product Teams," *Academy of Management Executive* (August 1999), pp. 50–63.

70. A. M. Townsend, S. M. DeMarie, and A. R. Hendrickson, "Virtual Teams' Technology and the Workplace of the Future," *Academy of Management Executive* (August 1998), pp. 17–29.

71. S. A. Furst, M. Reeves, B. Rosen, and R. S. Blackburn, "Managing the Life Cycle of Virtual Teams," *Academy of Management Executive* (May 2004), pp. 6–20; L. L. Martins, L. L. Gilson, and M. T. Maynard, "Virtual Teams: What Do We Know and Where Do We Go From Here?" *Journal of Management*, Vol. 30, No. 6 (2004), pp. 805–835.

72. C. B. Gibson and J. L. Gibbs, "Unpacking the Concept of Virtuality: The Effects of Geographic Dispersion, Electronic De-pendence, Dynamic Structure, and National Diversity on Team Innovation," *Administrative Science Quarterly* (September 2006), pp. 451–495.

73. T. D. Golden and J. F. Veiga, "The Impact of Extent of Telecommuting on Job Satisfaction: Resolving Inconsistent Findings," *Journal of Management* (April 2005), pp. 301–318.

74. M. Conlin, "The Easiest Commute of All," *Business Week* (December 12, 2005), pp. 78–80.

75. BPOIndia.org, BPO Industry in India- A Report, recovered on 25th Oct 2011, from http://www.bpoindia.org/research/bpo-in-india.shtml

76. BPO Watch News Desk, A global view of the BPO industry's future, posted on September 17, 2008, recovered on 25th Oct 2011, from India syndicate.com Pvt.Ltd. website http://www.bpowatchindia.com/bpo_industry_report/bpo_future/september-17-2008/bpo_future_global.html

77. Townsend, DeMarie, and Hendrickson, p. 18.

78. India-Labor Relations Size and Composition of the Work Force, recovered on 25th Oct 2011, from http://www.mongabay.com/history/india/india-labor_relations_size_and_composition_of_the_work_force.html

79. OUR BUREAU, Labour woes easing out: Survey, posted on NEW DELHI, FEB. 25 2011, recovered on 25th Oct 2011, from http://www.thehindubusinessline.com/industry-and-economy/article1490164.ece

80. DiGiacomo Gordon, Trade Unions and the Reform of the Quality of Work Life: Ergonomic and Other QWL Reforms Have Limited Goals and Are Held No Substitute for Labor Involvement, The American Journal of Economics and Sociology, Vol. 46, No. 4 (Oct., 1987), pp. 399-414.

81. Ghosh Piyali, Shefali Nandan & Ashish Gupta, The Changing Roles Of Trade Unions In India: A Case Study Of National Thermal Power Corporation (Ntpc), Unchahar, Asian Academy of Management Journal, Vol. 14, No. 1, 37–57, January 2009, recovered on 25th Oct, 2011, from http://web.usm.my/aamj/14.1.2009/AAMJ%2014-1-3.pdf

82. Ono Yukako, Why do fi rms use temporary workers?, Chicago Fed Letter, March 2009, Number 260, The Federal Reserve Bank of Chicago, recovered on 25th Oct 2011, from http://www.chicagofed.org/digital_assets/publications/chicago_fed_letter/2009/cflmarch2009_260.pdf

83. Economictimes, India Inc hiring temporary employees to cut cost, posted on December 30, 2008, 09:39:32 AM, recovered on 25th Oct 2011, from http://discuss.itacumens.com/index.php?topic=45972.0

84. Naurkihub.com, Temporary Staffing in Indian Companies, recovered on 25th Oct 2011, from http://www.naukrihub.com/hr-today/temporary-staffing.html

85. J. Muller, "A Ford Redesign," *Business Week* (November 13, 2000), Special Report.

86. O. C. Richard, B. P. S. Murthi, and K. Ismail, "The Impact of Racial Diversity on Intermediate and Long-Term Performance: The Moderating Role of Environmental Context," *Strategic Management Journal* (December 2007), pp. 1213–1233; G. Colvin, "The 50 Best Companies for Asians, Blacks, and Hispanics," *Fortune* (July 19, 1999), pp. 53–58.

87. V. Singh and S. Point, "Strategic Responses by European Companies to the Diversity Challenge: An Online Comparison," *Long Range Planning* (August 2004), pp. 295–318.

88. Singh and Point, p. 310.

89. J. Bachman, "Coke to Pay $192.5 Million to Settle Lawsuit," *The* (Ames) *Tribune* (November 20, 2000), p. D4.

90. O. Gottschalg and M. Zollo, "Interest Alignment and Competitive Advantage," *Academy of Management Review* (April 2007), pp. 418–437.

91. J. Lee and D. Miller, "People Matter: Commitment to Employees, Strategy, and Performance in Korean Firms," *Strategic Management Journal* (June 1999), pp. 579–593.

92. A. Cortese, "Here Comes the Intranet," *Business Week* (February 26, 1996), p. 76.

93. D. Bartholomew, "Blue-Collar Computing," *Information Week* (June 19, 1995), pp. 34–43.

94. J. Bughin, J. Manyika, A. Miller, and M. Cjhui, "Building the Web 2.0 Enterprise," *McKinsey Quarterly Online* (July 2008); J. Bughin, M. Chui, and B. Johnson, "The Next Step in Open Innovation," *McKinsey Quarterly Online* (June 2008), pp. 1–8.

95. C. C. Poirier, *Advanced Supply Chain Management* (San Francisco: Berrett-Koehler Publishers, 1999), p. 2.

96. J. H. Dyer and N. W. Hatch, "Relation-Specific Capabilities and Barriers to Knowledge Transfers: Creating Advantage through Network Relationships," *Strategic Management Journal* (August 2006), pp. 701–719.

97. D. Paulonis and S. Norton, "Managing Global Supply Chains," *McKinsey Quarterly Online* (August 2008).

98. M. Cook and R. Hagey, "Why Companies Flunk Supply-Chain 101: Only 33 Percent Correctly Measure Supply-Chain Performance; Few Use the Right Incentives," *Journal of Business Strategy*, Vol. 24, No. 4 (2003), pp. 35–42.

99. C. C. Poirer, pp. 3–5. For further information on RFID technology, see F. Taghaboni-Dutta and B. Velthouse, "RFID Technology is Revolutionary: Who Should Be Involved in This Game of Tag?" *Academy of Management Perspectives* (November 2006), pp. 65–78.

100. M. Arndt, "Everything Old Is New Again," *Business Week* (September 25, 2006), pp. 64–70.

101. R. Farzad, "Cash for Trash," *Business Week* (August 4, 2008), pp. 36–46.

Ending Case for Part Two

BOEING BETS THE COMPANY

The Boeing Company, a well-known U.S.-based manufacturer of commercial and military aircraft, faced a dilemma in 2004. Long the leader of the global airframe manufacturing industry, Boeing had been slowly losing market share since the 1990s to the European-based Airbus Industrie—now incorporated as the European Aeronautic & Space Company (EADS). In December 2001, the EADS board of directors had committed the corporation to an objective it had never before achieved—taking from Boeing the leadership of the commercial aviation industry by building the largest commercial jet plane in the world, the Airbus 380. The A380 would carry 481 passengers in a normal multiple-class seating configuration compared to the 416 passengers carried by Boeing's 747—400 in a similar seating configuration. The A380 would not only fly 621 miles farther than the 747, but it would cost airlines 15%–20% less per passenger to operate. With orders for 50 A380 aircraft in hand, the EADS board announced that the new plane would be ready for delivery during 2006. The proposed A380 program decimated the sales of Boeing's jumbo jet. Since 2000, airlines had ordered only 10 Boeing 747s configured for passengers.

Boeing was clearly a company in difficulty in 2004. Distracted by the 1996 acquisitions of McDonnell Douglas and Rockwell Aerospace, Boeing's top management had spent the next few years strengthening the corporation's historically weak position in aerospace and defense and had allowed its traditional competency in commercial aviation to deteriorate. Boeing, once the manufacturing marvel of the world, was now spending 10%–20% more than EADS (Airbus) to build a plane. The prices it asked for its planes were thus also higher. As a result, Boeing's estimated market share of the commercial market slid from nearly 70% in 1996 to less than half that by the end of 2003. EADS claimed to have delivered 300 aircraft to Boeing's 285 and to have won 56% of the 396 orders placed by airlines in 2003—quite an improvement from 1994, when EADS controlled only one-fifth of the market! This was quite an accomplishment, given that the A380 was so large that the modifications needed to accommodate it at airports would cost $80 to $100 million.

Even though defense sales now accounted for more than half of the company's revenues, Boeing's CEO realized that he needed to quickly act to regain Boeing's leadership of the commercial part of the industry. In December 2003, the board approved the strategic decision to promote a new commercial airplane, the Boeing 787, for sale to airlines. The 787 was a midrange aircraft, not a jumbo jet such as the A380. The 787 would

This case was written by J. David Hunger for *Strategic Management and Business Policy*, 12th edition and for *Concepts in Strategic Management and Business Policy*, 12th edition. Copyright © 2008 by J. David Hunger. Reprinted by permission. References available upon request.

carry between 220 and 250 passengers but consume 20% less fuel and be 10% cheaper to operate than its competitor, EADS' current midrange plane, the smaller wide-body A330-200. It was to be made from a graphite/epoxy resin instead of aluminum. It was designed to fly faster, higher, farther, cleaner, more quietly, and more efficiently than any other medium-sized jet. This was the first time since approving the 777 jet in 1990 that the company had launched an all-new plane program. Development costs were estimated at $8 billion over five years. Depending on the results of these sales efforts, the board would decide sometime during 2004 to either begin or cancel the 787 construction program. If approved, the planes could be delivered in 2008—two years after the delivery of the A380.

The Boeing 787 decision was based on a completely different set of assumptions from those used by the EADS board to approve the A380. EADS top management believed that the commercial market wanted even larger jumbo jets to travel long international routes. Airports in Asia, the Middle East, and Europe were becoming heavily congested. In these locations, the "hub-and-spoke" method of creating major airline hubs was flourishing. Using larger planes was a way of dealing with that congestion by flying more passengers per plane out of these hubs. EADS management believed that over the next 20 years, airlines and freight carriers would need a minimum of 1,500 more aircraft at least as big as the B747. EADS management had concluded that the key to controlling the future commercial market was by using larger, more expensive planes. The A380 was a very large bet on that future scenario. The A380 program would cost EADS almost $13 million before the first plane was delivered.

In contrast, Boeing's management believed in a very different future scenario. Noting the success of Southwest and JetBlue, among other airlines in North America, it concluded that no more than 320 extra-large planes would be sold in the future as the airline industry moved away from hub-and-spoke networks toward more direct flights between smaller airports. The fragmentation of the airline industry, with its emphasis on competing through lower costs was the primary rationale for Boeing's fuel-efficient 787. A secondary reason was to deal with increasing passenger complaints about shrinking legroom and seat room on current planes flown by cost-conscious airlines.

The 787 was designed with larger windows, seats, lavatories, and overhead bins. The plane was being designed in both short- and long-range versions. Boeing's management predicted a market for 2,000 to 3,000 such planes. Additional support for the midrange plane came from some industry analysts who predicted that the huge A380 would give new meaning to the term "cattle class." To reach necessary economies of scale, the A380 would likely devote a large portion of both of its decks to economy class, with passengers sitting three or four across, the same configuration as most of Boeing's 747s.

Boeing's strategy to regain industry leadership with its proposed 787 airplane meant that the company would have to increase its manufacturing efficiency in order to keep the price low. To significantly cut costs, management would be forced to implement a series of new programs:

- Outsource approximately 70% of manufacturing. Could it find suppliers who could consistently make the high-quality parts needed by Boeing?

- Reduce final assembly time to three days (compared to 20 for its 737 plane) by having suppliers build completed plane sections. Could this many suppliers meet Boeing's exacting deadlines?

- Use new, lightweight composite materials in place of aluminum to reduce inspection time. Would the plane be as dependable and as easy to maintain as Boeing's aluminum airplanes?

- Resolve poor relations with labor unions caused by downsizing and outsourcing. The machinists' union would have to be given a greater voice in specifying manufacturing procedures. Would Boeing's middle managers be willing to share power with an antagonistic union?

Which vision of the future was correct? The long-term fortunes of both Boeing and EADS depended on two contrasting strategic decisions, based on two very different assessments of the market. If EADS was correct, the market would continue to demand ever-larger airplanes. If Boeing was correct, the current wave of jumbo jets had crested, and a new wave of fuel-saving midrange jets would soon replace them. Which company's strategy had the best chance of succeeding?

PART 3

Strategy
Formulation

strategy formulation: situation analysis and Business Strategy

India, has a colorful and diverse range of food and tastes to offer. For centuries, Indian food and spices have been known far and wide for their authentic taste and rich quality. India has a variety of dishes, be it North Indian food or South Indian food, that use spices and herbs such as coriander, ginger, garlic, cinnamon, cardamoms, cloves, aniseed and asafetida – that are used in different combinations and flavors to enhance the pleasure of a meal.[1]

"Haldiram" – is a name associated with discerning consumers for sweets and namkeens for the past six decades in India and abroad. It made its modest start in the beginning way back in 1941 in Bikaner, a state of Rajasthan. Ganga Bishen Agarwal alias Haldiram Agarwal expertising in his skill of making *bhujias*, served the local clienteles on contract basis. He was the first to commercialize the name **Haldiram's** in 1958 and named his shop **Haldiram Bhujiawala**, dedicated to his legendary father.

Haldiram is successful because of its diversification strategy in a traditionally fragmented Indian sweets industry. The company which started off as a family run business, has products ranging from tin packed sweets to namkeens to dry fruits. Amongst the sweets and namkeens, Haldiram's modestly says "you *name it, we have it*". Soft drinks (*sharbats*) range includes exciting flavors like the royal badam, rose squash, *thandai* etc., which serve as energy supplements and coolants. Haldiram's also enjoys a strong market share in processed milk, bakery and ice creams. Recently, keeping in line with its corporate strategy, it ventured into ready- to- eat food segment as well.

Haldiram's transition from a one-counter sweet shop in Bikaner in the early 1940's to a full-fledged Indian snack foods company today has taken a lot of people by surprise. `Haldiram's' bagged the prestigious "International Food and Beverage Award" (1994), "Kashalkar Memorial Award" (1996) and "Brand Equity Award" (1998). The company also exports its products to various parts of the world viz. U.S.A., Canada, U.K., Europe, Middle East, Far East, Moscow, Australia, New Zealand, Sri Lanka, Nepal, Japan, Thailand, and in total more than 35 countries cross the world.

The company has grown as a result of its efforts to provide its customers quality product. For this, company has state- of- the- art machineries which maintain uniform level of production.

Learning Objectives

After reading this chapter, you should be able to:

- Organize environmental and organizational information using SWOT analysis and a SFAS matrix
- Generate strategic options by using the TOWS matrix
- Understand the competitive and cooperative strategies available to corporations

- List the competitive tactics that would accompany competitive strategies
- Identify the basic types of strategic alliances

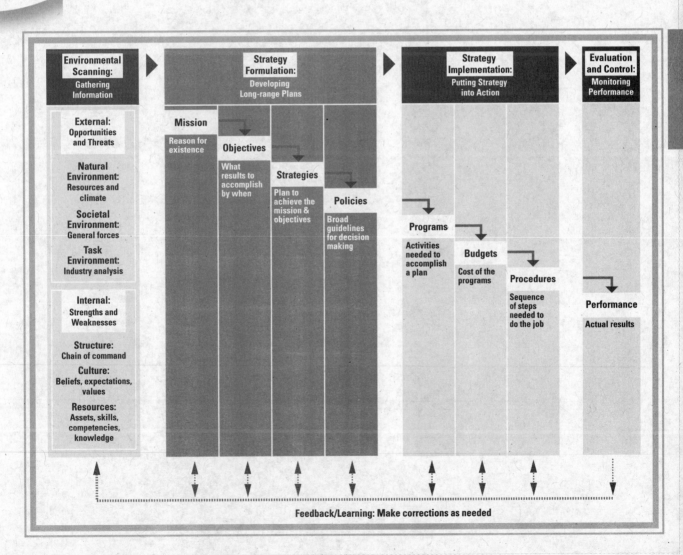

| Environmental Scanning: Gathering Information | Strategy Formulation: Developing Long-range Plans | Strategy Implementation: Putting Strategy into Action | Evaluation and Control: Monitoring Performance |

External: Opportunities and Threats

Natural Environment: Resources and climate

Societal Environment: General forces

Task Environment: Industry analysis

Internal: Strengths and Weaknesses

Structure: Chain of command

Culture: Beliefs, expectations, values

Resources: Assets, skills, competencies, knowledge

Mission — Reason for existence

Objectives — What results to accomplish by when

Strategies — Plan to achieve the mission & objectives

Policies — Broad guidelines for decision making

Programs — Activities needed to accomplish a plan

Budgets — Cost of the programs

Procedures — Sequence of steps needed to do the job

Performance — Actual results

Feedback/Learning: Make corrections as needed

No effort is spared at the shop floor to make sure that quality and other standards are adhered to. The company even has a full-fledged laboratory, which monitors the quality of the raw materials and regularly tests samples drawn from batches of daily production. It also has an exclusive R&D wing which is dedicated to improving quality, taste, packaging and shelf life of the products. Strenuous efforts are undertaken to reach the best of even the most perishable sweets in its original taste to any part of the world on client demand.

Haldiram's products inherit the matchless quality, zero impurity and world class packaging. Efficient supply chain management and distribution network are the hallmark of each and every Haldiram's product, and to top it up the trump card of reasonable prices and efficient marketing strategy are the key to success. By adopting diversification strategies it is posing a tough fight to its competitors which include not only Agarwal's, Nathu's and Bikanerwala, but also pizza chains like Pizza Hut, Mc Donald's etc. Reprinted with permission from Haldiram Pvt. Ltd.

6.1 Situational Analysis: SWOT Analysis

Strategy formulation, often referred to as strategic planning or long-range planning, is concerned with developing a corporation's mission, objectives, strategies, and policies. It begins with situation analysis: the process of finding a strategic fit between external opportunities and internal strengths while working around external threats and internal weaknesses. As shown in the Strategic Decision-Making Process in Figure 1–5, step 5(a) is analyzing strategic factors in light of the current situation using SWOT analysis. **SWOT** is an acronym used to describe the particular **S**trengths, **W**eaknesses, **O**pportunities, and **T**hreats that are strategic factors for a specific company. SWOT analysis should not only result in the identification of a corporation's distinctive competencies—the particular capabilities and resources that a firm possesses and the superior way in which they are used—but also in the identification of opportunities that the firm is not currently able to take advantage of due to a lack of appropriate resources. Over the years, SWOT analysis has proven to be the most enduring analytical technique used in strategic management. For example, in a 2007 McKinsey & Company global survey of 2,700 executives, 82% of the executives stated that the most relevant activities for strategy formulation were evaluating the strengths and weaknesses of the organization and identifying top environmental trends affecting business unit performance over the next three to five years.[2] A 2005 survey of competitive intelligence professionals found that SWOT analysis was used by 82.7% of the respondents, the second most frequently used technique, trailing only competitor analysis.[3]

It can be said that the essence of strategy is opportunity divided by capacity.[4] An opportunity by itself has no real value unless a company has the capacity (i.e., resources) to take advantage of that opportunity. This approach, however, considers only opportunities and strengths when considering alternative strategies. By itself, a distinctive competency in a key resource or capability is no guarantee of competitive advantage. Weaknesses in other resource areas can prevent a strategy from being successful. SWOT can thus be used to take a broader view of strategy through the formula $SA = O/(S - W)$ that is, (Strategic alternative *equals* Opportunity *divided* by Strengths *minus* Weaknesses). This reflects an important issue strategic managers face: Should we invest more in our strengths to make them even stronger (a distinctive competence) or should we invest in our weaknesses to at least make them competitive?

SWOT analysis, by itself, is not a panacea. Some of the primary criticisms of SWOT analysis are:

- It generates lengthy lists.
- It uses no weights to reflect priorities.
- It uses ambiguous words and phrases.
- The same factor can be placed in two categories (e.g., a strength may also be a weakness).
- There is no obligation to verify opinions with data or analysis.
- It requires only a single level of analysis.
- There is no logical link to strategy implementation.[5]

GENERATING A STRATEGIC FACTORS ANALYSIS SUMMARY (SFAS) MATRIX

The EFAS and IFAS Tables plus the SFAS Matrix have been developed to deal with the criticisms of SWOT analysis. When used together, they are a powerful analytical set of tools for strategic analysis. The **SFAS (Strategic Factors Analysis Summary) Matrix** summarizes an organization's strategic factors by combining the external factors from the EFAS Table with the internal factors from the IFAS Table. The EFAS and IFAS examples given of Maytag Corporation (as it was in 1995) in **Tables 4–5** and **5–2** list a total of 20 internal and external factors. These are too many factors for most people to use in strategy formulation. The SFAS Matrix requires a strategic decision maker to condense these strengths, weaknesses, opportunities, and threats into fewer than 10 strategic factors. This is done by reviewing and revising the weight given each factor. The revised weights reflect the priority of each factor as a determinant of the company's future success. The highest-weighted EFAS and IFAS factors should appear in the SFAS Matrix.

As shown in **Figure 6–1**, you can create an SFAS Matrix by following these steps:

1. In **Column 1** *(Strategic Factors)*, list the most important EFAS and IFAS items. After each factor, indicate whether it is a Strength (**S**), Weakness (**W**), an Opportunity (**O**), or a Threat (**T**).

2. In **Column 2** *(Weight)*, assign weights for all of the internal and external strategic factors. As with the EFAS and IFAS Tables presented earlier, the **weight column must total 1.00**. This means that the weights calculated earlier for EFAS and IFAS will probably have to be adjusted.

3. In **Column 3** *(Rating)*, assign a rating of how the company's management is responding to each of the strategic factors. These ratings will probably (but not always) be the same as those listed in the EFAS and IFAS Tables.

4. In **Column 4** *(Weighted Score)*, multiply the weight in **Column 2** for each factor by its rating in **Column 3** to obtain the factor's rated score.

5. In **Column 5** *(Duration)*, depicted in **Figure 6–1**, indicate **short-term** (less than one year), **intermediate-term** (one to three years), or **long-term** (three years and beyond).

6. In **Column 6** *(Comments)*, repeat or revise your comments for each strategic factor from the previous EFAS and IFAS Tables. **The total weighted score for the average firm in an industry is always 3.0.**

The resulting SFAS Matrix is a listing of the firm's external and internal strategic factors in one table. The example given in **Figure 6–1** is for Maytag Corporation in 1995, before the firm sold its European and Australian operations and it was acquired by Whirlpool. The SFAS Matrix includes only the most important factors gathered from environmental scanning and thus provides information that is essential for strategy formulation. The use of EFAS and IFAS Tables together with the SFAS Matrix deals with some of the criticisms of SWOT analysis. For example, the use of the SFAS Matrix reduces the list of factors to a manageable number, puts weights on each factor, and allows one factor to be listed as both a strength and a weakness (or as an opportunity and a threat).

FINDING A PROPITIOUS NICHE

One desired outcome of analyzing strategic factors is identifying a niche where an organization can use its core competencies to take advantage of a particular market opportunity. A niche is a need in the marketplace that is currently unsatisfied. The goal is to find a **propitious niche**—an extremely favorable niche—that is so well suited to the firm's internal and external environment that other corporations are not likely to challenge or dislodge it.[6] A niche is propitious to the extent that it currently is just large enough for one firm to satisfy its demand. After a firm has found and filled that niche, it is not worth a potential competitor's time or money to also go after the same niche. Such a niche may also be called a *strategic sweet spot* (see **Figure 6–2**)—where a company is able to satisfy customers' needs in a way that rivals cannot, given the context in which it operates.[7]

Finding such a niche or sweet spot is not always easy. A firm's management must be always looking for a *strategic window*—that is, a unique market opportunity that is available only for a particular time. The first firm through a strategic window can occupy a propitious niche and discourage competition (if the firm has the required internal strengths).

As a niche grows, so can a company within that niche—by increasing its operations' capacity or through alliances with larger firms. The key is to identify a market opportunity in which the first firm to reach that market segment can obtain and keep dominant market share. For example, Career Launcher, a niche company founded in 1995 by a group of IIM students, initially helped students to prepare for the CAT entrance exam. Small initial demand allowed this entrepreneurial venture to go after other niches that were too small to be noticed by established companies. This led the company to expand its product offerings to school and college students seeking admission to a broad range of professional courses. The company grew with the niche and today it plays a leading role in test preparation, K12, higher education, and vocational training markets.[8,9] Another example of a company growing with the niche is of "The Millenium School." Edu School is the school education subsidiary of Educomp Solutions. The subsidiary owns and operates K-12 schools and has already opened schools in Bangalore, Chennai, Delhi/NCR, and Mohali region under "The Millenium School" brand.[10] These schools adopt best practices in education with a proprietary Millennium Learning System (MLS).

Niches can also change—sometimes faster than a firm can adapt to that change. A company's management may discover in their situation analysis that they need to invest heavily in the firm's capabilities to keep them competitively strong in a changing niche. South African Breweries (SAB), for example, took this approach when management realized that the only way to keep competitors out of its market was to continuously invest in increased productivity and infrastructure in order to keep its prices very low.

6.2 Review of Mission and Objectives

A reexamination of an organization's current mission and objectives must be made before alternative strategies can be generated and evaluated. Even when formulating strategy, decision makers tend to concentrate on the alternatives—the action possibilities—rather than on a mission to be fulfilled and objectives to be achieved. This tendency is so attractive because it is much easier to deal with alternative courses of action that exist right here and now than to really think about what you want to accomplish in the future. The end result is that we often choose strategies that set our objectives for us rather than having our choices incorporate clear objectives and a mission statement.

Problems in performance can derive from an inappropriate statement of mission, which may be too narrow or too broad. If the mission does not provide a **common thread** (a unifying theme) for a corporation's businesses, managers may be unclear about where the company is heading. Objectives and strategies might be in conflict with each other. Divisions might be competing against one another rather than against outside competition—to the detriment of the corporation as a whole.

A company's objectives can also be inappropriately stated. They can either focus too much on short-term operational goals or be so general that they provide little real guidance. There may be a gap between planned and achieved objectives. When such a gap occurs, either the strategies have to be changed to improve performance or the objectives need to be adjusted downward to be more realistic. Consequently, objectives should be constantly reviewed to ensure their usefulness. This is what happened at Boeing when management decided to change its primary objective from being the largest in the industry to being the most profitable. This had a significant effect on its strategies and policies. Following its new objective, the company cancelled its policy of competing with Airbus on price and abandoned its commitment to maintaining a manufacturing capacity that could produce more than half a peak year's demand for airplanes.[11]

FIGURE 6–1   Strategic Factor Analysis Summary (SFAS) Matrix

Internal Strategic Factors	Weight	Rating	Weighted Score	Comments
	1	2	3	4	5
Strengths				
S1 Quality Maytag culture	.15	5.0	.75	Quality key to success
S2 Experienced top management	.05	4.2	.21	Know appliances
S3 Vertical integration	.10	3.9	.39	Dedicated factories
S4 Employee relations	.05	3.0	.15	Good, but deteriorating
S5 Hoover's international orientation	.15	2.8	.42	Hoover name in cleaners
Weaknesses				
W1 Process-oriented R&D	.05	2.2	.11	Slow on new products
W2 Distribution channels	.05	2.0	.10	Superstores replacing small dealers
W3 Financial position	.15	2.0	.30	High debt load
W4 Global positioning	.20	2.1	.42	Hoover weak outside the United Kingdom and Australia
W5 Manufacturing facilities	.05	4.0	.20	Investing now
Total Scores	1.00		3.05	

External Strategic Factors	Weight	Rating	Weighted Score	Comments
	1	2	3	4	5
Opportunities				
O1 Economic integration of European Community	.20	4.1	.82	Acquisition of Hoover
O2 Demographics favor quality appliances	.10	5.0	.50	Maytag quality
O3 Economic development of Asia	.05	1.0	.05	Low Maytag presence
O4 Opening of Eastern Europe	.05	2.0	.10	Will take time
O5 Trend to "Super Stores"	.10	1.8	.18	Maytag weak in this channel
Threats				
T1 Increasing government regulations	.10	4.3	.43	Well positioned
T2 Strong U.S. competition	.10	4.0	.40	Well positioned
T3 Whirlpool and Electrolux strong globally	.15	3.0	.45	Hoover weak globally
T4 New product advances	.05	1.2	.06	Questionable
T5 Japanese appliance companies	.10	1.6	.16	Only Asian presence is Australia
Total Scores	1.00		3.15	

*The most important external and internal factors are identified in the EFAS and IFAS tables as shown here by shading these factors.

Strategic Factors (Select the most important opportunities/threats from EFAS, Table 4–5 and the most important strengths and weaknesses from IFAS, Table 5–2)	1	2 Weight	3 Rating	4 Weighted Score	Duration SHORT	INTERMEDIATE	5 LONG	6 Comments
S1 Quality Maytag culture (S)		.10	5.0	.50			X	Quality key to success
S5 Hoover's international								
orientation (S)		.10	2.8	.28	X	X		Name recognition
W3 Financial position (W)		.10	2.0	.20	X	X		High debt
W4 Global positioning (W)		.15	2.2	.33		X	X	Only in N.A., U.K., and
								Australia
O1 Economic integration of								
European Community (O)		.10	4.1	.41			X	Acquisition of Hoover
O2 Demographics favor quality (O)		.10	5.0	.50		X		Maytag quality
O5 Trend to super stores (O + T)		.10	1.8	.18	X			Weak in this channel
T3 Whirlpool and Electrolux (T)		.15	3.0	.45	X			Dominate industry
T5 Japanese appliance								
companies (T)		.10	1.6	.16			X	Asian presence
Total Scores		1.00		3.01				

Notes:
1. List each of the most important factors developed in your IFAS and EFAS Tables in Column 1.
2. Weight each factor from 1.0 (Most Important) to 0.0 (Not Important) in Column 2 based on that factor's probable impact on the company's strategic position. **The total weights must sum to 1.00.**
3. Rate each factor from 5.0 (Outstanding) to 1.0 (Poor) in Column 3 based on the company's response to that factor.
4. Multiply each factor's weight times its rating to obtain each factor's weighted score in Column 4.
5. For duration in Column 5, check appropriate column (short term—less than 1 year; intermediate—1 to 3 years; long term—over 3 years).
6. Use Column 6 (comments) for rationale used for each factor.

SOURCE: T.L. Wheelen, J.D. Hunger, "Strategic Factor Analysis Summary (SFAS)." Copyright © 1987, 1988, 1989, 1990, 1991, 1992, 1993, 1994, 1995, 1996 and 2005 by T.L. Wheelen Copyright © 1997 and 2005 by Wheelen and Associates. Reprinted by permission.

6.3 Generating Alternative Strategies by Using a TOWS Matrix

Thus far we have discussed how a firm uses SWOT analysis to assess its situation. SWOT can also be used to generate a number of possible alternative strategies. The **TOWS Matrix** (TOWS is just another way of saying SWOT) illustrates how the external opportunities and threats facing a particular corporation can be matched with that company's internal strengths and weaknesses to result in four sets of possible strategic alternatives. (See **Figure 6–3**.) This is a good way to use brainstorming to create alternative strategies that might not otherwise be

FIGURE 6–2
The Strategic
Sweet Spot

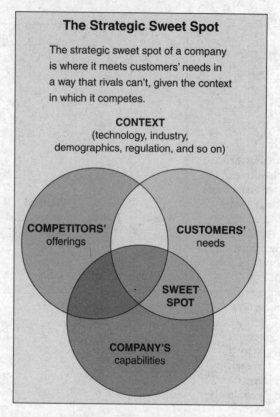

The Strategic Sweet Spot

The strategic sweet spot of a company is where it meets customers' needs in a way that rivals can't, given the context in which it competes.

CONTEXT
(technology, industry, demographics, regulation, and so on)

COMPETITORS' offerings

CUSTOMERS' needs

SWEET SPOT

COMPANY'S capabilities

FIGURE 6–2
The Strategic
Sweet Spot

SOURCE: D. J. Collis and M. G. Rukstad, "Can You Say What Your Strategy Is?" Reprinted by permission of Harvard Business Review. 'The Strategic Sweet Spot' from "Can You Say What Strategy is?" by D. J. Collis & M. G. Rukstad April 2008. Copyright © 2008 by the Harvard Business School Publishing Corporation. All rights reserved.

FIGURE 6–3
TOWS Matrix

INTERNAL FACTORS (IFAS) / EXTERNAL FACTORS (EFAS)	Strengths (S) List 5 – 10 *internal* strengths here	Weaknesses (W) List 5 – 10 *internal* weaknesses here
Opportunities (O) List 5 – 10 *external* opportunities here	**SO Strategies** Generate strategies here that use **strengths** to take **advantage** of **opportunities**	**WO Strategies** Generate strategies here that take **advantage** of **opportunities** by **overcoming weaknesses**
Threats (T) List 5 – 10 *external* threats here	**ST Strategies** Generate strategies here that use **strengths** to **avoid threats**	**WT Strategies** Generate strategies here that **minimize weaknesses** and **avoid threats**

SOURCE: *Reprinted from* Long-Range Planning, *Vol. 15, No. 2, 1982, Weihrich "The TOWS Matrix—A Tool For Situational Analysis," p. 60. Copyright © 1982 with permission of Elsevier.*

STRATEGY highlight 6.1

NATCO PHARMA INDIA: NICHE STRATEGY

The Indian pharmaceutical industry is one of the leading science-based industries in India with wide-ranging capabilities. It ranks very high in the third world, in terms of technology, quality, and range of medicines manufactured. Almost every type of medicine is now made indigenously in India.[1]

The industry structure of Indian pharma industry is highly fragmented. As per the Organization of Pharmaceutical Producers of India (OPPI) estimates, the industry is very fragmented, with over 20,000 registered unit[2] companies producing 400 bulk drugs and over 60,000 generic formulations.[3] This means that none of the generic players get big market shares. Strong presence of substitute and competitive generic drugs also means that the industry is susceptible to price competition.

Natco Pharama Limited is a niche company, which almost exclusively sells generics in oncology. Natco Pharma Limited was incorporated in Hyderabad in 1981 with an initial investment of INR 3.3 million and mere 20 employees.[4] Generally speaking, in India no insurance policy covers the cost of daily medicines, therefore, affordability of daily drugs becomes a key variable for the success of companies. The multinational products when sold in Indian markets are very highly priced and therefore, unaffordable by people. The company understood this aspect of consumer need and behavior and introduced generic drugs in oncology. These drugs can be bought at 1/10–1/20 the price of the original product.[5] Natco's business model is an alliance-based model. The company, using its strong technological capabilities develops a hard-to-make niche product. Then, it approaches a partner to help out with the litigation and the marketing. The company helps its MNC partner enter into markets with lesser costs where the volume makes profits rather than prices per unit. This niche-based business model has helped Natco Pharma business grow from one unit to five manufacturing facilities spread across India with more than 2,500 employees.[4]

1. Pharmaceutical Drug Manufacturers , Indian Pharmaceutical Industry, accessed on 25 Oct 2011, from http://www.pharmaceutical-drug-manufacturers.com/pharmaceutical-industry/

2. CCI, A Brief Report on Pharmaceutical Industry in India, Jan 2011, accessed on 25 Oct 2011, from http://www.cci.in/pdf/surveys_reports/indian-pharmaceuticals-industry.pdf

3. Overview, accessed on 25 Oct 2011, from http://info.shine.com/Industry-Information/Pharmaceuticals/819.aspx

4. Natco Pharma, Welcome to Natco Pharma Limited, accessed on 25 Oct 2011, from http://www.natcopharma.co.in/

5. Media Center, Interview with Rajeev Nannapaneni, Focus reports, accessed on 25 Oct 2011, from "http://www.pharma.focusreports.net/index.php" \I "state=InterviewDetail&id=1288" http://www.pharma.focusreports.net/index.php#state=InterviewDetail&id=1288

considered. It forces strategic managers to create various kinds of growth as well as retrenchment strategies. It can be used to generate corporate as well as business strategies. See **Strategy Highlight 6.1** to learn about Natco Pharma's niche strategy.

To generate a TOWS Matrix for Maytag Corporation in 1995, for example, use the External Factor Analysis Summary (EFAS) Table listed in **Table 4–5** from **Chapter 4** and the Internal Factor Analysis Summary (IFAS) Table listed in **Table 5–2** from **Chapter 5**. To build **Figure 6–4**, take the following steps:

1. In the **Opportunities (O)** block, list the external opportunities available in the company's or business unit's current and future environment from the EFAS Table (**Table 4–5**).

2. In the **Threats (T)** block, list the external threats facing the company or unit now and in the future from the EFAS Table (**Table 4–5**).

3. In the **Strengths (S)** block, list the specific areas of current and future strength for the company or unit from the IFAS Table (**Table 5–2**).

FIGURE 6–4 Generating a TOWS Matrix for Maytag Corporation

Internal Strategic Factors	Weight	Rating	Weighted Score	Comments
	1	2	3	4	5
Strengths				
S1 Quality Maytag culture	.15	5.0	.75	Quality key to success
S2 Experienced top management	.05	4.2	.21	Know appliances
S3 Vertical integration	.10	3.9	.39	Dedicated factories
S4 Employee relations	.05	3.0	.15	Good, but deteriorating
S5 Hoover's international orientation	.15	2.8	.42	Hoover name in cleaners
Weaknesses				
W1 Process-oriented R&D	.05	2.2	.11	Slow on new products
W2 Distribution channels	.05	2.0	.10	Superstores replacing small dealers
W3 Financial position	.15	2.0	.30	High debt load
W4 Global positioning	.20	2.1	.42	Hoover weak outside the United Kingdom and Australia
W5 Manufacturing facilities	.05	4.0	.20	Investing now
Total Scores	1.00		3.05	

External Strategic Factors	Weight	Rating	Weighted Score	Comments
	1	2	3	4	5
Opportunities				
O1 Economic integration of European Community	.20	4.1	.82	Acquisition of Hoover
O2 Demographics favor quality appliances	.10	5.0	.50	Maytag quality
O3 Economic development of Asia	.05	1.0	.05	Low Maytag presence
O4 Opening of Eastern Europe	.05	2.0	.10	Will take time
O5 Trend to "Super Stores"	.10	1.8	.18	Maytag weak in this channel
Threats				
T1 Increasing government regulations	.10	4.3	.43	Well positioned
T2 Strong U.S. competition	.10	4.0	.40	Well positioned
T3 Whirlpool and Electrolux strong globally	.15	3.0	.45	Hoover weak globally
T4 New product advances	.05	1.2	.06	Questionable
T5 Japanese appliance companies	.10	1.6	.16	Only Asian presence is Australia
Total Scores	1.00		3.15	

*The most important external and internal factors are identified in the EFAS and IFAS Tables as shown here by shading these factors.

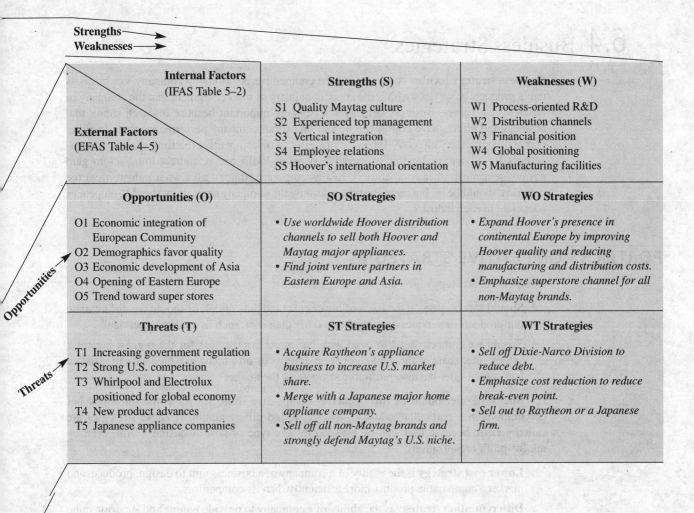

	Internal Factors (IFAS Table 5–2)	Strengths (S)	Weaknesses (W)
External Factors (EFAS Table 4–5)		S1 Quality Maytag culture S2 Experienced top management S3 Vertical integration S4 Employee relations S5 Hoover's international orientation	W1 Process-oriented R&D W2 Distribution channels W3 Financial position W4 Global positioning W5 Manufacturing facilities
Opportunities (O)		SO Strategies	WO Strategies
O1 Economic integration of European Community O2 Demographics favor quality O3 Economic development of Asia O4 Opening of Eastern Europe O5 Trend toward super stores		• *Use worldwide Hoover distribution channels to sell both Hoover and Maytag major appliances.* • *Find joint venture partners in Eastern Europe and Asia.*	• *Expand Hoover's presence in continental Europe by improving Hoover quality and reducing manufacturing and distribution costs.* • *Emphasize superstore channel for all non-Maytag brands.*
Threats (T)		ST Strategies	WT Strategies
T1 Increasing government regulation T2 Strong U.S. competition T3 Whirlpool and Electrolux positioned for global economy T4 New product advances T5 Japanese appliance companies		• *Acquire Raytheon's appliance business to increase U.S. market share.* • *Merge with a Japanese major home appliance company.* • *Sell off all non-Maytag brands and strongly defend Maytag's U.S. niche.*	• *Sell off Dixie-Narco Division to reduce debt.* • *Emphasize cost reduction to reduce break-even point.* • *Sell out to Raytheon or a Japanese firm.*

Strengths →
Weaknesses →
Opportunities
Threats

4. In the **Weaknesses (W)** block, list the specific areas of current and future weakness for the company or unit from the IFAS Table (**Table 5–2**).

5. Generate a series of possible strategies for the company or business unit under consideration based on particular combinations of the four sets of factors:
   - **SO Strategies** are generated by thinking of ways in which a company or business unit could use its strengths to take advantage of opportunities.
   - **ST Strategies** consider a company's or unit's strengths as a way to avoid threats.
   - **WO Strategies** attempt to take advantage of opportunities by overcoming weaknesses.
   - **WT Strategies** are basically defensive and primarily act to minimize weaknesses and avoid threats.

The TOWS Matrix is very useful for generating a series of alternatives that the decision makers of a company or business unit might not otherwise have considered. It can be used for the corporation as a whole (as is done in **Figure 6–4** with Maytag Corporation before it sold Hoover Europe), or it can be used for a specific business unit within a corporation (such as Hoover's floor care products). Nevertheless using a TOWS Matrix is only one of many ways to generate alternative strategies. Another approach is to evaluate each business unit within a corporation in terms of possible competitive and cooperative strategies.

6.4 Business Strategies

Business strategy focuses on improving the competitive position of a company's or business unit's products or services within the specific industry or market segment that the company or business unit serves. Business strategy is extremely important because research shows that business unit effects have double the impact on overall company performance than do either corporate or industry effects.[12] Business strategy can be competitive (battling against all competitors for advantage) and/or cooperative (working with one or more companies to gain advantage against other competitors). Just as corporate strategy asks what industry(ies) the company should be in, business strategy asks how the company or its units should compete or cooperate in each industry.

PORTER'S COMPETITIVE STRATEGIES

Competitive strategy raises the following questions:

- Should we compete on the basis of lower cost (and thus price), or should we differentiate our products or services on some basis other than cost, such as quality or service?

- Should we compete head to head with our major competitors for the biggest but most sought-after share of the market, or should we focus on a niche in which we can satisfy a less sought-after but also profitable segment of the market?

Michael Porter proposes two "generic" competitive strategies for outperforming other corporations in a particular industry: lower cost and differentiation.[13] These strategies are called generic because they can be pursued by any type or size of business firm, even by not-for-profit organizations:

- **Lower cost strategy** is the ability of a company or a business unit to design, produce, and market a comparable product more efficiently than its competitors.

- **Differentiation strategy** is the ability of a company to provide unique and superior value to the buyer in terms of product quality, special features, or after-sale service.

Porter further proposes that a firm's competitive advantage in an industry is determined by its **competitive scope**, that is, the breadth of the company's or business unit's target market. Before using one of the two generic competitive strategies (lower cost or differentiation), the firm or unit must choose the range of product varieties it will produce, the distribution channels it will employ, the types of buyers it will serve, the geographic areas in which it will sell, and the array of related industries in which it will also compete. This should reflect an understanding of the firm's unique resources. Simply put, a company or business unit can choose a broad target (that is, aim at the middle of the mass market) or a narrow target (that is, aim at a market niche). Combining these two types of target markets with the two competitive strategies results in the four variations of generic strategies depicted in **Figure 6–5**. When the lower-cost and differentiation strategies have a broad mass-market target, they are simply called *cost leadership* and *differentiation*. When they are focused on a market niche (narrow target), however, they are called *cost focus* and *differentiation focus*. Although research does indicate that established firms pursuing broad-scope strategies outperform firms following narrow-scope strategies in terms of ROA (Return on Assets), new entrepreneurial firms have a better chance of surviving if they follow a narrow-scope rather than a broad-scope strategy.[14]

Competitive Advantage

		Lower Cost	Differentiation
Competitive Scope	**Broad Target**	**Cost Leadership**	**Differentiation**
	Narrow Target	**Cost Focus**	**Differentiation Focus**

Cost leadership is a lower-cost competitive strategy that aims at the broad mass market and requires "aggressive construction of efficient-scale facilities, vigorous pursuit of cost reductions from experience, tight cost and overhead control, avoidance of marginal customer accounts, and cost minimization in areas like R&D, service, sales force, advertising, and so on."[15] Because of its lower costs, the cost leader is able to charge a lower price for its products than its competitors and still make a satisfactory profit. Although it may not necessarily have the lowest costs in the industry, it has lower costs than its competitors. Some companies successfully following this strategy are Wal-Mart (discount retailing), McDonald's (fast-food restaurants), Dell (computers), Alamo (rental cars), Aldi (grocery stores), Southwest Airlines, and Timex (watches). Big Bazaar is a hypermarket chain that combines the look and feel of Indian bazaars, with the aspects of modern retail such as choice, convenience, and hygiene. The store displays related products in an organized manner such as displaying shower curtains, towels, and ceramic bathroom accessories on one aisle. This arrangement encourages sale of "multiples" of related products. The attention to layout details helps the store shape shopper's attitude. The fun and colorful interiors buzz with energy and customer excitement. The store offers bargain prices and an assortment unlike other stores in India. The discounts offered range from 5% to 60% (discount stores is still a nascent concept in India) that makes it a cost-focus store. Many retailing executives consider it to be the Walmart of India. The store is apt at striking a delicate balance needed to convince customers that its prices are low without making the people feel that the store is cheap.[16]

Having a lower-cost position also gives a company or business unit a defense against rivals. Its lower costs allow it to continue to earn profits during times of heavy competition. Its high market share means that it will have high bargaining power relative to its suppliers (because it buys in large quantities). Its low price will also serve as a barrier to entry because few new entrants will be able to match the leader's cost-advantage. As a result, cost leaders are likely to earn above-average returns on investment.

Differentiation is aimed at the broad mass market and involves the creation of a product or service that is perceived throughout its industry as unique. The company or business unit may then charge a premium for its product. This specialty can be associated with design or brand image, technology, features, a dealer network, or customer service. Differentiation is a viable strategy for earning above-average returns in a specific business because the resulting brand loyalty lowers customers' sensitivity to price. Increased costs can usually be passed on to the buyers. Buyer loyalty also serves as an entry barrier; new firms must develop their own distinctive competence to differentiate their products in some way in order to compete successfully. Examples of companies that successfully use a differentiation strategy are Walt Disney Productions (entertainment), BMW (automobiles), Nike (athletic shoes), Apple Computer (computers and cell phones). Similarly Indian corporate sector has multiple examples of companies adopting differentiation strategy successfully. For example, ITC before entering the biscuits segment conducted extensive market research. The market research project helped ITC develop an understanding about the Indian consumers, who according to the company's findings, wished to taste new and innovative products (some competition had ignored). The company used DIFFERENTIATION as its USP and in 2003 launched Sunfeast with six ranges.

Hindustan Unilever Limited (HUL), India's largest FMCG Company, touches lives of two out of three Indians with its product. The company has over 20 product lines in home and personal care products and foods and beverages. These product lines contribute to company's portfolio with a scale of combined volumes of about 4 million tonnes and sales of nearly Rs 13,718 crores.[17] HUL has achieved such a successful portfolio by focusing on growth strategy and product line pruning. The company concentrated on brands that constitute most of the business. From marketing 110 brands in 2000, HUL reduced the product line to 35 power brands—such as Lifebuoy, Lux, Surf Excel, Rin, Wheel, Fair & Lovely, Pond's, Sunsilk, Clinic Plus, Pepsodent, Close-up, etc. These were chosen on basis of their scale and potential. The company has also divested or transferred non-core business. This has helped HUL achieve product differentiation and improvement in sales.[18]

Research does suggest that a differentiation strategy is more likely to generate higher profits than does a low-cost strategy because differentiation creates a better entry barrier. A low-cost strategy is more likely, however, to generate increases in market share.[19] For an example of a differentiation strategy based upon environmental sustainability, see the **Environmental Sustainability Issue** feature on Wipro.

Cost focus is a low-cost competitive strategy that focuses on a particular buyer group or geographic market and attempts to serve only this niche, to the exclusion of others. In using cost focus, the company or business unit seeks a cost advantage in its target segment. A good example of this strategy is Potlach Corporation, a manufacturer of toilet tissue. Rather than compete directly against Procter & Gamble's Charmin, Potlach makes the house brands for Albertson's, Safeway, Jewel, and many other grocery store chains. It matches the quality of the well-known brands, but keeps costs low by eliminating advertising and promotion expenses. As a result, Spokane-based Potlach makes 92% of the private-label bathroom tissue and one-third of all bathroom tissue sold in Western U.S. grocery stores.[20]

Differentiation focus, like cost focus, concentrates on a particular buyer group, product line segment, or geographic market. This is the strategy successfully followed by Midamar Corporation (distributor of halal foods), Morgan Motor Car Company (a manufacturer of classic British sports cars), Nickelodeon (a cable channel for children), Orphagenix (pharmaceuticals), and local ethnic grocery stores. In using differentiation focus, a company or business unit seeks differentiation in a targeted market segment. This strategy is valued by those who believe that a company or a unit that focuses its efforts is better able to serve the special needs of a narrow strategic target more effectively than can its competition. For example, Orphagenix is a small biotech pharmaceutical company that avoids head-to-head competition with big companies like AstraZenica and Merck by developing "orphan" drugs to target diseases that affect fewer than 200,000 people—diseases such as sickle cell anemia and spinal muscular atrophy that big drug makers are overlooking.[21]

Risks in Competitive Strategies

No one competitive strategy is guaranteed to achieve success, and some companies that have successfully implemented one of Porter's competitive strategies have found that they could not

ENVIRONMENTAL sustainability issue

WIPRO USES SUSTAINABILITY AS A STRATEGY

According to the International Association of Electronics Recyclers, about 400 million units of electronic junk, or "e-waste," is generated annually. The discarded electronic devices that enter the waste stream are called e-waste. Rest of it is thought to reside in consumers' closets and basements – as consumers become more reticent to send their gadgets to landfills, but have no clue how to responsibly dispose of them.

Such statistics aren't lost on Bangalore-based IT services firm Wipro Technologies which has adopted a differentiation strategy based on environmental sustainability. Following this strategy, the company aims at finding ways of working so that it and its stakeholders cause least harm to the environment. Mr. Azim Premji, Chairman, Wipro Limited, says, "We firmly believe business cannot be built at the cost of ecology. It is not sustainable. Ecological sustainability will increasingly be the defining force for society and business globally. Wipro believes ecological sustainability is the right thing to do – in fact is the only way forward." Wipro believes that enormous business opportunities lie for a business which builds itself and its profit motivations around ecological sustainability.

In June, the 96,000-employee firm launched a company-wide initiative called Eco Eye. The initiative attempts to engage with increasing levels of intensity with all stakeholders – Wipro's own employees, partners, suppliers, customers and immediate communities. According to Mr. Premji, Eco Eye is the "eye" through which the company attempts to see everything, and act for ecological sustainability.

The framework has five themes and seven goals identified for implementation. The five themes include being an ecological surplus organization, larger sustainability initiatives beyond Wipro, profitable investments, transparent reporting, risk planning and mitigation. The website http://www.wiprocorporate.com/ecoeye/ has various sections like Wipro Charter, city eco news, how green are you, eco-gallery, eco action, green tips, articles and feedback section which also reviews what others are saying.

Wipro aims to achieve a per capita GHG intensity of less than 1 ton of CO_2-e per capita by 2025 , 25 years ahead of the global target of 1 ton per capita by 2050. It aims to set new standards in recycling waste and facilitate employees achieve a higher ecological footprint in their personal lives. It also aims to achieve transparency in sustainability reporting and incorporate the expected effects of climate change and other areas of environmental degradation into Wipro's risk strategy.

Wipro has taken up several initiatives in ecological sustainability. Some of the initiatives adopted to make its internal operations green has resulted in 13% reduction in average electricity consumption in 2007–08 over 2001–02 (from 338 Kwh per person to 294 Kwh per person) and meet 52% of its water requirement with recycled water. Its campus at Gurgaon and Kochi are rated Platinum and Gold rated green buildings respectively by LEED. Its operations are ISO 14001 certified.

On the customer front, Wipro is at the forefront to build green data centers, launch Greenware PCs, India's first eco-friendly PC range, eco-friendly product engineering designs, e-waste disposal service and water treatment solutions.

The company is very proud of its reputation as a "Green Company", but also wants the firm to be economically sustainable as well. The company engages into these experiments to see if they can run it so its there 100 years from now and always makes best quality stuff.

....
Courtesy: Wipro Technologies Ltd.

sustain the strategy. As shown in **Table 6–1**, each of the generic strategies has risks. For example, a company following a differentiation strategy must ensure that the higher price it charges for its higher quality is not too far above the price of the competition; otherwise customers will not see the extra quality as worth the extra cost. This is what is meant in **Table 6.1** by the term *cost proximity*. For years, Deere & Company was the leader in farm machinery until low-cost competitors from India and other developing countries began making low-priced products. Deere responded by building high-tech flexible manufacturing plants using mass-customization to cut its manufacturing costs and using innovation to create differentiated products which, although higher-priced, reduced customers' labor and fuel expenses.[22]

TABLE 6–1	Risks of Generic Competitive Strategies	
Risks of Cost Leadership	**Risks of Differentiation**	**Risks of Focus**
Cost leadership is not sustained: ■ Competitors imitate. ■ Technology changes. ■ Other bases for cost leadership erode.	Differentiation is not sustained: ■ Competitors imitate. ■ Bases for differentiation become less important to buyers.	The focus strategy is imitated. The target segment becomes structurally unattractive: ■ Structure erodes. ■ Demand disappears.
Proximity in differentiation is lost.	Cost proximity is lost.	Broadly targeted competitors overwhelm the segment: ■ The segment's differences from other segments narrow. ■ The advantages of a broad line increase.
Cost focusers achieve even lower cost in segments.	Differentiation focusers achieve even greater differentiation in segments.	New focusers subsegment the industry.

Issues in Competitive Strategies

Porter argues that to be successful, a company or business unit must achieve one of the previously mentioned generic competitive strategies. Otherwise, the company or business unit is *stuck in the middle* of the competitive marketplace with no competitive advantage and is doomed to below-average performance. A classic example of a company that found itself stuck in the middle was K-Mart. The company spent a lot of money trying to imitate both Wal-Mart's low-cost strategy and Target's quality differentiation strategy—only to end up in bankruptcy with no clear competitive advantage. Although some studies do support Porter's argument that companies tend to sort themselves into either lower cost or differentiation strategies and that successful companies emphasize only one strategy,[23] other research suggests that some combination of the two competitive strategies may also be successful.[24]

The Toyota and Honda auto companies are often presented as examples of successful firms able to achieve both of these generic competitive strategies. Thanks to advances in technology, a company may be able to design quality into a product or service in such a way that it can achieve both high quality and high market share—thus lowering costs.[25] Although Porter agrees that it is possible for a company or a business unit to achieve low cost and differentiation simultaneously, he continues to argue that this state is often temporary.[26] Porter does admit, however, that many different kinds of potentially profitable competitive strategies exist. Although there is generally room for only one company to successfully pursue the mass-market cost leadership strategy (because it is so dependent on achieving dominant market share), there is room for an almost unlimited number of differentiation and focus strategies (depending on the range of possible desirable features and the number of identifiable market niches). Quality, alone, has eight different dimensions—each with the potential of providing a product with a competitive advantage (see **Table 6–2**).

Most entrepreneurial ventures follow focus strategies. The successful ones differentiate their product from those of other competitors in the areas of quality and service, and they focus the product on customer needs in a segment of the market, thereby achieving a dominant share of that part of the market. Adopting guerrilla warfare tactics, these companies go after opportunities in market niches too small to justify retaliation from the market leaders.

Industry Structure and Competitive Strategy

Although each of Porter's generic competitive strategies may be used in any industry, certain strategies are more likely to succeed than others in some instances. In a **fragmented industry**,

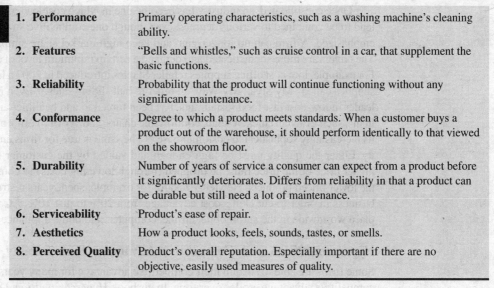

TABLE 6–2	1. **Performance**	Primary operating characteristics, such as a washing machine's cleaning ability.
The Eight Dimensions of Quality	2. **Features**	"Bells and whistles," such as cruise control in a car, that supplement the basic functions.
	3. **Reliability**	Probability that the product will continue functioning without any significant maintenance.
	4. **Conformance**	Degree to which a product meets standards. When a customer buys a product out of the warehouse, it should perform identically to that viewed on the showroom floor.
	5. **Durability**	Number of years of service a consumer can expect from a product before it significantly deteriorates. Differs from reliability in that a product can be durable but still need a lot of maintenance.
	6. **Serviceability**	Product's ease of repair.
	7. **Aesthetics**	How a product looks, feels, sounds, tastes, or smells.
	8. **Perceived Quality**	Product's overall reputation. Especially important if there are no objective, easily used measures of quality.

for example, where many small- and medium-sized local companies compete for relatively small shares of the total market, focus strategies will likely predominate. Fragmented industries are typical for products in the early stages of their life cycles. If few economies are to be gained through size, no large firms will emerge and entry barriers will be low—allowing a stream of new entrants into the industry. Chinese restaurants, veterinary care, used-car sales, ethnic grocery stores, and funeral homes are examples. Even though P.F. Chang's and the Panda Restaurant Group have firmly established themselves as chains in the United States, local, family-owned restaurants still comprise 87% of Asian casual dining restaurants.[27]

If a company is able to overcome the limitations of a fragmented market, however, it can reap the benefits of a broadly targeted cost-leadership or differentiation strategy. Until Pizza Hut was able to use advertising to differentiate itself from local competitors, the pizza fast-food business was a fragmented industry composed primarily of locally owned pizza parlors, each with its own distinctive product and service offering. Subsequently Domino's used the cost-leader strategy to achieve the market share.

As an industry matures, fragmentation is overcome, and the industry tends to become a **consolidated industry** dominated by a few large companies. Although many industries start out being fragmented, battles for market share and creative attempts to overcome local or niche market boundaries often increase the market share of a few companies. After product standards become established for minimum quality and features, competition shifts to a greater emphasis on cost and service. Slower growth, overcapacity, and knowledgeable buyers combine to put a premium on a firm's ability to achieve cost leadership or differentiation along the dimensions most desired by the market. R&D shifts from product to process improvements. Overall product quality improves, and costs are reduced significantly.

The *strategic rollup* was developed in the mid-1990s as an efficient way to quickly consolidate a fragmented industry. With the aid of money from venture capitalists, an entrepreneur acquires hundreds of owner-operated small businesses. The resulting large firm creates economies of scale by building regional or national brands, applies best practices across all aspects of marketing and operations, and hires more sophisticated managers than the small businesses could previously afford. Rollups differ from conventional mergers and acquisitions in three ways: (1) they involve large numbers of firms, (2) the acquired firms are typically owner operated, and (3) the objective is not to gain incremental advantage, but to reinvent an entire industry.[28]

Once consolidated, an industry has become one in which cost leadership and differentiation tend to be combined to various degrees, even though one competitive strategy may be primarily emphasized. A firm can no longer gain and keep high market share simply through low price. The buyers are more sophisticated and demand a certain minimum level of quality for price paid. For example, low-cost office supplies retailer Staples introduced in 2007 a line of premium office supplies called "My Style, My Way" in order to halt sliding sales.[29] Even McDonald's, long the leader in low-cost fast-food restaurants, has been forced to add healthier and more upscale food items, such as Asian chicken salad, comfortable chairs, and Wi-Fi Internet access in order to keep its increasingly sophisticated customer base.[30] The same is true for firms emphasizing high quality. Either the quality must be high enough and valued by the customer enough to justify the higher price or the price must be dropped (through lowering costs) to compete effectively with the lower priced products. Hewlett-Packard, for example, spent years restructuring its computer business in order to cut Dell's cost advantage from 20% to just 10%.[31] Consolidation is taking place worldwide in the automobile, airline, computer, and home appliance industries.

Hypercompetition and Competitive Advantage Sustainability

Some firms are able to sustain their competitive advantage for many years,[32] but most find that competitive advantage erodes over time. In his book *Hypercompetition*, D'Aveni proposes that it is becoming increasingly difficult to sustain a competitive advantage for very long. "Market stability is threatened by short product life cycles, short product design cycles, new technologies, frequent entry by unexpected outsiders, repositioning by incumbents, and tactical redefinitions of market boundaries as diverse industries merge."[33] Consequently, a company or business unit must constantly work to improve its competitive advantage. It is not enough to be just the lowest-cost competitor. Through continuous improvement programs, competitors are usually working to lower their costs as well. Firms must find new ways not only to reduce costs further but also to add value to the product or service being provided.

The same is true of a firm or unit that is following a differentiation strategy. Maytag Corporation, for example, was successful for many years by offering the most reliable brand in North American major home appliances. It was able to charge the highest prices for Maytag brand washing machines. When other competitors improved the quality of their products, however, it became increasingly difficult for customers to justify Maytag's significantly higher price. Consequently Maytag Corporation was forced not only to add new features to its products but also to reduce costs through improved manufacturing processes so that its prices were no longer out of line with those of the competition. D'Aveni's theory of hypercompetition is supported by developing research on the importance of building *dynamic capabilities* to better cope with uncertain environments (discussed previously in Chapter 5 in the resource-based approach to organization analysis).

D'Aveni contends that when industries become hypercompetitive, they tend to go through escalating stages of competition. Firms initially compete on cost and quality, until an abundance of high-quality, low-priced goods result. This occurred in the U.S. major home appliance industry by 1980. In a second stage of competition, the competitors move into untapped markets. Others usually imitate these moves until the moves become too risky or expensive. This epitomized the major home appliance industry during the 1980s and 1990s, as strong U.S. and European firms like Whirlpool, Electrolux, and Bosch-Siemens established presences in both Europe and the Americas and then moved into Asia. Strong Asian firms like LG and Haier likewise entered Europe and the Americas in the late 1990s.

According to D'Aveni, firms then raise entry barriers to limit competitors. Economies of scale, distribution agreements, and strategic alliances made it all but impossible for a new firm to enter the major home appliance industry by the end of the 20th century. After the established players have entered and consolidated all new markets, the next stage is for the remaining firms to attack and destroy the strongholds of other firms. Maytag's inability to hold onto its North American stronghold led to its acquisition by Whirlpool in 2006. Eventually, according

STRATEGY highlight 6.2

HYPERCOMPETITIVE TELECOM INDUSTRY OF INDIA

Indian telecom sector, till late 2000, was dominated by 4–5 big telecom service providers. These companies adopted product differentiation strategy and pretended to cater to customers who valued quality network and value-services over cheap tariff plans.[1]

However, this industry structure did not hold for long. Indian market numbers motivated many companies to make a beeline for the Indian telecom industry. At the end of September 2008, it was estimated that India had more than 315 million wireless connections and had already overtaken the United States to become the world's second-largest telecom market.[2] Such numbers motivated the companies to enter into Indian market.

Therefore, with entry of new players and advent of new telecom operators such as Tata DoCoMo, MTS, Maxis, Etisalat, etc., the industry structure evolved. Today, the sector has 12–13 players and is the fastest growing telecom market in the world in terms of subscribers per month with call rates that are cheaper than any other country in the world.

These newcomers understood that they needed to fight with incumbents such as Airtel and Vodafone to create a market presence and market share. These newcomers like Tata DoCoMo, changed the competitive dimensions of the industry by adopting a cost-leadership strategy. These companies introduced extremely low-priced plans (as low as 50 paise/minute) to attract customers. This cost leadership- based strategy tactically redefined the Indian telecom industry. The industry dimensions changed and the strategy led to erosion of all the competitive advantages. Price became the only differentiator between these 10 to 12 operators. The industry transformed into a hypercompetitive industry where the competitors competed on the basis of price and every player became a loser except for the Indian customer.[3] Today, though the Indian mobile telecom companies are, in the process, signing up 15 million customers every month, every new subscriber brings less than Rs 250 of business a month.[4] Therefore, these companies are operating on very thin margins.[5] The incumbents have managed to control their operating costs by outsourcing practically everything from management of IT functions to networks and call center operations and also sharing passive infrastructure such as telecom towers and generators.[6] However, it is not the cost that differentiates between the winners and losers. In the Indian telecom industry, the differentiation stems from the quality of high-speed mobile data services provided by the company. The incumbents have to offer quality services, i.e., high-speed mobile data services at lower prices to survive the hypercompetition.

Therefore, hypercompetition in an industry happens over a period of time and is characterized by erosion of competitive advantages, shortened product life cycles, shorter product design cycles, frequent introduction of new technologies, frequent entry by unexpected outsiders, repositioning by incumbents, and tactical redefinitions of the market. In such an industry, the business constantly works at improving their competitive advantage and reducing their costs.

1. Admin, The great Indian Telecom War, posted on 12 Oct 2009, accessed on 25 Oct 2011, from http://microreviews.org/the-great-indian-telecom-war/

2. Knowledge@Wharton, NTT DoCoMo's Tata Deal: Why Global Telecom Firms Want to Dial India, published on 27 Nov 2008 in India Knowledge@Wharton, accessed from http://knowledge.wharton.upenn.edu/india/article.cfm?articleid=4335

3. Admin, Indian Hypercompetitive Telecom Market – Has Consolidation started with Etisalat and Reliance Communication, posted on 2 Jun 2010, accessed on 25 Oct 2011, from http://www.greenworldinvestor.com/2010/06/02/indian-telecom-market-has-the-long-anticipated-consolidation-started-with-etisalat-and-reliance-communication/

4. Hindustan Times, A-roaming we will go, posted on 11 Oct 2011, Last Updated: 02:35 IST(12/10/2011), accessed on http://www.hindustantimes.com/StoryPage/Print/756183.aspx

5. Budget 2011: Telecom, accessed on 25 Oct 2011, from http://www.equitymaster.com/budget2011/sectors/telecom.asp

6. Knowledge @ Wharton, After the Telecom Price Wars, the Model Debate, Posted on 8 Sep 2011, accessed on 25 Oct 2011, from http://knowledgetoday.wharton.upenn.edu/2011/09/after-the-telecom-price-wars-the-model-debate/ .

to D'Aveni, the remaining large global competitors work their way to a situation of perfect competition in which no one has any advantage and profits are minimal.

Before hypercompetition, strategic initiatives provided competitive advantage for many years, perhaps for decades. Except for a few stable industries, this is no longer the case. According to D'Aveni, as industries become hypercompetitive, there is no such thing as a sustainable competitive advantage. Successful strategic initiatives in this type of industry typically last only months to a few years. According to D'Aveni, the only way a firm in this kind of dynamic industry can sustain any competitive advantage is through a continuous series of multiple short-term initiatives aimed at replacing a firm's current successful products with the next generation of products before the competitors can do so. Intel and Microsoft are taking this approach in the hypercompetitive computer industry.

Hypercompetition views competition, in effect, as a distinct series of ocean waves on what used to be a fairly calm stretch of water. As industry competition becomes more intense, the waves grow higher and require more dexterity to handle. Although a strategy is still needed to sail from point A to point B, more turbulent water means that a craft must continually adjust course to suit each new large wave. One danger of D'Aveni's concept of hypercompetition, however, is that it may lead to an overemphasis on short-term tactics (discussed in the next section) over long-term strategy. Too much of an orientation on the individual waves of hypercompetition could cause a company to focus too much on short-term temporary advantage and not enough on achieving its long-term objectives through building sustainable competitive advantage. Nevertheless, research supports D'Aveni's argument that sustained competitive advantage is increasingly a matter not of a single advantage maintained over time, but more a matter of sequencing advantages over time.[34] See **Strategy Highlight 6.2** to learn about the hypercompetition in telecom industry of India.

Which Competitive Strategy Is Best?

Before selecting one of Porter's generic competitive strategies for a company or business unit, management should assess its feasibility in terms of company or business unit resources and capabilities. Porter lists some of the commonly required skills and resources, as well as organizational requirements, in **Table 6–3**.

Competitive Tactics

Studies of decision making report that half the decisions made in organizations fail because of poor tactics.[35] A **tactic** is a specific operating plan that details how a strategy is to be implemented in terms of when and where it is to be put into action. By their nature, tactics are narrower in scope and shorter in time horizon than are strategies. Tactics, therefore, may be viewed (like policies) as a link between the formulation and implementation of strategy. Some of the tactics available to implement competitive strategies are timing tactics and market location tactics.

Timing Tactics: When to Compete

A **timing tactic** deals with *when* a company implements a strategy. The first company to manufacture and sell a new product or service is called the **first mover** (or pioneer). Some of the advantages of being a first mover are that the company is able to establish a reputation as an industry leader, move down the learning curve to assume the cost-leader position, and earn temporarily high profits from buyers who value the product or service very highly. A successful first mover can also set the standard for all subsequent products in the industry. A company that sets the standard "locks in" customers and is then able to offer further products based on that standard.[36] Microsoft was able to do this in software with its Windows operating system, and Netscape garnered over an 80% share of the Internet browser market by being first to commercialize the product successfully. Research does indicate that moving first or second into a new industry or foreign country results in greater market share and shareholder wealth than

TABLE 6–3	Requirements for Generic Competitive Strategies	
Generic Strategy	**Commonly Required Skills and Resources**	**Common Organizational Requirements**
Overall Cost Leadership	■ Sustained capital investment and access to capital ■ Process engineering skills ■ Intense supervision of labor ■ Products designed for ease of manufacture ■ Low-cost distribution system	■ Tight cost control ■ Frequent, detailed control reports ■ Structured organization and responsibilities ■ Incentives based on meeting strict quantitative targets
Differentiation	■ Strong marketing abilities ■ Product engineering ■ Creative flair ■ Strong capability in basic research ■ Corporate reputation for quality or technological leadership ■ Long tradition in the industry or unique combination of skills drawn from other businesses ■ Strong cooperation from channels	■ Strong coordination among functions in R&D, product development, and marketing ■ Subjective measurement and incentives instead of quantitative measures ■ Amenities to attract highly skilled labor, scientists, or creative people
Focus	■ Combination of the above policies directed at the particular strategic target	■ Combination of the above policies directed at the particular strategic target

SOURCE: Reprinted with the permission of The Free Press, a Division of Simon & Schuster, from *COMPETITIVE ADVANTAGE: Techniques for Analyzing Industries and Competitors* by Michael E. Porter. Copyright © 1980, 1998 by The Free Press. All rights reserved.

does moving later.[37] Being first provides a company profit advantages for about 10 years in consumer goods and about 12 years in industrial goods.[38] This is true, however, only if the first mover has sufficient resources to both exploit the new market and to defend its position against later arrivals with greater resources.[39] Gillette, for example, has been able to keep its leadership of the razor category (70% market share) by continuously introducing new products.[40]

Being a first mover does, however, have its disadvantages. These disadvantages can be, conversely, advantages enjoyed by late-mover firms. **Late movers** may be able to imitate the technological advances of others (and thus keep R&D costs low), keep risks down by waiting until a new technological standard or market is established, and take advantage of the first mover's natural inclination to ignore market segments.[41] Research indicates that successful late movers tend to be large firms with considerable resources and related experience.[42] Microsoft is one example. Once Netscape had established itself as the standard for Internet browsers in the 1990s, Microsoft used its huge resources to directly attack Netscape's position with its Internet Explorer. It did not want Netscape to also set the standard in the developing and highly lucrative intranet market inside corporations. By 2004, Microsoft's Internet Explorer dominated Web browsers, and Netscape was only a minor presence. Nevertheless, research suggests that the advantages and disadvantages of first and late movers may not always generalize across industries because of differences in entry barriers and the resources of the specific competitors.[43]

Market Location Tactics: Where to Compete

A **market location tactic** deals with *where* a company implements a strategy. A company or business unit can implement a competitive strategy either offensively or defensively. An *offensive tactic* usually takes place in an established competitor's market location. A *defensive tactic* usually takes place in the firm's own current market position as a defense against possible attack by a rival.[44]

Offensive Tactics. Some of the methods used to attack a competitor's position are:

- **Frontal assault:** The attacking firm goes head to head with its competitor. It matches the competitor in every category from price to promotion to distribution channel. To be successful, the attacker must have not only superior resources, but also the willingness to persevere. This is generally a very expensive tactic and may serve to awaken a sleeping giant, depressing profits for the whole industry. This is what Kimberly-Clark did when it introduced Huggies disposable diapers against P&G's market-leading Pampers. The resulting competitive battle between the two firms depressed Kimberly-Clark's profits.[45]

- **Flanking maneuver:** Rather than going straight for a competitor's position of strength with a frontal assault, a firm may attack a part of the market where the competitor is weak. Texas Instruments, for example, avoided competing directly with Intel by developing microprocessors for consumer electronics, cell phones, and medical devices instead of computers. Taken together, these other applications are worth more in terms of dollars and influence than are computers, where Intel dominates.[46]

- **Bypass attack:** Rather than directly attacking the established competitor frontally or on its flanks, a company or business unit may choose to change the rules of the game. This tactic attempts to cut the market out from under the established defender by offering a new type of product that makes the competitor's product unnecessary. For example, instead of competing directly against Microsoft's Pocket PC and Palm Pilot for the handheld computer market, Apple introduced the iPod as a personal digital music player. It was the most radical change to the way people listen to music since the Sony Walkman. By redefining the market, Apple successfully sidestepped both Intel and Microsoft, leaving them to play "catch-up."[47]

- **Encirclement:** Usually evolving out of a frontal assault or flanking maneuver, encirclement occurs as an attacking company or unit encircles the competitor's position in terms of products or markets or both. The encircler has greater product variety (e.g., a complete product line, ranging from low to high price) and/or serves more markets (e.g., it dominates every secondary market). For example, SAP is a leading manufacturer of enterprise applications in terms of software and software-related service revenues. SAP empowers people and organizations to work together more efficiently and uses business insight more effectively to stay ahead of the competition. Motivated by numbers, Oracle entered into the market of enterprise resource planning software. Initially, it tried to enter the market against the incumbent by moving beyond databases and other "infrastructure" software and break into enterprise applications with its own programs. When this failed, it decided to lead consolidation of the software industry and "surround" SAP with acquisitions.[48] Oracle surrounded SAP with acquisitions of companies such as BEA, PeopleSoft, Retex, etc.[49]

- **Guerrilla warfare:** Instead of a continual and extensive resource-expensive attack on a competitor, a firm or business unit may choose to "hit and run." Guerrilla warfare is characterized by the use of small, intermittent assaults on different market segments held by the competitor. In this way, a new entrant or small firm can make some gains without seriously threatening a large, established competitor and evoking some form of retaliation. To be successful, the firm or unit conducting guerrilla warfare must be patient enough to accept small gains and to avoid pushing the established competitor to the point that it must respond or else lose face.

Defensive Tactics. According to Porter, defensive tactics aim to lower the probability of attack, divert attacks to less threatening avenues, or lessen the intensity of an attack. Instead of increasing competitive advantage per se, they make a company's or business unit's competitive advantage more sustainable by causing a challenger to conclude that an attack is unattractive. These tactics deliberately reduce short-term profitability to ensure long-term profitability:[50]

■ **Raise structural barriers.** Entry barriers act to block a challenger's logical avenues of attack. Some of the most important, according to Porter, are to:

1. Offer a full line of products in every profitable market segment to close off any entry points (for example, Coca Cola offers unprofitable noncarbonated beverages to keep competitors off store shelves);
2. Block channel access by signing exclusive agreements with distributors;
3. Raise buyer switching costs by offering low-cost training to users;
4. Raise the cost of gaining trial users by keeping prices low on items new users are most likely to purchase;
5. Increase scale economies to reduce unit costs;
6. Foreclose alternative technologies through patenting or licensing;
7. Limit outside access to facilities and personnel;
8. Tie up suppliers by obtaining exclusive contracts or purchasing key locations;
9. Avoid suppliers that also serve competitors; and
10. Encourage the government to raise barriers, such as safety and pollution standards or favorable trade policies.

■ **Increase expected retaliation:** This tactic is any action that increases the perceived threat of retaliation for an attack. For example, management may strongly defend any erosion of market share by drastically cutting prices or matching a challenger's promotion through a policy of accepting any price-reduction coupons for a competitor's product. This counterattack is especially important in markets that are very important to the defending company or business unit. For example, when Clorox Company challenged P&G in the detergent market with Clorox Super Detergent, P&G retaliated by test marketing its liquid bleach, Lemon Fresh Comet, in an attempt to scare Clorox into retreating from the detergent market. Research suggests that retaliating quickly is not as successful in slowing market share loss as a slower, but more concentrated and aggressive response.[51]

■ **Lower the inducement for attack:** A third type of defensive tactic is to reduce a challenger's expectations of future profits in the industry. Like Southwest Airlines, a company can deliberately keep prices low and constantly invest in cost-reducing measures. With prices kept very low, there is little profit incentive for a new entrant.[52]

COOPERATIVE STRATEGIES

A company uses competitive strategies and tactics to gain competitive advantage within an industry by battling against other firms. These are not, however, the only business strategy options available to a company or business unit for competing successfully within an industry. A company can also use **cooperative strategies** to gain competitive advantage within an industry by working with other firms. The two general types of cooperative strategies are collusion and strategic alliances.

Collusion

Collusion is the active cooperation of firms within an industry to reduce output and raise prices in order to get around the normal economic law of supply and demand. Collusion may be explicit, in which case firms cooperate through direct communication and negotiation, or tacit, in which case firms cooperate indirectly through an informal system of signals. Explicit collusion is illegal in most countries and in a number of regional trade associations, such as the European Union. India also considers the collusion illegal. In India, Competition Commission of India (CCI) caters to collusion issues. CCI seeks to prohibit anti-competitive agreement, abuse of dominant position by an enterprise, and to regulate certain combinations, which include acquisition of shares, acquiring of control, and mergers/amalgamation between and among enterprises. In India, CCI has been set up to govern trade associations of sectors such as steel, cement, and shipping where government is of the view that these trade associations act in collusion to indulge in anti-competitive activities. CCI has asked companies to set up strict compliance standards for their employees to follow. CCI makes market-related discussions and pricing issues during their meetings with trade bodies and competitors, very risky.[53]

In case of suspicion, the CCI can order an enquiry. After an enquiry, in case the Commission finds that any agreement referred to in Section 3 or action of an enterprise in a dominant position is in contravention of Section 3 or Section 4, it may pass all or any of the following orders, namely:

i.   direction to discontinue and not to re-enter such agreement or discontinue abuse of dominance;
ii. impose penalty;
iii. direct modification of agreement;
iv. direction to abide by such other order including payment of costs; and
v.   pass such other order as it may deem fit.[54]

Indian Government makes most explicit efforts to control collusion in agri-based businesses. One such example is of wholesale grain market. Indian wholesale grain markets are characterized by large number of sellers, and a relatively small number of buyers. This imbalance provides ample opportunities for manipulation of the otherwise transparent price formation process. It leaves the system susceptible to collusion. It is only due to government intervention and continuous efforts that the extent of manipulation has been limited. The government has set up regulated markets where the rules of exchange are clearly spelled out. The study conducted by Banerjee and Meenakshi states that key institutional features of these grain markets are (a) sales through open ascending auctions; (b) presence of "commission agents" representing both buyers and sellers. The study found that the incentives of sellers and a subset of the large buyers were aligned; this along with a principal-agent slack between millers and commission agents facilitated the collusion. This in turn had huge influence on the market prices.[55]

Collusion can also be tacit, in which case there is no direct communication among competing firms. According to Barney, tacit collusion in an industry is most likely to be successful if (1) there are a small number of identifiable competitors, (2) costs are similar among firms, (3) one firm tends to act as the price leader, (4) there is a common industry culture that accepts cooperation, (5) sales are characterized by a high frequency of small orders, (6) large inventories and order backlogs are normal ways of dealing with fluctuations in demand, and (7) there are high entry barriers to keep out new competitors.[56]

Even tacit collusion can, however, be illegal. For example, when General Electric wanted to ease price competition in the steam turbine industry, it widely advertised its prices and publicly committed not to sell below those prices. Customers were even told that if GE reduced turbine prices in the future, it would give customers a refund equal to the price reduction. GE's message was not lost on Westinghouse, the major competitor in steam turbines. Both prices and profit margins remained stable for the next 10 years in this industry. The U.S. Department of Justice then sued both firms for engaging in "conscious parallelism" (following each other's lead to reduce the level of competition) in order to reduce competition.

Strategic Alliances

A **strategic alliance** is a long-term cooperative arrangement between two or more independent firms or business units that engage in business activities for mutual economic gain.[57] Alliances between companies or business units have become a fact of life in modern business. Some popular strategic alliances in India are Timex alliance with Indian watchmaker Titan Industries, which is a subsidiary of Tata Group; IBM strategic alliance agreement with Wipro to address customer needs in India and the Asia Pacific region; DreamWorks Animation formed a strategic alliance with tech major Thomson's Technicolor Services division to develop animation facilities for DreamWorks in India; Hero ITES has a strategic alliance with Live Bridge, USA—a U.S. $100 million per year contact center company specializing in inbound customer support and inbound sales for Fortune 500 corporations. For these and other reasons, around half of all alliances (including international alliances) perform unsatisfactorily. Others are more long lasting and may even be preludes to full mergers between companies.

Many alliances do increase profitability of the members and have a positive effect on firm value.[58] A study by Cooper & Lybrand found that firms involved in strategic alliances had 11% higher revenue and 20% higher growth rate than did companies not involved in alliances.[59] Forming and managing strategic alliances is a capability that is learned over time. Research reveals that the more experience a firm has with strategic alliances, the more likely that its alliances will be successful.[60] (There is some evidence, however, that too much partnering experience with the same partners generates diminishing returns over time and leads to reduced performance.)[61] Consequently, leading firms are making investments in building and developing their partnering capabilities.[62]

Companies or business units may form a strategic alliance for a number of reasons, including:

1. **To obtain or learn new capabilities:** For example, General Motors and Chrysler formed an alliance in 2004 to develop new fuel-saving hybrid engines for their automobiles.[63] Alliances are especially useful if the desired knowledge or capability is based on tacit knowledge or on new poorly-understood technology.[64] A study found that firms with strategic alliances had more modern manufacturing technologies than did firms without alliances.[65]

2. **To obtain access to specific markets:** Rather than buy a foreign company or build breweries of its own in other countries, Anheuser-Busch chose to license the right to brew and market Budweiser to other brewers, such as Labatt in Canada, Modelo in Mexico, and Kirin in Japan. As another example, U.S. defense contractors and aircraft manufacturers selling to foreign governments are typically required by these governments to spend a percentage of the contract/purchase value, either by purchasing parts or obtaining sub-contractors, in that country. This is often achieved by forming value-chain alliances with foreign companies either as parts suppliers or as sub-contractors.[66] In a survey by the *Economist Intelligence Unit*, 59% of executives stated that their primary reason for engaging in alliances was the need for fast and low-cost expansion into new markets.[67]

3. **To reduce financial risk:** Alliances take less financial resources than do acquisitions or going it alone and are easier to exit if necessary.[68] For example, because the costs of developing new large jet airplanes were becoming too high for any one manufacturer, Aerospatiale of France, British Aerospace, Construcciones Aeronáuticas of Spain, and Daimler-Benz Aerospace of Germany formed a joint consortium called Airbus Industrie to design and build such planes. Using alliances with suppliers is a popular means of outsourcing an expensive activity.

4. **To reduce political risk:** Forming alliances with local partners is a good way to overcome deficiencies in resources and capabilities when expanding into international markets.[69] To gain access to China while ensuring a positive relationship with the often restrictive Chinese government, Maytag Corporation formed a joint venture with the Chinese appliance maker, RSD.

Cooperative arrangements between companies and business units fall along a continuum from weak and distant to strong and close. (See **Figure 6–6**.) The types of alliances range from mutual service consortia to joint ventures and licensing arrangements to value-chain partnerships.[70]

FIGURE 6–6
Continuum of Strategic Alliances

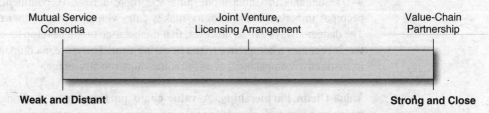

Mutual Service Consortia	Joint Venture, Licensing Arrangement	Value-Chain Partnership

Weak and Distant   **Strong and Close**

Mutual Service Consortia. A **mutual service consortium** is a partnership of similar companies in similar industries that pool their resources to gain a benefit that is too expensive to develop alone, such as access to advanced technology. For example, IBM established a research alliance with Sony Electronics and Toshiba to build its next generation of computer chips. The result was the "cell" chip, a microprocessor running at 256 gigaflops—around ten times the performance of the fastest chips currently used in desktop computers. Referred to as a "supercomputer on a chip," cell chips were to be used by Sony in its PlayStation 3, by Toshiba in its high-definition televisions, and by IBM in its super computers.[71] The mutual service consortia is a fairly weak and distant alliance—appropriate for partners that wish to work together but not share their core competencies. There is very little interaction or communication among the partners.

Joint Venture. A **joint venture** is a "cooperative business activity, formed by two or more separate organizations for strategic purposes, that creates an independent business entity and allocates ownership, operational responsibilities, and financial risks and rewards to each member, while preserving their separate identity/autonomy."[72] Along with licensing arrangements, joint ventures lie at the midpoint of the continuum and are formed to pursue an opportunity that needs a capability from two or more companies or business units, such as the technology of one and the distribution channels of another.

Joint ventures are the most popular form of strategic alliance. They often occur because the companies involved do not want to or cannot legally merge permanently. Joint ventures provide a way to temporarily combine the different strengths of partners to achieve an outcome of value to all. For example, Proctor & Gamble formed a joint venture with Clorox to produce food-storage wraps. P&G brought its cling-film technology and 20 full-time employees to the venture, while Clorox contributed its bags, containers, and wraps business.[73]

Extremely popular in international undertakings because of financial and political–legal constraints, forming joint ventures is a convenient way for corporations to work together without losing their independence. Around 30% to 55% of international joint ventures include three or more partners.[74] Disadvantages of joint ventures include loss of control, lower profits, probability of conflicts with partners, and the likely transfer of technological advantage to the partner. Joint ventures are often meant to be temporary, especially by some companies that may view them as a way to rectify a competitive weakness until they can achieve long-term dominance in the partnership. Partially for this reason, joint ventures have a high failure rate. Research indicates, however, that joint ventures tend to be more successful when both partners have equal ownership in the venture and are mutually dependent on each other for results.[75]

Licensing Arrangements. A **licensing arrangement** is an agreement in which the licensing firm grants rights to another firm in another country or market to produce and/or sell a product. The licensee pays compensation to the licensing firm in return for technical expertise. Licensing is an especially useful strategy if the trademark or brand name is well known but the MNC does not have sufficient funds to finance its entering the country directly. For example, Yum! Brands successfully used franchising and licensing to establish its KFC, Pizza Hut, Taco Bell, Long John Silvers, and A&W restaurants throughout the world. In 2007 alone, it opened 471 restaurants in China alone plus 852 more across six continents.[76] This strategy also becomes important if the country makes entry via investment either difficult or impossible. The danger always exists, however, that the licensee might develop its competence to the point that it becomes a competitor to the licensing firm. Therefore, a company should never license its distinctive competence, even for some short-run advantage.

Value-Chain Partnerships. A **value-chain partnership** is a strong and close alliance in which one company or unit forms a long-term arrangement with a key supplier or distributor for mutual advantage. Research suggests that suppliers that engage in long-term relationships are more profitable than suppliers with multiple short-term contracts.[77] For example, Tata Motors (previously known as TELCO) illustrates how a company in an emerging market can achieve success by developing close alliances with its suppliers and distributors. TATA motors, since 1983, was into manufacturing commercial vehicles. In 1990, it aspired to move into passenger cars. Though the two businesses shared the same Standard Industrial Classification (SIC) code, they were strategically different. The company's existing resources and capabilities were not enough to help it develop a passenger car. This motivated TATA to turn to its suppliers and distributors. The car was developed in 31 months and the bill totaled to Rs 1,700 crores as compared to an industry average of 48 months and U.S. $3 billion (Rs 12,750 crores).[80] For this venture, TATA outsourced 80% of the components (1,200 of its 1,500-plus parts), from 200-odd vendors.[78, 79, 81] Therefore, it was only through its value-chain partnerships that Tata Motors was able to introduce Indica as a small-cost leadership car in Indian markets.

All forms of strategic alliances involve uncertainty. Many issues need to be dealt with when an alliance is initially formed, and others, which emerge later. Many problems revolve around the fact that a firm's alliance partners may also be its competitors, either immediately or in the future. According to Peter Lorange, an authority in strategy, one thorny issue in any strategic alliance is how to cooperate without giving away the company or business unit's core competence: "Particularly when advanced technology is involved, it can be difficult for partners in an alliance to cooperate and openly share strategic know-how, but it is mandatory if the joint venture is to succeed."[82] It is therefore important that a company or business unit that is interested in joining or forming a strategic alliance consider the strategic alliance success factors listed in **Table 6–4**.

TABLE 6–4 Strategic Alliance Success Factors	<ul><li>Have a clear strategic purpose. Integrate the alliance with each partner's strategy. Ensure that mutual value is created for all partners.</li><li>Find a fitting partner with compatible goals and complementary capabilities.</li><li>Identify likely partnering risks and deal with them when the alliance is formed.</li><li>Allocate tasks and responsibilities so that each partner can specialize in what it does best.</li><li>Create incentives for cooperation to minimize differences in corporate culture or organization fit.</li><li>Minimize conflicts among the partners by clarifying objectives and avoiding direct competition in the marketplace.</li><li>In an international alliance, ensure that those managing it have comprehensive cross-cultural knowledge.</li><li>Exchange human resources to maintain communication and trust. Don't allow individual egos to dominate.</li><li>Operate with long-term time horizons. The expectation of future gains can minimize short-term conflicts.</li><li>Develop multiple joint projects so that any failures are counterbalanced by successes.</li><li>Agree on a monitoring process. Share information to build trust and keep projects on target. Monitor customer responses and service complaints.</li><li>Be flexible in terms of willingness to renegotiate the relationship in terms of environmental changes and new opportunities.</li><li>Agree on an exit strategy for when the partners' objectives are achieved or the alliance is judged a failure.</li></ul>

SOURCE: Compiled from B. Gomes-Casseres, "Do You Really Have an Alliance Strategy?" *Strategy & Leadership* (September/October 1998), pp. 6–11; L. Segil, "Strategic Alliances for the 21st Century," *Strategy & Leadership* (September/October 1998), pp. 12–16; and A. C. Inkpen and K-Q Li, "Joint Venture Formation: Planning and Knowledge Gathering for Success," *Organizational Dynamics* (Spring 1999), pp. 33–47. Inkpen and Li provide a checklist of 17 questions on p. 46.

Let's Summarize the Chapter with a Mind Map

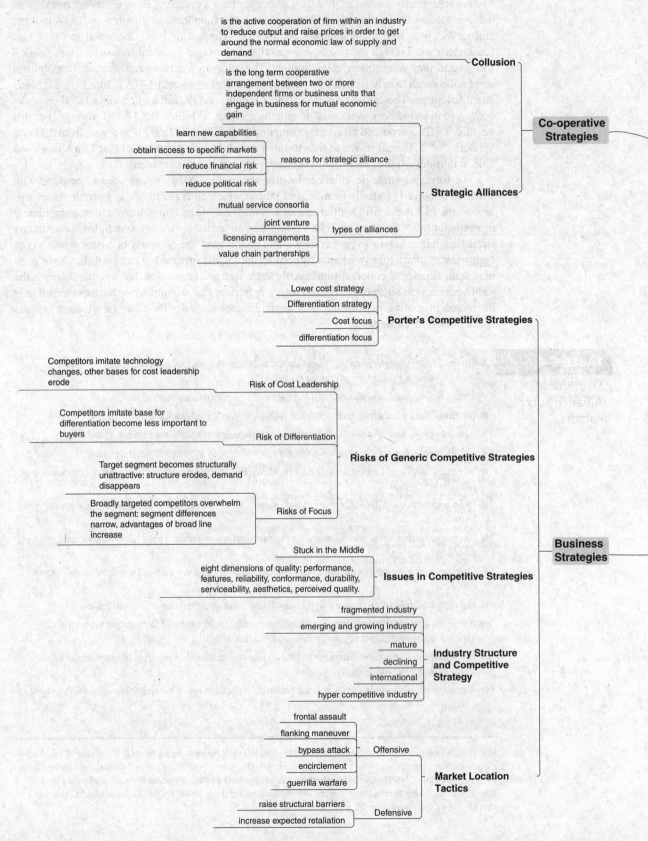

is the active cooperation of firm within an industry to reduce output and raise prices in order to get around the normal economic law of supply and demand — **Collusion**

is the long term cooperative arrangement between two or more independent firms or business units that engage in business for mutual economic gain

Co-operative Strategies

learn new capabilities
obtain access to specific markets
reduce financial risk
reduce political risk
reasons for strategic alliance

Strategic Alliances

mutual service consortia
joint venture
licensing arrangements
value chain partnerships
types of alliances

Lower cost strategy
Differentiation strategy
Cost focus
differentiation focus
Porter's Competitive Strategies

Competitors imitate technology changes, other bases for cost leadership erode — Risk of Cost Leadership

Competitors imitate base for differentiation become less important to buyers — Risk of Differentiation

Target segment becomes structurally unattractive: structure erodes, demand disappears

Broadly targeted competitors overwhelm the segment: segment differences narrow, advantages of broad line increase — Risks of Focus

Risks of Generic Competitive Strategies

Stuck in the Middle

eight dimensions of quality: performance, features, reliability, conformance, durability, serviceability, aesthetics, perceived quality. — **Issues in Competitive Strategies**

fragmented industry
emerging and growing industry
mature
declining
international
hyper competitive industry
Industry Structure and Competitive Strategy

Business Strategies

frontal assault
flanking maneuver
bypass attack
encirclement
guerrilla warfare
Offensive

raise structural barriers
increase expected retaliation
Defensive

Market Location Tactics

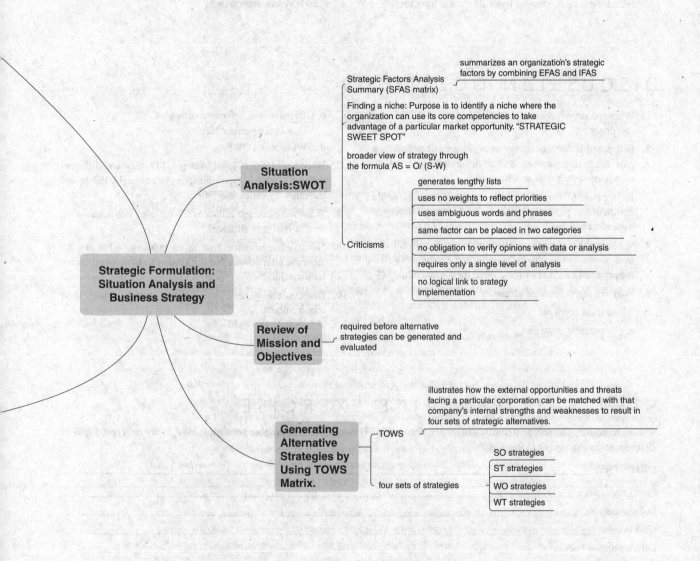

Strategic Formulation: Situation Analysis and Business Strategy

Situation Analysis:SWOT

Strategic Factors Analysis Summary (SFAS matrix) — summarizes an organization's strategic factors by combining EFAS and IFAS

Finding a niche: Purpose is to identify a niche where the organization can use its core competencies to take advantage of a particular market opportunity. "STRATEGIC SWEET SPOT"

broader view of strategy through the formula AS = O/ (S-W)

Criticisms
- generates lengthy lists
- uses no weights to reflect priorities
- uses ambiguous words and phrases
- same factor can be placed in two categories
- no obligation to verify opinions with data or analysis
- requires only a single level of analysis
- no logical link to srategy implementation

Review of Mission and Objectives — required before alternative strategies can be generated and evaluated

Generating Alternative Strategies by Using TOWS Matrix.

TOWS — illustrates how the external opportunities and threats facing a particular corporation can be matched with that company's internal strengths and weaknesses to result in four sets of strategic alternatives.

four sets of strategies
- SO strategies
- ST strategies
- WO strategies
- WT strategies

ECO-BITS

- Target became a certified organic produce retailer in 2006 and now offers more than 500 choices of organic certified food. The company reduces waste by giving away 7 million pounds of food annually.

- Home Depot offers more than 2,500 environmentally friendly products, ranging from all-natural insect repel-

lants to front-loading washing machines, specially tagged as Eco Options.

- Vowing to become "carbon neutral" by 2010, Timberland introduced Green Index tags, which rate its products on the use of greenhouse gas emissions, solvents, and organic materials.[83]

DISCUSSION QUESTIONS

1. What industry forces might cause a propitious niche to disappear?

2. Is it possible for a company or business unit to follow a cost leadership strategy and a differentiation strategy simultaneously? Why or why not?

3. Is it possible for a company to have a sustainable competitive advantage when its industry becomes hypercompetitive?

4. What are the advantages and disadvantages of being a first mover in an industry? Give some examples of first mover and late mover firms. Were they successful?

5. Why are many strategic alliances temporary?

6. Write short notes on:

   a. Cooperative strategies

   b. Offensive and defensive strategies

   c. Value-chain partnerships

   d. SWOT and TOWS.

7. What are business-level strategies? Outline and differentiate between two typologies, i.e., one given by Porter and the other by Miles and Snow.

8. What are strategic alliances? Why does a business unit form a business alliance?

9. Discuss hypercompetition in an industry. What are the strategic alternatives that a company in hypercompetitive industry has?

10. Discuss the generic competitive strategies and their requirements.

STRATEGIC PRACTICE EXERCISE

Select an industry to analyze. Identify companies for each of Porter's four competitive strategies. How many different kinds of differentiation strategies can you find?

INDUSTRY: _____

Cost Leadership: _____

Differentiation: _____

Cost Focus: _____

Differentiation Focus: _____

KEY TERMS

business strategy (p. 216)

collusion (p. 227)

common thread (p. 209)

competitive scope (p. 216)

competitive strategy (p. 216)

consolidated industry (p. 221)

cooperative strategy (p. 227)

cost focus (p. 218)

cost leadership (p. 217)

differentiation (p. 217)

differentiation focus (p. 218)

differentiation strategy (p. 216)

first mover (p. 224)

fragmented industry (p. 220)

joint venture (p. 230)

late mover (p. 225)

licensing arrangement (p. 230)

lower cost strategy (p. 216)

market location tactics (p. 225)

mutual service consortium (p. 230)

propitious niche (p. 208)

SFAS (Strategic Factors Analysis Summary) Matrix (p. 207)

strategic alliance (p. 228)

strategy formulation (p. 207)

SWOT (p. 207)

tactic (p. 224)

timing tactic (p. 224)

TOWS Matrix (p. 211)

value-chain partnership (p. 230)

NOTES

1. Indianetzone.com, Famous Sweet Makers:History & Specialities, recovered on 25th Oct 2011, from http://indianfood.indianetzone.com/1/famous_sweet_makers,_their_history_their_s pecialities.htm

2. J. Choi, D. Lovallo, and A. Tarasova, "Better Strategy for Business Units: A McKinsey Global Survey," *McKinsey Quarterly Online* (July 2007).

3. D. Fehringer, "Six Steps to Better SWOTs," *Competitive Intelligence Magazine* (January–February, 2007), p. 54.

4. T. Brown, "The Essence of Strategy," *Management Review* (April 1997), pp. 8–13.

5. T. Hill and R. Westbrook, "SWOT Analysis: It's Time for a Product Recall," *Long Range Planning* (February 1997), pp. 46–52.

6. W. H. Newman, "Shaping the Master Strategy of Your Firm," *California Management Review*, Vol. 9, No. 3 (1967), pp. 77–88.

7. D. J. Collis and M. G. Rukstad, "Can You Say What Your Strategy Is?" *Harvard Business Review* (April 2008), pp. 82–90.

8. Career launcher, About US, recovered on 25th Oct 2011, from http://www.careerlauncher.com/company/aboutcl/index.html

9. Gaja Capital, Portfolio, Career Launcher, recovered on 25th Oct 2011, from http://www.gajacapital.com/portfolio.aspx

10. Educomp, EDUSCHOOLS, recovered on 25th Oct 2011, from http://www.educomp.com/Services/EduSchools.aspx

11. D. J. Collis and M. G. Rukstad, "Can You Say What Your Strategy Is?" *Harvard Business Review* (April 2008), p. 86.

12. V. F. Misangyi, H. Elms, T. Greckhamer, and J. A Lepine, "A New Perspective on a Fundamental Debate: A Multilevel Approach to Industry, Corporate, and Business Unit Effects," *Strategic Management Journal* (June 2006), pp. 571–590.

13. M. E. Porter, *Competitive Strategy* (New York: The Free Press, 1980), pp. 34–41 as revised in M. E. Porter, *The Competitive Advantage of Nations* (New York: The Free Press, 1990), pp. 37–40.

14. J. O. DeCastro and J. J. Chrisman, "Narrow-Scope Strategies and Firm Performance: An Empirical Investigation," *Journal of Business Strategies* (Spring 1998), pp. 1–16; T. M. Stearns, N. M. Carter, P. D. Reynolds, and M. L. Williams, "New Firm Survival: Industry, Strategy, and Location," *Journal of Business Venturing* (January 1995), pp. 23–42.

15. Porter, *Competitive Strategy* (New York: The Free Press, 1980), p. 35.

16. L. J. Karjewski, L. P. Ritzman, and M. K. Malhotra, *Operations Management: Processes and Value Chains*. (New Delhi: Dorling Kindersley (India) Pvt. Ltd, 2008), pp. 316.

17. Hindustan Unilever Limited (HUL) recovered on 25th Oct 2011 from http://www.hul.co.in/knowus/present_stature.asp

18. India Brand Equity Foundation, Unilever: Fortune 500 Companies in India, pp. 168–171, Recovered on 25th Oct 2011 from http://ibef.org/attachdisplay.aspx?cat_id=60&art_id=6833

19. R. E. Caves, and P. Ghemawat, "Identifying Mobility Barriers," *Strategic Management Journal* (January 1992), pp. 1–12.

20. N. K. Geranios, "Potlach Aims to Squeeze Toilet Tissue Leaders," *Des Moines Register* (October 22, 2003), p. 3D.

21. "Company Targets 'Orphan Drugs,'" *St. Cloud (MN) Times* (May 9, 2007), p. 2A.

22. M. Arndt, "Deere's Revolution on Wheels," *Business Week* (July 2, 2007), pp. 78–79.

23. S. Thornhill and R. E. White, "Strategic Purity: A Multi-Industry Evaluation of Pure Vs. Hybrid Business Strategies," *Strategic Management Journal* (May 2007), pp. 553–561; M. Delmas, M. V. Russo, and M. J. Montes-Sancho, "Deregulation and Environmental Differentiation in the Electric Utility Industry," *Strategic Management Journal* (February 2007), pp. 189–209.

24. C. Campbell-Hunt, "What Have We Learned About Generic Competitive Strategy? A Meta Analysis," *Strategic Management Journal* (February 2000), pp. 127–154.

25. M. Kroll, P. Wright, and R. A. Heiens, "The Contribution of Product Quality to Competitive Advantage: Impacts on Systematic Variance and Unexplained Variance in Returns," *Strategic Management Journal* (April 1999), pp. 375–384.

26. R. M. Hodgetts, "A Conversation with Michael E. Porter: A 'Significant Extension' Toward Operational Improvement and Positioning," *Organizational Dynamics* (Summer 1999), pp. 24–33.

27. M. Rushlo, "P. F. Chang's Plans Succeed Where Others Have Failed," *Des Moines Register* (May 18, 2004), pp. 1D, 6D.

28. P. F. Kocourek, S. Y. Chung, and M. G. McKenna, "Strategic Rollups: Overhauling the Multi-Merger Machine," *Strategy + Business* (2nd Quarter 2000), pp. 45–53.

29. A. Pressman, "Upwardly Mobile Stationary," *Business Week* (March 17, 2008), pp. 60–61.

30. P. Gogoi, "Mickey D's McMakeover," *Business Week* (May 15, 2006), pp. 42–43.

31. N. Kumar, "Strategies to Fight Low-Cost Rivals," *Harvard Business Review* (December 2006), pp. 104–112.

32. J. C. Bou and A. Satorra, "The Presistence of Abnormal Returns at Industry and Firm Levels: Evidence from Spain," *Strategic Management Journal* (July 2007), pp. 707–722.

33. R. A. D'Aveni, *Hypercompetition* (New York: The Free Press, 1994), pp. xiii–xiv.

34. R. R. Wiggins and T. W. Ruefli, "Schumpeter's Ghost: Is Hypercompetition Making the Best of Times Shorter?" *Strategic Management Journal* (October 2005), pp. 887–911.

35. P. C. Nutt, "Surprising But True: Half the Decisions in Organizations Fail," *Academy of Management Executive* (November 1999), pp. 75–90.

36. Some refer to this as the economic concept of "increasing returns." Instead of the curve leveling off when the company reaches a point of diminishing returns when a product saturates a market, the curve continues to go up as the company takes advantage of setting the standard to spin off new products that use the new standard to achieve higher performance than competitors. See J. Alley, "The Theory That Made Microsoft," *Fortune* (April 29, 1996), pp. 65–66.

37. H. Lee, K. G. Smith, C. M. Grimm and A. Schomburg, "Timing, Order and Durability of New Product Advantages with Imitation," *Strategic Management Journal* (January 2000), pp. 23–30; Y. Pan and P. C. K. Chi, "Financial Performance and Survival of Multinational Corporations in China," *Strategic Management Journal* (April 1999), pp. 359–374; R. Makadok, "Can First-Mover and Early-Mover Advantages Be Sustained in an Industry with Low Barriers to Entry/Imitation?" *Strategic Management Journal* (July 1998), pp. 683–696); B. Mascarenhas, "The Order and Size of Entry into International Markets," *Journal of Business Venturing* (July 1997), pp. 287–299.

38. At these respective points, cost disadvantages vis-à-vis later entrants fully eroded the earlier returns to first movers. See W. Boulding and M. Christen, "Idea—First Mover Disadvantage," *Harvard Business Review*, Vol. 79, No. 9 (2001), pp. 20–21 as reported by D. J. Ketchen, Jr., C. C. Snow, and V. L. Hoover, "Research on Competitive Dynamics: Recent Accomplishments and Future Challenges," *Journal of Management*, Vol. 30, No. 6 (2004), pp. 779–804.

39. M. B. Lieberman and D. B. Montgomery, "First-Mover (Dis) Advantages: Retrospective and Link with the Resource-Based View," *Strategic Management Journal* (December, 1998), pp. 1111–1125; G. J. Tellis and P. N. Golder, "First to Market, First to Fail? Real Causes of Enduring Market Leadership," *Sloan Management Review* (Winter 1996), pp. 65–75.

40. J. Pope, "Schick Entry May Work Industry into a Lather," *Des Moines Register* (May 15, 2003), p. 6D.

41. S. K. Ethiraj and D. H. Zhu, "Performance Effects of Imitative Entry," *Strategic Management Journal* (August 2008), pp. 797–817; G. Dowell and A. Swaminathan, "Entry Timing, Exploration, and Firm Survival in the Early U.S. Bicycle Industry," *Strategic Management Journal* (December 2006), pp. 1159–1182. For an in-depth discussion of first and late mover advantages and disadvantages, see D. S. Cho, D. J. Kim, and D. K. Rhee, "Latecomer Strategies: Evidence from the Semiconductor Industry in Japan and Korea," *Organization Science* (July–August 1998), pp. 489–505.

42. J. Shamsie, C. Phelps, and J. Kuperman, "Better Late Than Never: A Study of Late Entrants in Household Electrical Equipment," *Strategic Management Journal* (January 2004), pp. 69–84.

43. T. S. Schoenecker and A. C. Cooper, "The Role of Firm Resources and Organizational Attributes in Determining Entry Timing: A Cross-Industry Study," *Strategic Management Journal* (December 1998), pp. 1127–1143.

44. Summarized from various articles by L. Fahey in *The Strategic Management Reader*, edited by L. Fahey (Englewood Cliffs, NJ: Prentice Hall, 1989), pp. 178–205.

45. M. Boyle, "Dueling Diapers," *Fortune* (February 17, 2003), pp. 115–116.

46. C. Edwards, "To See Where Tech Is Headed, Watch TI," *Business Week* (November 6, 2006), p. 74.

47. P. Burrows, "Show Time," *Business Week* (February 2, 2004), pp. 56–64.

48. The Economist, Programmed for a fight: Oracle and SAP are battling to dominate the business-software market, posted on 18th Oct 2007, recovered on 25th Oct 2011.

49. GCCRM market evaluation Guide, Siebel+Oracle > SAP: An Independent study on Siebel, Oracle and SAP, recovered on 25th Oct 2011, from http://www.realmarket.com/required/OracleSAP.pdf

50. This information on defensive tactics is summarized from M. E. Porter, *Competitive Advantage* (New York: The Free Press, 1985), pp. 482–512.

51. H. D. Hopkins, "The Response Strategies of Dominant U.S. Firms to Japanese Challengers," *Journal of Management*, Vol. 29, No. 1 (2003), pp. 5–25.

52. For additional information on defensive competitive tactics, see G. Stalk, "Curveball Strategies to Fool the Competition," *Harvard Business Review* (September 2006), pp. 115–122.

53. S. Souvik, "Checking Cartels: CCI Favours Compliance Code for Staff," *ET Bureau*, posted on 7th July 2008, recovered on 25th Oct 2011 from http://www.cci.gov.in/index.php?option=com_news&task=details&sid=17

54. Competition Commission of India, About Us, recovered on 25th Oct 2011 from http://www.cci.gov.in/index.php?option=com_content&task=view&exp=0&id=12

55. A. Banerji and J.V. Meenakshi, "Competition and Collusion in Grain Markets: Basmati Auctions in North India," Working papers 91, Centre for Development Economics, Delhi School of Economics, 2001.

56. Much of the content on cooperative strategies was summarized from J. B. Barney, *Gaining and Sustaining Competitive Advantage* (Reading, MA: Addison-Wesley, 1997), pp. 255–278.

57. A. C. Inkpen and E. W. K. Tsang, "Learning and Strategic Alliances," *Academy of Management Annals*, Vol. 1, edited by J. F. Walsh and A. F. Brief (December 2007), pp. 479–511.

58. N. K. Park, J. M. Mezias, and J. Song, "A Resource-based View of Strategic Alliances and Firm Value in the Electronic Marketplace," *Journal of Management*, Vol. 30, No. 1 (2004), pp. 7–27; T. Khanna and J. W. Rivkin, "Estimating the Performance Effects of Business Groups in Emerging Markets," *Strategic Management Journal* (January 2001), pp. 45–74; G. Garai, "Leveraging the Rewards of Strategic Alliances," *Journal of Business Strategy* (March–April 1999), pp. 40–43.

59. L. Segil, "Strategic Alliances for the 21st Century," *Strategy & Leadership* (September/October 1998), pp. 12–16.

60. R. C. Sampson, "Experience Effects and Collaborative Returns in R&D Alliances," *Strategic Management Journal* (November 2005), pp. 1009–1031; J. Draulans, A-P deMan, and H. W. Volberda, "Building Alliance Capability: Management Techniques for Superior Alliance Performance," *Long Range Planning* (April 2003), pp. 151–166; P. Kale, J. H. Dyer, and H. Singh, "Alliance Capability, Stock Market Response, and Long-Term Alliance Success: The Role of the Alliance Function," *Strategic Management Journal* (August 2002), pp. 747–767.

61. H. Hoang and F. T. Rothaermel, "The Effect of General and Partner-Specific Alliance Experience on Joint R&D Project Performance," *Academy of Management Journal* (April 2005), pp. 332–345; A. Goerzen, "Alliance Networks and Firm Performance: The Impact of Repeated Partnerships," *Strategic Management Journal* (May 2007), pp. 487–509.

62. A. MacCormack and T. Forbath, "Learning the Fine Art of Global Collaboration," *Harvard Business Review* (January 2008), pp. 24–26.

63. J. Porretto, "Rival Automakers Team Up to Catch Up," *Des Moines Register* (December 14, 2004), pp. 1D–2D.

64. H. Bapuji and M. Crossan, "Knowledge Types and Knowledge Management Strategies," in *Strategic Networks: Learning to Compete*, M. Gibbert and T. Durand, eds. (Malden, MA: Blackwell Publishing, 2007), pp. 8–25; F. T. Rothaermel and W. Boeker, "Old Technology Meets New Technology: Complementarities, Similarities, and Alliance Formation," *Strategic Management Journal* (January 2008), pp. 47–77.

65. M. M. Bear, "How Japanese Partners Help U.S. Manufacturers to Raise Productivity," *Long Range Planning* (December 1998), pp. 919–926.

66. According to M. J. Thome of Rockwell Collins in a June 26, 2008, e-mail, these are called "international offsets."

67. P. Anslinger and J. Jenk, "Creating Successful Alliances," *Journal of Business Strategy*, Vol. 25, No. 2 (2004), p. 18.

68. X. Yin and M. Shanley, "Industry Determinants of the 'Merger Versus Alliance' Decision," *Academy of Management Review* (April 2008), pp. 473–491.

69. J. W. Lu and P. W. Beamish, "The Internationalization and Performance of SMEs," *Strategic Management Journal* (June–July 2001), pp. 565–586.

70. R. M. Kanter, "Collaborative Advantage: The Art of Alliances," *Harvard Business Review* (July–August 1994), pp. 96–108.

71. "The Cell of the New Machine," *The Economist* (February 12, 2005), pp. 77–78.

72. R. P. Lynch, *The Practical Guide to Joint Ventures and Corporate Alliances* (New York: John Wiley and Sons, 1989), p. 7.

73. "Will She, Won't She? *The Economist* (August 11, 2007), pp. 61–63.

74. Y Gong, O Shenkar, Y. Luo, and M-K Nyaw, "Do Multiple Parents Help or Hinder International Joint Venture Performance? The Mediating Roles of Contract Completeness and Partner Cooperation," *Strategic Management Journal* (October 2007), pp. 1021–1034.

75. L. L. Blodgett, "Factors in the Instability of International Joint Ventures: An Event History Analysis," *Strategic Management Journal* (September 1992), pp. 475–481; J. Bleeke and D. Ernst, "The Way to Win in Cross-Border Alliances," *Harvard Business Review* (November–December 1991), pp. 127–135; J. M. Geringer, "Partner Selection Criteria for Developed Country Joint Ventures," in *International Management Behavior*, 2nd ed., edited by H. W. Lane and J. J. DiStephano (Boston: PWS-Kent, 1992), pp. 206–216.

76. 2007 Annual Report, *Yum! Brands*.

77. K. Z. Andrews, "Manufacturer/Supplier Relationships: The Supplier Payoff," *Harvard Business Review* (September–October 1995), pp. 14–15.

78. ICMR, Tata Indica: The Making of the Small Car, IBS center for management research, published 2003, 8 pages.

79. The Economic Times, Company History—Tata Motors Ltd, recovered on 25th Oct 2011, from http://economictimes.indiatimes.com/tata-motors-ltd/infocompanyhistory/companyid-12934.cms

80. The horoscope of INDICA, recovered on 25th Oct 2011, from http://ramsap.tripod.com/indica1.html

81. P. Tapan, A Case Study on the Indian Small Car Industry, recovered on 25th Oct 2011, from http://www.tapanpanda.com/doc/casestudy/indian%20small%20car%20industry.pdf

82. P. Lorange, "Black-Box Protection of Your Core Competencies in Strategic Alliances," in *Cooperative Strategies: European Perspectives*, edited by P. W. Beamish and J. P. Killing (San Francisco: The New Lexington Press, 1997), pp. 59–99.

83. J. O'Donnell and C. Dugas, "More Retailers Go for Green—the Eco Kind," *USA Today* (April 18, 2007), p. 3B.

CHAPTER 7

strategy formulation: corporate Strategy

What is the best way for a company to grow if its primary business is maturing? A study of 1,850 companies by Zook and Allen revealed two conclusions: First, the most sustained profitable growth occurs when a corporation pushes out of the boundary around its core business into adjacent businesses. Second, corporations that consistently outgrow their rivals do so by developing a formula for expanding those boundaries in a predicable, repeatable manner.[1]

Nike is a classic example of this process. Despite its success in athletic shoes, no one expected Nike to be successful when it diversified in 1995 from shoes into golf apparel, balls, and equipment. Only a few years later, it was acknowledged to be a major player in the new business. According to researchers Zook and Allen, the key to Nike's success was a formula for growth that the company had applied and adapted successfully in a series of entries into sports markets, from jogging to volleyball to tennis to basketball to soccer and, most recently, to golf. First, Nike established a leading position in athletic shoes in the target market, in this case, golf shoes. Second, Nike launched a clothing line endorsed by the sports' top athletes—in this case, Tiger Woods. Third, the company formed new distribution channels and contracts with key suppliers in the new business. Nike's reputation as a strong marketer of new products gave it credibility. Fourth, the company introduced higher-margin equipment into the new market. In the case of golf clubs, it started with irons and then moved to drivers. Once it had captured a significant share in the U.S. market, Nike's next step was global distribution.

Zook and Allen propose that this formula was the reason Nike moved past Reebok in the sporting goods industry. In 1987, Nike's operating profits were only $164 million compared to Reebok's much larger $309 million. Fifteen years later, Nike's operating profits had grown to $1.1 billion while Reebok's had declined to $247 million.[2] Reebok was subsequently acquired by Adidas in 2005 while Nike went on to generate operating profits of $2.4 billion in 2008.

Learning Objectives

After reading this chapter, you should be able to:

- Understand the three aspects of corporate strategy
- Apply the directional strategies of growth, stability, and retrenchment
- Understand the differences between vertical and horizontal growth as well as concentric and conglomerate diversification
- Identify strategic options to enter a foreign country
- Apply portfolio analysis to guide decisions in companies with multiple products and businesses
- Develop a parenting strategy for a multiple-business corporation

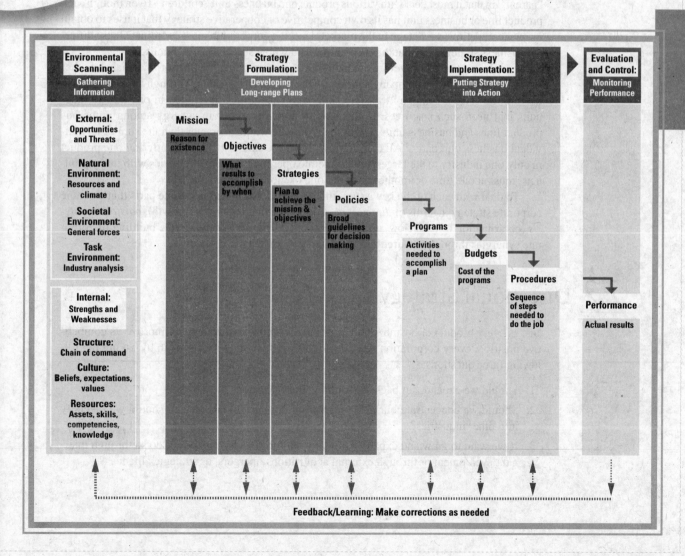

7.1 Corporate Strategy

The vignette about Nike illustrates the importance of corporate strategy to a firm's survival and success. Corporate strategy deals with three key issues facing the corporation as a whole:

1. The firm's overall orientation toward growth, stability, or retrenchment (**directional strategy**)

2. The industries or markets in which the firm competes through its products and business units (**portfolio analysis**)

3. The manner in which management coordinates activities and transfers resources and cultivates capabilities among product lines and business units (**parenting strategy**)

Corporate strategy is primarily about the choice of direction for a firm as a whole and the management of its business or product portfolio.[3] This is true whether the firm is a small company or a large multinational corporation (MNC). In a large multiple-business company, in particular, corporate strategy is concerned with managing various product lines and business units for maximum value. In this instance, corporate headquarters must play the role of the organizational "parent," in that it must deal with various product and business unit "children." Even though each product line or business unit has its own competitive or cooperative strategy that it uses to obtain its own competitive advantage in the marketplace, the corporation must coordinate these different business strategies so that the corporation as a whole succeeds as a "family."[4]

Corporate strategy, therefore, includes decisions regarding the flow of financial and other resources to and from a company's product lines and business units. Through a series of coordinating devices, a company transfers skills and capabilities developed in one unit to other units that need such resources. In this way, it attempts to obtain synergy among numerous product lines and business units so that the corporate whole is greater than the sum of its individual business unit parts.[5] All corporations, from the smallest company offering one product in only one industry to the largest conglomerate operating in many industries with many products, must at one time or another consider one or more of these issues.

To deal with each of the key issues, this chapter is organized into three parts that examine corporate strategy in terms of *directional strategy* (orientation toward growth), *portfolio analysis* (coordination of cash flow among units), and *corporate parenting* (the building of corporate synergies through resource sharing and development).[6]

7.2 Directional Strategy

Just as every product or business unit must follow a business strategy to improve its competitive position, every corporation must decide its orientation toward growth by asking the following three questions:

1. Should we expand, cut back, or continue our operations unchanged?

2. Should we concentrate our activities within our current industry, or should we diversify into other industries?

3. If we want to grow and expand nationally and/or globally, should we do so through internal development or through external acquisitions, mergers, or strategic alliances?

FIGURE 7–1
Corporate
Directional
Strategies

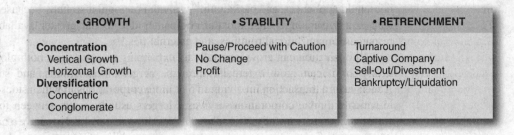

• GROWTH	• STABILITY	• RETRENCHMENT

Concentration
  Vertical Growth
  Horizontal Growth
Diversification
  Concentric
  Conglomerate
	Pause/Proceed with Caution
	No Change
	Profit
		Turnaround
		Captive Company
		Sell-Out/Divestment
		Bankruptcy/Liquidation

A corporation's **directional strategy** is composed of three general orientations (sometimes called *grand strategies*):

- **Growth strategies** expand the company's activities.
- **Stability strategies** make no change to the company's current activities.
- **Retrenchment strategies** reduce the company's level of activities.

Having chosen the general orientation (such as growth), a company's managers can select from several more specific corporate strategies such as concentration within one product line/industry or diversification into other products/industries. (See **Figure 7–1.**) These strategies are useful both to corporations operating in only one industry with one product line and to those operating in many industries with many product lines.

GROWTH STRATEGIES

By far the most widely pursued corporate directional strategies are those designed to achieve growth in sales, assets, profits, or some combination. Companies that do business in expanding industries must grow to survive. Continuing growth means increasing sales and a chance to take advantage of the experience curve to reduce the per-unit cost of products sold, thereby increasing profits. This cost reduction becomes extremely important if a corporation's industry is growing quickly or consolidating and if competitors are engaging in price wars in attempts to increase their shares of the market. Firms that have not reached "critical mass" (that is, gained the necessary economy of large-scale production) face large losses unless they can find and fill a small, but profitable, niche where higher prices can be offset by special product or service features. That is why Oracle acquired PeopleSoft, a rival software firm, in 2005. Although still growing, the software industry was maturing around a handful of large firms. According to CEO Larry Ellison, Oracle needed to double or even triple in size by buying smaller and weaker rivals if it was to compete with SAP and Microsoft.[7] It was growth that motivated the world's largest steel company, Mittal Steel, to merge with the second largest player, Arcelor SA, in 2006, to form a gigantic entity Arcelor Mittal Steel.[8] According to Mittal, the bid was only an extension of his growth strategy and the takeover of Arcelor (corporate jewel of Europe) would create an entity which would have a better bargaining power with suppliers and also entail synergies in marketing and manufacturing efficiencies.[9] The entity, ArcelorMittal is the world's number one steel company, present in more than 60 countries. It has led to the consolidation of the world steel industry and ranks as the global steel maker. ArcelorMittal is the **leader in all major global markets,** including automotive, construction, household appliances, and packaging.[10] Growth is a popular strategy because larger businesses tend to survive longer than smaller companies due to the greater availability of financial resources, organizational routines, and external ties.[11]

A corporation can grow internally by expanding its operations both globally and domestically, or it can grow externally through mergers, acquisitions, and strategic alliances. A **merger** is a transaction involving two or more corporations in which stock is exchanged but in which only one corporation survives. Mergers usually occur between firms of somewhat similar size and are usually "friendly." The resulting firm is likely to have a name derived from its composite firms. One example is the merging of Allied Corporation and Signal Companies to form Allied Signal. An **acquisition** is the purchase of a company that is completely absorbed as an operating subsidiary or division of the acquiring corporation. Procter & Gamble's (P&G's) purchase of Gillette is an example of a recent acquisition. Acquisitions usually occur between firms of different sizes and can be either friendly or hostile. Hostile acquisitions are often called *takeovers*.

Growth is a very attractive strategy for two key reasons:

- Growth based on increasing market demand may mask flaws in a company—flaws that would be immediately evident in a stable or declining market. A growing flow of revenue into a highly leveraged corporation can create a large amount of *organization slack* (unused resources) that can be used to quickly resolve problems and conflicts between departments and divisions. Growth also provides a big cushion for turnaround in case a strategic error is made. Larger firms also have more bargaining power than do small firms and are more likely to obtain support from key stakeholders in case of difficulty.

- A growing firm offers more opportunities for advancement, promotion, and interesting jobs. Growth itself is exciting and ego-enhancing for CEOs. The marketplace and potential investors tend to view a growing corporation as a "winner" or "on the move." Executive compensation tends to get bigger as an organization increases in size. Large firms are also more difficult to acquire than are smaller ones; thus an executive's job in a large firm is more secure.

The two basic growth strategies are **concentration** on the current product line(s) in one industry and **diversification** into other product lines in other industries.

Concentration

If a company's current product lines have real growth potential, concentration of resources on those product lines makes sense as a strategy for growth. The two basic concentration strategies are vertical growth and horizontal growth. Growing firms in a growing industry tend to choose these strategies before they try diversification.

Vertical Growth. **Vertical growth** can be achieved by taking over a function previously provided by a supplier or by a distributor. The company, in effect, grows by making its own supplies and/or by distributing its own products. This may be done in order to reduce costs, gain control over a scarce resource, guarantee quality of a key input, or obtain access to potential customers. This growth can be achieved either internally by expanding current operations or externally through acquisitions. Henry Ford, for example, used internal company resources to build his River Rouge plant outside Detroit. The manufacturing process was integrated to the point that iron ore entered one end of the long plant, and finished automobiles rolled out the other end, into a huge parking lot. In contrast, Cisco Systems, a maker of Internet hardware, chose the external route to vertical growth by purchasing Scientific-Atlanta Inc., a maker of set-top boxes for television programs and movies-on-demand. This acquisition gave Cisco access to technology for distributing television to living rooms through the Internet.[12]

Vertical growth results in **vertical integration**—the degree to which a firm operates vertically in multiple locations on an industry's value chain from extracting raw materials to manufacturing to retailing. More specifically, assuming a function previously provided by a supplier is called **backward integration** (going backward on an industry's value chain). For example, the Indian petrochemical giant Reliance Industries (before the split), went for backward integration into polyester fibers from textiles and petrochemicals. Reliance had, over the years, entered into oil and natural gas sector on one end and retail sector on the other. Nirma Limited is another example, which has successfully adopted backward integration strategy. Nirma, a pioneer in introducing low-cost detergents and soaps in India, achieved further cost economies and expansion in its market by adopting backward integration strategy.[13] In 2000, the company's backward integration strategy attempts led to establishing plants to produce linear alkyl benzene (LAB) in 1997 and soda ash in 2000. The company was able to benefit from this integration as more than 60% of the total cost of production was on account of these raw materials.[14] Assuming a function previously provided by a distributor is labeled as **forward integration** (going forward on an industry's value chain). FedEx, for example, used forward integration when it purchased Kinko's in order to provide store-front package drop-off and delivery services for the small-business market.[15] In the Indian context, there have been examples of small to medium-sized companies who sensed the retail opportunity and came up with innovative business models to emerge successfully.[16] One such example is of ABCTCL. Amalgamated Bean Coffee Trading Company (ABCTCL), better known as "ABC," is one of the largest exporters of green coffee from India since 1999.[17] ABCTCL today is more recognized by its chain of branded coffee outlets known as Café Coffee Day (CCD). The company has a complex and integrated value chain from presence in plantation activity to retailing. The company started off as a grower and exporter of coffee beans and later as a forward integration strategy started their retail operations. Today CCD is a chain of cafes in cities around India.[18] A lower pricing strategy, an equivalent product quality, and excellent service has made it the most successful coffee chain in India. Entry into retail has resulted in faster growth for ABCTCL vis-à-vis CCL products, an exporter of coffee.[19]

Vertical growth is a logical strategy for a corporation or business unit with a strong competitive position in a highly attractive industry—especially when technology is predictable and markets are growing.[20] To keep and even improve its competitive position, a company may use backward integration to minimize resource acquisition costs and inefficient operations as well as forward integration to gain more control over product distribution. The firm, in effect, builds on its distinctive competence by expanding along the industry's value chain to gain greater competitive advantage.

Although backward integration is often more profitable than forward integration (because of typical low margins in retailing), it can reduce a corporation's strategic flexibility. The resulting encumbrance of expensive assets that might be hard to sell could create an exit barrier, preventing the corporation from leaving that particular industry. Examples of single-use assets are blast furnaces and breweries. When demand drops in either of these industries (steel or beer), these assets have no alternative use, but continue to cost money in terms of debt payments, property taxes, and security expenses.

FIGURE 7–2
Vertical
Integration
Continuum

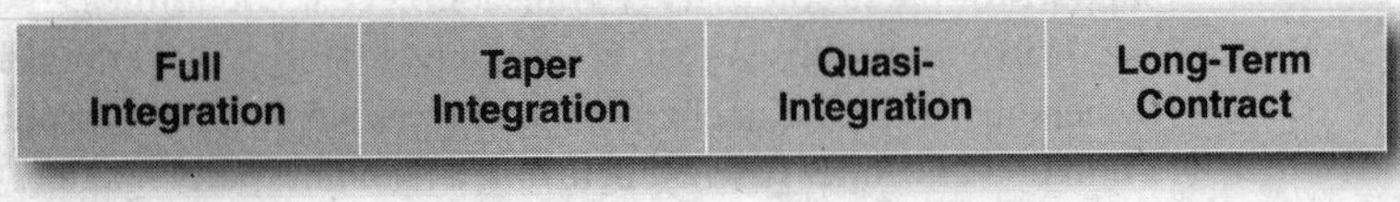

Full Integration	Taper Integration	Quasi-Integration	Long-Term Contract

SOURCE: *Suggested by K. R. Harrigan,* Strategies for Vertical Integration *(Lexington, Mass.: Lexington Books, D.C. Health, 1983), pp. 16–21.*

STRATEGY highlight 7.1

TRANSACTION COST ECONOMICS ANALYZES VERTICAL GROWTH STRATEGY

Why do corporations use vertical growth to permanently own suppliers or distributors when they could simply purchase individual items when needed on the open market? Transaction cost economics is a branch of institutional economics that attempts to answer this question. Transaction cost economics proposes that owning resources through vertical growth is more efficient than contracting for goods and services in the marketplace when the transaction costs of buying goods on the open market become too great. Transaction costs include the basic costs of drafting, negotiating, and safeguarding a market agreement (a contract) as well as the later managerial costs when the agreement is creating problems (goods aren't being delivered on time or quality is lower than needed), renegotiation costs (e.g., costs of meetings and phone calls), and the costs of settling disputes (e.g., lawyers' fees and court costs).

According to Williamson, three conditions must be met before a corporation will prefer internalizing a vertical transaction through ownership over contracting for the transaction in the marketplace: (1) a high level of uncertainty must surround the transaction, (2) assets involved in the transaction must be highly specialized to the transaction, and (3) the transaction must occur frequently. If there is a high level of uncertainty, it will be impossible to write a contract covering all contingencies, and it is likely that the contractor will act opportunistically to exploit any gaps in the written agreement—thus creating problems and increasing costs. If the assets being contracted for are highly specialized (e.g., goods or services with few alternate uses), there are likely to be few alternative suppliers—thus allowing the contractor to take advantage of the situation and increase costs. The more frequent the transactions, the more opportunity for the contractor to demand special treatment and thus increase costs further.

Vertical integration is not always more efficient than the marketplace, however. When highly vertically integrated firms become excessively large and bureaucratic, the costs of managing the internal transactions may become greater than simply purchasing the needed goods externally—thus justifying outsourcing over ownership. The usually hidden management costs (e.g., excessive layers of management, endless committee meetings needed for interdepartmental coordination, and delayed decision making due to excessively detailed rules and policies) add to the internal transaction costs—thus reducing the effectiveness and efficiency of vertical integration. The decision to own or to outsource is, therefore, based on the particular situation surrounding the transaction and the ability of the corporation to manage the transaction internally both effectively and efficiently.

SOURCES: O. E. Williamson and S. G. Winter, eds., *The Nature of the Firm: Origins, Evolution, and Development* (New York: Oxford University Press, 1991); E. Mosakowski, "Organizational Boundaries and Economic Performance: An Empirical Study of Entrepreneurial Computer Firms," *Strategic Management Journal* (February 1991), pp. 115–133; P. S. Ring and A. H. Van de Ven, "Structuring Cooperative Relationships Between Organizations," *Strategic Management Journal* (October 1992), pp. 483–498.

Transaction cost economics proposes that vertical integration is more efficient than contracting for goods and services in the marketplace when the transaction costs of buying goods on the open market become too great. When highly vertically integrated firms become excessively large and bureaucratic, however, the costs of managing the internal transactions may become greater than simply purchasing the needed goods externally—thus justifying outsourcing over vertical integration. This is why vertical integration and outsourcing are situation specific. Neither approach is best for all companies in all situations.[21] See the **Strategy Highlight 7.1** feature on how transaction cost economics helps explain why firms vertically integrate or outsource important activities. Research thus far provides mixed support for the predictions of transaction cost economics.[22]

Harrigan proposes that a company's degree of vertical integration can range from total ownership of the value chain needed to make and sell a product to no ownership at all.[23] (See **Figure 7–2**.) Under **full integration**, a firm internally makes 100% of its key supplies and completely controls its distributors. Large oil companies, such as British Petroleum and Royal Dutch Shell, are fully integrated. They own the oil rigs that pump the oil out of the ground, the ships and pipelines that transport the oil, the refineries that convert the oil to gasoline, and the trucks that deliver the gasoline to company-owned and franchised gas stations. Sherwin-Williams Company, which not only manufacturers paint, but also sells it in its own chain of 3,000 retail stores, is another example of a fully-integrated firm.[24] If a corporation does not want the disadvantages of full vertical integration, it may choose either taper or quasi-integration strategies.

With **taper integration** (also called concurrent sourcing), a firm internally produces less than half of its own requirements and buys the rest from outside suppliers (backward taper integration).[25] In the case of Smithfield Foods, its purchase of Carroll's allowed it to produce 27% of the hogs it needed to process into pork. In terms of forward taper integration, a firm sells part of its goods through company-owned stores and the rest through general wholesalers. Although Apple had 216 of its own retain stores in 2008, much of the company's sales continued to be through national chains such as Best Buy and through independent local and regional dealers.

With **quasi-integration**, a company does not make any of its key supplies but purchases most of its requirements from outside suppliers that are under its partial control (backward quasi-integration). A company may not want to purchase outright a supplier or distributor, but it still may want to guarantee access to needed supplies, new products, technologies, or distribution channels. An example of forward quasi-integration would be a paper company acquiring part interest in an office products chain in order to guarantee that its products had access to the distribution channel. Purchasing part interest in another company usually provides a company with a seat on the other firm's board of directors, thus guaranteeing the acquiring firm both information and control. For example, 24/7 Customer, an Indian company founded in 2000, is the first BPO company that provides integrated customer lifecycle management services through a multi-shore global delivery model. It focuses on predictable and sustainable business performance coupled with innovation.[26] To gain sustained competitive advantage, the company has a continuous demand for skilled labor. However, the company is also susceptible to inherent industry problem of high attrition rate. This has motivated the company to test quasi-integration strategy. To ensure good quality supply it has set up close relationships with universities and colleges they hope to hire from. The company even provides course content and at times faculty to these colleges. 24/7 works in this way with over 300 colleges across various states. As a result of this strategy, the company has reported significantly better retention rates with employees hired in this way.[27]

Long-term contracts are agreements between two firms to provide agreed-upon goods and services to each other for a specified period of time. This cannot really be considered to be vertical integration unless it is an *exclusive* contract that specifies that the supplier or distributor cannot have a similar relationship with a competitive firm. In that case, the supplier or distributor is really a *captive company* that, although officially independent, does most of its business with the contracted firm and is formally tied to the other company through a long-term contract.

Recently there has been a movement away from vertical growth strategies (and thus vertical integration) toward cooperative contractual relationships with suppliers and even with competitors.[28] These relationships range from *outsourcing*, in which resources are purchased from outsiders through long-term contracts instead of being made in-house (e.g. Hewlett-Packard bought its laser engines from Canon for HP's laser jet printers), to strategic alliances, in which partnerships, technology licensing agreements, and joint ventures supplement a firm's capabilities (e.g. Toshiba has used strategic alliances with GE, Siemens, Motorola, and Ericsson to become one of the world's leading electronic companies).[29]

Horizontal Growth. A firm can achieve **horizontal growth** by expanding its operations into other geographic locations and/or by increasing the range of products and services offered to current markets. Research indicates that firms that grow horizontally by broadening their product lines have high survival rates.[30] Horizontal growth results in **horizontal integration**— the degree to which a firm operates in multiple geographic locations at the same point on an industry's value chain. For example, Procter & Gamble (P&G) continually adds additional sizes and multiple variations to its existing product lines to reduce possible niches competitors may enter. In addition, it introduces successful products from one part of the world to other regions. P&G has been introducing into China a steady stream of popular American brands, such as Head & Shoulders, Crest, Olay, Tide, Pampers, and Whisper. By 2007, it had 6,300 employees in China and the extensive distribution network it needed to prosper in the world's fastest growing market.[31]

Horizontal growth can be achieved through internal development or externally through acquisitions and strategic alliances with other firms in the same industry. For example, Tata Tea Limited, a member of the Tata Group, bought all the brands of Tetley Tea of UK for 271 million ($431.3 million).[32] It was the first major takeover by an Indian corporate.[33] Tata Tea acquired Tetley to obtain access to foreign markets like UK, U.S., Canada, Australia, and Europe. The audacious acquisition of Tetley in 2000 has defined the growth of Tatas and of India. Tata Sons, has since acquired over 36 global corporations, investing nearly $30 billion and Indian companies have marched with the beat, acquiring since then over 400 companies across domains from steel to textiles, aircraft to toolkits, unleashing the Indian entrepreneurial spirit backed by the world's largest free market democracy.[34] For example, Delta Airlines acquired Northwest Airlines in 2008 to obtain access to Northwest's Asian markets and those American markets that Delta was not serving then. In contrast, many small commuter airlines engage in long-term contracts with major airlines to offer a complete arrangement for travelers.

Horizontal growth is increasingly being achieved in today's world through international expansion. American's Wal-Mart, France's Carrefour, and Britain's Tesco are examples of national supermarket discount chains expanding horizontally throughout the world. This type of growth can be achieved internationally through many different strategies.

International Entry Options for Horizontal Growth

Research indicates that growing internationally is positively associated with firm profitability.[35] A corporation can select from several strategic options the most appropriate method for entering a foreign market or establishing manufacturing facilities in another country. The options vary from simple exporting to acquisitions to management contracts.

Some of the most popular options for international entry are as follows:

- **Exporting:** A good way to minimize risk and experiment with a specific product is **exporting**, shipping goods produced in the company's home country to other countries for marketing. The company could choose to handle all critical functions itself, or it could contract these functions to an export management company. Exporting is becoming increasingly popular for small businesses because of the Internet, fax machines, toll-free numbers, and overnight express services, which reduce the once-formidable costs of going international.

- **Licensing:** Under a **licensing** agreement, the licensing firm grants rights to another firm in the host country to produce and/or sell a product. The licensee pays compensation to the licensing firm in return for technical expertise. This is an especially useful strategy if the trademark or brand name is well known, but the company does not have sufficient funds to finance its entering the country directly. Anheuser-Busch used this strategy to produce and market Budweiser beer in the United Kingdom, Japan, Israel, Australia, Korea, and the Philippines. This strategy is also important if the country makes entry via investment either difficult or impossible.

- **Franchising:** Under a **franchising** agreement, the franchiser grants rights to another company to open a retail store using the franchiser's name and operating system. In exchange, the franchisee pays the franchiser a percentage of its sales as a royalty. Franchising provides an opportunity for a firm to establish a presence in countries where the population or per capita spending is not sufficient for a major expansion effort.[36]

■ **Joint Ventures:** Forming a **joint venture** between a foreign corporation and a domestic company is the most popular strategy used to enter a new country.[37] Companies often form joint ventures to combine the resources and expertise needed to develop new products or technologies. A joint venture may be an association between a company and a firm in the host country or a government agency in that country. A quick method of obtaining local management, it also reduces the risks of expropriation and harassment by host country officials. A joint venture may also enable a firm to enter a country that restricts foreign ownership. The corporation can enter another country with fewer assets at stake and thus lower risk. Under Indian law, for example, foreign retailers are permitted to own no more than 51% of shops selling single-brand products, or to sell to others on a wholesale basis. These and other restrictions deterred supermarket giants Tesco and Carrefour from entering India. As a result, 97% of Indian retailing is composed of small, family-run stores. Eager to enter India, Wal-Mart's management formed an equal partnership joint venture in 2007 with Bharti Enterprises to start wholesale operations. Under the name Bharti-Mart, the new company planned to open a dozen small retail stores by 2015.[38]

■ **Acquisitions:** A relatively quick way to move into an international area is through acquisitions—purchasing another company already operating in that area. Synergistic benefits can result if the company acquires a firm with strong complementary product lines and a good distribution network. Research suggests that wholly owned subsidiaries are more successful in international undertakings than are strategic alliances, such as joint ventures.[39] This is one reason why firms more experienced in international markets take a higher ownership position when making a foreign investment.[40] In some countries, however, acquisitions can be difficult to arrange because of a lack of available information about potential candidates.

■ **Green-Field Development:** If a company doesn't want to purchase another company's problems along with its assets, it may choose **green-field development** and build its own manufacturing plant and distribution system. Research indicates that firms possessing high levels of technology, multinational experience, and diverse product lines prefer green-field development to acquisitions.[41] This is usually a far more complicated and expensive operation than acquisition, but it allows a company more freedom in designing the plant, choosing suppliers, and hiring a workforce. For example, Nissan, Honda, and Toyota built auto factories in rural areas of Great Britain and then hired a young workforce with no experience in the industry. BMW did the same thing when it built its auto plant in Spartanburg, South Carolina, to make its Z3 and Z4 sports cars.

■ **Production Sharing:** Coined by Peter Drucker, the term **production sharing** means the process of combining the higher labor skills and technology available in developed countries with the lower-cost labor available in developing countries. Often called *outsourcing*, one example is Maytag's moving some of its refrigeration production to a new plant in Reynosa, Mexico, in order to reduce labor costs. Many companies have moved data processing, programming, and customer service activities "offshore" to Ireland, India, Barbados, Jamaica, the Philippines, and Singapore, where wages are lower, English is spoken, and telecommunications are in place. As the number of technology services employees in India grew to be 15% of IBM's total tech services employees by 2007, the company has been able to eliminate 20,000 jobs in high-cost locations in the U.S., Europe, and Japan.[42]

■ **Turnkey Operations: Turnkey operations** are typically contracts for the construction of operating facilities in exchange for a fee. The facilities are transferred to the host country or firm when they are complete. For example, the construction division of Larsen and Toubro (L&T) is building (the contract was allotted to L&T in 2008) textile mills and spring mills complexes for Bombay Dyeing.[43] The turnkey project which is a Rs 2,000-crore order from Wadia Group flagship company, requires L&T to build approximately four million sq. ft. at the textile mills in Worli and five million sq. ft. at spring mills in Wadala. These were expected to be completed by the end of December 2011.[44] The customer is usually a government agency of, for example, a Middle Eastern country that has decreed that a particular product must be produced locally and under its control. For example, Fiat built an auto plant in Tagliatti, Russia, for the Soviet Union in the late 1960s to produce an older model of Fiat under the brand name of Lada. MNCs that perform turnkey operations are frequently industrial equipment manufacturers that supply some of their own equipment for the project and that commonly sell replacement parts and maintenance services to the host country. They thereby create customers as well as future competitors. Interestingly, Renault purchased in 2008 a 25% stake in the same Tagliatti factory built by Fiat to help the Russian carmaker modernize, using Renault's low cost Logan as the base for the plant's new Lada model.[45]

- **BOT Concept:** The **BOT (Build, Operate, Transfer) concept** is a variation of the turnkey operation. Instead of turning the facility (usually a power plant or toll road) over to the host country when completed, the company operates the facility for a fixed period of time during which it earns back its investment plus a profit. It then turns the facility over to the government at little or no cost to the host country.[46]

- **Management Contracts:** A large corporation operating throughout the world is likely to have a large amount of management talent at its disposal. **Management contracts** offer a means through which a corporation can use some of its personnel to assist a firm in a host country for a specified fee and period of time. Management contracts are common when a host government expropriates part or all of a foreign-owned company's holdings in its country. The contracts allow the firm to continue to earn some income from its investment and keep the operations going until local management is trained.[47]

Diversification Strategies

According to strategist Richard Rumelt, companies begin thinking about diversification when their growth has plateaued and opportunities for growth in the original business have been depleted.[48] This often occurs when an industry consolidates, becomes mature, and most of the surviving firms have reached the limits of growth using vertical and horizontal growth strategies. Unless the competitors are able to expand internationally into less mature markets, they may have no choice but to diversify into different industries if they want to continue growing. The two basic diversification strategies are concentric and conglomerate.

Concentric (Related) Diversification. Growth through **concentric diversification** into a related industry may be a very appropriate corporate strategy when a firm has a strong competitive position but industry attractiveness is low.

Research indicates that the probability of succeeding by moving into a related business is a function of a company's position in its core business. For companies in leadership positions, the chances for success are nearly three times higher than those for followers.[49] By focusing on the characteristics that have given the company its distinctive competence, the company uses those very strengths as its means of diversification. The firm attempts to secure strategic fit in a new industry where the firm's product knowledge, its manufacturing capabilities, and the marketing skills it used so effectively in the original industry can be put to good use.[50] The corporation's products or processes are related in some way: they possess some common thread.

The search is for **synergy**, the concept that two businesses will generate more profits together than they could separately. The point of commonality may be similar technology, customer usage, distribution, managerial skills, or product similarity. This is the rationale taken by Quebec-based Bombardier, the world's third-largest aircraft manufacturer. In the 1980s, the company expanded beyond snowmobiles into making light rail equipment. Defining itself as a transportation company, it entered the aircraft business in 1986, with its purchase of Canadair, then best known for its fire-fighting airplanes. It later bought Learjet, a well-known maker of business jets. Over a 14-year period, Bombardier launched 14 new aircraft. In July 2008, the company announced its C Series Aircraft Program to manufacture a 110–130-seat "green" single-aisle family of airplanes to directly compete with Airbus and Boeing.[51]

A firm may choose to diversify concentrically through either internal or external means. Bombardier, for example, diversified externally through acquisitions. Toro, in contrast, grew internally in North America by using its current manufacturing processes and distributors to make and market snow blowers in addition to lawn mowers. When considering concentric diversification alternatives, see the criteria presented in **Strategy Highlight 7.2.**

Conglomerate (Unrelated) Diversification. When management realizes that the current industry is unattractive and that the firm lacks outstanding abilities or skills that it could easily transfer to related products or services in other industries, the most likely strategy is **conglomerate diversification**—diversifying into an industry unrelated to its current one. Rather than maintaining a common thread throughout their organization, strategic managers who adopt this strategy are primarily concerned with financial considerations of cash flow or risk reduction. This is also a good strategy for a firm that is able to transfer its own excellent management system into less-well-managed acquired firms. General Electric and Berkshire Hathaway are examples of companies that have used conglomerate diversification to grow successfully. Managed by Warren Buffet, Berkshire Hathaway has interests in furniture retailing, razor blades, airlines, paper, broadcasting, soft drinks, and publishing.[52]

The emphasis in conglomerate diversification is on sound investment and value-oriented management rather than on the product-market synergy common to concentric diversification. A cash-rich company with few opportunities for growth in its industry might, for example, move into another industry where opportunities are great but cash is hard to find. Another instance of conglomerate diversification might be when a company with a seasonal and, therefore, uneven cash flow purchases a firm in an unrelated industry with complementing seasonal sales that will level out the cash flow.

STRATEGY highlight 7.2

SCREENING CRITERIA FOR CONCENTRIC DIVERSIFICATION

Market Attractiveness

1. Is the market large enough to be attractive?
2. Is the market growing faster than the economy?
3. Does it offer the potential to increase revenue from current customers?
4. Does it provide the ability to sell existing services to new customers?
5. Does it create a recurring revenue stream?
6. Are average earnings in the industry/market higher than in current businesses?
7. Is the market already taken by strong competitors?
8. Does it strengthen relationships with existing value-chain players?

Market Feasibility

1. Can the company enter the market within a year?
2. Are there any synergies in the geographic region where the market is located?
3. Can existing capabilities be leveraged for market entry?
4. Can existing assets be leveraged for market entry?
5. Can existing employees be used to support this opportunity?
6. Will current and future laws and regulations affect entry?
7. Is there a need for a strong brand in the new market?
8. If there is a need for partners, can the company secure and manage partner relationships?

SOURCE: Summarized from N. J. Kaplan, "Surviving and Thriving When Your Customers Contract," *Journal of Business Strategy* (January/February, 2003), p. 20.

CONTROVERSIES IN DIRECTIONAL GROWTH STRATEGIES

Is vertical growth better than horizontal growth? Is concentration better than diversification? Is concentric diversification better than conglomerate diversification? Research reveals that companies following a related diversification strategy appear to be higher performers and survive longer than do companies with narrower scope following a pure concentration strategy.[53] Although the research is not in complete agreement, growth into areas related to a company's current product lines is generally more successful than is growth into completely unrelated areas.[54] For example, one study of various growth projects examined how many were considered successful, that is, still in existence after 22 years. The results were vertical growth, 80%; horizontal growth, 50%; concentric diversification, 35%; and conglomerate diversification, 28%.[55] This supports the conclusion from a study of 40 successful European companies that companies should first exploit their existing assets and capabilities before exploring for new ones, but that they should also diversify their portfolio of products.[56]

In terms of diversification strategies, research suggests that the relationship between relatedness and performance is curvilinear in the shape of an inverted U-shaped curve. If a new business is very similar to that of the acquiring firm, it adds little new to the corporation and only marginally improves performance. If the new business is completely different from the acquiring company's businesses, there may be very little potential for any synergy. If, however, the new business provides new resources and capabilities in a different, but similar, business, the likelihood of a significant performance improvement is high.[57]

Is internal growth better than external growth? Corporations can follow the growth strategies of either concentration or diversification through the internal development of new products and services, or through external acquisitions, mergers, and strategic alliances. The value of global acquisitions and mergers has steadily increased from less than $1 trillion in 1990 to $3.5 trillion in 2000.[58] According to a McKinsey & Company survey, managers are primarily motivated to purchase other companies in order to add capabilities, expand geographically, and buy growth.[59] Research generally concludes, however, that firms growing through acquisitions do not perform financially as well as firms that grow through internal means.[60] For example, on September 3, 2001, the day *before* HP announced that it was purchasing Compaq, HP's stock was selling at $23.11. After the announcement, the stock price fell to $18.87. Three years later, on September 21, 2004, the shares sold at $18.70.[61] One reason for this poor performance may be that acquiring firms tend to spend less on R&D than do other firms.[62] Another reason may be the typically high price of the acquisition itself. Studies reveal that over half to two-thirds of acquisitions are failures primarily because the premiums paid were too high for them to earn their cost of capital.[63] Another reason for the poor stock performance is that 50% of the customers of a merged firm are less satisfied with the combined company's service two years after the merger.[64] It is likely that neither strategy is best by itself and that some combination of internal and external growth strategies is better than using one or the other.[65]

What can improve acquisition performance? For one thing, the acquisition should be linked to strategic objectives and support corporate strategy. In addition, a corporation must be prepared to identify roughly 100 candidates and conduct due diligence investigation on around 40 companies in order to ultimately purchase 10 companies. This kind of effort requires the capacity to sift through many candidates while simultaneously integrating previous acquisitions.[66] A study by Bain & Company of more than 11,000 acquisitions by companies throughout the world concluded that successful acquirers make small, low-risk acquisitions before moving on to larger ones.[67] Previous experience between an acquirer and a target firm in terms of R&D, manufacturing, or marketing alliances improves the likelihood of a successful acquisition.[68] Realizing that an acquired company must be carefully assimilated into the acquiring firm's operations, Cisco uses three criteria to judge whether a company is a suitable candidate for takeover:

■ It must be relatively small.

■ It must be comparable in organizational culture.

■ It must be physically close to one of the existing affiliates.[69]

STABILITY STRATEGIES

A corporation may choose stability over growth by continuing its current activities without any significant change in direction. Although sometimes viewed as a lack of strategy, the stability family of corporate strategies can be appropriate for a successful corporation operating in a reasonably predictable environment.[70] They are very popular with small business owners who have found a niche and are happy with their success and the manageable size of their firms. Stability strategies can be very useful in the short run, but they can be dangerous if followed for too long. Some of the more popular of these strategies are the pause/proceed-with-caution, no-change, and profit strategies.

Pause/Proceed with Caution Strategy

A **pause/proceed-with-caution strategy** is, in effect, a timeout—an opportunity to rest before continuing a growth or retrenchment strategy. It is a very deliberate attempt to make only incremental improvements until a particular environmental situation changes. It is typically conceived as a temporary strategy to be used until the environment becomes more hospitable or to enable a company to consolidate its resources after prolonged rapid growth. This was the strategy Dell followed after its growth strategy had resulted in more growth than it could handle. Explained CEO Michael Dell, "We grew 285% in two years, and we're having some growing pains." Selling personal computers by mail enabled Dell to underprice competitors, but it could not keep up with the needs of a $2 billion, 5,600-employee company selling PCs in 95 countries. Dell did not give up on its growth strategy; it merely put it temporarily in limbo until the company was able to hire new managers, improve the structure, and build new facilities.[71] This was a popular strategy in late-2008 during a U.S. financial crisis when banks were freezing their lending and awaiting a rescue package from the federal government.

No-Change Strategy

A **no-change strategy** is a decision to do nothing new—a choice to continue current operations and policies for the foreseeable future. Rarely articulated as a definite strategy, a no-change strategy's success depends on a lack of significant change in a corporation's situation. The relative stability created by the firm's modest competitive position in an industry facing little or no growth encourages the company to continue on its current course, making only small adjustments for inflation in its sales and profit objectives. There are no obvious opportunities or threats, nor is there much in the way of significant strengths or weaknesses. Few aggressive new competitors are likely to enter such an industry. The corporation has probably found a reasonably profitable and stable niche for its products. Unless the industry is undergoing consolidation, the relative comfort a company in this situation experiences is likely to encourage the company to follow a no-change strategy in which the future is expected to continue as an extension of the present. Many small-town businesses followed this strategy before Wal-Mart moved into their areas and forced them to rethink their strategy.

Profit Strategy

A **profit strategy** is a decision to do nothing new in a worsening situation but instead to act as though the company's problems are only temporary. The profit strategy is an attempt to artificially support profits when a company's sales are declining by reducing investment and short-term discretionary expenditures. Rather than announce the company's poor position to shareholders and the investment community at large, top management may be tempted to follow this very seductive strategy. Blaming the company's problems on a hostile environment (such as anti-business government policies, unethical competitors, finicky customers, and/or greedy lenders), management defers investments and/or cuts expenses (such as R&D, maintenance, and advertising) to stabilize profits during this period. It may even sell one of its product lines for the cash-flow benefits.

The profit strategy is useful only to help a company get through a temporary difficulty. It may also be a way to boost the value of a company in preparation for going public via an initial public offering (IPO). Unfortunately, the strategy is seductive and if continued long enough it will lead to a serious deterioration in a corporation's competitive position. The profit strategy is typically top management's passive, short-term, and often self-serving response to a difficult situation. In such situations, it is often better to face the problem directly by choosing a retrenchment strategy.

RETRENCHMENT STRATEGIES

A company may pursue retrenchment strategies when it has a weak competitive position in some or all of its product lines resulting in poor performance—sales are down and profits are becoming losses. These strategies impose a great deal of pressure to improve performance. In an attempt to eliminate the weaknesses that are dragging the company down, management may follow one of several retrenchment strategies, ranging from turnaround or becoming a captive company to selling out, bankruptcy, or liquidation.

Turnaround Strategy

Turnaround strategy emphasizes the improvement of operational efficiency and is probably most appropriate when a corporation's problems are pervasive but not yet critical. Research shows that poorly performing firms in mature industries have been able to improve their performance by cutting costs and expenses and by selling off assets.[72] Analogous to a weight-reduction diet, the two basic phases of a turnaround strategy are contraction and consolidation.[73]

Contraction is the initial effort to quickly "stop the bleeding" with a general, across-the-board cutback in size and costs. For example, when Howard Stringer was selected to be CEO of Sony Corporation in 2005, he immediately implemented the first stage of a turnaround plan by eliminating 10,000 jobs, closing 11 of 65 plants, and divesting many unprofitable electronics businesses.[74] The second phase, *consolidation*, implements a program to stabilize the now-leaner corporation. To streamline the company, plans are developed to reduce unnecessary overhead and to make functional activities cost-justified. This is a crucial time for the organization. If the consolidation phase is not conducted in a positive manner, many of the best people leave the organization. An overemphasis on downsizing and cutting costs coupled with a heavy hand by top management is usually counterproductive and can actually hurt performance.[75] If, however, all employees are encouraged to get involved in productivity improvements, the firm is likely to emerge from this retrenchment period a much stronger and better-organized company. It has improved its competitive position and is able once again to expand the business.[76] In India, the best example of turnaround strategy is that of Indian Railways. Indian Railways. The premier transport organization of the country is the largest rail network in Asia and the world's second largest under one management. It runs 11,000 trains everyday, of which 7,000 are passenger trains and employs 1.54 million Indians.[77]. In 2001, it was said that the Railways would declare a bankruptcy of $15 billion (Rs 61,000 crores) and that they were in a "terminal debt trap."[78] The turnaround was achieved by targeting improvement in the operational efficiency by adopting different strategies for different categories of stakeholders.

For freight customers, a whole host of schemes was put in place to attract the freight customer, since July 2005 [MOR, 2006-b]. These include initiatives of (i) increased axle load (ii) reduced wagon turnaround, and (iii) market oriented tariffs and schemes.[79]

For passengers, emphasis has been laid on service quality. Consequent to the above initiatives, the growth in number of passengers has been 7.5% in 2008.[80] The growth in the earlier three years ranged between 2.4% and 5.4% (opcit 76).

For value-added services such as parcel, catering, advertising, dividends from the public sector units under the ministry, a slew of initiatives on these areas have been implemented over the past two years, making it attractive for private parties to take advantage of the market opportunity that IR offers.

As a result of these initiatives, Shri Lalu Prasad, while introducing the Railway Budget in 2007–2008, quoted that the railways were poised to create history by generating a cash surplus before dividend of Rs 20,000 crore as against Rs 14,700 crore in the previous year; the same railway that defaulted on payment of dividend and whose fund balances dipped to Rs 359 crore in 2001.[81]

Captive Company Strategy

A **captive company strategy** involves giving up independence in exchange for security. A company with a weak competitive position may not be able to engage in a full-blown turnaround strategy. The industry may not be sufficiently attractive to justify such an effort from either the current management or investors. Nevertheless, a company in this situation faces poor sales and increasing losses unless it takes some action. Management desperately searches for an "angel" by offering to be a captive company to one of its larger customers in order to guarantee the company's continued existence with a long-term contract. In this way, the corporation may be able to reduce the scope of some of its functional activities, such as marketing, thus significantly reducing costs. The weaker company gains certainty of sales and production in return for becoming heavily dependent on another firm for at least 75% of its sales. For example, to become the sole supplier of an auto part to General Motors, Simpson Industries of Birmingham, Michigan, agreed to let a special team from GM inspect its engine parts facilities and books and interview its employees. In return, nearly 80% of the company's production was sold to GM through long-term contracts.[82]

Sell-Out/Divestment Strategy

If a corporation with a weak competitive position in an industry is unable either to pull itself up by its bootstraps or to find a customer to which it can become a captive company, it may have no choice but to sell out. The **sell-out strategy** makes sense if management can still obtain a good price for its shareholders and the employees can keep their jobs by selling the entire company to another firm. The hope is that another company will have the necessary resources and determination to return the company to profitability. Marginal performance in a troubled industry was one reason Northwest Airlines was willing to be acquired by Delta Airlines in 2008.

If the corporation has multiple business lines and it chooses to sell off a division with low growth potential, this is called **divestment**. This was the strategy Ford used when it sold its struggling Jaguar and Land Rover units to Tata Motors in 2008 for $2 billion. Ford had spent $10 billion trying to turn around Jaguar after spending $2.5 billion to buy it in 1990. In addition, Ford had paid $2.8 billion for Land Rover in 2000. Ford's management hoped to use the proceeds of the sale to help the company reach profitability in 2009.[83] General Electric's management used the same reasoning when it decided to sell or spin off its slow-growth appliance business in 2008.

Divestment is often used after a corporation acquires a multi unit corporation in order to shed the units that do not fit with the corporation's new strategy. This is why Whirlpool sold Maytag's Hoover vacuum cleaner unit after Whirlpool purchased Maytag. Divestment was also a key part of Lego's turnaround strategy when management decided to divest its theme parks to concentrate more on its core business of making toys.[84]

Bankruptcy/Liquidation Strategy

When a company finds itself in the worst possible situation with a poor competitive position in an industry with few prospects, management has only a few alternatives—all of them distasteful. Because no one is interested in buying a weak company in an unattractive industry, the firm must pursue a bankruptcy or liquidation strategy. **Bankruptcy** involves giving up management of the firm to the courts in return for some settlement of the corporation's obligations. Top management hopes that once the court decides the claims on the company, the company will be stronger and better able to compete in a more attractive industry.

In contrast to bankruptcy, which seeks to perpetuate a corporation, **liquidation** is the termination of the firm. When the industry is unattractive and the company too weak to be sold as a going concern, management may choose to convert as many saleable assets as possible to cash, which is then distributed to the shareholders after all obligations are paid. Liquidation is a prudent strategy for distressed firms with a small number of choices, all of which are problematic.[85] This was Circuit City's situation in 2008, when it liquidated its retail stores. The benefit of liquidation over bankruptcy is that the board of directors, as representatives of the shareholders, together with top management make the decisions instead of turning them over to the bankruptcy court, which may choose to ignore shareholders completely.

At times, top management must be willing to select one of these less desirable retrenchment strategies. Unfortunately, many top managers are unwilling to admit that their company has serious weaknesses for fear that they may be personally blamed. Even worse, top management may not even perceive that crises are developing. When these top managers eventually notice trouble, they are prone to attribute the problems to temporary environmental disturbances and tend to follow profit strategies. Even when things are going terribly wrong, top management is greatly tempted to avoid liquidation in the hope of a miracle. Top management enters a *cycle of decline,* in which it goes through a process of secrecy and denial, followed by blame and scorn, avoidance and turf protection, ending with passivity and helplessness.[86] Thus, a corporation needs a strong board of directors who, to safeguard shareholders' interests, can tell top management when to quit.

7.3 Portfolio Analysis

Chapter 6 dealt with how individual product lines and business units can gain competitive advantage in the marketplace by using competitive and cooperative strategies. Companies with multiple product lines or business units must also ask themselves how these various products and business units should be managed to boost overall corporate performance:

- How much of our time and money should we spend on our best products and business units to ensure that they continue to be successful?

- How much of our time and money should we spend developing new costly products, most of which will never be successful?

One of the most popular aids to developing corporate strategy in a multiple-business corporation is portfolio analysis. Although its popularity has dropped since the 1970s and 1980s, when more than half of the largest business corporations used portfolio analysis, it is still used by around 27% of Fortune 500 firms in corporate strategy formulation.[87] Portfolio analysis puts corporate headquarters into the role of an internal banker. In **portfolio analysis**, top management views its product lines and business units as a series of investments from which it expects a profitable return. The product lines/business units form a portfolio of investments that top management must constantly juggle to ensure the best return on the corporation's invested money. A McKinsey & Company study of the performance of the 200 largest U.S. corporations found that companies that actively managed their business portfolios through acquisitions and divestitures created substantially more shareholder value than those companies that passively held their businesses.[88] Given the increasing number of strategic alliances in today's corporations, portfolio analysis is also being used to evaluate the contribution of alliances to corporate and business unit objectives.

Two of the most popular portfolio techniques are the BCG Growth-Share Matrix and GE Business Screen.

BCG GROWTH-SHARE MATRIX

Using the **BCG (Boston Consulting Group) Growth-Share Matrix** depicted in **Figure 7–3** is the simplest way to portray a corporation's portfolio of investments. Each of the corporation's product lines or business units is plotted on the matrix according to both the growth rate of the industry in which it competes and its relative market share. A unit's relative competitive position is defined as its market share in the industry divided by that of the largest other competitor. By this calculation, a relative market share above 1.0 belongs to the market leader. The business growth rate is the percentage of market growth, that is, the percentage by which sales of a particular business unit classification of products have increased. The matrix assumes that, other things being equal, a growing market is attractive.

The line separating areas of high and low relative competitive position is set at 1.5 times. A product line or business unit must have relative strengths of this magnitude to ensure that it will have the dominant position needed to be a "star" or "cash cow." On the other hand, a product line or unit having a relative competitive position less than 1.0 has "dog" status.[89] Each product or unit is represented in Figure 7–3 by a circle. The area of the circle represents the relative significance of each business unit or product line to the corporation in terms of assets used or sales generated.

The BCG Growth-Share Matrix has a lot in common with the product life cycle. As a product moves through its life cycle, it is categorized into one of four types for the purpose of funding decisions:

- **Question marks** (sometimes called "problem children" or "wildcats") are new products with the potential for success, but they need a lot of cash for development. If such a product is to gain enough market share to become a market leader and thus a star, money must be taken from more mature products and spent on the question mark. This is a "fish or cut bait" decision in which management must decide if the business is worth the investment needed. For example, after years of fruitlessly experimenting with an electric car, General Motors finally decided in 2006 to take a chance on developing the Chevrolet Volt.[90] To learn more of GM's decision to build the electric car, see the **Environmental Sustainability Issue** feature.

FIGURE 7–3
BCG Growth-Share Matrix

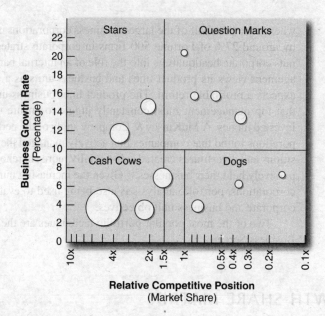

SOURCE: *Reprinted from* Long Range Planning, *Vol. 10, No. 2, 1977, Hedley, "Strategy and the Business Portfolio," p. 12. Copyright © 1977 with permission from Elsevier.*

- **Stars** are market leaders that are typically at the peak of their product life cycle and are able to generate enough cash to maintain their high share of the market and usually contribute to the company's profits. HP's printer business has been called HP's "crown jewel" because of its 41% market share in printers and its control of the replacement cartridge market. On its own, it accounted for more than half of HP's operating profit.[91] When a star's market growth rate slows, it becomes a cash cow.

- **Cash cows** typically bring in far more money than is needed to maintain their market share. In this declining stage of their life cycle, these products are "milked" for cash that will be invested in new question marks. Expenses such as advertising and R&D are reduced. Panasonic's video cassette recorders (VCRs) moved to this category when sales declined and DVD player/recorders replaced them. Question marks unable to obtain dominant market share (and thus become stars) by the time the industry growth rate inevitably slows become dogs.

- **Dogs** have low market share and do not have the potential (because they are in an unattractive industry) to bring in much cash. According to the BCG Growth-Share Matrix, dogs should be either sold off or managed carefully for the small amount of cash they can generate. For example, DuPont, the inventor of nylon, sold its textiles unit in 2003 because the company wanted to eliminate its low-margin products and focus more on its growing biotech business.[92] The same was true of IBM when it sold its PC business to China's Lenovo Group in order to emphasize its growing services business.

Underlying the BCG Growth-Share Matrix is the concept of the experience curve (discussed in **Chapter 5**). The key to success is assumed to be market share. Firms with the highest market share tend to have a cost leadership position based on economies of scale, among other things. If a company is able to use the experience curve to its advantage, it should be able to manufacture and sell new products at a price low enough to garner early market share leadership (assuming no successful imitation by competitors). Once the product becomes a star, it is destined to be very profitable, considering its inevitable future as a cash cow.

Having plotted the current positions of its product lines or business units on a matrix, a company can project its future positions, assuming no change in strategy. Present and

ENVIRONMENTAL sustainability issue

GENERAL MOTORS AND THE ELECTRIC CAR

In 2003, top management at General Motors (GM) decided to discontinue further work on its EV1 electric automobile. Working versions of the car had been leased to a limited number of people, but never sold. Environmentalists protested that GM stopped making the car just to send a message to government policy makers that an electric car was bad business. Management responded by stating that the car would never have made a profit.

In an April 2005 meeting of GM's top management team, Vice Chairman Robert Lutz suggested that it might be time to build another electric car. He noted that Toyota's Prius hybrid had made Toyota look environmentally sensitive; whereas, GM was viewed as making gas "hogs." The response was negative. Lutz recalled one executive saying, "We lost $1 billion on the last one. Do you want to lose $1 billion on the next one?"

Even though worldwide car ownership was growing 5% annually, rising fuel prices in 2005 reduced sales of GM's profitable SUVs—resulting in a loss of $11 billion. Board members began signaling that it was time for management to take some riskier bets to get the company out of financial trouble. In February 2006, management reluctantly approved developmental work on another electric car. At the time, no one in GM knew if batteries could be made small enough to power a car, but they knew that choices were limited. According to Larry Burns, Vice President of R&D and Strategic Planning, "This industry is 98% dependent on petroleum. GM has concluded that that's not sustainable."

Chairman and CEO Richard Wagoner, Jr. surprised the world at the January 2007 Detroit Auto Show with a vow to start developing an electric car called the Chevrolet Volt. It would plug into a regular electric outlet, leapfrog the competition, and be on sale in 2010. The company not only needed to build a radical new car, but had to convert as much as 75% of its current fleet to hybrid engines to meet fuel economy rules taking effect in 2017.

Management created a new team dedicated to getting hybrid and electric cars to market. The R&D budget was increased from $6.6 billion in 2006 to $8.1 billion in 2007. Several new models were canceled to free resources. The battery lab was under pressure to design batteries that could propel the Volt 40 miles before a small gasoline engine would re-charge the battery and extend the range to 600 miles. Douglas Drauch, battery lab manager, promised that the batteries would be ready on schedule. "We're making history," he said. "Fifty years from now, people will remember the Volt—like they remember a '53 Corvette."

....
SOURCES: D. Welch, "GM: Live Green or Die," *Business Week* (May 26, 2008), pp. 36–41; "The Drive for Low Emissions," *The Economist's Special Report on Business and Climate Change* (June 2, 2007), pp. 26–28.

projected matrixes can thus be used to help identify major strategic issues facing the organization. The goal of any company is to maintain a balanced portfolio so it can be self-sufficient in cash and always working to harvest mature products in declining industries to support new ones in growing industries.

The BCG Growth-Share Matrix is a very well-known portfolio concept with some clear advantages. It is quantifiable and easy to use. *Cash cow, dog, question mark,* and *star* are easy-to-remember terms for referring to a corporation's business units or products. Unfortunately, the BCG Growth-Share Matrix also has some serious limitations:

- The use of highs and lows to form four categories is too simplistic.
- The link between market share and profitability is questionable.[93] Low-share businesses can also be profitable.[94] For example, Olivetti is still profitably selling manual typewriters through mail-order catalogs.
- Growth rate is only one aspect of industry attractiveness.
- Product lines or business units are considered only in relation to one competitor: the market leader. Small competitors with fast-growing market shares are ignored.
- Market share is only one aspect of overall competitive position.

GE BUSINESS SCREEN

General Electric, with the assistance of the McKinsey & Company consulting firm, developed a more complicated matrix. As depicted in **Figure 7–4**, the **GE Business Screen** includes nine cells based on long-term industry attractiveness and business strength competitive position. The GE Business Screen, in contrast to the BCG Growth-Share Matrix, includes much more data in its two key factors than just business growth rate and comparable market share. For example, at GE, industry attractiveness includes market growth rate, industry profitability, size, and pricing practices, among other possible opportunities and threats. Business strength or competitive position includes market share as well as technological position, profitability, and size, among other possible strengths and weaknesses.[95]

The individual product lines or business units are identified by a letter and plotted as circles on the GE Business Screen. The area of each circle is in proportion to the size of the industry in terms of sales. The pie slices within the circles depict the market shares of the product lines or business units.

To plot product lines or business units on the GE Business Screen, follow these four steps:

1. Select criteria to rate the industry for each product line or business unit. Assess overall industry attractiveness for each product line or business unit on a scale from 1 (very unattractive) to 5 (very attractive).

2. Select the key factors needed for success in each product line or business unit. Assess business strength/competitive position for each product line or business unit on a scale of 1 (very weak) to 5 (very strong).

3. Plot each product line's or business unit's current position on a matrix as that depicted in **Figure 7–4.**

FIGURE 7–4
General Electric's Business Screen

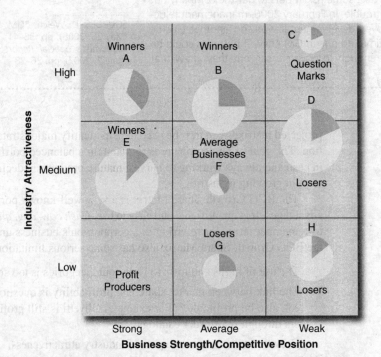

SOURCE: *Adapted from* Strategic Management in GE, *Corporate Planning and Development, General Electric Corporation, Reprinted by permission of General Electric Company.*

4. Plot the firm's future portfolio, assuming that present corporate and business strategies remain unchanged. Is there a performance gap between projected and desired portfolios? If so, this gap should serve as a stimulus to seriously review the corporation's current mission, objectives, strategies, and policies.

Overall, the nine-cell GE Business Screen is an improvement over the BCG Growth-Share Matrix. The GE Business Screen considers many more variables and does not lead to such simplistic conclusions. It recognizes, for example, that the attractiveness of an industry can be assessed in many different ways (other than simply using growth rate), and it thus allows users to select whatever criteria they feel are most appropriate to their situation. This portfolio matrix, however, does have some shortcomings:

- It can get quite complicated and cumbersome.
- The numerical estimates of industry attractiveness and business strength/competitive position give the appearance of objectivity, but they are in reality subjective judgments that may vary from one person to another.
- It cannot effectively depict the positions of new products or business units in developing industries.

ADVANTAGES AND LIMITATIONS OF PORTFOLIO ANALYSIS

Portfolio analysis is commonly used in strategy formulation because it offers certain *advantages:*

- It encourages top management to evaluate each of the corporation's businesses individually and to set objectives and allocate resources for each.
- It stimulates the use of externally oriented data to supplement management's judgment.
- It raises the issue of cash-flow availability for use in expansion and growth.
- Its graphic depiction facilitates communication.

Portfolio analysis does, however, have some very real *limitations* that have caused some companies to reduce their use of this approach:

- Defining product/market segments is difficult.
- It suggests the use of standard strategies that can miss opportunities or be impractical.
- It provides an illusion of scientific rigor when in reality positions are based on subjective judgments.
- Its value-laden terms such as cash cow and dog can lead to self-fulfilling prophecies.
- It is not always clear what makes an industry attractive or where a product is in its life cycle.
- Naively following the prescriptions of a portfolio model may actually reduce corporate profits if they are used inappropriately. For example, General Mills' Chief Executive H. Brewster Atwater cited his company's Bisquick brand of baking mix as a product that would have been written off years ago based on portfolio analysis. "This product is 57 years old. By all rights it should have been overtaken by newer products. But with the proper research to improve the product and promotion to keep customers excited, it's doing very well."[96]

MANAGING A STRATEGIC ALLIANCE PORTFOLIO

Just as product lines/business units form a portfolio of investments that top management must constantly juggle to ensure the best return on the corporation's invested money, strategic alliances can also be viewed as a portfolio of investments—investments of money, time, and energy. The way a company manages these intertwined relationships can significantly influence corporate competitiveness. Alliances are thus recognized as an important source of competitive advantage and superior performance.[97]

Managing groups of strategic alliances is primarily the job of the business unit. Its decisions may escalate, however, to the corporate level. Toman Corporation, for example, has 195 international joint ventures containing 422 alliance partners. According to a Toman executive, "If headquarters is trying to bring us and some other company closer together, they should understand not only our business unit, but also other business units. Sometimes the whole of our company may benefit (from an alliance) but it may not be good for one of our business units. And if it proceeds, headquarters must give some credit to our business unit so that we can agree. But it is not acceptable if they say to us that we are to lose something as a result of the alliance and now we have to make up the difference in one of our other businesses." In this instance the stage is set for negotiations across business units at the corporate level to achieve a broadly supported alliance network management system.[98]

A study of 25 leading European corporations found four tasks of multi alliance management that are necessary for successful alliance portfolio management:

1. **Developing and implementing a portfolio strategy for each business unit and a corporate policy for managing all the alliances of the entire company:** Alliances are primarily determined by business units. The corporate level develops general rules concerning when, how, and with whom to cooperate. The task of alliance policy is to strategically align all of the corporation's alliance activities with corporate strategy and corporate values. Every new alliance is thus checked against corporate policy before it is approved.

2. **Monitoring the alliance portfolio in terms of implementing business unit strategies and corporate strategy and policies:** Each alliance is measured in terms of achievement of objectives (e.g., market share), financial measures (e.g., profits and cash flow), contributed resource quality and quantity, and the overall relationship. The more a firm is diversified, the less the need for monitoring at the corporate level.

3. **Coordinating the portfolio to obtain synergies and avoid conflicts among alliances:** Because the interdependencies among alliances within a business unit are usually greater than among different businesses, the need for coordination is greater at the business level than at the corporate level. The need for coordination increases as the number of alliances in one business unit and the company as a whole increases, the average number of partners per alliance increases, and/or the overlap of the alliances increases.

4. **Establishing an alliance management system to support other tasks of multi alliance management:** This infrastructure consists of formalized processes, standardized tools and specialized organizational units. All but two of the 25 companies established centers of competence for alliance management. The centers were often part of a department for corporate development or a department of alliance management at the corporate level. In other corporations, specialized positions for alliance management were created at both the corporate and business unit levels or only at the business unit level. Most corporations prefer a system in which the corporate level provides the methods and tools to support alliances centrally, but decentralizes day-to-day alliance management to the business units.[99]

7.4 Corporate Parenting

Campbell, Goold, and Alexander, authors of *Corporate-Level Strategy: Creating Value in the Multibusiness Company*, contend that corporate strategists must address two crucial questions:

- What businesses should this company own and why?
- What organizational structure, management processes, and philosophy will foster superior performance from the company's business units?[100]

Portfolio analysis typically attempts to answer these questions by examining the attractiveness of various industries and by managing business units for cash flow, that is, by using cash generated from mature units to build new product lines. Unfortunately, portfolio analysis fails to deal with the question of what industries a corporation should enter or with how a corporation can attain synergy among its product lines and business units. As suggested by its name, portfolio analysis tends to primarily view matters financially, regarding business units and product lines as separate and independent investments.

Corporate parenting, in contrast, views a corporation in terms of resources and capabilities that can be used to build business unit value as well as generate synergies across business units. According to Campbell, Goold, and Alexander:

> *Multibusiness companies create value by influencing—or parenting—the businesses they own. The best parent companies create more value than any of their rivals would if they owned the same businesses. Those companies have what we call parenting advantage.*[101]

Corporate parenting generates corporate strategy by focusing on the core competencies of the parent corporation and on the value created from the relationship between the parent and its businesses. In the form of corporate headquarters, the parent has a great deal of power in this relationship. According to Campbell, Goold, and Alexander, if there is a good fit between the parent's skills and resources and the needs and opportunities of the business units, the corporation is likely to create value. If, however, there is not a good fit, the corporation is likely to destroy value.[102] Research indicates that companies that have a good fit between their strategy and their parenting roles are better performers than those companies that do not have a good fit.[103] This approach to corporate strategy is useful not only in deciding what new businesses to acquire but also in choosing how each existing business unit should be best managed. This appears to have been the secret to the success of General Electric under CEO Jack Welch. According to one analyst in 2000, "He and his managers really add value by imposing tough standards of profitability and by disseminating knowledge and best practice quickly around the GE empire. If some manufacturing trick cuts costs in GE's aero-engine repair shops in Wales, he insists it be applied across the group."[104]

The primary job of corporate headquarters is, therefore, to obtain synergy among the business units by providing needed resources to units, transferring skills and capabilities among the units, and coordinating the activities of shared unit functions to attain economies of scope (as in centralized purchasing).[105] This is in agreement with the concept of the learning organization discussed in **Chapter 1** in which the role of a large firm is to facilitate and transfer the knowledge assets and services throughout the corporation.[106] This is especially important given that 75% or more of a modern company's market value stems from its intangible assets—the organization's knowledge and capabilities.[107] At Proctor & Gamble, for example, the various business units are expected to work together to develop innovative products. Crest Whitestrips, which controls 68% of the at-home tooth-whitening market, was based on the P&G laundry division's knowledge of whitening agents.[108]

DEVELOPING A CORPORATE PARENTING STRATEGY

Campbell, Goold, and Alexander recommend that the search for appropriate corporate strategy involves three analytical steps:

1. **Examine each business unit (or target firm in the case of acquisition) in terms of its strategic factors:** People in the business units probably identified the strategic factors when they were generating business strategies for their units. One popular approach is to establish centers of excellence throughout the corporation. According to Frost, Birkinshaw, and Ensign, a *center of excellence* is "an organizational unit that embodies a set of capabilities that has been explicitly recognized by the firm as an important source of value creation, with the intention that these capabilities be leveraged by and/or disseminated to other parts of the firm."[109]

2. **Examine each business unit (or target firm) in terms of areas in which performance can be improved:** These are considered to be parenting opportunities. For example, two business units might be able to gain economies of scope by combining their sales forces. In another instance, a unit may have good, but not great, manufacturing and logistics skills. A parent company having world-class expertise in these areas could improve that unit's performance. The corporate parent could also transfer some people from one business unit who have the desired skills to another unit that is in need of those skills. People at corporate headquarters may, because of their experience in many industries, spot areas where improvements are possible that even people in the business unit may not have noticed. Unless specific areas are significantly weaker than the competition, people in the business units may not even be aware that these areas could be improved, especially if each business unit monitors only its own particular industry.

3. **Analyze how well the parent corporation fits with the business unit (or target firm):** Corporate headquarters must be aware of its own strengths and weaknesses in terms of resources, skills, and capabilities. To do this, the corporate parent must ask whether it has the characteristics that fit the parenting opportunities in each business unit. It must also ask whether there is a misfit between the parent's characteristics and the critical success factors of each business unit.

HORIZONTAL STRATEGY AND MULTIPOINT COMPETITION

A **horizontal strategy** is a corporate strategy that cuts across business unit boundaries to build synergy across business units and to improve the competitive position of one or more business units.[110] When used to build synergy, it acts like a parenting strategy. When used to improve the competitive position of one or more business units, it can be thought of as a corporate competitive strategy. In **multipoint competition,** large multi business corporations compete against other large multi business firms in a number of markets. These multipoint competitors are firms that compete with each other not only in one business unit, but also in a number of business units. At one time or another, a cash-rich competitor may choose to build its own market share in a particular market to the disadvantage of another corporation's business unit. Although each business unit has primary responsibility for its own business strategy, it may sometimes need some help from its corporate parent, especially if the competitor business unit is getting heavy financial support from its corporate parent. In this instance, corporate headquarters develops a horizontal strategy to coordinate the various goals and strategies of related business units.

For example, P&G, Kimberly-Clark, Scott Paper, and Johnson & Johnson (J&J) compete with one another in varying combinations of consumer paper products, from disposable diapers to facial tissue. If (purely hypothetically) J&J had just developed a toilet tissue with which it chose to challenge Procter & Gamble's high-share Charmin brand in a particular district, it might charge a low price for its new brand to build sales quickly. P&G might not choose to respond to this attack on its share by cutting prices on Charmin. Because of Charmin's high market share, P&G would lose significantly more sales dollars in a price war than J&J would with its initially low-share brand. To retaliate, P&G might thus challenge J&J's high-share baby shampoo with P&G's own low-share brand of baby shampoo in a different district. Once J&J had perceived P&G's response, it might choose to stop challenging Charmin so that P&G would stop challenging J&J's baby shampoo.

Multipoint competition and the resulting use of horizontal strategy may actually slow the development of hypercompetition in an industry. The realization that an attack on a market leader's position could result in a response in another market leads to mutual forbearance in which managers behave more conservatively toward multimarket rivals and competitive rivalry is reduced.[111] In one industry, for example, multipoint competition resulted in firms being less likely to exit a market. "Live and let live" replaced strong competitive rivalry.[112] Multipoint competition is likely to become even more prevalent in the future, as corporations become global competitors and expand into more markets through strategic alliances.[113]

Let's Summarize the Chapter with a Mind Map

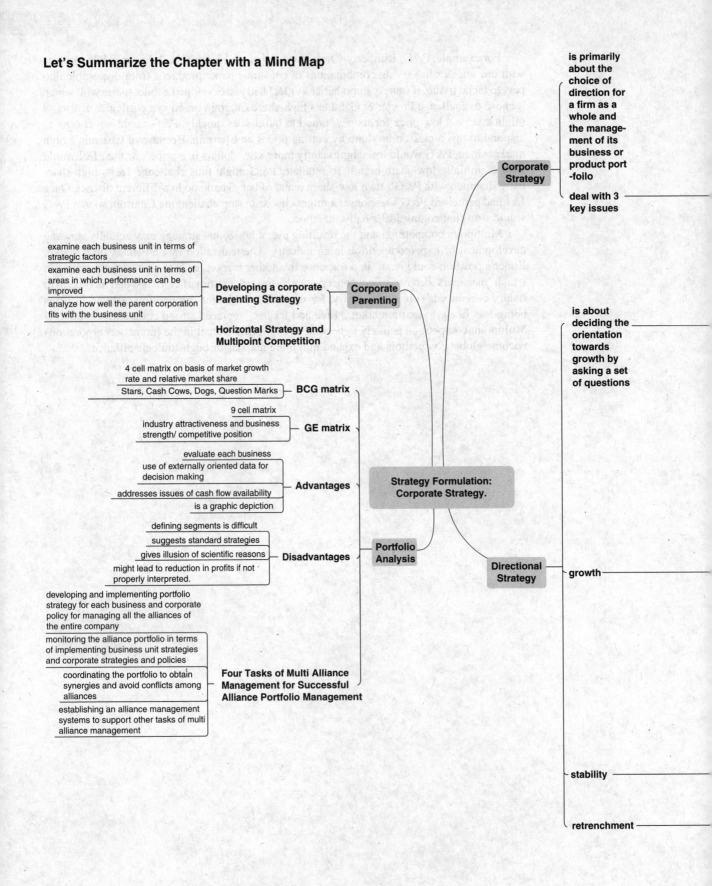

Corporate Strategy

- is primarily about the choice of direction for a firm as a whole and the management of its business or product port-foilo
- deal with 3 key issues

Corporate Parenting

- **Developing a corporate Parenting Strategy**
  - examine each business unit in terms of strategic factors
  - examine each business unit in terms of areas in which performance can be improved
  - analyze how well the parent corporation fits with the business unit
- **Horizontal Strategy and Multipoint Competition**

Portfolio Analysis

- **BCG matrix**
  - 4 cell matrix on basis of market growth rate and relative market share
  - Stars, Cash Cows, Dogs, Question Marks
- **GE matrix**
  - 9 cell matrix
  - industry attractiveness and business strength/ competitive position
- **Advantages**
  - evaluate each business
  - use of externally oriented data for decision making
  - addresses issues of cash flow availability
  - is a graphic depiction
- **Disadvantages**
  - defining segments is difficult
  - suggests standard strategies
  - gives illusion of scientific reasons
  - might lead to reduction in profits if not properly interpreted.
- **Four Tasks of Multi Alliance Management for Successful Alliance Portfolio Management**
  - developing and implementing portfolio strategy for each business and corporate policy for managing all the alliances of the entire company
  - monitoring the alliance portfolio in terms of implementing business unit strategies and corporate strategies and policies
  - coordinating the portfolio to obtain synergies and avoid conflicts among alliances
  - establishing an alliance management systems to support other tasks of multi alliance management

Strategy Formulation: Corporate Strategy.

Directional Strategy

- is about deciding the orientation towards growth by asking a set of questions
- growth
- stability
- retrenchment

directional strategy: Firm's orientation towards growth, stability or retrenchment

portfolio analysis: industries or markets in which the firm competes through its products and business units.

parenting strategy: the manner in which management coordinates activities and transfers resources and cultivates capabilities among product lines and business units.

should we expand, cut back or continue our opertions unchanged

should we concentrate our activities within our current industry or diversify into other industries

if we want to grow and expand nationally / globally should we go through international development or through external acquisitions, mergers or strategic alliances

on basis of external or internal growth — external growth — three ways
- mergers
- acquisitions
- strategic alliances

types

on basis of scope of portfolio

vertical growth: take over functions previously provided by supplier.

on basis of degree of functions
- forward integration
- backward integration

on basis of transaction cost economics
- full integration
- taper integration
- quasi integration
- long term contract

concentration: the company's current product lines have growth potential and therefore resources are concentrated on those product lines

horizontal growth: take over firms in similar business across different locations.
- exporting
- licensing
- franchising
- joint ventures
- acquisitions
- green field development
- production sharing
- turnkey operations
- BOT concept
- management contracts

diversification: when growth of the company has plateaued and opportunities for growth are depleted the company thinks about growing internationally and diversify into different industries
- concentric
- conglomerate

pause/proceed with caution

no change

profit

turnaround

captive company

sell-out/divestment

bankruptcy/liquidation

ECO-BITS

- Bosch Appliances, the German multinational corporation, was the only U.S. appliance manufacturer whose entire line of major appliances in 2008 was Energy Star qualified in the categories that the program rates. According to Bosch, if the more than 8 million U.S. consumers who purchased a new dishwasher in 2007 had bought a Bosch 800 model instead of a conventional unit, the lifetime energy savings would be equal to preventing 21 billion pounds of CO_2 emissions.[114]

- The green building industry is projected to grow from $2.2 billion in 2006 to $4.7 billion by 2011.[115]

DISCUSSION QUESTIONS

1. How does horizontal growth differ from vertical growth as a corporate strategy? From concentric diversification?

2. What are the tradeoffs between an internal and an external growth strategy? Which approach is best as an international entry strategy?

3. Is stability really a strategy or just a term for no strategy?

4. Compare and contrast SWOT analysis with portfolio analysis.

5. How is corporate parenting different from portfolio analysis? How is it alike? Is it a useful concept in a global industry?

6. Differentiate between portfolio analysis and corporate parenting.

7. What is corporate strategy? Discuss various types of corporate strategies.

8. Differentiate between full, taper, and quasi integrations.

9. What are the various international entry options available to a company for horizontal growth?

10. Write short notes on following:

   a. Diversification strategy

   b. Stability strategies

   c. Turnkey projects

   d. Retrenchment strategies

STRATEGIC PRACTICE EXERCISE

On March 14, 2000, Stephen King, the horror writer, published his new book, *Riding the Bullet*, on the Internet before it appeared in print. Within 24 hours, around 400,000 people had downloaded the book—even though most of them needed to download software in order to read the book. The unexpected demand crashed servers. According to Jack Romanos, president of Simon & Schuster, "I don't think anybody could have anticipated how many people were out there who are willing to accept the written word in a paperless format." To many, this announced the coming of the electronic novel. Environmentalists applauded that e-books would soon replace paper books and newspapers, thus reducing pollution coming from paper mills and landfills. The King book was easy to download and took less time than a trip to the bookstore. Critics argued that the King book used the Internet because at 66 pages, it was too short to be a standard printed novel. It was also free, so there was nothing to discourage natural curiosity. Some people in the industry estimated that 75% of those who downloaded the book did not read it.[116]

By 2008, HarperCollins and Random House were offering free online book content. Amazon was selling a $399 Kindle e-book reader for downloadable books costing $10 each, but Apple CEO Steve Jobs described the Kindle as something that filled no void and would "go nowhere." Sales in electronic trade books increased from $5.8 million in 2002 to $20 million in 2006 compared to total 2006 book sales of $25–$30 billion. Borders was market testing the downloading of digital purchases. Tim O'Reilly, coiner of the term *Web 2.0*, had been urging publishers to go digital since the early 1980s, but publishers and authors were still concerned with how they would be paid for the intellectual property they created. Om Malik, senior writer for *Business 2.0* magazine reported that the money earned from advertising clicks related to their blog content was barely enough to cover the costs of blogging. Flat World Knowledge, a new entrepreneurial digital textbook publisher, announced that in 2009 it planned to offer free online textbooks with the hope that the firm would make money selling supplementary materials like study guides. Publishers wondered how an industry built on a 15th century paper technology could make a profitable transition to a 21st century paperless electronic technology.[117]

1. Form into small groups in the class to discuss the future of Internet publishing.

2. Consider the following questions as discussion guides:
   - What are the pros and cons of electronic publishing?
   - What is the impact of electronic publishing on the environment?
   - Should newspaper and book publishers completely convert to electronic publishing over paper? (The *Wall Street Journal* and others publish in both paper and electronic formats. Is this a success?)
   - Would you prefer this textbook and others in an electronic format? How would you prefer to read the book?
   - What business model should publishers use to make money publishing on the Internet?

3. Present your group's conclusions to the class.

KEY TERMS

acquisition (p. 242)
backward integration (p. 243)
bankruptcy (p. 254)
BCG (Boston Consulting Group) Growth-Share Matrix (p. 255)
BOT (Build, Operate, Transfer) concept (p. 248)
captive company strategy (p. 253)
cash cows (p. 256)
concentration (p. 242)
concentric diversification (p. 248)
conglomerate diversification (p. 249)
corporate parenting (p. 261)
corporate strategy (p. 240)
directional strategy (p. 241)
diversification (p. 208)
divestment (p. 253)
dogs (p. 256)
exporting (p. 246)

forward integration (p. 243)
franchising (p. 246)
full integration (p. 244)
GE business screen (p. 258)
green-field development (p. 247)
growth strategy (p. 241)
horizontal growth (p. 245)
horizontal integration (p. 245)
horizontal strategy (p. 262)
joint venture (p. 247)
licensing (p. 246)
liquidation (p. 254)
long-term contracts (p. 245)
management contracts (p. 248)
merger (p. 242)
multipoint competition (p. 262)
no-change strategy (p. 251)
parenting strategy (p. 240)

pause/proceed with caution strategy (p. 251)
portfolio analysis (p. 255)
production sharing (p. 247)
profit strategy (p. 251)
quasi-integration (p. 245)
question marks (p. 255)
retrenchment strategies (p. 241)
sell-out strategy (p. 253)
stability strategy (p. 241)
stars (p. 256)
synergy (p. 248)
taper integration (p. 245)
transaction cost economics (p. 244)
turnaround strategy (p. 252)
turnkey operations (p. 247)
vertical growth (p. 242)
vertical integration (p. 243)

NOTES

1. C. Zook and J. Allen, "Growth Outside the Core," *Harvard Business Review* (December 2003), pp. 66–73.

2. Ibid., p. 67.

3. R. P. Rumelt, D. E. Schendel, and D. J. Teece, "Fundamental Issues in Strategy," in *Fundamental Issues in Strategy: A Research Agenda*, edited by R. P. Rumelt, D. E. Schendel, and D. J. Teece (Boston: HBS Press, 1994), p. 42.

4. This analogy of corporate parent and business unit children was initially proposed by A. Campbell, M. Goold, and M. Alexander. See "Corporate Strategy: The Quest for Parenting Advantage," *Harvard Business Review* (March–April, 1995), pp. 120–132.

5. M. E. Porter, "From Competitive Strategy to Corporate Strategy," in *International Review of Strategic Management*, Vol. 1, edited by D. E. Husey (Chicester, UK: John Wiley & Sons, 1990), p. 29.

6. This is in agreement with Toyohiro Kono when he proposes that corporate headquarters has three main functions: formulate corporate strategy, identify and develop the company's core competencies, and provide central resources. See T. Kono, "A Strong Head Office Makes a Strong Company," *Long Range Planning* (April 1999), pp. 225–236.

7. "Larry Ups the Ante," *Economist* (February 7, 2004), pp. 59–60.

8. Financial Express, "Mittal Captures Arcelor," posted from New Delhi, June 25: Posted: 2006-06-26 00:34:30+05:30 IST Updated: June 26, 2006 at 00:34 hrs IST, recovered on 28th Oct 2011, from http://www.financialexpress.com/news/mittal-captures-arcelor/88558/

9. D. J. Gayathri, The Mittal Arcelor Bid, IBS Case Development Centre, 2006, Case Code GBE0109C.

10. ArcelotMittal, recovered on 28th Oct 2011, from http://www.arcelormittal.com/index.php?lang=en&page=9

11. J. Bercovitz and W. Mitchell, "When Is More Better? The Impact of Business Scale and Scope on Long-term Business Survival, While Controlling for Profitability," *Strategic Management Journal* (January 2007), pp. 61–79.

12. "Cisco Inc. Buys Top Technology Innovator," *St. Cloud (MN) Times* (November 19, 2005), p. 6A.

13. Equitymaster Agora Research Private Limited, Nirma: Standing the test of time, posted on 17th October 2000, recovered on 28th Oct 2011, from http://www.equitymaster.com/detail.asp?date=10/17/2000&story=6

14. C. Manas and M. Philipose, "Mark to Market | Nirma: In FMCG or Chemicals? posted on Tuesday, November 27, 2007. 11:40 PM IST, recovered on 28th Oct 2011, from LIVEMINT HT media website http://www.livemint.com/2007/11/27233042/Mark-To-Market-Nirma-In-FMC.html

15. C. Woodyard, "FedEx Ponies Up $2.4B for Kinko's," *USA Today* (December 31, 2003), p. B1.

16. Tata Strategic Management Group, "Do You Have an 'R – Biz' Strategy for Your Company? recovered on 28th Oct 2011, from http://www.tsmg.com/download/article/Do%20you%20have%20a%20retail%20growth%20strategy.pdf

17. ABC Exports, recovered on 28th Oct 2011, from http://www.coffeeday.com/exports/about-us.html

18. Café Coffee Day, recovered on 28th Oct 2011, from http://www.cafecoffeeday.com/aboutus.htm

19. TATA Strategic Management, "Planning the Retail Strategy," Tata Review May 2008, pp. 78-80, recovered on 28th Oct 2011, from http://www.tata.com/pdf/strategy.pdf

20. J. W. Slocum, Jr., M. McGill, and D. T. Lei, "The New Learning Strategy: Anytime, Anything, Anywhere," *Organizational Dynamics* (Autumn 1994), p. 36.

21. M. J. Leiblein, J. J. Reuer, and F. Dalsace, "Do Make or Buy Decisions Matter? The Influence of Organizational Governance on Technological Performance," *Strategic Management Journal* (September 2002), pp. 817–833.

22. I. Geyskens, J-B. E. M. Steenkamp, and N. Kumar, "Make, Buy, or Ally: A Transaction Cost Theory Meta-Analysis," *Academy of Management Journal* (June 2006), pp. 519–543; R. Carter and G. M. Hodgson, "The Impact of Empirical Tests of Transaction Cost Economics on the Debate on the Nature of the Firm," *Strategic Management Journal* (May 2006), pp. 461–476; T. A. Shervani, G. Frazier, and G. Challagalla, "The Moderating Influence of Firm Market Power on the Transaction Cost Economics Model: An Empirical Test in a Forward Channel Integration Context," *Strategic Management Journal* (June 2007), pp. 635–652; K. J. Mayer and R. M. Solomon, "Capabilities, Contractual Hazards, and Governance: Integrating Resource-Based and Transaction Cost Perspectives," *Academy of Management Journal* (October 2006), pp. 942–959.

23. K. R. Harrigan, *Strategies for Vertical Integration* (Lexington, MA.: Lexington Books, 1983), pp. 16–21.

24. M. Arndt, "Who's Afraid of a Housing Slump?" *Business Week* (April 30, 2007), p. 76.

25. A. Parmigiani, "Why Do Firms Both Make and Buy? An Investigation of Concurrent Sourcing," *Strategic Management Journal* (March 2007), pp. 285–311; F. T. Rothaermel, M. A. Hitt, and L. A. Jobe, "Balancing Vertical Integration and Strategic Outsourcing: Effects on Product Portfolio, Product Success, and Firm Performance," *Strategic Management Journal* (November 2006), pp. 1033–1056.

26. 24/7 Customer, recovered 25th Oct 2011, from http://www.247customer.com/whoweare/aboutus.php

27. K. Nirmalya and P. Puranam, "High Wages, Attrition Compel IT Sector to Look Beyond India," *The Economic Time*, posted on 14 Febuary, 2008, recovered 25th Oct 2011, from http://www.nasscom.in/Nasscom/templates/NormalPage.aspx?id=53421

28. M. G. Jacobides, "Industry Change Through Vertical Disintegration: How and Why Markets Emerged in Mortgage Banking," *Academy of Management Journal* (June 2005), pp. 465–498.

29. For a discussion of the pros and cons of contracting versus vertical integration, see J. T. Mahoney, "The Choice of Organizational Form: Vertical Financial Ownership Versus Other Methods of Vertical Integration," *Strategic Management Journal* (November 1992), pp. 559–584.

30. G. Dowell, "Product Line Strategies of New Entrants in an Established Industry: Evidence from the U.S. Bicycle Industry," *Strategic Management Journal* (October 2006), pp. 959–979; C. Sorenson, S. McEvily, C. R. Ren, and R. Roy, "Niche Width Revisited: Organizational Scope, Behavior and Performance," *Strategic Management Journal* (October 2006), pp. 915–936.

31. D. Roberts, "Scrambling to Bring Crest to the Masses," *Business Week* (June 25, 2007), pp. 72–73.

32. Asia Times, Tata bags Tetley Tea, posted on February 29, 2000, recovered on 25th Oct 2011, from http://www.atimes.com/ind-pak/BB29Df02.html

33. Goldstein Andrea, The Internationalization of Indian Companies: The Case of Tata, CASI WORKING PAPER SERIES, Number 08-02, Published January 2008, recovered on 25th Oct 2011, from "http://www.sajaforum.org/files/AG-WP-final.pdf"

34. India Today, 2000-Tata Tea-Tetley merger: The cup that cheered, posted on December 25, 2009 | UPDATED 09:14 IST, recovered on 25th Oct 2011, from http://indiatoday.intoday.in/story/2000-Tata+Tea-Tetley+merger:+The+cup+that+cheered/1/76481.html

35. A. Delios and P. W. Beamish, "Geographic Scope, Product Diversification, and the Corporate Performance of Japanese Firms," Strategic Management Journal (August 1999), pp. 711–727.

36. E. Elango and V. H. Fried, "Franchising Research: A Literature Review and Synthesis," Journal of Small Business Management (July 1997), pp. 68–81.

37. J. E. McCann III, "The Growth of Acquisitions in Services," Long Range Planning (December 1996), pp. 835–841.

38. "Gently Does It," The Economist (August 11, 2007), p. 59.

39. B. Voss, "Strategic Federations Frequently Falter in Far East," Journal of Business Strategy (July/August 1993), p. 6; S. Douma, "Success and Failure in New Ventures," Long Range Planning (April 1991), pp. 54–60.

40. A. Delios and P. W. Beamish, "Ownership Strategy of Japanese Firms: Transactional, Institutional, and Experience Approaches," Strategic Management Journal (October 1999), pp. 915–933.

41. K. D. Brouthers and L. E. Brouthers, "Acquisition or Greenfield Start-up? Institutional, Cultural, and Transaction Cost Influences," Strategic Management Journal (January 2000), pp. 89–97.

42. M. Kripalani, "A Red-Hot Big Blue in India," Business Week (September 3, 2007), p. 52.

43. domain-b.com Corporate Bureau, L&T secures Rs 2,000-crore order from Bombay Dyeing, posted on 15 April 2008, recovered 25th Oct 2011, from http://www.domain-b.com/companies/companies_l/Larsen/20080415_bombay_dyeing.html

44. Financial Express Corporate Bureau, L&T clinches Rs 2,000 crore Bombay Dyeing turnkey project, Posted: 2008-04-16 01:00:30+05:30 IST Updated: April 16, 2008 at 01:00 hrs IST, recovered 25th Oct 2011, from http://www.financialexpress.com/news/l&t-clinches-rs-2-000-crore-bombay-dyeing-turnkey-project/297407/

45. C. Matlack, "Carlos Ghosn's Russian Gambit," Business Week (March 17, 2008), pp. 57–58.

46. J. Naisbitt, Megatrends Asia (New York: Simon & Schuster, 1996), p. 143.

47. For additional information on international entry modes, see D. F. Spulber, Global Competitive Strategy (Cambridge, UK: Cambridge University Press, 2007) and K. D. Brouthers and J-F Hennart, "Boundaries of the Firm: Insights from International Entry Mode Research," Journal of Management (June 2007), pp. 395–425.

48. D. P. Lovallo and L. T. Mendonca, "Strategy's Strategist: An Interview with Richard Rumelt," McKinsey Quarterly Online (2007, No. 4).

49. C. Zook, "Increasing the Odds of Successful Growth: The Critical Prelude to Moving 'Beyond the Core.'" Strategy & Leadership, Vol. 32, No. 4 (2004), pp. 17–23.

50. A. Y. Ilinich and C. P. Zeithaml, "Operationalizing and Testing Galbraith's Center of Gravity Theory," Strategic Management Journal (June 1995), pp. 401–410; H. Tanriverdi and N. Venkatraman, "Knowledge Relatedness and the Performance of Multibusiness Firms," Strategic Management Journal (February 2005), pp. 97–119.

51. "Flying into Battle," Economist (May 8, 2004), p. 60 and Corporate Web site (www.bombardier.com) accessed September 27, 2008.

52. R. F. Bruner, "Corporation Diversification May Be Okay After All," Batten Briefings (Spring 2003), pp. 2–3, 12.

53. J. Bercovitz and W. Mitchell, "When Is More Better? The Impact of Business Scale and Scope on Long-Term Business Survival, While Controlling for Profitability," Strategic Management Journal (January 2007), pp. 61–79; D. J. Miller, "Technological Diversity, Related Diversification, and Firm Performance," Strategic Management Journal (July 2006), pp. 601–619; C. Stadler, "The Four Principles of Enduring Success," Harvard Business Review (July–August 2007), pp. 62–72.

54. K. Carow, R. Heron, and T. Saxton, "Do Early Birds Get the Returns? An Empirical Investigation of Early-Mover Advantages in Acquisitions," Strategic Management Journal (June 2004), pp. 563–585; K. Ramaswamy, "The Performance Impact of Strategic Similarity in Horizontal Mergers: Evidence from the U.S. Banking Industry," Academy of Management Journal (July 1997), pp. 697–715; D. J. Flanagan, "Announcements of Purely Related and Purely Unrelated Mergers and Shareholder Returns: Reconciling the Relatedness Paradox," Journal of Management, Vol. 22, No. 6 (1996), pp. 823–835; D. D. Bergh, "Predicting Diversification of Unrelated Acquisitions: An Integrated Model of Ex Ante Conditions," Strategic Management Journal (October 1997), pp. 715–731.

55. J. M. Pennings, H. Barkema, and S. Douma, "Organizational Learning and Diversification," Academy of Management Journal (June 1994), pp. 608–640.

56. C. Stadler, "The Four Principles of Enduring Success," Harvard Business Review (July–August 2007), pp. 62–72.

57. L. E. Palich, L. B. Cardinal, and C. C. Miller, "Curvilinearity in the Diversification-Performance Linkage: An Examination of over Three Decades of Research," Strategic Management Journal (February 2000), pp. 155–174; M. S. Gary, "Implementation Strategy and Performance Outcomes in Related Diversification," Strategic Management Journal (July 2005), pp. 643–664; G. Yip and G. Johnson, "Transforming Strategy," Business Strategy Review (Spring 2007), pp. 11–15.

58. "The Great Merger Wave Breaks," The Economist (January 27, 2001), pp. 59–60.

59. R. N. Palter and D. Srinivasan, "Habits of Busiest Acquirers," McKinsey on Finance (Summer 2006), pp. 8–13.

60. D. R. King, D. R. Dalton, C. M. Daily, and J. G. Covin, "Meta-Analyses of Post-Acquisition Performance: Indications of Unidentified Moderators," Strategic Management Journal (February 2004), pp. 187–200; W. B. Carper, "Corporate Acquisitions and Shareholder Wealth: A Review and Exploratory Analysis" Journal of Management (December 1990), pp. 807–823; P. G. Simmonds, "Using Diversification as a Tool for Effective Performance," Handbook of Business Strategy, 1992/93 Yearbook, edited by H. E. Glass and M. A. Hovde (Boston: Warren, Gorham & Lamont, 1992), pp. 3.1–3.7; B. T. Lamont and C. A. Anderson, "Mode of Corporate Diversification and Economic Performance," Academy of Management Journal (December 1985), pp. 926–936.

61. "The HP–Compaq Merger Two Years Out: Still Waiting for the Upside," Knowledge @Wharton (October 6–19, 2004).

62. D. J. Miller, "Firms' Technological Resources and the Performance Effects of Diversification: A Longitudinal Study," *Strategic Management Journal* (November 2004), pp. 1097–1119.

63. A. Hinterhuber, "When Two Companies Become One," in *Financial Times Handbook of Management*, 3rd ed., S. Crainer and D. Dearlove, Eds. (Harlow, UK: Pearson Education, 2004), pp. 824–833; D. L. Laurie, Y. L. Doz, and C. P. Sheer, "Creating New Growth Platforms," *Harvard Business Review* (May 2006), pp. 80–90; R. Langford and C. Brown III, "Making M&A Pay: Lessons from the World's Most Successful Acquirers," *Strategy & Leadership*, Vol. 32, No. 1 (2004), pp. 5–14; J. G. Lynch and B. Lind, "Escaping Merger and Acquisition Madness," *Strategy & Leadership*, Vol. 30, No. 2 (2002), pp. 5–12; M. L. Sirower, *The Synergy Trap* (New York: Free Press, 1997); B. Jensen, "Make It Simple! How Simplicity Could Become Your Ultimate Strategy," *Strategy & Leadership* (March/April 1997), p. 35.

64. E. Thornton, "Why Consumers Hate Mergers," *Business Week* (December 6, 2004), pp. 58–64.

65. S. Karim and W. Mitchell, "Innovating through Acquisition and Internal Development: A Quarter-century of Boundary Evolution at Johnson & Johnson," *Long Range Planning* (December 2004), pp. 525–547; L. Selden and G. Colvin, "M&A Needn't Be a Loser's Game," *Harvard Business Review* (June 2003), pp. 70–79; E. C. Busija, H. M. O'Neill, and C. P. Zeithaml, "Diversification Strategy, Entry Mode, and Performance: Evidence of Choice and Constraints," *Strategic Management Journal* (April 1997), pp. 321–327; A. Sharma, "Mode of Entry and Ex-Post Performance," *Strategic Management Journal* (September 1998), pp. 879–900.

66. R. T. Uhlaner and A. S. West, "Running a Winning M&A Shop," *McKinsey Quarterly* (March 2008), pp.1–7.

67. S. Rovitt, D. Harding, and C. Lemire, "A Simple M&A Model for All Seasons," *Strategy & Leadership*, Vol. 32, No. 5 (2004), pp. 18–24.

68. P. Porrini, "Can a Previous Alliance Between an Acquirer and a Target Affect Acquisition Performance?" *Journal of Management*, Vol. 30, No. 4 (2004), pp. 545–562; L. Wang and E. J. Zajac, "Alliance or Acquisition? A Dyadic Perspective on Inter-firm Resource Combinations," *Strategic Management Journal* (December 2007), pp. 1291–1317.

69. F. Vermeulen, "Controlling International Expansion," *Business Strategy Review* (September 2001), pp. 29–36.

70. A. Inkpen and N. Choudhury, "The Seeking of Strategy Where It Is Not: Towards a Theory of Strategy Absence," *Strategic Management Journal* (May 1995), pp. 313–323.

71. P. Burrows and S. Anderson, "Dell Computer Goes Into the Shop," *Business Week* (July 12, 1993), pp. 138–140.

72. M. Brauer, "What Have We Acquired and What Should We Acquire in Divestiture Research? A Review and Research Agenda," Journal of Management (December 2006), pp. 751–785; J. L. Morrow, Jr., R. A. Johnson, and L. W. Busenitz, "The Effects of Cost and Asset Retrenchment on Firm Performance: The Overlooked Role of a Firm's Competitive Environment," *Journal of Management*, Vol. 30, No. 2 (2004), pp. 189–208.

73. J. A. Pearce II and D. K. Robbins, "Retrenchment Remains the Foundation of Business Turnaround," *Strategic Management Journal* (June 1994), pp. 407–417.

74. Y. Kageyama, "Sony Turnaround Plan Draws Yawns," *Des Moines Register* (September 23, 2005), p. 3D.

75. F. Gandolfi, "Reflecting on Downsizing: What Have We Learned?" *SAM Advanced Management Journal* (Spring 2008), pp. 46–55; C. Chadwick, L. W. Hunter, and S. L. Walston, "Effects of Downsizing Practices on the Performance of Hospitals," *Strategic Management Journal* (May 2004), pp. 405–427; J. R. Morris, W. F. Cascio, and C. E. Young, "Downsizing After All These Years," *Organizational Dynamics* (Winter 1999), pp. 78–87; P. H. Mirvis, "Human Resource Management: Leaders, Laggards, and Followers," *Academy of Management Executive* (May 1997), pp. 43–56; J. K. DeDee and D. W. Vorhies, "Retrenchment Activities of Small Firms During Economic Downturn: An Empirical Investigation," *Journal of Small Business Management* (July 1998), pp. 46–61.

76. C. Chadwick, L. W. Hunter, and S. L Walston, "Effects of Downsizing Practices on the Performance of Hospitals," *Strategic Management Journal* (May 2004), pp. 405–427.

77. Indian Railways, recovered 25th Oct 2011, from http://www.indianrailways.gov.in/

78. K. Sudhir, ISB insights, The Great Turnaround of Indian Railways, recovered 25th Oct 2011, from http://www.isb.edu/isbinsight/Insight_Sep07/The%20Great%20Turnaround.html

79. G. Raghuram, "Turnaround" of Indian Railways: A Critical Appraisal of Strategies and Processes, W.P. No.2007-02-03, February 2007, recovered 25th Oct 2011, from http://www.iimahd.ernet.in/publications/data/2007-02-03graghuram.pdf

80. IANS, Indian Railways posts 18.04 percent Q1 revenue growth, posted on July 21, 2008 7:58 pm ICT by IANS, recovered 25th Oct 2011, from http://www.thaindian.com/newsportal/business/indian-railways-posts-1804-percent-q1-revenue-growth_10074247.html

81. Introducing the Railway Budget 2007–2008, recovered 25th Oct 2011, from http://www.indianrailways.gov.in/Budget-2007/budget0708.htm

82. J. B. Treece, "U.S. Parts Makers Just Won't Say 'Uncle,'" *Business Week* (August 10, 1987), pp. 76–77.

83. S. S. Carty, "Ford Plans to Park Jaguar, Land Rover with Tata Motors," *USA Today* (March 26, 2008), p. 1B–2B.

84. For more on divestment, see C. Dexter and T. Mellewight, "Thirty Years After Michael E. Porter: What Do We Know about Business Exit?" *Academy of Management Perspectives* (May 2007), pp. 41–55.

85. D. D. Dawley, J. J. Hoffman, and B. T. Lamont, "Choice Situation, Refocusing, and Post-Bankruptcy Performance," *Journal of Management*, Vol. 28, No. 5 (2002), pp. 695–717.

86. R. M. Kanter, "Leadership and the Psychology of Turnarounds," *Harvard Business Review* (June 2003), pp. 58–67.

87. B. C. Reimann and A. Reichert, "Portfolio Planning Methods for Strategic Capital Allocation: A Survey of Fortune 500 Firms," *International Journal of Management* (March 1996), pp. 84–93; D. K. Sinha, "Strategic Planning in the Fortune 500," *Handbook of Business Strategy, 1991/92 Yearbook*, edited by H. E. Glass and M. A. Hovde (Boston: Warren, Gorham & Lamont, 1991), p. 9.6.

88. L. Dranikoff, T. Koller, and A. Schneider, "Divestiture: Strategy's Missing Link," *Harvard Business Review* (May 2002), pp. 74–83.

89. B. Hedley, "Strategy and the Business Portfolio," *Long Range Planning* (February 1977), p. 9.

90. D. Welch, "GM: Live Green or Die," *Business Week* (May 26, 2008), pp. 36–41.

91. P. Burrows and S. Hamm, "Tech Has a New Top Dog," *Business Week* (June 19, 2006), p. 60.

92. A. Fitzgerald, "Going Global," *Des Moines Register* (March 14, 2004), pp. 1M, 3M.

93. C. Anterasian, J. L. Graham, and R. B. Money, "Are U.S. Managers Superstitious About Market Share?" *Sloan Management Review* (Summer 1996), pp. 67–77.

94. D. Rosenblum, D. Tomlinson, and L. Scott, "Bottom-Feeding for Blockbuster Businesses," *Harvard Business Review* (March 2003), pp. 52–59.

95. R. G. Hamermesh, *Making Strategy Work* (New York: John Wiley & Sons, 1986), p. 14.

96. J. J. Curran, "Companies That Rob the Future," *Fortune* (July 4, 1988), p. 84.

97. W. H. Hoffmann, "Strategies for Managing a Portfolio of Alliances," *Strategic Management Journal* (August 2007), pp. 827–856; D. Lavie, "Alliance Portfolios and Firm Performance: A Study of Value Creation and Appropriation in the U.S. Software Industry," *Strategic Management Journal* (December 2007), pp. 1187–1212.

98. A. Goerzen, "Managing Alliance Networks: Emerging Practices of Multinational Corporations," *Academy of Management Executive* (May 2005), pp. 94–107; S. Lazzarini, "The Impact of Membership in Competing Alliance Constellations: Evidence on the Operational Performance of Global Airlines," *Strategic Management Journal* (April 2007), pp. 345–367.

99. W. H. Hoffmann, "How to Manage a Portfolio of Alliances," *Long Range Planning* (April 2005), pp. 121–143.

100. A. Campbell, M. Goold, and M. Alexander, *Corporate-Level Strategy: Creating Value in the Multibusiness Company* (New York: John Wiley & Sons, 1994). See also M. Goold, A. Campbell, and M. Alexander, "Corporate Strategy and Parenting Theory," *Long Range Planning* (April 1998), pp. 308–318, and M. Goold and A. Campbell, "Parenting in Complex Structures," *Long Range Planning* (June 2002), pp. 219–243.

101. A. Campbell, M. Goold, and M. Alexander, "Corporate Strategy: The Quest for Parenting Advantage," *Harvard Business Review* (March–April 1995), p. 121.

102. Ibid., p. 122.

103. A. van Oijen and S. Douma, "Diversification Strategy and the Roles of the Centre," *Long Range Planning* (August 2000), pp. 560–578.

104. "Jack's Gamble," *The Economist* (October 28, 2000), pp. 13–14.

105. D. J. Collis, "Corporate Strategy in Multibusiness Firms," *Long Range Planning* (June 1996), pp. 416–418; D. Lei, M. A. Hitt, and R. Bettis, "Dynamic Core Competencies Through Meta-Learning and Strategic Context," *Journal of Management*, Vol. 22, No. 4 (1996), pp. 549–569.

106. D. J. Teece, "Strategies for Managing Knowledge Assets: The Role of Firm Structure and Industrial Context," *Long Range Planning* (February 2000), pp. 35–54.

107. R. S. Kaplan and D. P. Norton, "The Strategy Map: Guide to Aligning Intangible Assets," *Strategy & Leadership*, Vol. 32, No. 5 (2004), pp. 10–17; L. Edvinsson, "The New Knowledge Economics," *Business Strategy Review* (September 2002), pp. 72–76; C. Havens and E. Knapp, "Easing into Knowledge Management," *Strategy & Leadership* (March/April 1999), pp. 4–9.

108. J. Scanlon, "Cross-Pollinators," *Business Week's Inside Innovation* (September 2007), pp. 8–11.

109. T. S. Frost, J. M. Birkinshaw, and P. C. Ensign, "Centers of Excellence in Multinational Corporations," *Strategic Management Journal* (November 2002), pp. 997–1018.

110. M. E. Porter, *Competitive Advantage* (New York: The Free Press, 1985), pp. 317–382.

111. H. R. Greve, "Multimarket Contact and Sales Growth: Evidence from Insurance," *Strategic Management Journal* (March 2008), pp. 229–249; L. Fuentelsaz and J. Gomez, "Multipoint Competition, Strategic Similarity and Entry Into Geographic Markets," *Strategic Management Journal* (May 2006), pp. 477–499; J. Gimeno, "Reciprocal Threats in Multimarket Rivalry: Staking Out 'Spheres of Influence' in the U.S. Airline Industry," *Strategic Management Journal* (February 1999), pp. 101–128; J. Baum and H. J. Korn, "Dynamics of Dyadic Competitive Interaction," *Strategic Management Journal* (March 1999), pp. 251–278; J. Gimeno and C. Y. Woo, "Hypercompetition in a Multimarket Environment: The Role of Strategic Similarity and Multimarket Contact in Competitive De-escalation," *Organization Science* (May/June 1996), pp. 322–341.

112. W. Boeker, J. Goodstein, J. Stephan, and J. P. Murmann, "Competition in a Multimarket Environment: The Case of Market Exit," *Organization Science* (March/April 1997), pp. 126–142.

113. J. Gimeno and C. Y. Woo, "Multimarket Contact, Economies of Scope, and Firm Performance," *Academy of Management Journal* (June 1999), pp. 239–259.

114. "Energy Efficiency Update," *Appliance Magazine Online* (April 2008).

115. "Sustainability Living Grows Up," *St. Cloud (MN) Times* (July 11, 2008), p. 5C.

116. "Learning to E-Read," *The Economist Survey E-Entertainment* (October 7, 2000), p. 22.

117. P. Tucker, "The 21st-Century Writer," *The Futurist* (July–August 2008), pp. 25–31; M. J. Perenson, "Amazon Kindles Interest in E-Books," *PC World* (February 2008), p. 64; M. R. Nelson, "E-Books in Higher Education: Nearing the End of the Era of Hype?" *EDUCAUSE Review* (March/April 2008), pp. 40–56.

CHAPTER 8

strategy formulation: functional strategy and Strategic Choice

Indian detergent market is roughly estimated to be Rs. 12,000 crore and is characterized by immense competition and high penetration levels. The Indian detergent segment is ruled by players such as Hindustan Unilever Limited, Nirma, Henkel, and Proctor & Gamble.[1] The fabric wash market consists of 2.2 million metric tonnes of synthetic detergents, with detergent cakes and bars accounting for 40% of the volume and the rest being the detergent powders.[2] Today, there are four price-based segments in Indian detergent market which has both organized players and unorganized ones.

However, the industry exhibited very different characteristics in 1960s and 1970s. Back then, the Indian detergent industry was dominated by few players and there was only premium segment.[3] The industry was revolutionized after the introduction of a homegrown brand, i.e., Nirma, which in 1969 was priced at Rs. 3 per kg as compared to Rs. 13 per kg against the cheapest brand in the market. Nirma is almost wholly responsible for creating the new market segment in this sector.

It began its life in the back alleys of Ahmedabad, in the summer of 1969, and went on to bring detergents within the reach of every household, thus expanding this market almost exponentially. Today, it is one of the few names—recognized as a true Indian brand, which took over mighty multinationals and rewrote the marketing rules to win the heart of consumers. This brand has been ranked as the "Most Widely Distributed Detergent Powder Brand in India" as per the All India Census of Retail Outlets carried out in 435 urban towns by the AIMS (Asian Information Marketing & Social) Research agency. Moreover, the A.C. Nielsen Retail Audit (2002–2003) has ranked Nirma as India's seventh largest consumer brand. It created the concept of value-for-money and made it a part of the Indian marketing lexicon. As a manufacturer of personal care and laundry products in India, saw an opportunity to target the low-income market with a new formulation, process, packaging, and distribution model focused towards the poor.

Result: By 1992, Nirma had sales of 333,000 tons p.a. and a market share of 55%.

How/what got Nirma here, in a market with very few players and dominated by multinational brands?

Dr Patel started the production of the brand in December 1969 in a small shed. He did not follow fixed business principles and defied all then existing business logics. He did not believe

Learning Objectives

After reading this chapter, you should be able to:

- Identify a variety of functional strategies that can be used to achieve organizational goals and objectives
- Understand what activities and functions are appropriate to outsource in order to gain or strengthen competitive advantage
- Recognize strategies to avoid and understand why they are dangerous
- Construct corporate scenarios to evaluate strategic options
- Use a stakeholder priority matrix to aid in strategic decision making
- Develop policies to implement corporate, business, and functional strategies

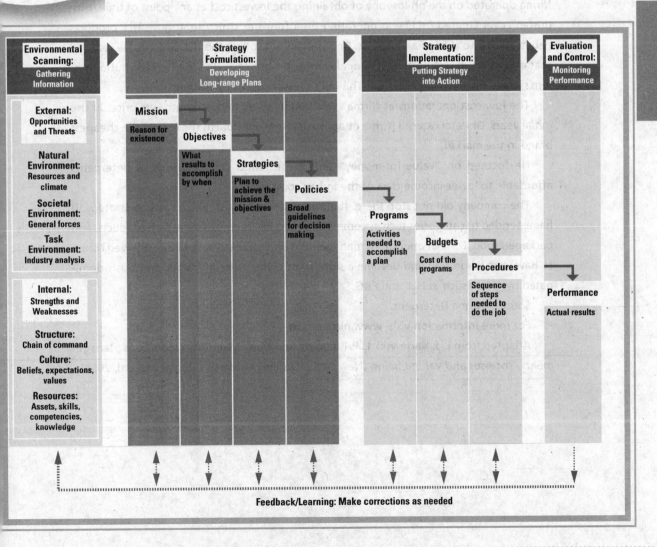

Environmental Scanning:	Strategy Formulation:	Strategy Implementation:	Evaluation and Control:
Gathering Information	Developing Long-range Plans	Putting Strategy into Action	Monitoring Performance

External:
Opportunities and Threats

Natural Environment:
Resources and climate

Societal Environment:
General forces

Task Environment:
Industry analysis

Internal:
Strengths and Weaknesses

Structure:
Chain of command

Culture:
Beliefs, expectations, values

Resources:
Assets, skills, competencies, knowledge

Mission
Reason for existence

Objectives
What results to accomplish by when

Strategies
Plan to achieve the mission & objectives

Policies
Broad guidelines for decision making

Programs
Activities needed to accomplish a plan

Budgets
Cost of the programs

Procedures
Sequence of steps needed to do the job

Performance
Actual results

Feedback/Learning: Make corrections as needed

that "better quality always demanded higher price." He concentrated on operational aspects such as production, packaging and a low-profile marketing. The result was an innovative and quality product: Nirma. Using lower fat to water ratio and indigenous oils used in formulating soap, the company dramatically cut production costs. As a result of its indigenous operational strategies, Nirma catered to the consumers at a fraction of price of the then leading brands. This managed to change the habits of Indian housewives for washing clothes. In the end, Nirma created an entirely new market segment in domestic marketplace, which eventually became the largest consumer product and quickly emerged as a dominating market player—a position it has never since relinquished. By creating a more environmentally sound product that was cheaper than any other product in the market, Nirma forced Hindustan Lever, the Indian subsidiary of Unilever, to recognize the need to create and market soaps and laundry detergents for India's poor.

Dr Patel's concentration on operational aspects helped him build an operation structure that was easily adapted to changing circumstances. For example, with transportation, Nirma operated on the philosophy of obtaining the lowest cost at any point of time. Hindustan Lever Limited (HLL) was operating on a four-tier structure. It gave HLL products penetration into the Indian markets. Dr Patel did not follow the HLL systems. He realized that more tiers in distribution system also meant more cost. He kept his distribution system simple, flexible, and effective. This led to lesser cost of operations for Nirma.

The low-cost operations at Nirma's resulted in an all time strength—its price. In the initial years, Dr Patel catered Nirma at approximately one-fourth the cost of the cheapest brand in the market.

He focused on "value-for-money" and made FMCG products such as detergents affordable to lower-income class of the Indian society.

The company did not stop there. It adopted an aggressive line extension strategy. It has extended to categories such as commodity food products, personal care products, and packaged food. Distinct operations management and robust infrastructure allowed Nirma to have cost leadership and become a significant competitor in market previously dominated by giants such as HLL and P&G.

Source: Nirma Detergent.

For more information visit: www.nirma.co.in

Adapted from L. J. Karjewski, L. P. Ritzman, and M. K. Malhotra, *Operations Management: Processes and Value Chains*, (New Delhi: Dorling Kindersley (India) Pvt. Ltd, 2008).

8.1 Functional Strategy

Functional strategy is the approach a functional area takes to achieve corporate and business unit objectives and strategies by maximizing resource productivity. It is concerned with developing and nurturing a distinctive competence to provide a company or business unit with a competitive advantage. Just as a multidivisional corporation has several business units, each with its own business strategy, each business unit has its own set of departments, each with its own functional strategy.

The orientation of a functional strategy is dictated by its parent business unit's strategy.[4] For example, a business unit following a competitive strategy of differentiation through high quality needs a manufacturing functional strategy that emphasizes expensive quality assurance processes over cheaper, high-volume production; a human resource functional strategy that emphasizes the hiring and training of a highly skilled, but costly, workforce; and a marketing functional strategy that emphasizes distribution channel "pull," using advertising to increase consumer demand, over "push," using promotional allowances to retailers. If a business unit were to follow a low-cost competitive strategy, however, a different set of functional strategies would be needed to support the business strategy.

Just as competitive strategies may need to vary from one region of the world to another, functional strategies may need to vary from region to region. After liberalization, Coca-Cola decided to re-enter the Indian market. Based on its experience, the company knew that the key to building a market and brand presence in India was a penetrative distribution network. The company opted to buy out Thumbs Up, which is India's most successful soft drink brand. Initial decision of the company was to discontinue Thumbs Up. However, the Thumbs Up brand recall motivated the company to re-launch it and it remained more popular than Coke for many years.

Similarly, Kellogg's decided to enter the Indian market in 1994. At that point of time, the Indian breakfast cereal market was very underdeveloped, and the concept of eating cereal was alien to Indian culture. The most common way to start the day in India was with parathas or a bowl of hot vegetables. The socio-cultural environment of India ensured that Kellogg's had few direct competitors. However, the attractiveness of lack of competitors was tided over by the fact that the company had to start from creating primary demand, educating people about the product, and changing their habits. After trying for a few years with strategies such as "Indianize" the brand, the company also experimented with launching biscuits to establish a brand and also marketing its product as mid-day snacks for kids.

MARKETING STRATEGY

Marketing strategy deals with pricing, selling, and distributing a product. Using a **market development** strategy, a company or business unit can (1) capture a larger share of an existing market for current products through market saturation and market penetration or (2) develop new uses and/or markets for current products. Consumer product giants such as P&G, Colgate-Palmolive, and Unilever are experts at using advertising and promotion to implement a market saturation/penetration strategy to gain the dominant market share in a product category. As seeming masters of the product life cycle, these companies are able to extend product life almost indefinitely through "new and improved" variations of product and packaging that appeal to most market niches. A company like Nestle had to follow market development strategy by finding alternate uses of its product Milkmaid. Initially launched in India as a substitute for milk, the product was unable to grasp customer attention. The company extended its lifecycle by introducing the product as a dessert ingredient and today the product has a wide range of recipes.

Using the **product development** strategy, a company or unit can (1) develop new products for *existing markets* or (2) develop new products for *new markets*. Church & Dwight has had great success by following the first product development strategy developing new products to sell to its current customers in its existing markets. Acknowledging the widespread appeal of its Milkmaid brand as a dessert ingredient, Nestle generated new uses for its product by reformulating it as a fruit yoghurt and funshakes. In another example, Lakme developed the concept of Lakme India Fashion Week to sell its products and educate the current customers. The company introduced latest season looks, makeup and fashion trends in the show. These makeup trends are then further advertised through its saloons across the country.

ITC, the most reputed brand in the Indian tobacco industry, has extended itself into almost every other product category such as cosmetics, match box, staples, hotels, etc. Dettol is another successful example of brand extension. Originally an antiseptic company, Dettol now sells shaving creams, soaps, etc.

There are numerous other marketing strategies. For advertising and promotion, for example, a company or business unit can choose between "push" and "pull" marketing strategies. Many large food and consumer products companies in the United States and Canada follow a *push strategy* by spending a large amount of money on trade promotion in order to gain or hold shelf space in retail outlets. Trade promotion includes discounts, in-store special offers, and advertising allowances designed to "push" products through the distribution system. The Kellogg Company decided a few years ago to change its emphasis from a push to a *pull strategy*, in which advertising "pulls" the products through the distribution channels. The company now spends more money on consumer advertising designed to build brand awareness so that shoppers will ask for the products. Research has found that a high level of advertising (a key part of a pull strategy) is beneficial to leading brands in a market.[5] Strong brands provide a competitive advantage to a firm because they act as entry barriers and usually generate high market share.[6]

Other marketing strategies deal with distribution and pricing. Should a company use distributors and dealers to sell its products, or should it sell directly to mass merchandisers or use the direct marketing model by selling straight to the consumers via the Internet? Companies are progressively opting for multiple distribution-channel strategy though it holds true for every industry. However, in banking and insurance, the trend is more common. For example, HDFC Bank is one of India's premier banks providing a wide range of financial products and services to over 15 million customers across hundreds of Indian cities using multiple distribution channels including a pan-India network of branches, ATMs, phone banking, net banking, and mobile banking. As of March 31, 2009, the bank had a distribution network with 1,412 branches and 3,295 ATMs in 528 cities.[7] According to the World Insurance Report, 2009 from Capgemini and the European Financial Management and Marketing Association (EFMA), multidistribution is the most effective way for insurers to attract new customers. According to the report, multidistribution helps insurers to generate additional revenues and improve network sales productivity, since lead generation and management are more tailored to "value-creating" relationships. As a result, cross-network cooperation can increase the sales conversion rate and, therefore, improve the sales productivity of networks—which consequently boosts revenues.[8] However, using multiple channels simultaneously can lead to problems. It can lead to cannibalization across distribution channels hence, increased competition and insufficient sales to stay in the business and thus discontent among distribution channel members. For example, many distributors across industries resent companies selling their products through big departmental stores such as Walmart, Big Bazaar, Home Depot, etc. Distributors fear that the ability of the big stores to underprice the product would lead to them becoming little more than repair facilities.

When pricing a new product, a company or business unit can follow one of two strategies. For new-product pioneers, *skim pricing* offers the opportunity to "skim the cream" from the top of the demand curve with a high price while the product is novel and competitors are few. *Penetration pricing*, in contrast, attempts to hasten market development and offers the pioneer the opportunity to use the experience curve to gain market share with a low price and then dominate the industry. Depending on corporate and business unit objectives and strategies, either of these choices may be desirable to a particular company or unit. Penetration pricing is, however, more likely than skim pricing to raise a unit's operating profit in the long term.[9] The use of the Internet to market goods directly to consumers allows a company to use *dynamic pricing*, a practice in which prices vary frequently based upon demand, market segment, and product availability.[10]

FINANCIAL STRATEGY

Financial strategy examines the financial implications of corporate and business-level strategic options and identifies the best financial course of action. It can also provide competitive advantage through a lower cost of funds and a flexible ability to raise capital to support a business strategy. Financial strategy usually attempts to maximize the financial value of a firm.

The trade-off between achieving the desired debt-to-equity ratio and relying on internal long-term financing via cash flow is a key issue in financial strategy. Many small and medium sized family owned companies try to avoid all external sources of funds in order to avoid outside entanglement, and to keep control of the company within the family. Few large publicly-held firms have no long-term debt and instead keep a large amount of money in cash and short-term investments. One of these is Apple, Inc. According to Apple's Chief Financial Officer, Peter Oppenheimer, "Our preference is to maintain a strong balance sheet in order to preserve our flexibility."[11] Many financial analysts believe, however, that only by financing through long-term debt can a corporation use financial leverage to boost earnings per share—thus raising stock price and the overall value of the company. Research indicates that higher debt levels not only deter takeover by other firms (by making the company less attractive) but also lead to improved productivity and improved cash flows by forcing management to focus on core businesses.[12] High debt can be a problem, however, when the economy falters and a company's cash flow drops.

Research reveals that a firm's financial strategy is influenced by its corporate diversification strategy. Equity financing, for example, is preferred for related diversification, whereas debt financing is preferred for unrelated diversification.[13] The trend away from unrelated to related acquisitions explains why the number of acquisitions being paid for entirely with stock increased from only 2% in 1988 to 50% in 1998.[14]

A very popular financial strategy is the leveraged buyout (LBO). During 2006 and 2007, for example, the total value of LBOs was $1.4 trillion, about one-third of all the buyouts ever done.[15] In a **leveraged buyout**, a company is acquired in a transaction financed largely by debt, usually obtained from a third party, such as an insurance company or an investment banker. Ultimately the debt is paid with money generated from the acquired company's operations or by sales of its assets. The acquired company, in effect, pays for its own acquisition. Management of the LBO is then under tremendous pressure to keep the highly leveraged company profitable. Unfortunately, the huge amount of debt on the acquired company's books may actually cause its eventual decline by focusing management's attention on short-term matters. For example, one year after the buyout, the cash flow of eight of the largest LBOs made during 2006–2007 was barely enough to cover interest payments.[16] One study of LBOs (also called MBOs—Management BuyOuts) revealed that the financial performance of the typical LBO usually falls below the industry average in the fourth year after the buyout. The firm declines because of inflated expectations, utilization of all slack, management burnout, and a lack of strategic management.[17] Often the only solutions are to sell the company or to again go public by selling stock to finance growth.[18]

The management of dividends and stock price is an important part of a corporation's financial strategy. Corporations in fast-growing industries such as computers and computer software often do not declare dividends. They use the money they might have spent on dividends to finance rapid growth. If the company is successful, its growth in sales and profits is reflected in a higher stock price, eventually resulting in a hefty capital gain when shareholders sell their common stock. Other corporations, such as Whirlpool Corporation, that do not face rapid growth, must support the value of their stock by offering consistent dividends. Instead of raising dividends when profits are high, a popular financial strategy is to use excess cash (or even use debt) to buy back a company's own shares of stock. For example, in 2007, Reliance Energy Ltd (REL) announced that its board of directors had given sanction to the buyback of its shares, valued at Rs 2,000 crore, in two different phases through open market purchases at a maximum price of Rs 1,600 per share.[19] The company stated that the buyback would slash the outstanding number of shares and raise its earnings per share (EPS), lessen floating stock, help in improving valuations and increase long-term price performance.[20] In October 2007, Hindustan Unilever Ltd set aside Rs 630 crore to buy back up to 25% of its stake at a price not exceeding Rs 230 per share and the buyback was implemented by way of open market purchases through the BSE and the NSE.[21] Analysts said that this buyback was implemented possibly due to two reasons. One to increase its stock price and secondly, to be in line with Unilever's (the Anglo-Dutch parent company) mega global plans, including a merger with Colgate worldwide.[22] DLF in 2008 allocated Rs 1,100 crore for the buyback scheme, which closed on July 9, 2009. Since October 17, 2008, DLF has bought a total of 38,65,767 shares so far, as per stock exchange statistics.[23]

A number of firms have been supporting the price of their stock by using *reverse stock splits*. Contrasted with a typical forward 2-for-1 stock split in which an investor receives an additional share for every share owned (with each share being worth only half as much), in a reverse 1-for-2 stock split, an investor's shares are split in half for the same total amount of money (with each share now being worth twice as much). Thus, 100 shares of stock worth $10 each are exchanged for 50 shares worth $20 each. A reverse stock split may successfully raise a company's stock price, but it does not solve underlying problems. A study by Credit Suisse First Boston revealed that almost all 800 companies that had reverse stock splits in a five-year period underperformed their peers over the long term.[24]

A rather novel financial strategy is the selling of a company's patents. Companies such as AT&T, Bellsouth, American Express, Kimberly Clark, and 3Com have been selling patents for products that they no longer wish to commercialize or are not a part of their core business. They use an intermediary, like Chicago-based Ocean Tomo, to group the patents into lots related to a common area and sell them to the highest bidder.[25]

RESEARCH AND DEVELOPMENT (R&D) STRATEGY

R&D strategy deals with product and process innovation and improvement. It also deals with the appropriate mix of different types of R&D (basic, product, or process) and with the question of how new technology should be accessed—through internal development, external acquisition, or strategic alliances.

One of the R&D choices is to be either a **technological leader**, pioneering an innovation, or a **technological follower**, imitating the products of competitors. Porter suggests that deciding to become a technological leader or follower can be a way of achieving either overall low cost or differentiation (see **Table 8–1**). To know about few of the successful, R&D strategies in India refer to **Strategy Highlight 8.1**.

STRATEGY highlight 8.1

R&D STRATEGY AND INDIA

India has come a long way since 1991. Initially known for low-level IT outsourcing and call centers, India has, over the past few years, become a destination known for outsourcing R&D in sophisticated areas such as semiconductor design, aerospace, automotive, network equipment, and medical devices.

Semiconductor Device R&D: Leading MNCs such as Microsoft, IBM, Oracle, AMD, NetApp, Adobe, Intel, EMC, Quantum, etc have R&D centers in India. These R&D centers are responsible for a significant portion of their product development. India's large skilled labor and end market competence are responsible for India's competence in this industry.[1] The competitiveness of the industry is judged from the fact that, approximately 20% of the Fortune 500 companies have their R&D operations in India and recruit managerial and engineering staff locally for their Indian operations.[2]

Aerospace R&D: India has a strong aerospace industry. Over the last 16 years, India has seen more engineering and R&D investments in aerospace than in the United States or Europe. India has a pool of qualified engineering professionals, high-tech/precision equipment, established production systems, a strong IT industry, a good network of aeronautical development labs, favorable geographical location, and manufacturing cost advantage.[3] Many companies have been motivated by these factors and have set up their units in India. For example, Honeywell Technology Solutions has set up an engineering facility, in Banglore, with over 5,500 engineers, while GE's Jack Welch Technology Centre has an extensive research lab with over 3,000 engineers.[4]

Automotive R&D: The use of high-end software in automobile design and R&D has created an edge for Indian companies over their European and American competitors. Hence, European and American car companies are setting up either their R&D services in India or entering into outsourcing agreements with Indian manufacturers. For example, in the year 2009, with the investment of Rs 4.8 billion, Mahindra and Mahindra opened its new automobile design and development facility called the Mahindra Research Valley (MRV) in Chennai.[5] Equally important is the arrival of Indian multinationals who are tackling global markets, such as Tata with its dirt cheap Nano car that the company is now positioning for a European market entry.[6]

In addition to MNCs setting up their R&D in India, local enterprises are using this strategy to capture market. For example, EnNatura, an IIT Delhi company started in 2006, is a clean materials company, developing specialty chemicals from renewable sources. The entrepreneurs have developed a resin platform for application in the printing ink industry, allowing for eco-friendly printing along with high-efficiency recycling of printed paper. The Clima print reduces hydrocarbon consumption and delivers high performance and environment-friendly attributes when applied in specialty chemicals. This also allows for economies in paper recycling.[7] Many more such examples of innovations exist in India; for example, India's R&D has been credited with the introduction of "World's Cheaptest Tablet" and "World's Cheapest Car."

1. P. Nivedan, "MNC R&D in India: Industry Perspective," posted on 25 May 2009, accessed on 1 Nov 2011, from http://www.expresscomputeronline.com/20090525/1000thissue07.shtml

2. IBEF, "Semiconductor Industry," posted on September 2009, accessed on 1 Nov 2011, from http://www.ibef.in/download/Semiconductor_171109.pdf

3. G. Siva, "Can India's Aerospace Manufacturers Step Up?" posted on 3 Feb 2009 12:00, accessed on 1 Nov 2011, from http://www.flightglobal.com/news/articles/can-indias-aerospace-manufacturers-step-up-321894/

4. S. Toby, "India's Aerospace industry to boost economy," posted on 11 Jan 2010 12:28 IST, accessed on 1 Nov 2011, from http://business.rediff.com/column/2010/jan/11/guest-india-aerospace-industry-to-boost-economy.htm

5. Editorial, "The Indian R&d Design for Cars," accessed on 1 Nov 2011, from http://www.streetdirectory.com/travel_guide/58017/car_focus/the_indian_rd_design_for_cars.html

6. V. Wadhwa, "India Is Morphing into a Global R&D Hub, but Can It Ever Take on Silicon Valley?" posted on 14 Nov 2009, from http://techcrunch.com/2009/11/14/india-rd-hub-silicon-valley/

7. Ennatura, ClimaPrint Solution, accessed on 1 Nov 2011, from http://ennatura.com/

TABLE 8–1		Technological Leadership	Technological Followership
Research and Development Strategy and Competitive Advantage	**Cost Advantage**	Pioneer the lowest-cost production design. Be the first down the learning curve. Create low cost ways of performing value activities.	Lower the cost of the product or value activities by learning from the leader's experience. Avoid R&D costs through imitation.
	Differentiation	Pioneer a unique product that increases buyer value. Innovate in other activities to increase buyer value.	Adapt the product or delivery system more closely to buyer needs by learning from the leader's experience.

SOURCE: Reprinted with the permission of The Free Press, a Division of Simon & Schuster, from *COMPETITIVE ADVANTAGE. Creating and Sustaining Superior Performance* by Michael E. Porter. Copyright © 1985, 1988 by The Free Press. All rights reserved.

One example of an effective use of the *leader* R&D functional strategy to achieve a differentiation competitive advantage is Nike, Inc. Nike spends more than most in the industry on R&D to differentiate the performance of its athletic shoes from that of its competitors. As a result, its products have become the favorite of serious athletes. An example of the use of the *follower* R&D functional strategy to achieve a low-cost competitive advantage is Dean Foods Company. "We're able to have the customer come to us and say, 'If you can produce X, Y, and Z product for the same quality and service, but at a lower price and without that expensive label on it, you can have the business,'" says Howard Dean, president of the company.[26]

An increasing number of companies are working with their suppliers to help them keep up with changing technology. They are beginning to realize that a firm cannot be competitive technologically only through internal development. For example, Chrysler Corporation's skillful use of parts suppliers to design everything from car seats to drive shafts has enabled it to spend consistently less money than its competitors to develop new car models. Using strategic technology alliances is one way to combine the R&D capabilities of two companies. Maytag Company worked with one of its suppliers to apply fuzzy logic technology to its IntelliSense™ dishwasher. The partnership enabled Maytag to complete the project in a shorter amount of time than if it had tried to do it alone.[27] One UK study found that 93% of UK auto assemblers and component manufacturers use their suppliers as technology suppliers.[28] See **Strategy Highlight 8.1** for R&D strategies in India.

A new approach to R&D is *open innovation*, in which a firm uses alliances and connections with corporate, government, academic labs, and even consumers to develop new products and processes. Indian companies are now willing to take the risk of investing big money in R&D. The last few years have seen a lot of companies such as Avesthagen, Dr Reddy's, Biocon, Dabur, Panacea Biotec, and Bharat Biotech making substantial investments in establishing, upgrading, and expanding their R&D infrastructure in an effort to ascend the research value chain and sustain global challenges, competitiveness, and avail the opportunities.[29] Tata Consultancy Services (TCS) over the years has forged academic alliances with various universities. While TCS does not own the university research that is sponsored, it is the first to gain access to it. Therefore, if there is any opportunity for commercial exploitation, TCS has the right to first refusal. The universities, in turn, benefit from having the funds to work in emerging fields and from getting a free hand to work on a larger canvas than they would otherwise have had.[30] Mattel, Walmart, and other toy manufacturers and retailers use idea brokers such as Big Idea Group to scout for new toy ideas. Big Idea Group invites inventors to submit ideas to its Web site (www.bigideagroup.net). It then refines and promotes to its clients the most promising ideas.[31] IBM adopted the open operating system Linux for some of its computer products and systems, drawing on a core code base that is continually improved and enhanced by a massive global community of software developers, of whom only a fraction work for IBM.[32] To open its own labs to ideas being generated elsewhere, P&G's CEO Art Lafley decreed that half of the company's ideas must come from outside, up from 10% in 2000. P&G instituted the use of *technology scouts* to search beyond the company for promising innovations. By 2007, the objective was achieved—50% of the company's innovations originated outside P&G.[33]

A slightly different approach to technology development is for a large firm such as IBM or Microsoft to purchase minority stakes in relatively new high-tech entrepreneurial ventures that need capital to continue operation. Investing corporate venture capital is one way to gain access to promising innovations at a lower cost than by developing them internally.[34]

OPERATIONS STRATEGY

Operations strategy determines how and where a product or service is to be manufactured, the level of vertical integration in the production process, the deployment of physical resources, and relationships with suppliers. It should also deal with the optimum level of technology the firm should use in its operations processes. See the **Global Issue** feature to see how differences in national conditions can lead to differences in product design and manufacturing facilities from one country to another.

Advanced Manufacturing Technology (AMT) is revolutionizing operations worldwide and should continue to have a major impact as corporations strive to integrate diverse business activities by using computer assisted design and manufacturing (CAD/CAM) principles. The use of CAD/CAM, flexible manufacturing systems, computer numerically controlled systems, automatically guided vehicles, robotics, manufacturing resource planning (MRP II), optimized production technology, and just-in-time techniques contribute to increased flexibility, quick response time, and higher productivity. Such investments also act to increase the company's fixed costs and could cause significant problems if the company is unable to achieve economies of scale or scope.

A firm's manufacturing strategy is often affected by a product's life cycle. As the sales of a product increase, there will be an increase in production volume ranging from lot sizes as low as one in a *job shop* (one-of-a-kind production using skilled labor) through *connected line batch flow* (components are standardized; each machine functions such as a job shop but is positioned in the same order as the parts are processed) to lot sizes as high as 100,000 or more per year for *flexible manufacturing systems* (parts are grouped into manufacturing families to produce a wide variety of mass-produced items) and *dedicated transfer lines* (highly automated assembly lines making one mass-produced product using little human labor). According to this concept, the product becomes standardized into a commodity over time in conjunction with increasing demand. Flexibility thus gives way to efficiency.[35]

Increasing competitive intensity in many industries has forced companies to switch from traditional mass production using dedicated transfer lines to a continuous improvement production strategy. A *mass-production* system was an excellent method to produce a large number of low-cost, standard goods and services. Employees worked on narrowly defined, repetitive tasks under close supervision in a bureaucratic and hierarchical structure. Quality, however, often tended to be fairly low. Learning how to do something better was the prerogative of management; workers were expected only to learn what was assigned to them. This system tended to dominate manufacturing until the 1970s. Under the *continuous improvement* system developed by Japanese firms, empowered cross-functional teams strive constantly to improve production processes. Managers are more like coaches than like bosses. The result is a large quantity of low-cost, standard goods and services, but with high quality. The key to continuous improvement is the acknowledgment that workers' experience and knowledge can

GLOBAL issue

INTERNATIONAL DIFFERENCES ALTER WHIRLPOOL'S OPERATIONS STRATEGY

To better penetrate the growing markets in developing nations, Whirlpool decided to build a "world washer." This new type of washing machine was to be produced in Brazil, Mexico, and India. Lightweight, with substantially fewer parts than its U.S. counterpart, its performance was to be equal to or better than anything on the world market while being competitive in price with the most popular models in these markets. The goal was to develop a complete product, process, and facility design package that could be used in different countries with low initial investment. Originally the plan had been to make the same low-cost washer in identical plants in each of the three countries.

Significant differences in each of the three countries forced Whirlpool to change its product design to adapt to each nation's situation. According to Lawrence Kremer, Senior Vice President of Global Technology and Operations, "Our Mexican affiliate, Vitromatic, has porcelain and glassmaking capabilities. Porcelain baskets made sense for them. Stainless steel became the preferred material for the others." Costs also affected decisions. "In India, for exam-

ple, material costs may run as much as 200% to 800% higher than elsewhere, while labor and overhead costs are comparatively minimal," added Kremer. Another consideration was the garments to be washed in each country. For example, saris—the 18-foot lengths of cotton or silk with which Indian women drape themselves—needed special treatment in an Indian washing machine, forcing additional modifications.

Manufacturing facilities also varied from country to country. Brastemp, Whirlpool's Brazilian partner, built its plant of precast concrete to address the problems of high humidity. In India, however, the construction crew cast the concrete, allowed it to cure, and then using chain, block, and tackle, five or six men raised each three-ton slab into place. Instead of using one building, Mexican operations used two, one housing the flexible assembly lines and stamping operations, and an adjacent facility housing the injection molding and extrusion processes.

SOURCE: WHEELEN, TOM; HUNGER, J. DAVID, STRATEGIC MANAGEMENT AND BUSINESS POLICY, 9th Edition, © 2004, p. 172. Reprinted by permission of Pearson Education, Inc. Upper Saddle River, NJ.

---

help managers solve production problems and contribute to tightening variances and reducing errors. Because continuous improvement enables firms to use the same low-cost competitive strategy as do mass-production firms but at a significantly higher level of quality, it is rapidly replacing mass production as an operations strategy.

The automobile industry is currently experimenting with the strategy of *modular manufacturing* in which preassembled subassemblies are delivered as they are needed (i.e., Just-in-Time) to a company's assembly-line workers, who quickly piece the modules together into a finished product. For example, General Motors built a new automotive complex in Brazil to make its new subcompact, the Celta. Sixteen of the 17 buildings were occupied by suppliers, including Delphi, Lear, and Goodyear. These suppliers delivered preassembled modules (which comprised 85% of the final value of each car) to GM's building for assembly. In a process new to the industry, the suppliers acted as a team to build a single module comprising the motor, transmission, fuel lines, rear axle, brake-fluid lines, and exhaust system, which was then installed as one piece. GM hoped that this manufacturing strategy would enable it to produce 100 vehicles annually per worker compared to the standard rate of 30 to 50 autos per worker.[36] Ford and Chrysler have also opened similar modular facilities in Brazil.

The concept of a product's life cycle eventually leading to one-size-fits-all mass production is being increasingly challenged by the new concept of mass customization. Appropriate for an ever-changing environment, *mass customization* requires that people, processes, units, and technology reconfigure themselves to give customers exactly what they want, when they want it. In the case of Dell Computer, customers use the Internet to design their own computers. In contrast to continuous improvement, mass customization requires flexibility and quick

STRATEGY highlight 8.2

THEORY OF CONSTRAINTS IN INDIA

Many companies across industries are adopting the theory of constraints (TOC) to accelerate process improvement in manufacturing and project operations. It states that "The throughput of any system is determined by one constraint."[1] TOC is philosophy of management and improvement, originally developed by Eliyahu M. Goldratt and introduced in his book in 1984, *The Goal*.[2] The philosophy states that in a production process, there is usually one aspect of that system that limits the ability of the system to achieve more of its goal. A constraint is anything that prevents the system from achieving more of its goal. These could be internal or external. Types of (internal) constraints may be equipment, people, or policy. An external constraint exists when the system can produce more than the market can bear.

Therefore, for that system to attain any significant improvement, the constraint must be identified and the whole system must be managed with it in mind. The essence of the TOC approach is that if you want more of your goal, you must:

- Identify your constraint
- Focus on the constraint
- Follow it through.[3]

For example, Nat Steels, a manufacturer and exporter of hospital autoclaves, laundry, and canteen equipment from Bombay, India, benefitted from this philosophy. The company, before discovering TOC, was facing acute problems with late deliveries and large outstanding debts, etc. in 2001. In 2002–2003, i.e., within one year of adopting TOC, the company saw the following:

- On-time deliveries increased from 5% to 95%
- Lead time decreased from 13 to 2 weeks

- Order inflow rate increased by 25%
- Sales increased by 25%
- Receivables down by 33%
- Inventory down by 20%
- Supplier payments reduced from 3 to 1 month
- Bank borrowings reduced by 40%[4]

Similar results were seen at Eicher Demm Ltd. a part of Eicher Motors Limited, which comprises the automotive businesses of the Eicher Group. The results were visible within two months of adopting the TOC line of thinking. Almost immediately, bloated inventories began to dry up. The company was able to meet the line of their budget after five years for the first half of the financial year 2003–2004, which was over 29% growth over the last year.5

1. Nayima bvba, "The Theory of Constraints," accessed on 1 Nov 2011, from http://www.nayima.be/about/TheoryOfConstraints.html

2. Focused Performance, "What Is the Theory of Constraints?" accessed on 1 Nov 2011, from http://www.focusedperformance.com/toc01.html

3. Value Based Management.net, "Theory of Constraints-Goldratt, Eliyahu," accessed on 1 Nov 2011, from http://www.valuebasedmanagement.net/methods_goldratt_theory_of_constraints.html

4. L. J. Karjewski, L. P. Ritzman, and M. K. Malhotra, *Operations Management: Processes and Value Chains*, (New Delhi: Dorling Kindersley (India) Pvt. Ltd, 2008), p. 253.

5. L. J. Karjewski, L. P. Ritzman, and M. K. Malhotra, *Operations Management: Processes and Value Chains*, (New Delhi: Dorling Kindersley (India) Pvt. Ltd, 2008), p. 258.

responsiveness. Managers coordinate independent, capable individuals. An efficient linkage system is crucial. The result is low-cost, high-quality, customized goods and services appropriate for a large number of market niches. See **Strategy Highlight 8.2.**

A contentious issue for manufacturing companies throughout the world is the availability of resources needed to operate a modern factory. The increasing cost of oil during 2007 and 2008 drastically boosted costs, only some of which could be passed on to the customers in a competitive environment. The likelihood that fresh water could become an equally scarce resource is causing many companies to rethink water-intensive manufacturing processes. To learn how companies are beginning to deal with increasing fresh water scarcity, see the **Environmental Sustainability Issue** feature.

PURCHASING STRATEGY

Purchasing strategy deals with obtaining the raw materials, parts, and supplies needed to perform the operations function. Purchasing strategy is important because materials and components purchased from suppliers comprise 50% of total manufacturing costs of manufacturing companies in the United Kingdom, United States, Australia, Belgium, and Finland.[37] The basic purchasing choices are multiple, sole, and parallel sourcing. Under *multiple sourcing,* the purchasing company orders a particular part from several vendors. Multiple sourcing has traditionally been considered superior to other purchasing approaches because (1) it forces suppliers to compete for the business of an important buyer, thus reducing purchasing costs, and (2) if one supplier cannot deliver, another usually can, thus guaranteeing that parts and supplies are always on hand when needed. Multiple sourcing has been one way for a purchasing firm to control the relationship with its suppliers. So long as suppliers can provide evidence that they can meet the product specifications, they are kept on the purchaser's list of acceptable vendors for specific parts and supplies. Unfortunately, the common practice of accepting the lowest bid often compromises quality.

W. Edward Deming, a well-known management consultant, strongly recommended *sole sourcing* as the only manageable way to obtain high supplier quality. Sole sourcing relies on only one supplier for a particular part. Given his concern with designing quality into a product in its early stages of development, Deming argued that the buyer should work closely with the supplier at all stages. This reduces both cost and time spent on product design and it also improves quality. It can also simplify the purchasing company's production process by using the *Just-In-Time* (JIT) concept of having the purchased parts arrive at the plant just when they are needed rather than keeping inventories. The concept of sole sourcing is taken one step further in JIT II, in which vendor sales representatives actually have desks next to the purchasing company's factory floor, attend production status meetings, visit the R&D lab, and analyze the purchasing company's sales forecasts. These in-house suppliers then write sales orders for which the purchasing company is billed. Developed by Lance Dixon at Bose Corporation, JIT II is also being used at IBM, Honeywell, and Ingersoll-Rand. Karen Dale, purchasing manager for Honeywell's office supplies, said she was very concerned about confidentiality when JIT II was first suggested to her. Soon she had five suppliers working with her 20 buyers and reported few problems.[38]

Sole sourcing reduces transaction costs and builds quality by having the purchaser and supplier work together as partners rather than as adversaries. With sole sourcing, more companies will have longer relationships with fewer suppliers. Research has found that buyer-supplier collaboration and joint problem solving with both parties dependent upon the other results in the development of competitive capabilities, higher quality, lower costs, and better scheduling.[39] Sole sourcing does, however, have limitations. If a supplier is unable to deliver a part, the purchaser has no alternative but to delay production. Multiple suppliers can provide the purchaser with better information about new technology and performance capabilities. The limitations of sole sourcing have led to the development of parallel sourcing. In *parallel sourcing*, two suppliers are the sole suppliers of two different parts, but they are also backup suppliers for each other's parts. If one vendor cannot supply all of its parts on time, the other vendor is asked to make up the difference.[40]

The Internet is being increasingly used both to find new sources of supply and to keep inventories replenished. For example, Hewlett-Packard introduced a Web-based procurement system to enable its 84,000 employees to buy office supplies from a standard set of suppliers. The new system enabled the company to save $60 to $100 million annually in purchasing costs.[41] Research indicates that companies using Internet-based technologies are able to lower administrative costs and purchase prices.[42]

ENVIRONMENTAL sustainability issue

OPERATIONS NEED FRESH WATER AND LOTS OF IT!

The U.S. Department of Energy (DOE) plans to build a rail line more than 300 miles long through the Nevada wilderness to move spent nuclear fuel from 121 sites in 39 states to a geologic repository at Yucca Mountain. One of the biggest issues to overcome will be water supply. The DOE estimates that the construction phase would require 5,500 acre feet of water for earthwork compaction, 370 acre-feet for construction personnel, 200 acre-feet for dust control along access roads, and 30 acre-feet for quarry operations, totaling 6,100 acre-feet, or two billion gallons, of water to support a four-year construction period. To meet this need, DOE wants to drill 150 to 176 new wells. The state of Nevada, however, has rejected a permit request to use water for drilling on the Yucca Mountain site, stating that water has to be used for the benefit of the public. Negotiations continue.

This is just one of the ways that organizations need fresh water for their operations. Nestlé, Unilever, Coca-Cola, Anheuser-Busch, and Danone consume almost 575 billion liters of water a year, enough to satisfy the daily water needs of every person on the planet. It takes about 13 cubic meters of freshwater to produce a single 200 mm semiconductor wafer. As a result, chip making is believed to account for 25% of the water consumption in Silicon Valley. According to Jose Lopez, Nestlé's COO, it takes four liters of water to make one liter of product in Nestlé's factories, but 3,000 liters of water are needed to grow the agricultural produce that supplies them. Each year, around 40% of the freshwater withdrawn from lakes and aquifers in America is used to cool power plants. Separating one liter of oil from Canada's tar sands requires up to five liters of water!

"Water is the oil of the 21st century," contends Andrew Liveris, CEO of the chemical company Dow. Like oil, supplies of clean, easily accessible fresh water are under a growing strain because of the growing population and widespread improvements in living standards. Industrialization in developing nations is contaminating rivers and aquifers. Climate change is altering the patterns of fresh water availability so that droughts are more likely in many parts of the world. According to a survey by the Marsh Center for Risk Insights, 40% of Fortune 1000 companies stated that the impact of a water shortage on their business would be "severe" or "catastrophic," but only 17% said that they were prepared for such a crisis. Of Nestlé's 481 factories worldwide, 49 are located in water-scarce regions. Environmental activists have attacked PepsiCo and Coca-Cola for allegedly depleting groundwater in India to make bottled drinks.

There are a number of companies that are taking action to protect their future supply of freshwater. Dow has reduced the amount of water it uses by over a third since 1995. During 1997–2006, when Nestle almost doubled the volume of food it produced, it reduced the amount of water used by 29%. By 2008, Coca-Cola had achieved 85% of its objective to clean all of the wastewater generated at its bottling plants by 2010. China's Elion Chemical is working with General Electric to recycle 90% of its wastewater to comply with the government's new "zero-liquid" discharge rules.

SOURCE: K. Kube, "Into the Wild Brown Yonder," *Trains* (November 2008), pp. 68–73; "Running Dry," *The Economist* (August 23, 2008), pp. 53–54.

LOGISTICS STRATEGY

Logistics strategy deals with the flow of products into and out of the manufacturing process. India's logistics cost of 13% of the gross domestic product (GDP) is among the highest in the world as a percentage of GDP. This is compared to 11% in Japan; 10% in Europe, and 9% in the United States.[43] In India, transportation accounts for almost 40% of the logistics cost.[44] To stay competitive, companies need to cater to a strategy that allows the company to deliver right product at the right time, at the right place, and to the right consumer. Three trends related to this strategy are evident: centralization, outsourcing, and the use of the Internet. To gain logistical synergies across business units, corporations began centralizing logistics in the headquarters group. This centralized logistics group usually contains specialists with expertise in different transportation modes such as rail or trucking. They work to aggregate shipping volumes across the entire corporation to gain better contracts with shippers. Companies view logistics function as an important way to differentiate themselves from the competition, add value, and reduce costs. It is because of this logic that Walmart's fully owned logistics arm Gazeley is looking after Walmart and Bharti's retail venture. They are closely studying various logistics providers such as Radhakrishnan Foods, before they finally close on a model for the Indian market. The Future Group (includes Pantaloons, Big Bazaar, Central Food Bazaar, etc.) understood that in retail business, logistics forms a critical business activity. The company, therefore, launched another subsidiary, i.e., Future Logistics Solutions Limited (FLSL). FLSL, a specialized subsidiary, offers strategic, focused, and consolidated approach to meet the group's large supply chain requirements as well as those of select supply and business partners. For instance, DCM Shriram Consolidated Ltd (DSCL) is in the process of tying up with various retail chains such as Future Group's Food Bazaar, south-based Subhiksha, and RPG's Spencer to meet their sourcing requirements. The new tie-ups would help the company operate on economies of scale and all over the country.

Many companies are using the Internet to simplify their logistical system. For example, Ace Hardware created an online system for its retailers and suppliers. An individual hardware store can now see on the Web site that ordering 210 cases of wrenches is cheaper than ordering 200 cases. Because a full pallet is composed of 210 cases of wrenches, an order for a full pallet means that the supplier doesn't have to pull 10 cases off a pallet and repackage them for storage. There is less chance that loose cases will be lost in delivery, and the paperwork doesn't have to be redone. As a result, Ace's transportation costs are down 18%, and warehouse costs have been cut 28%.[45]

HUMAN RESOURCE MANAGEMENT (HRM) STRATEGY

HRM strategy, among other things, addresses the issue of whether a company or business unit should hire a large number of low-skilled employees who receive low pay, perform repetitive jobs, and are most likely quit after a short time (the McDonald's restaurant strategy) or hire skilled employees who receive relatively high pay and are cross-trained to participate in *self-managing work teams*. As work increases in complexity, the more suited it is for teams, especially in the case of innovative product development efforts. Multinational corporations are increasingly using self-managing work teams in their foreign affiliates as well as in home-country operations.[46] Research indicates that the use of work teams leads to increased quality and productivity as well as to higher employee satisfaction and commitment.[47]

Companies following a competitive strategy of differentiation through high quality use input from subordinates and peers in performance appraisals to a greater extent than do firms following other business strategies.[48] A complete *360-degree appraisal*, in which input is gathered from multiple sources, is now being used by more than 10% of U.S. corporations and has become one of the most popular and effective tools in developing employees and new managers.[49] One Indian company, HCL Technologies, publishes the appraisal ratings for the top 20 managers on the company's intranet for all to see.[50]

Companies are finding that having a *diverse workforce* can be a competitive advantage. Research reveals that firms with a high degree of racial diversity following a growth strategy have higher productivity than do firms with less racial diversity.[51] Avon Company, for example, was able to turn around its unprofitable inner-city markets by putting African-American and Hispanic managers in charge of marketing to these markets.[52] Diversity in terms of age and national origin also offers benefits. DuPont's use of multinational teams has helped the company develop and market products internationally. McDonald's has discovered that older workers perform as well as, if not better than, younger employees. According to Edward Rensi, CEO of McDonald's USA, "We find these people to be particularly well motivated, with a sort of discipline and work habits hard to find in younger employees."[53]

INFORMATION TECHNOLOGY STRATEGY

Corporations are increasingly using **information technology strategy** to provide business units with competitive advantage. When FedEx first provided its customers with PowerShip computer software to store addresses, print shipping labels, and track package location, its sales jumped significantly. UPS soon followed with its own MaxiShips software. Viewing its information system as a distinctive competency, FedEx continued to push for further advantage over UPS by using its Web site to enable customers to track their packages. FedEx uses this competency in its advertisements by showing how customers can track the progress of their shipments. Soon thereafter, UPS provided the same service. Although it can be argued that information technology has now become so pervasive that it no longer offers companies a competitive advantage, corporations worldwide continue to spend over $2 trillion annually on information technology.[54]

Multinational corporations are finding that having a sophisticated intranet allows employees to practice *follow-the-sun management*, in which project team members living in one country can pass their work to team members in another country in which the work day is just beginning. Thus, night shifts are no longer needed.[55] The development of instant translation software is also enabling workers to have online communication with co-workers in other countries who use a different language.[56] For example, Mattel has cut the time it takes to develop new products by 10% by enabling designers and licensees in other countries to collaborate on toy design. IBM uses its intranet to allow its employees to collaborate and improve their skills, thus reducing its training and travel expenses.[57]

Many companies, such as Lockheed Martin, General Electric, and Whirlpool, use information technology to form closer relationships with both their customers and suppliers through sophisticated extranets. For example, General Electric's Trading Process Network allows suppliers to electronically download GE's requests for proposals, view diagrams of parts specifications, and communicate with GE purchasing managers. According to Robert Livingston, GE's head of worldwide sourcing for the Lighting Division, going on the Web reduces processing time by one-third.[58] Thus, the use of information technology through extranets makes it easier for a company to buy from others (outsource) rather than make it themselves (vertically integrate).[59]

8.2 The Sourcing Decision: Location of Functions

For a functional strategy to have the best chance of success, it should be built on a distinctive competency residing within that functional area. If a corporation does not have a distinctive competency in a particular functional area, that functional area could be a candidate for outsourcing.

Outsourcing is purchasing from someone else a product or service that had been previously provided internally. Thus, it is the reverse of vertical integration. Outsourcing is becoming an increasingly important part of strategic decision making and an important way to increase efficiency and often quality. In a study of 30 firms, outsourcing resulted on average in a 9% reduction in costs and a 15% increase in capacity and quality.[60] For example, Boeing used outsourcing as a way to reduce the cost of designing and manufacturing its new 787 Dreamliner. Up to 70% of the plane was outsourced. In a break from past practice, suppliers make large parts of the fuselage, including plumbing, electrical, and computer systems, and ship them to Seattle for assembly by Boeing. Outsourcing enabled Boeing to build a 787 in 4 months instead of the usual 12.[61]

According to an American Management Association survey of member companies, 94% of the responding firms outsource at least one activity. The outsourced activities are general and administrative (78%), human resources (77%), transportation and distribution (66%), information systems (63%), manufacturing (56%), marketing (51%), and finance and accounting (18%). The survey also reveals that 25% of the respondents have been disappointed in their outsourcing results. Fifty-one percent of the firms reported bringing an outsourced activity back in-house. Nevertheless, authorities not only expect the number of companies engaging in outsourcing to increase, they also expect companies to outsource an increasing number of functions, especially those in customer service, bookkeeping, financial/clerical, sales/telemarketing, and the mailroom.[62] It is estimated that 50% of U.S. manufacturing will be outsourced to firms in 28 developing countries by 2015.[63]

Offshoring is the outsourcing of an activity or a function to a wholly owned company or an independent provider in another country. Offshoring is a global phenomenon that has been supported by advances in information and communication technologies, the development of stable, secure, and high-speed data transmission systems, and logistical advances like containerized shipping. According to Bain & Company, 51% of large firms in North America, Europe, and Asia outsource offshore.[64] Although India currently has 70% of the offshoring market, countries such as Brazil, China, Russia, the Phillipines, Malaysia, Hungary, the Czech Republic, and Israel are growing in importance. These countries have low-cost qualified labor and an educated workforce. These are important considerations because more than 93% of offshoring companies do so to reduce costs.[65] For example, Mexican assembly line workers average $3.50 an hour plus benefits compared to $27 an hour plus benefits at a GM or Ford plant in the U.S. Less skilled Mexican workers at auto parts makers earn as little as $1.50 per hour with fewer benefits.[66]

Software programming and customer service, in particular, are being outsourced to India. For example, General Electric's back-office services unit, GE Capital International Services, is one of the oldest and biggest of India's outsourcing companies. From only $26 million in 1999, its annual revenues grew to over $420 million by 2004.[67] As part of this trend, IBM acquired Daksh eServices Ltd., one of India's biggest suppliers of remote business services.[68]

Outsourcing, including offshoring, has significant disadvantages. For example, mounting complaints forced Dell Computer to stop routing corporate customers to a technical support call center in Bangalore, India.[69] GE's introduction of a new washing machine was delayed three weeks because of production problems at a supplier's company to which it had contracted out key work. Some companies have found themselves locked into long-term contracts with outside suppliers that were no longer competitive.[70] Some authorities propose that the cumulative effects of continued outsourcing steadily reduces a firm's ability to learn new skills and to develop new core competencies.[71] One survey of 129 outsourcing firms revealed that half the outsourcing projects undertaken in one year failed to deliver anticipated savings. This is in agreement with a survey by Bain & Company in which 51% of large North American, European, and Asian firms stated that outsourcing (including offshoring) did not meet their expectations.[72] Another survey of software projects, by MIT, found that the median Indian project had 10% more software bugs than did comparable U.S. projects.[73] During 2007–2008, tainted goods made by Chinese manufacturers, ranging from lead paint on toys, contaminated heparin, and melamine-laced milk caused their customers to reevaluate the manner in which they engaged in offshore outsourcing.[74] The increasing cost of oil was making offshoring less economical. Since 2003, crude oil increased in price from $28 to over $100 a barrel in 2008, causing the cost to ship a standard 40-foot container to triple. By 2008 it cost about $100 to ship a ton of iron from Brazil to China, more than the cost of the mineral itself.[75]

A study of 91 outsourcing efforts conducted by European and North American firms found seven major errors that should be avoided:

1. **Outsourcing activities that should not be outsourced:** Companies failed to keep core activities in-house.
2. **Selecting the wrong vendor:** Vendors were not trustworthy or lacked state-of-the-art processes.
3. **Writing a poor contract:** Companies failed to establish a balance of power in the relationship.
4. **Overlooking personnel issues:** Employees lost commitment to the firm.
5. **Losing control over the outsourced activity:** Qualified managers failed to manage the outsourced activity.[76]

6. **Overlooking the hidden costs of outsourcing:** Transaction costs overwhelmed other savings.

7. **Failing to plan an exit strategy:** Companies failed to build reversibility clauses into the contract.[77]

The key to outsourcing is to purchase from outside only those activities that are not key to the company's distinctive competencies. Otherwise, the company may give up the very capabilities that made it successful in the first place—thus putting itself on the road to eventual decline. This is supported by research reporting that companies that have more experience with a particular manufacturing technology tend to keep manufacturing in-house.[78] J. P. Morgan Chase & Company terminated a seven-year technology outsourcing agreement with IBM because the bank's management realized that information technology (IT) was too important strategically to be outsourced.[79]

In determining functional strategy, the strategist must:

- Identify the company's or business unit's core competencies
- Ensure that the competencies are continually being strengthened
- Manage the competencies in such a way that best preserves the competitive advantage they create

An outsourcing decision depends on the fraction of total value added that the activity under consideration represents and on the amount of potential competitive advantage in that activity for the company or business unit. See the outsourcing matrix in **Figure 8–1**. A firm should consider outsourcing any activity or function that has low potential for competitive advantage. If that activity constitutes only a small part of the total value of the firm's products or services, it should be purchased on the open market (assuming that quality providers of the activity are plentiful). If, however, the activity contributes highly to the company's products or services, the firm should purchase it through long-term contracts with trusted suppliers or distributors. A firm should always produce at least some of the activity or function (i.e., taper vertical integration) if that activity has the potential for providing the company some competitive advantage. However, full vertical integration should be considered only when that activity or function adds significant value to the company's products or services in addition to providing competitive advantage.[80]

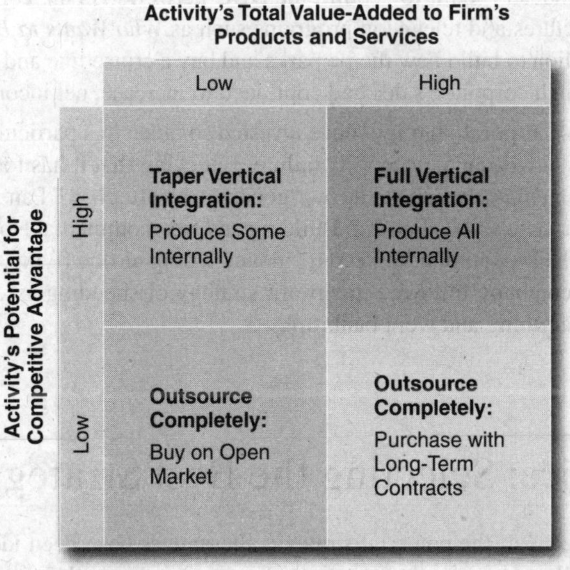

Activity's Total Value-Added to Firm's Products and Services

	Low	High
High (Activity's Potential for Competitive Advantage)	**Taper Vertical Integration:** Produce Some Internally	**Full Vertical Integration:** Produce All Internally
Low (Activity's Potential for Competitive Advantage)	**Outsource Completely:** Buy on Open Market	**Outsource Completely:** Purchase with Long-Term Contracts

FIGURE 8–1
Proposed
Outsourcing
Matrix

8.3 Strategies to Avoid

Several strategies, that could be considered corporate, business, or functional are very dangerous. Managers who have made poor analyses or lack creativity may be trapped into considering some of the following strategies to avoid:

- **Follow the leader:** Imitating a leading competitor's strategy might seem to be a good idea, but it ignores a firm's particular strengths and weaknesses and the possibility that the leader may be wrong. Fujitsu Ltd., the world's second-largest computer maker, had been driven since the 1960s by the sole ambition of catching up to IBM. Like IBM, Fujitsu competed primarily as a mainframe computer maker. So devoted was it to catching IBM, however, that it failed to notice that the mainframe business had reached maturity by 1990 and was no longer growing.

- **Hit another home run:** If a company is successful because it pioneered an extremely successful product, it tends to search for another super product that will ensure growth and prosperity. As in betting on long shots in horse races, the probability of finding a second winner is slight. Polaroid spent a lot of money developing an "instant" movie camera, but the public ignored it in favor of the camcorder.

- **Arms race:** Entering into a spirited battle with another firm for increased market share might increase sales revenue, but that increase will probably be more than offset by increases in advertising, promotion, R&D, and manufacturing costs. Since the deregulation of airlines, price wars and rate specials have contributed to the low profit margins and bankruptcies of many major airlines, such as Eastern, Pan American, TWA, and United.

- **Do everything:** When faced with several interesting opportunities, management might tend to leap at all of them. At first, a corporation might have enough resources to develop each idea into a project, but money, time, and energy are soon exhausted as the many projects demand large infusions of resources. The Walt Disney Company's expertise in the entertainment industry led it to acquire the ABC network. As the company churned out new motion pictures and television programs such as *Who Wants to Be a Millionaire*? it spent $750 million to build new theme parks and buy a cruise line and a hockey team. By 2000, even though corporate sales had continued to increase, net income was falling.[81]

- **Losing hand:** A corporation might have invested so much in a particular strategy that top management is unwilling to accept its failure. Believing that it has too much invested to quit, management may continue to throw "good money after bad." Pan American Airlines, for example, chose to sell its Pan Am Building and Intercontinental Hotels, the most profitable parts of the corporation, to keep its money-losing airline flying. Continuing to suffer losses, the company followed this profit strategy of shedding assets for cash until it had sold off everything and went bankrupt.

8.4 Strategic Choice: Selecting the Best Strategy

After the pros and cons of the potential strategic alternatives have been identified and evaluated, one must be selected for implementation. By now, it is likely that many feasible alternatives will have emerged. How is the best strategy determined?

Perhaps the most important criterion is the capability of the proposed strategy to deal with the specific strategic factors developed earlier, in the SWOT analysis. If the alternative doesn't take advantage of environmental opportunities and corporate strengths/competencies, and lead away from environmental threats and corporate weaknesses, it will probably fail.

Another important consideration in the selection of a strategy is the ability of each alternative to satisfy agreed-on objectives with the least resources and the fewest negative side effects. It is, therefore, important to develop a tentative implementation plan in order to address the difficulties that management is likely to face. This should be done in light of societal trends, the industry, and the company's situation based on the construction of scenarios.

CONSTRUCTING CORPORATE SCENARIOS

Corporate scenarios are *pro forma* (estimated future) balance sheets and income statements that forecast the effect each alternative strategy and its various programs will likely have on division and corporate return on investment. In a survey of Fortune 500 firms, 84% reported using computer simulation models in strategic planning. Most of these were simply spreadsheet-based simulation models dealing with what-if questions.[82]

The recommended scenarios are simply extensions of the industry scenarios. If, for example, industry scenarios suggest the probable emergence of a strong market demand in a specific country for certain products, a series of alternative strategy scenarios can be developed. The alternative of acquiring another firm having these products in that country can be compared with the alternative of a green-field development (e.g., building new operations in that country). Using three sets of estimated sales figures (Optimistic, Pessimistic, and Most Likely) for the new products over the next five years, the two alternatives can be evaluated in terms of their effect on future company performance as reflected in the company's probable future financial statements. Pro forma balance sheets and income statements can be generated with spreadsheet software, such as Excel, on a personal computer. Pro forma statements are based on financial and economic scenarios.

To construct a corporate scenario, follow these steps:

1. Use industry scenarios to develop a set of assumptions about the task environment (in the specific country under consideration). For example, 3M requires the general manager of each business unit to describe annually what his or her industry will look like in 15 years. List *optimistic, pessimistic*, and *most likely* assumptions for key economic factors such as the GDP (Gross Domestic Product), CPI (Consumer Price Index), and prime interest rate and for other key external strategic factors such as governmental regulation and industry trends. This should be done for every country/region in which the corporation has significant operations that will be affected by each strategic alternative. These same underlying assumptions should be listed for each of the alternative scenarios to be developed.

2. Develop common-size financial statements for the company's or business unit's previous years, to serve as the basis for the trend analysis projections of pro forma financial statements. Use the *Scenario Box* form shown in **Table 8–2**:

    a. Use the historical common-size percentages to estimate the level of revenues, expenses, and other categories in estimated pro forma statements for future years.

    b. Develop for each strategic alternative a set of *Optimistic(O)*, *Pessimistic(P)*, and *Most Likely(ML)* assumptions about the impact of key variables on the company's future financial statements.

    c. Forecast three sets of sales and cost of goods sold figures for at least five years into the future.

   d. Analyze historical data and make adjustments based on the environmental assumptions listed earlier. Do the same for other figures that can vary significantly.
   e. Assume for other figures that they will continue in their historical relationship to sales or some other key determining factor. Plug in expected inventory levels, accounts receivable, accounts payable, R&D expenses, advertising and promotion expenses, capital expenditures, and debt payments (assuming that debt is used to finance the strategy), among others.
   f. Consider not only historical trends but also programs that might be needed to implement each alternative strategy (such as building a new manufacturing facility or expanding the sales force).

3. Construct detailed pro forma financial statements for each strategic alternative:
   a. List the actual figures from this year's financial statements in the left column of the spreadsheet.
   b. List to the right of this column the optimistic figures for years 1 through 5.
   c. Go through this same process with the same strategic alternative, but now list the pessimistic figures for the next five years.
   d. Do the same with the most likely figures.
   e. Develop a similar set of *optimistic* (O), *pessimistic* (P), and *most likely* (ML) pro forma statements for the second strategic alternative. This process generates six different pro forma scenarios reflecting three different situations (O, P, and ML) for two strategic alternatives.
   f. Calculate financial ratios and common-size income statements, and create balance sheets to accompany the pro forma statements.

TABLE 8–2 Scenario Box for Use in Generating Financial Pro Forma Statements

Factor	Last Year	Historical Average	Trend Analysis	200–			200–			200–			Comments
				O	P	ML	O	P	ML	O	P	ML	
GDP													
CPI													
Other													
Sales units													
Dollars													
COGS													
Advertising and marketing													
Interest expense													
Plant expansion													
Dividends													
Net profits													
EPS													
ROI													
ROE													
Other													

NOTE 1: **O** = Optimistic; **P** = Pessimistic; **ML** = Most Likely.

SOURCE: T. L. Wheelen and J. D. Hunger. Copyright © 1987, 1988, 1989, 1990, 1992, 2005, and 2009 by T. L. Wheelen. Copyright © 1993 and 2005 by Wheelen and Hunger Associates. Reprinted with permission.

g. Compare the assumptions underlying the scenarios with the financial statements and ratios to determine the feasibility of the scenarios. For example, if cost of goods sold drops from 70% to 50% of total sales revenue in the pro forma income statements, this drop should result from a change in the production process or a shift to cheaper raw materials or labor costs rather than from a failure to keep the cost of goods sold in its usual percentage relationship to sales revenue when the predicted statement was developed.

The result of this detailed scenario construction should be anticipated net profits, cash flow, and net working capital for each of three versions of the two alternatives for five years into the future. A strategist might want to go further into the future if the strategy is expected to have a major impact on the company's financial statements beyond five years. The result of this work should provide sufficient information on which forecasts of the likely feasibility and probable profitability of each of the strategic alternatives could be based.

Obviously, these scenarios can quickly become very complicated, especially if three sets of acquisition prices and development costs are calculated. Nevertheless, this sort of detailed what-if analysis is needed to realistically compare the projected outcome of each reasonable alternative strategy and its attendant programs, budgets, and procedures. Regardless of the quantifiable pros and cons of each alternative, the actual decision will probably be influenced by several subjective factors such as those described in the following sections.

Management's Attitude Toward Risk

The attractiveness of a particular strategic alternative is partially a function of the amount of risk it entails. **Risk** is composed not only of the *probability* that the strategy will be effective but also of the *amount of assets* the corporation must allocate to that strategy and the *length of time* the assets will be unavailable for other uses. Because of variation among countries in terms of customs, regulations, and resources, companies operating in global industries must deal with a greater amount of risk than firms operating only in one country.[83] The greater the assets involved and the longer they are committed, the more likely top management is to demand a high probability of success. Managers with no ownership position in a company are unlikely to have much interest in putting their jobs in danger with risky decisions. Research indicates that managers who own a significant amount of stock in their firms are more likely to engage in risk-taking actions than are managers with no stock.[84]

A high level of risk was why Intel's board of directors found it difficult to vote for a proposal in the early 1990s to commit $5 billion to making the Pentium microprocessor chip—five times the amount of money needed for its previous chip. In looking back on that board meeting, then-CEO Andy Grove remarked, "I remember people's eyes looking at that chart and getting big. I wasn't even sure I believed those numbers at the time." The proposal committed the company to building new factories—something Intel had been reluctant to do. A wrong decision would mean that the company would end up with a killing amount of overcapacity. Based on Grove's presentation, the board decided to take the gamble. Intel's resulting manufacturing expansion eventually cost $10 billion but resulted in Intel's obtaining 75% of the microprocessor business and huge cash profits.[85]

Risk might be one reason that significant innovations occur more often in small firms than in large, established corporations. A small firm managed by an entrepreneur is often willing to accept greater risk than is a large firm of diversified ownership run by professional managers.[86] It is one thing to take a chance if you are the primary shareholder and are not concerned with periodic changes in the value of the company's common stock. It is something else if the corporation's stock is widely held and acquisition-hungry competitors or takeover artists surround the company like sharks every time the company's stock price falls below some external assessment of the firm's value.

A new approach to evaluating alternatives under conditions of high environmental uncertainty is to use real-options theory. According to the **real-options** approach, when the future is highly uncertain, it pays to have a broad range of options open. This is in contrast to using *net present value (NPV)* to calculate the value of a project by predicting its payouts, adjusting them for risk, and subtracting the amount invested. By boiling everything down to one scenario, NPV doesn't provide any flexibility in case circumstances change. NPV is also difficult to apply to projects in which the potential payoffs are currently unknown. The real-options approach, however, deals with these issues by breaking the investment into stages. Management allocates a small amount of funding to initiate multiple projects, monitors their development, and then cancels the projects that aren't successful and funds those that are doing well.[87] This approach is very similar to the way venture capitalists fund an entrepreneurial venture in stages of funding based on the venture's performance.

A survey of 4,000 CFOs found that 27% of them always or almost always used some sort of options approach to evaluating and deciding upon growth opportunities.[88] Research indicates that the use of the real-options approach does improve organizational performance.[89] Some of the corporations using the real-options approach are Chevron for bidding on petroleum reserves, Airbus for calculating the costs of airlines changing their orders at the last minute, and the Tennessee Valley Authority for outsourcing electricity generation instead of building its own plant. Because of its complexity, the real-options approach is not worthwhile for minor decisions or for projects requiring a full commitment at the beginning.[90]

Pressures from Stakeholders

The attractiveness of a strategic alternative is affected by its perceived compatibility with the key stakeholders in a corporation's task environment. Creditors want to be paid on time. Unions exert pressure for comparable wage and employment security. Governments and interest groups demand social responsibility. Shareholders want dividends. All these pressures must be given some consideration in the selection of the best alternative.

Stakeholders can be categorized in terms of their (1) interest in the corporation's activities and (2) relative power to influence the corporation's activities. As shown in **Figure 8–2**, each stakeholder group can be shown graphically based on its *level of interest* (from low to high) in

FIGURE 8–2
**Stakeholder
Priority Matrix**

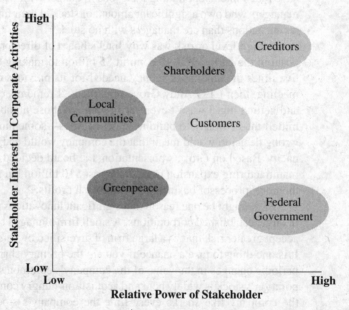

SOURCE: Based on C. Anderson, "Values-Based Management," *Academy of Management Executive* (November 1997), pp. 25–46.

a corporation's activities and on its *relative power* (from low to high) to influence a corporation's activities.

Strategic managers should ask four questions to assess the importance of stakeholder concerns in a particular decision:

1. How will this decision affect each stakeholder, especially those given high and medium priority?

2. How much of what each stakeholder wants is he or she likely to get under this alternative?

3. What are the stakeholders likely to do if they don't get what they want?

4. What is the probability that they will do it?

Strategy makers should choose strategic alternatives that minimize external pressures and maximize the probability of gaining stakeholder support. Managers may, however, ignore or take some stakeholders for granted—leading to serious problems later. The Tata Group, for example, failed to consider the unwillingness of farmers in Singur, India, to accept the West Bengal government's compensation for expropriating their land so that Tata could build its Nano auto plant. Farmers formed rallies against the plant, blocked roads, and even assaulted an employee of a Tata supplier.[92]

Top management can also propose a political strategy to influence its key stakeholders. A **political strategy** is a plan to bring stakeholders into agreement with a corporation's actions. Some of the most commonly used political strategies are constituency building, political action committee contributions, advocacy advertising, lobbying, and coalition building. Research reveals that large firms, those operating in concentrated industries, and firms that are highly dependent upon government regulation are more politically active.[93] Political support can be critical in entering a new international market, especially in transition economies where free market competition did not previously exist.[94]

Pressures from the Corporate Culture

If a strategy is incompatible with a company's corporate culture, the likelihood of its success is very low. Foot-dragging and even sabotage will result as employees fight to resist a radical change in corporate philosophy. Precedents from the past tend to restrict the kinds of objectives and strategies that are seriously considered.[95] The "aura" of the founders of a corporation can linger long past their lifetimes because their values are imprinted on a corporation's members.

In evaluating a strategic alternative, strategy makers must consider pressures from the corporate culture and assess a strategy's compatibility with that culture. If there is little fit, management must decide if it should:

■ Take a chance on ignoring the culture

■ Manage around the culture and change the implementation plan

■ Try to change the culture to fit the strategy

■ Change the strategy to fit the culture

Further, a decision to proceed with a particular strategy without a commitment to change the culture or manage around the culture (both very tricky and time consuming) is dangerous. Nevertheless, restricting a corporation to only those strategies that are completely compatible with its culture might eliminate from consideration the most profitable alternatives. (See **Chapter 10** for more information on managing corporate culture.)

Needs and Desires of Key Managers

Even the most attractive alternative might not be selected if it is contrary to the needs and desires of important top managers. Personal characteristics and experience affect a person's assessment of an alternative's attractiveness.[96] For example, one study found that narcissistic (self-absorbed and arrogant) CEOs favor bold actions that attract attention, like many large acquisitions—resulting in either big wins or big losses.[97] A person's ego may be tied to a particular proposal to the extent that all other alternatives are strongly lobbied against. As a result, the person may have unfavorable forecasts altered so that they are more in agreement with the desired alternative.[98] In a study by McKinsey & Company of 2,507 executives from around the world, 36% responded that managers hide, restrict, or misrepresent information at least "somewhat" frequently when submitting capital-investment proposals. In addition, an executive might influence other people in top management to favor a particular alternative so that objections to it are overruled. In the same McKinsey study of global executives, more than 60% of the managers reported that business unit and divisional heads form alliances with peers or lobby someone more senior in the organization at least "somewhat" frequently when resource allocation decisions are being made.[99]

Industry and cultural backgrounds affect strategic choice. For example, executives with strong ties within an industry tend to choose strategies commonly used in that industry. Other executives who have come to the firm from another industry and have strong ties outside the industry tend to choose different strategies from what is being currently used in their industry.[100] Country of origin often affects preferences. For example, Japanese managers prefer a cost-leadership strategy more than do United States managers.[101] Research reveals that executives from Korea, the U.S., Japan, and Germany tend to make different strategic choices in similar situations because they use different decision criteria and weights. For example, Korean executives emphasize industry attractiveness, sales, and market share in their decisions; whereas, U.S. executives emphasize projected demand, discounted cash flow, and ROI.[102]

There is a tendency to maintain the status quo, which means that decision makers continue with existing goals and plans beyond the point when an objective observer would recommend a change in course.[103] Some executives show a self-serving tendency to attribute the firm's problems not to their own poor decisions but to environmental events out of their control, such as government policies or a poor economic climate.[104] For example, a CEO is more likely to divest a poorly performing unit when its poor performance does not incriminate that same CEO who had acquired it.[105] Negative information about a particular course of action to which a person is committed may be ignored because of a desire to appear competent or because of strongly held values regarding consistency. It may take a crisis or an unlikely event to cause strategic decision makers to seriously consider an alternative they had previously ignored or discounted.[106] For example, it wasn't until the CEO of ConAgra, a multinational food products company, had a heart attack that ConAgra started producing the Healthy Choice line of low-fat, low-cholesterol, low-sodium frozen-food entrees.

PROCESS OF STRATEGIC CHOICE

There is an old story told at General Motors:

> At a meeting with his key executives, CEO Alfred Sloan proposed a controversial strategic decision. When asked for comments, each executive responded with supportive comments and praise. After announcing that they were all in apparent agreement, Sloan stated that they were not going to proceed with the decision. Either his executives didn't know enough to point out potential downsides of the decision, or they were agreeing to avoid upsetting the boss and disrupting the cohesion of the group. The decision was delayed until a debate could occur over the pros and cons.[107]

Strategic choice is the evaluation of alternative strategies and selection of the best alternative. According to Paul Nutt, an authority in decision making, half of the decisions made by managers are failures.[108] After analyzing 400 decisions, Nutt found that failure almost always stems from the actions of the decision maker, not from bad luck or situational limitations. In these instances, managers commit one or more key blunders: (1) their desire for speedy actions leads to a rush to judgment, (2) they apply failure-prone decision-making practices such as adopting the claim of an influential stakeholder, and (3) they make poor use of resources by investigating only one or two options. These three blunders cause executives to limit their search for feasible alternatives and look for quick consensus. Only 4% of the 400 managers set an objective and considered several alternatives. The search for innovative options was attempted in only 24% of the decisions studied.[109] Another study of 68 divestiture decisions found a strong tendency for managers to rely heavily on past experience when developing strategic alternatives.[110]

There is mounting evidence that when an organization is facing a dynamic environment, the best strategic decisions are not arrived at through **consensus** when everyone agrees on one alternative. They actually involve a certain amount of heated disagreement, and even conflict.[111] Many diverse opinions are presented, participants trust in one another's abilities and competences, and conflict is task-oriented, not personal.[112] This is certainly the case for firms operating in global industries. Because unmanaged conflict often carries a high emotional cost, authorities in decision making propose that strategic managers use "programmed conflict" to raise different opinions, regardless of the personal feelings of the people involved.[113] Two techniques help strategic managers avoid the consensus trap that Alfred Sloan found:

1. **Devil's advocate:** The idea of the **devil's advocate** originated in the medieval Roman Catholic Church as a way of ensuring that impostors were not canonized as saints. One trusted person was selected to find and present all the reasons why a person should not be canonized. When this process is applied to strategic decision making, a devil's advocate (who may be an individual or a group) is assigned to identify potential pitfalls and problems with a proposed alternative strategy in a formal presentation.

2. **Dialectical inquiry:** The dialectical philosophy, which can be traced back to Plato and Aristotle and more recently to Hegel, involves combining two conflicting views—the thesis and the antithesis—into a synthesis. When applied to strategic decision making, **dialectical inquiry** requires that two proposals using different assumptions be generated for each alternative strategy under consideration. After advocates of each position present and debate the merits of their arguments before key decision makers, either one of the alternatives or a new compromise alternative is selected as the strategy to be implemented.

Research generally supports the conclusion that the devil's advocate and dialectical inquiry methods are equally superior to consensus in decision making, especially when the firm's environment is dynamic. The debate itself, rather than its particular format, appears to improve the quality of decisions by formalizing and legitimizing constructive conflict and by encouraging critical evaluation. Both lead to better assumptions and recommendations and to a higher level of critical thinking among the people involved.[114]

Regardless of the process used to generate strategic alternatives, each resulting alternative must be rigorously evaluated in terms of its ability to meet four criteria:

1. **Mutual Exclusivity:** Doing any one alternative would preclude doing any other.

2. **Success:** It must be feasible and have a good probability of success.

3. **Completeness:** It must take into account all the key strategic issues.

4. **Internal Consistency:** It must make sense on its own as a strategic decision for the entire firm and not contradict key goals, policies, and strategies currently being pursued by the firm or its units.[115]

8.5 Developing Policies

The selection of the best strategic alternative is not the end of strategy formulation. The organization must then engage in developing policies. Policies define the broad guidelines for implementation. Flowing from the selected strategy, policies provide guidance for decision making and actions throughout the organization. They are the principles under which the corporation operates on a day-to-day basis. At General Electric, for example, Chairman Jack Welch initiated the policy that any GE business unit must be Number One or Number Two in whatever market it competes. This policy gave clear guidance to managers throughout the organization. Another example of such a policy is Casey's General Stores' policy that a new service or product line may be added to its stores only when the product or service can be justified in terms of increasing store traffic.

When crafted correctly, an effective policy accomplishes three things:

- It forces trade-offs between competing resource demands.
- It tests the strategic soundness of a particular action.
- It sets clear boundaries within which employees must operate while granting them freedom to experiment within those constraints.[116]

Policies tend to be rather long lived and can even outlast the particular strategy that created them. These general policies—such as "The customer is always right" (Nordstrom) or "Low prices, every day" (Wal-Mart)—can become, in time, part of a corporation's culture. Such policies can make the implementation of specific strategies easier. They can also restrict top management's strategic options in the future. Thus a change in strategy should be followed quickly by a change in policies. Managing policy is one way to manage the corporate culture.

ECO-BITS

- In the two-day period after joining the U.S. Environmental Protection Agency's voluntary Climate Leader's initiative, which requires members to reduce or offset emissions over the next 5 to 10 years, the average company's stock price dropped 0.9% more than it would have from normal market factors.[117]

- General Motors states that its facilities recycle 89% of the waste they generate and that GM is one of the world's largest industrial users of solar power.[118]

DISCUSSION QUESTIONS

1. Are functional strategies interdependent, or can they be formulated independently of other functions?

2. Why is penetration pricing more likely than skim pricing to raise a company's or a business unit's operating profit in the long run?

3. How does mass customization support a business unit's competitive strategy?

4. When should a corporation or business unit outsource a function or an activity?

5. What is the relationship of policies to strategies?

6. What is functional strategy? Discuss the different types of functional strategies.

7. What is value chain analysis? Discuss its importance for business and functional-level strategies and explain how it is different.

8. Discuss in detail three examples from Indian industry that have used logistics strategy to gain competitive advantage.

STRATEGIC PRACTICE EXERCISE

Pierre Omidyar founded a sole proprietorship in September 1995 called Auction Web to allow people to buy and sell goods over the Internet. The new venture was based on the idea of developing a community-driven process, where an organic, evolving, self-organizing web of individual relationships, formed around shared interests, would handle tasks that other companies handle with customer service operations. By May 1996, Omidyar had added Jeff Skoll as a partner and the venture was incorporated as eBay. Two years later, Omidyar asked Meg Whitman to direct corporate strategy to continue the accelerated growth rate of the company. Whitman brought to the company global management and marketing experience and soon became President and CEO. In almost no time, the company became one of the Web's most successful sites, with 233 million registered users. By 2007, the average eBay user spent nearly two hours a month on the site—more than five times the time spent on Amazon.com.[119]

Whitman expanded the company's operations and spent more than $6 billion to acquire companies, such as Internet-phone operation Skype, online payments service PayPal, ticket reseller StubHub, property rental and roommate search firm Rent.com, comparison shopping site Shopping.com, Web site recommender Stumbleupon, and 25% interest in Craigslist. Expansion and diversification provided revenue and profit growth plus stock price appreciation. Although financial analysts wondered how all these businesses would fit together, Whitman argued that she wanted eBay to be everywhere users wanted to be. At developer conferences, company representatives unveiled new services that let buyers shop for and purchase eBay items outside of the core eBay.com site.

By 2008, eBay was in trouble. Its stock price had lost half its value over the past three years. The core auction and retail businesses, which accounted for the majority of revenue, were showing signs of weakness. The number of active users had been flat for three quarters, at 83 million. The number of new products listed on the site had increased only 4% from the previous year. The number of stores selling goods at fixed prices on eBay declined from a year earlier to 532,000. The company had not done a good job of integrating Skype with its main business. Since its acquisition, Skype's service had actually deteriorated.[120] Competition had increased as rival Web sites, particularly Amazon, now provided similar Web services and eroded eBay's competitive advantage.

On January 23, 2008, CEO Whitman announced that John Donahoe would take over as the company's CEO. Donahoe stated that his first priority would be to revitalize eBay's core business, even at the expense of investors. "We need to aggressively change our product, our customer approach, and our business model," announced the new CEO.[121]

1. What is eBay's problem?

2. Which marketing strategy was eBay following: market development or product development? Do you agree with it?

3. What decision-making process should CEO Donahoe utilize to make the decisions necessary to change the company's product, customer approach, and business model?

KEY TERMS

consensus (p. 297)

corporate scenarios (p. 291)

devil's advocate (p. 297)

dialectical inquiry (p. 277)

financial strategy (p. 277)

functional strategy (p. 275)

HRM strategy (p. 286)

information technology strategy (p. 287)

leveraged buyout (p. 277)

logistics strategy (p. 285)

market development (p. 275)

marketing strategy (p. 275)

offshoring (p. 288)

operations strategy (p. 281)

outsourcing (p. 287)

political strategy (p. 295)

product development (p. 276)

purchasing strategy (p. 284)

R&D strategy (p. 278)

real-options (p. 294)

risk (p. 293)

Stakeholder Priority Matrix (p. 294)

strategic choice (p. 296)

technological follower (p. 278)

technological leader (p. 278)

Let's Summarize the Chapter with a Mind Map

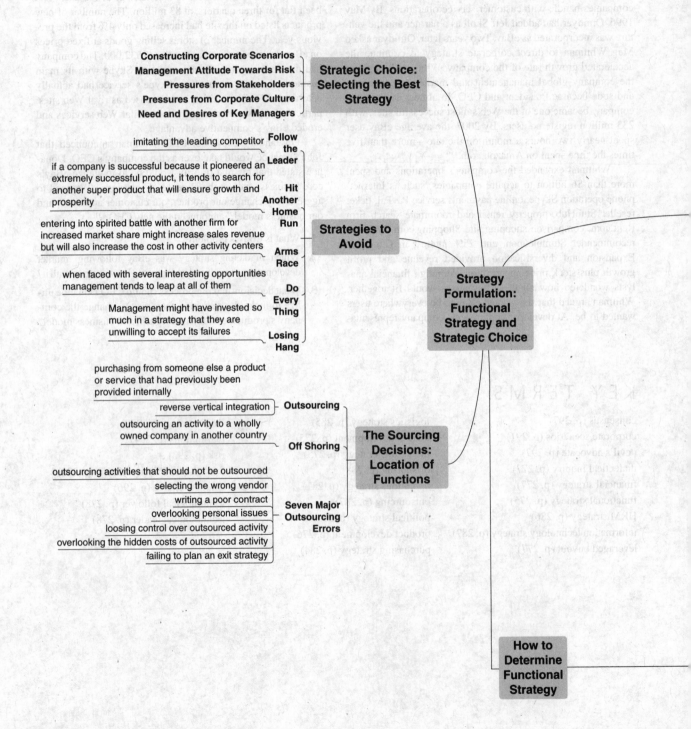

Constructing Corporate Scenarios
Management Attitude Towards Risk
Pressures from Stakeholders
Pressures from Corporate Culture
Need and Desires of Key Managers

Strategic Choice: Selecting the Best Strategy

imitating the leading competitor — **Follow the Leader**

if a company is successful because it pioneered an extremely successful product, it tends to search for another super product that will ensure growth and prosperity — **Hit Another Home Run**

entering into spirited battle with another firm for increased market share might increase sales revenue but will also increase the cost in other activity centers — **Arms Race**

when faced with several interesting opportunities management tends to leap at all of them — **Do Every Thing**

Management might have invested so much in a strategy that they are unwilling to accept its failures — **Losing Hang**

Strategies to Avoid

Strategy Formulation: Functional Strategy and Strategic Choice

purchasing from someone else a product or service that had previously been provided internally

reverse vertical integration — **Outsourcing**

outsourcing an activity to a wholly owned company in another country — **Off Shoring**

The Sourcing Decisions: Location of Functions

outsourcing activities that should not be outsourced
selecting the wrong vendor
writing a poor contract
overlooking personal issues — **Seven Major Outsourcing Errors**
loosing control over outsourced activity
overlooking the hidden costs of outsourced activity
failing to plan an exit strategy

How to Determine Functional Strategy

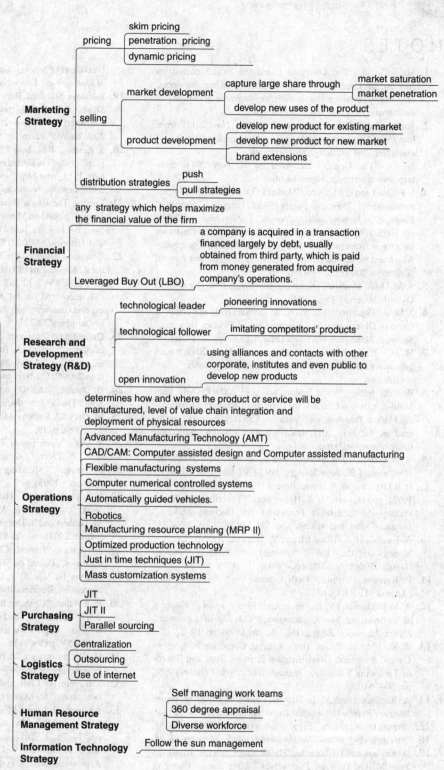

Functional Strategy: is the approach a fuctional area takes to achieve corporate and business unit objectives.

Marketing Strategy

pricing
- skim pricing
- penetration pricing
- dynamic pricing

selling
- market development
  - capture large share through
    - market saturation
    - market penetration
  - develop new uses of the product
- product development
  - develop new product for existing market
  - develop new product for new market
  - brand extensions

distribution strategies
- push
- pull strategies

Financial Strategy

any strategy which helps maximize the financial value of the firm

Leveraged Buy Out (LBO) — a company is acquired in a transaction financed largely by debt, usually obtained from third party, which is paid from money generated from acquired company's operations.

Research and Development Strategy (R&D)

- technological leader — pioneering innovations
- technological follower — imitating competitors' products
- open innovation — using alliances and contacts with other corporate, institutes and even public to develop new products

Operations Strategy

determines how and where the product or service will be manufactured, level of value chain integration and deployment of physical resources

- Advanced Manufacturing Technology (AMT)
- CAD/CAM: Computer assisted design and Computer assisted manufacturing
- Flexible manufacturing systems
- Computer numerical controlled systems
- Automatically guided vehicles.
- Robotics
- Manufacturing resource planning (MRP II)
- Optimized production technology
- Just in time techniques (JIT)
- Mass customization systems

Purchasing Strategy
- JIT
- JIT II
- Parallel sourcing

Logistics Strategy
- Centralization
- Outsourcing
- Use of internet

Human Resource Management Strategy
- Self managing work teams
- 360 degree appraisal
- Diverse workforce

Information Technology Strategy
- Follow the sun management

Identify the Company's Core Competence

Ensure that the Competencies are Continually Being Strengthened

Manage the Competencies in Such a Way That They Best Preserve the Competitive Advantage They Create

NOTES

1. MapsofIndia, "Top Detergent Brands in India," posted on June 20, 2011, recovered on 1st Nov 2011, from http://business.mapsofindia.com/top-brands-india/top-detergent-brands-in-india.html

2. Superbrands, "Nirma," recovered on 1st Nov 2011, from http://www.superbrandsindia.com/images/brand_pdf/consumer_2nd_edition_2007/Nirma.pdf

3. Nirma, "The Gensis," recovered on 1st Nov 2011, from http://www.nirma.co.in/genesis.htm

4. S. F. Slater and E. M. Olson, "Market's Contribution to the Implementation of Business Strategy: An Empirical Analysis," *Strategic Management Journal* (November 2001), pp. 1055–1067; B. C. Skaggs and T. R. Huffman, "A Customer Interaction Approach to Strategy and Production Complexity Alignment in Service Firms," *Academy of Management Journal* (December 2003), pp. 775–786.

5. S. M. Oster, *Modern Competitive Analysis*, 2nd ed. (New York: Oxford University Press, 1994), p. 93.

6. J. M. de Figueiredo and M. K. Kyle, "Surviving the Gales of Creative Destruction: The Determinants of Product Turnover," *Strategic Management Journal* (March 2006), pp. 241–264.

7. HDFC Bank Ltd., recovered on 1st Nov 2011, from http://www.hdfcbank.com/aboutus/awards/Asian_Banker_Awards.htm

8. Banknet India, "World Insurance Report 2009 Reveals Vital Multi-distribution Channels for Capturing Growth in a Challenging Market: Transformation Strategies Can Help Insurers, recovered on 1st Nov 2011, from http://www.banknetindia.com/finance/insreport09.htm.

9. W. Redmond, "The Strategic Pricing of Innovative Products," *Handbook of Business Strategy, 1992/1993 Yearbook*, edited by H. E. Glass and M. A. Hovde (Boston: Warren, Gorham & Lamont, 1992), pp. 16.1–16.13; A. Hinterhuber, "Towards Value-Based Pricing—An Integrative Framework for Decision Making," *Industrial Marketing Management*, Vol. 33 (2004), pp. 765–778.

10. A. Kambil, H. J. Wilson III, and V. Agrawal, "Are You Leaving Money on the Table?" *Journal of Business Strategy* (January/February 2002), pp. 40–43.

11. P. Burrows, "Apple's Cash Conundrum," *Business Week* (August 11, 2008), p. 32.

12. A. Safieddine and S. Titman in April 1999 *Journal of Finance*, as summarized by D. Champion, "The Joy of Leverage," *Harvard Business Review* (July–August 1999), pp. 19–22.

13. R. Kochhar and M. A. Hitt, "Linking Corporate Strategy to Capital Structure: Diversification Strategy, Type and Source of Financing," *Strategic Management Journal* (June 1998), pp. 601–610.

14. A. Rappaport and M. L. Sirower, "Stock or Cash?" *Harvard Business Review* (November–December 1999), pp. 147–158.

15. "Private Investigations," *The Economist* (July 5, 2008), pp. 84–85.

16. "Private Investigations," *The Economist* (July 5, 2008), pp. 84–85.

17. D. Angwin and I. Contardo, "Unleashing Cerberus: Don't Let Your MBOs Turn on Themselves," *Long Range Planning* (October 1999), pp. 494–504.

18. For information on different types of LBOs, see M. Wright, R. E. Hoskisson, and L. W. Busenitz, "Firm Rebirth: Buyouts as Facilitators of Strategic Growth and Entrepreneurship," *Academy of Management Executive* (February 2001), pp. 111–125.

19. Business Standard Reporter in Mumbai, "REL to Buyback Shares at Rs 1,600," posted on March 06, 2008 11:33 IST, recovered on 1st Nov 2011, from http://in.rediff.com/money/2008/mar/06rel.htm

20. S. Keshav, "REL Board Sanctions Rs 2,000 Cr Share Buyback Plan," posted on Thursday, 03/06/2008 - 04:35, recovered on 1st Nov 2011 from http://www.topnews.in/rel-board-sanctions-rs-2-000-cr-share-buyback-plan-224254.

21. Bureau, The Hindu Business Line, "HUL Closes Buyback of Shares," posted on Mumbai, January 31, 2008, recovered on 1st Nov 2011, from http://www.thehindubusinessline.com/2008/02/01/stories/2008020152221700.htm

22. Corporate Bureau, The Financial Express, "HUL Share Buyback May Be Part of Unilever Global Plans," posted: 2007-07-22 00:00:00+05:30 IST Updated: July 22, 2007 at 0215 hrs IST, recovered on 1st Nov 2011, from http://www.financialexpress.com/news/hul-share-buyback-may-be-part-of-unilever-global-plans/206227/

23. OnlineEquityCalls.com, "DLF Buyback Just Rs 86 Crore Worth of Shares," posted on Tuesday, January 20, 2009 at 8:42 AM, recovered on 1st Nov 2011, from http://www.onlineequitycalls.com/2009/01/dlf-buys-back-just-rs-86-crore-worth-of-shares/

24. B. Deener, "Back Up and Look at Reasons for Reverse Stock Split," *The (St. Petersburg, FL) Times* (December 29, 2002), p. 3H.

25. M. Orey, "A Sotheby's for Investors," *Business Week* (February 13, 2006), p. 39.

26. T. Due, "Dean Foods Thrives on Regional Off-Brand Products," *Wall Street Journal* (September 17, 1987), p. A6.

27. S. Stevens, "Speeding the Signals of Change," *Appliance* (February 1995), p. 7.

28. L-E. Gadde and H. Hakansson, "Teaching in Supplier Networks," in *Strategic Networks: Learning to Compete*, by M. Gibbert and T. Durand, eds. (Malden, MA: Blackwell Publishing, 2007), pp. 40–57.

29. J. Parveen, "Biotech Companies Keen on Setting Up R&D Factories," Posted on Wednesday, November 05, 2008, recovered on 1st Nov 2011, from http://biospectrumindia.ciol.com/content/BioBusiness/10811051.asp

30. R. Cynthia, "Creating Intellectual Assets," posted on January 2007, recovered on 1st Nov 2011, from Tata Sons Ltd website http://www.tata.com/innovation/articles/inside.aspx?artid=c5V1pxVwRaI=

31. H. W. Chesbrough, "A Better Way to Innovate," *Harvard Business Review* (July 2003), pp. 12–13.

32. J. Bughin, M. Chui, and B. Johnson, "The Next Step in Open Innovation," *McKinsey Quarterly* (June 2008), pp. 1–8.

33. J. Greene, J. Carey, M. Arndt, and O. Port, "Reinventing Corporate R&D," *Business Week* (September 22, 2003), pp. 74–76; J. Birkinshaw, S. Crainer, and M. Mol, "From R&D to Connect + Develop at P&G," *Business Strategy Review* (Spring 2007), pp. 66–69; L. Huston and N. Sakkab, "Connect and Develop: Inside Proctor & Gamble's New Model for Innovation," *Harvard Business Review* (March 2006), pp. 58–66.

34. G. Dushnitsky and M. J. Lenox, "When Do Firms Undertake R&D by Investing in New Ventures?" Paper presented to annual meeting of the *Academy of Management*, Seattle, WA (August 2003).

35. J. R. Williams and R. S. Novak, "Aligning CIM Strategies to Different Markets," *Long Range Planning* (February 1990), pp. 126–135.

36. J. Wheatley, "Super Factory—or Super Headache," *Business Week* (July 31, 2000), p. 66.

37. M. Tayles and C. Drury, "Moving from Make/Buy to Strategic Sourcing: The Outsource Decision Process," *Long Range Planning* (October 2001), pp. 605–622.

38. F. R. Bleakley, "Some Companies Let Supplies Work on Site and Even Place Orders," *Wall Street Journal* (January 13, 1995), pp. A1, A6.

39. M. Hoegl and S. M. Wagner, "Buyer-Supplier Collaboration in Product Development Projects," *Journal of Management* (August 2005), pp. 530–548; B. McEvily and A. Marcus, "Embedded Ties and the Acquisition of Competitive Capabilities," *Strategic Management Journal* (November 2005), pp. 1033–1055; R. Gulati and M. Sytch, "Dependence Asymmetry and Joint Dependence in Interorganizational Relationships: Effects of Embeddedness on a Manufacturer's Performance in Procurement Relationships," *Administrative Science Quarterly* (March 2007), pp. 32–69.

40. J. Richardson, "Parallel Sourcing and Supplier Performance in the Japanese Automobile Industry," *Strategic Management Journal* (July 1993), pp. 339–350.

41. S. Roberts-Witt, "Procurement: The HP Way," *PC Magazine* (November 21, 2000), pp. 21–22.

42. D. H. Pearcy, D. B. Parker, and L. C. Giunipero, "Using Electronic Procurement to Facilitate Supply Chain Integration: An Exploratory Study of U.S.-based Firms," *American Journal of Business* (Spring 2008), pp. 23–35.

43. T. E. Raja Simhan, "Logistics Providers Must Innovate to Retain Their Edge," recovered on 20th May 2009, from http://www.thehindubusinessline.com/bline/2007/10/01/stoies/20071001506 90600.htm

44. Equity Master, "Indian Logistics Sector: An Overview," posted May 13, 2009, recovered on 20th May 2009, from http://www.equitymaster.com/detail.asp?date=5/13/2009&story=3

45. F. Keenan, "Logistics Gets a Little Respect," *Business Week* (November 20, 2000), pp. 112–116.

46. B. L. Kirkman and Debra L. Shapiro, "The Impact of Cultural Values on Employee Resistance to Teams: Toward a Model of Globalized Self-Managing Work Team Effectiveness," *Academy of Management Review* (July 1997), pp. 730–757.

47. R. D. Banker, J. M. Field, R. G. Schroeder, and K. K. Sinha, "Impact of Work Teams on Manufacturing Performance: A Longitudinal Field Study," *Academy of Management Journal* (August 1996), pp. 867–890; B. L. Kirkman and B. Rosen, "Beyond Self-Management: Antecedents and Consequences of Team Empowerment," *Academy of Management Journal* (February 1999), pp. 58–74.

48. V. Y. Haines III, S. St. Onge, and A. Marcoux, "Performance Management Design and Effectiveness in Quality-Driven Organizations," *Canadian Journal of Administrative Sciences* (June 2004), pp. 146–160.

49. A. S. DeNisi and A. N. Kluger, "Feedback Effectiveness: Can 360-Degree Appraisals Be Improved?" *Academy of Management Executive* (February 2000), pp. 129–139; G. Toegel and J. A. Conger, "360-Degree Assessment: Time for Reinvention," *Academy of Management Learning and Education* (September 2003), pp. 297–311; F. Shipper, R. C. Hoffman, and D. M. Rotondo, "Does the 360 Feedback Process Create Actionable Knowledge Equally Across Cultures?" *Academy of Management Learning & Education* (March 2007), pp. 33–50.

50. J. McGregor, "The Employee Is Always Right," *Business Week* (November 19, 2007), pp. 80–82.

51. O. C. Richard, "Racial Diversity, Business Strategy, and Firm Performance: A Resource-Based View," *Academy of Management Journal* (April 2000), pp. 164–177.

52. G. Robinson and K. Dechant, "Building a Business Case for Diversity," *Academy of Management Executive* (August 1997), pp. 21–31.

53. K. Labich, "Making Diversity Pay," *Fortune* (September 9, 1996), pp. 177–180.

54. N. G. Carr, "IT Doesn't Matter," *Harvard Business Review* (May 2003), pp. 41–50.

55. J. Greco, "Good Day Sunshine," *Journal of Business Strategy* (July/August 1998), pp. 4–5.

56. W. Howard, "Translate Now," *PC Magazine* (September 19, 2000), p. 81.

57. H. Green, "The Web Smart 50," *Business Week* (November 24, 2003), p. 84.

58. T. Smart, "Jack Welch's Cyber-Czar," *Business Week* (August 5, 1996), p. 83.

59. S. M. Kim and J. T. Mahoney, "Mutual Commitment to Support Exchange: Relation-Specific IT System as a Substitute for Managerial Hierarchy," *Strategic Management Journal* (May 2006), pp. 401–423.

60. B. Kelley, "Outsourcing Marches On," *Journal of Business Strategy* (July/August 1995), p. 40.

61. S. Holmes and M. Arndt, "A Plane that Could Change the Game," *Business Week* (August 9, 2004), p. 33.

62. J. Greco, "Outsourcing: The New Partnership," *Journal of Business Strategy* (July/August 1997), pp. 48–54.

63. W. M. Fitzpatrick and S. A. DiLullo, "Outsourcing and the Personnel Paradox," *SAM Advanced Management Journal* (Summer 2007), pp. 4–12.

64. Outsourcing: Time to Bring It Back Home?" *The Economist* (March 5, 2005), p. 63.

65. A. Y. Lewin and C. Peeters, "Offshoring Work: Business Hype or the Onset of Fundamental Transformation?" *Long Range Planning* (June 2006), pp. 221–239; A. Y. Lewing and C. Peeters, "The Top-Line Allure of Offshoring," *Harvard Business Review* (March 2006), pp. 22–24.

66. G. Smith, "Factories Go South; So Does Pay," *Business Week* (April 9, 2007), p. 76.

67. "Out of Captivity," *Economist* (November 13, 2004), p. 68.

68. "IBM's Plan to Buy India Firm Points to Demand for Outsourcing," *Des Moines Register* (April 11, 2004), p. 2D.

69. A. Castro, "Complaints Push Dell to Use U.S. Call Centers," *Des Moines Register* (November 25, 2003), p. 1D.

70. J. A. Byrne, "Has Outsourcing Gone Too Far?" *Business Week* (April 1, 1996), pp. 26–28.

71. R. C. Insinga and M. J. Werle, "Linking Outsourcing to Business Strategy," *Academy of Management Executive* (November 2000), pp. 58–70; D. Lei and M. A. Hitt, "Strategic Restructuring and Outsourcing: The Effect of Mergers and Acquisitions and LBOs on Building Firm Skills and Capabilities," *Journal of Management*, Vol. 21, No. 5 (1995), pp. 835–859.

72. "Outsourcing: Time to Bring It Back Home*?*" *The Economist* (May 5, 2005), p. 63.

73. S. E. Ante, "Shifting Work Offshore? Outsourcer Beware," *Business Week* (January 12, 2004), pp. 36–37.

74. J. Carey, "Not Made in China," *Business Week* (July 30, 2007), pp. 41–43; "The Poison Spreads," *The Economist* (September 27, 2008), pp. 77–78; "Plenty of Blame to Go Around," *The Economist* (September 29, 2007), pp. 68–70; J. Schmit, "Heparin Plant in China Passed 'In-Depth' Review," *USA Today* (April 30, 2008), p. B1.

75. A. Goel, N. Moussavi, and V. N. Srivatsan, "Time to Rethink Offshoring?" *McKinsey Quarterly* (September 2008), pp. 1–5.

76. A. Takeishi, "Bridging Inter- and Intra-Firm Boundaries: Management of Supplier Involvement in Automobile Product Development," *Strategic Management Journal* (May 2001), pp. 403–433.

77. J. Barthelemy, "The Seven Deadly Sins of Outsourcing," *Academy of Management Executive* (May 2003), pp. 87–98.

78. M. J. Leiblein and D. J. Miller, "An Empirical Examination of Transaction and Firm-Level Influences on the Vertical Boundaries of the Firm," *Strategic Management Journal* (September 2003), pp. 839–859.

79. S. Hamm, "Is Outsourcing on the Outs?" *Business Week* (October 4, 2004), p. 42.

80. For further information on effective offshoring, see R. Aron and J. V. Singh, "Getting Offshoring Right," *Harvard Business Review* (December 2005), pp. 135–143.

81. R. Grover and D. Polek, "Millionaire Buys Disney Time," *Business Week* (June 26, 2000), pp. 141–144.

82. D. K. Sinha, "Strategic Planning in the Fortune 500," *Handbook of Business Strategy, 1991/1992 Yearbook*, edited by H. E. Glass and M. A. Hovde (Boston: Warren, Gorham & Lamont, 1991), pp. 9.6–9.8.

83. N. Checa, J. Maguire, and J. Berry, "The New World Disorder," *Harvard Business Review* (August 2003), pp. 70–79.

84. T. B. Palmer and R. M. Wiseman, "Decoupling Risk Taking from Income Stream Uncertainty: A Holistic Model of Risk," *Strategic Management Journal* (November 1999), pp. 1037–1062; W. G. Sanders and D. C. Hambrick, "Swinging for the Fences: The Effects of CEO Stock Options on Company Risk Taking and Performance," *Academy of Management Journal* (October 2007), pp. 1055–1078.

85. D. Clark, "All the Chips: A Big Bet Made Intel What It Is Today; Now It Wagers Again," *Wall Street Journal* (June 6, 1995), pp. A1, A5.

86. L. W. Busenitz and J. B. Barney, "Differences Between Entrepreneurs and Managers in Large Organizations: Biases and Heuristics in Strategic Decision-Making," *Journal of Business Venturing* (January 1997), pp. 9–30.

87. J. J. Janney and G. G. Dess, "Can Real-Options Analysis Improve Decision-Making? Promises and Pitfalls," *Academy of Management Executive* (November 2004), pp. 60–75; S. Maklan, S. Knox, and L. Ryals, "Using Real Options to Help Build the Business Case for CRM Investment," *Long Range Planning* (August 2005), pp. 393–410.

88. T. Copeland and P. Tufano, "A Real-World Way to Manage Real Options," *Harvard Business Review* (March 2004), pp. 90–99.

89. J. Rosenberger and K. Eisenhardt, "What Are Real Options: A Review of Empirical Research," Paper presented to annual meeting of the *Academy of Management*, Seattle, WA (August 2003).

90. P. Coy, "Exploiting Uncertainty," *Business Week* (June 7, 1999), pp. 118–124. For further information on real options, see M. Amram and N. Kulatilaka, *Real Options* (Boston, Harvard University Press, 1999). For a simpler summary, see R. M. Grant, *Contemporary Strategy Analysis*, 5th edition (Malden, MA: Blackwell Publishing, 2005), pp. 48–50.

91. C. Anderson, "Values-Based Management," *Academy of Management Executive* (November 1997), pp. 25–46.

92. "Nano Wars," *The Economist* (August 30, 2008), p. 63.

93. J-P. Bonardi, A. J. Hillman, and G. D. Keim, "The Attractiveness of Political Markets: Implications for Firm Strategy," *Academy of Management Review* (April 2005), pp. 397–413.

94. J. G. Frynas, K. Mellahi, and G. A. Pigman, "First Mover Advantages in International Business and Firm-Specific Political Resources," *Strategic Management Journal* (April 2006), pp. 321–345. For additional information about political strategies, see C. Oliver and I. Holzinger, "The Effectiveness of Strategic Political Management: A Dynamic Capabilities Framework," *Academy of Management Review* (April 2008), pp. 496–520.

95. H. M. O'Neill, R. W. Pouder, and A. K. Buchholtz, "Patterns in the Diffusion of Strategies Across Organizations: Insights from the Innovation Diffusion Literature," *Academy of Management Executive* (January 1998), pp. 98–114; C. G. Gilbert, "Unbundling the Structure of Inertia: Resource Versus Routine Rigidity," *Academy of Management Journal* (October 2005), pp. 741–763.

96. B. B. Tyler and H. K. Steensma. "Evaluating Technological Collaborative Opportunities: A Cognitive Modeling Perspective," *Strategic Management Journal* (Summer 1995), pp. 43–70; D. Duchan, D. P. Ashman, and M. Nathan, "Mavericks, Visionaries, Protestors, and Sages: Toward a Typology of Cognitive Structures for Decision Making in Organizations," *Journal of Business Strategies* (Fall 1997), pp. 106–125; P. Chattopadhyay, W. H. Glick, C. C. Miller, and G. P. Huber, "Determinants of Executive Beliefs: Comparing Functional Conditioning and Social Influence," *Strategic Management Journal* (August 1999), pp. 763–789; B. Katey and G. G. Meredith, "Relationship Among Owner/Manager Personal Values, Business Strategies, and Enterprise Performance," *Journal of Small Business Management* (April 1997), pp. 37–64.

97. A. Chatterjee and D. C. Hambrick, "It's All About Me: Narcissistic Executive Officers and Their Effects on Company Strategy and Performance," *Administrative Science Quarterly* (September 2007), pp. 351–386.

98. C. S. Galbraith and G. B. Merrill, "The Politics of Forecasting: Managing the Truth," *California Management Review* (Winter 1996), pp. 29–43.

99. M. Garbuio, D. Lovallo, and P. Viguerie, "How Companies Spend Their Money: A McKinsey Global Survey," *McKinsey Quarterly Online* (June 2007).

100. M. A. Geletkanycz and D. C. Hambrick, "The External Ties of Top Executives: Implications for Strategic Choice and Performance," *Administrative Science Quarterly* (December 1997), pp. 654–681.

101. M. Song, R. J. Calantone, and C. A. Di Benedetto, "Competitive Forces and Strategic Choice Decisions: An Experimental Investigation in the United States and Japan," *Strategic Management Journal* (October 2002), pp. 969–978.

102. M. A. Hitt, M. T. Dacin, B. B. Tyler, and D. Park, "Understanding the Differences in Korean and U.S. Executives' Strategic Orientation," *Strategic Management Journal* (February 1997), pp. 159–167; L. G. Thomas III and G. Waring, "Competing Capitalisms: Capital Investment in American, German, and Japanese Firms," *Strategic Management Journal* (August 1999), pp. 729–748.

103. M. H. Bazerman and D. Chugh, "Decisions Without Blinders," *Harvard Business Review* (January 2006), pp. 88–97.

104. J. A. Wagner III and R. Z. Gooding, "Equivocal Information and Attribution: An Investigation of Patterns of Managerial Sensemaking," *Strategic Management Journal* (April 1997), pp. 275–286; K. Shimizu and M. A. Hitt, "Strategic Flexibility: Organizational Preparedness to Reverse Ineffective Strategic Decisions," *Academy of Management Executive* (November 2004), pp. 44–59.

105. M. L. A. Hayward and K. Shimizu, "De-Commitment to Losing Strategic Action: Evidence from the Divestiture of Poorly Performing Acquisitions," *Strategic Management Journal* (June 2006), pp. 541–557.

106. J. Ross and B. M. Staw, "Organizational Escalation and Exit: Lessons from the Shoreham Nuclear Power Plant," *Academy of Management Journal* (August 1993), pp. 701–732; P. W. Mulvey, J. F. Veiga, and P. M. Elsass, "When Teammates Raise a White Flag," *Academy of Management Executive* (February 1996), pp. 40–49.

107. R. A. Cosier and C. R. Schwenk, "Agreement and Thinking Alike: Ingredients for Poor Decisions," *Academy of Management Executive* (February 1990), p. 69.

108. P. C. Nutt, *Why Decisions Fail* (San Francisco: Berrett-Koehler, 2002).

109. P. C. Nutt, "Expanding the Search for Alternatives During Strategic Decision-Making," *Academy of Management Executive* (November 2004), pp. 13–28.

110. K. Shimizu, "Prospect Theory, Behavioral Theory, and the Threat-Rigidity Thesis: Combinative Effects on Organizational Decisions to Divest Formerly Acquired Units," *Academy of Management Journal* (December 2007), pp. 1495–1514.

111. G. P. West III and G. D. Meyer, "To Agree or Not to Agree? Consensus and Performance in New Ventures," *Journal of Business Venturing* (September 1998), pp. 395–422; L. Markoczy, "Consensus Formation During Strategic Change," *Strategic Management Journal* (November 2001), pp. 1013–1031.

112 B. J. Olson, S. Parayitam, and Y. Bao, "Strategic Decision Making: The Effects of Cognitive Diversity, Conflict, and Trust on Decision Outcomes," *Journal of Management* (April 2007), pp. 196–222.

113. A. C. Amason, "Distinguishing the Effects of Functional and Dysfunctional Conflict on Strategic Decision Making: Resolving a Paradox for Top Management Teams," *Academy of Management Journal* (February 1996), pp. 123–148; A. C. Amason and H. J. Sapienza, "The Effects of Top Management Team Size and Interaction Norms on Cognitive and Affective Conflict," *Journal of Management*, Vol. 23, No. 4 (1997), pp. 495–516.

114. D. M. Schweiger, W. R. Sandberg, and P. L. Rechner, "Experiential Effects of Dialectical Inquiry, Devil's Advocacy, and Consensus Approaches to Strategic Decision Making," *Academy of Management Journal* (December 1989), pp. 745–772; G. Whyte, "Decision Failures: Why They Occur and How to Prevent Them," *Academy of Management Executive* (August 1991), pp. 23–31; R. L. Priem, D. A. Harrison, and N. K. Muir, "Structured Conflict and Consensus Outcomes in Group Decision Making," *Journal of Management*, Vol. 21, No. 4 (1995), pp. 691–710.

115. S. C. Abraham, "Using Bundles to Find the Best Strategy," *Strategy & Leadership* (July/August/September 1999), pp. 53–55.

116. O. Gadiesh and J. L Gilbert, "Transforming Corner-Office Strategy into Frontline Action," *Harvard Business Review* (May 2001), pp. 73–79.

117. "Losing Green By Going Green," *Business Week* (June 30, 2008), p. 61.

118. Advertisement by General Motors appearing in *National Geographic Magazine* (June 2008).

119. C. Holahan, "Going, Going...Everywhere," *Business Week* (June 18, 2007), pp. 62–64.

120. "The Skype Hyper," *The Economist* (October 6, 2007), p. 80.

121. C. Holahan, "EBay's New Tough Love CEO," *Business Week* (February 4, 2008), pp. 58–59.

Ending Case for Part Three

KMART AND SEARS: STILL STUCK IN THE MIDDLE?

On January 22, 2002, Kmart Corporation became the largest retailer in U.S. history to seek bankruptcy protection. In Kmart's petition for reorganization under Chapter 11 of the U.S. Bankruptcy Code, Kmart management announced that they would outline a plan for repaying Kmart's creditors, reducing its size, and restructuring its business so that it could leave court protection as a viable competitor in discount mass-market retailing. Emerging from bankruptcy in May 2003, Kmart still lacked a business strategy to succeed in an extremely competitive marketplace.

The U.S. discount department store industry had reached maturity by 2004 and Kmart no longer possessed a clearly-defined position within that industry. Its primary competitors were Wal-Mart, Sears, Target, Kohl's, and J.C. Penney, with secondary competitors in certain categories. Wal-Mart, an extremely efficient retailer, was known for consistently having the lowest costs (reflected in low prices) and the highest sales in the industry. Having started in rural America, Wal-Mart was now actively growing internationally. Sears, with the second-highest annual sales, had a strong position in hard goods, such as home appliances and tools. Around 40% of all major home appliance sales continued to be controlled by Sears. Nevertheless, Sears was struggling with slumping sales as customers turned from Sears mall stores to stand-alone, big-box retailers, such as Lowe's and Home Depot, to buy their hard goods. Target, third in sales but second in profits, behind Wal-Mart, had distinguished itself as a merchandiser of stylish upscale products. Along with Wal-Mart, Target had flourished to such an extent that Dayton-Hudson, its parent company, had changed its corporate name to Target. Kohl's, a relatively new entrant to the industry, operated 420 family-oriented stores in 32 states. J.C. Penney operated more than 1,000 stores in all 50 states. Both Kohl's and J.C. Penney emphasized soft goods, such as clothing and related items.

This case was written by J. David Hunger for *Strategic Management and Business Policy*, 12th edition and for *Concepts in Strategic Management and Business Policy*, 12th edition. Copyright © 2008 by J. David Hunger. Reprinted by permission. References available upon request.

Kmart was also challenged by "category killers" that competed in only one or a few industry categories, but in greater depth within any category than could any department store. Some of these were Toys "R" Us, Home Depot, Lowe's, and drug stores such as Rite Aid, CVS, Eckerd, and Walgreens.

Kmart had been established in 1962 by its parent company S.S. Kresge as a discount department store offering the most variety of goods at the lowest prices. Unlike Sears, the company chose not to locate in large shopping malls but to establish its discount stores in highly visible corner locations. During the 1960s, '70s, and '80s, Kmart prospered. By 1990, however, when Wal-Mart first surpassed Kmart in annual sales, Kmart's stores had become dated and lost their appeal. Other well-known discount stores, such as Korvette's, Grant's, Woolco, Ames, Bradlees, and Montgomery Ward, had gone out of business as the industry had consolidated and reached maturity. Attempting to avoid this fate, Kmart management updated and enlarged the stores, added name brands, and hired Martha Stewart as its lifestyle consultant. None of these changes improved Kmart's financial situation. By the time it declared bankruptcy, it had lost money in five of the past 10 years.

Out of bankruptcy, Kmart became profitable—primarily by closing or selling (to Sears and Home Depot) around 600 of its retail stores. Management had been unable to invigorate sales in its stores. Declared guilty of insider trading, Martha Stewart went to prison just before the 2004 Christmas season. In a surprise move, Edward Lampert, Kmart's Chairman of the Board and a controlling shareholder of Kmart, initiated the acquisition of Sears by Kmart for $11 billion in November 2004. The new company was to be called Sears Holdings Corporation. Even though management predicted that the combined company's costs could be reduced by $500 million annually within three years through supplier and administrative economies, analysts wondered how these two struggling firms could ever be successful.

By the end of 2007, the stock of Sears Holdings had fallen to 111 from its peak of 195 earlier in the year. Like many retailers, both Sears and Kmart struggled to attract shoppers in an overcrowded industry and a slumping economy. Sears Holdings did, however, have $1.5 billion in cash, a significant advantage during lean times, and more than its rivals J.C. Penney, Kohl's, and Macy's combined. The company's debt load was only

25% of the total capital on its balance sheet, compared to 46% for Penney's and 53% for Macy's. It also had significant real estate assets on its balance sheet. For example, Sears owned outright 518 of its 816 locations and many of the Kmart stores were located in strip malls close to large cities. Since fewer shopping malls were now being built, it was becoming harder to find space for "big-box" retailers in metropolitan areas.

The most recent quarterly results for 2007 of Sears Holdings reported the third straight quarter of deteriorating profit margins and same-store sales. After months of cutting the number of employees and reducing other expenses, industry analysts felt that there was little left to cut. They were also concerned that management had failed to invest in store improvements. Sears Holdings had just launched a bid in November 2007 to purchase Restoration Hardware, a home-goods retailer. Even though Restoration Hardware was also facing sluggish sales, it was thought that Sears' management could use the acquisition to create an upscale boutique within its stores.

PART 4

Strategy

Implementation

and

Control

strategy implementation: organizing for Action

AT Kearney, the well-known international management consultancy firm, annually ranks emerging market economies based on more than 25 macroeconomic and retail-specific variables through their Global Retail Development Index (GRDI). In its 2011 edition, it has ranked India on fourth position indicating that the country is one of the most attractive market for global retailers to enter.[1] However, given the unique cultural characteristics of India, the global players are plagued by the question of not only choice of business model and strategy but also their implementation. One company that has been able to penetrate the Indian retail market is Pantaloons Retail (India) Limited.

Pantaloons Retail (India) Limited is the flagship company of Future Group. It is India's retail pioneer with presence across multiple lines of businesses. The company owns and manages multiple retail formats such as Pantaloons, Big Bazaar, HomeTown, Food Bazaar, Ezone, and Central. These formats cater to a wide cross section of the Indian society and are able to capture almost the entire consumption basket of the Indian consumer.[2]

The successful Indian retailer did not mimic models that have worked elsewhere in the world, but based its stores and merchandise on an in-depth understanding of Indian consumers. The design team was inspired more by traditional Indian retail models than by western retail models. In launching Big Bazaar, the team visited many Indian neighborhood markets and incorporated elements of these markets into their stores. Big Bazaar's success could be traced to its "Indianness." Understanding the customer needs and site selection for each store played a crucial role in interpreting concepts that have worked overseas for Indian consumers.

Pantaloons Retail forayed into modern retail in 1997 with the launch of fashion retail chain, Pantaloons in Kolkata. In 2001, it launched Big Bazaar, a hypermarket chain that combines the look and feel of Indian bazaars, with aspects of modern retail such as choice, convenience, and hygiene. These stores offer products and services such as a chemist, a photography shop, a bakery, financial products, automobile accessories, bicycles and electrical hardware among other items. The range is vast and practically fulfills every need of the consumer under one roof. With wide aisles, less-cramped racks and attractive displays, the store looks like a departmental store rather than a discounted hypermarket store. The store displays related products in an organized

Learning Objectives

After reading this chapter, you should be able to:

- Develop programs, budgets, and procedures to implement strategic change
- Understand the importance of achieving synergy during strategy implementation
- List the stages of corporate development and the structure that characterizes each stage
- Identify the blocks to changing from one stage to another

- Construct matrix and network structures to support flexible and nimble organizational strategies
- Decide when and if programs such as reengineering, Six Sigma, and job redesign are appropriate methods of strategy implementation
- Understand the centralization versus decentralization issue in multinational corporations

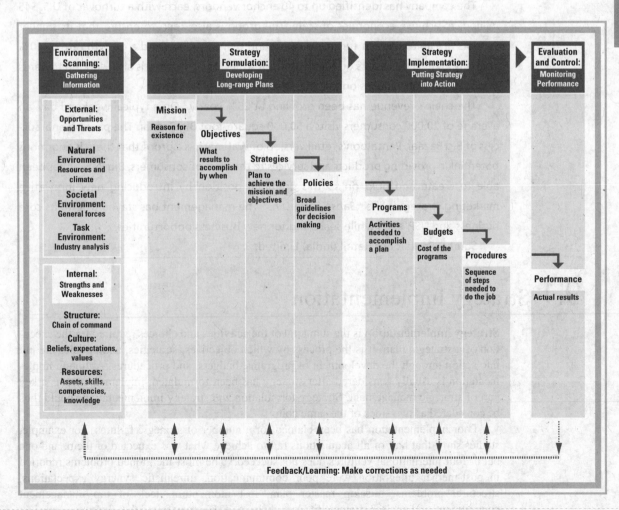

manner such as displaying shower curtains, towels, and ceramic bathroom accessories on one aisle. This arrangement encourages sale of "multiple" of related products. The attention to layout details helps the store shape shopper's attitude. The fun and colorful interiors buzz with energy and customer excitement.

However, the company's USP is not only convenience and hygiene but also basic worth allied with reasonable pricing. The store offers bargain prices and an assortment unlike other stores in India. The discounts offered ranges from 5% to 60% (discount stores is still a nascent concept in India). Many retailing executives consider it to be the Walmart of India. The store is apt at striking a delicate balance between convincing customers that its prices are low and also not making people feel that the store is cheap.

The promoter of Pantaloons Retail, Mr. Kishore Biyani's management philosophy was to find strong managers and give them near-total control of their businesses. Many analysts felt that Biyani's deep and intuitive understanding of Indian consumers combined with his firm's ability to execute operationally was the major reason for success for PRIL. At operational level, 10–20% discounts on products, innovative advertising, and brand-building exercises coupled with innovative logistics activities led to the success of Big Bazaar.

The company has identified up to 40 anchor vendors, each with a turnover of U.S. $45 million, to achieve economies of scale. The group is also keen to ensure that its smaller vendors are able to reach turnovers of around U.S. $1 million and a growth rate of 40% annually, to be able to pass on the benefits of scales. The company is also working towards bringing its 1,200 vendors online, like Wal-mart.

The chain's revenue has been growing at 25% yearly.[3] On a typical weekend day, an average of 20,000 consumers visits a 50,000-square-foot Big Bazaar. The phenomenal success of Big Bazaar, Pantaloon's retail version of Wal-mart, is a proof that there is enormous potential in providing products and services to this class of consumers. Big Bazaar has been able to create and hold on to this premium position by introducing new innovative marketing strategies like "*Sabse Sasta Din.*" The management has stayed true to its core business and USP, even while searching for new business opportunities.

Source: Pantaloons Retail (India) Limited.

9.1 Strategy Implementation

Strategy implementation is the sum total of the activities and choices required for the execution of a strategic plan. It is the process by which objectives, strategies, and policies are put into action through the development of programs, budgets, and procedures. Although implementation is usually considered after strategy has been formulated, implementation is a key part of strategic management. Strategy formulation and strategy implementation should thus be considered as two sides of the same coin.

Poor implementation has been blamed for a number of strategic failures. For example, studies show that half of all acquisitions fail to achieve what was expected of them, and one out of four international ventures does not succeed.[4] The most-mentioned problems reported in post-merger integration were poor communication, unrealistic synergy expectations, structural problems, missing master plan, lost momentum, lack of top management commitment, and unclear strategic fit. A study by A. T. Kearney found that a company has just two years in which to make an acquisition perform. After the second year, the window of opportunity for forging synergies has mostly closed. Kearney's study was supported by further independent research by Bert, MacDonald, and Herd. Among the most successful acquirers studied, 70% to 85% of all merger synergies were realized within the first 12 months, with the remainder being realized in year two.[5]

To begin the implementation process, strategy makers must consider these questions:

- *Who* are the people who will carry out the strategic plan?
- *What* must be done to align the company's operations in the new intended direction?
- *How* is everyone going to work together to do what is needed?

These questions and similar ones should have been addressed initially when the pros and cons of strategic alternatives were analyzed. They must also be addressed again before appropriate implementation plans can be made. Unless top management can answer these basic questions satisfactorily, even the best planned strategy is unlikely to provide the desired outcome.

A survey of 93 Fortune 500 firms revealed that more than half of the corporations experienced the following 10 problems when they attempted to implement a strategic change. These problems are listed in order of frequency:

1. Implementation took more time than originally planned.
2. Unanticipated major problems arose.
3. Activities were ineffectively coordinated.
4. Competing activities and crises took attention away from implementation.
5. The involved employees had insufficient capabilities to perform their jobs.
6. Lower-level employees were inadequately trained.
7. Uncontrollable external environmental factors created problems.
8. Departmental managers provided inadequate leadership and direction.
9. Key implementation tasks and activities were poorly defined.
10. The information system inadequately monitored activities.[6]

9.2 Who Implements Strategy?

Depending on how a corporation is organized, those who implement strategy will probably be a much more diverse set of people than those who formulate it. In most large, multi-industry corporations, the implementers are everyone in the organization. Vice presidents of functional areas and directors of divisions or strategic business units (SBUs) work with their subordinates to put together large-scale implementation plans. Plant managers, project managers, and unit heads put together plans for their specific plants, departments, and units. Therefore, every operational manager down to the first-line supervisor and every employee is involved in some way in the implementation of corporate, business, and functional strategies.

Many of the people in the organization who are crucial to successful strategy implementation probably had little to do with the development of the corporate and even business strategy. Therefore, they might be entirely ignorant of the vast amount of data and work that went into the formulation process. Unless changes in mission, objectives, strategies, and policies and their importance to the company are communicated clearly to all operational managers, there can be a lot of resistance and foot-dragging. Managers might hope to influence top management into abandoning its new plans and returning to its old ways. This is one reason why involving people from all organizational levels in the formulation and implementation of strategy tends to result in better organizational performance.[7]

9.3 What Must Be Done?

The managers of divisions and functional areas work with their fellow managers to develop programs, budgets, and procedures for the implementation of strategy. They also work to achieve synergy among the divisions and functional areas in order to establish and maintain a company's distinctive competence.

DEVELOPING PROGRAMS, BUDGETS, AND PROCEDURES

Strategy implementation involves establishing programs to create a series of new organizational activities, budgets to allocate funds to the new activities, and procedures to handle the day-to-day details.

Programs

The purpose of a **program** is to make a strategy action oriented. For example, when Wipro required improvement in product performance of a telecom application and wanted to focus on quality of services provided, it implemented a program called Six Sigma. The program was developed to identify and improve the alignment of business operations with customer needs while resulting in cost saving and overall performance improvement. The result of the program was that, the company was able to reduce data transfer time, avoid interruption due to LAN/WAN downtime, and adopt crises planning methodologies such as switching to administrative tasks during LAN/WAN downtime. Today, Wipro has one of the most mature Six Sigma programs in the Indian software industry ensuring that 91% of the projects are completed on schedule, much above the industry average of 55%[8] (Six Sigma is explained later in this chapter).

Most corporate headquarters have around 10–30 programs in effect at any one time.[9] One of the programs initiated by Ford Motor Company was to find an organic substitute for petroleum-based foam being used in vehicle seats. For more information on Ford's innovative soybean seat program, see the **Environment Sustainability Issue** feature.

One way to examine the likely impact new programs will have on an existing organization is to compare proposed programs and activities with current programs and activities. Brynjolfsson, Renshaw, and Van Alstyne proposed a **matrix of change** to help managers decide how quickly change should proceed, in what order changes should take place, whether to start at a new site, and whether the proposed systems are stable and coherent. As shown in **Figure 9–1**, target practices for the software firm Unistar Outsourcing India Pvt. Ltd are drawn on the vertical axis and existing practices are drawn on the horizontal axis. Use the following steps to create the matrix:

1. Compare the new programs/target practices with each other to see if they are complementary (+), interfering (−), or have no effect on each other (leave blank).

2. Examine existing practices/activities for their interactions with each other using the same symbols as in step 1.

3. Compare each new program/target practice with each existing practice/activity for any interaction effects. Place the appropriate symbols in the cells in the lower-right part of the matrix.

4. Evaluate each program/activity in terms of its relative importance to achieving the strategy or getting the job accomplished.

5. Examine the overall matrix to identify problem areas where proposed programs are likely to either interfere with each other or with existing practices/activities. Note in **Figure 9–1** that the proposed program of installing flexible equipment interferes with the proposed program

STRATEGY highlight 9.1

MATRIX OF CHANGE FOR UNISTAR OUTSOURCING PVT. LTD

a. Existing Processes (horizontal matrix)
- Run an efficient and low-cost operation
  - i. Narrow job function.
  - ii. Functional groups.
  - iii. Permanent employees make all the decisions.
  - iv. Temporary employees carry them out.
- Meet quality and quantity product requirements
  - i. Through regular inspection and test run by the management (vertical hierarchy).
  - ii. Performance-based pay.
  - iii. Understanding of the customer with the top management.
- Hierarchical entrepreneurial structure
  - i. Vertical structure.
  - ii. Entrepreneurial-based firm.
  - iii. Distant and frequently changing suppliers.

b. Target Practices (vertical matrix)
- Energized, empowered organization
  - i. Flexible equipments and jobs.
  - ii. Systematic problem solving.
  - iii. All employees contribute ideas.
- Control requirements
  - i. Operators responsible for quality.
  - ii. All operators paid same flat rate.
  - iii. Vision given from top.
  - iv. 24-hour customer respond time.
  - v. Elimination of all non value-adding costs.
  - vi. Database connectivity.

ENVIRONMENTAL sustainability issue

FORD'S SOYBEAN SEAT FOAM PROGRAM

The Model T Ford once contained 60 pounds of soybeans in its paint and molded plastic parts. Since that time, petroleum has become the primary ingredient in most plastic parts, including the foam currently used in car and truck seats. Nevertheless, today's manufacturers are looking for ways to replace petroleum-based products with ones made from agricultural crops, as the political, environmental, and economic costs of oil increase. According to Larry Johnson, Director of the Center for Crops Utilization Research at Iowa State University, soy is usually cheaper and more environmentally friendly than petroleum and comes from a renewable agricultural source. With this in mind, Ford's management initiated a program in 2001 with seat supplier Lear Corporation to research soy-based foam as a possible substitute for petroleum-based foam. The program was a huge success. A complete seating system, including suspension systems, contains about 20% soy oil. The new seats were used in the Mustang and other Ford vehicles delivered to auto showrooms beginning August 2007.

Sears Manufacturing Company, a seat supplier to Deere and other companies, licensed the Ford technology to work with Deere in developing soy-based foam for seats on Deere's farm and construction equipment. Deere was already using soy-based materials for parts such as hoods, side panels, and doors on some models of tractors, combines, cotton pickers, and backhoes. According to John Koutsky, Vice President of Product Development, Sears started commercial production of the new seats in 2009 and planned to use soy foam throughout its product line being sold to heavy truck manufacturers like Freightliner and International. "It's good to be green," commented Koutsky.

SOURCE: "Manufacturers Turn to Soy for Cushy Seats," *St. Cloud* (MN) *Times* (January 26, 2008), p. 3A, and Ford Motor Company Web site (www.Ford.com).

FIGURE 9–1
The Matrix of Change

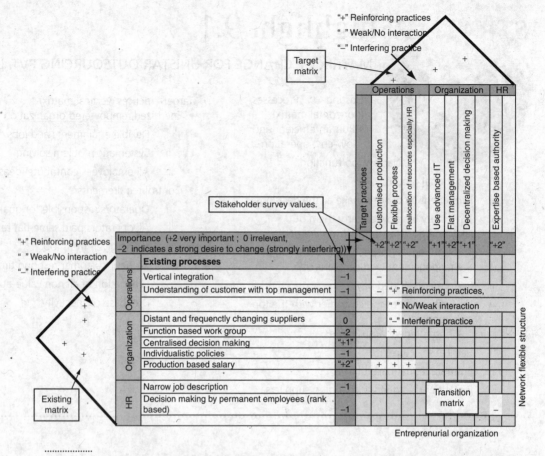

SOURCE: Reprinted from The Matrix of Change by E. Brynjolfsson, A.A. Renshaw, and M. Van Alstyne. *Sloan Management Review,* Winter 1997, pp. 168-181. From MIT Sloan Management Review © 1997 by Massachusetts Institute of Technology. All rights reserved. Distributed by Tribune Media Services.

of assembly line rationalization. The two new programs need to be changed so that they no longer conflict with each other. Note also that the amount of change necessary to carry out the proposed implementation programs (target practices) is a function of the number of times each program interferes with existing practices/activities. That is, the more minus signs and the fewer plus signs in the matrix, the more implementation problems can be expected.

The matrix of change can be used to address the following types of questions:

- **Feasibility:** Do the proposed programs and activities constitute a coherent, stable system? Are the current activities coherent and stable? Is the transition likely to be difficult?

- **Sequence of execution:** Where should the change begin? How does the sequence affect success? Are there reasonable stopping points?

- **Location:** Are we better off instituting the new programs at a new site, or can we reorganize the existing facilities at a reasonable cost?

- **Pace and nature of change:** Should the change be slow or fast, incremental or radical? Which blocks of current activities must be changed at the same time?

- **Stakeholder evaluations:** Have we overlooked any important activities or interactions? Should we get further input from interested stakeholders? Which new programs and current activities offer the greatest sources of value?

The matrix offers useful guidelines on where, when, and how fast to implement change.[10]

The matrix was used by the company to address feasibility and sequence of execution questions. In the existing matrix, no competing practices were identified; this suggests that the existing system at Unistar solutions is a stable unit. Similarly, in the target triangular matrix there were no competing practices either. The transition matrix helped the company evaluate the degree of difficulty in shifting from existing to target practices. The company wanted to address control requirements from its clients and create an empowered organization. The stakeholders were surveyed and the company found that the stakeholders were in strong favor for changing to customized production and flexible processes. A large majority of activities in the target system were complimenting the original system, therefore, making it easy for the company to change. However, there was some conflict between vertical integration with customized production and decentralized decision making, understanding of customer with top management and customized production and decision making by the permanent employees and target strategy of expertise-based authority. Unistar Outsourcing Private Limited devised strategies for change based on the inputs it received from the matrix of change by starting with those processes that opposed other existing practices and then moving to other ones. See **Strategy Highlight 9.1** to learn more about Unistar Outsourcing Pvt. Ltd.

Budgets

After programs have been developed, the **budget** process begins. Planning a budget is the last real check a corporation has on the feasibility of its selected strategy. An ideal strategy might be found to be completely impractical only after specific implementation programs are costed in detail. As an example, once Cadbury Schweppes' management realized how dependent the company was on cocoa from Ghana to continue the company's growth strategy, it developed a program to show cocoa farmers how to increase yields using fertilizers and by working with each other. Ghana produced 70% of Cadbury's worldwide supply of the high-quality cocoa necessary to provide the distinctive taste of Dairy Milk, Crème Egg, and other treats. Management introduced the "Cadbury Cocoa Partnership" on January 28, 2008, and budgeted $87 million for this program over a 10-year period.[11]

Procedures

After the program, divisional, and corporate budgets are approved, **procedures** must be developed. Often called *Standard Operating Procedures (SOPs),* they typically detail the various activities that must be carried out to complete a corporation's programs. Also known as *organizational routines*, procedures are the primary means by which organizations accomplish much of what they do.[12] Once in place, procedures must be updated to reflect any changes in technology as well as in strategy. For example, a company following a differentiation competitive strategy manages its sales force more closely than does a firm following a low-cost strategy. Differentiation requires long-term customer relationships created out of close interaction with the sales force. An in-depth understanding of the customer's needs provides the foundation for product development and improvement.[13] For example, at ICICI Lombard General Insurance Company (ILGIC), SOPs have enabled the company to develop long-term relationship with its customers and sales force while exploiting the benefits of a cost-leadership strategy (**Strategy Highlight 9.2**).

In a retail store, procedures ensure that the day-to-day store operations will be consistent over time (that is, next week's work activities will be the same as this week's) and consistent among stores (that is, each store will operate in the same manner as the others). Properly planned procedures can help eliminate poor service by making sure that employees do use not excuses to justify poor behavior toward customers. Even though McDonald's, the fast-food restaurant, has developed very detailed procedures to ensure that customers have high quality service, not every business is so well managed. See **Strategy Highlight 9.3** for the top 10 excuses for bad service.

STRATEGY highlight 9.2

SOPS AT ICICI LOMBARD GENERAL INSURANCE COMPANY (ILGIC)

ICICI Lombard General Insurance Company (ILGIC) Limited is a 74:26 joint venture between ICICI Bank Limited and the Canada-based $26 billion Fairfax Financial Holdings Limited. ICICI Bank is India's second largest bank, whereas Fairfax Financial Holdings is a diversified financial corporate engaged in general insurance, reinsurance, insurance claims management, and investment management.

ILGIC started commercial operations in August 2001 and is India 's number one private general insurance company with a market share of 13% and growing at over 80% year on year. ILGIC attributes its growth to innovative processes and procedures, which are adopted as Standard Operating Procedures (SOPs). The SOPs are designed with single-minded focus, i.e., meeting customer needs proactively through innovative product and service solutions, backed by robust processes and systems.

ILGIC SOPs target three variables for transparency namely, speed, convenience, and availability. This allows the company to maintain long-term relationship, and close interaction with their sales force at a comparatively lower cost.

Transparency and Speed

Traditionally filing for a claim was perceived as a complex, subjective process fraught with delays and unnecessary demand for documents from insurance companies. To counter these inadequacies and to enhance the customer experience, the company developed a standardized procedure for claims settlement. Some examples of the changes made are highlighted below:

- Business acquisition processes were designed where most information was collected from the customer at the time of policy issuance versus claim settlement.

- In motor and health insurances (which account for over 80% of the industry claims), the payment was made cashless to the customer and the settlement was done directly at the garage and hospital.

- Through a 24x7 call center and dedicated claims service representatives, the company ensured that their surveyor was on-site within 24 hours of any claim being reported.

Convenience and Availability

Traditionally, customers were expected to visit the branches of insurance companies for policy issuance and claims servicing. Further, the processes adopted by the industry had high-cost manual processes. These manual processes acted as deterrent for insurance companies to innovate and distribute low-cost insurance product. ILGIC leveraged technology to deliver customer convenience. The technology enabled process-empowered customers to instantly issue policies. This direct distribution channel offers instant policy issuance with an option of dial-a-policy 24x7 through toll free numbers for India, US, UK, and Canada. Additionally, ILGIC employees could track the claim status online. This helped in eliminating poor service and chances of employees using excuses to justify poor behavior toward customer.

These SOPs facilitate delivery of product at a fraction of the cost for the company. Moreover, they empower the customer and intermediaries with greater control, confidence and convenience. The ILGIC processes and system are designed to ensure seamless fulfillment and high-grade customer service at all the above channels.

With its relentless effort and focus on continuous improvement, it has attained the current scale with enhanced quality service provided to the customers. It is the only general insurance company in India to be ISO 9001:2000 certified. ILGIC covers 300 of India's top 1,000 corporates, insures over 100 million Indians, issues 10,000 policies per day, and settles over 2,000 claims daily. ICICI Lombard was also voted among the top three general insurers across Asia in the 10th Asia Insurance Industry Awards.

....
Courtesy: ICICI Lombard General Insurance Company (ILGIC)

Before a new strategy can be successfully implemented, current procedures may need to be changed. For example, in order to implement Home Depot's strategic move into services, such as kitchen and bathroom installation, the company had to first improve its productivity. Store managers were drowning in paperwork designed for a smaller and simpler company. "We'd get a fax, an e-mail, a call, and a memo, all on the same project," reported store manager Michael Jones. One executive used just three weeks of memos to wallpaper an entire conference room, floor to ceiling, windows included. CEO Robert Nardelli told his top managers to eliminate duplicate communications and streamline work projects. Directives not

STRATEGY highlight 9.3

THE TOP TEN EXCUSES FOR BAD SERVICE

Corporations may have official policies stating that the "customer is always right" or "customer is number one," but these quickly become meaningless platitudes unless procedures are developed and communicated to all employees for them to follow when confronted with a problem or a question from a customer. Beware of the top ten excuses for bad service. They can sabotage a company's strategy and send valued customers to the competition. How many times have you heard the following excuses when you received poor service? Or even worse, how many times have you personally given one or all of these excuses?

#10. Customer complaint: Why do I have to wait so long for service? **Excuse:** To get service as good as ours, sometimes you have to wait; our guests expect that.

#9. Customer complaint: Why didn't your service meet what I expected? **Excuse:** Nobody's perfect; we simply can't make every customer happy.

#8. Customer complaint: Why didn't you let us have it "our way?" **Excuse:** We're sorry, but if we did it "your way" for all our customers, we would crash our systems and overextend our already overworked employees.

#7. Customer complaint: Service wasn't as good this time as it was the last time we were here. **Excuse:** Everybody has good days and bad days; we're doing our best to please you, but we can't always be perfect.

#6. Customer complaint: Your place is dirty, dated, and worn. **Excuse:** We do our best to keep it clean and up to date, but we can't afford to follow every customer around to make sure we pick up everything, nor can we refurbish our place all the time.

#5. Customer complaint: I placed my order a while ago, why is it taking so long? **Excuse:** Sorry, but we are very busy right now. You came at our "busy" time and you must be patient.

#4. Customer complaint: Your server did not seem to know what he/she was doing and made a mess of my experience. **Excuse:** Unfortunately, with all the turnover we are having right now, we just didn't have the time to train everyone up to our standards.

#3. Customer complaint: Your employee was rude to me and has a bad attitude. **Excuse:** We do apologize for the unfortunate attitude of a few employees.

#2. Customer complaint: The server didn't seem to be interested in doing what he/she was supposed to do. Why can't she/he do it the right way? **Excuse:** We are sorry. While we trained them to do it the right way, sometimes they just seem to ignore what we taught them.

#1. Customer complaint: We expected something different from your company and we are really disappointed. **Excuse:** You must be misinformed, as we have been successful for a long time and obviously know exactly what our customers want and need.

SOURCE: D. Dickson, R. C. Ford, and B. Laval, "The Top Ten Excuses for Bad Service (and How to Avoid Needing Them)" *Organizational Dynamics*, Vol. 34, No. 2 (2005), pp. 168–181.

related to work orders had to be sent separately and only once a month. The company also spent $2 million on workload-management software.[14]

ACHIEVING SYNERGY

One of the goals to be achieved in strategy implementation is synergy between and among functions and business units. This is the reason corporations commonly reorganize after an acquisition. **Synergy** is said to exist for a divisional corporation if the return on investment (ROI) of each division is greater than what the return would be if each division were an independent business. According to Goold and Campbell, synergy can take place in one of six forms:

■ **Shared know-how:** Combined units often benefit from sharing knowledge or skills. This is a leveraging of core competencies. One reason that Procter & Gamble purchased

Gillette was to combine P&G's knowledge of the female consumer with Gillette's knowledge of the male consumer.

- **Coordinated strategies:** Aligning the business strategies of two or more business units may provide a corporation significant advantage by reducing inter-unit competition and developing a coordinated response to common competitors (horizontal strategy). The merger between Arcelor and Mittal Steel, for example, gave the combined company enhanced R&D capabilities and wider global coverage while presenting a common face to the market.

- **Shared tangible resources:** Combined units can sometimes save money by sharing resources, such as a common manufacturing facility or R&D lab. The alliance between Renault and Nissan allowed it to build new factories that would build both Nissan and Renault vehicles.

- **Economies of scale or scope:** Coordinating the flow of products or services of one unit with that of another unit can reduce inventory, increase capacity utilization, and improve market access. This was a reason Delta Airlines bought Northwest Airlines.

- **Pooled negotiating power:** Combined units can combine their purchasing to gain bargaining power over common suppliers to reduce costs and improve quality. The same can be done with common distributors.

- **New business creation:** Exchanging knowledge and skills can facilitate new products or services by extracting discrete activities from various units and combining them in a new unit or by establishing joint ventures among internal business units. Oracle, for example, purchased a number of software companies in order to create a suite of software code-named "Project Fusion" to help corporations run everything from accounting and sales to customer relations and supply-chain management.[15]

9.4 How Is Strategy to Be Implemented? Organizing for Action

Before plans can lead to actual performance, a corporation should be appropriately organized, programs should be adequately staffed, and activities should be directed toward achieving desired objectives. (Organizing activities are reviewed briefly in this chapter; staffing, directing, and control activities are discussed in **Chapters 10** and **11**.)

Any change in corporate strategy is very likely to require some sort of change in the way an organization is structured and in the kind of skills needed in particular positions. Managers must, therefore, closely examine the way their company is structured in order to decide what, if any, changes should be made in the way work is accomplished. Should activities be grouped differently? Should the authority to make key decisions be centralized at headquarters or decentralized to managers in distant locations? Should the company be managed like a "tight ship" with many rules and controls, or "loosely" with few rules and controls? Should the corporation be organized into a "tall" structure with many layers of managers, each having a narrow span of control (that is, few employees per supervisor) to better control his or her subordinates; or should it be organized into a "flat" structure with fewer layers of managers, each having a wide span of control (that is, more employees per supervisor) to give more freedom to his or her subordinates?

STRUCTURE FOLLOWS STRATEGY

In a classic study of large U.S. corporations such as DuPont, General Motors, Sears, and Standard Oil, Alfred Chandler concluded that **structure follows strategy**—that is, changes in corporate strategy lead to changes in organizational structure.[16] He also concluded that organizations follow a pattern of development from one kind of structural arrangement to another as they expand. According to Chandler, these structural changes occur because the old structure, having been pushed too far, has caused inefficiencies that have become too obviously detrimental to bear. Chandler, therefore, proposed the following as the sequence of what occurs:

1. New strategy is created.
2. New administrative problems emerge.
3. Economic performance declines.
4. New appropriate structure is invented.
5. Profit returns to its previous level.

Chandler found that in their early years, corporations such as DuPont tend to have a centralized functional organizational structure that is well suited to producing and selling a limited range of products. As they add new product lines, purchase their own sources of supply, and create their own distribution networks, they become too complex for highly centralized structures. To remain successful, this type of organization needs to shift to a decentralized structure with several semiautonomous divisions (referred to in **Chapter 5** as *divisional structure*).

Alfred P. Sloan, past CEO of General Motors, detailed how GM conducted such structural changes in the 1920s.[17] He saw decentralization of structure as "centralized policy determination coupled with decentralized operating management." After top management had developed a strategy for the total corporation, the individual divisions (Chevrolet, Buick, and so on) were free to choose how to implement that strategy. Patterned after DuPont, GM found the decentralized multidivisional structure to be extremely effective in allowing the maximum amount of freedom for product development. Return on investment was used as a financial control. (ROI is discussed in more detail in **Chapter 11**.)

Research generally supports Chandler's proposition that structure follows strategy (as well as the reverse proposition that structure influences strategy).[18] As mentioned earlier, changes in the environment tend to be reflected in changes in a corporation's strategy, thus leading to changes in a corporation's structure. In 2008, Arctic Cat, the recreational vehicles firm, reorganized its ATV (all terrain vehicles), snowmobile and parts, and garments and accessories product lines into three separate business units, each led by a general manager focused on expanding the business. True to Chandler's findings, the restructuring of Arctic Cat came after seven consecutive years of record growth followed by its first loss in 25 years.

Strategy, structure, and the environment need to be closely aligned; otherwise, organizational performance will likely suffer.[19] For example, a business unit following a differentiation strategy needs more freedom from headquarters to be successful than does another unit following a low-cost strategy.[20]

Although it is agreed that organizational structure must vary with different environmental conditions, which, in turn, affect an organization's strategy, there is no agreement about an optimal organizational design. What was appropriate for DuPont and General Motors in the 1920s might not be appropriate today. Firms in the same industry do, however, tend to organize themselves similarly to one another. For example, automobile manufacturers tend to emulate General Motors' divisional concept, whereas consumer-goods producers tend to emulate the brand-management concept (a type of matrix structure) pioneered by Procter & Gamble Company. The general conclusion seems to be that firms following similar strategies in similar industries tend to adopt similar structures.

STAGES OF CORPORATE DEVELOPMENT

Successful corporations tend to follow a pattern of structural development as they grow and expand. Beginning with the simple structure of the entrepreneurial firm (in which everybody does everything), successful corporations usually get larger and organize along functional lines, with marketing, production, and finance departments. With continuing success, the company adds new product lines in different industries and organizes itself into interconnected divisions. The differences among these three structural **stages of corporate development** in terms of typical problems, objectives, strategies, reward systems, and other characteristics are specified in detail in **Table 9–1.**

Stage I: Simple Structure

Stage I is typified by the entrepreneur, who founds a company to promote an idea (a product or a service). The entrepreneur tends to make all the important decisions personally and is involved in every detail and phase of the organization. The Stage I company has little formal structure, which allows the entrepreneur to directly supervise the activities of every employee (see **Figure 5–4** for an illustration of the simple, functional, and divisional structures). Planning is usually short range or reactive. The typical managerial functions of planning, organizing, directing, staffing, and controlling are usually performed to a very limited degree, if at all. The greatest strengths of a Stage I corporation are its flexibility and dynamism. The drive of the entrepreneur energizes the organization in its struggle for growth. Its greatest weakness is its extreme reliance on the entrepreneur to decide general strategies as well as detailed procedures. If the entrepreneur falters, the company usually flounders. This is labeled by Greiner as a *crisis of leadership.*[21]

Stage I describes Oracle Corporation, the computer software firm, under the management of its co-founder and CEO Lawrence Ellison. The company adopted a pioneering approach to retrieving data, called Structured Query Language (SQL). When IBM made SQL its standard, Oracle's success was assured. Unfortunately, Ellison's technical wizardry was not sufficient to manage the company. Often working at home, he lost sight of details outside his technical interests. Although the company's sales were rapidly increasing, its financial controls were so weak that management had to restate an entire year's results to rectify irregularities. After the company recorded its first loss, Ellison hired a set of functional managers to run the company while he retreated to focus on new product development.

Stage II: Functional Structure

Stage II is the point when the entrepreneur is replaced by a team of managers who have functional specializations. The transition to this stage requires a substantial managerial style change for the chief officer of the company, especially if he or she was the Stage I entrepreneur. He or she must learn to delegate; otherwise, having additional staff members yields no benefits to the organization. The previous example of Ellison's retreat from top management at Oracle Corporation to new product development manager is one way that technically brilliant founders are able to get out of the way of the newly empowered functional managers. In Stage II, the corporate strategy favors protectionism through dominance of the industry, often through vertical and horizontal growth. The great strength of a Stage II corporation lies in its concentration and specialization in one industry. Its great weakness is that all its eggs are in one basket.

By concentrating on one industry while that industry remains attractive, a Stage II company, such as Oracle Corporation in computer software, can be very successful. Once a functionally structured firm diversifies into other products in different industries, however, the advantages of the functional structure break down. A *crisis of autonomy* can now develop, in which people managing diversified product lines need more decision-making freedom than top management is willing to delegate to them. The company needs to move to a different structure.

TABLE 9–1	Factors Differentiating Stage I, II, and III Companies		
Function	**Stage I**	**Stage II**	**Stage III**
1. Sizing up: Major problems	Survival and growth dealing with short-term operating problems.	Growth, rationalization, and expansion of resources, providing for adequate attention to product problems.	Trusteeship in management and investment and control of large, increasing, and diversified resources. Also, important to diagnose and take action on problems at division level.
2. Objectives	Personal and subjective.	Profits and meeting functionally oriented budgets and performance targets.	ROI, profits, earnings per share.
3. Strategy	Implicit and personal; exploitation of immediate opportunities seen by owner-manager.	Functionally oriented moves restricted to "one product" scope; exploitation of one basic product or service field.	Growth and product diversification; exploitation of general business opportunities.
4. Organization: Major characteristic of structure	One unit, "one-man show."	One unit, functionally specialized group.	Multiunit general staff office and decentralized operating divisions.
5. (a) Measurement and control	Personal, subjective control based on simple accounting system and daily communication and observation.	Control grows beyond one person; assessment of functional operations necessary; structured control systems evolve.	Complex formal system geared to comparative assessment of performance measures, indicating problems and opportunities and assessing management ability of division managers.
5. (b) Key performance indicators	Personal criteria, relationships with owner, operating efficiency, ability to solve operating problems.	Functional and internal criteria such as sales, performance compared to budget, size of empire, status in group, personal, relationships, etc.	More impersonal application of comparisons such as profits, ROI, P/E ratio, sales, market share, productivity, product leadership, personnel development, employee attitudes, public responsibility.
6. Reward-punishment system	Informal, personal, subjective; used to maintain control and divide small pool of resources for key performers to provide personal incentives.	More structured; usually based to a greater extent on agreed policies as opposed to personal opinion and relationships.	Allotment by "due process" of a wide variety of different rewards and punishments on a formal and systematic basis. Companywide policies usually apply to many different classes of managers and workers with few major exceptions for individual cases.

SOURCE: D. H. Thain, "Stages of Corporate Development," *Ivey Business Quarterly,* Winter 1969, p. 37. © 1969 Ivey Management Services. One time Permission to reproduce granted by Ivey Management Services.

Stage III: Divisional Structure

Stage III is typified by the corporation's managing diverse product lines in numerous industries; it decentralizes the decision-making authority. Stage III organizations grow by diversifying their product lines and expanding to cover wider geographical areas. They move to a divisional structure with a central headquarters and decentralized operating divisions—with each division or business unit a functionally organized Stage II company. They may also use a conglomerate structure if top management chooses to keep its collection of Stage II subsidiaries operating autonomously. A *crisis of control* can now develop, in which the various units act to optimize their own sales and profits without regard to the overall corporation, whose headquarters seems far away and almost irrelevant.

Recently, divisions have been evolving into SBUs to better reflect product-market considerations. Headquarters attempts to coordinate the activities of its operating divisions or SBUs through performance- and results-oriented control and reporting systems and by stressing corporate planning techniques. The units are not tightly controlled but are held responsible for their own performance results. Therefore, to be effective, the company has to have a decentralized decision process. The greatest strength of a Stage III corporation is its almost unlimited resources. Its most significant weakness is that it is usually so large and complex that it tends to become relatively inflexible. General Electric, DuPont, and General Motors are examples of Stage III corporations.

Stage IV: Beyond SBUs

Even with its evolution into SBUs during the 1970s and 1980s, the divisional structure is not the last word in organizational structure. The use of SBUs may result in a *red tape crisis* in which the corporation has grown too large and complex to be managed through formal programs and rigid systems, and procedures take precedence over problem solving.[22] For example, Pfizer's acquisitions of Warner-Lambert and Pharmacia resulted in 14 layers of management between scientists and top executives and forced researchers to spend most of their time in meetings.[23] Under conditions of (1) increasing environmental uncertainty, (2) greater use of sophisticated technological production methods and information systems, (3) the increasing size and scope of worldwide business corporations, (4) a greater emphasis on multi-industry competitive strategy, and (5) a more educated cadre of managers and employees, new advanced forms of organizational structure are emerging. These structures emphasize collaboration over competition in the managing of an organization's multiple overlapping projects and developing businesses.

The matrix and the network are two possible candidates for a fourth stage in corporate development—a stage that not only emphasizes horizontal over vertical connections between people and groups but also organizes work around temporary projects in which sophisticated information systems support collaborative activities. According to Greiner, it is likely that this stage of development will have its own crisis as well—a sort of *pressure-cooker crisis*. He predicts that employees in these collaborative organizations will eventually grow emotionally and physically exhausted from the intensity of teamwork and the heavy pressure for innovative solutions.[24]

Blocks to Changing Stages

Corporations often find themselves in difficulty because they are blocked from moving into the next logical stage of development. Blocks to development may be internal (such as lack of resources, lack of ability, or refusal of top management to delegate decision making to others) or external (such as economic conditions, labor shortages, and lack of market growth). For example, Chandler noted in his study that the successful founder/CEO in one stage was rarely the person who created the new structure to fit the new strategy, and as a result, the transition from one stage to another was often painful. This was true of General Motors Corporation under the management of William Durant, Ford Motor Company under Henry Ford I, Polaroid Corporation under Edwin Land, Apple Computer under Steven Jobs, and Sun Microsystems under Scott McNealy.

Entrepreneurs who start businesses generally have four tendencies that work very well for small new ventures but become Achilles' heels for these same individuals when they try to manage a larger firm with diverse needs, departments, priorities, and constituencies:

- **Loyalty to comrades:** This is good at the beginning but soon becomes a liability as "favoritism."

- **Task oriented:** Focusing on the job is critical at first but then becomes excessive attention to detail.

- **Single-mindedness:** A grand vision is needed to introduce a new product but can become tunnel vision as the company grows into more markets and products.

- **Working in isolation:** This is good for a brilliant scientist but disastrous for a CEO with multiple constituencies.[25]

This difficulty in moving to a new stage is compounded by the founder's tendency to maneuver around the need to delegate by carefully hiring, training, and grooming his or her own team of managers. The team tends to maintain the founder's influence throughout the organization long after the founder is gone. This is what happened at Walt Disney Productions when the family continued to emphasize Walt's policies and plans long after he was dead. Although this may often be an organization's strength, it may also be a weakness—to the extent that the culture supports the status quo and blocks needed change.

ORGANIZATIONAL LIFE CYCLE

Instead of considering stages of development in terms of structure, the organizational life cycle approach places the primary emphasis on the dominant issue facing the corporation. Organizational structure is only a secondary concern. The **organizational life cycle** describes how organizations grow, develop, and eventually decline. It is the organizational equivalent of the product life cycle in marketing. These stages are Birth (Stage I), Growth (Stage II), Maturity (Stage III), Decline (Stage IV), and Death (Stage V). The impact of these stages on corporate strategy and structure is summarized in **Table 9–2**. Note that the first three stages of the organizational life cycle are similar to the three commonly accepted stages of corporate development mentioned previously. The only significant difference is the addition of the Decline and Death stages to complete the cycle. Even though a company's strategy may still be sound, its aging structure, culture, and processes may be such that they prevent the strategy from being executed properly. Its core competencies become *core rigidities* that are no longer able to adapt to changing conditions—thus the company moves into Decline.[26]

Movement from Growth to Maturity to Decline and finally to Death is not, however, inevitable. A Revival phase may occur sometime during the Maturity or Decline stages. The corporation's life cycle can be extended by managerial and product innovations.[27] Developing new combinations of existing resources to introduce new products or acquiring new resources through acquisitions can enable firms with declining performance to regain growth—so long as the action is valuable and difficult to imitate.[28] This can occur during the implementation of a turnaround strategy.[29] Nevertheless, the fact that firms in decline are less likely to search for new technologies suggests that it is difficult to revive a company in decline.[30]

Eastman Kodak is an example of a firm in decline that has been attempting to develop new combinations of its existing resources to introduce new products, and thus, revive the corporation. When Antonio Perez left Hewlett-Packard to become Kodak's President in 2003, Kodak was in the midst of its struggle to make the transition from chemical film technology

TABLE 9–2	Organizational Life Cycle				
	Stage I	**Stage II**	**Stage III***	**Stage IV**	**Stage V**
Dominant Issue	Birth	Growth	Maturity	Decline	Death
Popular Strategies	Concentration in a niche	Horizontal and vertical growth	Concentric and conglomerate diversification	Profit strategy followed by retrenchment	Liquidation or bankruptcy
Likely Structure	Entrepreneur dominated	Functional management emphasized	Decentralization into profit or investment centers	Structural surgery	Dismemberment of structure

NOTE: *An organization may enter a Revival phase either during the Maturity or Decline stages and thus extend the organization's life.

to digital technology and digital cameras. Instead of focusing the company's efforts on acquisitions to find growth, Perez looked at technologies that Kodak already owned, but was not utilizing. He noticed that Kodak scientists had developed new ink to yield photo prints with vivid colors that would last a lifetime. He suddenly realized that Kodak's distinctive competence was not in digital photography, where other competitors led the market, but in color printing. Perez initiated project *Goza* to go head to head with HP in the consumer inkjet printer business. In 2007, Kodak unveiled its new line of multipurpose machines that not only handled photographs and documents, but also made copies and sent faxes. The printers were designed to print high-quality photos with ink that would stay vibrant for 100 rather than the usual 15 years. Most importantly, replacement ink cartridges would cost half the price of competitors' cartridges. According to Perez, "We think it will give us the opportunity to disrupt the industry's business model and address consumers' key dissatisfaction: the high cost of ink." Perez then predicted that Kodak's inkjet printers would become a multibillion-dollar product line.[31]

Unless a company is able to resolve the critical issues facing it in the Decline stage, it is likely to move into Stage V, Death—also known as bankruptcy. This is what happened to Montgomery Ward, Pan American Airlines, Macy's Department Stores, Baldwin-United, Eastern Airlines, Colt's Manufacturing, Orion Pictures, and Wheeling-Pittsburgh Steel, as well as many other firms. As in the cases of Johns-Manville, International Harvester, Macy's, and Kmart—all of which went bankrupt—a corporation can rise like a phoenix from its own ashes and live again under the same or a different name. The company may be reorganized or liquidated, depending on individual circumstances. For example, Kmart emerged from **Chapter 11** bankruptcy in 2003 with a new CEO and a plan to sell a number of its stores to Home Depot and Sears. These sales earned the company close to $1 billion. Although store sales continued to erode, Kmart had sufficient cash reserves to continue with its turnaround.[32] It used that money to acquire Sears in 2005. Unfortunately, however, fewer than 20% of firms entering **Chapter 11** bankruptcy in the United States emerge as going concerns; the rest are forced into liquidation.[33]

Few corporations will move through these five stages in order. Some corporations, for example, might never move past Stage II. Others, such as General Motors, might go directly from Stage I to Stage III. A large number of entrepreneurial ventures jump from Stage I or II directly into Stage IV or V. Hayes Microcomputer Products, for example, went from the Growth to Decline stage under its founder Dennis Hayes. The key is to be able to identify indications that a firm is in the process of changing stages and to make the appropriate strategic and structural adjustments to ensure that corporate performance is maintained or even improved.

ADVANCED TYPES OF ORGANIZATIONAL STRUCTURES

The basic structures (simple, functional, divisional, and conglomerate) are discussed in **Chapter 5** and summarized under the first three stages of corporate development in this chapter. A new strategy may require more flexible characteristics than the traditional functional or divisional structure can offer. Today's business organizations are becoming less centralized with a greater use of cross-functional work teams. **Table 9–3** depicts some of the changing structural characteristics of modern corporations. Although many variations and hybrid structures contain these characteristics, two forms stand out: the matrix structure and the network structure.

Matrix Structure

Most organizations find that organizing around either functions (in the functional structure) or products and geography (in the divisional structure) provides an appropriate organizational structure. The matrix structure, in contrast, may be very appropriate when organizations conclude that neither functional nor divisional forms, even when combined with horizontal linking mechanisms such as SBUs, are right for their situations. In **matrix structures,** functional and product forms are combined simultaneously at the same level of the organization. (See **Figure 9–2.**) Employees have two superiors, a product or project manager, and a functional manager. The "home" department—that is, engineering, manufacturing, or sales—is usually functional and is reasonably permanent. People from these functional units are often assigned temporarily to one or more product units or projects. The product units or projects are usually temporary and act like divisions in that they are differentiated on a product-market basis.

Pioneered in the aerospace industry, the matrix structure was developed to combine the stability of the functional structure with the flexibility of the product form. The matrix structure is very useful when the external environment (especially its technological and market aspects) is very complex and changeable. It does, however, produce conflicts revolving around duties, authority, and resource allocation. To the extent that the goals to be achieved are vague and the technology used is poorly understood, a continuous battle for power between product and functional managers is likely. The matrix structure is often found in an organization or SBU when the following three conditions exist:

- Ideas need to be cross-fertilized across projects or products.
- Resources are scarce.
- Abilities to process information and to make decisions need to be improved.[34]

TABLE 9–3	Old Organization Design	New Organization Design
Changing Structural Characteristics of Modern Corporations	One large corporation	Minibusiness units and cooperative relationships
	Vertical communication	Horizontal communication
	Centralized, top-down decision making	Decentralized participative decision making
	Vertical integration	Outsourcing and virtual organizations
	Work/quality teams	Autonomous work teams
	Functional work teams	Cross-functional work teams
	Minimal training	Extensive training
	Specialized job design focused on individuals	Value-chain team-focused job design

SOURCE: Reprinted from *RESEARCH IN ORGANIZATIONAL CHANGE AND DEVELOPMENT*, Vol. 7, No. 1, 1993, Macy and Izumi, "Organizational Change, Design, and Work Innovation: A Meta-Analysis of 131 North American Field Studies—1961–1991," p. 298. Copyright © 1993 with permission.

FIGURE 9–2
Matrix
and Network
Structures

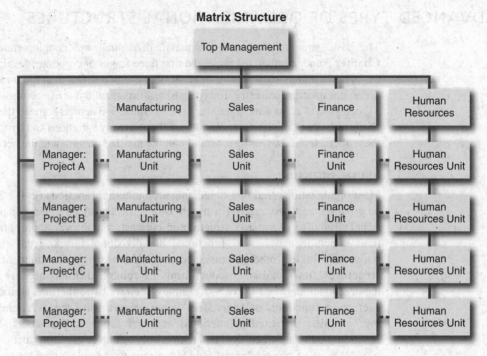

Matrix Structure

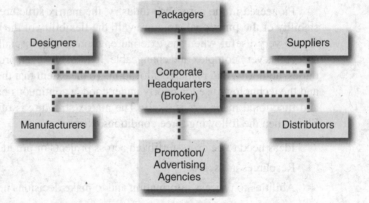

Network Structure

Davis and Lawrence, authorities on the matrix form of organization, propose that *three distinct phases* exist in the development of the matrix structure:[35]

1. **Temporary cross-functional task forces:** These are initially used when a new product line is being introduced. A project manager is in charge as the key horizontal link. J&J's experience with cross-functional teams in its drug group led it to emphasize teams crossing multiple units.

2. **Product/brand management:** If the cross-functional task forces become more permanent, the project manager becomes a product or brand manager and a second phase begins. In this arrangement, function is still the primary organizational structure, but product or brand managers act as the integrators of semi-permanent products or brands. Considered by many a key to the success of P&G, brand management has been widely imitated by other consumer products firms around the world.

3. **Mature matrix:** The third and final phase of matrix development involves a true dual-authority structure. Both the functional and product structures are permanent. All employees are connected to both a vertical functional superior and a horizontal product manager. Functional and product managers have equal authority and must work well together to resolve disagreements over resources and priorities. Boeing, Philips, and TRW Systems are example of companies that use a mature matrix.

Network Structure–The Virtual Organization

A newer and somewhat more radical organizational design, the **network structure** (see **Figure 9–2**) is an example of what could be termed a "non structure" because of its virtual elimination of in-house business functions. Many activities are outsourced. A corporation organized in this manner is often called a **virtual organization** because it is composed of a series of project groups or collaborations linked by constantly changing nonhierarchical, cobweb-like electronic networks.[36]

The network structure becomes most useful when the environment of a firm is unstable and is expected to remain so.[37] Under such conditions, there is usually a strong need for innovation and quick response. Instead of having salaried employees, the company may contract with people for a specific project or length of time. Long-term contracts with suppliers and distributors replace services that the company could provide for itself through vertical integration. Electronic markets and sophisticated information systems reduce the transaction costs of the marketplace, thus justifying a "buy" over a "make" decision. Rather than being located in a single building or area, the organization's business functions are scattered worldwide. The organization is, in effect, only a shell, with a small headquarters acting as a "broker," electronically connected to some completely owned divisions, partially owned subsidiaries, and other independent companies. In its ultimate form, a network organization is a series of independent firms or business units linked together by computers in an information system that designs, produces, and markets a product or service.[38]

Entrepreneurial ventures often start out as network organizations. For example, Randy and Nicole Wilburn of Dorchester, Massachusetts, run real estate, consulting, design, and baby food companies out of their home. Nicole, a stay-at-home mom and graphic designer, farms out design work to freelancers and cooks her own line of organic baby food. For $300, an Indian artist designed the logo for Nicole's "Baby Fresh Organic Baby Foods." A London freelancer wrote promotional materials. Instead of hiring a secretary, Randy hired "virtual assistants" in Jerusalem to transcribe voice mail, update his Web site, and design PowerPoint graphics. Retired brokers in Virginia and Michigan deal with his real estate paperwork.[39]

Large companies such as Nike, Reebok, and Benetton use the network structure in their operations function by subcontracting (outsourcing) manufacturing to other companies in low-cost locations around the world. For control purposes, the Italian-based Benetton maintains what it calls an "umbilical cord" by assuring production planning for all its subcontractors, planning materials requirements for them, and providing them with bills of labor and standard prices and costs, as well as technical assistance to make sure their quality is up to Benetton's standards.

The network organizational structure provides an organization with increased flexibility and adaptability to cope with rapid technological change and shifting patterns of international trade and competition. It allows a company to concentrate on its distinctive competencies, while gathering efficiencies from other firms that are concentrating their efforts in their areas of expertise. The network does, however, have disadvantages. Some believe that the network is really only a transitional structure because it is inherently unstable and subject to tensions.[40] The availability of numerous potential partners can be a source of trouble. Contracting out individual activities to separate suppliers/distributors may keep the firm from discovering any internal synergies by combining these activities. If a particular firm overspecializes on only a few functions, it runs the risk of choosing the wrong functions and thus becoming noncompetitive.

Cellular/Modular Organization: A New Type of Structure?

Some authorities in the field propose that the evolution of organizational forms is leading from the matrix and the network to the cellular (also called modular) organizational form. According to Miles and Snow et al., "a **cellular organization** is composed of cells (self-managing teams, autonomous business units, etc.) which can operate alone but which can interact with other cells to produce a more potent and competent business mechanism." This combination of independence and interdependence allows the cellular/modular organizational form to generate and share the knowledge and expertise needed to produce continuous innovation. The cellular/modular form includes the dispersed entrepreneurship of the divisional structure, customer responsiveness of the matrix, and self-organizing knowledge and asset sharing of the network.[41] Bombardier, for example, broke up the design of its Continental business jet into 12 parts provided by internal divisions and external contractors. The cockpit, center, and forward fuselage were produced in-house, but other major parts were supplied by manufacturers spread around the globe. The cellular/modular structure is used when it is possible to break up a company's products into self-contained modules or cells and where interfaces can be specified such that the cells/modules work when they are joined together.[42] The cellular/modular structure is similar to a current trend in industry of using internal joint ventures to temporarily combine specialized expertise and skills within a corporation to accomplish a task which individual units alone could not accomplish.[43]

The impetus for such a new structure is the pressure for a continuous process of innovation in all industries. Each cell/module has an entrepreneurial responsibility to the larger organization. Beyond knowledge creation and sharing, the cellular/modular form adds value by keeping the firm's total knowledge assets more fully in use than any other type of structure.[44] It is beginning to appear in firms that are focused on rapid product and service innovation—providing unique or state-of-the-art offerings in industries such as automobile manufacture, bicycle production, consumer electronics, household appliances, power tools, computing products, and software.[45]

REENGINEERING AND STRATEGY IMPLEMENTATION

Reengineering is the radical redesign of business processes to achieve major gains in cost, service, or time. It is not in itself a type of structure, but it is an effective program to implement a turnaround strategy.

Business process reengineering strives to break away from the old rules and procedures that develop and become ingrained in every organization over the years. They may be a combination of policies, rules, and procedures that have never been seriously questioned because they were established years earlier. These may range from "Credit decisions are made by the credit department" to "Local inventory is needed for good customer service." These rules of organization and work design may have been based on assumptions about technology, people, and organizational goals that may no longer be relevant. Rather than attempting to fix existing problems through minor adjustments and fine-tuning of existing processes, the key to reengineering is asking "If this were a new company, how would we run this place?"

Michael Hammer, who popularized the concept of reengineering, suggests the following principles for reengineering:

- **Organize around outcomes, not tasks:** Design a person's or a department's job around an objective or outcome instead of a single task or series of tasks.

- **Have those who use the output of the process perform the process:** With computer-based information systems, processes can now be reengineered so that the people who need the result of the process can do it themselves.

- **Subsume information-processing work into the real work that produces the information:** People or departments that produce information can also process it for use instead of just sending raw data to others in the organization to interpret.

- **Treat geographically dispersed resources as though they were centralized:** With modern information systems, companies can provide flexible service locally while keeping the actual resources in a centralized location for coordination purposes.

- **Link parallel activities instead of integrating their results:** Instead of having separate units perform different activities that must eventually come together, have them communicate while they work so that they can do the integrating.

- **Put the decision point where the work is performed and build control into the process:** The people who do the work should make the decisions and be self-controlling.

- **Capture information once and at the source:** Instead of having each unit develop its own database and information processing activities, the information can be put on a network so that all can access it.

Studies of the performance of reengineering programs show mixed results. Several companies have had success with business process reengineering. For example, Mahindra and Mahindra (M&M) farm equipment sector (as it is called since organizational restructuring in 1994) is the largest manufacturer of tractors in India with sustained leadership of over 19 years. Attaining and maintaining this leadership has required commitment and relentless pursuit of quality. In very initial years of its business, the shop floor simply fitted out various parts of the tractor. The quality of the product was only at the final stage, i.e., at the factory level or customer level. If the product showed any flaws, it was sent back to the shop floor. This led to wastage in terms of both time and resources and had no sustained quality improvement. This prompted the management to reengineer the production process. The company concentrated on improving the manufacturing quality through process control and components quality. It aimed at reducing cost of poor quality (COPQ) by solving chronic cross-functional quality problems and by standardization of operations.

The benefits of process reengineering were reduction in rework and rejections at suppliers' end as well as at receipt stage at M&M. It also led to decrease in number of consumer complaints during the first 250/500/1000/2000 hours of tractor operation.[46]

One study of North American financial firms found that "the average reengineering project took 15 months, consumed 66 person-months of effort, and delivered cost savings of 24%."[47] In a survey of 782 corporations using reengineering, 75% of the executives said their companies had succeeded in reducing operating expenses and increasing productivity.[48] A study of 134 large and small Canadian companies found that reengineering programs resulted in (1) an increase in productivity and product quality, (2) cost reductions, and (3) an increase in overall organizational quality, for both large and small firms.[49] Other studies report, however, that anywhere from 50% to 70% of reengineering programs fail to achieve their objectives.[50] Reengineering thus appears to be more useful for redesigning specific processes like order entry, than for changing an entire organization.[51]

SIX SIGMA

Originally conceived by Motorola as a quality improvement program in the mid-1980s, Six Sigma has become a cost-saving program for all types of manufacturers. Briefly, **Six Sigma** is an analytical method for achieving near-perfect results on a production line. Although the emphasis is on reducing product variance in order to boost quality and efficiency, it is increasingly being applied to accounts receivable, sales, and R&D. In statistics, the Greek letter *sigma* denotes variation in the standard bell-shaped curve. One sigma equals 690,000 defects per 1 million. Most companies are able to achieve only three sigma, or 66,000 errors per million. Six Sigma reduces the defects to only 3.4 per million—thus saving money by preventing waste. The process of Six Sigma encompasses five steps.

1. *Define* a process where results are poorer than average.
2. *Measure* the process to determine exact current performance.
3. *Analyze* the information to pinpoint where things are going wrong.
4. *Improve* the process and eliminate the error.
5. *Establish* controls to prevent future defects from occurring.[52]

Savings attributed to Six Sigma programs have ranged from 1.2% to 4.5% of annual revenue for a number of Fortune 500 firms. For example, Dr. Reddy's has implemented Six Sigma successfully. Founded in 1984, Dr. Reddy's is one of the largest companies in India, with presence in more than 50 countries.[53] Dr. Reddy's, has in the past streamlined its new product development process, by adopting Six Sigma, so as to help the business in managing large portfolio projects. It also helped Dr. Reddy's remote research teams to collaborate. This helped the management in faster decision making and decrease in response time to enable better risk management.[54] Another company that pioneers in Six Sigma is WIPRO Corp. Six Sigma was adopted in WIPRO Corp. with the help from personnel from Motorola University in Chicago.[55] Within 15 months of implementation, WIPRO Corp. reported elimination of unnecessary steps and decreased rework, leading to a gain of eight times the initial investment. Today, Six Sigma is an umbrella initiative covering all business units and divisions resulting in the overall productivity and reduction in cycle time.[56] Other companies include Maruti Udyog Limited (MUL), Satyam, Reliance, HBL, etc. About 35% of U.S. companies now have a Six Sigma program in place.[57] At Dow Chemical, each Six Sigma project has resulted in cost savings of $500,000 in the first year. According to Jack Welch, GE's past CEO, Six Sigma is an appropriate change program for the entire organization.[58] Six Sigma experts at 3M have been able to speed up R&D and analyze why its top sales people sold more than others. A disadvantage of the program is that training costs in the beginning may outweigh any savings. The expense of compiling and analyzing data, especially in areas where a process cannot be easily standardized, may exceed what is saved.[59] Another disadvantage is that Six Sigma can lead to less-risky incremental innovation based on previous work than on riskier "blue-sky" projects.[60]

A new program called *Lean Six Sigma* is becoming increasingly popular in companies. This program incorporates the statistical approach of Six Sigma with the lean manufacturing program originally developed by Toyota. Like reengineering, it includes the removal of unnecessary steps in any process and fixing those that remain. This is the "lean" addition to Six Sigma. Xerox used Lean Six Sigma to resolve a problem with a $500,000 printing press it had just introduced. Teams from supply, manufacturing, and R&D used Lean Six Sigma to find the cause of the problem and to resolve it by working with a supplier to change the chemistry of the oil on a roller.[61]

DESIGNING JOBS TO IMPLEMENT STRATEGY

Organizing a company's activities and people to implement strategy involves more than simply redesigning a corporation's overall structure; it also involves redesigning the way jobs are done. With the increasing emphasis on reengineering, many companies are beginning to rethink their work processes with an eye toward phasing unnecessary people and activities out of the process. Process steps that have traditionally been performed sequentially can be improved by performing them concurrently using cross-functional work teams. Harley-Davidson, for example, has managed to reduce total plant employment by 25%

while reducing by 50% the time needed to build a motorcycle. Restructuring through needing fewer people requires broadening the scope of jobs and encouraging teamwork. The design of jobs and subsequent job performance are, therefore, increasingly being considered as sources of competitive advantage.

Job design refers to the study of individual tasks in an attempt to make them more relevant to the company and to the employee(s). To minimize some of the adverse consequences of task specialization, corporations have turned to new job design techniques: *job enlargement* (combining tasks to give a worker more of the same type of duties to perform), *job rotation* (moving workers through several jobs to increase variety), and *job enrichment* (altering the jobs by giving the worker more autonomy and control over activities). The *job characteristics model* is a good example of job enrichment. (See **Strategy Highlight 9.4**.) Although each of these methods has its adherents, no one method seems to work in all situations.

A good example of modern job design is the introduction of team-based production by the glass manufacturer Corning Inc. in its Blacksburg, Virginia, plant. With union approval, Corning reduced job classifications from 47 to 4 to enable production workers to rotate jobs after learning new skills. The workers were divided into 14-member teams that, in effect, managed themselves. The plant had only two levels of management: Plant Manager Robert Hoover and two line leaders who only advised the teams. Employees worked demanding 12 ½-hour shifts, alternating three-day and four-day weeks. The teams made managerial decisions, imposed discipline on fellow workers, and were required to learn three "skill modules" within two years or else lose their jobs. As a result of this new job design, a Blacksburg team, made up of workers with interchangeable skills, can retool a line to produce a different type of filter in only 10 minutes—six times faster than workers in a traditionally designed filter plant. The Blacksburg plant earned a $2 million profit in its first eight months of production instead of losing the $2.3 million projected for the startup period. The plant performed so well that Corning's top management acted to convert the company's 27 other factories to team-based production.[62]

STRATEGY highlight 9.4

DESIGNING JOBS WITH THE JOB CHARACTERISTICS MODEL

The job characteristics model is an advanced approach to job design based on the belief that tasks can be described in terms of certain objective characteristics and that these characteristics affect employee motivation. In order for a job to be motivating, (1) the worker needs to feel a sense of responsibility, feel the task to be meaningful, and receive useful feedback on his or her performance, and (2) the job has to satisfy needs that are important to the worker. The model proposes that managers follow five principles for redesigning work:

1. Combine tasks to increase task variety and to enable workers to identify with what they are doing.

2. Form natural work units to make a worker more responsible and accountable for the performance of the job.

3. Establish client relationships so the worker will know what performance is required and why.

4. Vertically load the job by giving workers increased authority and responsibility over their activities.

5. Open feedback channels by providing workers with information on how they are performing.

Research supports the job characteristics model as a way to improve job performance through job enrichment. Although there are several other approaches to job design, practicing managers seem increasingly to follow the prescriptions of this model as a way of improving productivity and product quality.

SOURCE: J. R. Hackman and G. R. Oldham, *Work Redesign* (Reading, MA: Addison-Wesley, 1980), pp. 135–141; G. Johns, J. L. Xie, and Y. Fang, "Mediating and Moderating Effects in Job Design," *Journal of Management* (December 1992), pp. 657–676; R. W. Griffin, "Effects of Work Redesign on Employee Perceptions, Attitudes, and Behaviors: A Long-Term Investigation," *Academy of Management Journal* (June 1991), pp. 425–435.

9.5 International Issues in Strategy Implementation

An international company is one that engages in any combination of activities, from exporting/importing to full-scale manufacturing, in foreign countries. A **multinational corporation (MNC)**, in contrast, is a highly developed international company with a deep involvement throughout the world, plus a worldwide perspective in its management and decision making. For an MNC to be considered global, it must manage its worldwide operations as if they were totally interconnected. This approach works best when the industry has moved from being *multidomestic* (each country's industry is essentially separate from the same industry in other countries) to *global* (each country is a part of one worldwide industry).

The global MNC faces the dual challenge of achieving scale economies through standardization while at the same time responding to local customer differences. According to Spulber in his book, *Global Competitive Strategy*, the forces pushing for *standardization* are:

■ Convergence in customer preferences and income across target countries.

■ Competition from successful global products.

■ Growing customer awareness of international brands.

■ Economies of scale.

■ Falling trading costs across countries.

■ Cultural exchange and business interactions among countries.

The forces pushing for *customization* to local markets are:

■ Persistent differences in customer preferences.

■ Persistent differences in customer incomes.

■ The need to build local brand reputation.

■ Competition from successful, innovative domestic companies.

■ Variations in trading costs across countries.

■ Local regulatory requirements.[63]

The design of an organization's structure is strongly affected by the company's stage of development in international activities and the types of industries in which the company is involved. Strategic alliances may complement or even substitute for an internal functional activity. The issue of centralization versus decentralization becomes especially important for an MNC operating in both multidomestic and global industries.

INTERNATIONAL STRATEGIC ALLIANCES

Strategic alliances, such as joint ventures and licensing agreements, between an MNC and a local partner in a host country are becoming increasingly popular as a means by which a corporation can gain entry into other countries, especially less developed countries. The key to the successful implementation of these strategies is the selection of the local partner. Each party needs to assess not only the strategic fit of each company's project strategy but also the fit of each company's respective resources. A successful joint venture may require as much as two years of prior contacts between the parties. A prior relationship helps to develop a level of trust, which facilitates openness in sharing knowledge and a reduced fear of opportunistic behavior by the alliance partners. This is especially important when the environmental uncertainty is high.[64] Research reveals that firms favor past partners when forming new alliances.[65] Key drivers for strategic fit between alliance partners are the following:

- Partners must agree on fundamental values and have a shared vision about the potential for joint value creation.
- Alliance strategy must be derived from business, corporate, and functional strategy.
- The alliance must be important to both partners, especially to top management.
- Partners must be mutually dependent for achieving clear and realistic objectives.
- Joint activities must have added value for customers and the partners.
- The alliance must be accepted by key stakeholders.
- Partners contribute key strengths but protect core competencies.[66]

STAGES OF INTERNATIONAL DEVELOPMENT

Corporations operating internationally tend to evolve through five common stages, both in their relationships with widely dispersed geographic markets and in the manner in which they structure their operations and programs. These **stages of international development** are:

- **Stage 1 (Domestic company):** The primarily domestic company exports some of its products through local dealers and distributors in the foreign countries. The impact on the organization's structure is minimal because an export department at corporate headquarters handles everything.

- **Stage 2 (Domestic company with export division):** Success in Stage 1 leads the company to establish its own sales company with offices in other countries to eliminate the middlemen and to better control marketing. Because exports have now become more important, the company establishes an export division to oversee foreign sales offices.

- **Stage 3 (Primarily domestic company with international division):** Success in earlier stages leads the company to establish manufacturing facilities in addition to sales and service offices in key countries. The company now adds an international division with responsibilities for most of the business functions conducted in other countries.

- **Stage 4 (Multinational corporation with multidomestic emphasis):** Now a full-fledged MNC, the company increases its investments in other countries. The company establishes a local operating division or company in the host country, such as Ford of Britain, to better serve the market. The product line is expanded, and local manufacturing capacity is established. Managerial functions (product development, finance, marketing, and so on) are organized locally. Over time, the parent company acquires other related businesses, broadening the base of the local operating division. As the subsidiary in the host country successfully develops a strong regional presence, it achieves greater autonomy and self-sufficiency. The operations in each country are, nevertheless, managed separately as if each is a domestic company.

- **Stage 5 (MNC with global emphasis):** The most successful MNCs move into a fifth stage in which they have worldwide human resources, R&D, and financing strategies. Typically operating in a global industry, the MNC denationalizes its operations and plans product design, manufacturing, and marketing around worldwide considerations. Global considerations now dominate organizational design. The global MNC structures itself in a matrix form around some combination of geographic areas, product lines, and functions. All managers are responsible for dealing with international as well as domestic issues.

Research provides some support for stages of international development, but it does not necessarily support the preceding sequence of stages. For example, a company may initiate

GLOBAL issue

MULTIPLE HEADQUARTERS: A SIXTH STAGE OF INTERNATIONAL DEVELOPMENT?

In what could be a sixth stage of international development, an increasing number of MNCs are relocating their headquarters and headquarters functions at multiple locations around the world. Of the 800 corporate headquarters established in 2002, 200 of them were in developing nations. The antivirus software company Trend Micro, for example, spreads its top executives, engineers, and support staff throughout the world to improve its ability to respond to new virus threats. "With the Internet, viruses became global. To fight them, we had to become a global company," explained Chairman Steve Chang. Trend Micro's financial headquarters is in Tokyo, where it went public. Its product development is in Taiwan, and its sales headquarters is in America's Silicon Valley.

C. K. Prahalad, strategy professor at the University of Michigan, proposes that this is a new stage of international development. "There is a fundamental rethinking about what is a multinational company. Does it have a home country? What does headquarters mean? Can you fragment your corporate functions globally?" Corporate headquarters are now becoming virtual with executives and core corporate functions dispersed throughout various world regions. These primarily technology companies are using geography to obtain competitive advantage through the availability of talent or capital, low costs, or proximity to most important customers. Logitech, for example, has its manufacturing headquarters in Taiwan to capitalize on low-cost Asian manufacturing, its business-development headquarters in Switzerland where it has a series of strategic technology partnerships, and a third headquarters in Fremont, California.

SOURCES: S. Hamm, "Borders Are So 20th Century," *Business Week* (January 22, 2003), pp. 68–70; "Globalization from the Top Down," *Futurist* (November–December 2003), p. 13.

---

production and sales in multiple countries without having gone through the steps of exporting or having local sales subsidiaries. In addition, any one corporation can be at different stages simultaneously, with different products in different markets at different levels. Firms may also leapfrog across stages to a global emphasis. In addition, most firms that are considered to be stage 5 global MNCs are actually regional. Around 88% of the world's biggest MNCs derive at least half of their sales from their home regions. Just 2% (a total of nine firms) derive 20% or more of their sales from each of the North American, European, and Asian regions.[67]

Developments in information technology are changing the way business is being done internationally. See the **Global Issue** feature for a possible sixth stage of international development, in which an MNC locates its headquarters and key functions at multiple locations around the world.[68] Nevertheless, the stages concept provides a useful way to illustrate some of the structural changes corporations undergo when they increase their involvement in international activities.

CENTRALIZATION VERSUS DECENTRALIZATION

A basic dilemma an MNC faces is how to organize authority centrally so that it operates as a vast interlocking system that achieves synergy and at the same time decentralize authority so that local managers can make the decisions necessary to meet the demands of the local market or host government.[69] To deal with this problem, MNCs tend to structure themselves either along product groups or geographic areas. They may even combine both in a matrix structure—the design chosen by 3M Corporation, Philips, and Asea Brown Boveri (ABB), among others.[70] One side of 3M's matrix represents the company's product divisions; the other side includes the company's international country and regional subsidiaries.

Two examples of the usual international structure are Nestlé and American Cyanamid. Nestlé's structure is one in which significant power and authority have been decentralized to geographic entities. This structure is similar to that depicted in **Figure 9–3,** in which each

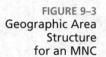

FIGURE 9–3
Geographic Area
Structure
for an MNC

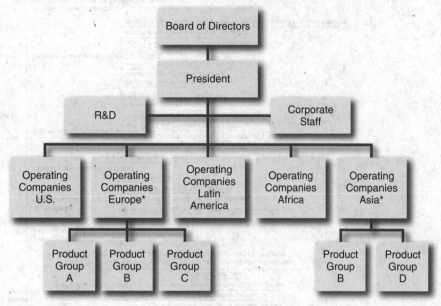

*NOTE: Because of space limitations, product groups for only Europe and Asia are shown here.

geographic set of operating companies has a different group of products. In contrast, American Cyanamid has a series of centralized product groups with worldwide responsibilities. To depict Cyanamid's structure, the geographical entities in **Figure 9–3** would have to be replaced by product groups or SBUs.

The **product-group structure** of American Cyanamid enables the company to introduce and manage a similar line of products around the world. This enables the corporation to centralize decision making along product lines and to reduce costs. The **geographic-area structure** of Nestlé, in contrast, allows the company to tailor products to regional differences and to achieve regional coordination. For instance, Nestlé markets 200 different varieties of its instant coffee, Nescafé. The geographic-area structure decentralizes decision making to the local subsidiaries.

As industries move from being multidomestic to more globally integrated, MNCs are increasingly switching from the geographic-area to the product-group structure. Nestlé, for example, has found that its decentralized area structure had become increasingly inefficient. As a result, operating margins at Nestlé have trailed those at rivals Unilever, Group Danone, and Kraft Foods by as much as 50%. CEO Peter Brabeck-Letmathe acted to eliminate country-by-country responsibilities for many functions. In one instance, he established five centers worldwide to handle most coffee and cocoa purchasing. Nevertheless, Nestlé is still using three different versions of accounting, planning, and inventory software for each of its main regions—Europe, the Americas, and Asia, Oceania, and Africa.[71]

Simultaneous pressures for decentralization to be locally responsive and centralization to be maximally efficient are causing interesting structural adjustments in most large corporations. This is what is meant by the phrase "think globally, act locally." Companies are attempting to decentralize those operations that are culturally oriented and closest to the customers—manufacturing, marketing, and human resources. At the same time, the companies are consolidating less visible internal functions, such as research and development, finance, and information systems, where there can be significant economies of scale.

Let's Summarize the Chapter with a Mind Map

Strategy Implementation: Organizing for Action

International Issues in Strategy Implementation

Scale of Economies VS Standardization and Customization Trade off

Forces for Standardization
- Convergence of customer preferences and income across target countries
- competition from sucessful global products
- growing customer awareness of international brands
- economies of scale
- falling trading costs across countries
- cultural exchange and business interaction among countries

Forces for Customization
- differences in customer preferences
- differences in customer incomes
- the need to build local brand reputation
- competition from local brand reputation
- competition from successful, innovative domestic companies
- varlations in trading costs across countries
- legal regulatory requirements

International Strategic Alliances

Stages of International Development
- domestic company
- domestic company with export division
- primarily domestic company with international division
- multinational corporation with multidomestic emphasis
- MNC with global emphasis

Centralization vs Decentralization

How Strategy is to be Implemented

Structure Follows Strategy

structural changes occur because the old structure, having been pushed too far, has caused inefficiencies that have become too obviously detrimental to bear.

Chandler says that in an organization sequence of change is
- new strategy is created
- new administrative promblems emerge
- economic performance declines
- new appropriate structure is invented
- profit returns to its previous levels

Stages of Corporate Development

STAGE I: simple structure
- typified by entrepreneur, who founds a company to promote an idea.

STAGE II: functional structure
- is the point where the entrepreneur is replaced by a team of managers who have functional specialization

STAGE III: divisional structure
- is typified by the corporations managing diverse product lines in numerous industries, it decentralizes the decision making authority.

matrix structure
- appropriate when neither divisional nor functional structure works for the organization.
- functional and product forms are combined simultaneously at the same level of the organization.

networking structure
- kind of nonstructure
- there is virtual elimination of in house functions
- radical organizational design
- many activities are outsourced
- organized series of project groups or collaborations linked by constantly changing nonhierarchical cobweb like electronic networks.

cellular modular organizations
- is composed of cells which can operate alone and interact with other cells to produce a more potent and competent business medium.

STAGE IV: beyond SBUs
- these structures emphasize collaboration over competition in the managing of an organization's multiple overlapping projects and developing buisnesses.

Blocks for Changing Stages in Terms of Entrepreneurs' Attitude.
- loyalty to comrades
- task oriented
- single mindedness
- working in isolation

Organizational Life Cycle.
- describe how organizations grow, develop and eventually decline.
- 5 stages
  - birth
  - growth
  - maturlty
  - decline
  - death

Reengineering and Strategy Implementation
- reengineering is radical redesign of buisness processes to achieve major gains in cost service or time.

principles of reengineering
- organize around outcomes and not tasks
- have those who use the output of the process perform the process
- information processing work into the real work that produces the information
- treat geographically dispersed resources as though they were centralized
- link parallel activities instead of integrating their results
- put the decision point where the work is performed and build control into the process
- capture information once at the source

Six Sigma
- concieved by Motorola
- is an analytical method for achieving near perfect results on the production lines

Designing Jobs to Implement Strategy

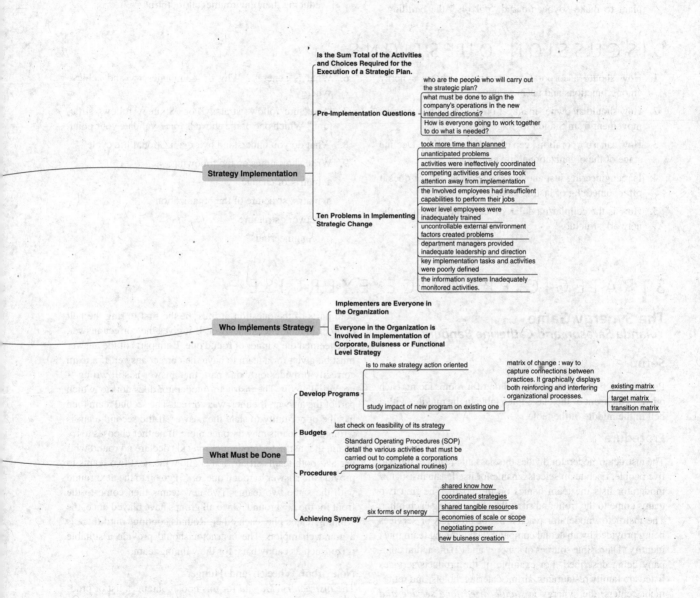

Strategy Implementation

Is the Sum Total of the Activities and Choices Required for the Execution of a Strategic Plan.

Pre-Implementation Questions
- who are the people who will carry out the strategic plan?
- what must be done to align the company's operations in the new intended directions?
- How is everyone going to work together to do what is needed?

Ten Problems in Implementing Strategic Change
- took more time than planned
- unanticipated problems
- activities were ineffectively coordinated
- competing activities and crises took attention away from implementation
- the Involved employees had insufficient capabilities to perform their jobs
- lower level employees were inadequately trained
- uncontrollable external environment factors created problems
- department managers provided inadequate leadership and direction
- key implementation tasks and activities were poorly defined
- the information system Inadequately monitored activities.

Who Implements Strategy

Implementers are Everyone in the Organization

Everyone in the Organization is Involved in Implementation of Corporate, Buisness or Functional Level Strategy

What Must be Done

Develop Programs
- is to make strategy action oriented
- study impact of new program on existing one
  - matrix of change : way to capture connections between practices. It graphically displays both reinforcing and interfering organizational processes.
    - existing matrix
    - target matrix
    - transition matrix

Budgets
- last check on feasibility of its strategy

Procedures
- Standard Operating Procedures (SOP) detail the various activities that must be carried out to complete a corporations programs (organizational routines)

Achieving Synergy
- six forms of synergy
  - shared know how
  - coordinated strategies
  - shared tangible resources
  - economies of scale or scope
  - negotiating power
  - new buisness creation

ECO-BITS

- Only 5% of the 30 million tons of annual plastic waste in the U.S. is currently being recycled.[72]
- Cargill is building the first large-scale manufacturing plant to make soybean-based "polyols," the building blocks of polyurethane. The company says that the use of polyols is a more sustainable option for manufacturers of plastic and ultimately for consumers interested in reducing their environmental footprint.[73]

DISCUSSION QUESTIONS

1. How should a corporation attempt to achieve synergy among functions and business units?

2. How should an owner-manager prepare a company for its movement from Stage I to Stage II?

3. How can a corporation keep from sliding into the Decline stage of the organizational life cycle?

4. Is reengineering just another management fad, or does it offer something of lasting value?

5. How is the cellular/modular structure different from the network structure?

6. What is synergy? Why do companies try and achieve synergy?

7. "Structure follows strategy" or "Strategy follows structure." Which one of the above is true? Validate your point.

8. What do you understand by organizational life cycle?

9. Write short notes on the following:

   a. matrix of change

   b. matrix structure of the organization

   c. network structure

   d. reengineering.

STRATEGIC PRACTICE EXERCISE

The Synergy Game
Yolanda Sarason and Catherine Banbury

Setup

Put three to five chairs on either side of a room, facing each other, in the front of the class. Put a table in the middle, with a bell in the middle of the table.

Procedure

The instructor/moderator divides the class into teams of three to five people. Each team selects a name for itself. The instructor/moderator lists the team names on the board. The first two teams come to the front and sit in the chairs facing each other. The instructor/moderator reads a list of products or services being provided by an actual company. The winning team must identify (1) possible sources of synergy and (2) the actual company being described. For example, if the products/services listed are family restaurants, airline catering, hotels, and retirement centers, the synergy is **standardized food service and hospitality settings** and the company is **The Marriott Corporation**. The first team to successfully name the company *and* the synergy wins the round.

After one practice session, the game begins. Each of the teams is free to discuss the question with other team members. When one of the two teams thinks that it has the answer to both parts of the question, it must be the first to ring the bell in order to announce its answer. If it gives the correct answer, it is deemed the winner of round one. Both parts of the answer must be given for a team to have the correct answer. If a team correctly provides only one part, that answer is still wrong—no partial credit. The instructor/moderator does not say which part of the answer, if either, was correct. The second team then has the opportunity to state the answer. If the second team is wrong, both teams may try once more. If neither chooses to try again, the instructor/moderator may (1) declare no round winner and both teams sit down, (2) allow the next two teams to provide the answer to round one, or (3) go on to the next round with the same two teams. Two new teams then come to the front for the next round. Once all groups have played once, the winning teams play each other. Rounds continue until there is a grand champion. The instructor should provide a suitable prize, such as candy bars, for the winning team.

Note from Wheelen and Hunger

The *Instructors' Manual* for this book contains a list of products and services with their synergy and the name of the company. In case your instructor does not use this exercise, try the following examples:

Example 1: Motorcycles, autos, lawn mowers, generators

Example 2: Athletic footwear, Rockport shoes, Greg Norman clothing, sportswear

For each example, did you guess the company providing these products/services and the synergy obtained? The answers are printed here, upside-down:

Example 1: Engine technology by Honda

Example 2: Marketing and distribution for the athletically-oriented by Reebok

SOURCE: This exercise was developed by Professors Yolanda Sarason of Colorado State University and Catherine Banbury of St. Mary's College and Purdue University and presented at the Organizational Behavior Teaching Conference, June 1999. Copyright © 1999 by Yolanda Sarason and Catherine Banbury. Adapted with permission.

KEY TERMS

budget (p. 317)

cellular organization (p. 330)

geographic-area structure (p. 337)

job design (p. 333)

matrix of change (p. 314)

matrix structure (p. 327)

multinational corporation (MNC) (p. 334)

network structure (p. 329)

organizational life cycle (p. 325)

procedure (p. 317)

product-group structure (p. 337)

program (p. 314)

reengineering (p. 330)

Six Sigma (p. 331)

stages of corporate development (p. 322)

stages of international development (p. 335)

strategy implementation (p. 312)

structure follows strategy (p. 321)

synergy (p. 319)

virtual organization (p. 329)

NOTES

1. ITP Division, Ministry of External Affairs, Government of India, Industry & Services: Retailing, recovered on 2nd Nov 2011, from http://www.indiainbusiness.nic.in/industry-infra-structure/service-sectors/retailing.htm

2. Pantaloons Retail, recovered on 2nd Nov 2011, from http://www.retail.in/about-us/overview-retail.html

3. M. Nivedita, "Big Bazaar Sees No Growth Problem, Upbeat on Demand," posted on March 5, 2011, 0:54 IST, New Delhi, recovered on 2nd Nov 2011, from http://www.business-standard.com/india/news/big-bazaar-sees-no-growth-problem-upbeatdemand/427366/

4. J. W. Gadella, "Avoiding Expensive Mistakes in Capital Investment," Long Range Planning (April 1994), pp. 103–110; B. Voss, "World Market Is Not for Everyone," Journal of Business Strategy (July/August 1993), p. 4.

5. A. Bert, T. MacDonald, and T. Herd, "Two Merger Integration Imperatives: Urgency and Execution," Strategy & Leadership, Vol. 31, No. 3 (2003), pp. 42–49.

6. L. D. Alexander, "Strategy Implementation: Nature of the Problem," International Review of Strategic Management, Vol. 2, No. 1, edited by D. E. Hussey (New York: John Wiley & Sons, 1991), pp. 73–113. See also L. G. Hrebiniak, "Obstacles to Effective Strategy Implementation," Organizational Dynamics, Vol. 35, Issue 1 (2006), pp. 12–31 for six obstacles to implementation.

7. L. G. Hrebiniak (2006).

8. S. Manisha, K. Pandla, and P. Gupta, "Six Sigma at Wipro Technologies: Thrust on Quality," recovered on 2nd Nov 2011, from http://www.iitk.ac.in/infocell/announce/convention/papers/Changing%20Playfield-04-Manisha%20Sharma,%20Kapil%20Pandla,%20Prasanth%20Gupta.pdf

9. J. Darragh and A. Campbell, "Why Corporate Initiatives Get Stuck?" Long Range Planning (February 2001), pp. 33–52.

10. E. Brynjolfsson, A. A. Renshaw, and M. Van Alstyne, "The Matrix of Change," Sloan Management Review (Winter 1997), pp. 37–54.

11. "Cocoa Farming: Fair Enough?" The Economist (February 2, 2008), p. 74.

12. M. S. Feldman and B. T. Pentland, "Reconceptualizing Organizational Routines as a Source of Flexibility and Change," Administrative Science Quarterly (March 2003), pp. 94–118.

13. S. F. Slater and E. M. Olson, "Strategy Type and Performance: The Influence of Sales Force Management," Strategic Management Journal (August 2000), pp. 813–829.

14. B. Grow, "Thinking Outside the Box," Business Week (October 25, 2004), pp. 70–72.

15. M. Goold and A. Campbell, "Desperately Seeking Synergy," Harvard Business Review (September–October 1998), pp. 131–143.

16. A. D. Chandler, Strategy and Structure (Cambridge, MA: MIT Press, 1962).

17. A. P. Sloan, Jr., My Years with General Motors (Garden City, NY: Doubleday, 1964).

18. T. L. Amburgey and T. Dacin, "As the Left Foot Follows the Right? The Dynamics of Strategic and Structural Change," Academy of Management Journal (December 1994), pp. 1427–1452; M. Ollinger, "The Limits of Growth of the Multidivisional Firm: A Case Study of the U.S. Oil Industry from 1930–90," Strategic Management Journal (September 1994), pp. 503–520.

19. D. F. Jennings and S. L. Seaman, "High and Low Levels of Organizational Adaptation: An Empirical Analysis of Strategy, Structure, and Performance," Strategic Management Journal (July 1994), pp. 459–475; L. Donaldson, "The Normal Science of Structured Contingency Theory," in Handbook of Organization Studies, edited by S. R. Clegg, C. Hardy, and W. R. Nord (London: Sage Publications, 1996), pp. 57–76.

20. A. K. Gupta, "SBU Strategies, Corporate-SBU Relations, and SBU Effectiveness in Strategy Implementation," Academy of Management Journal (September 1987), pp. 477–500.

21. L. E. Greiner, "Evolution and Revolution As Organizations Grow," Harvard Business Review (May–June 1998), pp. 55–67. This is an updated version of Greiner's classic 1972 article.

22. K. Shimizu and M. A. Hitt, "What Constrains or Facilitates Divestitures of Formerly Acquired Firms? The Effects of Organizational Inertia," *Journal of Management* (February 2005), pp. 50–72.

23. A. Weintraub, "Can Pfizer Prime the Pipeline?" *Business Week* (December 31, 2007), pp. 90–91.

24. Ibid, p. 64. Although Greiner simply labeled this as the *"?" crisis*, the term *pressure-cooker* seems apt.

25. J. Hamm, "Why Entrepreneurs Don't Scale," *Harvard Business Review* (December 2002), pp. 110–115. See also C. B. Gibson and R. M. Rottner, "The Social Foundations for Building a Company Around an Inventor," *Organizational Dynamics*, Vol. 37, Issue 1 (January–March 2008), pp. 21–34.

26. W. P. Barnett, "The Dynamics of Competitive Intensity," *Administrative Science Quarterly* (March 1997), pp. 128–160; D. Miller, *The Icarus Paradox: How Exceptional Companies Bring About Their Own Downfall* (New York: Harper Business, 1990).

27. D. Miller and P. H. Friesen, "A Longitudinal Study of the Corporate Life Cycle," *Management Science* (October 1984), pp. 1161–1183.

28. J. L. Morrow, Jr., D. G. Sirmon, M. A. Hitt, and T. R. Holcomb, "Creating Value in the Face of Declining Performance: Firm Strategies and Organizational Recovery," *Strategic Management Journal* (March 2007), pp. 271–283; C. Zook, "Finding Your Next Core Business," *Harvard Business Review* (April 2007), pp. 66–75.

29. J. P. Sheppard and S. D. Chowdhury, "Riding the Wrong Wave: Organizational Failure as a Failed Turnaround," *Long Range Planning* (June 2005), pp. 239–260.

30. W-R. Chen and K. D. Miller, "Situational and Institutional Determinants of Firms' R&D Search Intensity," *Strategic Management Journal* (April 2007), pp. 369–381.

31. S. Hamm, "Kodak's Moment of Truth," *Business Week* (February 19, 2007), pp. 42–49.

32. R. Berner, "Turning Kmart into a Cash Cow," *Business Week* (July 12, 2004), p. 81.

33. H. Tavakolian, "Bankruptcy: An Emerging Corporate Strategy," *SAM Advanced Management Journal* (Spring 1995), p. 19.

34. L. G. Hrebiniak and W. F. Joyce, *Implementing Strategy* (New York: Macmillan, 1984), pp. 85–86.

35. S. M. Davis and P. R. Lawrence, *Matrix* (Reading, MA: Addison-Wesley, 1977), pp. 11–24.

36. J. G. March, "The Future Disposable Organizations and the Rigidities of Imagination," *Organization* (August/November 1995), p. 434.

37. M. A. Schilling and H. K. Steensma, "The Use of Modular Organizational Forms: An Industry-Level Analysis," *Academy of Management Journal* (December 2001), pp. 1149–1168.

38. M. P. Koza and A. Y. Lewin, "The Coevolution of Network Alliances: A Longitudinal Analysis of an International Professional Service Network," *Organization Science* (September/October 1999), pp. 638–653.

39. P. Engardio, "Mom-and-Pop Multinationals," *Business Week* (July 14 & 21, 2008), pp. 77–78.

40. For more information on managing a network organization, see G. Lorenzoni and C Baden-Fuller, "Creating a Strategic Center to Manage a Web of Partners," *California Management Review* (Spring 1995), pp. 146–163.

41. R. E. Miles, C. C. Snow, J. A. Mathews, G. Miles, and H. J. Coleman, Jr., "Organizing in the Knowledge Age: Anticipating the Cellular Form," *Academy of Management Executive* (November 1997), pp. 7–24.

42. N. Anand and R. L. Daft, "What Is the Right Organization Design?" *Organizational Dynamics*, Vol. 36, No. 4 (2007), pp. 329–344.

43. J. Naylor and M. Lewis, "Internal Alliances: Using Joint Ventures in a Diversified Company," *Long Range Planning* (October 1997), pp. 678–688.

44. G. Hoetker, "Do Modular Products Lead to Modular Organizations?" *Strategic Management Journal* (June 2006), pp. 501–518.

45. Anand and Daft, pp. 336–338.

46. L. J. Karjewski, L. P. Ritzman, and M. K. Malhotra, *Operations Management: Processes and Value Chains*, (New Delhi: Dorling Kindersley (India) Pvt. Ltd, 2008), p. 211.

47. D. Paper, "BPR: Creating the Conditions for Sucess," *Long Range Planning* (June 1998), pp. 426–435.

48. S. Drew, "BPR in Financial Services: Factors for Success," *Long Range Planning* (October 1994), pp. 25–41.

49. "Do As I Say, Not As I Do," *Journal of Business Strategy* (May/June 1997), pp. 3–4.

50. L. Raymond and S. Rivard, "Determinants of Business Process Reengineering Success in Small and Large Enterprises: An Empirical Study in the Canadian Context," *Journal of Small Business Management* (January 1998), pp. 72–85.

51. K. Grint, "Reengineering History: Social Resonances and Business Process Reengineering," *Organization* (July 1994), pp. 179–201; A. Kleiner, "Revisiting Reengineering," *Strategy + Business* (3rd Quarter 2000), pp. 27–31.

52. E. A. Hall, J. Rosenthal, and J. Wade, "How to Make Reengineering *Really* Work," McKinsey Quarterly (1994, No.2), pp. 107–128.

53. "Dr. Reddy's Laboratories Streamlines New Product Development Process and Improves Insight, Visibility, and Control via Six Sigma", recovered on 2nd Nov 2011, from http://www.microsoft.com/resources/casestudies/CaseStudy.asp?CaseStudyID=15139

54. "Dr. Reddy's Laboratories Limited", Referred on 1st Feb 2005, from www.drreddys.com Rastogi, P. N. "Unlocking Profit Potentials Is Knowledge the Key?" General Management Review, recovered on 2nd Nov 2011, from http://www.etgmr.com/gmrjan-mar3/art2.html

55. "Wipro Grows in Quality Consulting", The Hindu Business Line: Internet Edition (23rd May 2004), referred on 2nd Nov 2011, from http://www.thehindubusinessline.com/2004/05/24/stories/2004052401400200.htm

56. "Chopping Costs with Six Sigma", referred on 2nd Nov 2011, from http://www.expresscomputeronline.com/20041122/technologylife01.shtml

57. Arndt, p. 73.

58. B. Hindo, "At 3M, A Struggle Between Efficiency and Creativity," *Business Week IN* (June 11, 2007), pp. 8–16.

59. F. Arner and A. Aston, "How Xerox Got Up to Speed," *Business Week* (May 3, 2004), pp. 103–104.

60. J. Hoerr, "Sharpening Minds for a Competitive Edge," *Business Week* (December 17, 1990), pp. 72–78.

61. D. Spulberg, *Global Competitive Strategy* (Cambridge, UK: Cambridge University Press, 2007), p. 257; See also A. K. Gupta, V. Govindarajan, and H. Wang, *The Quest for Global Dominance*, 2nd ed. (San Francisco: Jossey-Bass, 2007) for a similar set of forces.

62. R. Krishnan, X. Martin, and N. G. Noorderhaven, "When Does Trust Matter to Alliance Performance," *Academy of Management Journal* (October 2006), pp. 894–917.

63. S. X. Li and T. J. Rowley, "Inertia and Evaluation Mechanisms in Interorganizational Partner Selection: Syndicate Formation Among U.S. Investment Banks," *Academy of Management Journal* (December 2002), pp. 1104–1119.

64. M. U. Douma, J. Bilderbeek, P. J. Idenburg, and J. K. Loise, "Strategic Alliances: Managing the Dynamics of Fit," *Long Range Planning* (August 2000), pp. 579–598; W. Hoffmann and R. Schlosser, "Success Factors of Strategic Alliances in Small and Medium-Sized Enterprises—An Empirical Survey," *Long Range Planning* (June 2001), pp. 357–381; Y. Luo, "How Important Are Shared Perceptions of Procedural Justice in Cooperative Alliances?" *Academy of Management Journal* (August 2005), pp. 695–709.

65. Alan M. Rugman, *The Regional Multinationals* (Cambridge, UK: Cambridge University Press, 2005); P. Ghemawat, "Regional Strategies for Global Leadership," *Harvard Business Review* (December 2005), pp. 98–108.

66. J. Birkinshaw, P. Braunerhjelm, U. Holm, and S. Terjesen, "Why Do Some Multinational Corporations Relocate Their Headquarters Overseas?" *Strategic Management Journal* (July 2006), pp. 681–700.

67. J. H. Taggart, "Strategy Shifts in MNC Subsidiaries," *Strategic Management Journal* (July 1998), pp. 663–681.

68. C. A. Bartlett and S. Ghoshal, "Beyond the M-Form: Toward a Managerial Theory of the Firm," *Strategic Management Journal* (Winter 1993), pp. 23–46.

69. C. Matlack, "Nestle Is Starting to Slim Down at Last," *Business Week* (October 27, 2003), pp. 56–57; "Daring, Defying to Grow," *Economist* (August 7, 2004), pp. 55–58.

70. J. Sterling, "Translating Strategy into Effective Implementation: Dispelling the Myths and Highlighting What Works," *Strategy & Leadership*, Vol. 31, No. 3 (2003), pp. 27–34.

71. "Rebirth of a Carmaker," *The Economist* (April 26, 2008), pp. 87–89.

72. M. Der Hovanesian, "I Have One Word for You: Bioplastics," *Business Week* (June 30, 2008), pp. 44–47.

73. "Cargill Begins to Build Chicago Plant," *St. Cloud* (MN) *Times* (July 9, 2008), p. 3A.

strategy implementation: staffing and Directing

Have you heard of Enterprise Rent-A-Car? Hertz, Avis, and National Car Rental operations are much more visible at airports. Yet Enterprise owns more cars and operates in more locations than Hertz or Avis. Enterprise began operations in St. Louis in 1957, but didn't locate at an airport until 1995. It is the largest rental car company in North America, but only 230 out of its 7,000 worldwide offices are at airports. In virtually ignoring the highly competitive airport market, Enterprise has chosen a cost-leadership competitive strategy by marketing to people in need of a spare car at neighborhood locations. Its offices are within 15 miles of 90% of the U.S. population. Instead of locating many cars at a few high-priced locations at airports, Enterprise sets up inexpensive offices throughout metropolitan areas. As a result, cars are rented for 30% less than they cost at airports. As soon as one branch office grows to about 150 cars, the company opens another rental office a few miles away. People are increasingly renting from Enterprise even when their current car works fine. According to CEO Andy Taylor, "We call it a 'virtual car.' Small-business people who have to pick up clients call us when they want something better than their own car." Why is this competitive strategy so successful for Enterprise even though its locations are now being imitated by Hertz and Avis?

The secret to Enterprise's success is its well-executed strategy implementation. Clearly laid out programs, budgets, and procedures support the company's competitive strategy by making Enterprise stand out in the mind of the consumer. It was ranked on *Business Week*'s list of "Customer Service Champs" in both 2007 and 2008. When a new rental office opens, employees spend time developing relationships with the service managers of every auto dealership and body shop in the area. Enterprise employees bring pizza and doughnuts to workers at the auto garages across the country. Enterprise forms agreements with dealers to provide replacements for cars brought in for service. At major accounts, the company actually staffs an office at the dealership and has cars parked outside so customers don't have to go to an Enterprise office to complete paperwork.

One key to implementation at Enterprise is *staffing*—hiring and promoting a certain kind of person. Virtually every Enterprise employee is a college graduate, usually from the bottom half of the class. According to COO Donald Ross, "We hire from the half of the college class that

Learning Objectives

After reading this chapter, you should be able to:

- Understand the link between strategy and staffing decisions
- Match the appropriate manager to the strategy
- Understand how to implement an effective downsizing program
- Discuss important issues in effectively staffing and directing international expansion
- Assess and manage the corporate culture's fit with a new strategy
- Decide when and if programs such as MBO and TQM are appropriate methods of strategy implementation
- Formulate action plans

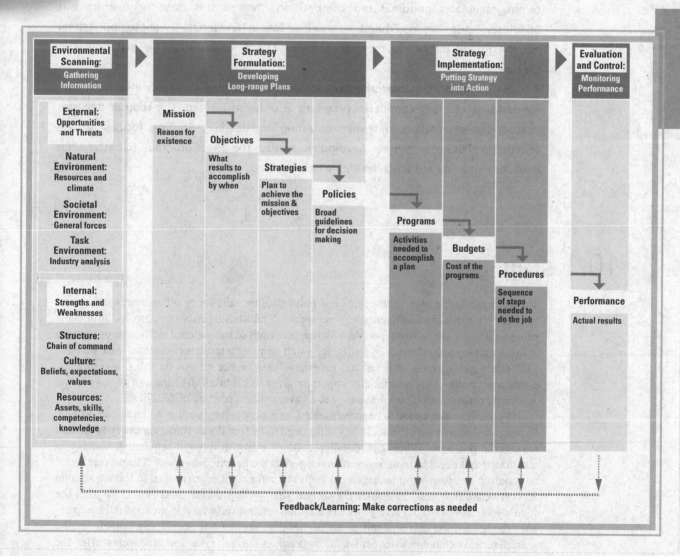

| Environmental Scanning: Gathering Information | Strategy Formulation: Developing Long-range Plans | Strategy Implementation: Putting Strategy into Action | Evaluation and Control: Monitoring Performance |

External: Opportunities and Threats

Natural Environment: Resources and climate

Societal Environment: General forces

Task Environment: Industry analysis

Internal: Strengths and Weaknesses

Structure: Chain of command

Culture: Beliefs, expectations, values

Resources: Assets, skills, competencies, knowledge

Mission — Reason for existence

Objectives — What results to accomplish by when

Strategies — Plan to achieve the mission & objectives

Policies — Broad guidelines for decision making

Programs — Activities needed to accomplish a plan

Budgets — Cost of the programs

Procedures — Sequence of steps needed to do the job

Performance — Actual results

Feedback/Learning: Make corrections as needed

makes the upper half possible. We want athletes, fraternity types—especially fraternity presidents and social directors. People people." These new employees begin as management trainees. Instead of regular raises, their pay is tied to branch office profits.

Another key to implementation at Enterprise is *leading*—specifying clear performance objectives and promoting a team-oriented corporate culture. The company stresses promotion from within and advancement based on performance. Every Enterprise employee, including top executives, starts at the bottom. As a result, a bond of shared experience connects all employees and managers. Enterprise was included in *Business Week*'s "50 Best Places to Launch a Career" three years in a row. To reinforce a cohesive culture of camaraderie, senior executives routinely do "grunt work" at branch offices. Even Andy Taylor, the CEO, joins the work. "We were visiting an office in Berkeley and it was mobbed, so I started cleaning cars," says Taylor. "As it was happening, I wondered if it was a good use of my time, but the effect on morale was tremendous." Because the financial results of every branch office and every region are available to all, the collegial culture stimulates good-natured competition. "We're this close to beating out Middlesex," grins Woody Erhardt, an area manager in New Jersey. "I want to pound them into the ground. If they lose, they have to throw a party for us, and we get to decide what they wear."[1]

This example from Enterprise Rent-A-Car illustrates how a strategy must be implemented with carefully considered programs in order to succeed. This chapter discusses strategy implementation in terms of staffing and leading. **Staffing** focuses on the selection and use of employees. **Leading** emphasizes the use of programs to better align employee interests and attitudes with a new strategy.

10.1 Staffing

The implementation of new strategies and policies often calls for new human resource management priorities and a different use of personnel. Such staffing issues can involve hiring new people with new skills, firing people with inappropriate or substandard skills, and/or training existing employees to learn new skills. Research demonstrates that companies with enlightened talent-management policies and programs have higher returns on sales, investments, assets, and equity.[2] This is especially important given that it takes an average of 48 days for an American company to fill a job vacancy at an average cost per hire of $3,270.[3]

If growth strategies are to be implemented, new people may need to be hired and trained. Experienced people with the necessary skills need to be found for promotion to newly created managerial positions. When a corporation follows a growth through acquisition strategy, it may find that it needs to replace several managers in the acquired company. The percentage of an acquired company's top management team that either quit or was asked to leave is around 25% after the first year, 35% after the second year, 48% after the third year, 55% after the fourth year, and 61% after five years.[4] In addition, executives who join an acquired company after the acquisition quit at significantly higher-than-normal rates beginning in their second year. Executives continue to depart at higher-than-normal rates for nine years after the acquisition.[5] Turnover rates of executives in firms acquired by foreign firms are significantly higher than for firms acquired by domestic firms, primarily in the fourth and fifth years after the acquisition.[6]

It is one thing to lose excess employees after a merger, but it is something else to lose highly skilled people who are difficult to replace. In a study of 40 mergers, 90% of the acquiring companies in the 15 successful mergers identified key employees and targeted them for retention within 30 days after the announcement. In contrast, this task was carried out only in one-third of the unsuccessful acquisitions.[7] To deal with integration issues such as these, some companies are appointing special **integration managers** to shepherd companies through the implementation process. The job of the integrator is to prepare a competitive profile of the combined company in terms of its strengths and weaknesses, draft an ideal profile of what the combined company should look like, develop action plans to close the gap between the actuality and the ideal, and establish training programs to unite the combined company and to make it more competitive.[8] To be a successful integration manager, a person should have (1) a deep knowledge of the acquiring company, (2) a flexible management style, (3) an ability to work in cross-functional project teams, (4) a willingness to work independently, and (5) sufficient emotional and cultural intelligence to work well with people from all backgrounds.[9]

If a corporation adopts a retrenchment strategy, however, a large number of people may need to be laid off or fired (in many instances, being laid off is the same as being fired); and top management, as well as the divisional managers, needs to specify the criteria to be used in making these personnel decisions. Should employees be fired on the basis of low seniority or on the basis of poor performance? Sometimes corporations find it easier to close or sell off an entire division than to choose which individuals to fire.

STAFFING FOLLOWS STRATEGY

As in the case of structure, staffing requirements are likely to follow a change in strategy. For example, promotions should be based not only on current job performance but also on whether a person has the skills and abilities to do what is needed to implement the new strategy.

Changing Hiring and Training Requirements

Having formulated a new strategy, a corporation may find that it needs to either hire different people or retrain current employees to implement the new strategy. Consider the introduction of team-based production at Corning's filter plant mentioned in **Chapter 9**. Employee selection and training were crucial to the success of the new manufacturing strategy. Plant Manager Robert Hoover sorted through 8,000 job applications before hiring 150 people with the best problem-solving ability and a willingness to work in a team setting. Those selected received extensive training in technical and interpersonal skills. During the first year of production, 25% of all hours worked were devoted to training, at a cost of $750,000.[10]

One way to implement a company's business strategy, such as overall low cost, is through training and development. According to the American Society of Training and Development, the average annual expenditure per employee on corporate training and development is $1,000 per employee.[11] A study of 51 corporations in the UK found that 71% of "leading" companies rated staff learning and training as important or very important compared to 62% of the other companies.[12] Another study of 155 U.S. manufacturing firms revealed that those with training programs had 19% higher productivity than did those without such programs. Another study found that a doubling of formal training per employee resulted in a 7% reduction in scrap.[13] Training is especially important for a differentiation strategy emphasizing quality or customer service. The Indian training industry seems to have come of age. Surprisingly, no official data on the market for corporate training in India exists. The market is unofficially estimated to be anywhere between Rs 3,000 crore to Rs 6,000 crore.[14]

India Inc. is suffering from severe manpower shortage and inflicted companies are leaving no stone unturned to fill the void in employable talent. For example, Infosys Technologies Ltd (NASDAQ: INFY) was started in 1981 by seven people with U.S. $250. Today, it is a global leader in the "next generation" of IT and consulting with revenues of over U.S. $4 billion.[15] To deal with skilled manpower shortage, Infy has set up Infosys' Global Education Centre. The centre trains all the prospective employees of Infy. As a company policy, all its employees before joining the job go through a mandatory residential training-cum-foundation program. Similarly, Tata Consultancy Services' employees go through a training and development program at TCS Learning and Development Centre. TCS, the largest white-collar recruiter in the country with an employee base of nearly 89,500, spends 4% of its turnover on training and education annually (for more on innovative hiring strategies, see **Strategy Highlight 10.1**).[16]

STRATEGY highlight 10.1

CHANGING HIRING AND TRAINING REQUIREMENTS IN INDIA

In India and across Asia today, one of the important topics discussed across industries is talent management. Due to shortage of appropriate talent across Asia, companies are now looking for factors beyond pay to motivate and retain good talent.[1] It is due to this changed scenario that human resource function today has assumed the importance and stature it deserves. In India till early 2000, HR was considered as a function dealing only with transactional and administrative kinds of activities.[2] Talent crises have led the companies to realize the importance of hiring, training, retaining, and rewarding their employees. Companies are adopting innovative hiring and training strategies. Following are some examples from Indian landscape:

1. TESCO: Tesco, the British retail giant, set up its service support arm in Bangalore in 2004. Being a new entrant in India, its presence as an employer was not there and the prospective recruits did not have shopping experience in foreign markets to know Tesco's repute as an employer. Therefore, in order to build its employer brand and to attract the right kind of talent, it spent a huge chunk of its recruitment budget on hoardings. The company not only altered the medium but also the message.[3]

2. ABB: As one of the world's leading engineering companies, it helps customers use electrical power effectively and to increase industrial productivity in a sustainable way.[4] ABB manufactures across 14 facilities across India. During the early days of its operations, it was having trouble in locating qualified engineers. Therefore, in July 2005, it adopted an innovative hiring strategy, i.e., a web-based recruiting drive. As a result of this drive, students across India took a simultaneous written online test. The best of the candidates were offered jobs instantly.[5] The strategy helped the company not only hire the best talent but also train to alleviate human resource pool to the level of an asset.

More and more Indian companies are realizing this and are trying to compensate employees through other methods such as employee development. Companies such as Infosys, Wipro, Aditya Birla Group, and HCL are all taking innovative steps at hiring and retaining the best talent.

1. Rediff.com, "India Faces Massive Talent Shortage," posted on 06 Feb 2007 11:28 IST, accessed on 4 Nov 2011, from http://www.rediff.com/money/2007/feb/06inter.htm

2. Krishna, Saroja, "To Outsource or Not to Outsource HR and Payroll," accessed on 4 Nov 2011, from http://www.chillibreeze.com/articles_various/outsourcing-HR-and-payroll-711.asp

3. Bajpai, Vimarsh, "Innovative Hiring Strategies," posted on Monday, 07 Jul 2008 17:59, Strategy—Human Resources and Recruitment, accessed on 4 Nov 2011, from Http://Dare.Co.In/Strategy/Human-Resources-Recruitment/Innovative-Hiring-Strategies.Htm

4. ABB, "About U.S.," accessed on 4 Nov 2011, from http://www.abb.co.in/cawp/inabb506/e045ebb7761757c6652571d5003158a4.aspx and http://www02.abb.com/global/inabb/inabb506.nsf/bf177942f19f4a98c1257148003b7a0a/a30dbe7fc0f8120c65257754003ad04c/$FILE/ABB+India+Presentation.pdf

5. *Asia Business Week,* "India: Desperately Seeking Talent," posted on 7 Nov 2005, accessed on 4 Nov 2011, from http://www.businessweek.com/magazine/content/05_45/b3958050.htm

For example, Motorola, with annual sales of $17 billion, spends 4% of its payroll on training by providing at least 40 hours of training a year to each employee. There is a very strong connection between strategy and training at Motorola. For example, after setting a goal to reduce product development cycle time, Motorola created a two-week course to teach its employees how to accomplish that goal. It brought together marketing, product development, and manufacturing managers to create an action learning format in which the managers worked together instead of separately. The company is especially concerned with attaining the highest quality possible in all its operations. Realizing that it couldn't hit quality targets with poor parts, Motorola developed a class for its suppliers on statistical process control. The company estimates that every $1 it spends on training delivers $30 in productivity gains within three years.[17]

Training is also important when implementing a retrenchment strategy. As suggested earlier, successful downsizing means that a company has to invest in its remaining employees. General Electric's Aircraft Engine Group used training to maintain its share of the market even though it had cut its workforce from 42,000 to 33,000 in the 1990s.[18]

Matching the Manager to the Strategy

Executive characteristics influence strategic outcomes for a corporation.[19] It is possible that a current CEO may not be appropriate to implement a new strategy. Research indicates that there may be a career life cycle for top executives. During the early years of executives' tenure, for example, they tend to experiment intensively with product lines to learn about their business. This is their learning stage. Later, their accumulated knowledge allows them to reduce experimentation and increase performance. This is their harvest stage. They enter a decline stage in their later years, when they reduce experimentation still further, and performance declines. Thus, there is an inverted U-shaped relationship between top executive tenure and the firm's financial performance. Some executives retire before any decline occurs. Others stave off decline longer than their counterparts. Because the length of time spent in each stage varies among CEOs, it is up to the board to decide when a top executive should be replaced.[20]

The most appropriate type of general manager needed to effectively implement a new corporate or business strategy depends on the desired strategic direction of that firm or business unit. Executives with a particular mix of skills and experiences may be classified as an **executive type** and paired with a specific corporate strategy. For example, a corporation following a concentration strategy emphasizing vertical or horizontal growth would probably want an aggressive new chief executive with a great deal of experience in that particular industry—a *dynamic industry expert*. A diversification strategy, in contrast, might call for someone with an analytical mind who is highly knowledgeable in other industries and can manage diverse product lines—an *analytical portfolio manager*. A corporation choosing to follow a stability strategy would probably want as its CEO a *cautious profit planner*, a person with a conservative style, a production or engineering background, and experience with controlling budgets, capital expenditures, inventories, and standardization procedures.

Weak companies in a relatively attractive industry tend to turn to a type of challenge-oriented executive known as a *turnaround specialist* to save the company. For example, when former IHOP (International House of Pancakes) waitress Julia Stewart left Applebee's restaurant chain to become CEO of IHOP, she worked to rebuild the company with better food, better ads, and better atmosphere. Six years later, a much improved IHOP acquired the struggling Applebee's restaurant chain. CEO Stewart vowed to turnaround Applebee's within a year by improving service, food quality and focusing the menu on what the restaurant does best: riblets, burgers, and salads. She wanted Applebee's to again be the friendly, neighborhood bar and grill that it once was.[21]

If a company cannot be saved, a *professional liquidator* might be called on by a bankruptcy court to close the firm and liquidate its assets. This is what happened to Montgomery Ward, Inc., the nation's first catalog retailer, which closed its stores for good in 2001, after declaring bankruptcy for the second time.[22] Research tends to support the conclusion that as a firm's environment changes, it tends to change the type of top executive to implement a new strategy.[23] For example, during the 1990s when the emphasis was on growth in a company's core products/services, the most desired background for a U.S. CEO was either in marketing or international experience. With the current decade's emphasis on mergers, acquisitions, and divestitures, the most desired background is finance. Currently, one out of five American and UK CEOs are former Chief Financial Officers, twice the percentage during the previous decade.[24]

This approach is in agreement with Chandler, who proposes (see **Chapter 9**) that the most appropriate CEO of a company changes as a firm moves from one stage of development to another. Because priorities certainly change over an organization's life, successful corporations need to select managers who have skills and characteristics appropriate to the organization's particular stage of development and position in its life cycle. For example, founders of firms tend to have functional backgrounds in technological specialties, whereas successors tend to have backgrounds in marketing and administration.[25] A change in the environment leading to a change in a company's strategy also leads to a change in the top management team. For example, a change in the U.S. utility industry's environment in 1992 supporting internally focused, efficiency-oriented strategies, led to top management teams being dominated by older managers with longer company and industry tenure, with efficiency-oriented backgrounds in operations, engineering, and accounting.[26] Research reveals that executives having a specific personality characteristic (external locus of control) are more effective in regulated industries than are executives with a different characteristic (internal locus of control).[27]

Other studies have found a link between the type of CEO and a firm's overall strategic type. (Strategic types were presented in **Chapter 4**). For example, successful prospector firms tended to be headed by CEOs from research/engineering and general management backgrounds. High performance defenders tended to have CEOs with accounting/finance, manufacturing/production, and general management experience. Analyzers tended to have CEOs with a marketing/sales background.[28]

A study of 173 firms over a 25-year period revealed that CEOs in these companies tended to have the same functional specialization as the former CEO, especially when the past CEO's strategy continued to be successful. This may be a pattern for successful corporations.[29] In particular, it explains why so many prosperous companies tend to recruit their top executives from one particular area. At Procter & Gamble (P&G)—a good example of an analyzer firm—for example, the route to the CEO's position has traditionally been through brand management, with a strong emphasis on marketing—and more recently international experience. In other firms, the route may be through manufacturing, marketing, accounting, or finance—depending on what the corporation has always considered its core capability (and its overall strategic orientation).

SELECTION AND MANAGEMENT DEVELOPMENT

Selection and development are important not only to ensure that people with the right mix of skills and experiences are initially hired but also to help them grow on the job so that they might be prepared for future promotions.

Executive Succession: Insiders versus Outsiders

Executive succession is the process of replacing a key top manager. The average tenure of a chief executive of a large U.S. company declined from nearly nine years in 1980 to six years in 2006.[30] Given that two-thirds of all major corporations worldwide replace their CEO at least once in a five-year period, it is important that the firm plan for this eventuality.[31] It is especially important for a company that usually promotes from within to prepare its current managers for promotion. For over a century, family-run business empires have dominated the Indian business portfolio. Names such as Tata, Birla, Godrej, and Reliance dominate the scene and their business ranges from steel to concrete, autos, telecoms, and petrochemicals. Some of India's largest conglomerates are still family affairs. Stakeholders of these companies, over the years, have seen these companies implode, as the founders died, and their children squabbled over their business empire inheritance.[32]

Such companies are known to throw discretion to the winds and spend time on dividing the family fortune rather than grooming the successor. Many Indian companies are now beginning to appreciate the importance of planning successions carefully. For example, L&T, one of India's leading engineering companies, hires HR consulting firms to list the positions falling vacant and the required competencies to fill them.[33]

Companies known for being excellent training grounds for executive talent are AlliedSignal, Bain & Company, Bankers Trust, Bristol Myers Squibb, Cititcorp, General Electric, Hewlett-Packard, McDonald's, McKinsey & Company, Microsoft, Nike, PepsiCo, Pfizer, and P&G. For example, one study showed that hiring 19 GE executives into CEO positions added $24.5 billion to the share prices of the companies that hired them. After people from GE started their new jobs, one year after, 11 of the 19 companies they joined were outperforming their competitors and the overall market.[34]

Some of the best practices for top management succession are encouraging boards to help the CEO create a succession plan, identifying succession candidates below the top layer, measuring internal candidates against outside candidates to ensure the development of a comprehensive set of skills, and providing appropriate financial incentives.[35] Succession planning has become the most important topic discussed by boards of directors.[36] See **Strategy Highlight 10.2** to see how Hewlett-Packard identifies those with potential for executive leadership positions.

Prosperous firms tend to look outside for CEO candidates only if they have no obvious internal candidates.[37] For example, 85% of the CEOs selected to run S&P 500 companies in 2006 were insiders, according to executive search firm Spencer Stuart.[38] Hiring an outsider to be a CEO is a risky gamble. CEOs from the outside tend to introduce significant change and high turnover among the current top management.[39] For example, in one study, the percentage of senior executives that left a firm after a new CEO took office was 20% when the new CEO was an insider, but increased to 34% when the new CEO was an outsider.[40] CEOs hired from outside the firm tend to have a low survival rate. According to RHR International, 40% to 60% of high-level executives brought in from outside a company failed within two years.[41] A study of 392 large U.S. firms revealed that only 16.6% of them had hired outsiders to be their CEOs. The outsiders tended to perform slightly worse than insiders but had a very high variance in performance. Compared to that of insiders, the performance of outsiders tended to be either very good or very poor. Although outsiders performed much better (in terms of shareholder returns) than insiders in the first half of their tenures, they did much worse in their second half. As a result, the average tenure of an outsider was significantly less than for insiders.[42]

Firms in trouble, however, overwhelmingly choose outsiders to lead them.[43] For example, one study of 22 firms undertaking turnaround strategies over a 13-year period found that the CEO was replaced in all but two companies. Of 27 changes of CEO (several firms had more than one CEO during this period), only seven were insiders—20 were outsiders.[44] The probability of an outsider being chosen to lead a firm in difficulty increases if there is no internal heir apparent, if the last CEO was fired, and if the board of directors is composed of a large percentage of outsiders.[45] Boards realize that the best way to force a change in strategy is to hire a new CEO who has no connections to the current strategy.[46] For example, outsiders have been found to be very effective in leading strategic change for firms in **Chapter 11** bankruptcy.[47]

STRATEGY highlight 10.2

HOW HEWLETT-PACKARD IDENTIFIES POTENTIAL EXECUTIVES

Hewlett-Packard identifies those with high potential for executive leadership by looking for six broad competencies that the company believes are necessary:

1. *Practice the HP Way* by building trust and respect, focusing on achievement, demonstrating integrity, being innovative with customers, contributing to the community, and developing organizational decision making.

2. *Lead change and learning* by recognizing and acting on signals for change, leading organizational change, learning from organizational experience, removing barriers to change, developing self, and challenging and developing others.

3. *Know the internal and external environments* by anticipating global trends, acting on trends, and learning from others.

4. *Lead strategy setting* by inspiring breakthrough business strategy, leading the strategy-making process, committing to business vision, creating long-range strategies, building financial strategies, and defining a business-planning system.

5. *Align the organization* by working across boundaries, implementing competitive cost structures, developing alliances and partnerships, planning and managing core business, and designing the organization.

6. *Achieve results* by building a track record, establishing accountability, supporting calculated risks, making tough individual decisions, and resolving performance problems.

....

SOURCE: Summarized from R. M. Fulmer, P. A. Gibbs, and M. Goldsmith, "The New HP Way: Leveraging Strategy with Diversity, Leadership Development and Decentralization," *Strategy & Leadership* (October/November/December, 1999), pp. 21–29.

Identifying Abilities and Potential

A company can identify and prepare its people for important positions in several ways. One approach is to establish a sound *performance appraisal system* to identify good performers with promotion potential. A survey of 34 corporate planners and human resource executives from 24 large U.S. corporations revealed that approximately 80% made some attempt to identify managers' talents and behavioral tendencies so that they could place a manager with a likely fit to a given competitive strategy.[48] Companies select those people with promotion potential to be in their executive development training program. Approximately 10,000 of GE's 276,000 employees take at least one class at the company's famous Leadership Development Center in Crotonville, New York.[49] Doug Pelino, chief talent officer at Xerox, keeps a list of about 100 managers in middle management and at the vice presidential levels who have been selected to receive special training, leadership experience, and mentorship to become the next generation of top management.[50] Aditya Birla Group, a U.S. $35 billion corporation, is an Indian company considered to be in the league of Fortune 500 companies. It has an extraordinary force of 133,000 employees, belonging to 42 different nationalities. The company has an exhaustive talent management process in line with its belief that talent is "omnipresent." The company's talent management program and processes facilitate and enable managers to plan career moves, which leverage their strengths. It helps managers focus on areas of development that would prepare them in the best possible way for leadership roles. The company uses combination of developmental assignments, classroom training, coaching, and participation in special project teams to enable employees to continuously learn and develop.[51] Other companies such as Infosys and Wipro are all taking steps in this direction. In industries such as pharma, too, companies are clearly looking at more stable methods of finding and retaining talent.[52]

A company should examine its human resource system to ensure not only that people are being hired without regard to their racial, ethnic, or religious background, but also that they are being identified for training and promotion in the same manner. Management diversity could be a competitive advantage in a multiethnic world. With more women in the workplace, an increasing number are moving into top management, but are demanding more flexible career ladders to allow for family responsibilities.

Many large organizations are using *assessment centers* to evaluate a person's suitability for an advanced position. Corporations such as AT&T, Standard Oil, IBM, Sears, and GE have successfully used assessment centers. Because each is specifically tailored to its corporation, these assessment centers are unique. They use special interviews, management games, in-basket exercises, leaderless group discussions, case analyses, decision-making exercises, and oral presentations to assess the potential of employees for specific positions. Promotions into these positions are based on performance levels in the assessment center. Assessment centers have generally been able to accurately predict subsequent job performance and career success.[53]

Job rotation—moving people from one job to another—is also used in many large corporations to ensure that employees are gaining the appropriate mix of experiences to prepare them for future responsibilities. Rotating people among divisions is one way that a corporation can improve the level of organizational learning. General Electric, for example, routinely rotates its executives from one sector to a completely different one to learn the skills of managing in different industries. Jeffrey Immelt, who took over as CEO from Jack Welch, had managed businesses in plastics, appliances, and medical systems.[54] Companies that pursue related diversification strategies through internal development make greater use of interdivisional transfers of people than do companies that grow through unrelated acquisitions. Apparently, the companies that grow internally attempt to transfer important knowledge and skills throughout the corporation in order to achieve some sort of synergy.[55]

STRATEGY highlight 10.3

SUCCESSION PLANNING AMONG PROSPEROUS FAMILY BUSINESSES IN INDIA

Preparing the business for such transitions is possible via the use of succession planning. The process involves an evolution in responsibility and decision-making authority for the successor, with a corresponding decline in authority for the incumbent.

In a study conducted across 252 family-business executives across India, results found that succession planning in Indian family businesses is typically an unplanned affair. Results indicated that there was a strong correlation between the dimensions of retirement and succession planning. Retiree well being, wealth management and transfer, continuity and viability, leadership succession and development, and relationship with family were important and influencing variables on succession planning. The analysis further indicated that very few Indian family-firm CEOs proactively address the issue of leadership succession.

Therefore, though the successful retirement depended on several factors related to ownership and organizational governance of the family firm, yet the CEOs were reluctant to pass ownership interest to the successor. Instead, founder CEOs of family businesses in India generally intend to maintain ownership control of their firms until their death or disability. This unwillingness to "let go of control" motivates incumbent CEOs to postpone their retirement planning and also succession planning process as long as possible. When coupled with cultural (e.g., male) and emotional (e.g., blood relative) preferences, the result, often is a very limited pool of qualified candidates being considered as potential successors to the incumbent CEO.

Excerpts from results of research project conducted by Dr. Purva Kansal on Succession Planning among Family Businesses in India with a team of researchers from Baylor University, Texas, USA, i.e., Jamie Collins, William Worthington, Prof. Schoen from Baylor University.

PROBLEMS IN RETRENCHMENT

On January 28, 2009, Starbucks announced that it was closing 300 stores in addition to the 600 closures it had announced earlier and thus reduce its workforce by 7,000 people. On May 15, 2009, Jet Airways (India) said that it would retrench its excess staff to tackle the financial crisis it was facing following the global slowdown.[56] Meanwhile, Hershey Foods closed six plants in the U.S. and Canada and eliminated 3,000 U.S. jobs. Like other companies at the time, both firms were experiencing declining sales and profits and attempting to cut costs. Due to a poor economy, more than 2.1 million U.S. workers were laid off in 2008. **Downsizing** (sometimes called "rightsizing" or "resizing") refers to the planned elimination of positions or jobs. This program is often used to implement retrenchment strategies. Because the financial community is likely to react favorably to announcements of downsizing from a company in difficulty, such a program may provide some short-term benefits such as raising the company's stock price. If not done properly, however, downsizing may result in less, rather than more, productivity. One study found that a 10% reduction in people resulted in only a 1.5% reduction in costs, profits increased in only half the firms downsizing, and the stock prices of downsized firms increased over three years, but not as much as did those of firms that did not downsize.[57] Why were the results so marginal? See **Strategy Highlight 10.3** for succession planning.

A study of downsizing at automobile-related U.S. industrial companies revealed that at 20 out of 30 companies, either the wrong jobs were eliminated or blanket offers of early retirement prompted managers, even those considered invaluable, to leave. After the layoffs, the remaining employees had to do not only their work but also the work of the people who had gone. Because the survivors often didn't know how to do the departeds' work, morale and productivity plummeted.[58] Downsizing can seriously damage the learning capacity of organizations.[59] Creativity drops significantly (affecting new product development), and it becomes very difficult to keep high performers from leaving the company.[60] In addition, cost-conscious executives tend to defer maintenance, skimp on training, delay new product introductions, and avoid risky new businesses—all of which leads to lower sales and eventually to lower profits.[61] These are some of the reasons why layoffs worry customers and have a negative effect on a firm's reputation.[62]

A good retrenchment strategy can thus be implemented well in terms of organizing but poorly in terms of staffing. A situation can develop in which retrenchment feeds on itself and acts to further weaken instead of strengthen the company. Research indicates that companies undertaking cost-cutting programs are four times more likely than others to cut costs again, typically by reducing staff.[63] This happened at Eastman Kodak, Xerox, Ford, and General Motors during the 1990s, but 10 years later the companies were still downsizing and working to regain their profitable past performance. In contrast, successful downsizing firms undertake a strategic reorientation, not just a bloodletting of employees. Research shows that when companies use downsizing as part of a larger restructuring program to narrow company focus, they enjoy better performance.[64]

Consider the following guidelines that have been proposed for successful downsizing:

- **Eliminate unnecessary work instead of making across-the-board cuts:** Spend the time to research where money is going and eliminate the task, not the workers, if it doesn't add value to what the firm is producing. Reduce the number of administrative levels rather than the number of individual positions. Look for interdependent relationships before eliminating activities. Identify and protect core competencies.

- **Contract out work that others can do cheaper:** For example, Bankers Trust of New York contracted out its mailroom and printing services and some of its payroll and accounts payable activities to a division of Xerox. Outsourcing may be cheaper than vertical integration.

- **Plan for long-run efficiencies:** Don't simply eliminate all postponable expenses, such as maintenance, R&D, and advertising, in the unjustifiable hope that the environment will become more supportive. Continue to hire, grow, and develop—particularly in critical areas.

- **Communicate the reasons for actions:** Tell employees not only why the company is downsizing but also what the company is trying to achieve. Promote educational programs.

- **Invest in the remaining employees:** Because most "survivors" in a corporate downsizing will probably be doing different tasks from what they were doing before the change, firms need to draft new job specifications, performance standards, appraisal techniques, and compensation packages. Additional training is needed to ensure that everyone has the proper skills to deal with expanded jobs and responsibilities. Empower key individuals/groups and emphasize team building. Identify, protect, and mentor people who have leadership talent.

- **Develop value-added jobs to balance out job elimination:** When no other jobs are currently available within the organization to transfer employees to, management must consider other staffing alternatives. For example, Harley-Davidson worked with the company's unions to find other work for surplus employees by moving into Harley plants work that had previously been done by suppliers.[65]

INTERNATIONAL ISSUES IN STAFFING

Implementing a strategy of international expansion takes a lot of planning and can be very expensive. Nearly 80% of midsize and larger companies send their employees abroad, and 45% plan to increase the number they have on foreign assignment. A complete package for one executive working in another country costs from $300,000 to $1 million annually. Nevertheless, between 10% and 20% of all U.S. managers sent abroad returned early because of job dissatisfaction or difficulties in adjusting to a foreign country. Of those who stayed for the duration of their assignment, nearly one-third did not perform as well as expected. One-fourth of those completing an assignment left their company within one year of returning home—often leaving to join a competitor.[66] One common mistake is failing to educate the person about the customs and values in other countries.

Because of cultural differences, managerial style and human resource practices must be tailored to fit the particular situations in other countries. Because only 11% of human resource managers have ever worked abroad, most have little understanding of a global assignment's unique personal and professional challenges and thus fail to develop the training necessary for such an assignment.[67] Ninety percent of companies select employees for an international assignment based on their technical expertise while ignoring other areas.[68] A lack of knowledge of national and ethnic differences can make managing an international operation extremely difficult. For example, the three ethnic groups living in Malaysia (Malay, Chinese, and Indian) share different religions, attend different schools, and do not like to work in the same factories with each other. Because of the importance of cultural distinctions such as these, multinational corporations (MNCs) are now putting more emphasis on intercultural training for managers being sent on an assignment to a foreign country. This type of training is one of the commonly cited reasons for the lower expatriate failure rates—6% or less—for European and Japanese MNCs, which have emphasized cross-cultural experiences, compared with a 35% failure rate for U.S.-based MNCs.[69]

To improve organizational learning, many MNCs are providing their managers with international assignments lasting as long as five years. Upon their return to headquarters, these expatriates have an in-depth understanding of the company's operations in another part of the world. This has value to the extent that these employees communicate this understanding to others in decision-making positions. Research indicates that an MNC performs at a higher level when its CEO has international experience.[70] Global MNCs, in particular, emphasize international experience, have a greater number of senior managers who have been expatriates, and have a strong focus on leadership development through the expatriate experience.[71] Unfortunately, not all corporations appropriately manage international assignments. While out of the country, a person may be overlooked for an important promotion (out of sight, out of mind). Upon his or her return to the home country, co-workers may deprecate the out-of country experience as a waste of time. The perceived lack of organizational support for international assignments increases the likelihood that an expatriate will return home early.[72]

From their study of 750 U.S., Japanese, and European companies, Black and Gregersen found that the companies that do a good job of managing foreign assignments follow three general practices:

- When making international assignments, they focus on transferring knowledge and developing global leadership.

- They make foreign assignments to people whose technical skills are matched or exceeded by their cross-cultural abilities.

- They end foreign assignments with a deliberate repatriation process, with career guidance and jobs where the employees can apply what they learned in their assignments.[73]

Once a corporation has established itself in another country, it hires and promotes people from the host country into higher-level positions. For example, most large MNCs attempt to fill managerial positions in their subsidiaries with well-qualified citizens of the host countries. Unilever and IBM have traditionally taken this approach to international staffing. This policy serves to placate nationalistic governments and to better attune management practices to the host country's culture. The danger in using primarily foreign nationals to staff managerial positions in subsidiaries is the increased likelihood of suboptimization (the local subsidiary ignores the needs of the larger parent corporation). This makes it difficult for an MNC to meet its long-term, worldwide objectives. To a local national in an MNC subsidiary, the corporation as a whole is an abstraction. Communication and coordination across subsidiaries become more difficult. As it becomes harder to coordinate the activities of several international subsidiaries, an MNC will have serious problems operating in a global industry.

Another approach to staffing the managerial positions of MNCs is to use people with an "international" orientation, regardless of their country of origin or host country assignment. This is a widespread practice among European firms. For example, Electrolux, a Swedish firm, had a French director in its Singapore factory. Using third-country "nationals" can allow for more opportunities for promotion than does Unilever's policy of hiring local people, but it can also result in more misunderstandings and conflicts with the local employees and with the host country's government.

Some corporations take advantage of immigrants and their children to staff key positions when negotiating entry into another country and when selecting an executive to manage the company's new foreign operations. For example, when General Motors wanted to learn more about business opportunities in China, it turned to Shirley Young, a Vice President of Marketing at GM. Born in Shanghai and fluent in Chinese language and customs, Young was instrumental in helping GM negotiate a $1 billion joint venture with Shanghai Automotive to build a Buick plant in China. With other Chinese-Americans, Young formed a committee to advise GM on relations with China. Although just a part of a larger team of GM employees working on the joint venture, Young coached GM employees on Chinese customs and traditions.[74]

MNCs with a high level of international interdependence among activities need to provide their managers with significant international assignments and experiences as part of their training and development. Such assignments provide future corporate leaders with a series of valuable international contacts in additional to a better personal understanding of international issues and global linkages among corporate activities.[75] Research reveals that corporations using cross-national teams, whose members have international experience and communicate frequently with overseas managers, have greater product development capabilities than others.[76] Executive recruiters report that more major corporations are now requiring candidates to have international experience.[77] To increase its own top management's global expertise, Cisco Systems introduced a staffing program in 2007 with the objective of locating 20% of its senior managers at its new Bangalore, India, Globalization Center by 2010.[78]

Since an increasing number of multinational corporations are primarily organized around business units and product lines instead of geographic areas, product and SBU managers who are based at corporate headquarters are often traveling around the world to work personally with country managers. These managers and other mobile workers are being called *stealth expatriates* because they are either cross-border commuters (especially in the EU) or the accidental expatriate who goes on many business trips or temporary assignments due to offshoring and/or international joint ventures.[79]

10.2 Leading

Implementation also involves leading through coaching people to use their abilities and skills most effectively and efficiently to achieve organizational objectives. Without direction, people tend to do their work according to their personal view of what tasks should be done, how, and in what order. They may approach their work as they have in the past or emphasize those tasks that they most enjoy—regardless of the corporation's priorities. This can create real problems, particularly if the company is operating internationally and must adjust to customs and traditions in other countries. This direction may take the form of management leadership, communicated norms of behavior from the corporate culture, or agreements among workers in autonomous work groups. It may be accomplished more formally through action planning or through programs, such as Management By Objectives and Total Quality Management. Procedures can be changed to provide incentives to motivate employees to align their behavior with corporate objectives. For an example of Abbott Laboratories' new procedures to motivate employees to drive carbon neutral autos, see the **Environmental Sustainability Issue** feature.

MANAGING CORPORATE CULTURE

Because an organization's culture can exert a powerful influence on the behavior of all employees, it can strongly affect a company's ability to shift its strategic direction. A problem for a strong culture is that a change in mission, objectives, strategies, or policies is not likely to be successful if it is in opposition to the accepted culture of the company. Corporate culture has a strong tendency to resist change because its very reason for existence often rests on preserving stable relationships and patterns of behavior. For example, when Robert Nardelli became CEO at Home Depot in 2000, he changed the corporate strategy to growing the company's small professional supply business (sales to building contractors) through acquisitions and making the mature retail business cost-effective. He attempted to replace the old informal entrepreneurial collaborative culture with one of military efficiency. Before Nardelli's arrival, most store managers had based their decisions upon their personal knowledge of their customers' preferences. Under Nardelli, they were instead given weekly sales and profit targets.

ENVIRONMENTAL sustainability issue

ABBOTT LABORATORIES' NEW PROCEDURES FOR GREENER COMPANY CARS

Abbott Laboratories, which provides its sales staff with 6,000 vehicles, has changed its procedures for mileage reimbursement in order to make its car fleet more carbon neutral. Under previous rules, Abbott's employees reimbursed the company for *personal* use of company cars at 17.3¢ per mile. Starting January 2009, those choosing SUVs were required to pay **72.3¢** per mile. As a result, 48% of the sales reps selected sedans compared to only 25% in 2008. Requests for SUVs dropped from 44% of the sales reps the previous year to 29% in 2009. Requests for hybrid autos increased from 6% in 2008 to 18% in 2009.

....

SOURCE: Summarized from D. Kiley, "Steering Workers into the Green Lane," *Business Week* (October 27, 2008), p. 18.

Underperforming managers were asked to leave the company. The once-heavy ranks of full-time employees were replaced with cheaper part-timers. In this "culture of fear," morale fell and Home Depot's customer satisfaction score dropped to last place among major U.S. retailers. By 2007, Nardelli was asked to leave the company.

There is no one best corporate culture. An optimal culture is one that best supports the mission and strategy of the company of which it is a part. This means that *corporate culture should support the strategy*. Unless strategy is in complete agreement with the culture, any significant change in strategy should be followed by a modification of the organization's culture. Although corporate culture can be changed, it may often take a long time, and it requires much effort. At Home Depot, for example, CEO Nardelli attempted to change the corporate culture by hiring GE veterans like himself into top management positions, hiring ex-military officers as store managers, and instituting a top-down command structure.

A key job of management involves managing corporate culture. In doing so, management must evaluate what a particular change in strategy means to the corporate culture, assess whether a change in culture is needed, and decide whether an attempt to change the culture is worth the likely costs.

Assessing Strategy-Culture Compatibility

When implementing a new strategy, a company should take the time to assess *strategy-culture compatibility*. (See **Figure 10–1**.) Consider the following questions regarding a corporation's culture:

1. **Is the proposed strategy compatible with the company's current culture?** *If yes*, full steam ahead. Tie organizational changes into the company's culture by identifying how the new strategy will achieve the mission better than the current strategy does. *If not . . .*

2. **Can the culture be easily modified to make it more compatible with the new strategy?** *If yes,* move forward carefully by introducing a set of culture-changing activities such as minor structural modifications, training and development activities, and/or hiring new managers who are more compatible with the new strategy. When Procter & Gamble's top management decided to implement a strategy aimed at reducing costs, for example, it made some changes in how things were done, but it did not eliminate its brand-management system. The culture adapted to these modifications over a couple years and productivity increased. *If not . . .*

FIGURE 10–1 Assessing Strategy–Culture Compatibility

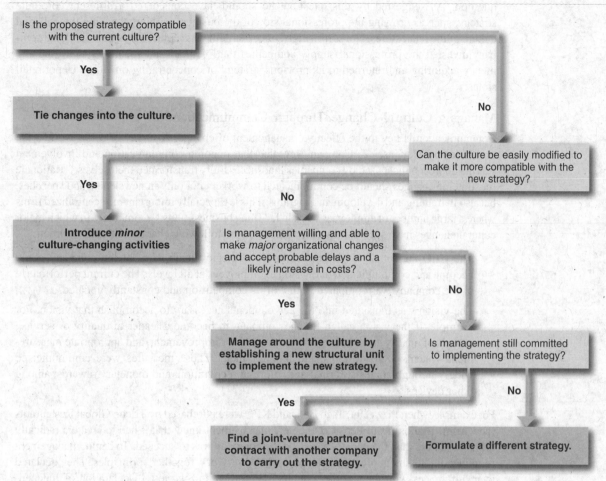

3. **Is management willing and able to make major organizational changes and accept probable delays and a likely increase in costs?** *If yes*, manage around the culture by establishing a new structural unit to implement the new strategy. At General Motors, for example, top management realized the company had to make some radical changes to be more competitive. Because the current structure, culture, and procedures were very inflexible, management decided to establish a completely new Saturn division (GM's first new division since 1918) to build its new auto. In cooperation with the United Auto Workers, an entirely new labor agreement was developed, based on decisions reached by consensus. Carefully selected employees received from 100 to 750 hours of training, and a whole new culture was built, piece by piece. *If not . . .*

4. **Is management still committed to implementing the strategy?** *If yes*, find a oint-venture partner or contract with another company to carry out the strategy. *If not*, formulate a different strategy.

Based on Robert Nardelli's decisions when he initially started as Home Depot's CEO, he probably answered "no" to the first question and "yes" to the second question—thus justifying his many changes in staffing and leading. Unfortunately, these changes didn't work very well.

Instead, he should have replied "no" to the first and second questions and stopped at the third question. As suggested by this question, he should have considered a different corporate strategy, such as growing the professional side of the business without changing the collegial culture of the retail stores. Not surprisingly, once Nardelli was replaced by a new CEO, the company divested the professional supply companies that Nardelli had spent so much time and money acquiring and returned to its previous strategy of concentrating on Home Depot retail stores.

Managing Cultural Change Through Communication

Communication is key to the effective management of change. A survey of 3,199 world-wide executives by McKinsey & Company revealed that ongoing communication and involvement was the approach most used by companies that successfully transformed themselves.[80] Rationale for strategic changes should be communicated to workers not only in newsletters and speeches, but also in training and development programs. This is especially important in decentralized firms where a large number of employees work in far-flung business units.[81] Companies in which major cultural changes have successfully taken place had the following characteristics in common:

- The CEO and other top managers had a strategic vision of what the company could become and communicated that vision to employees at all levels. The current performance of the company was compared to that of its competition and constantly updated.

- The vision was translated into the key elements necessary to accomplish that vision. For example, if the vision called for the company to become a leader in quality or service, aspects of quality and service were pinpointed for improvement, and appropriate measurement systems were developed to monitor them. These measures were communicated widely through contests, formal and informal recognition, and monetary rewards, among other devices.[82]

For example, when Pizza Hut, Taco Bell, and KFC were purchased by Tricon Global Restaurants (now Yum! Brands) from PepsiCo, the new management knew that it had to create a radically different culture than the one at PepsiCo if the company was to succeed. To begin, management formulated a statement of shared values—"How We Work Together" principles. They declared their differences with the "mother country" (PepsiCo) and wrote a "Declaration of Independence" stating what the new company would stand for. Restaurant managers participated in team-building activities at the corporate headquarters and finished by signing the company's "Declaration of Independence" as "founders" of the company. Since then, "Founder's Day" has become an annual event celebrating the culture of the company. Headquarters was renamed the "Restaurant Support Center," signifying the cultural value that the restaurants were the central focus of the company. People measures were added to financial measures and customer measures, reinforcing the "putting people first" value. In an unprecedented move in the industry, restaurant managers were given stock options and added to the list of performance incentives. The company created values-focused 360-degree performance reviews, which were eventually pushed to the restaurant manager level.[83]

Managing Diverse Cultures Following an Acquisition

When merging with or acquiring another company, top management must give some consideration to a potential clash of corporate cultures. According to a Hewitt Associates survey of 218 major U.S. corporations, integrating culture was a top challenge for 69% of the reporting companies.[84] Cultural differences are even more problematic when a company acquires a firm in another country. DaimlerChrysler's purchase of a controlling interest in Mitsubishi Motors in 2001 was insufficient to overcome Mitsubishi's resistance to change. After investing $2 billion to cut Mitsubishi's costs and improve its product development, DaimlerChrysler gave up.[85] It's dangerous to assume that the firms can simply be integrated into the same reporting

STRATEGY highlight 10.4

CORPORATE CULTURE AND COMPETITIVE ADVANTAGE: CASE STUDY OF INDIAN BANKING SECTOR

A study conducted across 100 managers regarding ownership in Indian banks explored the controllable nature of the organizational culture. A questionnaire was used to simulate the organizational scenario involving members' interaction with their faith and passion; discipline, belief, and focus for their colleagues, top management, and their subordinates.

Results indicated existence of significant difference in mean perception of employees across three dimensions of organizational culture for private and public sector banks, i.e., stability, people orientation and detail orientation. Results also highlighted that, from earlier years of its operation to late 1990s, although these public sector banks had a detailed oriented culture, yet the culture was easy going (mean = 2.94), calmer (mean = 3.26), and reflective (mean = 3.04) kind of culture. However, of late, the organizational culture in these public sector banks has become one which encourages more team orientation, innovativeness, and opportunistic behavior hence indicating that public sector banks were redefining their organizational culture.

The study also highlighted that organizational culture is neither static nor non imitable. It needs to be changed according to the changed consumer needs and expectations and competition, i.e., business environment. The government targeted stability, people orientation, and detail orientation as characteristics of public sector banks. In 1969, these were positive characteristics for a public sector bank. However, with changed industry environment, these very characteristics became limitations for the public sector banks and led to competitive rigidity. This created a gap where private sector banks could gain competitive advantage and therefore, penetrate the market.

Today, the history is repeating itself. Private sector and foreign banks may have taken the leap on new products and better service, but public sector banks are fast catching up by adopting an innovative and an opportunistic stance supported by their culture. The results showed that though private sector banks had a more favorable over all organizational culture, the public sector banks had better ingredients.

Therefore, to compete with public sector banks, the private and foreign banks need to rethink about their organizational culture and come up with a new, unique mix to differentiate themselves in an industry where strategy imitation is name of the game.

The case study indicated that corporate culture was an acquired capability and could lead to competitive advantage as well as rigidity.

Excerpts from results of research project conducted by Dr. Purva Kansal on Effects of Organization Culture in the Dynamic Context of the Indian Banking Industry. Results presented in National Conference on Emerging Trends in Management Practices Conference at Tolani Institute of Management Studies, Adipur, Kachchh, India, 4-5 December 2010. Awarded Best Paper in HR category.

structure. The greater the gap between the cultures of the acquired firm and the acquiring firm, the faster executives in the acquired firm quit their jobs and valuable talent is lost. In 2008, Infosys announced plans to acquire UK-based Axon Group plc. One of the key areas of concern was cultural integration. It was to allow smooth integration of two diverse corporate cultures, that as a part of the deal, the Axon management committed to stay for 2 years.[86] Conversely, when corporate cultures are similar, performance problems are minimized.[87]

There are four general methods of managing two different cultures. (See **Figure 10–2**.) The choice of which method to use should be based on (1) *how much members of the acquired firm value preserving their own culture* and (2) *how attractive they perceive the culture of the acquirer to be.*[88]

1. *Integration* involves a relatively balanced give-and-take of cultural and managerial practices between the merger partners, and no strong imposition of cultural change on either company. It merges the two cultures in such a way that the separate cultures of both firms are preserved in the resulting culture. This is what occurred when France's Renault purchased a controlling interest in Japan's Nissan Motor Company and installed Carlos Ghosn as Nissan's new CEO to turn around the company. Ghosn was very sensitive to Nissan's

FIGURE 10–2
Methods
of Managing
the Culture
of an
Acquired Firm

Integration

Equal merger of both cultures into a new corporate culture

Assimilation

Acquiring firm's culture kept intact, but subservient to that of acquiring firm's corporate culture

Separation

Conflicting cultures kept intact, but kept separate in different units

Deculturation

Forced replacement of conflicting acquired firm's culture with that of the acquiring firm's culture

SOURCE: Based on A. R. Malezadeh and A. Nahavandi, "Making Mergers Work in Managing Cultures," *Journal of Business Strategy* (May/June 1990), pp. 53–57 and "Acculturation in Mergers and Acquisitions," *Academy of Management Review* (January 1988), pp. 79–90.

culture and allowed the company room to develop a new corporate culture based on the best elements of Japan's national culture. His goal was to form one successful auto group from two very distinct companies.[89]

2. *Assimilation* involves the domination of one organization over the other. The domination is not forced, but it is welcomed by members of the acquired firm, who may feel for many reasons that their culture and managerial practices have not produced success. The acquired firm surrenders its culture and adopts the culture of the acquiring company. This was the case when Maytag Company (now part of Whirlpool) acquired Admiral. Because Admiral's previous owners had not kept the manufacturing facilities up to date, quality had drastically fallen over the years. Admiral's employees were willing to accept the dominance of Maytag's strong quality-oriented culture because they respected it and knew that without significant changes at Admiral, they would soon be out of work. In turn, they expected to be treated with some respect for their skills in refrigeration technology.

3. *Separation* is characterized by a separation of the two companies' cultures. They are structurally separated, without cultural exchange. When Boeing acquired McDonnell-Douglas, known for its expertise in military aircraft and missiles, Boeing created a separate unit to house both McDonnell's operations and Boeing's own military business. McDonnell executives were given top posts in the new unit and other measures were taken to protect the strong McDonnell culture. On the commercial side, where Boeing had the most expertise, McDonnell's commercial operations were combined with Boeing's in a separate unit managed by Boeing executives.[90] See **Strategy Highlight 10.4** for case study on Indian banking sector.

4. *Deculturation* involves the disintegration of one company's culture resulting from unwanted and extreme pressure from the other to impose its culture and practices. This is the most common and most destructive method of dealing with two different cultures. It is often accompanied by much confusion, conflict, resentment, and stress. This is a primary reason why so many executives tend to leave after their firm is acquired. Such a merger typically results in poor performance by the acquired company and its eventual divestment. This is what happened when AT&T acquired NCR Corporation in 1990 for its computer business. It replaced NCR managers with an AT&T management team, reorganized sales, forced

employees to adhere to the AT&T code of values (called the "Common Bond"), and even dropped the proud NCR name (successor to National Cash Register) in favor of a sterile GIS (Global Information Solutions) nonidentity. By 1995, AT&T was forced to take a $1.2 billion loss and lay off 10,000 people.[91] The NCR unit was consequently sold.

ACTION PLANNING

Activities can be directed toward accomplishing strategic goals through action planning. At a minimum, an **action plan** states what actions are going to be taken, by whom, during what time frame, and with what expected results. After a program has been selected to implement a particular strategy, an action plan should be developed to put the program in place. **Table 10–1** shows an example of an action plan for a new advertising and promotion program.

TABLE 10–1   Example of an Action Plan

Action Plan for Jan Lewis, Advertising Manager, and Rick Carter, Advertising Assistant, Ajax Continental

Program Objective: To Run a New Advertising and Promotion Campaign for the Combined Jones Surplus/Ajax Continental Retail Stores for the Coming Christmas Season within a Budget of $XX.

Program Activities:
1. Identify Three Best Ad Agencies for New Campaign.
2. Ask Three Ad Agencies to Submit a Proposal for a New Advertising and Promotion Campaign for Combined Stores.
3. Agencies Present Proposals to Marketing Manager.
4. Select Best Proposal and Inform Agencies of Decision.
5. Agency Presents Winning Proposal to Top Management.
6. Ads Air on TV and Promotions Appear in Stores.
7. Measure Results of Campaign in Terms of Viewer Recall and Increase in Store Sales.

Action Steps	Responsibility	Start–End
1. A. Review previous programs	Lewis & Carter	1/1–2/1
B. Discuss with boss	Lewis & Smith	2/1–2/3
C. Decide on three agencies	Lewis	2/4
2. A. Write specifications for ad	Lewis	1/15–1/20
B. Assistant writes ad request	Carter	1/20–1/30
C. Contact ad agencies	Lewis	2/5–2/8
D. Send request to three agencies	Carter	2/10
E. Meet with agency acct. execs	Lewis & Carter	2/16–2/20
3. A. Agencies work on proposals	Acct. Execs	2/23–5/1
B. Agencies present proposals	Carter	5/1–5/15
4. A. Select best proposal	Lewis	5/15–5/20
B. Meet with winning agency	Lewis	5/22–5/30
C. Inform losers	Carter	6/1
5. A. Fine-tune proposal	Acct. Exec	6/1–7/1
B. Presentation to management	Lewis	7/1–7/3
6. A. Ads air on TV	Lewis	9/1–12/24
B. Floor displays in stores	Carter	8/20–8/30
7. A. Gather recall measures of ads	Carter	9/1–12/24
B. Evaluate sales data	Carter	1/1–1/10
C. Prepare analysis of campaign	Carter	1/10–2/15

Take the example of a company choosing forward vertical integration through the acquisition of a retailing chain as its growth strategy. Once it owns its own retail outlets, it must integrate the stores into the company. One of the many programs it would have to develop is a new advertising program for the stores. The resulting action plan to develop a new advertising program should include much of the following information:

1. **Specific actions to be taken to make the program operational:** One action might be to contact three reputable advertising agencies and ask them to prepare a proposal for a new radio and newspaper ad campaign based on the theme "Jones Surplus is now a part of Ajax Continental. Prices are lower. Selection is better."

2. **Dates to begin and end each action:** Time would have to be allotted not only to select and contact three agencies, but to allow them sufficient time to prepare a detailed proposal. For example, allow one week to select and contact the agencies plus three months for them to prepare detailed proposals to present to the company's marketing director. Also allow some time to decide which proposal to accept.

3. **Person (identified by name and title) responsible for carrying out each action:** List some-one—such as Jan Lewis, advertising manager—who can be put in charge of the program.

4. **Person responsible for monitoring the timeliness and effectiveness of each action:** Indicate that Jan Lewis is responsible for ensuring that the proposals are of good quality and are priced within the planned program budget. She will be the primary company contact for the ad agencies and will report on the progress of the program once a week to the company's marketing director.

5. **Expected financial and physical consequences of each action:** Estimate when a completed ad campaign will be ready to show top management and how long it will take after approval to begin to air the ads. Estimate also the expected increase in store sales over the six-month period after the ads are first aired. Indicate whether "recall" measures will be used to help assess the ad campaign's effectiveness plus how, when, and by whom the recall data will be collected and analyzed.

6. **Contingency plans:** Indicate how long it will take to get an acceptable ad campaign to show top management if none of the initial proposals is acceptable.

Action plans are important for several reasons. First, action plans serve as a link between strategy formulation and evaluation and control. Second, the action plan specifies what needs to be done differently from the way operations are currently carried out. Third, during the evaluation and control process that comes later, an action plan helps in both the appraisal of performance and in the identification of any remedial actions, as needed. In addition, the explicit assignment of responsibilities for implementing and monitoring the programs may contribute to better motivation.

MANAGEMENT BY OBJECTIVES

Management By Objectives (MBO) is a technique that encourages participative decision making through shared goal setting at all organizational levels and performance assessment based on the achievement of stated objectives.[92] MBO links organizational objectives and the behavior of individuals. Because it is a system that links plans with performance, it is a powerful implementation technique.

The MBO process involves:

1. Establishing and communicating organizational objectives.

2. Setting individual objectives (through superior-subordinate interaction) that help implement organizational ones.

3. Developing an action plan of activities needed to achieve the objectives.

4. Periodically (at least quarterly) reviewing performance as it relates to the objectives and including the results in the annual performance appraisal.[93]

MBO provides an opportunity for the corporation to connect the objectives of people at each level to those at the next higher level. MBO, therefore, acts to tie together corporate, business, and functional objectives, as well as the strategies developed to achieve them. Although MBO originated the 1950s, 90% of surveyed practicing managers feel that MBO is applicable today.[94] The principles of MBO are a part of self-managing work teams and quality circles.[95]

One of the real benefits of MBO is that it can reduce the amount of internal politics operating within a large corporation. Political actions within a firm can cause conflict and create divisions between the very people and groups who should be working together to implement strategy. People are less likely to jockey for position if the company's mission and objectives are clear and they know that the reward system is based not on game playing, but on achieving clearly communicated, measurable objectives.

TOTAL QUALITY MANAGEMENT

Total Quality Management (TQM) is an operational philosophy committed to *customer satisfaction* and *continuous improvement*. TQM is committed to quality/excellence and to being the best in all functions. Because TQM aims to reduce costs and improve quality, it can be used as a program to implement an overall low-cost or a differentiation business strategy. About 92% of manufacturing companies and 69% of service firms have implemented some form of quality management practices.[96] Not all TQM programs have been successes. Nevertheless, a recent survey of 325 manufacturing firms in Canada, Hungary, Italy, Lebanon, Taiwan, and the United States revealed that total quality management and just-in-time were the two highest-ranked improvement programs to improve company performance. This study agreed with a 2004 Census of Manufacturing survey that identified total quality management and lean manufacturing as the top improvement methodologies in both the U.S. and China.[97] An analysis of the successes and failures of TQM concluded that the key ingredient is top management. Successful TQM programs occur in those companies in which "top managers move beyond defensive and tactical orientations to embrace a developmental orientation."[98]

TQM has four objectives:

1. Better, less variable quality of the product and service,

2. Quicker, less variable response in processes to customer needs,

3. Greater flexibility in adjusting to customers' shifting requirements, and

4. Lower cost through quality improvement and elimination of nonvalue-adding work.[99]

According to TQM, faulty processes, not poorly motivated employees, are the cause of defects in quality. The program involves a significant change in corporate culture, requiring strong leadership from top management, employee training, empowerment of lower-level employees (giving people more control over their work), and teamwork in order to succeed in a company. TQM emphasizes prevention, not correction. Inspection for quality still takes place, but the emphasis is on improving the process to prevent errors and deficiencies. Thus, quality circles or quality improvement teams are formed to identify problems and to suggest how to improve the processes that may be causing the problems. An organization which has successfully adopted TQM Strategy to gain competitive advantage is Mahindra & Mahindra. Refer to **Strategy Highlight 10.5.**

TQM's essential ingredients are:

■ **An intense focus on customer satisfaction:** Everyone (not just people in the sales and marketing departments) understands that their jobs exist only because of customer

STRATEGY highlight 10.5

MAHINDRA AND MAHINDRA: USING TQM FOR COMPETITIVE ADVANTAGE

Mahindra and Mahindra's (M&M) Farm Equipment Sector (FES) is a part of the U.S. $6.7 billion Mahindra Group, which is among the top 10 industrial houses in India. The Mahindra Group's Farm Equipment Sector (FES) is among the top three tractor brands in the world. It has won the Japan Quality Medal in 2007. FES is the first tractor company worldwide to win these honors. This shows the strong focus of FES on quality and customer satisfaction.[1]

Attaining and maintaining this leadership required commitment and relentless pursuit of quality at Mahindra and Mahindra's Farm Equipment Sector.

In the very initial years of its business, the shop floor simply fitted out various parts of the tractor. It was only at the final test stage, i.e., at the factory or customer level, that the quality of the product was tested. If the product showed any flaws, it was sent back to the shop floor. The management found this as wasteful, time and resource consuming and, most importantly, did not lead to sustained qualitative improvement in the manufacturing process.

This prompted the management to develop a long-term vision.[2] To achieve this, total quality management was implemented in M&M's Farm Equipment Sector. The TQM journey was made in three phases at M&M:[3]

■ Introduction phase: 1990–1994

In this phase, M&M introduced initiatives such as Juran's process of quality improvement (JQI), statistical process control (SPC), supplier support activity, and business process reengineering (BPR). It concentrated on:

(a) improving manufacturing quality through process control,
(b) improving the quality of bought-out components, and
(c) increasing productivity and reducing the cost of poor quality (COPQ) by solving chronic cross-functional quality problems.

■ Promotion phase: 1995–1999

In this phase, the stress was on standardization of operations as per the international guidelines and to improve upon them. To facilitate its journey, M&M obtained ISO 9000 certification, the automotive sector specific standard QS 9000 (for both Mumbai and Nagpur locations), and ISO 14001.

■ Development phase: from 2000 onwards

The company has been working on creating dominance in local market and building substantial presence in international market by aggressive use of the Deming Prize guidelines and also winning the coveted medal before 2004.

The benefits of M&M's commitment and relentless pursuit of quality are as follows:

(a) reduction in rework, rejections,
(b) reduction in rejection at suppliers' end as well as at receipt stage at M&M units,
(c) improvement in field quality indicated by the number of consumer complaints during the first 250/500/1000/2000 hours of tractor operation,
(d) increased productivity, customer satisfaction, and employee involvement in continuous improvement, and
(e) introduction of new models—15 models in three years.[4]

Today, the sector's entire business process is designed to create consistent customer delight. Each stage of its product and process development follows a system that includes customer feedback mechanism, i.e., an in-depth and focused customer interview, and continuous feedback from suppliers, trade partners, customers, etc.[5]

Its products are exported to the United States, South Africa, Sri Lanka, Bangladesh, Nepal, Zimbabwe and several European countries. The Mahindra FES enjoys the trust of lakhs of Indian farmers.[6] As a validation for its efforts, it was awarded the coveted Japan Quality Medal on October 16, 2007, by the Union of Japanese Scientists and Engineers (JUSE), Tokyo.[7]

1. Mahindra and Mahindra, accessed on 3 Nov 2011, from http://www.mahindra.com/Farm_Equ_sec/farm-equipment-manufacturers.html

2. DasGupta, Arundhati, "The Deming Prize—The End of the Beginning," *Indian Management*, Vol. 43, No. 5 (2004), pp. 16–20.

3. J. Venkatachari, "Rich harvest," 23 Dec 2003, accessed on 3 Nov 2011, from http://www.domain-b.com/companies/companies_m/mahindra/20031223_harvest.html

4. L. J. Karjewski, L. P. Ritzman, and M. K. Malhotra, *Operations Management: Processes and Value Chains*, (New Delhi: Dorling Kindersley (India) Pvt. Ltd, 2008), p. 211.

5. Arjun, Mahindra's Farm Equipment Sector wins Japan Quality Medal, Mechanist.in, posted on Tuesday, 23 Oct 2007, accessed on 3 Nov 2011, from http://machinist.in/index.php?option=com_content&task=view&id=420&Itemid=2

6. PR domain Register M&M Tractors awarded the Deming for excellence in quality posted on 13 Oct 2003, accessed on 3 Nov 2011, from http://www.prdomain.com/companies/M/Mahindra&Mahindra/newsreleases/2003101820570.htm

7. Mahindra and Mahindra, Mahindra's Farm Equipment Sector to Accept the 2007 Japan Quality Medal, accessed on 3 Nov 2011, from http://www.mahindrausa.com/news.php?nID=105

needs. Thus all jobs must be approached in terms of how they will affect customer satisfaction.

- **Internal as well as external customers:** An employee in the shipping department may be the internal customer of another employee who completes the assembly of a product, just as a person who buys the product is a customer of the entire company. An employee must be just as concerned with pleasing the internal customer as in satisfying the external customer.

- **Accurate measurement of every critical variable in a company's operations:** This means that employees have to be trained in what to measure, how to measure, and how to interpret the data. A rule of TQM is that *you only improve what you measure.*

- **Continuous improvement of products and services:** Everyone realizes that operations need to be continuously monitored to find ways to improve products and services.

- **New work relationships based on trust and teamwork:** Important is the idea of empowerment—giving employees wide latitude in how they go about achieving the company's goals. Research indicates that the keys to TQM success lie in executive commitment, an open organizational culture, and employee empowerment.[100]

INTERNATIONAL CONSIDERATIONS IN LEADING

In a study of 53 different national cultures, Hofstede found that each nation's unique culture could be identified using five dimensions. He found that national culture is so influential that it tends to overwhelm even a strong corporate culture. (See the numerous sociocultural societal variables that compose another country's culture that are listed in **Table 4–3**.) In measuring the differences among these **dimensions of national culture** from country to country, he was able to explain why a certain management practice might be successful in one nation but fail in another:[101]

1. **Power distance (PD)** is the extent to which a society accepts an unequal distribution of power in organizations. Malaysia and Mexico scored highest, whereas Germany and Austria scored lowest. People in those countries scoring high on this dimension tend to prefer autocratic to more participative managers.

2. **Uncertainty avoidance (UA)** is the extent to which a society feels threatened by uncertain and ambiguous situations. Greece and Japan scored highest on disliking ambiguity, whereas the United States and Singapore scored lowest. People in those nations scoring high on this dimension tend to want career stability, formal rules, and clear-cut measures of performance.

3. **Individualism-collectivism (I-C)** is the extent to which a society values individual freedom and independence of action compared with a tight social framework and loyalty to the group. The United States and Canada scored highest on individualism, whereas Mexico and Guatemala scored lowest. People in nations scoring high on individualism tend to value individual success through competition, whereas people scoring low on individualism (thus high on collectivism) tend to value group success through collective cooperation.

4. **Masculinity-femininity (M-F)** is the extent to which society is oriented toward money and things (which Hofstede labels masculine) or toward people (which Hofstede labels feminine). Japan and Mexico scored highest on masculinity, whereas France and Sweden scored lowest (thus highest on femininity). People in nations scoring high on masculinity tend to value clearly defined sex roles where men dominate, and to emphasize performance and independence, whereas people scoring low on masculinity (and thus high on femininity) tend to value equality of the sexes where power is shared, and to emphasize the quality of life and interdependence.

5. **Long-term orientation (LT)** is the extent to which society is oriented toward the long- versus the short-term. Hong Kong and Japan scored highest on long-term

orientation, whereas Pakistan scored the lowest. A long-term time orientation emphasizes the importance of hard work, education, and persistence as well as the importance of thrift. Nations with a long-term time orientation tend to value strategic planning and other management techniques with a long-term payback.

Hofstede's work was extended by Project GLOBE, a team of 150 researchers who collected data on cultural values and practices and leadership attributes from 18,000 managers in 62 countries. The project studied the nine cultural dimensions of assertiveness, future orientation, gender differentiation, uncertainty avoidance, power distance, institutional emphasis on collectivism versus individualism, in-group collectivism, performance orientation, and humane orientation.[102]

The dimensions of national culture help explain why some management practices work well in some countries but not in others. For example, MBO, which originated in the United States, succeeded in Germany, according to Hofstede, because the idea of replacing the arbitrary authority of the boss with the impersonal authority of mutually agreed-upon objectives fits the low power distance that is a dimension of the German culture. It failed in France, however, because the French are used to high power distances; they are used to accepting orders from a highly personalized authority. In countries with high levels of uncertainty avoidance, such as Switzerland and Austria, communication should be clear and explicit, based on facts. Meetings should be planned in advance and have clear agendas. In contrast, in low-uncertainty-avoidance countries such as Greece or Russia, people are not used to structured communication and prefer more open-ended meetings. Because Thailand has a high level of power distance, Thai managers feel that communication should go from the top to the bottom of a corporation. As a result, 360-degree performance appraisals are seen as dysfunctional.[103] Some of the difficulties experienced by U.S. companies in using Japanese-style quality circles in TQM may stem from the extremely high value U.S. culture places on individualism. The differences between the United States and Mexico in terms of the power distance (Mexico 104 vs. U.S. 46) and individualism-collectivism (U.S. 91 vs. Mexico 30) dimensions may help explain why some companies operating in both countries have difficulty adapting to the differences in customs.[104] In addition, research has found that technology alliance formation is strongest in countries that value cooperation and avoid uncertainty.[105]

When one successful company in one country merges with another successful company in another country, the clash of corporate cultures is compounded by the clash of national cultures. For example, when two companies, one from a high-uncertainty-avoidance society and one from a low-uncertainty-avoidance country, are considering a merger, they should investigate each other's management practices to determine potential areas of conflict. Given the growing number of cross-border mergers and acquisitions, the management of cultures is becoming a key issue in strategy implementation. See the **Global Issue** feature to learn how differences in national and corporate cultures created conflict when Upjohn Company of the United States and Pharmacia AB of Sweden merged.

MNCs must pay attention to the many differences in cultural dimensions around the world and adjust their management practices accordingly. Cultural differences can easily go unrecognized by a headquarters staff that may interpret these differences as personality defects, whether the people in the subsidiaries are locals or expatriates. When conducting strategic planning in an MNC, top management must be aware that the process will vary based upon the national culture where a subsidiary is located. For example, in one MNC, the French expect concepts and key questions and answers. North American managers provide heavy financial analysis. Germans give precise dates and financial analysis. Information is usually late from Spanish and Moroccan operations and quotas are typically inflated. It is up to management to adapt to the differences.[106] The values embedded in his or her national culture have a profound and enduring effect on an executive's orientation, regardless of the impact of industry experience or corporate culture.[107] Hofstede and Bond conclude: "Whether they like it or not, the headquarters of multinationals are in the business of multicultural management."[108]

GLOBAL issue

CULTURAL DIFFERENCES CREATE IMPLEMENTATION PROBLEMS IN MERGER

When Upjohn Pharmaceuticals of Kalamazoo, Michigan, and Pharmacia AB of Stockholm, Sweden, merged in 1995, employees of both sides were optimistic for the newly formed Pharmacia & Upjohn, Inc. Both companies were second-tier competitors fighting for survival in a global industry. Together, the firms would create a global company that could compete scientifically with its bigger rivals.

Because Pharmacia had acquired an Italian firm in 1993, it also had a large operation in Milan. U.S. executives scheduled meetings throughout the summer of 1996—only to cancel them when their European counterparts could not attend. Although it was common knowledge in Europe that most Swedes take the entire month of July for vacation and that Italians take off all of August, this was not common knowledge in Michigan. Differences in management styles became a special irritant. Swedes were used to an open system, with autonomous work teams. Executives sought the whole group's approval before making an important decision. Upjohn executives followed the more traditional American top-down approach. Upon taking command of the newly merged firm, Dr Zabriskie (who had been Upjohn's CEO), divided the company into departments reporting to the new London headquarters. He required frequent reports, budgets, and staffing updates. The Swedes reacted negatively to this top-down management hierarchical style. "It was degrading," said Stener Kvinnsland, head of Pharmacia's cancer research in Italy before he quit the new company.

The Italian operations baffled the Americans, even though the Italians felt comfortable with a hierarchical management style. Italy's laws and unions made layoffs difficult. Italian data and accounting were often inaccurate. Because the Americans didn't trust the data, they were constantly asking for verification. In turn, the Italians were concerned that the Americans were trying to take over Italian operations. At Upjohn, all workers were subject to testing for drug and alcohol abuse. Upjohn also banned smoking. At Pharmacia's Italian business center, however, waiters poured wine freely every afternoon in the company dining room. Pharmacia's boardrooms were stocked with humidors for executives who smoked cigars during long meetings. After a brief attempt to enforce Upjohn's policies, the company dropped both the no-drinking and no-smoking policies for European workers.

Although the combined company had cut annual costs by $200 million, overall costs of the merger reached $800 million, some $200 million more than projected. Nevertheless, Jan Eckberg, CEO of Pharmacia before the merger, remained confident of the new company's ability to succeed. He admitted, however, that "we have to make some smaller changes to release the full power of the two companies."

SOURCE: Summarized from R. Frank and T. M. Burton, "Cross-Border Merger Results in Headaches for a Drug Company," *Wall Street Journal* (February 4, 1997), pp. A1, A12.

Let's Summarize the Chapter with a Mind Map

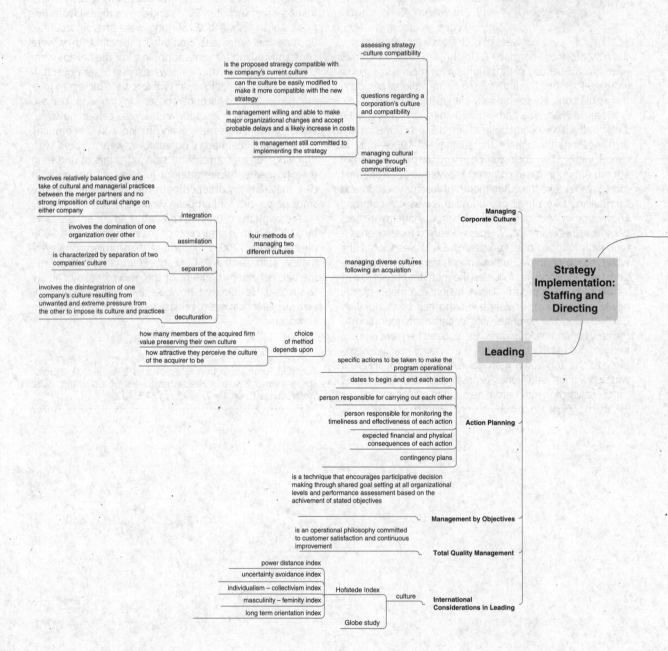

assessing strategy
-culture compatibility

is the proposed strategy compatible with the company's current culture

can the culture be easily modified to make it more compatible with the new strategy

questions regarding a corporation's culture and compatibility

is management willing and able to make major organizational changes and accept probable delays and a likely increase in costs

is management still committed to implementing the strategy

managing cultural change through communication

Managing Corporate Culture

involves relatively balanced give and take of cultural and managerial practices between the merger partners and no strong imposition of cultural change on either company

integration

involves the domination of one organization over other

assimilation

four methods of managing two different cultures

is characterized by separation of two companies' culture

separation

managing diverse cultures following an acquistion

involves the disintegratrion of one company's culture resulting from unwanted and extreme pressure from the other to impose its culture and practices

deculturation

how many members of the acquired firm value preserving their own culture

choice of method depends upon

how attractive they perceive the culture of the acquirer to be

specific actions to be taken to make the program operational

dates to begin and end each action

person responsible for carrying out each other

person responsible for monitoring the timeliness and effectiveness of each action

Action Planning

expected financial and physical consequences of each action

contingency plans

is a technique that encourages participative decision making through shared goal setting at all organizational levels and performance assessment based on the achivement of stated objectives

Management by Objectives

is an operational philosophy committed to customer satisfaction and continuous improvement

Total Quality Management

power distance index

uncertainty avoidance index

individualism – collectivism index

masculinity – feminity index

Hofstede Index

culture

International Considerations in Leading

long term orientation index

Globe study

Leading

Strategy Implementation: Staffing and Directing

Staffing

- **Issues**
  - hiring new people with new skills
  - firing people with inappropriate skills
  - firing people with substandard skills
  - training existing employees to learn new skills

- **Staffing Follows Strategy**
  - changing hiring and training requirements

- **Selection of Management Development**
  - matching the manager to the strategy
    - career life cycle of executives
      - learning stage: experiment intensively with product lines and learn about their business
      - harvest stage: with thier accumulated knowledge they are able to reduce the amount of experimentation required and increase the performance.
      - decline stage: executives reduce their experimentation even further and performance declines
    - executive type
      - dynamic industry expert
        - adequate for a company following concentration strategy emphasizing vertical or horizontal growth and requires aggressive CEO with great deal of experience in the industry
      - analytical portfolio manager
        - for diversification strategy requires a CEO with an analytical mind who is highly knowledgeable in other industries and can manage diverse product lines
      - cautious profit planner
        - for satbility strategy requires CEO with conservative style, a production or engineering background, an experience with controlling budgets, capital expenditures, inventories and standardization procedures.
      - turnaround strategist.
        - for weak companies in relatively attractive industries.
      - professional liquidator
        - for companies which cannot be saved.

- **Problems in Retrenchement**
  - executive succession: insiders versus outsiders
    - executive succession is there process of replacing a key top manager
  - identifying abilities and potential — ways
    - performance appraisal systems
    - assessment centers
    - job rotation
  - downsizing — refers to the planned elimination of positions and jobs — guidelines
    - eliminate unnecessary work instead of making across the board cuts
    - contact out work that others can do cheaper
    - plan for long run efficiencies
    - communicate the reasons for actions
    - invest in the remaining employees
    - develop value added jobs to balance out job elimination

- **International Issues in Staffing**
  - expensive
  - managerial style and human resources practices must be tailored to fit particular situations in other countries
  - hiring and training people from host country into higher positions
  - transferring people from home country into higher positions in host country

ECO-BITS

- The U.S. Climate Action Partnership (USCAP), composed of General Electric, Caterpillar, Alcoa, General Motors, Chrysler, and Duke Energy plus 21 other major corporations, endorses reducing greenhouse gas emissions by 10% to 30% within 15 years and 60% to 80% by 2050 to avert the severest consequences of global warming. 😣

- General Electric, Caterpillar, and Alcoa also sit on the board of the Center for Energy & Economic Development (CEED), an organization that opposes a federal climate bill requiring a 65% reduction in emissions by 2050. 😣

- USCAP members General Motors and Chrysler are also members of the Heartland Institute, an organization that disputes humanity's role in global warming. 😣

- Duke Energy, a USCAP member, is currently building two coal-burning power plants and also belongs to Americans for Balanced Energy Choices, a group that advocates expanded coal use.[109] 😣

DISCUSSION QUESTIONS

1. What skills should a person have for managing a business unit following a differentiation strategy? Why? What should a company do if no one is available internally and the company has a policy of promotion from within?

2. When should someone from outside a company be hired to manage the company or one of its business units?

3. What are some ways to implement a retrenchment strategy without creating a lot of resentment and conflict with labor unions?

4. How can corporate culture be changed?

5. Why is an understanding of national cultures important in strategic management?

STRATEGIC PRACTICE EXERCISE

Staffing involves finding the person with the right blend of characteristics, such as personality, training, and experience, to implement a particular strategy. The Keirsey Temperament Sorter is designed to identify different kinds of personality temperament. It is similar to other instruments derived from Carl Jung's theory of psychological types, such as the Myers-Briggs, the Singer-Loomis, and the Grey-Wheelright. The questionnaire identifies four temperament types: **Guardian (SJ), Artisan (SP), Idealist (NF), and Rational (NT)**. *Guardians* have natural talent in managing goods and services. They are dependable and trustworthy. *Artisans* have keen senses and are at home with tools, instruments, and vehicles. They are risk-takers and like action. *Idealists* are concerned with growth and development and like to work with people. They prefer friendly cooperation over confrontation and conflict. *Rationalists* are problem solvers who like to know how things work. They work tirelessly to accomplish their goals. Each of these four types has four variants.[110]

Keirsey challenges the assumption that people are basically the same in the ways that they think, feel, and approach problems. Keirsey argues that it is far less desirable to attempt to change others (because it has little likelihood of success) than to attempt to understand, work with, and take advantage of normal differences. Companies can use this type of questionnaire to help team members understand how each person can contribute to team performance. For example, Lucent Technology used the Myers-Briggs Type Indicator to help build trust and understanding among 500 engineers in 13 time zones and three continents in a distributed development project.

1. Access the Keirsey Temperament Sorter using your Internet browser. Type in the following URL: **www.advisorteam.com**

2. Complete and score the questionnaire. Print the description of your personality type.

3. Read the information on the Web site about each personality type. Become familiar with each.

4. Bring to class a sheet of paper containing your name and your personality type: *Guardian, Artisan, Idealist,* or *Rational*. Your instructor will either put you into a group containing people with the same predominant style or into a group with representatives from each type. He or she may then give each group a number. The instructor will then give the teams a task to accomplish. Each group will have approximately 30 minutes to do the task. It may be to solve a problem, analyze a short case, or propose a new entrepreneurial venture. The instructor will provide you with very little guidance other than to form and number the groups, give them a task, and keep track of time. He or she may move from group to group to sit in on each team's progress. When the time is up, the instructor will ask a spokesperson from each group to (1) describe the process

the group went through and (2) present orally each group's ideas. After each group makes its presentation, the instructor may choose one or more of the following:

- On a sheet of paper, each person in the class identifies his/her personality type and votes which team did the best on the assignment.

- The class as a whole tries to identify each group's dominant decision-making style in terms of how they did their assignment. See how many people vote for one of the four types for each team.

- Each member of a group guesses if she/he was put into a team composed of the same personality types or in one composed of all four personality types.

KEY TERMS

action plan (p. 363)

dimensions of national culture (p. 367)

downsizing (p. 354)

executive succession (p. 350)

executive type (p. 349)

individualism-collectivism (I-C) (p. 367)

integration manager (p. 347)

leading (p. 346)

long-term orientation (LT) (p. 368)

Management By Objectives (MBO) (p. 364)

masculinity-femininity (M-F) (p. 367)

power distance (PD) (p. 367)

staffing (p. 346)

Total Quality Management (TQM) (p. 365)

uncertainty avoidance (UA) (p. 367)

NOTES

1. B. O'Reilly, "The Rent-A-Car Jocks Who Made Enterprise #1," *Fortune* (October 28, 1996), pp. 125–128; J. Schlereth, "Putting People First," an interview with Andrew Taylor, *BizEd* (July/August 2003), pp. 16–20; P. Lehman, "A Clear Road to the Top," *Business Week* (September 18, 2006), p. 72; Company Web site at www.enterprise.com.

2. S. Caudron, "How HR Drives Profits," *Workforce Management* (December 2001), pp. 26–31 as reported by L. L. Bryan, C. I. Joyce, and L. M. Weiss in "Making a Market in Talent," *McKinsey Quarterly* (2006, No. 2), pp. 1–7.

3. "The Stat," *Business Week* (October 24, 2005), p. 16.

4. The numbers are approximate averages from three separate studies of top management turnover after mergers. See M. Lubatkin, D. Schweiger, and Y. Weber, "Top Management Turnover in Related M&Ss: An Additional Test of the Theory of Relative Standing," *Journal of Management*, Vol. 25, No. 1 (1999), pp. 55–73.

5. J. A. Krug, "Executive Turnover in Acquired Firms: A Longitudinal Analysis of Long-Term Interaction Effects," paper presented to annual meeting of *Academy of Management*, Seattle, WA (2003).

6. J. A. Krug and W. H. Hegarty, "Post-Acquisition Turnover Among U.S. Top Management Teams: An Analysis of the Effects of Foreign vs. Domestic Acquisitions of U.S. Targets," *Strategic Management Journal* (September 1997), pp. 667–675; J. A. Jrug and W. H. Hegarty, "Predicting Who Stays and Leaves After an Acquisition: A Study of Top Managers in Multinational Firms," *Strategic Management Journal* (February 2001), pp. 185–196.

7. D. Harding and T. Rouse, "Human Due Diligence," *Harvard Business Review* (April 2007), pp. 124–131.

8. A. Hinterhuber, "Making M&A Work," *Business Strategy Review* (September 2002), pp. 7–9.

9. R. N. Ashkenas and S. C. Francis, "Integration Managers: Special Leaders for Special Times," *Harvard Business Review* (November–December 2000), pp. 108–116.

10. J. Hoerr, "Sharpening Minds for a Competitive Edge," *Business Week* (December 17, 1990), pp. 72–78.

11. K. Hess and N. J. Nentl, "Strategic Training for Managers," *SAM Management in Practice* (2006, No. 4).

12. "Training and Human Resources," *Business Strategy News Review* (July 2000), p. 6.

13. *High Performance Work Practices and Firm Performance* (Washington, DC: U.S. Department of Labor, Office of the American Workplace, 1993), pp. i, 4.

14. IndiaMART InterMESH Limited, Economic Notes, posted on July 25, 2005, accessed on 3rd Nov 2011, from http://news.indiamart.com/news-analysis/economic-notes-9984.html.

15. Infosys Technologies Limited, accessed on 3rd Nov 2011, from http://www.infosys.com/about/what-we-do/default.asp.

16. D. Nandita, "A Headstart on Lesson 101," *Outlook Business*, posted on August 05, 2007 Print Edition, accessed on 3rd Nov 2011, from http://business.outlookindia.com/inner.aspx?articleid=243&editionid=15&catgid=9&subcatgid=513.

17. T. T. Baldwin, C. Danielson, and W. Wiggenhorn, "The Evolution of Learning Strategies in Organizations: From Employee Development to Business Redefinition," *Academy of Management Executive* (November 1997), pp. 47–58; K. Kelly, "Motorola: Training for the Millennium," *Business Week* (March 28, 1996), pp. 158–161.

18. R. Henkoff, "Companies That Train Best," *Fortune* (March 22, 1993), pp. 62–75.

19. D. C. Hambrick, "Upper Echelons Theory: An Update," *Academy of Management Review* (April 2007), pp. 334–343.

20. D. Miller and J. Shamsie, "Learning Across the Life Cycle: Experimentation and Performance Among the Hollywood Studio Heads," *Strategic Management Journal* (August 2001), pp. 725–745). An exception to these findings may be the computer software industry in which CEOs are at their best when they start their jobs and steadily decline during their tenures. See A. D. Henderson, D. Miller, and D. C. Hambrick, "How Quickly Do CEOs Become Obsolete? Industry Dynamism, CEO Tenure, and Company Performance," *Strategic Management Journal* (May 2006), pp. 447–460.

21. B. Hrowvitz, "New CEO Puts Comeback on the Menu at Applebee's," *USA Today* (April 28, 2008), pp. 1B, 2B.

22. A study of former General Electric executives who became CEOs categorized them as cost controllers, growers, or cycle

managers on the basis of their line experience at GE. See B. Groysberg, A. N. McLean, and N. Nohria, "Are Leaders Portable?" *Harvard Business Review* (May 2006), pp. 92–100.

23. D. K. Datta and N. Rajagopalan, "Industry Structure and CEO Characteristics: An Empirical Study of Succession Events," *Strategic Management Journal* (September 1998), pp. 833–852; A. S. Thomas and K. Ramaswamy, "Environmental Change and Management Staffing: A Comment," *Journal of Management* (Winter 1993), pp. 877–887; J. P. Guthrie, C. M. Grimm, and K. G. Smith, "Environmental Change and Management Staffing: An Empirical Study," *Journal of Management* (December 1991), pp. 735–748.

24. J. Greco, "The Search Goes On," *Journal of Business Strategy* (September/October 1997), pp. 22–25; W. Ocasio and H. Kim, "The Circulation of Corporate Control: Selection of Functional Backgrounds on New CEOs in Large U.S. Manufacturing Firms, 1981–1992," *Administrative Science Quarterly* (September 1999), pp. 532–562; R. Dobbs, D. Harris, and A. Rasmussen, "When Should CFOs Take the Helm?" *McKinsey Quarterly Online* (November 2006); "How to Get to the Top," *The Economist* (May 31, 2008), p. 70.

25. R. Drazin and R. K. Kazanjian, "Applying the Del Technique to the Analysis of Cross-Classification Data: A Test of CEO Succession and Top Management Team Development," *Academy of Management Journal* (December 1993), pp. 1374–1399; W. E. Rothschild, "A Portfolio of Strategic Leaders," *Planning Review* (January/February 1996), pp. 16–19.

26. R. Subramanian and C. M. Sanchez, "Environmental Change and Management Staffing: An Empirical Examination of the Electric Utilities Industry," *Journal of Business Strategies* (Spring 1998), pp. 17–34.

27. M. A. Carpenter and B. R. Golden, "Perceived Managerial Discretion: A Study of Cause and Effect," *Strategic Management Journal* (March 1997), pp. 187–206.

28. J. A. Parnell, "Functional Background and Business Strategy: The Impact of Executive-Strategy Fit on Performance," *Journal of Business Strategies* (Spring 1994), pp. 49–62.

29. M. Smith and M. C. White, "Strategy, CEO Specialization, and Succession," *Administrative Science Quarterly* (June 1987), pp. 263–280.

30. "Making Companies Work," *Economist* (October 25, 2003), p. 14; C. H. Mooney, C. M. Dalton, D. R. Dalton, and S. T. Certo, "CEO Succession as a Funnel: The Critical, and Changing Role of Inside Directors," *Organizational Dynamics*, Vol. 36, No. 4 (2007), pp. 418–428. Note, however, that the tenures of CEOs of family firms typically exceed 15 years. See I. Le Breton-Miller and D. Miller, "Why Do Some Family Businesses Out-Compete? Governance, Long-Term Orientations, and Sustainable Capability," *Entrepreneurship Theory and Practice* (November 2006), pp. 731–746.

31. A. Bianco, L. Lavelle, J. Merrit, and A. Barrett, "The CEO Trap," *Business Week* (December 11, 2000), pp. 86–92.

32. The Economic Times, "India's Corporate Empires Grapple with Succession," posted on October 13, 2008, 12:15 hrs IST, REUTERS, recovered on 3rd Nov 2011, from Bennett Coleman & Co. Ltd website http://economictimes.indiatimes.com/articleshow/msid-3588749, prtpage-1.cms

33. A. V. Vedpuriswar, "Strategic Issues in Succession Planning," *Effective Executive*, November 2001, ICFAI PRESS, recovered on 3rd Nov 2011, from http://www.vedpuriswar.org/book_review/Strategic%20Issues%20in%20succession%20planning.PDF

34. "Coming and Going," Survey of Corporate Leadership, *Economist* (October 25, 2003), pp. 12–14.

35. D. C. Carey and D. Ogden, *CEO Succession: A Window on How Boards Do It Right When Choosing a New Chief Executive* (New York: Oxford University Press, 2000).

36. "The King Lear Syndrome," *Economist* (December 13, 2003), p. 65.

37. Y. Zang and N. Rajagopalan, "Grooming for the Top Post and Ending the CEO Succession Crisis," *Organizational Dynamics*, Vol. 35, Issue 1 (2006), pp. 96–105.

38. J. Weber, "The Accidental CEO," *Business Week* (April 23, 2007), pp. 64–72.

39. M. S. Kraatz and J. H. Moore, "Executive Migration and Institutional Change," *Academy of Management Journal* (February 2002), pp. 120–143; Y. Zhang and N. Rajagopalan, "When the Known Devil Is Better Than an Unknown God: An Empirical Study of the Antecedents and Consequences of Relay CEO Succession," *Academy of Management Journal* (August 2004), pp. 483–500; W. Shen and A. A. Cannella, Jr., "Revisiting the Performance Consequences of CEO Succession: The Impacts of Successor Type, Post-Succession Senior Executive Turnover, and Departing CEO Tenure," *Academy of Management Journal* (August 2002), pp. 717–733.

40. K. P. Coyne and E. J. Coyne, Sr., "Surviving Your New CEO," *Harvard Business Review* (May 2007), pp. 62–69.

41. N. Byrnes and D. Kiley, "Hello, You Must Be Going," *Business Week* (February 12, 2007), pp. 30–32.

42. C. Lucier and J. Dyer, "Hiring an Outside CEO: A Board's Best Moves," *Directors & Boards* (Winter 2004), pp. 36–38. These findings are supported by a later study by Booz Allen Hamilton in which 1,595 worldwide companies during 1995 to 2005 showed the same results. See J. Webber, "The Accidental CEO," *Business Week* (April 23, 2007), pp. 64–72.

43. Q. Yue, "Antecedents of Top Management Successor Origin in China," paper presented to the annual meeting of the *Academy of Management*, Seattle, WA (2003); A. A. Buchko and D. DiVerde, "Antecedents, Moderators, and Consequences of CEO Turnover: A Review and Reconceptualization," Paper presented to *Midwest Academy of Management* (Lincoln, NE: 1997), p. 10; W. Ocasio, "Institutionalized Action and Corporate Governance: The Reliance on Rules of CEO Succession," *Administrative Science Quarterly* (June 1999), pp. 384–416.

44. C. Gopinath, "Turnaround: Recognizing Decline and Initiating Intervention," *Long Range Planning* (December 1991), pp. 96–101.

45. K. B. Schwartz and K. Menon, "Executive Succession in Failing Firms," *Academy of Management Journal* (September 1985), pp. 680–686; A. A. Cannella Jr., and M. Lubatkin, "Succession as a Sociopolitical Process: Internal Impediments to Outsider Selection," *Academy of Management Journal* (August 1993), pp. 763–793; W. Boeker and J. Goodstein, "Performance and Succession Choice: The Moderating Effects of Governance and Ownership," *Academy of Management Journal* (February 1993), pp. 172–186.

46. W. Boeker, "Executive Migration and Strategic Change: The Effect of Top Manager Movement on Product-Market Entry," *Administrative Science Quarterly* (June 1997), pp. 213–236.

47. E. Brockmann, J. J. Hoffman, and D. Dawley, "A Contingency Theory of CEO Successor Choice and Post-Bankruptcy Strategic Change," Paper presented to annual meeting of *Academy of Management*, Seattle, WA (2003).

48. P. Lorange, and D. Murphy, "Bringing Human Resources Into Strategic Planning: System Design Characteristics," in *Strategic Human Resource Management*, edited by C. J. Fombrun, N. M. Tichy, and M. A. Devanna (New York: John Wiley & Sons, 1984), pp. 281–283.

49. M. Leuchter, "Management Farm Teams," *Journal of Business Strategy* (May/June 1998), pp. 29–32.

50. S. Armour, "Playing the Succession Game," *USA Today* (November 24, 2003), p. 3B.

51. Aditya Birla Management Corporation Ltd, recovered on 3rd Nov 2011, from http://www.adityabirla.com/careers/talent-management.asp

52. Rediff.com India Limited, "India Faces Massive Talent Shortage," posted on February 06, 2007, recovered on 3rd Nov 2011, from http://www.indiaabroad.rediff.com/money/2007/feb/06 inter.htm

53. D. A. Waldman and T. Korbar, "Student Assessment Center Performance in the Prediction of Early Career Success," *Academy of Management Learning and Education* (June 2004), pp. 151–167.

54. "Coming and Going," Survey of Corporate Leadership, *Economist* (October 25, 2003), pp. 12–14.

55. R. A. Pitts, "Strategies and Structures for Diversification," *Academy of Management Journal* (June 1997), pp. 197–208.

56. Times of India, "Jet to Retrench Excess Staff, Blames Slowdown," posted on 15 May 2009, 17:38 hrs IST, IANS, recovered on 3rd Nov 2011, from Bennett Coleman & Co. Ltd. Website http://timesofindia.indiatimes.com/Business/India-Business/Jet-to-retrench-excess-staff-blames-slowdown/articleshow/4535546.cms

57. K. E. Mishra, G. M. Spreitzer, and A. K. Mishra, "Preserving Employee Morale During Downsizing," *Sloan Management Review* (Winter 1998), pp. 83–95.

58. B. O'Reilly, "Is Your Company Asking Too Much?" *Fortune* (March 12, 1990), p. 41. For more information on the emotional reactions of survivors of downsizing, see C. R. Stoner and R. I. Hartman, "Organizational Therapy: Building Survivor Health & Competitiveness," *SAM Advanced Management Journal* (Summer 1997), pp. 15–31, 41.

59. S. R. Fisher and M. A. White, "Downsizing in a Learning Organization: Are There Hidden Costs?" *Academy of Management Review* (January 2000), pp. 244–251.

60. T. M. Amabile and R. Conti, "Changes in the Work Environment for Creativity During Downsizing," *Academy of Management Journal* (December 1999), pp. 630–640; A. G. Bedeian and A. A. Armenakis, "The Cesspool Syndrome: How Dreck Floats to the Top of Declining Organizations," *Academy of Management Executive* (February 1998), pp. 58–67.

61. For a more complete listing of the psychological and behavioral reactions to downsizing, see M. L. Marks and K. P. De Meuse, "Resizing the Organization: Maximizing the Gain While Minimizing the Pain of Layoffs, Divestitures, and Closings," *Organizational Dynamics*, Vol. 34, No. 1 (2005), pp. 19–35.

62. D. J. Flanagan and K. C. O'Shaughnessy, "The Effect of Layoffs on Firm Reputation," *Journal of Management* (June 2005), pp. 445–463.

63. *Wall Street Journal* (December 22, 1992), p. B1.

64. R. D. Nixon, M. A. Hitt, H. Lee, and E. Jeong, "Market Reactions to Announcements of Corporate Downsizing Actions and Implementation Strategies," *Strategic Management Journal* (November 2004), pp. 1121–1129; G. D. Bruton, J. K. Keels, and C. L. Shook, "Downsizing the Firm: Answering the Strategic Questions," *Academy of Management Executive* (May 1996), pp. 38–45; E. G. Love and N. Nohria, "Reducing Slack: The Performance Consequences of Downsizing by Large Industrial Firms, 1977–93," *Strategic Management Journal* (December 2005), pp. 1087–1108; C. D. Zatzick and R. D. Iverson, "High-Involvement Management and Workforce Reduction: Competitive Advantage or Disadvantage?" *Academy of Management Journal* (October 2006), pp. 999–1015.

65. M. A. Hitt, B. W. Keats, H. F. Harback, and R. D. Nixon, "Rightsizing: Building and Maintaining Strategic Leadership and Long-Term Competitiveness," *Organizational Dynamics* (Autumn 1994), pp. 18–32. For additional suggestions, see W. F. Cascio, "Strategies for Responsible Restructuring," *Academy of Management Executive* (August 2002), pp. 80–91, and T. Mroczkowski and M. Hanaoka, "Effective Rightsizing Strategies in Japan and America: Is There a Convergence of Employment Practices?" *Academy of Management Executive* (May 1997), pp. 57–67. For an excellent list of cost-reduction programs for use in short, medium, and long-term time horizons, see F. Gandolfi, "Cost Reductions, Downsizing-related Layoffs, and HR Practices," *SAM Advanced Management Journal* (Spring 2008), pp. 52–58.

66. J. S. Black and H. B. Gregersen, "The Right Way to Manage Expats," *Harvard Business Review* (March–April 1999), pp. 52–61.

67. Ibid, p. 54.

68. J. I. Sanchez, P. E. Spector, and C. L. Cooper, "Adapting to a Boundaryless World: A Developmental Expatriate Model," *Academy of Management Executive* (May 2000), pp. 96–106.

69. R. L. Tung, *The New Expatriates* (Cambridge, MA.: Ballinger, 1988); J. S. Black, M. Mendenhall, and G. Oddou, "Toward a Comprehensive Model of International Adjustment: An Integration of Multiple Theoretical Perspectives," *Academy of Management Review* (April 1991), pp. 291–317.

70. M. A. Carpenter, W. G. Sanders, and H. B. Gregersen, "Bundling Human Capital with Organizational Context: The Impact of International Assignment Experience on Multinational Firm Performance and CEO Pay," *Academy of Management Journal* (June 2001), pp. 493–511.

71. P. M. Caligiuri and S. Colakoglu, "A Strategic Contingency Approach to Expatriate Assignment Management," *Human Resource Management Journal*, Vol. 17, No. 4 (2007), pp. 393–410.

72. M. A. Shaffer, D. A. Harrison, K. M. Gilley, and D. M. Luk, "Struggling for Balance Amid Turbulence on International Assignments: Work-Family Conflict, Support, and Commitment," *Journal of Management*, Vol. 27, No. 1 (2001), pp. 99–121.

73. J. S. Black and H. B. Gregersen, "The Right Way to Manage Expats," *Harvard Business Review* (March–April 1999), p. 54.

74. G. Stern, "GM Executive's Ties to Native Country Help Auto Maker Clinch Deal in China," *Wall Street Journal* (November 2, 1995), p. B7.

75. K. Roth, "Managing International Interdependence: CEO Characteristics in a Resource-Based Framework," *Academy of Management Journal* (February 1995), pp. 200–231.

76. M. Subramaniam and N. Venkatraman, "Determinants of Transnational New Product Development Capability: Testing the Influence of Transferring and Deploying Tacit Overseas Knowledge," *Strategic Management Journal* (April 2001), pp. 359–378.

77. J. S. Lublin, "An Overseas Stint Can Be a Ticket to the Top," *Wall Street Journal* (January 29, 1996), pp. B1, B2.

78. "Cisco Shifts Senior Executives to India," *St. Cloud* (MN) *Times* (January 13, 2007), p. 6A.

79. "Expatriate Employees: In Search of Stealth," *The Economist* (April 23, 2005), pp. 62–64.

80. M. Meaney, C. Pung, and S. Kamath, "Creating Organizational Transformations," *McKinsey Quarterly Online* (September 10, 2008).

81. L. G. Love, R. L. Priem, and G. T. Lumpkin, "Explicitly Articulated Strategy and Firm Performance Under Alternative Levels of Centralization," *Journal of Management*, Vol. 28, No. 5 (2002), pp. 611–627.

82. G. G. Gordon, "The Relationship of Corporate Culture to Industry Sector and Corporate Performance," in *Gaining Control of the Corporate Culture,* edited by R. H. Kilmann, M. J. Saxton, R. Serpa, and Associates (San Francisco: Jossey-Bass, 1985), p. 123; T. Kono, "Corporate Culture and Long-Range Planning," *Long Range Planning* (August 1990), pp. 9–19.

83. B. Mike and J. W. Slocum, Jr., "Changing Culture at Pizza Hut and Yum! Brands," *Organizational Dynamics*, Vol. 32, No. 4 (2003), pp. 319–330.

84. T. J. Tetenbaum, "Seven Key Practices That Improve the Chance for Expected Integration and Synergies," *Organizational Dynamics* (Autumn 1999), pp. 22–35.

85. B. Bremner and G. Edmondson, "Japan: A Tale of Two Mergers," *Business Week* (May 10, 2004), p. 42.

86. S. Dhiren, "Infosys to Thrive on Axon Boost," posted on September 01, 2008, recovered on 3rd Nov 2011, from http://www.rediff.com/money/2008/sep/01infy.htm

87. P. Very, M. Lubatkin, R. Calori, and J. Veiga, "Relative Standing and the Performance of Recently Acquired European Firms," *Strategic Management Journal* (September 1997), pp. 593–614.

88. A. R. Malekzadeh and A. Nahavandi, "Making Mergers Work by Managing Cultures," *Journal of Business Strategy* (May/June 1990), pp. 53–57; A. Nahavandi, and A. R. Malekzadeh, "Acculturation in Mergers and Acquisitions," *Academy of Management Review* (January 1988), pp. 79–90.

89. C. Ghosn, "Saving the Business Without Losing the Company," *Harvard Business Review* (January 2002), pp. 37–45; B. Bremner, G. Edmondson, C. Dawson, D. Welch, and K. Kerwin, "Nissan's Boss," *Business Week* (October 4, 2004), pp. 50–60.

90. D. Harding and T. Rouse, "Human Due Diligence," *Harvard Business Review* (April 2007), pp. 124–131.

91. J. J. Keller, "Why AT&T Takeover of NCR Hasn't Been a Real Bell Ringer," *Wall Street Journal* (September 19, 1995), pp. A1, A5.

92. J. W. Gibson and D. V. Tesone, "Management Fads: Emergence, Evolution, and Implications for Managers," *Academy of Management Executive* (November 2001), pp. 122–133.

93. For additional information, see S. J. Carroll, Jr., and M. L. Tosi, Jr., *Management by Objectives: Applications and Research* (New York: Macmillan, 1973), and A. P. Raia, *Managing by Objectives* (Glenview, IL: Scott, Foresman, and Company, 1974).

94. J. W. Gibson, D. V. Tesone, and C. W. Blackwell, "Management Fads: Here Yesterday, Gone Today?" *SAM Advanced Management Journal* (Autumn 2003), pp. 12–17.

95. J. W. Gibson and D. V. Tesone, "Management Fads: Emergence, Evolution, and Implications for Managers,"

Academy of Management Executive (November 2001), p. 125.

96. S. S. Masterson, and M. S. Taylor, "Total Quality Management and Performance Appraisal: An Integrative Perspective," *Journal of Quality Management*, Vol. 1, No. 1 (1996), pp. 67–89.

97. R. J. Vokurka, R. R. Lummus, and D. Krumwiede, "Improving Manufacturing Flexibility: The Enduring Value of JIT and TQM," *SAM Advanced Management Journal* (Winter 2007), pp. 14–21.

98. T. Y. Choi and O. C. Behling, "Top Managers and TQM Success: One More Look After All These Years," *Academy of Management Executive* (February 1997), pp. 37–47.

93. R. J. Schonberger, "Total Quality Management Cuts a Broad Swath—Through Manufacturing and Beyond," *Organizational Dynamics* (Spring 1992), pp. 16–28.

100. T. C. Powell, "Total Quality Management as Competitive Advantage: A Review and Empirical Study," *Strategic Management Journal* (January 1995), pp. 15–37.

101. G. Hofstede, "Culture's Recent Consequences: Using Dimensional Scores in Theory and Research," *International Journal of Cross Cultural Management*, Vol. 1, No. 1 (2001), pp. 11–17; G. Hofstede, *Cultures and Organizations: Software of the Mind* (London: McGraw-Hill, 1991); G. Hofstede and M. H. Bond, "The Confucius Connection: From Cultural Roots to Economic Growth," *Organizational Dynamics* (Spring 1988), pp. 5–21; R. Hodgetts, "A Conversation with Geert Hofstede," *Organizational Dynamics* (Spring 1993), pp. 53–61.

102. M. Javidan and R. J. House, "Cultural Acumen for the Global Manager: Lessons from Project GLOBE," *Organizational Dynamics*, Vol. 29, No. 4 (2001), pp. 289–305; R. J. House, P. J. Hanges, M. Javidan, P. W. Dorfman, and V. Gupta, eds., *Culture, Leadership and Organizations: The GLOBE Study of 62 Societies* (Thousand Oaks, CA: Sage, 2004).

103. M. Javidan and R. J. House, "Cultural Acumen for the Global Manager: Lessons from Project GLOBE," *Organizational Dynamics*, Vol. 29, No. 4 (2001), p. 303.

104. See G. Hofstede and M. H. Bond, "The Confucius Connection, From Cultural Roots to Economic Growth," *Organizational Dynamics,* (Spring 1988), pp. 12–13.

105. H. K. Steensma, L. Marino, K. M. Weaver, and P. H. Dickson, "The Influence of National Culture on the Formation of Technology Alliances by Entrepreneurial Firms," *Academy of Management Journal* (October 2000), pp. 951–973.

106. T. T. Herbert, "Multinational Strategic Planning: Matching Central Expectations to Local Realities," *Long Range Planning* (February 1999), pp. 81–87.

107. M. A. Geletkancz, "The Salience of 'Culture's Consequences': The Effects of Cultural Values on Top Executive Commitment to the Status Quo," *Strategic Management Journal* (September 1997), pp. 615–634.

108. G. Hofstede and M. H. Bond, "The Confucius Connection, From Cultural Roots to Economic Growth," *Organizational Dynamics,* (Spring 1988), p. 20.

109. B. Elgin, "Green—Up to a Point," *Business Week* (March 3, 2008), pp. 25–26.

110. D. Keirsey, *Please Understand Me II* (Del Mar, CA: Prometheus Nemesis Book Co., 1998).

evaluation and Control

> A significant player in the global tyre industry and a brand of choice,
> providing customer delight and continuously enhancing stakeholder value.
>
> **Vision statement of Apollo Tyres Ltd.**

Apollo Tyres Ltd. is one of the most successful tyre manufacturers in India. It manufactures automotive tyres and its accessories (tubes, flaps) and ships them to more than 150 locations. In 2006, Apollo Tyres acquired Dunlop Tyres International in South Africa and Zimbabwe, making Apollo the first Indian multinational tyre company. Apollo decided to deploy high-end information systems, comprehensive business process automation, and highly available network solutions to work smarter and maintain control and visibility over all its resources.

The company tried to keep focus on what really mattered—bottom-line performance and long-term survival through ethical practices and care for all its stakeholders.

The company uses IT for control and evaluation purposes that allows its shop floor to talk to its dealers and its customer assembly lines, thereby, vulcanizing Apollo's customer relationships. The company has kept its vision statements simple and clutter free. The company's competitive strategy is to build manufacturing facilities economically and operate them efficiently so as to be able to produce more for less money.

IT-based systems gave the company more control over developmental process and test environments. This was earlier a major expense centre for the company. The company had to incur infrastructure and maintenance expenses to manage multiple test systems for different in-house projects in order to maintain its competitive edge.

In India, transportation accounts for almost 40% of the logistics cost. Apollo works through a hired fleet of trucks. Since these vehicles are not dedicated, it was very important for Apollo to manage, control, and measure the performance of the transporters across all sectors where the vehicles were plying. IT-based systems have increased efficiency and effectiveness of logistics systems. As a result of these processes, the total transaction processing time reduced from 30 to 8 min per truck load, errors related to communication were eliminated because of standardization of the processes, order-processing related errors were eliminated (from 4 in a week to 0 in a week), and truck turnaround time (gate in to gate out) reduced from 12 to 7.5 h.

The evaluation and control process ensures that the company achieves what it set out to accomplish.

Source: Apollo Tyres Ltd. (India)

Learning Objectives

After reading this chapter, you should be able to:

- Understand the basic control process
- Choose among traditional measures, such as ROI, and shareholder value measures, such as economic value added, to properly assess performance
- Use the balanced scorecard approach to develop key performance measures

- Apply the benchmarking process to a function or an activity
- Understand the impact of problems with measuring performance
- Develop appropriate control systems to support specific strategies

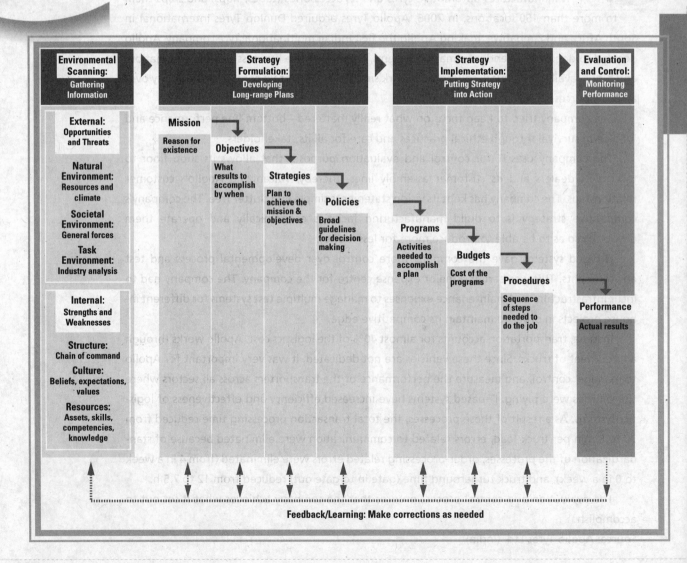

Environmental Scanning: Gathering Information	Strategy Formulation: Developing Long-range Plans	Strategy Implementation: Putting Strategy into Action	Evaluation and Control: Monitoring Performance

External: Opportunities and Threats

Natural Environment: Resources and climate

Societal Environment: General forces

Task Environment: Industry analysis

Internal: Strengths and Weaknesses

Structure: Chain of command

Culture: Beliefs, expectations, values

Resources: Assets, skills, competencies, knowledge

Mission
Reason for existence

Objectives
What results to accomplish by when

Strategies
Plan to achieve the mission & objectives

Policies
Broad guidelines for decision making

Programs
Activities needed to accomplish a plan

Budgets
Cost of the programs

Procedures
Sequence of steps needed to do the job

Performance
Actual results

Feedback/Learning: Make corrections as needed

11.1 Evaluation and Control in Strategic Management

Evaluation and control information consists of performance data and activity reports (gathered in Step 3 in **Figure 11–1**). If undesired performance results because the strategic management processes were inappropriately used, operational managers must know about it so that they can correct the employee activity. Top management need not be involved. If, however, undesired performance results from the processes themselves, top managers, as well as operational managers, must know about it so that they can develop new implementation programs or procedures. Evaluation and control information must be relevant to what is being monitored. One of the obstacles to effective control is the difficulty in developing appropriate measures of important activities and outputs.

An application of the control process to strategic management is depicted in **Figure 11–2**. It provides strategic managers with a series of questions to use in evaluating an implemented strategy. Such a strategy review is usually initiated when a gap appears between a company's financial objectives and the expected results of current activities. After answering the proposed set of questions, a manager should have a good idea of where the problem originated and what must be done to correct the situation.

11.2 Measuring Performance

Performance is the end result of activity. Select measures to assess performance based on the organizational unit to be appraised and the objectives to be achieved. The objectives that were established earlier in the strategy formulation part of the strategic management process (dealing with profitability, market share, and cost reduction, among others) should certainly be used to measure corporate performance once the strategies have been implemented.

APPROPRIATE MEASURES

Some measures, such as return on investment (ROI) and earnings per share (EPS), are appropriate for evaluating a corporation's or a division's ability to achieve a profitability objective. This type of measure, however, is inadequate for evaluating additional corporate objectives such as social responsibility or employee development. Even though profitability is a

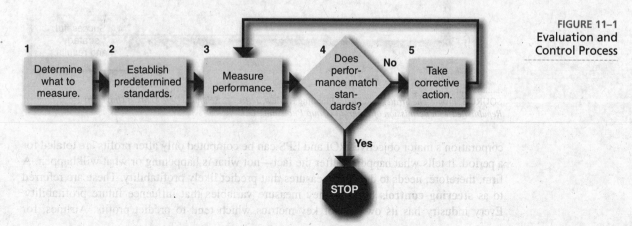

FIGURE 11–1
Evaluation and
Control Process

FIGURE 11–2
Evaluating an
Implemented
Strategy

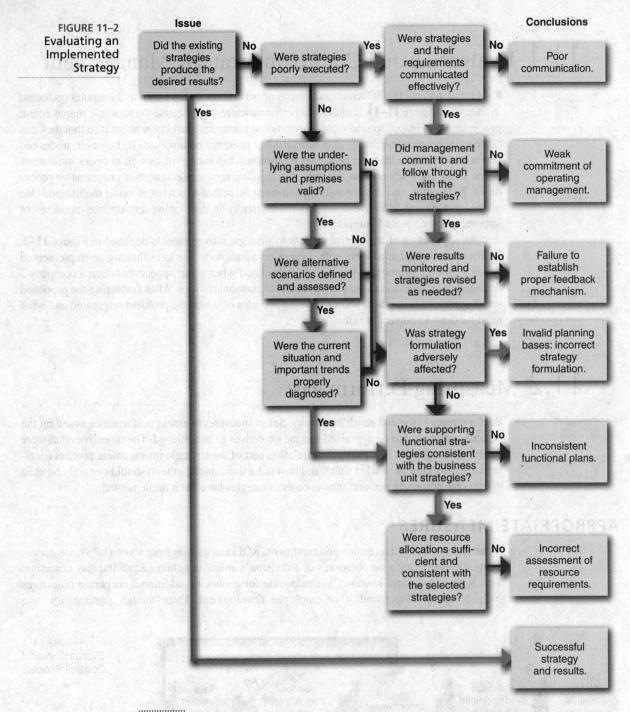

SOURCE: *From "The Strategic Review," Planning Review, Jeffrey A. Schmidt, 1998 © MCB University Press Limited. Republished with permission of Emerald Group Publishing Ltd.*

corporation's major objective, ROI and EPS can be computed only after profits are totaled for a period. It tells what happened after the fact—not what is happening or what will happen. A firm, therefore, needs to develop measures that predict likely profitability. These are referred to as **steering controls** because they measure variables that influence future profitability. Every industry has its own set of key metrics which tend to predict profits. Airlines, for example, closely monitor cost per passenger mile. In the 1990s, Southwest's cost per passenger mile was 6.43¢, the lowest in the industry, contrasted with American's 12.95¢, the highest in the industry.[2] Its low costs gave Southwest a significant competitive advantage.

An example of a steering control used by retail stores is the *inventory turnover ratio*, in which a retailer's cost of goods sold is divided by the average value of its inventories. This measure shows how hard an investment in inventory is working; the higher ratio, the better. Not only does quicker moving inventory tie up less cash in inventories, it also reduces the risk that the goods will grow obsolete before they're sold—a crucial measure for computers and other technology items. For example, Office Depot increased its inventory turnover ratio from 6.9 in one year to 7.5 the next year, leading to improved annual profits.[1]

Another steering control is customer satisfaction. Research reveals that companies that score high on the *American Customer Satisfaction Index (ACSI)*, a measure developed by the University of Michigan's National Research Center, have higher stock returns and better cash flows than do those companies that score low on the ACSI. A change in a firm's customer satisfaction typically works its way through a firm's value chain and is eventually reflected in quarterly profits.[2] Other approaches to measuring customer satisfaction include Oracle's use of the ratio of quarterly sales divided by customer service requests and the total number of hours that technicians spend on the phone solving customer problems. To help executives keep track of important steering controls, Netsuite developed *dashboard* software that displays critical information in easy-to-read computer graphics assembled from data pulled from other corporate software programs.[3]

TYPES OF CONTROLS

Controls can be established to focus on actual performance results (output), the activities that generate the performance (behavior), or on resources that are used in performance (input). **Output controls** specify what is to be accomplished by focusing on the end result of the behaviors through the use of objectives and performance targets or milestones. **Behavior controls** specify how something is to be done through policies, rules, standard operating procedures, and orders from a superior. **Input controls** emphasize resources, such as knowledge, skills, abilities, values, and motives of employees.[4]

Output, behavior, and input controls are not interchangeable. Output controls (such as sales quotas, specific cost-reduction or profit objectives, and surveys of customer satisfaction) are most appropriate when specific output measures have been agreed on but the cause–effect connection between activities and results is not clear. Behavior controls (such as following company procedures, making sales calls to potential customers, and getting to work on time) are most appropriate when performance results are hard to measure, but the cause–effect connection between activities and results is clear. Input controls (such as number of years of education and experience) are most appropriate when output is difficult to measure and there is no clear cause–effect relationship between behavior and performance (such as in college teaching). Corporations following the strategy of conglomerate diversification tend to emphasize output controls with their divisions and subsidiaries (presumably because they are managed independently of each other), whereas, corporations following concentric diversification use all three types of controls (presumably because synergy is desired).[5] Even if all three types of control are used, one or two of them may be emphasized more than another depending on the circumstances. For example, Muralidharan and Hamilton propose that as a multinational corporation moves through its stages of development, its emphasis on control should shift from being primarily output at first, to behavioral, and finally to input control.[6]

Examples of increasingly popular behavior controls are the ISO 9000 and 14000 Standards Series on quality and environmental assurance, developed by the International Standards Association of Geneva, Switzerland. Using the **ISO 9000 Standards Series** (composed of five sections from 9000 to 9004) is a way of objectively documenting a company's high level of quality operations. Using the **ISO 14000 Standards Series** is a way to document the company's impact on the environment. A company wanting ISO 9000 certification would document its process for product introductions, among other things. ISO 9001 would require this firm to separately document design input, design process, design output, and design verification—a large amount of work. ISO 14001 would specify how companies should establish, maintain and continually improve an environmental management system. Although the average total cost for a company to be ISO 9000 certified is close to $250,000, the annual savings are around $175,000 per company.[7] Overall, ISO 14001-related savings are about equal to the costs, reports Tim Delawder, Vice President of SWD, Inc., a metal finishing company in Addison, Illinois.[8]

Many corporations view ISO 9000 certification as assurance that a supplier sells quality products. Firms such as DuPont, Hewlett-Packard, and 3M have facilities registered to ISO standards. Companies in more than 60 countries, including Canada, Mexico, Japan, the United States (including the entire U.S. auto industry), and the European Union, require ISO 9000 certification of their suppliers.[9] The same is happening for ISO 14000. Both Ford and General

STRATEGY highlight 11.1

INDIAN PIONEERING COMPANIES AND TYPES OF CONTROLS

Popular behavior control mechanisms include ISO 9000 and ISO 14000 standard series on quality and environment assurance, developed by International Standards Association of Geneva, Switzerland. ISO 9000 is a way of objectively documenting a company's high level of quality operations and ISO 14000 is a way of documenting the company's impact on the environment. In order to make itself competitive, various companies in India are adopting these standards and these are also being internationally recognized for their efforts. Following are some examples:

TVS Group: This group is a pioneer in adopting different types of controls. Various companies in portfolio, i.e., Axles India Limited, India Japan Lighting Pvt Ltd., Harita TVS Technologies Limited, India Nippon Electricals Limited, etc. all have some sort of ISO control. For example, Brakes India, a joint venture with Lucas Industries, UK, manufactures braking equipment for automotive and non automotive applications and has ISO 14001, ISO 9002, TS 16949, and QS 9000 standards. Besides exporting products to 35 countries worldwide, Brakes India caters to over 60% of the domestic OEM market. The foundry division received the prestigious Deming Prize and Award for TPM excellence. Similarly, Delphi-TVS, a joint venture with Delphi Corporation, USA, manufactures diesel fuel injection equipment for cars, sports utility and multi utility vehicles, light commercial vehicles, tractors, single and two cylinder engines, and has ISO/TS 16949 and ISO 14000 certifications. The company has now won the JIPM TPM Excellence Award (first category).[1]

Tata Group: The Tata Group is one of the biggest and most renowned business conglomerates in India. Founded in the mid-19th century, the group has operations in more than 80 countries across six continents and a set of five core values to guide it namely, integrity, understanding, excellence, unity, and responsibility. In a bid to stay true to its core values every year, every company in Tata Group portfolio is assessed to ensure that processes are clearly defined and adhered to, and progress is made towards superior performance. To achieve this objective, the company adopts and follows quality management systems such as ISO 9000, ISO 14000, OHSAS 18000, TS 16949, and ISO 27000.[2] For example, all the major production units of Tata Steel are certified to ISO 9001 quality management system. The flat-products division has been certified to ISO/TS 16949, supporting the growing supply business to global automotive OEMs. Tata Motors has also obtained ISO/TS 16949 (2002). Furthermore, companies in TATA Group portfolio are ISO 20000 certified, demonstrating that all the operational processes are aligned to information technology service management (ITSM) standards for delivering consistent and quality service.

1. TVS Group, accessed on 3 Nov 2011, from http://www.tvsgroup.com/pages/group.htm

2. TATA Group, following International Standards Helps Our Companies Build Competitive Positions in the Global Marketplace, posted on September 2008, I sourced from ISO Focus, accessed on 3 Nov 2011, from http://www.tata.com/media/interviews/inside.aspx?artid=mSJsSpP9ILc=

Motors require their suppliers to follow ISO 14001. In a survey of manufacturing executives, 51% of the executives found that ISO 9000 certification increased their international competitiveness. Other executives noted that it signaled their commitment to quality and gave them a strategic advantage over noncertified competitors.[10]

Since its ISO 14000 certification, SWD Inc. has become a showplace for environmental awareness. According to SWD's Delawder, ISO 14000 certification improves environmental awareness among employees, reduces risks of violating regulations, and improves the firm's image among customers and the local community.[11]

Another example of a behavior control is a company's monitoring of employee phone calls and PCs to ensure that employees are behaving according to company guidelines. In a study by the American Management Association, nearly 75% of U.S. companies actively monitored their workers' communications and on-the-job activities. Around 54% tracked individual employees' Internet connections and 38% admitted storing and reviewing their employees' e-mail. About 45% of the companies surveyed had disciplined workers (16% had fired them). For example, Xerox fired 40 employees for visiting pornographic Web sites.[12] See **Strategy Highlight 11.1** for types of control adopted by Indian companies.

ACTIVITY-BASED COSTING

Activity-based costing (ABC) is a recently developed accounting method for allocating indirect and fixed costs to individual products or product lines based on the value-added activities going into that product.[13] This accounting method is thus very useful in doing a value-chain analysis of a firm's activities for making outsourcing decisions. Traditional cost accounting, in contrast, focuses on valuing a company's inventory for financial reporting purposes. To obtain a unit's cost, cost accountants typically add direct labor to the cost of materials. Then they compute overhead from rent to R&D expenses, based on the number of direct labor hours it takes to make a product. To obtain unit cost, they divide the total by the number of items made during the period under consideration.

Traditional cost accounting is useful when direct labor accounts for most of total costs and a company produces just a few products requiring the same processes. This may have been true of companies during the early part of the twentieth century, but it is no longer relevant today, when overhead may account for as much as 70% of manufacturing costs. According to Bob Van Der Linde, CEO of a contract manufacturing services firm in San Diego, California: "Overhead is 80% to 90% in our industry, so allocation errors lead to pricing errors, which could easily bankrupt the company."[14] The appropriate allocation of indirect costs and overhead has thus become crucial for decision making. The traditional volume-based cost-driven system systematically understates the cost per unit of products with low sales volumes and products with a high degree of complexity. Similarly, it overstates the cost per unit of products with high sales volumes and a low degree of complexity.[15] When Chrysler used ABC, it discovered that the true cost of some of the parts used in making cars was 30 times what the company had previously estimated.[16]

ABC accounting allows accountants to charge costs more accurately than the traditional method because it allocates overhead far more precisely. For example, imagine a production line in a pen factory where black pens are made in high volume and blue pens in low volume. Assume that it takes eight hours to retool (reprogram the machinery) to shift production from one kind of pen to the other. The total costs include supplies (the same for both pens), the direct labor of the line workers, and factory overhead. In this instance, a very significant part of the overhead cost is the cost of reprogramming the machinery to switch from one pen to another. If the company produces 10 times as many black pens as blue pens, 10 times the cost of the reprogramming expenses will be allocated to the black pens as to the blue pens under traditional cost accounting methods. This approach underestimates, however, the true cost of making the blue pens.

The ABC accounting, in contrast, first breaks down pen manufacturing into its activities. It is then very easy to see that it is the activity of changing pens that triggers the cost of retooling. The ABC accountant calculates an average cost of setting up the machinery and charges it against each batch of pens that requires retooling, regardless of the size of the run. Thus a product carries only those costs for the overhead it actually consumes. Management is now able to discover that its blue pens cost almost twice as much as do the black pens. Unless the company is able to charge a higher price for its blue pens, it cannot make a profit on these pens. Unless there is a strategic reason why it must offer blue pens (such as a key customer who must have a small number of blue pens with every large order of black pens or a marketing trend away from black to blue pens), the company will earn significantly greater profits if it completely stops making blue pens.[17]

ENTERPRISE RISK MANAGEMENT

Enterprise Risk Management (ERM) is a corporatewide, integrated process for managing the uncertainties that could negatively or positively influence the achievement of the corporation's objectives. In the past, managing risk was done in a fragmented manner within functions or business units. Individuals would manage process risk, safety risk, and insurance, financial, and other assorted risks. As a result of this fragmented approach, companies would take huge risks in some areas of the business while over-managing substantially smaller risks in other areas. ERM is being adopted because of the increasing amount of environmental uncertainty that can affect an entire corporation. As a result, the position Chief Risk Officer is one of the fastest growing executive positions in U.S. corporations.[18] Microsoft uses scenario analysis to identify key business risks. According to Microsoft's treasurer, Brent Callinicos, "The scenarios are really what we're trying to protect against."[19] The scenarios were the possibility of an earthquake in the Seattle region and a major downturn in the stock market.

The process of rating risks involves three steps:

1. Identify the risks using scenario analysis or brainstorming or by performing risk self-assessments.

2. Rank the risks, using some scale of impact and likelihood.

3. Measure the risks, using some agreed-upon standard.

Some companies are using value at risk, or VAR (effect of unlikely events in normal markets), and stress testing (effect of plausible events in abnormal markets) methodologies to measure the potential impact of the financial risks they face. DuPont uses earnings at risk (EAR) measuring tools to measure the effect of risk on reported earnings. It can then manage risk to a specified earnings level based on the company's "risk appetite." With this integrated view, DuPont can view how risks affect the likelihood of achieving certain earnings targets.[20] Research has shown that companies with integrative risk management capabilities achieve superior economic performance.[21]

PRIMARY MEASURES OF CORPORATE PERFORMANCE

The days when simple financial measures such as ROI or EPS were used alone to assess overall corporate performance are coming to an end. Analysts now recommend a broad range of methods to evaluate the success or failure of a strategy. Some of these methods are stakeholder measures, shareholder value, and the balanced scorecard approach. Even though each of these methods has supporters as well as detractors, the current trend is clearly toward more complicated financial measures and an increasing use of non financial measures of corporate performance. For example, research indicates that companies pursuing strategies founded on innovation and new product development now tend to favor non financial over financial measures.[22]

TABLE 11–1 Advantages and Limitations of Using ROI as a Measure of Corporate Performance	Before using Return on Investment (ROI) as a measure of corporate performance, consider its advantages and limitations. **Advantages** ■ ROI is a single, comprehensive number that includes all revenues, costs, and expenses. ■ It can be used to evaluate the performance of a general manager of a division or SBU. ■ It can be compared across companies to see which firms are performing better. ■ It provides an incentive to use current assets efficiently and to acquire new assets only when they would increase profits significantly. **Limitations** ■ ROI is very sensitive to depreciation policy. ROI can be increased by writing down the value of assets through accelerated depreciation. ■ It can discourage investment in new facilities or the upgrading of old ones. Older plants with depreciated assets have an advantage over newer plants in earning a higher ROI. ■ It provides an incentive for division managers to set transfer prices for goods sold to other divisions as high as possible and to lobby for corporate policy favoring in-house transfers over purchases from other firms. ■ Managers tend to focus more on ROI in the short-run over its use in the long-run. This provides an incentive for goal displacement and other dysfunctional consequences. ■ ROI is not comparable across industries which operate under different conditions of favorability. ■ It is influenced by the overall economy and will tend to be higher in prosperity and lower in a recession.

SOURCE: From Higgins, *Organizational Policy and Strategic Management*, 2nd Edition, © 1983 South-Western, a part of Cengage Learning, Inc. Reproduced by permission. www.cengage.com/permissions

Traditional Financial Measures

The most commonly used measure of corporate performance (in terms of profits) is **Return On Investment (ROI).** It is simply the result of dividing net income before taxes by the total amount invested in the company (typically measured by total assets). Although using ROI has several advantages, it also has several distinct limitations. (See **Table 11–1.**) Although ROI gives the impression of objectivity and precision, it can be easily manipulated.

Earnings Per Share (EPS), which involves dividing net earnings by the amount of common stock, also has several deficiencies as an evaluation of past and future performance. First, because alternative accounting principles are available, EPS can have several different but equally acceptable values, depending on the principle selected for its computation. Second, because EPS is based on accrual income, the conversion of income to cash can be near term or delayed. Therefore, EPS does not consider the time value of money. **Return On Equity (ROE),** which involves dividing net income by total equity, also has limitations because it is also derived from accounting-based data. In addition, EPS and ROE are often unrelated to a company's stock price.

Operating cash flow, the amount of money generated by a company before the cost of financing and taxes, is a broad measure of a company's funds. This is the company's net income plus depreciation, depletion, amortization, interest expense, and income tax expense.[23] Some takeover specialists look at a much narrower **free cash flow**: the amount of money a new owner can take out of the firm without harming the business. This is net income plus depreciation, depletion, and amortization less capital expenditures and dividends. The free cash flow ratio is very useful in evaluating the stability of an entrepreneurial venture.[24] Although cash flow may be harder to manipulate than earnings, the number can be increased by selling accounts receivable, classifying outstanding checks as accounts payable, trading securities, and capitalizing certain expenses, such as direct-response advertising.[25]

Because of these and other limitations, ROI, EPS, ROE, and operating cash flow are not by themselves adequate measures of corporate performance. At the same time, these traditional financial measures are very appropriate when used with complementary financial and non financial measures. For example, some non–financial performance measures often used by Internet business ventures are *stickiness* (length of Web site visit), *eyeballs* (number of people who visit a Web site), and *mindshare* (brand awareness). Mergers and acquisitions may be priced on multiples of *MUUs* (monthly unique users) or even on registered users.

Stakeholder Measures

Each stakeholder has its own set of criteria to determine how well the corporation is performing. These criteria typically deal with the direct and indirect impacts of corporate activities on stakeholder interests. Top management should establish one or more stakeholder measures for each stakeholder category so that it can keep track of stakeholder concerns. (See **Table 11–2**.)

TABLE 11–2 A Sample Scorecard for "Keeping Score" with Stakeholders

Stakeholder Category	Possible Near-Term Measures	Possible Long-Term Measures
Customers	Sales ($ and volume) New customers Number of new customer needs met ("tries")	Growth in sales Turnover of customer base Ability to control price

Suppliers	Cost of raw material
	 Delivery time
	 Inventory
	 Availability of raw material
		Growth rates of:
		  Raw material costs
		  Delivery time
		  Inventory
		 New ideas from suppliers

Financial community	EPS Stock price Number of "buy" lists ROE	Ability to convince Wall Street of strategy Growth in ROE
Employees	Number of suggestions Productivity Number of grievances	Number of internal promotions Turnover
Congress	Number of new pieces of legislation that affect the firm Access to key members and staff	Number of new regulations that affect industry Ratio of "cooperative" vs. "competitive" encounters
Consumer advocate (CA)	Number of meetings Number of "hostile" encounters Number of times coalitions formed Number of legal actions	Number of changes in policy due to CA Number of CA-initiated "calls for help"
Environmentalists	Number of meetings Number of hostile encounters Number of times coalitions formed Number of EPA complaints Number of legal actions	Number of changes in policy due to environmentalists Number of environmentalist "calls for help"

SOURCE: R. E. Freeman, *Strategic Management: A Stakeholder Approach* (Boston: Ballinger Publishing Company, 1984), p. 179. Copyright © 1984 by R. E. Freeman. Reprinted by permission of R. Edward Freeman.

Shareholder Value

Because of the belief that accounting-based numbers such as ROI, ROE, and EPS are not reliable indicators of a corporation's economic value, many corporations are using shareholder value as a better measure of corporate performance and strategic management effectiveness.

Shareholder value can be defined as the present value of the anticipated future stream of cash flows from the business plus the value of the company if liquidated. Arguing that the purpose of a company is to increase shareholder wealth, shareholder value analysis concentrates on cash flow as the key measure of performance. The value of a corporation is thus the value of its cash flows discounted back to their present value, using the business's cost of capital as the discount rate. As long as the returns from a business exceed its cost of capital, the business will create value and be worth more than the capital invested in it. For example, Deere and Company charges each business unit a cost of capital of 1% of assets a month. Each business unit is required to earn a shareholder value-added profit margin of 20% on average over the business cycle. Financial rewards are linked to this measure.[26]

The New York consulting firm Stern Stewart & Company devised and popularized two shareholder value measures: economic value added (EVA) and market value added (MVA). A basic tenet of EVA and MVA is that businesses should not invest in projects unless they can generate a profit above the cost of capital. Stern Stewart argues that a deficiency of traditional accounting-based measures is that they assume the cost of capital to be zero.[27] Well-known companies, such as Coca-Cola, General Electric, AT&T, Whirlpool, Quaker Oats, Eli Lilly, Georgia-Pacific, Polaroid, Sprint, Teledyne, and Tenneco have adopted MVA and/or EVA as the best yardstick for corporate performance.

Economic Value Added (EVA) has become an extremely popular shareholder value method of measuring corporate and divisional performance and may be on its way to replacing ROI as the standard performance measure. EVA measures the difference between the pre-strategy and post-strategy values for the business. Simply put, EVA is after-tax operating income minus the total annual cost of capital. The formula to measure EVA is:

$$\text{EVA} = \text{after tax operating income} - (\text{investment in assets} \times \text{weighted average cost of capital})[28]$$

The cost of capital combines the cost of debt and equity. The annual cost of borrowed capital is the interest charged by the firm's banks and bondholders. To calculate the cost of equity, assume that shareholders generally earn about 6% more on stocks than on government bonds. If long-term treasury bills are selling at 7.5%, the firm's cost of equity should be 13.5%—more if the firm is in a risky industry. A corporation's overall cost of capital is the weighted-average cost of the firm's debt and equity capital. The investment in assets is the total amount of capital invested in the business, including buildings, machines, computers, and investments in R&D and training (allocating costs annually over their useful life). Because the typical balance sheet understates the investment made in a company, Stern Stewart has identified 150 possible adjustments, before EVA is calculated.[29] Multiply the firm's total investment in assets by the weighted-average cost of capital. Subtract that figure from after-tax operating income. If the difference is positive, the strategy (and the management employing it) is generating value for the shareholders. If it is negative, the strategy is destroying shareholder value.[30]

Roberto Goizueta, past-CEO of Coca-Cola, explained, "We raise capital to make concentrate, and sell it at an operating profit. Then we pay the cost of that capital. Shareholders pocket the difference."[31] Managers can improve their company's or business unit's EVA by: (1) earning more profit without using more capital, (2) using less capital, and (3) investing capital in high-return projects. Studies have found that companies using EVA outperform their median competitor by an average of 8.43% of total return annually.[32] EVA does, however, have some limitations. For one thing, it does not control for size differences across plants or divisions. As with ROI, managers can manipulate the numbers. As with ROI, EVA is an after-the-fact measure and cannot be used like a steering control.[33] Although proponents of EVA argue that EVA (unlike Return on Investment, Equity, or Sales) has a strong relationship to stock price, other studies do not support this contention.[34]

Market Value Added (MVA) is the difference between the market value of a corporation and the capital contributed by shareholders and lenders. Like net present value, it measures the stock market's estimate of the net present value of a firm's past and expected capital investment projects. As such, MVA is the present value of future EVA.[35] To calculate MVA,

1. Add all the capital that has been put into a company—from shareholders, bondholders, and retained earnings.

2. Reclassify certain accounting expenses, such as R&D, to reflect that they are actually investments in future earnings. This provides the firm's total capital. So far, this is the same approach taken in calculating EVA.

3. Using the current stock price, total the value of all outstanding stock, adding it to the company's debt. This is the company's market value. If the company's market value is greater than all the capital invested in it, the firm has a positive MVA—meaning that management (and the strategy it is following) has created wealth. In some cases, however, the market value of the company is actually less than the capital put into it, which means shareholder wealth is being destroyed.

Microsoft, General Electric, Intel, and Coca-Cola have tended to have high MVAs in the United States, whereas, General Motors and RJR Nabisco have had low ones.[36] Studies have shown that EVA is a predictor of MVA. Consecutive years of positive EVA generally lead to a soaring MVA.[37] Research also reveals that CEO turnover is significantly correlated with MVA and EVA, whereas ROA and ROE are not. This suggests that EVA and MVA may be more appropriate measures of the market's evaluation of a firm's strategy and its management than are the traditional measures of corporate performance.[38] Nevertheless, these measures consider only the financial interests of the shareholder and ignore other stakeholders, such as environmentalists and employees.

Climate change is likely to lead to new regulations, technological remedies, and shifts in consumer behavior. It will thus have a significant impact on the financial performance of many corporations. To learn how global warming is likely to affect different industrial sectors and corporations, see the **Environmental Sustainability Issue** feature.

Balanced Scorecard Approach: Using Key Performance Measures

Rather than evaluate a corporation using a few financial measures, Kaplan and Norton argue for a "balanced scorecard," that includes non-financial as well as financial measures.[39] This approach is especially useful given that research indicates that non-financial assets explain 50% to 80% of a firm's value.[40] The **balanced scorecard** combines financial measures that tell the results of actions already taken with operational measures on customer satisfaction, internal processes, and the corporation's innovation and improvement activities—the drivers of future financial performance. Thus steering controls are combined with output controls. In the balanced scorecard, management develops goals or objectives in each of four areas:

1. **Financial:** How do we appear to shareholders?

2. **Customer:** How do customers view us?

3. **Internal business perspective:** What must we excel at?

4. **Innovation and learning:** Can we continue to improve and create value?[41]

ENVIRONMENTAL sustainability issue

HOW GLOBAL WARMING COULD AFFECT CORPORATE VALUATION

How will global warming affect the value of a corporation's stock? To answer this question, the U.S.-based consulting firm McKinsey & Company undertook a joint project with the Carbon Trust, a UK research organization. The resulting research found that the large reductions in greenhouse gas emissions needed to stop climate change will create significant opportunities and risks for most companies. Well-positioned, forward-thinking corporations could, for example, increase company value (stock price × number of shares outstanding) by up to 80%. The research found that as much as 65% of company value was at risk in some industrial sectors.

The joint study investigated the industrial sectors of aluminum, automotive, oil and gas, consumer electronics, building materials, and beer. It quantified the impacts on each industrial sector and found that the impact of climate change will vary by sector. The resulting report lists both the maximum value creation opportunity for a prepared company and the maximum company value at risk for a company that fails to adapt.

Note that the oil and gas sectors will have very few opportunities (especially in exploration and production), but many risks. This overall negative impact will mean falling cash flows and stock prices for the companies in those sectors. In contrast, the building materials sector will benefit from rising demand for improved energy efficiency and insulation products, leading to increasing cash flows and stock prices. The consumer electronics sector is also in a good position. Using current technology, consumer electronics companies can make their products significantly more energy efficient (by reducing active and standby power consumption) at low and diminishing costs. Automobile companies, in contrast, face both a high level of opportunities and threats. The better prepared companies should do well, but the laggards will likely face serious cash flow problems and falling stock prices.

Tom Delay, Carbon Trust's CEO warns: "We have a short window of opportunity to act but at present business and investor actions are way out of step with the need to tackle climate change. They must be urgently re-aligned by developing new business and investment strategies and by working with governments to develop policy frameworks that reward early and effective action to rapidly reduce carbon emissions."

Industrial Sector	Maximum Company Value Creation Opportunity for Prepared Company	Maximum Company Value at Risk for a Company Failing to Adapt
Aluminum	30%	65%
Automotive	60%	65%
Oil & Gas (Exploration & Production)	0%	35%
Oil & Gas (Refining)	7%	30%
Consumer Electronics	35%	7%
Building Materials	80%	20%
Beer	0%	15%

SOURCES: M. W. Brinkman, N. Hoffman, J. M. Oppenheim, "How Climate Change Could Affect Corporate Valuations," *McKinsey Quarterly* (Autumn 2008), pp. 1–7; "Climate Change: The Trillion Dollar Wake-Up Call," *Carbon Trust* Web site (September 22, 2008), www.carbontrust.com.

Each goal in each area (for example, avoiding bankruptcy in the financial area) is then assigned one or more measures, as well as a target and an initiative. These measures can be thought of as **key performance measures**—measures that are essential for achieving a desired strategic option.[42] For example, a company could include cash flow, quarterly sales growth, and ROE as measures for success in the financial area. It could include market share (competitive position goal), customer satisfaction, and percentage of new sales coming from new products (customer acceptance goal) as measures under the customer perspective. It could include cycle time and unit cost (manufacturing excellence goal) as measures under the internal business perspective. It could include time to develop next generation products (technology leadership objective) under the innovation and learning perspective.

A survey by Bain & Company reported that 50% of *Fortune 1,000* companies in North America and about 40% in Europe use a version of the balanced scorecard.[43] Another survey reported that the balanced scorecard is used by over half of *Fortune's Global 1000* companies.[44] A study of the *Fortune 500* firms in the U.S. and the *Post 300* firms in Canada revealed the most popular non-financial measures to be customer satisfaction, customer service, product quality, market share, productivity, service quality, and core competencies. New product development, corporate culture, and market growth were not far behind.[45] DuPont's Engineering Polymers Division uses the balanced scorecard to align employees, business units, and shared services around a common strategy involving productivity improvements and revenue growth.[46] Corporate experience with the balanced scorecard reveals that a firm should tailor the system to suit its situation, not just adopt it as a cookbook approach. When the balanced scorecard complements corporate strategy, it improves performance. Using the method in a mechanistic fashion without any link to strategy hinders performance and may even decrease it.[47]

Evaluating Top Management and the Board of Directors

Through its strategy, audit, and compensation committees, a board of directors closely evaluates the job performance of the CEO and the top management team. The vast majority of American (91%), European (75%), and Asian (75%) boards review the CEO's performance using a formalized process.[48] Objective evaluations of the CEO by the board are very important given that CEOs tend to evaluate senior management's performance significantly more positively than do other executives.[49] The board is concerned primarily with overall corporate profitability as measured quantitatively by ROI, ROE, EPS, and shareholder value. The absence of short-run profitability certainly contributes to the firing of any CEO. The board, however, is also concerned with other factors.

Members of the compensation committees of today's boards of directors generally agree that a CEO's ability to establish strategic direction, build a management team, and provide leadership are more critical in the long run than are a few quantitative measures. The board should evaluate top management not only on the typical output-oriented quantitative measures, but also on behavioral measures—factors relating to its strategic management practices. According to a survey by Korn/Ferry International, the criteria used by American boards are financial (81%), ethical behavior (63%), thought leadership (58%), corporate reputation (32%), stock price performance (22%), and meeting participation (10%).[50] The specific items that a board uses to evaluate its top management should be derived from the objectives that both the board and top management agreed on earlier. If better relations with the local community and improved safety practices in work areas were selected as objectives for the year (or for five years), these items should be included in the evaluation. In addition, other factors that tend to lead to profitability might be included, such as market share, product quality, or investment intensity.

Performance evaluations of the overall board's performance are standard practice for 87% of directors in the Americas, 72% in Europe, and 62% in Asia.[51] Evaluations of individual directors are less common. According to a PriceWaterhouseCoopers survey of 1,100 directors, 77% of the directors agreed that individual directors should be appraised regularly on their performance, but only 37% responded that they actually do so.[52] Corporations that have successfully used board performance appraisal systems are Target, Radio Shack, Eastman Chemical Company, Bell South, Raytheon, and Gillette.[53] However, in India, the move towards board reviews has been relatively slow and there continues to be some resistance by older or more senior directors, in particular, to the idea of individual director appraisals. Independent surveys have found that only one out of five companies appraises the board's performance in India.[54] In India, many companies have voluntarily developed board appraisal systems. One of the pioneers in this field was **Colgate-Palmolive (India) Ltd**. It introduced a formal board evaluation procedure in

1997. Its board committees conduct self-evaluations which are then reviewed by the board and the company complements this with evaluations for individual directors.[55] In 2004, Dabur India Ltd. implemented a process of performance evaluation system for its board of directors. The committee evaluates the board in three areas, namely guiding strategy, monitoring management performance and development/compensation, and statutory compliance and corporate governance.[56] Cognizant Technologies has empowered its Compensation Committee to evaluate its senior executives. The Compensation Committee in conjunction with the Audit Committee is responsible for such evaluation.[57] At **Infosys Technologies Ltd,** its board evaluates the performance of nonexecutive/independent directors through a peer evaluation process every year, whereas at **Wipro Limited**, the board governance and compensation committees oversee an annual performance evaluation where the performance of individuals is also evaluated and the chairman of the board communicates the results to each director.[58]

Chairman-CEO Feedback Instrument. An increasing number of companies are evaluating their CEO by using a 17-item questionnaire developed by Ram Charan, an authority on corporate governance. The questionnaire focuses on four key areas: (1) company performance, (2) leadership of the organization, (3) team-building and management succession, and (4) leadership of external constituencies.[59] After taking an hour to complete the questionnaire, the board of KeraVision, Inc. used it as a basis for a lengthy discussion with the CEO, Thomas Loarie. The board criticized Loarie for "not tempering enthusiasm with reality" and urged Loarie to develop a clear management succession plan. The evaluation caused Loarie to more closely involve the board in setting the company's primary objectives and discussing "where we are, where we want to go, and the operating environment."[60]

Management Audit. **Management audits** are very useful to boards of directors in evaluating management's handling of various corporate activities. Management audits have been developed to evaluate activities such as corporate social responsibility, functional areas such as the marketing department, and divisions such as the international division. These can be helpful if the board has selected particular functional areas or activities for improvement.

Strategic Audit. The strategic audit, presented in the **Chapter 1 Appendix 1.A**, is a type of management audit. The strategic audit provides a checklist of questions, by area or issue, that enables a systematic analysis of various corporate functions and activities to be made. It is a type of management audit and is extremely useful as a diagnostic tool to pinpoint corporate-wide problem areas and to highlight organizational strengths and weaknesses.[61] A strategic audit can help determine why a certain area is creating problems for a corporation and help generate solutions to the problem. As such, it can be very useful in evaluating the performance of top management.

PRIMARY MEASURES OF DIVISIONAL AND FUNCTIONAL PERFORMANCE

Companies use a variety of techniques to evaluate and control performance in divisions, strategic business units (SBUs), and functional areas. If a corporation is composed of SBUs or divisions, it will use many of the same performance measures (ROI or EVA, for instance) that it uses to assess overall corporate performance. To the extent that it can isolate specific functional units such as R&D, the corporation may develop responsibility centers. It will also use typical functional measures, such as market share and sales per employee (marketing), unit costs and percentage of defects (operations), percentage of sales from new products and number of patents (R&D), and turnover and job satisfaction (HRM). For example, FedEx uses Enhanced Tracker software with its COSMOS database to track the progress of its 2.5 to 3.5

million shipments daily. As a courier is completing her or his day's activities, the Enhanced Tracker asks whether the person's package count equals the Enhanced Tracker's count. If the count is off, the software helps reconcile the differences.[62]

During strategy formulation and implementation, top management approves a series of programs and supporting *operating budgets* from its business units. During evaluation and control, actual expenses are contrasted with planned expenditures, and the degree of variance is assessed. This is typically done on a monthly basis. In addition, top management will probably require *periodic statistical reports* summarizing data on such key factors as the number of new customer contracts, the volume of received orders, and productivity figures.

Responsibility Centers

Control systems can be established to monitor specific functions, projects, or divisions. Budgets are one type of control system that is typically used to control the financial indicators of performance. **Responsibility centers** are used to isolate a unit so that it can be evaluated separately from the rest of the corporation. Each responsibility center, therefore, has its own budget and is evaluated on its use of budgeted resources. It is headed by the manager responsible for the center's performance. The center uses resources (measured in terms of costs or expenses) to produce a service or a product (measured in terms of volume or revenues). There are five major types of responsibility centers. The type is determined by the way the corporation's control system measures these resources and services or products.

1. **Standard cost centers: Standard cost centers** are primarily used in manufacturing facilities. Standard (or expected) costs are computed for each operation on the basis of historical data. In evaluating the center's performance, its total standard costs are multiplied by the units produced. The result is the *expected* cost of production, which is then compared to the *actual* cost of production.

2. **Revenue centers:** With **revenue centers**, production, usually in terms of unit or dollar sales, is measured without consideration of resource costs (for example, salaries). The center is thus judged in terms of effectiveness rather than efficiency. The effectiveness of a sales region, for example, is determined by comparing its actual sales to its projected or previous year's sales. Profits are not considered because sales departments have very limited influence over the cost of the products they sell.

3. **Expense centers:** Resources are measured in dollars, without consideration for service or product costs. Thus budgets will have been prepared for engineered expenses (costs that can be calculated) and for discretionary expenses (costs that can be only estimated). Typical **expense centers** are administrative, service, and research departments. They cost a company money, but they only indirectly contribute to revenues.

4. **Profit centers:** Performance is measured in terms of the difference between revenues (which measure production) and expenditures (which measure resources). A **profit center** is typically established whenever an organizational unit has control over both its resources and its products or services. By having such centers, a company can be organized into divisions of separate product lines. The manager of each division is given autonomy to the extent that he or she is able to keep profits at a satisfactory (or better) level.

   Some organizational units that are not usually considered potentially autonomous can, for the purpose of profit center evaluations, be made so. A manufacturing department, for example, can be converted from a standard cost center (or expense center) into a profit center; it is allowed to charge a transfer price for each product it "sells" to the sales department. The difference between the manufacturing cost per unit and the agreed-upon transfer price is the unit's "profit."

Transfer pricing is commonly used in vertically integrated corporations and can work well when a price can be easily determined for a designated amount of product. Even though most experts agree that market-based transfer prices are the best choice, only 30%–40% of companies use market price to set the transfer price. (Of the rest, 50% use cost; 10%–20% use negotiation.)[63] When a price cannot be set easily, however, the relative bargaining power of the centers, rather than strategic considerations, tends to influence the agreed-upon price. Top management has an obligation to make sure that these political considerations do not overwhelm the strategic ones. Otherwise, profit figures for each center will be biased and provide poor information for strategic decisions at both the corporate and divisional levels.

5. **Investment centers:** Because many divisions in large manufacturing corporations use significant assets to make their products, their asset base should be factored into their performance evaluation. Thus it is insufficient to focus only on profits, as in the case of profit centers. An **investment center's** performance is measured in terms of the difference between its resources and its services or products. For example, two divisions in a corporation made identical profits, but one division owns a $3 million plant, whereas the other owns a $1 million plant. Both make the same profits, but one is obviously more efficient; the smaller plant provides the shareholders with a better return on their investment. The most widely used measure of investment center performance is ROI.

Most single-business corporations, such as Apple, tend to use a combination of cost, expense, and revenue centers. In these corporations, most managers are functional specialists and manage against a budget. Total profitability is integrated at the corporate level. Multidivisional corporations with one dominating product line (such as Anheuser-Busch), that have diversified into a few businesses but that still depend on a single product line (such as beer) for most of their revenue and income, generally use a combination of cost, expense, revenue, and profit centers. Multidivisional corporations, such as General Electric, tend to emphasize investment centers—although in various units throughout the corporation other types of responsibility centers are also used. One problem with using responsibility centers, however, is that the separation needed to measure and evaluate a division's performance can diminish the level of cooperation among divisions that is needed to attain synergy for the corporation as a whole. (This problem is discussed later in this chapter, under "Suboptimization.")

Using Benchmarking to Evaluate Performance

According to Xerox Corporation, the company that pioneered this concept in the United States, **benchmarking** is "the continual process of measuring products, services, and practices against the toughest competitors or those companies recognized as industry leaders."[64] Benchmarking, an increasingly popular program, is based on the concept that it makes no sense to reinvent something that someone else is already using. It involves openly learning how others do something better than one's own company so that the company not only can imitate, but perhaps even improve on its techniques. The benchmarking process usually involves the following steps:

1. Identify the area or process to be examined. It should be an activity that has the potential to determine a business unit's competitive advantage.

2. Find behavioral and output measures of the area or process and obtain measurements.

3. Select an accessible set of competitors and best-in-class companies against which to benchmark. These may very often be companies that are in completely different industries, but perform similar activities. For example, when Xerox wanted to improve its order

fulfillment, it went to L. L. Bean, the successful mail order firm, to learn how it achieved excellence in this area.

4. Calculate the differences among the company's performance measurements and those of the best-in-class and determine why the differences exist.

5. Develop tactical programs for closing performance gaps.

6. Implement the programs and then compare the resulting new measurements with those of the best-in-class companies.

Benchmarking has been found to produce best results in companies that are already well managed. Apparently poorer performing firms tend to be overwhelmed by the discrepancy between their performance and the benchmark—and tend to view the benchmark as too difficult to reach.[65] Nevertheless, a survey by Bain & Company of 460 companies of various sizes across all U.S. industries indicated that more than 70% were using benchmarking in either a major or limited manner.[66] Cost reductions range from 15% to 45%.[67] Benchmarking can also increase sales, improve goal setting, and boost employee motivation.[68] The average cost of a benchmarking study is around $100,000 and involves 30 weeks of effort.[69] Manco, Inc., a small Cleveland-area producer of duct tape regularly benchmarks itself against Wal-Mart, Rubbermaid, and Pepsico to enable it to better compete with giant 3M. APQC (American Productivity & Quality Center), a Houston research group, established the Open Standards Benchmarking Collaborative database, composed of more than 1,200 commonly used measures and individual benchmarks, to track the performance of core operational functions. Firms can submit their performance data to this online database to learn how they compare to top performers and industry peers (see www.apqc.org).

INTERNATIONAL MEASUREMENT ISSUES

The three most widely used techniques for international performance evaluation are ROI, budget analysis, and historical comparisons. In one study, 95% of the corporate officers interviewed stated that they use the same evaluation techniques for foreign and domestic operations. Rate of return was mentioned as the single most important measure.[70] However, ROI can cause problems when it is applied to international operations: Because of foreign currencies, different accounting systems, different rates of inflation, different tax laws, and the use of transfer pricing, both the net income figure and the investment base may be seriously distorted.[71] To deal with different accounting systems throughout the world, the London-based International Accounting Standards Board developed International Financial Reporting Standards (IFRS) to harmonize accounting practices. Over 100 countries have thus far adopted the rules. Foreign-based companies operating in the U.S. have a choice starting 2009 of using IFRS accounting standards or continuing the costly process translating their accounts using America's Generally Accepted Accounting Principles (GAAP). Nevertheless, enforcement and cultural interpretations of the international rules can still vary by country and may undercut what is hoped to be a uniform accounting system.[72]

A study of 79 MNCs revealed that *international transfer pricing* from one country unit to another is primarily used not to evaluate performance but to minimize taxes.[73] Taxes are an important issue for MNCs, given that corporate tax rates vary from 55% in Kuwait, 41% in Japan, 40% in the United States, and 34% in Canada and India, to 28% in the UK, South Korea, and Mexico, 25% in China, 18% in Singapore, 10% in Albania, and 0% in Bahrain and the Cayman Islands.[74] For example, the U.S. Internal Revenue Service contended in the early 1990s that many Japanese firms doing business in the United States artificially inflated the value of

U.S. deliveries in order to reduce the profits and thus the taxes of their American subsidiaries.[75] Parts made in a subsidiary of a Japanese MNC in a low-tax country such as Singapore could be shipped to its subsidiary in a high-tax country such as the United States at such a high price that the U.S. subsidiary reports very little profit (and thus pays few taxes), while the Singapore subsidiary reports a very high profit (but also pays few taxes because of the lower tax rate). A Japanese MNC could, therefore, earn more profit worldwide by reporting less profit in high-tax countries and more profit in low-tax countries. Transfer pricing can thus be one way the parent company can reduce taxes and "capture profits" from a subsidiary. Other common ways of transferring profits to the parent company (often referred to as the *repatriation of profits*) are through dividends, royalties, and management fees.[76]

Among the most important barriers to international trade are the different standards for products and services. There are at least three categories of standards: safety/environmental, energy efficiency, and testing procedures. Existing standards have been drafted by such bodies as the British Standards Institute (BSI-UK) in the United Kingdom, Japanese Industrial Standards Committee (JISC), AFNOR in France, DIN in Germany, CSA in Canada, and American Standards Institute in the United States. These standards traditionally created entry barriers that served to fragment various industries, such as major home appliances, by country. The International Electrotechnical Commission (IEC) standards were created to harmonize standards in the European Union and eventually to serve as worldwide standards, with some national deviations to satisfy specific needs. Because the European Union (EU) was the first to harmonize the many different standards of its member countries, the EU is shaping standards for the rest of the world. In addition, the International Organization for Standardization (ISO) is preparing and publishing international standards. These standards provide a foundation for regional associations to build upon. CANENA, the Council for Harmonization of Electrotechnical Standards of the Nations of the Americas, was created in 1992 to further coordinate the harmonization of standards in North and South America. Efforts are also under way in Asia to harmonize standards.[77]

An important issue in international trade is counterfeiting/piracy. Firms in developing nations around the world make money by making counterfeit/pirated copies of well-known name-brand products and selling them globally as well as locally. See the **Global Issue** feature to learn how this is being done.

Authorities in international business recommend that the control and reward systems used by a global MNC be different from those used by a multidomestic MNC.[78] A *multidomestic MNC* should use loose controls on its foreign units. The management of each geographic unit should be given considerable operational latitude, but it should be expected to meet some performance targets. Because profit and ROI measures are often unreliable in international operations, it is recommended that the MNC's top management, in this instance, emphasize budgets and non-financial measures of performance such as market share, productivity, public image, employee morale, and relations with the host country government.[79] Multiple measures should be used to differentiate between the worth of the subsidiary and the performance of its management.

A *global MNC*, however, needs tight controls over its many units. To reduce costs and gain competitive advantage, it is trying to spread the manufacturing and marketing operations of a few fairly uniform products around the world. Therefore, its key operational decisions must be centralized. Its environmental scanning must include research not only into each of the national markets in which the MNC competes but also into the "global arena" of the interaction between markets. Foreign units are thus evaluated more as cost centers, revenue centers, or expense centers than as investment or profit centers because MNCs operating in a global industry do not often make the entire product in the country in which it is sold.

GLOBAL issue

COUNTERFEIT GOODS & PIRATED SOFTWARE: A GLOBAL PROBLEM

"We know that 15 to 20 percent of all goods in China are counterfeit," states Dan Chow, a law professor at Ohio State University. This includes products from Tide detergent and Budweiser beer to Marlboro cigarettes. There is a saying in Shanghai, China: "We can copy everything except your mother." Yamaha estimates that five out of every six bikes bearing its brand name are fake. Fake Cisco network routers (known as "Chiscos") and counterfeit Nokia mobile phones can be easily found throughout China. Procter & Gamble estimates that 15% of the soaps and detergents under its Head & Shoulders, Vidal Sassoon, Safeguard, and Tide brands in China are counterfeit, costing the company $150 million in lost sales.

In Yiwu, a few hours from Shanghai, one person admitted to a *60 Minutes* reporter that she could make 1,000 pairs of counterfeit Nike shoes in 10 days for $4.00 a pair. According to the market research firm Automotive Resources, the profit margins on counterfeit shock absorbers can reach 80% versus only 15% for the real ones. The World Custom Organization estimates that 7% of the world's merchandise is bogus.

Tens of thousands of counterfeiters are active in China. They range from factories mixing shampoo and soap in back rooms to large state-owned enterprises making copies of soft drinks and beer. Other factories make everything from car batteries to automobiles. Mobile CD factories with optical disc-mastering machines counterfeit music and software. *60 Minutes* found a small factory in Donguan making fake Callaway golf clubs and bags at a rate of 500 bags per week. Factories in southern Guangdong or Fujian provinces truck their products to a central distribution center, such as the one in Yiwu. They may also be shipped across the border into Russia, Pakistan, Vietnam, or Burma. Chinese counterfeiters have developed a global reach through their connections with organized crime.

As much as 35% of software on personal computers worldwide is pirated, according to the Business Software Alliance and ISDC, a market research firm. The worldwide cost of software piracy was around $34 billion in 2005. For example, 21% of the software sold in the United States is pirated. That figure increases to 26%–30% in the European Union, 83% in Russia, Algeria, and Bolivia, to 86% in China, 87% in Indonesia, and 90% in Vietnam.

....

SOURCES: "The Sincerest Form of Flattery," *The Economist* (April 7, 2007), pp. 64–65; F. Balfour, "Fakes!" Business Week (February 7, 2005), pp. 54–64; "PC Software Piracy," *The Economist* (June 10, 2006), p. 102; "The World's Greatest Fakes," *60 Minutes*, CBS News (August 8, 2004); "Business Software Piracy," *Pocket World in Figures 2004* (London: Economist & Profile Book, 2003), p. 60; D. Roberts, F. Balfour, P. Magnusson, P. Engardio, and J. Lee, "China's Piracy Plague," *Business Week* (June 5, 2000), pp. 44–48.

11.3 Strategic Information Systems

Before performance measures can have any impact on strategic management, they must first be communicated to the people responsible for formulating and implementing strategic plans. Strategic information systems can perform this function. They can be computer based or manual, formal or informal. One of the key reasons given for the bankruptcy of International Harvester was the inability of the corporation's top management to precisely determine income by major class of similar products. Because of this inability, management kept trying to fix ailing businesses and was unable to respond flexibly to major changes and unexpected events. In contrast, one of the key reasons for the success of Wal-Mart has been management's use of the company's sophisticated information system to control purchasing decisions. Cash registers in Wal-Mart retail stores transmit information hourly to computers at company headquarters. Consequently, managers know every morning exactly how many of each item were sold the day before, how many have been sold so far in the year, and how this year's sales compare to last year's. The information system allows all reordering to be done automatically by computers, without any managerial input. It also allows the company to experiment with new products without committing to big orders in advance. In effect, the system allows the customers to decide through their purchases what gets reordered.

ENTERPRISE RESOURCE PLANNING (ERP)

Many corporations around the world have adopted **enterprise resource planning (ERP)** software. ERP unites all of a company's major business activities, from order processing to production, within a single family of software modules. The system provides instant access to critical information to everyone in the organization, from the CEO to the factory floor worker. Because of the ability of ERP software to use a common information system throughout a company's many operations around the world, it is becoming the business information systems' global standard. The major providers of this software are SAP AG, Oracle (including People-Soft), J. D. Edwards, Baan, and SSA.

The German company SAP AG originated the concept with its R/3 software system. Microsoft, for example, used R/3 to replace a tangle of 33 financial tracking systems in 26 subsidiaries. Even though it cost the company $25 million and took 10 months to install, R/3 annually saves Microsoft $18 million. Coca-Cola uses the R/3 system to enable a manager in Atlanta to use her personal computer to check the latest sales of 20-ounce bottles of Coke Classic in India. Owens-Corning envisioned that its R/3 system allowed salespeople to learn what was available at any plant or warehouse and to quickly assemble orders for customers.

ERP may not fit every company, however. The system is extremely complicated and demands a high level of standardization throughout a corporation. Its demanding nature often forces companies to change the way they do business. There are three reasons ERP could fail: (1) insufficient tailoring of the software to fit the company, (2) inadequate training, and (3) insufficient implementation support.[80] Over the two-year period of installing R/3, Owens-Corning had to completely overhaul its operations. Because R/3 was incompatible with Apple's very organic corporate culture, the company was able to apply it only to its order management and financial operations, but not to manufacturing. Other companies that had difficulty installing and using ERP are Whirlpool, Hershey Foods, Volkswagen, and Stanley Works. At Whirlpool, SAP's software led to missed and delayed shipments, causing Home Depot to cancel its agreement for selling Whirlpool products.[81] In India, Tata Power was the first utility company to implement an industry-specific ERP solution in early 2001. The company formed a team for each functional area. It then tied up with Tata Technologies to assist in implementation of the processes. SAP R/3 implementation covered all generations including distribution across all 28 locations; complete supply chain; centralized procurement; vendor management; cash cycle; centralized accounting; project management, budgeting, and monitoring; plant defect notification and work order management; HR organizational and personnel administration and customer management: and bill processing.[82] One survey found that 65% of executives believed that ERP had a moderate chance of hurting their business because of implementation problems. Nevertheless, the payoff from ERP software is likely to be worth the effort. ERP is a key ingredient for gaining competitive advantage, streamlining operations, and managing a lean manufacturing system.[83]

RADIO FREQUENCY IDENTIFICATION (RFID)

Radio frequency identification (RFID) is an electronic tagging technology used in a number of companies to improve supply-chain efficiency. By tagging containers and items with tiny chips, companies use the tags as wireless bar-codes to track inventory more efficiently. Both Wal-Mart and the U.S. Department of Defense began requiring their largest suppliers to incorporate RFID tags in their goods in 2003. Although Tesco has experimented with RFID in Europe, full-scale use of the technology proved unfeasible because of incompatible standards. Nevertheless, some suppliers and retailers of expensive consumer products view the cost of the tag as worthwhile because it reduces losses from counterfeiting and theft. RFID technology is currently in wide use as wireless commuter passes for toll roads, tunnels, and bridges. Even though RFID standards may vary among companies, individual firms like Audi, Sony, and Dole Food use the tags to track goods within their own factories and warehouses.[84] According to Dan Mullen of AIM Global, "RFID will go through a process similar to what happened in bar code technology 20 years ago. . . . As companies implement the technology deeper within their operations, the return on investment will grow and applications will expand."[85]

DIVISIONAL AND FUNCTIONAL IS SUPPORT

At the divisional or SBU level of a corporation, the information system should be used to support, reinforce, or enlarge its business-level strategy through its decision support system. An SBU pursuing a strategy of overall cost leadership could use its information system to reduce costs either by improving labor productivity or improving the use of other resources such as inventory or machinery. Merrill Lynch took this approach when it developed PRISM software to provide its 500 U.S. retail offices with quick access to financial information in order to boost brokers' efficiency. Another SBU, in contrast, might want to pursue a differentiation strategy. It could use its information system to add uniqueness to the product or service and contribute to quality, service, or image through the functional areas. FedEx wanted to use superior service to gain a competitive advantage. It invested significantly in several types of information systems to measure and track the performance of its delivery service. Together, these information systems gave FedEx the fastest error-response time in the overnight delivery business.

11.4 Problems in Measuring Performance

The measurement of performance is a crucial part of evaluation and control. The lack of quantifiable objectives or performance standards and the inability of the information system to provide timely and valid information are two obvious control problems. According to Meg Whitman, past-CEO of eBay, "If you can't measure it, you can't control it." That's why eBay has a multitude of measures, from total revenues and profits to *take rate*, the ratio of revenues to the value of goods traded on the site.[86] Without objective and timely measurements, it would be extremely difficult to make operational, let alone strategic, decisions. Nevertheless, the use of timely, quantifiable standards does not guarantee good performance. The very act of monitoring and measuring performance can cause side effects that interfere with overall corporate performance. Among the most frequent negative side effects are a short-term orientation and goal displacement.

SHORT-TERM ORIENTATION

Top executives report that in many situations, they analyze neither the long-term implications of present operations on the strategy they have adopted nor the operational impact of a strategy on the corporate mission. Long-run evaluations may not be conducted because executives (1) don't realize their importance, (2) believe that short-run considerations are more important than long-run considerations, (3) aren't personally evaluated on a long-term basis, or (4) don't have the time to make a long-run analysis.[87] There is no real justification for the first and last reasons. If executives realize the importance of long-run evaluations, they make the time needed to conduct them. Even though many chief executives point to immediate pressures from the investment community and to short-term incentive and promotion plans to support the second and third reasons, evidence does not always support their claims.[88]

At one international heavy-equipment manufacturer, managers were so strongly motivated to achieve their quarterly revenue target that they shipped unfinished products from their plant in England to a warehouse in the Netherlands for final assembly. By shipping the incomplete products, they were able to realize the sales before the end of the quarter—thus fulfilling their budgeted objective and making their bonuses. Unfortunately, the high cost of assembling the goods at a distant location (requiring not only the renting the warehouse but also paying additional labor) ended up reducing the company's overall profit.[89]

Many accounting-based measures, such as EPS and ROI, encourage a **short-term orientation** in which managers consider only current tactical or operational issues and ignore long-term strategic ones. Because growth in EPS (earnings per share) is an important driver of near-term stock price, top managers are biased against investments that might reduce short-term EPS.[90] This is compounded by pressure from financial analysts and investors for quarterly *earnings guidance*, that is, estimates of future corporate earnings.[91] For example, in a $303 million law suit settled in 2008, General Motors admitted that its top managers and auditor had misstated its revenue, earnings, and cash flow in order to artificially inflate the company's stock price and debt securities.[92]

Table 11.1 indicates that one of the limitations of ROI as a performance measure is its short-term nature. In theory, ROI is not limited to the short run, but in practice it is often difficult to use this measure to realize long-term benefits for a company. Because managers can often manipulate both the numerator (earnings) and the denominator (investment), the resulting ROI figure can be meaningless. Advertising, maintenance, and research efforts can be reduced. Estimates of pension-fund profits, unpaid receivables, and old inventory, are easy to adjust. Optimistic estimates of returned products, bad debts, and obsolete inventory inflate the present year's sales and earnings.[93] Expensive retooling and plant modernization can be delayed as long as a manager can manipulate figures on production defects and absenteeism. In a recent survey of financial executives, 80% of the managers stated that they would decrease spending on research and development, advertising, maintenance, and hiring in order to meet earnings targets. More than half said that they would delay a new project even if it meant sacrificing value.[94]

Mergers can be undertaken that will do more for the present year's earnings (and the next year's paycheck) than for the division's or corporation's future profits. For example, research on 55 firms that engaged in major acquisitions revealed that even though the firms performed poorly after the acquisition, the acquiring firms' top management still received significant increases in compensation.[95] Determining CEO compensation on the basis of firm size rather than performance is typical and is particularly likely for firms that are not monitored closely by independent analysts.[96]

Research supports the conclusion that many CEOs and their friends on the board of directors' compensation committee manipulate information to provide themselves a pay raise.[97] For example, CEOs tend to announce bad news—thus reducing the company's stock price—just before the issuance of stock options. Once the options are issued, the CEOs tend to announce good news—thus raising the stock price and making their options more valuable.[98] Board compensation committees tend to expand the peer group comparison outside their industry to include lower-performing firms to justify a high raise to the CEO. They tend to do this when the company performs poorly, the industry performs well, the CEO is already highly paid, and shareholders are powerful and active.[99]

GOAL DISPLACEMENT

If not carefully done, monitoring and measuring of performance can actually result in a decline in overall corporate performance. **Goal displacement** is the confusion of means with ends and occurs when activities originally intended to help managers attain corporate objectives become ends in themselves—or are adapted to meet ends other than those for which they were intended. Two types of goal displacement are behavior substitution and suboptimization.

Behavior Substitution

Behavior substitution refers to a phenomenon when people substitute activities that do not lead to goal accomplishment for activities that do lead to goal accomplishment because the wrong activities are being rewarded. Managers, like most other people, tend to focus more of their attention on behaviors that are clearly measurable than on those that are not. Employees often receive little or no reward for engaging in hard-to-measure activities such as cooperation and initiative. However, easy-to-measure activities might have little or no relationship to the desired good performance. Rational people, nevertheless, tend to work for the rewards that the system has to offer. Therefore, people tend to substitute behaviors that are recognized and rewarded for behaviors that are ignored, without regard to their contribution to goal accomplishment. A research study of 157 corporations revealed that most of the companies made little attempt to identify areas of non-financial performance that might advance their chosen strategy. Only 23% consistently built and verified cause-and-effect relationships between intermediate controls (such as number of patents filed or product flaws) and company performance.[100]

A U.S. Navy quip sums up this situation: "What you inspect (or reward) is what you get." If the reward system emphasizes quantity while merely asking for quality and cooperation, the system is likely to produce a large number of low-quality products and unsatisfied customers.[101] A proposed law governing the effect of measurement on behavior is that *quantifiable measures drive out non-quantifiable measures*.

A classic example of behavior substitution happened a few years ago at Sears. Sears' management thought that it could improve employee productivity by tying performance to rewards. It, therefore, paid commissions to its auto shop employees as a percentage of each repair bill. Behavior substitution resulted as employees altered their behavior to fit the reward system. The results were over-billed customers, charges for work never done, and a scandal that tarnished Sears' reputation for many years.[102]

Suboptimization

Suboptimization refers to the phenomenon of a unit optimizing its goal accomplishment to the detriment of the organization as a whole. The emphasis in large corporations on developing separate responsibility centers can create some problems for the corporation as a whole. To the extent that a division or functional unit views itself as a separate entity, it might refuse to cooperate with other units or divisions in the same corporation if cooperation could in some way negatively affect its performance evaluation. The competition between divisions to achieve a high ROI can result in one division's refusal to share its new technology or work process improvements. One division's attempt to optimize the accomplishment of its goals can cause other divisions to fall behind and thus negatively affect overall corporate performance. One common example of suboptimization occurs when a marketing department approves an early shipment date to a customer as a means of getting an order and forces the manufacturing department into overtime production for that one order. Production costs are raised, which reduces the manufacturing department's overall efficiency. The end result might be that, although marketing achieves its sales goal, the corporation as a whole fails to achieve its expected profitability.[103]

11.5 Guidelines for Proper Control

In designing a control system, top management should remember that controls should follow strategy. Unless controls ensure the use of the proper strategy to achieve objectives, there is a strong likelihood that dysfunctional side effects will completely undermine the implementation of the objectives. The following guidelines are recommended:

1. **Control should involve only the minimum amount of information needed to give a reliable picture of events:** Too many controls create confusion. Focus on the strategic factors by following the **80/20 rule**: *Monitor those 20% of the factors that determine 80% of the results.* See **Strategy Highlight 11.2** for some additional rules of thumb used by strategists.

STRATEGY highlight 11.2

SOME RULES OF THUMB IN STRATEGY

Managers use many *rules of thumb,* such as the 80/20 rule, in making strategic decisions. These "rules" are primarily approximations based on years of practical experience by many managers. Although most of these rules have no objective data to support them, they are often accepted by practicing managers as a way of estimating the cost or time necessary to conduct certain activities. They may be useful because they can help narrow the number of alternatives into a shorter list for more detailed analysis. Some of the rules of thumb used by experienced strategists are described here.

INDIRECT COSTS OF STRATEGIC INITIATIVES

■ The R&D *Rule of Sevens* is that for every $1 spent in developing a new prototype, $7 will be needed to get a product ready for market, and $7 additional dollars will be required to get to the first sale. These estimates don't cover working capital requirements for stocking distributor inventories.

■ First-year costs for promoting a new consumer goods product are 33% of anticipated first-year sales. Second-year costs should be 20%, and third-year costs 15%.

■ A reasonably successful patent-based innovation will require $2 million in legal defense costs.

SAFETY MARGINS FOR NEW BUSINESS INITIATIVES

■ A new manufacturing business should have sufficient startup capital to cover one year of costs.

■ A new consumer goods business should have sufficient capital to cover two years of business.

■ A new professional services business should have sufficient capital to cover three years of costs.

SOURCE: R. West and F. Wolek, "Rules of Thumb in Strategic Thinking," *Strategy & Leadership* (March/April 1999), p. 34. Copyright © 1999 by Emerald Group Publishing Ltd. Reprinted by permission.

2. **Controls should monitor only meaningful activities and results, regardless of measurement difficulty:** If cooperation between divisions is important to corporate performance, some form of qualitative or quantitative measure should be established to monitor cooperation.

3. **Controls should be timely so that corrective action can be taken before it is too late:** Steering controls, controls that monitor or measure the factors influencing performance, should be stressed so that advance notice of problems is given.

4. **Long-term *and* short-term controls should be used:** If only short-term measures are emphasized, a short-term managerial orientation is likely.

5. **Controls should aim at pinpointing exceptions:** Only activities or results that fall outside a predetermined tolerance range should call for action.

6. **Emphasize the reward of meeting or exceeding standards rather than punishment for failing to meet standards:** Heavy punishment of failure typically results in goal displacement. Managers will "fudge" reports and lobby for lower standards.

If corporate culture complements and reinforces the strategic orientation of a firm, there is less need for an extensive formal control system. In their book *In Search of Excellence*, Peters and Waterman state that "the stronger the culture and the more it was directed toward the marketplace, the less need was there for policy manuals, organizational charts, or detailed procedures and rules. In these companies, people way down the line know what they are supposed to do in most situations because the handful of guiding values is crystal clear."[104] For example, at Eaton Corporation, the employees are expected to enforce the rules themselves. If someone misses too much work or picks fights with co-workers, other members of the production team point out the problem. According to Randy Savage, a long-time Eaton employee, "They say there are no bosses here, but if you screw up, you find one pretty fast."[105]

11.6 Strategic Incentive Management

To ensure congruence between the needs of a corporation as a whole and the needs of the employees as individuals, management and the board of directors should develop an incentive program that rewards desired performance. This reduces the likelihood of the agency problems (when employees act to feather their own nests instead of building shareholder value) mentioned earlier in **Chapter 2**. Incentive plans should be linked in some way to corporate and divisional strategy. Research reveals that firm performance is affected by its compensation policies.[106] Companies using different strategies tend to adopt different pay policies. For example, a survey of 600 business units indicates that the pay mix associated with a growth strategy emphasizes bonuses and other incentives over salary and benefits, whereas the pay mix associated with a stability strategy has the reverse emphasis.[107] Research indicates that SBU managers having long-term performance elements in their compensation program favor a long-term perspective and thus greater investments in R&D, capital equipment, and employee training.[108] Although the typical CEO pay package is composed of 21% salary, 27% short-term annual incentives, 16% long-term incentives, and 36% stock options,[109] there is some evidence that stock options are being replaced by greater emphasis on performance-related pay.[110]

The following three approaches are tailored to help match measurements and rewards with explicit strategic objectives and time frames:[111]

1. **Weighted-factor method:** The weighted-factor method is particularly appropriate for measuring and rewarding the performance of top SBU managers and group-level executives when performance factors and their importance vary from one SBU to another. Using portfolio analysis, one corporation's measurements might contain the following variations: the performance of high-performing (star) SBUs is measured equally in terms of ROI, cash flow, market share, and progress on several future-oriented strategic projects; the performance of low-growth, but strong (cash cow) SBUs, in contrast, is measured in terms of ROI, market share, and cash generation; and the performance of developing (question marks) SBUs is measured in terms of development and market share growth with no weight on ROI or cash flow. (Refer to **Figure 11.3.**)

2. **Long-term evaluation method:** The **long-term evaluation method** compensates managers for achieving objectives set over a multiyear period. An executive is promised some company stock or "performance units" (convertible into money or stock) in amounts to be based on long-term performance. A board of directors, for example, might set a particular objective in terms of growth in earnings per share during a five-year period. The giving of awards would be contingent on the corporation's meeting that objective within the designated time. Any executive who leaves the corporation before the objective is met receives nothing. The typical emphasis on stock prices makes this approach more applicable to top management than to business unit managers. Because rising stock markets tend to raise the stock price of mediocre companies, there is a developing trend to index stock options to competitors or to the *Standard & Poor's 500*.[112] General Electric, for example, offered its CEO 250,000 performance share units (PSUs) tied to performance targets achieved over five years. Half of the PSUs convert into GE stock only if GE achieves 10% average annual growth in operations. The other half converts to stock only if total shareholder return meets or beats the *S&P 500*.[113]

3. **Strategic-funds method:** The **strategic-funds method** encourages executives to look at developmental expenses as being different from expenses required for current operations. The accounting statement for a corporate unit enters strategic funds as a separate entry below the current ROI. It is, therefore, possible to distinguish between expense dollars

Business Strength/Competitive Position

FIGURE 11–3
Weighted-Factor
Approach to
Strategic Incentive
Management

	High	Low
High	**Star** ROI (25%) Cash Flow (25%) Strategic Funds (25%) Market Share (25%)	**Question Mark** ROI (0%) Cash Flow (0%) Strategic Funds (50%) Market Share Growth (50%)
Low	**Cash Cow** ROI (20%) Cash Flow (60%) Strategic Funds (0%) Market Share (20%)	**DOG** ROI (50%) Cash Flow (50%) Strategic Funds (0%) Market Share (0%)

Industry Attractiveness (vertical axis label)

SOURCE: Based on Paul J. Stonich, "The Performance Measurement and Reward System: Critical to Strategic Management," *Organizational Dynamics*, (Winter 1984), pp. 45–57.

consumed in the generation of current revenues and those invested in the future of a business. Therefore, a manager can be evaluated on both a short- and a long-term basis and has an incentive to invest strategic funds in the future. For example, begin with the total sales of a unit ($12,300,000). Subtract cost of goods sold ($6,900,000) leaving a gross margin of $5,400,000. Subtract general and administrative expenses ($3,700,000) leaving an operating profit/ROI of $1,700,000. So far, this is standard accounting procedure. The strategic-funds approach goes one step further by subtracting an additional $1,000,000 for "strategic funds/development expenses." This results in a pretax profit of $700,000. This strategic-funds approach is a good way to ensure that the manager of a high-performing unit (e.g., star) not only generates $700,000 in ROI, but also invests $1 million in the unit for its continued growth. It also ensures that a manager of a developing unit is appropriately evaluated on the basis of market share growth and product development and not on ROI or cash flow.

An effective way to achieve the desired strategic results through a reward system is to combine the three approaches:

1. Segregate strategic funds from short-term funds, as is done in the strategic-funds method.

2. Develop a weighted-factor chart for each SBU.

3. Measure performance on three bases: The pretax profit indicated by the strategic-funds approach, the weighted factors, and the long-term evaluation of the SBUs' and the corporation's performance.

Genentech, General Electric, Adobe, IBM, and Textron are some firms in which top management compensation is contingent upon the company's achieving strategic objectives.[114]

The board of directors and top management must be careful to develop a compensation plan that achieves the appropriate objectives. One reason why top executives are often criticized for being overpaid (the ratio of CEO to average worker pay is currently 400 to 1)[115] is that in a large number of corporations the incentives for sales growth exceed those for shareholder wealth, resulting in too many executives pursuing growth to the detriment of shareholder value.[116]

Let's Summarize the Chapter with a Mind Map

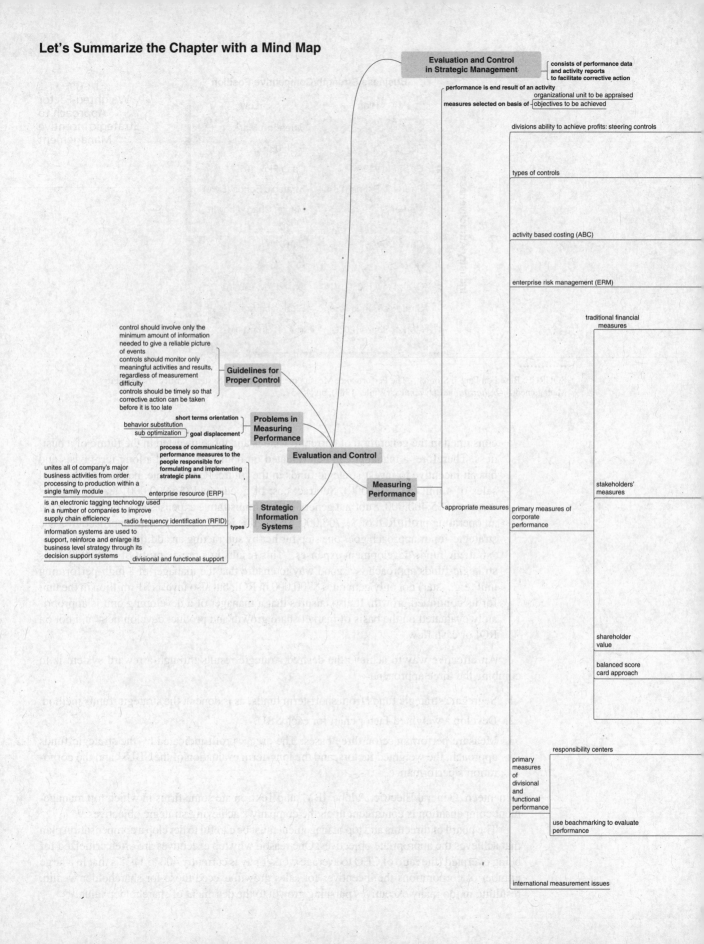

Evaluation and Control in Strategic Management
- consists of performance data and activity reports to facilitate corrective action
- performance is end result of an activity
- measures selected on basis of
  - organizational unit to be appraised
  - objectives to be achieved

Evaluation and Control

Guidelines for Proper Control
- control should involve only the minimum amount of information needed to give a reliable picture of events
- controls should monitor only meaningful activities and results, regardless of measurement difficulty
- controls should be timely so that corrective action can be taken before it is too late

Problems in Measuring Performance
- short terms orientation
- behavior substitution
- sub optimization — goal displacement

Strategic Information Systems
- enterprise resource (ERP)
  - unites all of company's major business activities from order processing to production within a single family module
- radio frequency identification (RFID)
  - is an electronic tagging technology used in a number of companies to improve supply chain efficiency
- types
- divisional and functional support
  - information systems are used to support, reinforce and enlarge its business level strategy through its decision support systems
- process of communicating performance measures to the people responsible for formulating and implementing strategic plans

Measuring Performance
- appropriate measures
- primary measures of corporate performance
  - traditional financial measures
  - stakeholders' measures
  - shareholder value
  - balanced score card approach
- types of controls
  - divisions ability to achieve profits: steering controls
- activity based costing (ABC)
- enterprise risk management (ERM)
- primary measures of divisional and functional performance
  - responsibility centers
  - use beachmarking to evaluate performance
- international measurement issues

return on investment (ROI)
earnings per share (EPS)
inventory turnover ratio
American customer satisfaction index

output controls — specify what is to be accomplished by focusing on the end result of the behaviors through use of objectives and performance targets or milestones

behavior controls — specify how something is to be done through policies, rules, standard operating procedures and orders from superiors

ISO 9000
ISO 14000

sales quotas
specific cost reduction
profit objectives
surveys of customer satisfaction

input controls — emphasize resources, such as knowledge, skills, abilities, values and motives of employees

accounting method for allocating indirect and fixed costs to individual products or product lines based on the value added activities going into that product

useful for doing value chain analysis and making outsourcing decisions

is a corporate wide, intergrated process for managing uncertainties that could negatively or positively influence the achievement of the corporations' objectives

adopted because of increasing amount of environment uncertainty

process of rating risks involves three steps
- identify risks using scenario analysis or brainstorming or by performing risk self assessment
- rank the risks using some scale of impact and likelihood
- measure the risks, using some agreed upon standard

ROI
EPS
operating cash flow
return on equity (ROE)

customer
- near term measures — sales, new customers, number of new customer needs met
- long term measures — growth in sales, turnover of customer base, ability to control prices

supplier
- near term measures — cost of raw materials, delivery time, inventory, availability of raw material
- long term measures — growth rates of raw material costs; delivery time; inventory, new ideas from suppliers

financial community
- near term measures — EPS, stock prices, number of buy lists, ROE
- long term measures — Ability to convince stock market of strategy, Growth in ROE

employees
- near term measures — number of suggestions, productivity, number of grievances
- long term measures — number of internal promotions, turnover

government
- near term measures — number of new pieces of regulations and laws that effect the firm, access to key members and staff
- long term measures — number of new regulations that effect the industry, ratio of cooperative vs. competitive encounters

consumer advocate
- near term measures — number of meetings, number of hostile encounters, number of times coalitions formed, number of legal actions
- long term measures — number of changes in policy due to a CA, number of CA initiated calls for help

environmentalists
- near term measures — number of meetings, number of hostile encounters, number of times coalitions were formed, number of EPA complaints and number of legal actions.
- long term measures — number of changes in policy due to environmentalists, number of environmentalists called for help

economic value added
market value added

financial
customer
internal business perspective
innovation and learning

evaluating top management and board of directors
- formalized process
- related to overall company performance
- chairman, CEO feedback instrument
- tools
  - management audit
  - strategic audit

standard cost centers
revenue centers
expense centers
profit centers
investment centers

identify the area or process to be examined
find behavioral and output measures of the area or process and obtain measurements
select an accessible set of competitors and best in class companies against which to benchmark
calculate differences among the company's performance measurements and those of best in class and determine why the differences exist
develope tactical programs for closing performance gaps
implement the programs and then compare the resulting new measurements with those of the best in class companies.

ECO-BITS

- In 2007, 64% of the Fortune Global 100 published a Corporate Social Responsibility report explaining their economic, environmental, and social performance.

- More than 4,000 organizations from over 100 countries are members of the United Nations Global Compact. Three of the 10 principles are:

- Support a precautionary approach to environmental challenges.

- Undertake initiatives to promote greater environmental responsibility.

- Encourage the development and diffusion of environmentally friendly technologies.[117]

DISCUSSION QUESTIONS

1. Is Figure 11–1 a realistic model of the evaluation and control process?

2. What are some examples of behavior controls? Output controls? Input controls?

3. Is EVA an improvement over ROI, ROE, or EPS?

4. How much faith can a manager place in a transfer price as a substitute for a market price in measuring a profit center's performance?

5. Is the evaluation and control process appropriate for a corporation that emphasizes creativity? Are control and creativity compatible?

STRATEGIC PRACTICE EXERCISE

Each year, *Fortune* magazine publishes an article entitled, "America's Most Admired Companies." It lists the 10 most admired companies in the United States and in the world. *Fortune*'s rankings are based on scoring publicly held companies on what it calls "eight key attributes of reputation": innovation, people management, use of corporate assets, social responsibility, quality of management, financial soundness, long-term investment value, and quality of products/services. In 2008, *Fortune* asked Hay Group to survey more than 3,700 people from multiple industries. Respondents were asked to choose the companies they admired most, regardless of industry. *Fortune* has been publishing this list since 1982. The *2008 Fortune* list of the top 10 most admired U.S. companies were (starting with #1): Apple, Berkshire Hathaway, General Electric, Google, Toyota Motor, Starbucks, FedEx, Procter & Gamble, Johnson & Johnson, and Goldman Sachs Group. The next 10 most admired were (from 11 to 20): Target, Southwest Airlines, American Express, BMW, Costco Wholesale, Microsoft, United Parcel Service, Cisco Systems, 3M, and Nordstrom.[118]

Four years earlier in 2004, the list of 10 most admired U.S. companies was: Wal-Mart, Berkshire Hathaway, Southwest Airlines, General Electric, Dell Computer, Microsoft, Johnson & Johnson, Starbucks, FedEx, and IBM.[119]

- Why did the most admired U.S. firm in 2004 (Wal-Mart) drop off the 10 listing in 2008?

- Why did Apple go from not even being on the 10 U.S. listing in 2004 to No. 1 in 2008?

- Which firms appeared on both top 10 lists? Why?

- Why did some firms drop off the list from 2004 to 2008 and why did others get included?

- What companies should be on the most admired list this year? Why?

Try One of These Exercises

1. Go to the library and find a "Most Admired Companies" *Fortune* article from the 1980s or early 1990s and compare that list to the latest one. (See www.fortune.com for the latest list.) Which companies have fallen out of the top 10? Pick one of the companies and investigate why it is no longer on the list.

2. Given the likely impact of global warming on various industrial sectors, which companies are likely to be on *Fortune*'s "Most Admired Companies" in 10 years?

3. Compare *Fortune*'s list to that compiled by the Reputation Institute (www.reputationinstitute.com). Why is there a difference between the ratings?

KEY TERMS

80/20 rule (p. 400)

activity-based costing (ABC) (p. 383)

balanced scorecard (p. 388)

behavior control (p. 381)

behavior substitution (p. 399)

benchmarking (p. 393)

earnings per share (EPS) (p. 385)

economic value added (EVA) (p. 387)

enterprise resource planning (ERP) (p. 397)

enterprise risk management (ERM) (p. 384)

expense center (p. 392)

free cash flow (p. 385)

goal displacement (p. 399)

input control (p. 381)

investment center (p. 393)

ISO 9000 Standards Service (p. 381)

ISO 14000 Standards Service (p. 382)

key performance measures (p. 389)

long-term evaluation method (p. 402)

management audit (p. 391)

market value added (MVA) (p. 388)

operating cash flow (p. 385)

output control (p. 381)

performance (p. 379)

profit center (p. 392)

responsibility center (p. 392)

return on equity (ROE) (p. 385)

return on investment (ROI) (p. 385)

revenue center (p. 392)

shareholder value (p. 387)

short-term orientation (p. 399)

standard cost center (p. 392)

steering control (p. 380)

strategic-funds method (p. 402)

suboptimization (p. 400)

transfer pricing (p. 393)

weighted-factor method (p. 402)

NOTES

1. R. Barker, "A Surprise in Office Depot's In-Box," *Business Week* (October 25, 2004), p. 122.

2. C. W. Hart, "Customer Service: Beating the Market with Customer Satisfaction," *Harvard Business Review* (March 2007), pp. 30–32.

3. S. E. Ante, "Giving the Boss the Big Picture," *Business Week* (February 13, 2006), pp. 48–51.

4. R. Muralidharan and R. D. Hamilton III, "Aligning Multinational Control Systems," *Long Range Planning* (June 1999), pp. 352–361. These types are based on W. G. Ouchi, "The Relationship Between Organizational Structure and Organizational Control," *Administrative Science Quarterly*, Vol. 20 (1977), pp. 95–113 and W. G. Ouchi, "A Conceptual Framework for the Design of Organizational Control Mechanisms," *Management Science*, Vol. 25 (1979), pp. 833–848. Muralidhara and Hamilton refer to Ouchi's clan control as input control.

5. W. G. Rowe and P. M. Wright, "Related and Unrelated Diversification and Their Effect on Human Resource Management Controls," *Strategic Management Journal* (April 1997), pp. 329–338.

6. R. Muralidharan and R. D. Hamilton III, "Aligning Multinational Control Systems," *Long Range* Planning (June 1999) pp. 356–359.

7. F. C. Barnes, "ISO 9000 Myth and Reality: A Reasonable Approach to ISO 9000," *SAM Advanced Management Journal* (Spring 1998), pp. 23–30.

8. M. Henricks, "A New Standard," *Entrepreneur* (October 2002), pp. 83–84.

9. M. V. Uzumeri, "ISO 9000 and Other Metastandards: Principles for Management Practice?" *Academy of Management Executive* (February 1997), pp. 21–36.

10. A. M. Hormozi, "Understanding and Implementing ISO 9000: A Manager's Guide," *SAM Advanced Management Journal* (Autumn 1995), pp. 4–11.

11. M. Henricks, "A New Standard," *Entrepreneur* (October 2002) p. 84.

12. L. Armstrong, "Someone to Watch Over You," *Business Week* (July 10, 2000), pp. 189–190.

13. J. K. Shank and V. Govindarajan, *Strategic Cost Management* (New York: The Free Press, 1993).

14. S. S. Rao, "ABCs of Cost Control," *Inc. Technology*, No. 2 (1997), pp. 79–81.

15. R. Gruber, "Why You Should Consider Activity-Based Costing," *Small Business Forum* (Spring 1994), pp. 20–36.

16. "Easier Than ABC," *Economist* (October 25, 2003), p. 56.

17. T. P. Pare, "A New Tool for Managing Costs," *Fortune* (June 14, 1993), pp. 124–129. For further information on the use of ABC with EVA, see T. L. Pohlen and B. J. Coleman, "Evaluating Internal Operations and Supply Chain Performance Using EVA and ABC," *SAM Advanced Management Journal* (Spring 2005), pp. 45–58.

18. K. Hopkins, "The Risk Agenda," *Business Week*, Special Advertising Section (November 22, 2004), pp. 166–170.

19. T. L. Barton, W. G. Shenkir, and P. L. Walker, "Managing Risk: An Enterprise-wide Approach," *Financial Executive* (March/April 2001), p. 51.

20. T. L. Barton, W. G. Shenkir, and P. L. Walker, "Managing Risk: An Enterprise-Wide Approach," *Financial Executive* (March/April 2001), pp. 48–51; P. L. Walker, W. G. Shenkir, and T. L. Barton, "Enterprise Risk Management: Putting It All Together," *Internal Auditor* (August 2003), pp. 50–55.

21. T. J. Andersen, "The Performance Relationship of Effective Risk Management: Exploring the Firm-Specific Investment Rationale," *Long Range Planning* (April 2008), pp. 155–176.

22. C. K. Brancato, *New Corporate Performance* Measures (New York: Conference Board, 1995); C. D. Ittner, D. F. Larcker, and M. V. Rajan, "The Choice of Performance Measures in Annual Bonus Contracts," working paper reported by K. Z. Andrews in "Executive Bonuses," *Harvard Business Review* (January–February 1996), pp. 8–9; J. Low and T. Siesfeld, "Measures That Matter: Wall Street Considers Non-Financial Performance More Than You Think," *Startegy & Leadership* (March/April 1998), pp. 24–30.

23. A similar measure, EBITDA (Earnings Before Interest, Taxes, Depreciation, and Amortization), is sometimes used, but is *not* determined in accordance with generally accepted accounting principles and is thus subject to varying calculations.

24. J. M. Laderman, "Earnings, Schmernings: Look at the Cash," *Business Week* (July 24, 1989), pp. 56–57.

25. H. Greenberg, "Don't Count on Cash Flow," *Fortune* (May 13, 2002), p. 176; A. Tergesen, "Cash-Flow Hocus-Pocus," *Business Week* (July 15, 2002), pp. 130–132.

26. "Green Revolutionary," *The Economist* (April 7, 2007), p. 66.

27. E. H. Hall, Jr., and J. Lee, "Diversification Strategies: Creating Value of Generating Profits?" paper presented to the annual meeting of the *Decision Sciences Institute*, Orlando, FL (November 18–21, 2000).

28. P. C. Brewer, G. Chandra, and C. A. Hock, "Economic Value Added (EVA): Its Uses and Limitations," SAM *Advanced Management Journal* (Spring 1999), pp. 4–11.

29. D. J. Skyrme and D. M. Amidon, "New Measures of Success," *Journal of Business Strategy* (January/February 1998), p. 23.

30. G. B. Stewart III, "EVA Works—But Not if You Make These Common Mistakes," *Fortune* (May 1, 1995), pp. 117–118.

31. S. Tully, "The Real Key to Creating Wealth," *Fortune* (September 20, 1993), p. 38.

32. A. Ehrbar, "Using EVA to Measure Performance and Assess Strategy," *Strategy & Leadership* (May/June 1999), pp. 20–24.

33. P. C. Brewer, G. Chandra, and C. A. Hock, "Economic Value Added (EVA): Its Uses and Limitations," *SAM Advanced Management Journal* (Spring 1999), pp. 7–9.

34. Pro: K. Lehn, and A. K. Makhija, "EVA & MVA As Performance Measures and Signals for Strategic Change," *Strategy & Leadership* (May/June 1996), pp. 34–38. Con: D. I. Goldberg, "Shareholder Value Debunked," *Strategy & Leadership* (January/February 2000), pp. 30–36.

35. A. Ehrbar, "Using EVA to Measure Performance and Assess Strategy," *Strategy &* Leadership (May/June 1999), p. 21.

36. S. Tully, "America's Wealth Creators," *Fortune* (November 22, 1999), pp. 275–284; A. B. Fisher, "Creating Stockholder Wealth: Market Value Added," *Fortune* (December 11, 1995), pp. 105–116.

37. A. B. Fisher, "Creating Stockholder Wealth: Market Value Added," *Fortune* (December 11, 1995), pp. 105–116.

38. K. Lehn and A. K. Makhija, "EVA & MVA As Performance Measures and Signals for Strategic Change," *Strategy & Leadership* (May/June, 1996), p. 37.

39. R. S. Kaplan and D. P. Norton, "Using the Balanced Scorecard as a Strategic Management System," *Harvard Business Review* (January–February 1996), pp. 75–85; R. S. Kaplan and D. P. Norton, "The Balanced Scorecard—Measures That Drive Performance," *Harvard Business Review* (January–February, 1992), pp. 71–79.

40. D. I. Goldenberg, "Shareholder Value Debunked," *Strategy &* Leadership (January/February 2000), p. 34.

41. In later work, Kaplan and Norton used the term "perspectives" and replaced "internal business perspective" with "process perspective" and "innovation and learning" to "learning and growth perspective." See R. S. Norton and D. P. Norton, "How to Implement a New Strategy Without Disrupting Your Organization," *Harvard Business Review* (March 2006), pp. 100–109.

42. C. K. Brancato, *New Performance Measures* (New York: Conference Board, 1995).

43. A. Gumpus and B. Lyons, "The Balanced Scorecard at Philips Electronics," *Strategic Finance*, Vol. 84 (2002), pp. 92–101.

44. P. D. Heaney, "Can Performance Be Measured?" *Progressive Grocer*, Vol. 82 (2003), pp. 11–13.

45. B. P. Stivers and T. Joyce, "Building a Balanced Performance Management System," *SAM Advanced Management Journal* (Spring 2000), pp. 22–29.

46. Kaplan and Norton (March, 2006), p. 107.

47. G. J. M. Braam and E. Nijssen, "Performance Effects of Using the Balanced Scorecard: A Note on the Dutch Experience," *Long Range Planning* (August 2004), pp. 335–349; H. Ahn, "Applying the Balanced Scorecard Concept: An Experience Report," *Long Range Planning* (August 2001), pp. 441–461.

48. S. P. Mader, D. Vuchot, and S. Fukushima of Korn/Ferry International, *33rd Annual Board of Directors Study* (2006), p. 9.

49. R. M. Rosen and F. Adair, "CEOs Misperceive Top Teams' Performance," *Harvard Business Review* (September 2007), p. 30.

50. S. P. Mader, D. Vuchot, and S. Fukushima of Korn/Ferry International, *33rd Annual Board of Directors Study* (2006), p. 33.

51. Ibid., p. 9.

52. J. L. Kerr and W. B. Werther, Jr., "The Next Frontier in Corporate Governance: Engaging the Board in Strategy," *Organizational Dynamics*, Vol. 37, No. 2 (2008), pp. 112–124. This agrees with figures (73% and 38%, respectively) reported by Korn/Ferry International in its *33rd Annual Board of Directors Study* from data gathered in 2006, p. 8.

53. J. M. Ivancevich, T. N. Duening, J. A. Gilbert, and R. Konopaske, "Deterring White-Collar Crime," *Academy of Management Executive* (May 2003), pp. 114–127. Also Kerr and Werther (2008).

54. M. Shyamal, "Is Your Board Competent Enough?" posted on October 19, 2006, accessed on 2nd May 2009, from http://www.rediff.com/money/2006/oct/19guest.htm.

55. B. Anjali, "Spencer Stuart Perspectives | Board Review: An Effective Tool" posted on Monday, August 11, 2008. 10:46 AM IST, accessed on 2nd May 2009, from HT Media website http://www.livemint.com/boardreview.htm.

56. The Indian Express Limited, Dabur India to Evaluate Board of Directors, posted on 2004-01-19 00:00:00+05:30 IST, accessed on 2nd May 2009, from http://www.financialexpress.com/news/Dabur-India-To-Evaluate-Board-Of-Directors/97569/.

57. Cognizant Technology Solutions Corporation, accessed on 2nd May 2009, from http://www.cognizant.com/html/content/aboutus/CompensationCommitteeCharter.pdf.

58. Majumdar, Shyamal *op.cit*

59. R. Charan, *Boards at Work* (San Francisco: Jossey-Bass, 1998), pp. 176–177.

60. T. D. Schellhardt, "Directors Get Tough: Inside a CEO Performance Review," *Wall Street Journal Interactive Edition* (April 27, 1998).

61. T. L. Wheelen and J. D. Hunger, "Using the Strategic Audit," *SAM Advanced Management Journal* (Winter 1987), pp. 4–12; G. Donaldson, "A New Tool for Boards: The Strategic Audit," *Harvard Business Review* (July–August 1995), pp. 99–107.

62. H. Threat, "Measurement Is Free," *Strategy & Leadership* (May/June 1999), pp. 16–19.

63. Z. U. Khan, S. K. Chawla, M. F. Smith, and M. F. Sharif, "Transfer Pricing Policy Issues in Europe 1992," *International Journal of Management* (September 1992), pp. 230–241.

64. H. Rothman, "You Need Not Be Big to Benchmark," *Nation's Business* (December 1992), p. 64.

65. C. W. Von Bergen and B. Soper, "A Problem with Benchmarking: Using Shaping as a Solution," *SAM Advanced Management Journal* (Autumn 1995), pp. 16–19.

66. "Tool Usage Rates," *Journal of Business Strategy* (March/April 1995), p. 12.

67. R. J. Kennedy, "Benchmarking and Its Myths," *Competitive Intelligence Magazine* (April–June 2000), pp. 28–33.

68. "Just the Facts: Numbers Runners," *Journal of Business Strategy* (July/August 2002), p. 3; L. Mann, D. Samson, and D. Dow, "A Field Experiment on the Effects of Benchmarking & Goal Setting on Company Sales Performance," *Journal of Management*, Vol. 24, No. 1 (1998), pp. 73–96.

69. S. A. W. Drew, "From Knowledge to Action: The Impact of Benchmarking on Organizational Performance," *Long Range Planning* (June 1997), pp. 427–441.

70. S. M. Robbins and R. B. Stobaugh, "The Bent Measuring Stick for Foreign Subsidiaries," *Harvard Business Review* (September–October 1973), p. 82.

71. J. D. Daniels and L. H. Radebaugh, *International Business*, 5th ed. (Reading, MA: Addison-Wesley, 1989), pp. 673–674.

72. D. Henry, "A Better Way to Keep the Books," *Business Week* (September 15, 2008), p. 35; "International Accounting: Speaking in Tongues," *The Economist* (May 19, 2007), pp. 77–78.

73. W. A. Johnson and R. J. Kirsch, "International Transfer Pricing and Decision Making in United States Multinationals," *International Journal of Management* (June 1991), pp. 554–561.

74. L. Hickey, *KPMG's Corporate and Indirect Tax Rate Survey 2008*, pp. 11 & 13.

75. "Fixing the Bottom Line," *Time* (November 23, 1992), p. 20.

76. J. M. L. Poon, R. Ainuddin, and H. Affrim, "Management Policies and Practices of American, British, European, and Japanese Subsidiaries in Malaysia: A Comparative Study," *International Journal of Management* (December 1990), pp. 467–474.

77. M. Egan, "Setting Standards: Strategic Advantages in International Trade," *Business Strategy Review*, Vol. 13, No. 1 (2002), pp. 51–64; L. Swatkowski, "Building Towards International Standards," *Appliance* (December 1999), p. 30.

78. C. W. L. Hill, P. Hwang, and W. C. Kim, "An Eclectic Theory of the Choice of International Entry Mode," *Strategic Management Journal* (February 1990), pp. 117–128; D. Lei, J. W. Slocum, Jr., and R. W. Slater, "Global Strategy and Reward Systems: The Key Roles of Management Development and Corporate Culture," *Organizational Dynamics* (Autumn 1990), pp. 27–41; W. R. Fannin, and A. F. Rodriques, "National or Global?—Control vs. Flexibility," *Long Range Planning* (October 1986), pp. 84–188.

79. A. V. Phatak, *International Dimensions of Management*, 2nd ed. (Boston: Kent, 1989), pp. 155–157.

80. S. McAlary, "Three Pitfalls in ERP Implementation," *Strategy & Leadership* (October/November/December 1999), pp. 49–50.

81. J. B. White, D. Clark, and S. Ascarelli, "This German Software Is Complex, Expensive—And Wildly Popular," *Wall Street Journal* (March 14, 1997), pp. A1, A8; D. Ward, "Whirlpool Takes a Dive with Software Snarl," *Des Moines Register* (April 29, 2000), p. 8D.

82. Lal, Aparna, "The ERP Behind Tata Power's Success," accessed on 2nd May 2009, from CyberMedia India Online Ltd. Website http://www.ciol.com/Ciol-Techportal/Content/ERP/Interviews/2006/2060804644.asp.

83. J. Verville, R. Palanisamy, C. Bernadas, and A. Halingten, "ERP Acquisition Planning: A Critical Dimension for Making the Right Choice," *Long Range Planning* (February 2007), pp. 45–63.

84. "Radio Silence," *The Economist* (June 9, 2007), pp. 20–21.

85. C. Krivda, "RFID After Compliance: Integration and Payback," Special Advertising Section, *Business Week* (December 20, 2004), pp. 91–98.

86. A. Lashinsky, "Meg and the Machine," *Fortune* (September 1, 2003), pp. 68–78.

87. R. M. Hodgetts and M. S. Wortman, *Administrative Policy*, 2nd ed. (New York: John Wiley & Sons, 1980), p. 128.

88. J. R. Wooldridge and C. C. Snow, "Stock Market Reaction to Strategic Investment Decisions," *Strategic Management Journal* (September 1990), pp. 353–363.

89. M. C. Jensen, "Corporate Budgeting Is Broken—Let's Fix It," *Harvard Business Review* (November 2001), pp. 94–101.

90. C. M. Christensen, S. P. Kaufman, and W. C. Smith, "Innovation Killers: How Financial Tools Destroy Your Capacity to Do New Things," *Harvard Business Review* (January 2008), pp. 98–105.

91. P. Hsieh, T. Koller, and S. R. Rajan, "The Misguided Practice of Earnings Guidance," *McKinsey Quarterly* (Spring 2006), pp. 1–5.

92. "GM, Auditor Will Pay $303 Million in Suit," *Saint Cloud* (MN) *Times* (August 9, 2008), p. 3A.

93. D. Henry "Fuzzy Numbers," *Business Week* (October 4, 2004), pp. 79–88.

94. A. Rappaport, "10 Ways to Create Shareholder Value," *Harvard Business Review* (September 2006), pp. 66–77.

95. D. R. Schmidt and K. L. Fowler, "Post-Acquisition Financial Performance and Executive Compensation," *Strategic Management Journal* (November–December 1990), pp. 559–569.

96. H. L. Tosi, S. Werner, J. P. Katz, and L. R. Gomez-Mejia, "How Much Does Performance Matter? A Meta-Analysis of CEO Pay Studies," *Journal of Management*, Vol. 26, No. 2 (2000), pp. 301–339.; P. Wright, M. Kroll, and D. Elenkov, "Acquisition Returns, Increase in Firm Size, and Chief Executive Officer Compensation: The Moderating Role of Monitoring," *Academy of Management Journal* (June 2002), pp. 599–608; S. Werner, H. L. Tosi, and L. Gomez-Mejia, "Organizational Governance and Employee Pay: How Ownership Structure Affects the Firm's Compensation Strategy," *Strategic Management Journal* (April 2005), pp. 377–384.

97. X. Zhang, K. M. Bartol, K. G. Smith, M. D. Pfarrer, and D. M. Khanin, "CEOs on the Edge: Earnings Manipulation and Stock-based Incentive Misalignment," *Academy of Management Journal* (April 2008), pp. 241–258; L. Bebchuk and J. Fried, *Pay Without Performance: The Unfulfilled Promise of Executive Compensation* (Boston: Harvard University Press, 2004); L. A. Benchuk and J. M. Fried, "Pay Without Performance: Overview of the Issues," *Academy of Management Perspectives* (February 2006), pp. 5–24.

98. D. Jones, "Bad News Can Enrich Executives," *Des Moines Register* (November 26, 1999), p. 8S.

99. J. F. Porac, J. B. Wade, and T. G. Pollock, "Industry Categories and the Politics of the Comparable Firm in CEO Compensation," *Administrative Science Quarterly* (March 1999), pp. 112–144. For summaries of current research on executive compensation and performance, see C. E. Devers, A. A. Cannella Jr., G. P. Reilly, and M. E. Yoder, "Executive Compensation: A Multidisciplinary Review of Recent Developments," *Journal of Management* (December 2007), pp. 1016–1072; M. Chan, "Executive Compensation," *Business and Society Review* (March 2008), pp. 129–161; and S. N. Kaplan, "Are CEOs Overpaid?" *Academy of Management Perspective* (May 2008), pp. 5–20.

100. C. D. Ittner and D. F. Larcker, "Coming Up Short," *Harvard Business Review* (November 2003), pp. 88–95.

101. See the classic article by S. Kerr, "On the Folly of Rewarding A, While Hoping for B," *Academy of Management Journal*, Vol. 18 (December 1975), 769–783.

102. W. Zellner, E. Schine, and G. Smith, "Trickle-Down Is Trickling Down at Work," *Business Week* (March 18, 1996), p. 34.

103. For more information on how goals can have dysfunctional side effects, see D. C. Kayes, "The Destructive Pursuit of Idealized Goals," *Organizational Dynamics*, Vol. 34, Issue 4 (2005), pp. 391–401.

104. T. J. Peters and R. H. Waterman, *In Search of Excellence* (New York: HarperCollins, 1982), pp. 75–76.

105. T. Aeppel, "Not All Workers Find Idea of Empowerment as Neat as It Sounds," *Wall Street Journal* (September 8, 1997), pp. A1, A13.

106. R. S. Allen and M. M. Helms, "Employee Perceptions of the Relationship Between Strategy, Rewards, and Organizational Performance," *Journal of Business Strategies* (Fall 2002), pp. 115–140; M. A. Carpenter, "The Price of Change: The Role of CEO Compensation in Strategic Variation and Deviation from Industry Strategy Norms," *Journal of Management*, Vol. 26, No. 6 (2000), pp. 1179–1198; M. A. Carpenter and W. G. Sanders, "The Effects of Top Management Team Pay and Firm Internationalization on MNC Performance," *Journal of Management*, Vol. 30, No. 4 (2004), pp. 509–528; J. D. Shaw, N. Gupta, and J. E. Delery, "Congruence Between Technology and Compensation Systems: Implications for Strategy Implementation," *Strategic Management Journal* (April 2001), pp. 379–386; E. F. Montemazon, "Congruence Between Pay Policy and Competitive Strategy in High-Performing Organizations," *Journal of Management*, Vol. 22, No. 6 (1996), pp. 889–908.

107. D. B. Balkin and L. R. Gomez-Mejia, "Matching Compensation and Organizational Strategies," *Strategic Management Journal* (February 1990), pp. 153–169.

108. C. S. Galbraith, "The Effect of Compensation Programs and Structure on SBU Competitive Strategy: A Study of Technology-Intensive Firms," *Strategic Management Journal* (July 1991), pp. 353–370.

109. T. A. Stewart, "CEO Pay: Mom Wouldn't Approve," *Fortune* (March 31, 1997), pp. 119–120.

110. "The Politics of Pay," *The Economist* (March 24, 2007), pp. 71–72.

111. P. J. Stonich, "The Performance Measurement and Reward System: Critical to Strategic Management," *Organizational Dynamics* (Winter 1984), pp. 45–57.

112. A. Rappaport, "New Thinking on How to Link Executive Pay with Performance," *Harvard Business Review* (March–April 1999), pp. 91–101.

113. Motley Fool, "Fool's School: Hooray for GE," *The (Ames, IA) Tribune* (October 27, 2003), p. 1D.

114. E. Iwata and B. Hansen, "Pay, Performance Don't Always Add Up," *USA Today* (April 30, 2004), pp. 1B–2B; W. Grossman and R. E. Hoskisson, "CEO Pay at the Crossroads of Wall Street and Main: Toward the Strategic Design of Executive Compensation," *Academy of Management Executive* (February 1998), pp. 43–57.

115. M. Chan, "Executive Compensation," *Business and Society Review* (March 2008), pp. 129–161.

116. S. E. O'Byrne and S. D. Young, "Why Executive Pay Is Failing," *Harvard Business Review* (June 2006), p. 28.

117. P. A. Heslin and J. D. Ochoa, "Understanding and Developing Strategic Corporate Social Responsibility," *Organizational Dynamics* (April–June 2008), pp. 125–144.

118. *Fortune* magazine Web site accessed on November 7, 2008 at http://money.cnn.com/magazines/fortune/mostadmired/2008/top20/index.html.

119. A. Harrington, "America's Most Admired Companies," *Fortune* (March 8, 2004), pp. 80–81.

Ending Case for Part Four

HEWLETT-PACKARD BUYS EDS

On May 13, 2008, Hewlett-Packard (HP) announced its $13.9 billion acquisition of Electronic Data Systems (EDS), a technology services company. Together, HP and EDS formed a formidable tech services provider with $38 billion in revenues. It enabled HP to better compete with IBM, which controlled more than 7% market share of the $748 billion market for services. Tech services included managing the data centers of large companies and governments, or handling entire functions such as personnel or claims processing. At the time of the acquisition, IBM was the leading firm in the area, with EDS in second place with much lower profit margins, and HP following in fifth place.

Founded by Ross Perot in 1962, EDS pioneered the business of outsourced data management. Perot sold EDS to General Motors (GM) in 1984, but GM was unable to obtain any synergy with the purchase and spun off the company in 1996. EDS profits turned to losses during the technology downturn in 2000. The company eventually became profitable once again, but with smaller margins. EDS had been slow to respond to the threat of Indian rivals offering services at sharply lower prices. The company did increase its overseas hiring and bought control of MphasiS, an Indian services company. Since MphasiS was allowed to operate independently, with its own sales force and customer base, EDS did not gain much synergy from the acquisition. By 2008, EDS had 45,000 people working offshore and planned to hire more. Nevertheless, the best services companies had a large, low-cost workforce with tightly integrated operations so that employees with diverse skills could collaborate smoothly. This was the case with IBM, Accenture, and Indian companies like Tata Consultancy Services, but not with EDS or HP. Commenting on HP's purchase of EDS, N. Venkat Venktraman, chair of the Information Systems Department at Boston University's School of Management said, "The services sector is going through a shift, and this merger doesn't address the global service-delivery challenges that HP faces."

....

This case was written by J. David Hunger for *Strategic Management and Business Policy*, 12th edition and for *Concepts in Strategic Management and Business Policy*, 12th edition. Copyright © 2008 by J. David Hunger. Reprinted by permission.

Founded in 1940 by Dave Packard and Bill Hewlett in a garage in Palo Alto, California, Hewlett-Packard soon developed a reputation for making high-quality testing and measurement devices. Emphasizing their engineering roots, the two founders worked hard to develop the company's strong corporate culture. Their philosophy of managing became known as the "HP Way," composed of five basic values:

- We have trust and respect for individuals.
- We focus on a high level of achievement and contribution.
- We focus on a high level of business with uncompromising integrity.
- We achieve our common objectives through teamwork.
- We encourage flexibility and innovation.

These values continued to be emphasized by the CEOs following in the founder's footsteps. Until Carleton (Carly) Fiorina was hired as CEO in 1999, HP had been primarily known for its engineering excellence, but not for its marketing. For example, it developed the first handheld calculator, a quality product long cherished by engineers, but never developed or priced for the mass market. Fiorina lamented that Dell offered information technology products that were "low-tech and low cost; and IBM offered "high-tech and high cost," but HP was stuck somewhere in between them. She wanted to offer customers "high-tech and low cost" by improving the marketing of the company's outstanding products. During her tenure, HP acquired Compaq, the personal computer company. She also tried to buy the computer services unit of PriceWaterhouseCoopers in 2000, but lost out to IBM. Problems with integrating Compaq's middle-market orientation with HP's top-end orientation led to her firing by the board in 2005.

Fiorina was replaced by Mark Hurd, known to be a disciplined operations manager, who vowed to focus on implementation. Hurd had come to the company from Dayton, Ohio's NCR, where he had been President and CEO. Hurd dumped the matrix management structure initiated by Fiorina and gave responsibility back to the business unit managers. According to Hurd, "the more accountable I can make you, the easier it is for you to show you're a great performer. The more I use a matrix, the easier I make it to blame someone else." He also broke up the centralized sales force and assigned sales people to each business unit. The SBUs now controlled over 70% of their own budget expenses, up from just 30% under Fiorina. Among other changes, Hurd hired executives from outside the company and cut costs by laying off 14,500 workers from a workforce of 150,000. Prith Banerjee, HP's new director of R&D, worked to make HP's famed research lab more efficient by cutting the number of projects from 150 to 20 or 30. Researchers would now be competing for money and manpower by proposing projects, complete with business plans to a central review board. Hurd knew that he had to make further changes to improve HP's competitive position. HP's corporate computing business seemed incapable of competing against IBM and Dell. Margins were slipping in the printer business, the source of 85% of HP's profits.

Hewlett-Packard was organized into three main groups: Imaging & Printing (27% of revenues), Personal Systems (35%), and Technology Solutions, which was composed of the Enterprise Storage & Servers segment (18%), HP Services segment (16%), and HP Software segment (2%). An additional business segment was Financial Services & Other (2% of revenues).

Even though Hurd was working hard to change the company by tightening up HP's operations, many of HP's middle managers still subscribed to the gentle, collegiate "HP Way." This culture fit the relaxed and casual style common to California's Silicon Valley and was part of the company's soul. People ate ahi tuna in the cafeteria. In contrast, EDS was founded in Plano, Texas, by the hard-charging entrepreneur, Ross Perot, who ran for U.S. president as an independent in 1992 and 1996. Reflecting Perot's no-nonsense style, the EDS corporate culture was military, buttoned-down, and staid. People wore ties and ate steak and fries in the EDS cafeteria.

One advantage of EDS was that it was the largest services firm that was independent of any hardware or software vendor. According to CEO Hurd, even though EDS would continue to advise clients to buy systems from all vendors, those clients would now be more likely to pay more attention when the boxes came from HP. Nevertheless, one disadvantage of the acquisition was the likely culture clash that would result from integrating EDS into HP's operations. Even though one analyst commented that Hurd's operations style made him "an EDS guy sitting on top of the HP Way," others wondered if the EDS acquisition would be as problematic as was the Compaq merger.

strategic issues in managing technology and Innovation

Most people have tasted Pepsi Cola, Lay's Potato Chips, and Frito's Corn Chips, but have they tried Quaker Soy Crisps or Gatorade Xtremo Thirst Quencher? These are just 2 of the more than 200 new product variations that PepsiCo annually adds to its already large global portfolio of products. Why does PepsiCo introduce so many new products when its current products are still in demand? According to PepsiCo's Chairman and CEO, Steven Reinemund, "Innovation is what consumers are looking for, particularly in the small, routine things of their life." This emphasis on product development seems to be paying off. PepsiCo's double-digit earnings have been consistent over the years and show no sign of slowing. (Its earnings increased 19% from 2002 to 2003 on a 7% increase in sales.) In 2004, PepsiCo was included in *Business Week*'s list of the 50 best-performing public companies.

PepsiCo constantly monitors its environment for changing tastes and fashions. It then tailors its products to suit those changes. When the public became concerned with obesity, its Frito-Lay division developed several low-fat chips and led its competitors by removing all trans fats from its Lay's, Ruffles, and Doritos brands. In June 2004, it introduced "low-carb" Doritos, Cheetos, and Tostitos. The company looks for new products both internally and externally. To capitalize on the growing market for New Age herbal-enhanced beverages, it acquired SoBe Beverages in 2001. Since then, PepsiCo has used brand extension to offer the energy drink SoBe No Fear to the school-aged market and SoBe Fuerte to the Hispanic market. Noting that the foreign-born segment of the 46 million U.S. Hispanic market didn't like PepsiCo's Latin-flavored versions of Lay's and Doritos chips, the company looked to its Mexican subsidiary, Sabritas. Not wanting to cannibalize Frito-Lay's core U.S. brands, the company limited the distribution of products such as Sabritones chile and lime puffed wheat snacks to smaller retail stores in Mexican-dominated areas. Despite no advertising and minimal distribution, U.S. sales of Sabritas brands doubled from $50 million in 2002 to $100 million in 2004. Distribution increased from 10% to one-third of the U.S. population. Because they were marketed as an ethnic specialty rather than as a Frito-Lay line extension, the Sabritas brands were able to win extra shelf space in grocery stores. Analysts agree that PepsiCo has developed a strong capability in product development. According to Robert van Brugge of Sanford C. Bernstein & Company, "They have been early to see trends and aggressive in targeting them."[1]

Learning Objectives

After reading this chapter, you should be able to:

- List the differences between successful and unsuccessful innovations
- Understand the importance of lead users and market research as sources of new ideas
- Assess the importance of product and process R&D for success within an industry

- Decide when to innovate internally and when to use alliances
- Propose an appropriate structure and culture to support innovative ideas and products
- Apply appropriate techniques and measures to manage new product development

PepsiCo is a good example of a company successfully using its resources to create new products for new and existing markets. Properly managing technology and innovation is crucial in a fast-moving global environment. In the high-pressure toys and games industry, for example, about 40% of all products on the market are less than one year old.[2] Over the past 15 years, the top 20% of firms in an annual innovation poll conducted by *Fortune* magazine achieved double the shareholder returns of their peers.[3] Nevertheless, many large firms find it difficult to be continually innovative. A recent survey of business executives reveals that a significant majority are concerned that their companies are losing growth opportunities because they are not able to properly manage new technology (see **Table 12–1**).[4] A survey of 700 companies by Arthur D. Little found that 85% of the executives were "dissatisfied with their ability to manage innovation."[5] Even innovative established companies, such as 3M, Procter & Gamble (P&G), and Rubbermaid, have experienced a slowing in their rate of successful new product introductions.[6]

In this chapter, we examine strategic issues in technology and innovation as they affect environmental scanning, strategy formulation, strategy implementation, and evaluation and control.

12.1 The Role of Management

Due to increased competition and accelerated product development cycles, innovation and the management of technology are becoming crucial to corporate success. Research conducted by Forbes, Ernst & Young, and the Wharton School of Business found the most important driver of corporate value for both durable and non-durable companies to be innovation.[7] New product development is positively associated with corporate performance.[8] Approximately half the profits of all U.S. companies come from products launched in the previous 10 years.[9] What is less obvious is how a company can generate a significant return from investment in R&D as

	TABLE 12–1

Executives Fear Their Companies Are Becoming Less Innovative

A survey of business executives conducted by *Fortune* with the consulting firm Integral, Inc., revealed the percentages of those responding either **agree** or **strongly agree** to the following five statements:

Your company has recently lost relatively low-value customers in small market niches or low-end market segments.	55%
Your organization passes up growth opportunities it would have pursued when the company was smaller because the opportunities are now "too small to be interesting."	60%
There is a disconnect between the kind of innovations your frontline troops suggest and the types of innovations upper management invests in.	64%
When your organization sees a potentially disruptive technology, it defines it as a technical problem ("Will our customers accept the product?") instead of a market problem.	58%
New entrants have exploited opportunities where uncertainty over market size and customer needs resulted in inaction by your company.	68%

SOURCE: "Don't Leave Us Behind," *Fortune* (April 3, 2000), p. 250. *Fortune Magazine.* Copyright © 2000 Time Inc. All rights reserved.

well as an overall sense of enthusiasm for innovative behavior and risk-taking. One way is to include innovation in the corporation's mission statement. See **Strategy Highlight 12.1** for mission statements from well-known companies. Another way is by establishing policies that support the innovative process. For example, 3M has a policy of generating at least 25% of its revenue from products introduced in the preceding three years. To support this policy, this $13 billion corporation annually spends nearly $1 billion.[10]

The importance of technology and innovation must be emphasized by people at the very top and reinforced by people throughout a corporation. If top management and the board are not interested in these topics, managers below them tend to echo their lack of interest. When growth in sales and profits stalled at P&G several years ago, the new CEO, Art Lafley, realized that product development was no longer a core competency of the company. In 2002, just

STRATEGY highlight 12.1

EXAMPLES OF INNOVATION EMPHASIS IN MISSION STATEMENTS

To emphasize the importance of technology, creativity, and innovation to overall future corporate success, some well-known firms have added sections to this effect in their published mission statements. Some of these are listed here:

Intel: "Delight our customers, employees, and shareholders by relentlessly delivering the platform and technology advancements that become essential to the way we work and live."

Merck & Co: "The mission of Merck is to provide society with superior products and services by developing innovations and solutions that improve the quality of life and satisfy customer needs, and to provide employees with meaningful work and advancement opportunities, and investors with a superior return."

SOURCES: Intel: All rights reserved. Intel Corporation, 2200 Mission College Blvd., Santa Clara, CA 95052-8119, USA. Used with permission. Reprinted by permission of Merck and Company.

12 of the firm's 250-some brands generated half of P&G's sales and an even larger percentage of its profits.[11] Lafley urged product groups to "connect and develop" by pulling in experts from unrelated brands to help with new product creation. One example of the impact of Lafley's directive was the decision to enter the home car-care business. Instead of a project team trying to develop a new product on its own, P&G looked for and found expertise in different parts of the company. The company's PuR unit's water filter experts knew how to deionize water to get rid of minerals. Its Cascade brand unit already had a compound in its dishwasher detergent that reduced water spots. The project team combined both technologies to make the Mr. Clean AutoDry handheld sprayer, a device that sprays soap on cars and then rinses them without spotting. The result was a doubling of Mr. Clean brand sales in a year.[12]

Management has an obligation to not only encourage new product development but also develop a system to ensure that technology is being used most effectively, with the consumer in mind. Between 33% and 60% of all new products that reach the market fail to make a profit.[13] A study by Chicago consultants Kuczmarski & Associates of 11,000 new products marketed by 77 manufacturing, service, and consumer-product firms revealed that only 56% of all newly introduced products were still being sold five years later. Only 1 in 13 new product ideas ever made it into test markets. Although some authorities argue that this percentage of successful new products needs to be improved, others contend that too high a percentage means that a company isn't taking the risks necessary to develop a really new product.[14]

A study of 111 successful and 86 unsuccessful product innovations found that the *successful innovations* had some or all of the following features:

- They were moderately new to the market.
- They were based on tried-and-tested technology.
- They saved money, met customers' needs, and supported existing practices.

In contrast, the *unsuccessful innovations* had a different set of characteristics:

- They were based on cutting-edge or untested technology.
- They followed a "me-too" approach.
- They were created with no clearly defined solution in mind.[15]

The importance of top management's providing appropriate direction is exemplified by Steve Jobs' management of Apple Computer. Ever since he co-founded the company, Jobs has pushed Apple to provide not just a product but a complete system. For example, Apple decided in 2001 to make a digital music player, the iPod, that would be as easy to use for digital media as the Sony Walkman was for cassette tapes. Jobs realized, however, that the company could not succeed by just making and selling hardware. The digital player would be worthless without an online download store. By painstakingly negotiating digital-rights issues with reluctant record companies, he achieved something never before accomplished: providing easy, legal access to over 1 million songs. By 2004, Apple sold 3.7 million iPods valued at $1 billion in sales. Commenting on the iPod's success, Jobs explained, "We can invent a complete solution that works."[16]

12.2 Environmental Scanning

Issues in innovation and technology influence both external and internal environmental scanning.

EXTERNAL SCANNING

Corporations need to continually scan their external societal and task environments for new developments in technology that may have some application to their current or potential products. Research reveals that firms that scan their external environment are more innovative than those that focus inward on their core competencies as a way to generate new products or processes.[17] Stakeholders, especially customers, can be important participants in the new product development process.

Technological Developments

Motorola, a company well known for its ability to invest in profitable new technologies and manufacturing improvements, has a sophisticated scanning system. Its intelligence department monitors the latest technological developments introduced at scientific conferences, in journals, and in trade gossip. This information helps it build "technology roadmaps" that assess where breakthroughs are likely to occur, when they can be incorporated into new products, how much money their development will cost, and which of the developments is being worked on by the competition.[18]

A company's focusing its scanning efforts too closely on its current product line is dangerous. Most new developments that threaten existing business practices and technologies do not come from existing competitors or even from within traditional industries. A new technology that can substitute for an existing technology at a lower cost and provide higher quality can change the very basis for competition in an industry. Managers therefore need to actively scan the periphery for new product ideas because this is where breakthrough innovations will be found.[19] Consider, for example, the impact of Internet technology on the personal computer software industry. Microsoft Corporation had ignored the developing Internet technology during the 1980s and early 1990s while battling successfully with IBM, Lotus, and WordPerfect to dominate operating system software via Windows 95 as well as word processing and spreadsheet programs via Microsoft Office. Ironically, just as Microsoft introduced its new Windows 95 operating system, newcomer Netscape used Java applets in its user-friendly, graphically oriented browser program with the potential to make operating systems unnecessary. By the time Microsoft realized the significance of this threat, Netscape had already established itself as the industry standard for browsers. Microsoft was forced to spend huge amounts of time and resources trying to catch up to Netscape's dominant market share with its own Internet Explorer browser.

One way to learn about new technological developments in an industry is to locate part of a company's R&D or manufacturing in those locations making a strong impact on product development. Large multinational corporations (MNCs) undertake between 5% and 25% of their R&D outside their home country.[20] For example, automobile companies like to have design centers in southern California and in Italy, key areas for automotive styling. Software companies throughout the world know that they must have a programming presence in California's Silicon Valley if they are to compete on the leading edge of technology. The same is true of the semiconductor industry in terms of manufacturing.[21]

Impact of Stakeholders on Innovation

A company should look to its stakeholders, especially its customers, suppliers, and distributors, for sources of product and service improvements. These groups of people have the most to gain from innovative new products or services. Under certain circumstances, they may propose new directions for product development. Some of the methods of gathering information from key stakeholders are using lead users, market research, and new product experimentation.

Lead Users. Research by Von Hippel indicates that customers are a key source of innovation in many industries. For example, 77% of the innovations developed in the scientific instruments industry came from the users of the products. Suppliers are often important sources as well. Suppliers accounted for 36% of innovations in the thermoplastics industry, according to Von Hippel.[22] One way to commercialize a new technology is through early and in-depth involvement with a firm's customers in a process called co-development.[23] This type of customer is called a "lead user."

Von Hipple proposes that companies should look to lead users for help in product development, especially in high-technology industries where things move so quickly that a product is becoming obsolete by the time it arrives on the market. These **lead users** are "companies, organizations, or individuals that are well ahead of market trends and have needs that go far beyond those of the average user."[24] They are the first to adopt a product because they benefit significantly from its use—even if it is not fully developed. At Dow Chemical, for example, scientists solicit feedback from customers before developing a new product in the lab. Once the product is ready for commercialization, Dow gives its lead users the first opportunity to use the product and suggest further development.[25]

At 3M, a product development team in 3M's Medical Surgical Markets Division was charged with creating a breakthrough in the area of surgical drapes—the material that prevents infections from spreading during surgery. At the time, 3M dominated the market but had not developed a new product improvement in almost a decade. After spending six weeks learning about the cause and prevention of infections, the project team spent six more weeks investigating trends in infection control. The team then worked to identify lead users—doctors in developing nations and veterinarians who couldn't afford the current expensive drapes. The team invited several lead users to a 2½-day workshop focused on "Can we find a revolutionary, low-cost approach to infection control?" The workshop generated concepts for six new product lines and a radical new approach to infection control. The team chose the three strongest concepts for presentation to senior management. 3M has successfully applied the lead user method in 8 of its 55 divisions.

Lead user teams are typically composed of four to six people from marketing and technical departments, with one person serving as project leader. Team members usually spend 12 to 15 hours per week on the project for its duration. For planning purposes, a team should allow four to six weeks for each phase and four to six months for the entire project. The four phases of the lead user process are:

1. **Lay the Foundation:** Identify target markets and the type and level of innovations desired.

2. **Determine the Trends:** Research the field and talk with experts who have a broad view of emerging technologies and leading-edge applications.

3. **Identify Lead Users:** Talk with users at the leading edge of the target and related markets to understand their needs.

4. **Develop the Breakthrough:** Host a two- to three-day workshop with several lead users and a half-dozen marketing and technical people. Participants first work in small groups and then as a whole to design the final concepts that fit the company's and the users' needs.[26]

Market Research. A more traditional method of obtaining new product ideas is to use **market research** to survey current users regarding what they would like in a new product. This method has been successfully used by companies, such as P&G, to identify consumer preferences. It is especially useful in directing incremental improvements to existing products. For example, the auto maker BMW solicits suggestions from BMW owners to improve its current offerings and to obtain ideas for new products.

Market research may not, however, necessarily provide the information needed for truly innovative products or services (radical innovation). According to Sony executive Kozo

Ohsone, "When you introduce products that have never been invented before, what good is market research?" For example, Hal Sperlich took the concept of the minivan from Ford to Chrysler when Ford refused to develop the concept. According to Sperlich,

> [Ford] lacked confidence that a market existed because the product didn't exist. The auto industry places great value on historical studies of market segments. Well, we couldn't prove there was a market for the minivan because there was no historical segment to cite. In Detroit most product-development dollars are spent on modest improvements to existing products, and most market research money is spent on studying what customers like among available products. In ten years of developing the minivan we never once got a letter from a housewife asking us to invent one. To the skeptics, that proved there wasn't a market out there.[27]

A heavy emphasis on being customer driven could actually prevent companies from developing innovative new products. A study of the impact of technological discontinuity (explained in **Chapter 5**) in various industries revealed that the leading firms failed to switch to the new technology not because management was ignorant of the new development but because they listened too closely to their current customers. In all of these firms, a key task of management was to decide which of the many product and development programs continually being proposed to them should receive financial resources. The criterion used for the decision was the total return perceived in each project, adjusted by the perceived riskiness of the project. Projects targeted at the known needs of key customers in established markets consistently won the most resources. Sophisticated systems for planning and compensation favored this type of project every time. As a result, the leading companies continued to use the established technology to make the products its current customers demanded, allowing smaller entrepreneurial competitors to develop the new, more risky technology.[28]

Because the market for the innovative products based on the new technology was fairly small at first, new ventures had time to fine-tune product design, build sufficient manufacturing capacity, and establish the product as the industry standard (as Netscape did with its Internet browser). As the marketplace began to embrace the new standard, the customers of the leading companies began to ask for products based on the new technology. Although some established manufacturers were able to defend their market share positions through aggressive product development and marketing activity (as Microsoft did against Netscape), many firms, finding that the new entrants had developed insurmountable advantages in manufacturing cost and design experience, were forced out of the market. Even the established manufacturers that converted to the new technology were unable to win a significant share of the new market.[29]

New Product Experimentation and Acquisition. Instead of using lead users or market research to test the potential of innovative products, some successful companies are using speed and flexibility to gain market information. These companies have developed their products by probing potential markets with early versions of the products, learning from the probes, and probing again.[30] For example, Seiko's only market research is surprisingly simple. The company introduces hundreds of new models of watches into the marketplace. It makes more of the models that sell; it drops those that don't.

The consulting firm Arthur D. Little found that the use of standard market research techniques has resulted in a success rate of only 8% for new cereals—92% of all new cereals fail. As a result, innovative firms, such as Keebler and the leading cereal makers, are reducing their expenditures for market research and working to reduce the cost of launching new products by making their manufacturing processes more flexible.[31]

Microsoft has successfully followed a strategy of monitoring the competition for new developments. It follows an *embrace and extend* strategy of imitating new products developed by pioneers, refining them, and outmarketing the competition. (This approach is nothing new.

P&G used Mr. Clean to defeat the newly introduced Lestoil.) Microsoft's distinctive competency is its ability to change directions and adjust priorities when the market changes.[32] Another approach to new product development is to simply acquire new technology from others. Cisco Systems, for example, kept itself on the cutting edge of making and selling Internet routers by buying a number of high-tech startups. In effect, Cisco outsourced its R&D to California's venture capitalists.[33]

INTERNAL SCANNING

In addition to scanning the external environment, strategists should also assess their company's ability to innovate effectively by asking the following questions:

1. Has the company developed the resources needed to try new ideas?
2. Do the managers allow experimentation with new products or services?
3. Does the corporation encourage risk-taking and tolerate mistakes?
4. Are people more concerned with new ideas or with defending their turf?
5. Is it easy to form autonomous project teams?[34]

In addition to answering these questions, strategists should assess how well company resources are internally allocated and evaluate the organization's ability to develop and transfer new technology in a timely manner into the generation of innovative products and services. These issues are important, given that it takes on average seven ideas to generate a new commercial product, according to the Product and Development Management Association.[35]

Resource Allocation Issues

A company must make available the resources necessary for effective research and development. Research indicates that a company's **R&D intensity** (its spending on R&D as a percentage of sales revenue) is a principal means of gaining market share in global competition.[36] The amount of money spent on R&D often varies by industry. For example, the computer software and drug industries spend an average of 11% to 13% of their sales revenue for R&D. Others, such as the food and the containers and packaging industries, spend less than 1%. A good rule of thumb for R&D spending is that a corporation should spend at a "normal" rate for that particular industry, unless its competitive strategy dictates otherwise.[37] Research indicates that consistency in R&D strategy and resource allocation across lines of business improves corporate performance by enabling the firm to better develop synergies among product lines and business units.[38]

Simply spending money on R&D or new projects does not, however, guarantee useful results. One study found that although large firms spent almost twice as much per R&D patent than did smaller firms, the smaller firms used more of their patents. The innovation rate of small businesses was 322 innovations per million employees versus 225 per million for large companies.[39] A recent study by the U.S. Small Business Administration reported that patents obtained by small firms were twice as likely to be among the top 1% of the most widely cited patents as patents obtained by large firms.[40] One explanation for this phenomenon is that large (especially older) firms tend to spend development money on extensions of their current products (incremental innovation) or to increase the efficiency of existing performance.[41] In contrast, small firms tend to apply technology to improving effectiveness through developing completely new products (radical innovation).[42] Other studies reveal that the maximum innovator in various industries often was the middle-sized firm. These firms were generally more effective and efficient than others in technology transfer. Very small firms often do not have sufficient resources to exploit new concepts (unless supported by venture capitalists with deep pockets), whereas the bureaucracy present in large firms rewards consistency over creativity.[43] From these studies,

Hitt, Hoskisson, and Harrison propose the existence of an inverted U-shaped relationship between size and innovation. According to Hitt et al., "This suggests that organizations are flexible and responsive up to some threshold size but encounter inertia after that point."[44]

In some cases, firms waste their R&D spending. For example, between 1950 and 1979, the U.S. steel industry spent 20% more on plant maintenance and upgrading for each ton of production capacity added or replaced than did the Japanese steel industry. Nevertheless, the top management of U.S. steel firms failed to recognize and adopt two breakthroughs in steelmaking—the basic oxygen furnace and continuous casting. Their hesitancy to adopt new technology caused them to lose the world steel market.[45]

Time-to-Market Issues

In addition to money, another important consideration in the effective management of R&D is **time to market**. During the 1980s, the time from inception to profitability of a specific R&D program was generally accepted to be 7 to 11 years. According to Karlheinz Kaske, CEO of Siemens AG, however, the time available to complete the cycle is getting shorter. Companies no longer can assume that competitors will allow them the number of years needed to recoup their investment. In the past, Kaske says, "ten to fifteen years went by before old products were replaced by new ones . . . now, it takes only four or five years."[46] Time to market is an important issue because 60% of patented innovations are generally imitated within four years at 65% of the cost of innovation.[47] In the 1980s, Japanese auto manufacturers gained incredible competitive advantage over U.S. manufacturers by reducing new products' time to market to only three years. (U.S. auto companies needed five years.)[48]

12.3 Strategy Formulation

R&D strategy deals not only with the decision to be a leader or a follower in terms of technology and market entry (discussed in **Chapter 8**, in the R&D strategy section) but also with the source of the technology. Should a company develop its own technology or purchase it from others? The strategy also takes into account a company's particular mix of basic versus applied and product versus process R&D (discussed in **Chapter 5**). The particular mix should suit the level of industry development and the firm's particular corporate and business strategies.

PRODUCT VERSUS PROCESS R&D

As illustrated in **Figure 12–1**, the proportion of product and process R&D tends to vary as a product moves along its life cycle. In the early stages, **product innovations** are most important because the product's physical attributes and capabilities most affect financial performance. Later, **process innovations** such as improved manufacturing facilities, increasing product quality, and faster distribution become important to maintaining the product's economic returns. Generally, product R&D has been key to achieving differentiation strategies, whereas process R&D has been at the core of successful cost-leadership strategies.

Historically, U.S. corporations have not been as skillful at process innovations as have German and Japanese companies. The primary reason has been a function of the amount of money invested in each form of R&D. U.S. firms spend, on the average, 70% of their R&D budgets on product R&D and only 30% on process R&D; German firms, 50% on each form; and Japanese firms, 30% on product and 70% on process R&D.[49] The traditionally heavy emphasis by U.S. major home appliance manufacturers on process R&D is one reason they have such a strong position in the North American market. The emphasis on quality and durability, coupled with a reluctance to make major design changes simply for the sake of

FIGURE 12–1
Product and
Process R&D
in the Product
Life Cycle

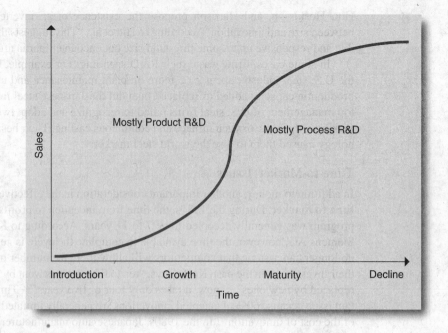

FIGURE 12–1
Product and Process R&D in the Product Life Cycle

change, has resulted in products with an average life expectancy of 20 years for refrigerators and 15 years for washers and dryers. Even though quality has improved significantly over the past 20 years, the average washer, dryer, and refrigerator cost no more than they did 20 years ago and yet last almost twice as long.

To be competitive, companies must find the proper mix of product and process R&D. Research indicates that too much emphasis by a firm on efficiency-oriented process R&D can drive out product R&D.[50] Even though the key to the success of the U.S. major home appliance industry has been its emphasis on process innovation, significant product innovation is more likely to result in a first-mover advantage.[51] For example, Maytag's introduction of the Neptune, a new type of front-loading washing machine, gave it a significant marketing advantage even after Whirlpool and General Electric introduced their versions of the new product.

TECHNOLOGY SOURCING

Technology sourcing, typically a make-or-buy decision, can be important in a firm's R&D strategy. Although in-house R&D has traditionally been an important source of technical knowledge (resulting in valuable patents) for companies, firms can also tap the R&D capabilities of competitors, suppliers, and other organizations through contractual agreements (such as licensing, R&D agreements, and joint ventures) or acquisitions. Each approach has advantages and disadvantages.[52] One example of technology acquisition was Motorola's purchase in 2004 of MeshNetworks, Inc., to obtain a Wi-Fi technology needed in Motorola's government contracting business.[53] When technological cycles were longer, a company was more likely to choose an independent R&D strategy not only because it gave the firm a longer lead time before competitors copied it but also because it was more profitable in the long run. In today's world of shorter innovation life cycles and global competition, a company may no longer have the luxury of waiting to reap a long-term profit.

Firms that are unable to finance alone the huge costs of developing a new technology may coordinate their R&D with other firms through a **strategic R&D alliance**. By the 1990s, more than 150 cooperative alliances involving 1,000 companies were operating in the United States, and many more were operating throughout Europe and Asia.[54] These alliances can be (1) joint programs or contracts to develop a new technology, (2) joint ventures establishing a separate company to take a new product to market, or (3) minority investments in innovative firms wherein the innovator obtains needed capital and the investor obtains access to valuable research. For example, the biotech company Amgen uses strategic alliances as part of its growth strategy. It uses its collegial corporate culture to court entrepreneurial ventures that are normally shy of big companies. "We're trying to have a small company feel," explains Amgen CEO Kevin Sharer. By 2003, Amgen had formed partnerships with 100 companies. It developed its latest drug, Cinacalcet, a treatment for a kidney-related condition called secondary hyperparathyroidism, from a license with one of its partners, NPS Pharmaceuticals.[55]

When should a company buy or license technology from others instead of developing it internally? Following the resource-based view of the firm discussed in **Chapter 5**, a company should buy technologies that are commonly available but make (and protect) those that are rare, valuable, and hard to imitate and that have no close substitutes. In addition, outsourcing technology may be appropriate when:

- The technology is of low significance to competitive advantage.
- The supplier has proprietary technology.
- The supplier's technology is better and/or cheaper and reasonably easy to integrate into the current system.
- The company's strategy is based on system design, marketing, distribution, and service—not on development and manufacturing.
- The technology development process requires special expertise.
- The technology development process requires new people and new resources.[56]

Licensing technology to other companies may be an excellent R&D strategy—especially in a turbulent high-tech environment where being the first firm to establish the standard dominant design may bring competitive advantage.[57] Matsushita successfully used this strategy to overcome the technologically superior Sony beta format with the VHS format for VCRs. When Matsushita freely licensed the VHS format to all other VCR makers, Sony was relegated to a minority position in the market, and Matsushita (through its Panasonic brand) became a dominant VCR manufacturer.[58] Licensing enables a company to enter foreign markets that might not otherwise be possible due to high tariffs, import prohibitions and restrictions, or the high cost and risk of investing in foreign factories. Licensing is an alternative international strategy in situations when exports or local production through a subsidiary or joint venture are impracticable.[59]

A serious issue in the sourcing of new technology is the use of another company's intellectual property without paying for it. **Intellectual property** is special knowledge used in a new product or process developed by a company for its own use and is usually protected by a patent, copyright, trademark, or trade secret. It can be licensed to another firm for a fee. As mentioned earlier, making and selling an imitation of someone else's product (such as Nike shoes) is considered to be piracy. Both the recording industry and the motion picture industry are extremely threatened by the illegal duplication of their products.

The number of patents being issued in the United States is growing at 6% annually and running at nearly twice the level of a decade ago. Similar growth is happening elsewhere in the world. Patents are global. Although a U.S. patent does not function outside the United States,

GLOBAL issue

USE OF INTELLECTUAL PROPERTY AT HUAWEI TECHNOLOGIES

Xu Danhua, chief of the pre-research department at Huawei Technologies, works to develop products for digital homes. He uses technologies to link PCs, TVs, stereos, and other devices to the Internet and to each other throughout a building or an apartment. "I like to face the challenges of new technology," says Xu. "Huawei is a company that very quickly takes on the trends of the industry." This is a relatively new direction for a company that until recently was a low-cost manufacturer of equipment developed elsewhere. Huawei intends to sell sophisticated electronic products to international customers. According to the company's head of R&D, "Huawei is a global company with global markets in mind." To take advantage of skilled people in other parts of the world, it builds development centers in Europe, India, and the United States.

Cisco Systems, a maker of networking equipment, launched a lawsuit against Huawei in December 2002, alleging patent and copyright infringement and asking for an injunction to remove certain Huawei products from the market. Cisco had already lined up support from the Chinese government. Having just joined the World Trade Organization (WTO) in 2001, China was eager to shed its image as the world's leading haven for pirated goods. According to an official with China's Ministry of Information Industry, "The government will not give any political help to Huawei."

Huawei protested its innocence but soon announced a global joint venture with Cisco's rival, 3Com Corporation. The venture provides Huawei with 3Com's distribution system, along with a strong base in the United States. When Cisco's Executive Vice President, Charles Giancarlo, was informed of the Huawei–3Com alliance, he said, "I was so mad I couldn't speak for three days." Keeping up the pressure, Cisco filed another suit in east Texas, near Huawei's Dallas office. Huawei typically undersells Western rivals by 30% or more and has a reputation for selling products that look and feel like Cisco's products. It was a major competitor in DSL equipment. "Huawei is a threat to everyone," says Christine Heckart, Vice President for Marketing at Juniper Networks. "They bid on everything that moves."

For Huawei, the lawsuits were part of a painful and risky transition from a position of cheap labor, government support, and lax intellectual property protection in China to the tougher rules of global markets. Eager to shed its "me-too" reputation, Huawei agreed to settle the lawsuit with Cisco Systems in 2004.

....

SOURCES: Summarized from P. Burrows and B. Einhorn, "Cisco: In Hot Pursuit of a Chinese Rival," *Business Week* (May 19, 2003), pp. 62–63, and B. Einhorn, M. Kripalani, and J. Ewing, "Huawei: More Than a Local Hero," *Business Week* (October 11, 2004), pp. 180–184.

the same idea cannot in theory be patented anywhere else.[60] Countries joining the World Trade Organization (WTO) must agree to Trips (trade-related aspects of intellectual property rights), an international agreement that establishes minimum standards for the legal protection of intellectual property.[61] Because China has recently joined the WTO, a number of companies are attempting to enforce their patents in that country. See the **Global Issue** feature for an example of a Chinese company that was sued by Cisco Systems for intellectual property violations.

IMPORTANCE OF TECHNOLOGICAL COMPETENCE

Firms that emphasize growth through acquisitions over internal development tend to be less innovative than others in the long run.[62] Research suggests that companies must have at least a minimal R&D capability if they are to correctly assess the value of technology developed by others. This is called a company's "absorptive capacity" and is a valuable by-product of routine in-house R&D activity.[63] **Absorptive capacity** is a firm's ability to recognize, assimilate, and utilize new external knowledge.[64] Firms that have absorptive capacity are able to use knowledge obtained externally to increase the productivity of their research expenditures.[65] Further, without this capacity, firms could become locked out in their ability to assimilate the technology at a later time. Therefore, a company's absorptive capacity is a dynamic capability that influences the nature and sustainability of that company's competitive advantage.[66]

A corporation that purchases an innovative technology must have the **technological competence** to make good use of it. Some companies that introduce the latest technology into their processes do not adequately assess the competence of their people to handle it. For example, a survey conducted in the United Kingdom in the 1980s found that 44% of all companies that started to use robots met with initial failure, and that 22% of those firms abandoned the use of robots altogether, mainly because of inadequate technological knowledge and skills.[67] One U.S. company built a new plant equipped with computer-integrated manufacturing and statistical process controls, but the employees could not operate the equipment because 25% of them were illiterate.[68]

CATEGORIES OF INNOVATION

Innovation can range from incremental to radical. As shown in **Figure 12–2**, a corporation's *capabilities* (existing or new) interact with its *strategic scope* (limited or unlimited) to form four basic categories of innovation. A corporation may emphasize one of these categories or operate in all of them.[69]

Quadrant 1: Improving Core Businesses: This type of innovation focuses on incremental innovations that can be developed rapidly and inexpensively. It includes line extensions and more convenient packaging and is often a part of a horizontal growth strategy. Its potential weakness is market myopia—its emphasis on current products and customers. As illustrated earlier in this chapter, PepsiCo is the master of this type of innovation.

Quadrant 2: Exploiting Strategic Advantages: This type of innovation focuses on taking existing brands and product lines to new customers and markets without requiring major change in current capabilities. It means moving beyond the company's current strategic

FIGURE 12–2
Categories of Innovation

Improve Core Businesses

Use existing capabilities and limited strategic scope for incremental innovations

Exploit Strategic Advantages

Use existing capabilities and unlimited strategic scope to develop new markets

Develop New Capabilities

Use new capabilities and limited strategic scope to expand and refine current product offerings

Create Revolutionary Change

Use new capabilities and unlimited scope in product development to generate radical innovations

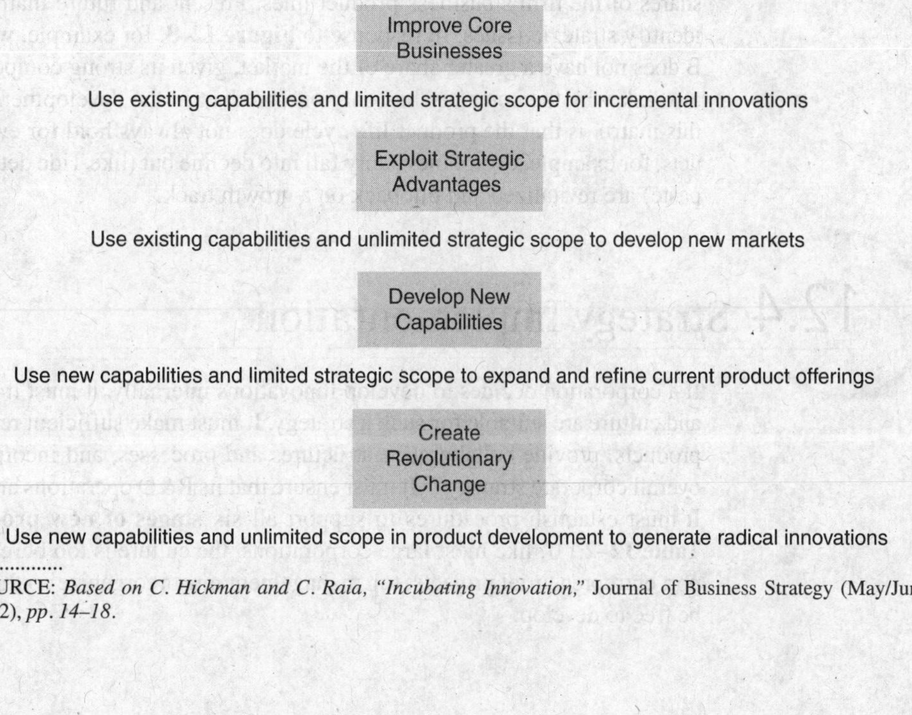

SOURCE: *Based on C. Hickman and C. Raia, "Incubating Innovation,"* Journal of Business Strategy (May/June 2002), *pp. 14–18.*

scope by leveraging capabilities by spreading them across a broader range of markets and customers via concentric diversification. Its potential weakness is the relative ease with which competitors with similar capabilities can imitate the innovation. Coleman and Toro are examples of companies that have leveraged their capabilities in camping (Coleman) and lawn (Toro) equipment to move into new products and new markets, such as Coleman gas grills and Toro snow blowers.

Quadrant 3: Developing New Capabilities: This type of innovation focuses on deepening customer satisfaction and loyalty to the brand or product line by adding new organizational capabilities without introducing major changes in strategic scope. The company may develop or purchase new technologies, talents, or businesses to better serve the firm's current scope of customers and markets. It may involve a vertical growth strategy. Its potential weakness is the investment cost and implementation time. Microsoft follows an embrace-and-extend policy to either acquire or imitate a new product in order to offer it to its current customers in the next version of Windows or Office software.

Quadrant 4: Creating Revolutionary Change: This type of innovation focuses on radical innovations that transcend current product lines or brands to make fundamental changes in both its strategic scope and its capabilities. This can mean a new business model and a revolutionary new future for the company. Its potential weakness is a high risk of failure. Sony Corporation is the master of radical innovation. Its pioneering products, such as the Walkman, the Airboard, and the robo-pet Aibo, introduce whole new product categories.

PRODUCT PORTFOLIO

Developed by Hofer and based on the product life cycle, the 15-cell **product/market evolution matrix** (shown in **Figure 12–3**) depicts the types of developing products that cannot be easily shown on other portfolio matrixes. Products are plotted in terms of their competitive positions and their stages of product/market evolution. As on the GE Business Screen, the circles represent the sizes of the industries involved, and the pie wedges represent the market shares of the firm's business product lines. Present and future matrixes can be developed to identify strategic issues. In response to **Figure 12–3**, for example, we could ask why Product B does not have a greater share of the market, given its strong competitive position. We could also ask why the company has only one product in the developmental stage. A limitation of this matrix is that the product life cycle does not always hold for every product. Many products, for example, do not inevitably fall into decline but (like Tide detergent and Colgate toothpaste) are revitalized and put back on a growth track.

12.4 Strategy Implementation

If a corporation decides to develop innovations internally, it must make sure that its structure and culture are suitable for such a strategy. It must make sufficient resources available for new products, provide collaborative structures and processes, and incorporate innovation into its overall corporate strategy.[70] It must ensure that its R&D operations are managed appropriately. It must establish procedures to support all six **stages of new product development**. (See **Table 12–2**.) If, like most large corporations, the culture is too bureaucratic and rigid to support entrepreneurial projects, top management must reorganize so that innovative projects can be free to develop.

FIGURE 12–3
Product/Market Evolution Portfolio Matrix

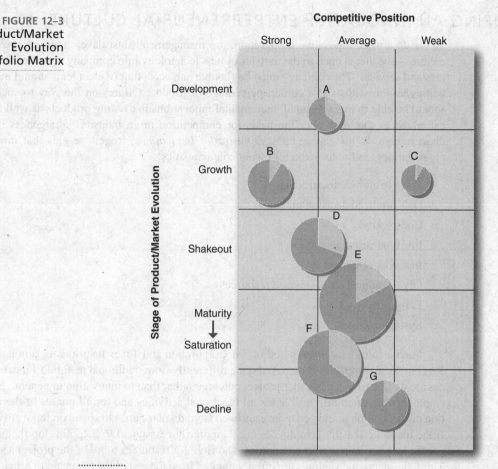

SOURCE: *C. W. Hofer and D. Schendel, Strategy Formulation: Analytical Concepts (St. Paul, MN: West Publishing Co., 1978), p. 34. From C. W. Hofer, "Conceptual Constructs for Formulating Corporate and Business Strategies" (Dover, MA: Case Publishing), no. BP-0041, p. 3. Copyright © 1977 by Charles W. Hofer. Reprinted by permission.*

TABLE 12–2

Six Stages of New Product Development

1. **Idea Generation.** New product concepts are identified and refined.

2. **Concept Evaluation.** Screening techniques are used to determine the concept's validity and market opportunity. Preliminary market research is conducted, and a strategy is developed. A business plan is developed to present to management.

3. **Preliminary Design.** A new venture team is formed to prepare desired product specifications.

4. **Prototype Build and Test.** A functioning model of the product is built and subjected to numerous tests.

5. **Final Design and Pilot Production.** Final product and process designs are developed to produce small numbers of the product for use in test marketing. Suggestions from the users are fed back to the design team for possible inclusion in the final product.

6. **New Business Development.** The entire company is energized to launch the product.

SOURCE: *Managing Corporate Culture, Innovation, and Intrapreneurship,* Howard W. Oden. Copyright © 1997 by Quorum Books. Reproduced with permission of Greenwood Publishing, Inc., Westport, CT.

DEVELOPING AN INNOVATIVE ENTREPRENEURIAL CULTURE

To create a more innovative corporation, top management must develop an entrepreneurial culture—one that is open to the transfer of new technology into company activities and products and services. The company must be flexible and accepting of change. It should include a willingness to withstand a certain percentage of product failures on the way to success. It should be able to manage small, incremental innovations in existing products as well as radical advances that may alter the basis for competition in an industry.[71] Largeness is not a disadvantage. In his classic book *Diffusion of Innovations*, Rogers reveals that innovative organizations tend to have the following characteristics:

- Positive attitude toward change
- Decentralized decision making
- Complexity
- Informal structure
- Interconnectedness
- Organizational slack (unused resources)
- Large size
- System openness[72]

Such a culture has been noted in 3M Corporation and Texas Instruments, among others. R&D in these companies is managed quite differently from traditional methods. First, employees are dedicated to a particular project outcome rather than to innovation in general. Second, employees are often responsible for all functional activities and for all phases of the innovation process. Time is allowed to be sacrificed from regular duties to spend on innovative ideas. If the ideas are feasible, employees are temporarily reassigned to help develop them. These people may become project champions who fight for resources to make the project a success. Third, these internal ventures are often separated from the rest of the company to provide them with greater independence, freedom for short-term pressures, different rewards, improved visibility, and access to key decision makers.[73]

The innovative process often involves individuals at different organizational levels who fulfill three different types of entrepreneurial roles: product champion, sponsor, and orchestrator. A **product champion** is a person who generates a new idea and supports it through many organizational obstacles. A **sponsor** is usually a department manager who recognizes the value of the idea, helps obtain funding to develop the innovation, and facilitates its implementation. An **orchestrator** is someone in top management who articulates the need for innovation, provides funding for innovating activities, creates incentives for middle managers to sponsor new ideas, and protects idea/product champions from suspicious or jealous executives. Unless all these roles are present in a company, major innovations are unlikely to occur.[74]

Companies are finding that one way to overcome the barriers to successful product innovation is by using multifunctional teams with significant autonomy dedicated to a project. In a survey of 701 companies from Europe, the United States, and Japan, 85% of the respondents have used this approach, with 62% rating it as successful.[75] Research reveals that cross-functional teams are best for designing and developing innovative new products, whereas the more traditional bureaucratic structures seem to be best for developing modifications to existing products, line extensions, and me-too products.[76] Chrysler Corporation was able to reduce the development time for new vehicles by 40% by using cross-functional teams and by developing a partnership approach to new projects.[77] International Specialty Products, a maker of polymers, used "product express" teams composed of chemists and representatives from manufacturing and engineering to cut development time in half. "Instead of passing a baton, we bring everyone into the commercialization process at the same time," explained John Tancredi, vice president for R&D. "We are moving laterally, like rugby players, instead of like runners in a relay race."[78]

ORGANIZING FOR INNOVATION: CORPORATE ENTREPRENEURSHIP

Corporate entrepreneurship (also called intrapreneurship) is defined by Guth and Ginsberg as "the birth of new businesses within existing organizations, that is, internal innovation or venturing; and the transformation of organizations through renewal of the key ideas on which they are built, that is, strategic renewal."[79] A large corporation that wants to encourage innovation and creativity within its firm must choose a structure that will give the new business unit an appropriate amount of freedom while maintaining some degree of control at headquarters. Research reveals that corporate entrepreneurship has a positive impact on a company's financial performance.[80]

Burgelman proposes (see **Figure 12–4**) that the use of a particular organizational design should be determined by (1) the strategic importance of the new business to the corporation and (2) the relatedness of the unit's operations to those of the corporation.[81] The combination of these two factors results in nine organizational designs for corporate entrepreneurship:

1. **Direct Integration:** A new business with a great deal of strategic importance and operational relatedness must be a part of the corporation's mainstream. Product champions—people who are respected by others in the corporation and who know how to work the system—are needed to manage these projects. Janiece Webb championed the incorporation of Internet web browsers in Motorola's mobile phones and is now in charge of Motorola's Personal Networks Group. Because Webb's unit only makes software, she works with other divisions to shape their "product maps," which show what they hope to bring to market and when.[82]

FIGURE 12–4

Organizational Designs for Corporate Entrepreneurship

	Strategic Importance		
Operational Relatedness	Very Important	Uncertain	Not Important
Unrelated	**3** Special Business Units	**6** Independent Business Units	**9** Complete Spin-off
Partly Related	**2** New Product Business Department	**5** New Venture Division	**8** Contracting
Strongly Related	**1** Direct Integration	**4** Micro New Ventures Department	**7** Nurturing and Contracting

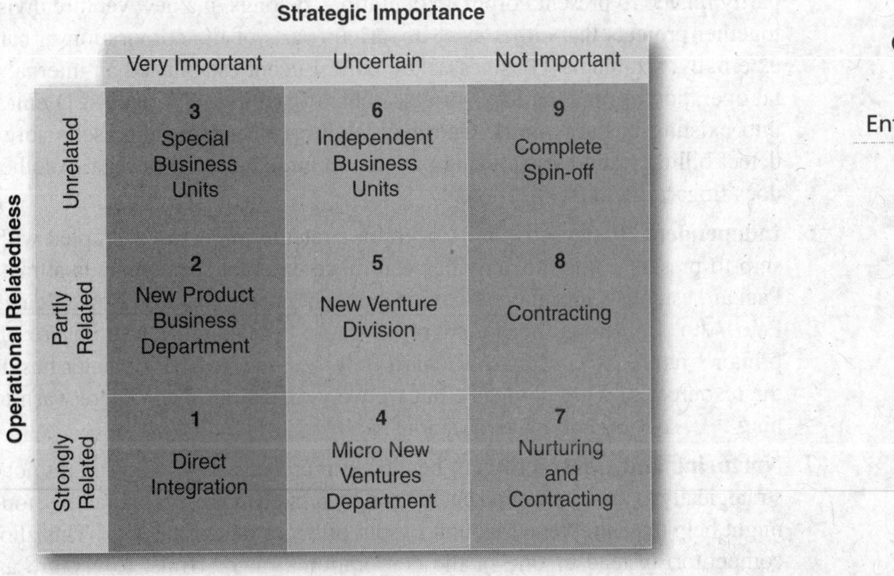

SOURCE: *Reprinted from R. A. Burgelman, "Designs for Corporate Entrepreneurship in Established Firms." Copyright © 1984, by the Regents of the University of California. Reprinted from the* California Management Review, *Vol. 26, No. 3. By permission of The Regents. All rights reserved.*

2. **New Product Business Department:** A new business with a great deal of strategic importance and partial operational relatedness should be a separate department, organized around an entrepreneurial project in the division where skills and capabilities can be shared. Maytag Corporation did this when it built a new plant near its current Newton, Iowa, washer plant to manufacture the wholly new Neptune line of energy- and water-efficient front-loading washing machines.

3. **Special Business Units:** A new business with a great deal of strategic importance and low operational relatedness should be a special new business unit with specific objectives and time horizons. Teradyne tried this with a new product called Integra. The new product was based on a new, low-cost technology—something that might be good enough in a few years to replace Teradyne's current technology. Because the technology wasn't good enough for Teradyne's high-end applications, Teradyne's management treated Integra like an entrepreneurial venture. Integra's general manager, Marc Levine, reported to a board of directors composed of Teradyne's top executives. Instead of a budget, Levine had a business plan and venture capital (from Teradyne). This governance structure allowed Integra to operate autonomously by recruiting and purchasing from outside the company. According to Levine, "The idea was to think of this as a business from the start, not an R&D project. The board setup allows more of a coaching attitude." Says Teradyne's Vice President, Edward Rogas, "A division is always pressed to do the next logical thing—and make it compatible with the existing line. We told Marc: Be aggressive on the technology; do something no one else has done."[83]

4. **Micro New Ventures Department:** A new business with uncertain strategic importance and high operational relatedness should be a peripheral project that is likely to emerge in the operating divisions on a continuous basis. Each division thus has its own new ventures department. Xerox Corporation, for example, uses its SBUs to generate and nurture new ideas. Small product-synthesis teams within each SBU test the feasibility of new ideas. Those concepts receiving a "go" are managed by an SBU product-delivery team, headed by a chief engineer, that takes the prototype from development through manufacturing.

5. **New Venture Division:** A new business with uncertain strategic importance that is only partly related to present corporate operations belongs in a new venture division. It brings together projects that either exist in various parts of the corporation or can be acquired externally; sizable new businesses are built. Lucent established an internal venture capital operation to fund the ideas of researchers from its Bell Labs R&D unit that didn't fit into existing business units. One new venture, Visual Insights, sells software that can detect billing fraud by analyzing patterns in large amounts of data. Another, Veridicom, does fingerprint authentication.[84]

6. **Independent Business Units:** Uncertain strategic importance coupled with no relationship to present corporate activities can make external arrangements attractive. Hewlett-Packard established printers as an independent business unit in Boise, Idaho (far from its Palo Alto, California, headquarters), because management was unsure of the desktop printer's future. According to Richard Belluzzo, head of HP's printer business, "We had the resources of a big company, but we were off on our own. There wasn't central planning . . . , so we could make decisions really fast."[85]

7. **Nurturing and Contracting:** When an entrepreneurial proposal might not be important strategically to the corporation but is strongly related to present operations, top management might help the entrepreneurial unit to spin off from the corporation. This allows a friendly competitor, instead of one of the corporation's major rivals, to capture a small niche. Techtronix has extensively used this approach. Because of research revealing that related spin-offs tend to be poorer performers than nonrelated spin-offs (presumably owing to the

loss of benefits enjoyed with a larger company), it is especially important that the parent company continue to support the development of the spun-off unit in this cell.[86]

8. **Contracting:** As the required capabilities and skills of the new business are less related to those of the corporation, the parent corporation may spin off the strategically unimportant unit yet keep some relationship through a contractual arrangement with the new firm. The connection is useful in case the new firm eventually develops something of value to the corporation. For example, B.F. Goodrich offered manufacturing rights plus a long-term purchasing agreement to a couple of its managers for a specific raw material Goodrich still used (in declining quantities) in its production process but no longer wanted to manufacture internally.

9. **Complete Spin-off:** If both the strategic importance and the operational relatedness of the new business are negligible, the corporation is likely to completely sell off the business to another firm or to the present employees in some form of Employee Stock Ownership Plan (ESOP). The corporation could also sell off the unit through a leveraged buyout (executives of the unit buy the unit from the parent company with money from a third source, to be repaid out of the unit's anticipated earnings). Because 3M wanted to focus its development money on areas with more profit potential, it decided to spin off its money-losing data storage and medical imaging divisions as a new company called Imation.

Organizing for innovation has become especially important for corporations that want to become more innovative but whose age and size have made them highly bureaucratic, with a culture that discourages creative thinking. These new structural designs for corporate entrepreneurship cannot work by themselves, however. The entrepreneurial units must also have the support of management and sufficient resources. They must also have employees who are risk-takers, willing to purchase an ownership interest in the new venture, and a corporate culture that supports new ventures. This is in contrast to corporations in which top management makes only a superficial commitment to innovation by demanding new ideas without providing the culture necessary to support their development. See **Strategy Highlight 12.2** for how *not* to develop an innovative organization.

STRATEGY highlight 12.2

HOW *NOT* TO DEVELOP AN INNOVATIVE ORGANIZATION

In their book *Corporate Venturing*, researchers Block and MacMillan state that fostering an organizationwide commitment to new business development means more than paying lip service to innovation. They argue that a superficial commitment is almost worse than no commitment at all. They noted that unsuccessful companies tend to follow the following "rules of the road to certain failure":

1. Announce to the company that from now on, it is going to "become entrepreneurial."

2. Create a separate venture department charged with the job of developing new businesses. Hold no one else responsible.

3. Bring in a horde of consultants and self-professed experts to harangue management and employees at all levels to aggressively seek new business ideas.

4. Hold several one-day senior management retreats to discuss the need to become more entrepreneurial.

5. Make no further changes in management practices or the behavior of senior managers.

12.5 Evaluation and Control

For innovations to succeed, appropriate evaluation and control techniques must be used to ensure that the end product is what was originally planned. Some of these techniques are the stage-gate process and the house of quality. Appropriate measures are also needed to evaluate the effectiveness of the R&D process. Today's global information technology enables executives to continually assess performance as a product moves from the idea to the finished product stage.

EVALUATION AND CONTROL TECHNIQUES

The **stage-gate process** is a method of managing new product development to increase the likelihood of launching new products quickly and successfully. The process is a series of steps to move products through the six stages of new product development listed in **Table 12–2**. A new concept cannot move beyond any stage until it has been evaluated thoroughly. The stage-gate process is used by companies such as IBM, 3M, General Motors, Corning, and P&G. Corning's managers believe that the process enables them to better estimate the potential payback of any project under consideration. They report that the stage-gate process reduces development time, allows identification of questionable projects, and increases the ratio of internally generated products that result in commercially successful products. It is especially useful for a major platform project (such as a line of new cars) that could be used to create multiple derivative products.[87]

The **house of quality** is another method of managing new product development.[88] Originally developed at Mitsubishi's Kobe shipyards, it is a tool to help project teams make important design decisions by getting them to think about what users want and how to get it to them most effectively.[89] It enhances communication and coordination among engineering, marketing, and manufacturing and ensures better product/customer fit. The house of quality is a tool to map customer requirements against product attributes. The first step is to identify product requirements and to weight their relative importance from the customer's perspective. For example, market research might identify five attributes that customers want from a car door. The second step is to identify the engineering attributes in measurable terms. For example, engineering might list four attributes of the door. In the third step, the team looks at the interaction between each engineering attribute and customer requirement. The team might find a negative interaction between "easy to open" (customer requirement) and "weight of the door" (engineering attribute), indicating that heavy doors are generally harder to open. The fourth step is to identify the interaction between design parameters. Thus, a negative interaction between door weight and hinge stiffness would indicate that a heavy door reduces the stiffness of the hinge. The final bit of information is a summary of the company's existing product compared with that of its competitors.

The house of quality provides a common framework within which the project team can interact. It makes the relationship between customer requirements and product attributes clear, emphasizes design tradeoffs, highlights the competitive shortcomings of current products, and helps identify what steps should be taken to improve the design. It is very useful for cross-functional project teams and a good technique to ensure that both the customer's desires and production feasibility are included in the end result.[90]

EVALUATION AND CONTROL MEASURES

Companies want to gain more productivity at a faster pace from their R&D activities. But how do we measure the effectiveness or efficiency of a company's R&D? This is a problem, given that a company shouldn't expect more than one in seven product ideas from basic research to make it to the marketplace. Some companies measure the proportion of their sales attributable to new products. For example, Hewlett-Packard measures how much of its revenues come from products introduced in the past three years.[91] At BellCore, the effectiveness of basic research is measured by how often the lab's research is cited in other scientists' work. This measure is compiled and published by the Institute for Scientific Information. Other companies judge the quality of research by counting how many patents they file annually.

Pittiglio Rabin Todd & McGrath (PRTM), a high-tech consulting firm, proposes an **index of R&D effectiveness**. The index is calculated by dividing the percentage of total revenue spent on R&D into new product profitability, which is expressed as a percentage. When this measure was applied to 45 large electronics manufacturers, only 9 companies scored 1.0 or higher, indicating that only 20% received a positive payback from their R&D

1. Corporate and business unit strategies are well defined and clearly communicated.	**TABLE 12–3**
2. Core technologies are defined and communicated to R&D.	Thirteen "Best Practices" for Improving R&D
3. Investments are made in developing multinational R&D capabilities to tap ideas throughout the world.	
4. Funding for basic research comes from corporate sources to ensure a long-term focus; funding for development comes from business units to ensure accountability.	
5. Basic and applied research are performed either at a central facility or at a small number of labs, each focused on a particular discipline of science or technology. Development work is usually performed at business unit sites.	
6. Formal, cross-functional teams are created for basic, applied, and developmental projects.	
7. Formal mechanisms exist for regular interaction among scientists, and between R&D and other functions.	
8. Analytical tools are used for selecting projects as well as for ongoing project evaluation.	
9. The transfer of technology to business units is the most important measure of R&D performance.	
10. Effective measures of career development are in place at all levels of R&D.	
11. Recruiting of new people is from diverse universities and from other companies when specific experience or skills are required that would take a long time to develop internally.	
12. Some basic research is performed internally, but there are also many university and third-party relationships.	
13. Formal mechanisms are used for monitoring external technological developments.	

SOURCE: From "Benchmarking R&D Productivity," I. Krause and J. Liu, 1993 © MCB University Press Limited. Republished with permission of Emerald Group Publishing Ltd.

spending. The top companies kept spending on marginal products to a minimum by running frequent checks on product versus market opportunities and canceling questionable products quickly. They also moved new products to market in half the time of the others. As a result, revenue growth among the top 20% of the companies was double the average of all 45 companies.[92]

A study of 15 multinational companies with successful R&D operations focused on three measures of R&D success: (1) improving technology transfer from R&D to business units, (2) accelerating time to market for new products and processes, and (3) institutionalizing cross-functional participation in R&D. The companies participated in basic, applied, and developmental research activities. The study revealed 13 **best practices** that all the companies followed.[93] Listed in **Table 12–3**, they provide a benchmark for a company's R&D activities.

INFO-BITS

- Japan is the world's robotics leader, with 350,000 industrial robots in 2003. Germany is second, with 105,000, and the United States is third, with 104,000 robots.[94]

- In 2004, 607,000 household robots were in use. Most of these were vacuum cleaner and lawn mower robots. The

UN Commission for Europe and the International Federation of Robotics predict that 4.1 million domestic robots will be in use by the end of 2007.[95]

- In 2004, 692,000 companion or entertainment robots, such as Sony's dog-like Aibo, were in use throughout the world.[96]

DISCUSSION QUESTIONS

1. How should a corporation scan the external environment for new technological developments? Who should be responsible?

2. What is technology research and how does it differ from market research?

3. What is the importance of product and process R&D to competitive strategy?

4. What factors help determine whether a company should outsource a technology?

5. How can a company develop an entrepreneurial culture?

STRATEGIC PRACTICE EXERCISE

How Creative Is Your Organization?
One of the keys to managing technology and innovation is to have a creative organization in which people are free to propose and try new ideas. The following questionnaire is taken from "Building a Creative Hothouse" by Barton Kunstler in the January–February 2001 issue of *The Futurist*. It is a simplified version of the Hothouse Assessment Instrument presented in greater detail in the Spring 2000 issue of *Futures*

Research Quarterly. This version describes many of the elements of a highly creative organization.

If you work or have worked full time in an organization, answer this questionnaire in light of your experience with that organization. If you have not worked full time anywhere, find someone who is working full time and ask that person to complete this questionnaire. Then discuss the person's answers with him or her.

To assess the level of creativity in your organization's culture, score your level of agreement or disagreement with the statements below as follows: **Strongly Agree** (5 points), **Mildly Agree** (4 points), **Neutral** (3 points), **Mildly Disagree** (2 points), **Strongly Disagree** (1 point).

(1) VALUES

1. ___ We believe that our work can change the world.

2. ___ The organization actively promotes a positive quality of life in our surrounding communities.

3. ___ People here really believe our products and services are vital to others' well-being.

4. ___ Virtually all who work here continually study and question the basic nature of their job and the technologies—human, organizational, technical—they work with.

5. ___ Working here fills me with a sense of personal well-being and commitment to my higher values.

(2) MISSION AND VISION

6. ___ Principles of justice and compassion directly and significantly influence strategy, design, and development.

7. ___ We explore the fundamental practices and principles of our industry and its disciplines as a source of creativity, values, and purpose.

8. ___ We can fail without fear for our jobs.

9. ___ My organization takes the long view.

10. ___ Employees are free to develop their own vision of what their jobs entail.

(3) IDEAS

11. ___ This organization cultivates the growth of knowledge into wisdom and views wisdom as a guide to action.

12. ___ Organizational structure is shaped by innovative, idea-driven approaches to our challenges and tasks.

13. ___ Organizational responses to crises are thoughtful and imaginative, not reactive and typical.

14. ___ The organization respects thinkers.

15. ___ I am respected for all my talents, whether or not they contribute to the bottom line.

(4) EXCHANGE

16. ___ My organization rewards those who display mastery at their jobs and seeks their advice, whatever their title or position.

17. ___ Institutionalized procedures enable anyone to make suggestions or raise objections.

18. ___ Intellectually exciting and stimulating conversation directly influences product development and delivery.

19. ___ "Idea people" share their vision with other employees and invite feedback.

20. ___ The group uses conflict as an opportunity for personal and organizational growth.

(5) PERCEPTION

21. ___ How we perceive our tasks, our expertise, and the group itself is a legitimate object of inquiry.

22. ___ Whole-minded thinking, including activities based on movement and heightening awareness of the five senses, is encouraged.

23. ___ Employees are taught and encouraged to think creatively.

24. ___ We continually re-vision our group's place within its industry and society as a whole.

25. ___ Clear problem-solving algorithms are taught, practiced, developed, and applied wherever a need is perceived, without regard to concerns of status, tradition, or company politics.

(6) LEARNING

26. ___ To be viewed as a "continuous learner" at work benefits one's career.

27. ___ We regularly challenge group norms, and anyone can initiate this process.

28. ___ My organization is constantly engaged in learning about itself and the environments in which it operates.

29. ___ The organization allocates resources toward employee involvement in cultural events as attendees, participants, or learners.

30. ___ Projects are undertaken by integrated teams whose members bring multiple disciplines and diverse perspectives to the task.

(7) SOCIAL

31. ___ Our relationships at work are relaxed, irreverent, warm, and crackling with ideas.

32. ___ People from different departments and organizational levels socialize together, either during or after work.

33. ___ Committee meetings are reasonably productive and amicable.

34. ___ When we form teams to work on special projects, the work is integrated into our day-to-day schedules.

35. ___ We always produce effective leadership when and where we need it.

Let's Summarize the Chapter with a Mind Map

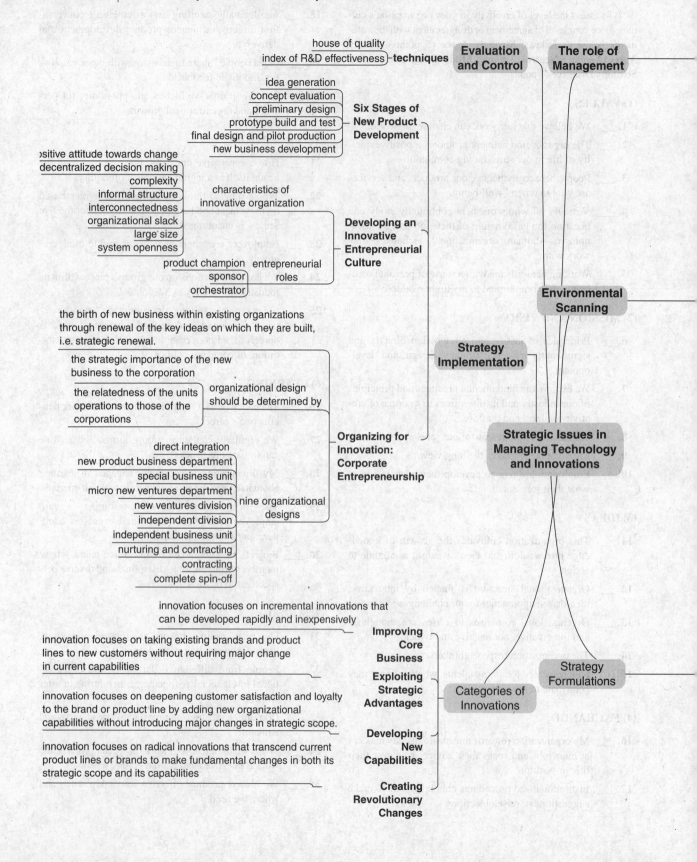

house of quality

index of R&D effectiveness — techniques

Evaluation and Control

The role of Management

idea generation
concept evaluation
preliminary design
prototype build and test
final design and pilot production
new business development

Six Stages of New Product Development

positive attitude towards change
decentralized decision making
complexity
informal structure
interconnectedness
organizational slack
large size
system openness

characteristics of innovative organization

Developing an Innovative Entrepreneurial Culture

product champion
sponsor
orchestrator

entrepreneurial roles

Environmental Scanning

the birth of new business within existing organizations through renewal of the key ideas on which they are built, i.e. strategic renewal.

Strategy Implementation

the strategic importance of the new business to the corporation

the relatedness of the units operations to those of the corporations

organizational design should be determined by

Organizing for Innovation: Corporate Entrepreneurship

Strategic Issues in Managing Technology and Innovations

direct integration
new product business department
special business unit
micro new ventures department
new ventures division
independent division
independent business unit
nurturing and contracting
contracting
complete spin-off

nine organizational designs

innovation focuses on incremental innovations that can be developed rapidly and inexpensively

Improving Core Business

innovation focuses on taking existing brands and product lines to new customers without requiring major change in current capabilities

Exploiting Strategic Advantages

Categories of Innovations

Strategy Formulations

innovation focuses on deepening customer satisfaction and loyalty to the brand or product line by adding new organizational capabilities without introducing major changes in strategic scope.

Developing New Capabilities

innovation focuses on radical innovations that transcend current product lines or brands to make fundamental changes in both its strategic scope and its capabilities

Creating Revolutionary Changes

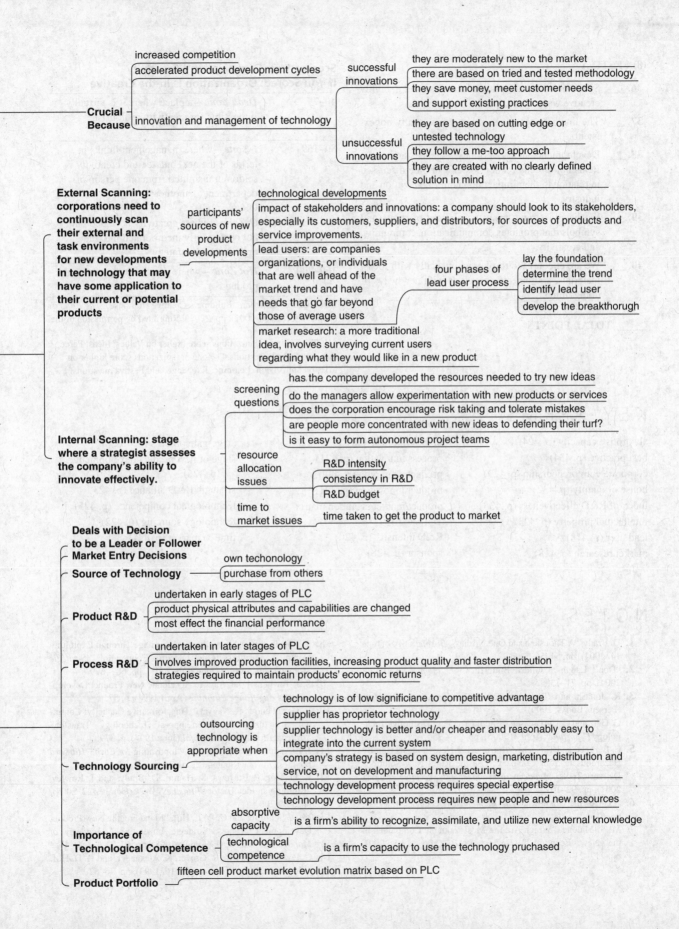

Crucial Because
- increased competition
- accelerated product development cycles
- innovation and management of technology

successful innovations
- they are moderately new to the market
- there are based on tried and tested methodology
- they save money, meet customer needs and support existing practices

unsuccessful innovations
- they are based on cutting edge or untested technology
- they follow a me-too approach
- they are created with no clearly defined solution in mind

External Scanning: corporations need to continuously scan their external and task environments for new developments in technology that may have some application to their current or potential products

participants' sources of new product developments
- technological developments
- impact of stakeholders and innovations: a company should look to its stakeholders, especially its customers, suppliers, and distributors, for sources of products and service improvements.
- lead users: are companies organizations, or individuals that are well ahead of the market trend and have needs that go far beyond those of average users
- market research: a more traditional idea, involves surveying current users regarding what they would like in a new product

four phases of lead user process
- lay the foundation
- determine the trend
- identify lead user
- develop the breakthorugh

Internal Scanning: stage where a strategist assesses the company's ability to innovate effectively.

screening questions
- has the company developed the resources needed to try new ideas
- do the managers allow experimentation with new products or services
- does the corporation encourage risk taking and tolerate mistakes
- are people more concentrated with new ideas to defending their turf?
- is it easy to form autonomous project teams

resource allocation issues
- R&D intensity
- consistency in R&D
- R&D budget

time to market issues
- time taken to get the product to market

Deals with Decision to be a Leader or Follower
Market Entry Decisions

Source of Technology
- own techonology
- purchase from others

Product R&D
- undertaken in early stages of PLC
- product physical attributes and capabilities are changed
- most effect the financial performance

Process R&D
- undertaken in later stages of PLC
- involves improved production facilities, increasing product quality and faster distribution
- strategies required to maintain products' economic returns

Technology Sourcing

outsourcing technology is appropriate when
- technology is of low significiane to competitive advantage
- supplier has proprietor technology
- supplier technology is better and/or cheaper and reasonably easy to integrate into the current system
- company's strategy is based on system design, marketing, distribution and service, not on development and manufacturing
- technology development process requires special expertise
- technology development process requires new people and new resources

Importance of Technological Competence
- **absorptive capacity** is a firm's ability to recognize, assimilate, and utilize new external knowledge
- **technological competence** is a firm's capacity to use the technology pruchased

Product Portfolio
- fifteen cell product market evolution matrix based on PLC

(8) FESTIVA

36. ___   Social occasions are planned and designed in highly creative ways.

37. ___   The line between work and play is virtually nonexistent.

38. ___   Developments in art, politics, science, and other fields not directly related to our work are discussed in relation to their impact upon our organization and industry.

39. ___   We have a strong group vocabulary of terms and symbols that promotes communication, community, and creativity.

40. ___   We are encouraged to play whimsically with ideas, materials, and objects as well as with new ways of doing things.

_____   **TOTAL POINTS**

Scoring Your Organization's Creativity
If You Scored: Organization Is in the Creative . . .

40–79	**Dead Zone**—a place where it is virtually impossible for creativity to flourish
80–159	**I-Zone**—where management thinks in terms of the next quarter and creativity is seldom transmitted from one person or department to another* OR . . . **O-Zone**—where creativity is valued but not consistently incorporated into the organization's strategy*
160–200	**Hot Zone**—where creativity is intense and productive

SOURCE: B. Kunstler, "Building a Creative Hothouse," *The Futurist* (January–February 2001), pp. 22–29. Reprinted by permission of the World Future Society.
*NOTE: I-Zone organizations score higher on Values, Ideas, Perception, and Social questions. O-Zone organizations score higher on Mission and Vision, Learning, Exchange, and Festiva questions.

KEY TERMS

absorptive capacity (p. 424)

best practice (p. 434)

corporate entrepreneurship (p. 429)

house of quality (p. 432)

index of R&D effectiveness (p. 433)

intellectual property (p. 423)

lead user (p. 418)

market research (p. 418)

orchestrator (p. 428)

process innovation (p. 421)

product champion (p. 428)

product innovation (p. 421)

product/market evolution matrix (p. 426)

R&D intensity (p. 420)

sponsor (p. 428)

stage-gate process (p. 432)

stage of new product development (p. 426)

strategic R&D alliance (p. 423)

technological competence (p. 425)

technology sourcing (p. 422)

time to market (p. 421)

NOTES

1. D. Brady, "A Thousand and One Noshes," *Business Week* (June 14, 2004), pp. 54–56.

2. "Don't Laugh at Gilded Butterflies," *Economist* (April 24, 2004), pp. 71–73.

3. R. Jonash and T. Sommerlatte, *The Innovation Premium* (Perseus Books, 1999).

4. G. Getz and C. Christensen, "Should You Fear Disruptive Technology?" *Fortune* (April 3, 2000), pp. 249–250.

5. E. Berggen and T. Nacher, "Introducing New Products Can Be Hazardous to Your Company: Use the Right New-Solutions Delivery Tools," *Academy of Management Executive* (August 2001), pp. 92–101.

6. "Fear of the Unknown," *The Economist* (December 4, 1999), pp. 61–62.

7. M. S. Malone, "Which Are the Most Valuable Companies in the New Economy?" *Forbes ASAP* (May 29, 2000), pp. 212–214.

8. F. T. Rothaermel, "Incumbent's Advantage Through Exploiting Complementary Assets via Interfirm Cooperation," *Strategic Management Journal* (June–July 2001), pp. 687–699.

9. S. J. Towner, "Four Ways to Accelerate New Product Development," *Long Range Planning* (April 1994), p. 57.

10. R. Garud and P. R. Nayyar, "Transformative Capacity: Continual Structuring by Intertemporal Technology Transfer," *Strategic Management Journal* (June 1994), p. 379.

11. J. P. Andrew and H. L. Sirkin, "Innovating for Cash," *Harvard Business Review* (September 2003), pp. 76–83.

12. R. D. Hof, P. Burrows, S. Hamm, D. Brady, and I. Rowley, "Building an Idea Factory," *Business Week* (October 22, 2004), pp. 194–200.

13. M. A. Schilling and C. W. L. Hill, "Managing the New Product Development Process: Strategic Imperatives," *Academy of Management Executive* (August 1998), pp. 67–81.

14. C. Power, K. Kerwin, R. Grover, K. Alexander, and R. D. Hof, "Flops," *Business Week* (August 16, 1993), pp. 76–82.

15. "Expect the Unexpected," *Economist* (September 6, 2003), p. 5. This article summarizes research reported in *Why Innovation Fails* by Carl Franklin (London: Spiro Press, 2003).

16. R. D. Hof, P. Burrows, S. Hamm, D. Brady, and I. Rowley, "Building an Idea Factory," *Business Week* (October 22, 2004), p. 196.

17. L. Rosenkopf and A. Nerkar, "Beyond Local Search: Boundary-Spanning, Exploration, and Impact in the Optical Disk Industry," *Strategic Management Journal* (April 2001), pp. 287–306.

18. G. C. Hill and K. Yamada, "Motorola Illustrates How an Aged Giant Can Remain Vibrant," *Wall Street Journal* (December 9, 1992), pp. A1, A14.

19. L. Huston, "Mining the Periphery for New Products," *Long Range Planning* (April 2004), pp. 191–196; N. Snyder, "Environmental Volatility, Scanning Intensity and Organizational Performance," *Journal of Contemporary Business* (September 1981), p. 16.

20. R. Nobel and J. Birkinshaw, "Innovations in MNCs: Control and Communication Patterns in International R&D Operations," *Strategic Management Journal* (May 1998), pp. 479–496.

21. J. Kerstetter, "An Old Hotbed with New Crops," *Business Week* (October 11, 2004), pp. 164–170; P. Almeida, "Knowledge Sourcing by Foreign Multinationals: Patent Citation Analysis in the U.S. Semiconductor Industry," *Strategic Management Journal* (December 1996), pp. 155–165.

22. E. Von Hippel, *The Sources of Innovation* (Oxford, UK: Oxford University Press, 1988), p. 4. See also S. Thomke and E. Von Hippel, "Customers As Innovators: A New Way to Create Value," *Harvard Business Review* (April 2002), pp. 74–81.

23. M. R. Neale and D. R. Corkindale, "Co-Developing Products: Involving Customer Earlier and More Deeply," *Long Range Planning* (June 1998), pp. 418–425.

24. E. Von Hippel, *The Sources of Innovation* (Oxford, UK: Oxford University Press, 1988), p. 107; E. Von Hippel, S. Thomke, and M. Sonnack, "Creating Breakthroughs at 3M," *Harvard Business Review* (September–October 1999), p. 48.

25. L. Lavelle, "Inventing to Order," *Business Week* (July 5, 2004), pp. 84–85.

26. E. Von Hippel, S. Thomke, and M. Sonnack, "Creating Breakthroughs at 3M," *Harvard Business Review* (September–October 1999), p. 52.

27. G. Hamel and C. K. Prahalad, "Seeing the Future First," *Fortune* (September 5, 1995), p. 70.

28. C. M. Christensen, *The Innovator's Dilemma* (Boston: HBS Press, 1997); J. Wade, "A Community-Level Analysis of Sources and Rates of Technological Variation in the Microprocessor Market," *Academy of Management Journal* (October 1996), pp. 1218–1244.

29. C. M. Christensen and J. L. Bower, "Customer Power, Strategic Investment, and the Failure of Leading Firms," *Strategic Management Journal* (March 1996), pp. 197–218.

30. G. S. Lynn, J. G. Morone, and A. S. Paulson, "Marketing and Discontinuous Innovation: The Probe and Learn Process," *California Management Review* (Spring 1996), pp. 8–37.

31. W. I. Zangwill, "When Customer Research Is a Lousy Idea," *Wall Street Journal* (March 8, 1993), p. A10.

32. S. Baker, "What Every Business Should Learn from Microsoft," *Journal of Business Strategy* (September/October 1998), pp. 36–41.

33. "Don't Laugh at Gilded Butterflies," *Economist* (April 24, 2004), pp. 71–73.

34. D. F. Kuratko, J. S. Hornsby, D. W. Naffziger, and R. V. Montagno, "Implement Entrepreneurial Thinking in Established Organizations," *SAM Advanced Management Journal* (Winter 1993), p. 29.

35. "Business Bulletin," *Wall Street Journal* (May 1, 1997), p. A1. The number improved from 58 ideas in 1967 to 11 in 1990, to 7 in 1995.

36. L. G. Franko, "Global Corporate Competition: Who's Winning, Who's Losing, and the R&D Factor as One Reason Why," *Strategic Management Journal* (September–October 1989), pp. 449–474; See also P. S. Chan, E. J. Flynn, and R. Chinta, "The Strategies of Growing and Turnaround Firms: A Multiple Discriminant Analysis," *International Journal of Management* (September 1991), pp. 669–675.

37. M. J. Chussil, "How Much to Spend on R&D?" *The PIMS-letter of Business Strategy*, No. 13 (Cambridge, MA: The Strategic Planning Institute, 1978), p. 5.

38. J. S. Harrison, E. H. Hall, Jr., and R. Nargundkar, "Resource Allocation as an Outcropping of Strategic Consistency: Performance Implications," *Academy of Management Journal* (October 1993), pp. 1026–1051.

39. S. B. Graves and N. S. Langowitz, "Innovative Productivity and Returns to Scale in the Pharmaceutical Industry," *Strategic Management Journal* (November 1993), pp. 593–605; A. Brady, "Small Is As Small Does," *Journal of Business Strategy* (March/April 1995), pp. 44–52.

40. "Small Firms Make More Than Their Share of Big Inventions," *The Small Business Advocate* (March 2003), pp. 1, 4.

41. J. B. Sorensen and T. E. Stuart, "Aging, Obsolescence, and Organizational Innovation," *Administrative Science Quarterly* (March 2000), pp. 81–112.

42. D. H. Freedman, "Through the Looking Glass," in "The State of Small Business," *Inc.* (May 21, 1996), pp. 48–54.

43. N. Nohria and R. Gulati, "Is Slack Good or Bad for Innovation?" *Academy of Management Journal* (October 1996), pp. 1245–1264.

44. M. A. Hitt, R. E. Hoskisson, and J. S. Harrison, "Strategic Competitiveness in the 1990s: Challenges and Opportunities for U.S. Executives," *Academy of Management Executive* (May 1991), p. 13.

45. T. F. O'Boyle, "Steel's Management Has Itself to Blame," *Wall Street Journal* (May 17, 1983), p. 32.

46. M. Silva and B. Sjogren, *Europe 1992 and the New World Power Game* (New York: John Wiley & Sons, 1990), p. 231.

47. E. Mansfield, M. Schwartz, and S. Wagner, "Imitation Costs and Patents: An Empirical Study," *Economic Journal* (December 1981), pp. 907–918.

48. G. Stalk, Jr., and A. M. Webber, "Japan's Dark Side of Time," *Harvard Business Review* (July–August 1993), p. 99.

49. M. Robert, "Market Fragmentation versus Market Segmentation," *Journal of Business Strategy* (September/October 1992), p. 52.

50. M. J. Benner and M. Tushman, "Process Management and Technological Innovation: A Longitudinal Study of the Photography and Paint Industries," *Administrative Science Quarterly* (December 2002), pp. 676–706.

51. W. T. Robinson and J. Chiang, "Product Development Strategies for Established Market Pioneers, Early Followers, and Late Entrants," *Strategic Management Journal* (September 2002), pp. 855–866.

52. C. L. Nicholls-Nixon and C. Y. Woo, "Technology Sourcing and Output of Established Firms in a Regime of Encompassing

Technological Change," *Strategic Management Journal* (July 2003), pp. 651–666.

53. "Business Briefcase," *Des Moines Register* (November 17, 2004), p. 3D.

54. M. Silva and B. Sjogren, *Europe 1992 and the New World Power Game* (New York: John Wiley & Sons), pp. 239–241. See also P. Nueno and J. Oosterveld, "Managing Technology Alliances," *Long Range Planning* (June 1988), pp. 11–17.

55. M. Krantz, "Amgen Thinks Small to Grow," *USA Today* (October 23, 2003), p. 3B.

56. P. R. Nayak, "Should You Outsource Product Development?" *Journal of Business Strategy* (May/June 1993), pp. 44–45.

57. C. W. L. Hill, "Establishing a Standard: Competitive Strategy and Technological Standards in Winner-Take-All Industries," *Academy of Management Executive* (May 1997), pp. 7–25.

58. M. H. Roy and S. S. Dugal, "The Effect of Technological Environment and Competitive Strategy on Licensing Decisions," *American Business Review* (June 1999), pp. 112–118.

59. T. M. Apke, "International Licensing of Technology: Protecting Your Interests," paper presented to the annual meeting of the *Western Decision Sciences Institute* (Honolulu, HI, April 15–19, 2003).

60. "The Cost of Ideas," *Economist* (November 13, 2004), p. 71; "Patent Wars," *Economist* (April 8, 2000), pp. 75–78.

61. "The Right to Good Ideas," *Economist* (June 23, 2001), pp. 21–23.

62. M. A. Hitt, R. E. Hoskisson, R. A. Johnson, and D. D. Moesel, "The Market for Corporate Control and Firm Innovation," *Academy of Management Journal* (October 1996), pp. 1084–1119.

63. W. M. Cohen and D. A. Levinthal, "Absorptive Capacity: A New Perspective on Learning and Innovation," *Administrative Science Quarterly* (March 1990), pp. 128–152.

64. P. J. Lane and M. Lubatkin, "Absorptive Capacity and Interorganizational Learning," *Strategic Management Journal* (May 1998), pp. 461–477.

65. M. B. Heeley, "Appropriating Rents from External Knowledge: The Impact of Absorptive Capacity on Firm Sales Growth and Research Productivity," paper presented to *Babson Entrepreneurship Research Conference* (Wellesley, MA, 1997).

66. S. A. Zahra and G. George, "Absorptive Capacity: A Review, Reconceptualization, and Extension," *Academy of Management Review* (April 2002), pp. 185–203.

67. "The Impact of Industrial Robotics on the World of Work," *International Labour Review*, Vol. 125, No. 1 (1986). Summarized in "The Risks of Robotization," *The Futurist* (May–June 1987), p. 56.

68. M. A. Hitt, R. E. Hoskisson, and J. S. Harrison, "Strategic Competitiveness in the 1990s: Challenges and Opportunities for U.S. Executives,"*Academy of Management Executive* (May 1991), p. 9.

69. C. Hickman and C. Raia, "Incubating Innovation," *Journal of Business Strategy* (May/June 2002), pp. 14–18.

70. D. Dougherty and C. Hardy, "Sustained Product Innovation in Large, Mature Organizations: Overcoming Innovation-to-Organization Problems," *Academy of Management* (October 1996), pp. 1120–1153.

71. C. A. O'Reilly III and M. L. Tushman, "The Ambidextrous Organization," *Harvard Business Review* (April 2004), pp. 74–81.

72. E. M. Rogers, *Diffusion of Innovations*, 4th edition (New York: The Free Press, 1995).

73. C. A. Lengnick-Hall, "Innovation and Competitive Advantage: What We Know and What We Need to Know," *Journal of Management* (June 1992), pp. 399–429.

74. J. R. Galbraith, "Designing the Innovative Organization," *Organizational Dynamics* (Winter 1982), pp. 5–25.

75. P. R. Nayak, "Product Innovation Practices in Europe, Japan, and the U.S.," *Journal of Business Strategy* (May/June 1992), pp. 62–63.

76. E. M. Olson, O. C. Walker, Jr., and R. W. Ruekert, "Organizing for Effective New Product Development: The Moderating Role of Product Innovativeness," *Journal of Marketing* (January 1995), pp. 48–62.

77. D. Rowe, "Up and Running," *Journal of Business Strategy* (May/June 1993), pp. 48–50.

78. N. Freundlich and M. Schroeder, "Getting Everybody Into the Act," *Business Week* (Quality 1991 edition), p. 152.

79. W. D. Guth and A. Ginsberg, "Corporate Entrepreneurship," *Strategic Management Journal* (Summer 1990), p. 5.

80. S. A. Zahra and J. G. Covin, "Contextual Measures on the Corporate Entrepreneurship–Performance Relationship: A Longitudinal Analysis," *Journal of Business Venturing*, Vol. 10 (1995), pp. 43–58.

81. R. A. Burgelman, "Designs for Corporate Entrepreneurship," *California Management Review* (Spring 1984), pp. 154–166; R. A. Burgelman and L. R. Sayles, *Inside Corporate Innovation* (New York: The Free Press, 1986).

82. W. J. Holstein, "Remaking Motorola Isn't Easy," *U.S. News & World Report* (October 23, 2000), p. 52; R. O. Crockett, "A New Company Called Motorola," *Business Week* (April 17, 2000), pp. 86–92.

83. T. A. Stewart, "How Teradyne Solved the Innovator's Dilemma," *Fortune* (June 10, 2000), pp. 188–190.

84. J. Carey, "An Ivory Tower That Spins Pure Gold," *Business Week* (April 19, 1999), pp. 167–170.

85. S. K. Yoder, "How H-P Used Tactics of the Japanese to Beat Them at Their Game," *Wall Street Journal* (September 8, 1994), pp. A1, A6.

86. C. Y. Woo, G. E. Willard, and S. M. Beckstead, "Spin-Offs: What Are the Gains?" *Journal of Business Strategy* (March–April 1989), pp. 29–32.

87. M. A. Schilling and C. W. L. Hill, "Managing the New Product Development Process: Strategic Imperatives," *Academy of Management Executive* (August 1998), pp. 67–81.

88. J. R. Hauser and D. Clausing, "The House of Quality," *Harvard Business Review* (May-June 1988), pp. 63–73.

89. E. H. Kessler, P. E. Bierly, III, and S. Gopalakrishnan, "Vasa Syndrome: Insights from a 17th-Century New-Product Disaster," *Academy of Management Executive* (August 2001), pp. 80–91.

90. M. A. Schilling and C. W. L. Hill, "Managing the New Product Development Process: Strategic Imperatives," *Academy of Management Executive* (August 1998), pp. 67–81.

91. J. B. Levin and R. D. Hof, "Has Philips Found Its Wizard?" *Business Week* (September 6, 1993), pp. 82–84.

92. O. Port, "Rating R&D: How Companies Get the Biggest Bang for the Buck," *Business Week* (July 5, 1993), p. 98.

93. I. Krause and J. Liu, "Benchmarking R&D Productivity," *Planning Review* (January/February 1993), pp. 16–21, 52–53.

94. "Robots," *Economist* (October 18, 2003), p. 98.

95. J. Fowler, "Vacuums Lead Surge in Household Robots," *Des Moines Register* (October 21, 2004), p. 3D.

96.. Ibid., p. 30.

CHAPTER 13

strategic issues in entrepreneurial ventures and Small Businesses

One night while attending a professional basketball game, Vincent Norment noticed a problem on the court. As the game progressed, sweat-soaked headbands kept creeping down into the players' eyes. The athletes seemed to be constantly adjusting their headbands and were distracted from playing their best. Norment concluded that all that was needed to solve the problem was to put a thick strap across the top of the headband. The strap could be made of the same super-absorbent material as the rest of the headband. With this strap, a headband would not only absorb more of the athlete's sweat but also stay in place. With a background in sports-related products, Norment suggested his idea to headband manufacturers. "They looked at the product and said it wouldn't work," reported Norment.

When a patent search found nothing similar on the market, Norment patented his idea for DBands and planned to sell them through his own company, DApparel, Inc. Knowing that the key to success was getting the product used by athletes, Norment promoted DBands at the three-point shooting contest of the 2003 March Madness collegiate basketball playoffs. He asked players for their opinions and persuaded one player to wear the headband on ESPN. Thanks to the exposure, Norment got endorsements from Ron Artest of the Indiana Pacers and Brad Miller of the Sacramento Kings, among others. Now that DBands was starting to get the attention of the market, the next step was securing distribution.

DBands arrived in sporting goods stores such as The Athlete's Foot and Foot Locker in spring 2005, priced between $9.99 and $14.99. Norment expected to sell 50,000 to 100,000 DBands by December 2005. His goal was to make the DApparel brand a household name, one head at the time.[1]

Learning Objectives

After reading this chapter, you should be able to:

- Differentiate between an entrepreneurial venture and a small business
- Use the strategic decision-making process to form a new venture
- Differentiate between an idea and an opportunity
- Identify sources of innovative concepts
- List the characteristics of the typical entrepreneur

- Understand the importance of moving through the substages of small-business development
- Avoid pitfalls in assessing the financial statements of a small, privately owned company

13.1 Importance of Small Business and Entrepreneurial Ventures

Strategic management as a field of study typically deals with large, established business corporations. However, small business cannot be ignored. There are approximately 23 million small businesses—over 99% of all businesses—in the United States. They generate 60% to 80% of net new jobs annually and produce almost 30% of known export value. Studies by the Global Entrepreneurship Monitor have found a strong correlation between national economic growth and the level of entrepreneurial activity in prior years.[2] Research reveals that not only do small firms spend almost twice as much of their R&D budget on fundamental research as do large firms, but also, small companies are roughly 13 times more innovative per employee than large firms.[3] The National Science Foundation estimates that 98% of "radical" product developments result from the research done in the labs of small companies.[4] Nevertheless, not every country is as supportive of new ventures as is the United States. See the **Global Issue** feature to learn how different countries support entrepreneurship.

Despite the overall success of small businesses, however, every year tens of thousands of small companies fail. Figures from the U.S. Small Business Administration indicate that 50% of businesses founded in any one year are not in business four years later.[5] Similar rates occur in the United Kingdom, the Netherlands, Japan, Taiwan, and Hong Kong.[6] Although an increasing number of studies are more positive regarding the survival rate of new entrepreneurial ventures, new businesses are definitely considered risky.[7] The causes of small-business failure (depending on the study cited) range from inadequate accounting systems to inability to cope with growth. The underlying problem appears to be an overall lack of strategic management—beginning with an inability to plan a strategy to reach the customer and ending with a failure to develop a system of controls to keep track of performance.[8]

GLOBAL issue

ENTREPRENEURSHIP: SOME COUNTRIES ARE MORE SUPPORTIVE THAN OTHERS

Entrepreneurship is becoming increasingly important throughout the world. True to economist Joseph Schumpeter's view of entrepreneurship as "creative destruction," much of the world from Eastern Europe to South America to Asia envisions entrepreneurial ventures as the means to build successful free market economies. New entrepreneurial ventures are emerging daily in these countries. Unfortunately, not every country makes it easy to start a new business.

According to the World Bank, countries range from easy to difficult in terms of starting an entrepreneurial venture. The amount of difficulty is usually a function of government requirements and paperwork and can be measured in the number of days it takes to start a new venture. The *quickest* in days are Australia (2), Canada (3), New Zealand (3), Denmark (4), the United States (4), Puerto Rico (6), Singapore (8), Hong Kong (11), Latvia (11), and the Netherlands (11). The *slowest* in days are Zaire (215), Haiti (203), Laos (198), Indonesia (168), Mozambique (153), Brazil (152), Angola (146), Burkina Faso (136), Zimbabwe (122), and Venezuela (119). Not surprisingly, the World Bank analysis of 130 countries concludes that onerous regulation retards economic growth.

Even though entrepreneurship is more difficult in many other parts of the world than in the United States, the situation is changing. For example, investors are flocking to young, fast-growing companies in Europe. Politicians are beginning to see entrepreneurs as part of a solution to unemployment rather than as grasping exploiters. Venture capital is becoming more available. The EASDAQ, founded in 1996, is Europe's version of the NASDAQ. Companies can be listed on the EASDAQ regardless of size or history, so long as they agree to international accounting standards and U.S.-style financial reporting.

There is still an ingrained cultural aversion to the risk-taking so necessary to entrepreneurship. The contradiction between the Marxist ideology and private ownership in China means that business entrepreneurs are not perceived as legitimate. The social stigma attached to business failure is deeply entrenched in many countries. According to Christophe Sapet, the French founder of a computer game company called Infogrames, "When you earn money, (French) people are jealous. They think you have done something wrong."

SOURCES: "Down to Business," *The Economist* (October 11, 2003), p. 9; J. Kahn, "Suddenly, Startups Are Chic," *Fortune* (February 15, 1999), p. 110; "Financial Indicators," *The Economist* (October 16, 1999), p. 109; "Emerging-Market Indicators," *The Economist* (September 23, 2000), p. 128; E. W. K. Tsang, "In Search of Legitimacy: The Private Entrepreneur in China," *Entrepreneurship Theory and Practice* (Fall 1996), pp. 21–30.

DEFINITION OF SMALL-BUSINESS FIRMS AND ENTREPRENEURIAL VENTURES

The most commonly accepted definition of a small-business firm in the United States is one that employs fewer than 500 people and that generates sales of less than $20 million annually.

Although the meanings of the terms *small business* and *entrepreneurship* overlap considerably, the concepts are different. A **small-business firm** is independently owned and operated, is not dominant in its field, and does not engage in innovative practices. An **entrepreneurial venture**, in contrast, is any business whose primary goals are profitability and growth and that can be characterized by innovative strategic practices.[9] The basic difference between a small-business firm and an entrepreneurial venture, therefore, lies not in the type of goods or services provided, but in their fundamental views on growth and innovation. According to Donald Sexton, an authority on entrepreneurship, this explains why strategic planning is more likely to be present in an entrepreneurial venture than in a typical small-business firm:

Most firms start with just a single product. Those oriented toward growth immediately start looking for another one. It's that planning approach that separates the entrepreneur from the small-business owner.[10]

THE ENTREPRENEUR AS STRATEGIST

Often defined as a person who organizes and manages a business undertaking and who assumes risk for the sake of a profit, an **entrepreneur** is the ultimate strategist. He or she makes all the strategic as well as operational decisions. All three levels of strategy—corporate, business, and functional—are the concerns of this founder and owner–manager of a company. This is typical of a new venture, which is usually a Stage I company (discussed in **Chapter 9**, in the stages of corporate development section). As one entrepreneur puts it: "Entrepreneurs are strategic planners without realizing it."

The development of DBands described earlier captures the key elements of an entrepreneurial venture: a basic business idea that has not yet been successfully tried and a gutsy entrepreneur who, while working on borrowed capital and a shoestring budget, creates a new business through a lot of trial and error and persistent hard work. Similar stories can be told of other people, such as Debbie Fields, who created Mrs. Fields Cookies, and Will Parish, who founded National Energy Associates. Both were ridiculed at one time or another for their desire to start businesses. Friends and family members told Fields that starting a business to sell chocolate chip cookies "was a stupid idea." Will Parish, who built a power plant in California's Imperial Valley that burns "pasture patties," was called an "entre-manure." Every day the plant burned 900 tons of manure collected from nearby feedlots to generate 15 megawatts of electricity—enough to light 20,000 homes. The power was sold to Southern California Edison. Parish got the idea from a trip to India, where the fuel used to heat a meal was cow dung. Once the plant was earning a profit, Parish planned to build a larger plant nearby that would burn wheat straw and other crop wastes. The plants provide an environmentally sound as well as profitable way to dispose of waste. Very interested in conservation, Parish says, "I wanted to combine doing well with doing good."[11]

13.2 Use of Strategic Planning and Strategic Management

Research shows that strategic planning is strongly related to small-business financial performance.[12] A survey of the high-growth *Inc. 500* firms revealed that 86% performed strategic planning. Of those performing strategic planning, 94% reported improved profits.[13] Nevertheless, many small companies still do not use the process.[14] A study of 131 firms filing for bankruptcy revealed that 72% lacked mission statements and objectives for their businesses.[15] Around 40% of existing small family-owned businesses do not have written strategic plans.[16] The reasons often cited for the apparent lack of strategic planning practices in many small-business firms are fourfold:

- **Not enough time:** Day-to-day operating problems take up the time necessary for long-term planning. It's relatively easy to justify avoiding strategic planning on the basis of day-to-day crisis management. Some will ask: "How can I be expected to do strategic planning when I don't know if I'm going to be in business next week?"
- **Unfamiliar with strategic planning:** A small-business CEO may be unaware of strategic planning or may view it as irrelevant to the small-business situation. Planning may be viewed as a straitjacket that limits flexibility.

■ **Lack of skills:** Small-business managers often lack the skills necessary to begin strategic planning and do not have or want to spend the money necessary to import trained consultants. Future uncertainty may be used to justify a lack of planning. One entrepreneur admits, "Deep down, I know I should plan. But I don't know what to do. I'm the leader, but I don't know how to lead the planning process."

■ **Lack of trust and openness:** Many small-business owner–managers are very sensitive regarding key information about the business and are thus unwilling to share strategic planning with employees or outsiders. For this reason, boards of directors are often composed only of close friends and relatives of the owner–manager—people unlikely to provide an objective viewpoint or professional advice.

DEGREE OF FORMALITY

Research generally concludes that the strategic planning process can be far more informal in small companies than it is in large corporations.[17] Some studies have even found that too much formalization of the strategic planning process may actually result in reduced performance.[18] Strategic planning is often forced on an entrepreneur by banks and venture capitalists when the entrepreneur is searching for capital to launch or expand the new venture. It is possible that a heavy emphasis on structured, written plans can be dysfunctional to the small entrepreneurial firm because it detracts from the very flexibility that is a benefit of small size. The process of strategic planning, not the plan itself, is probably the key to improving business performance. Research does show, however, that as an entrepreneurial firm matures, its strategic planning process tends to become more formal.[19]

These observations suggest that new entrepreneurial ventures begin life in Mintzberg's *entrepreneurial mode* of strategic planning (explained in **Chapter 1**) and move toward the *planning mode* as the company becomes established and wants to continue its strong growth. If, after becoming successfully established, the entrepreneur instead chooses stability over growth, the venture moves more toward the *adaptive mode* so common to many small businesses.

USEFULNESS OF THE STRATEGIC MANAGEMENT MODEL

The model of strategic management is also relevant to entrepreneurial ventures and small businesses. This basic model holds for both an established small company and a new entrepreneurial venture. As the research mentioned earlier concluded, small and developing companies increase their chances of success if they make a serious attempt to work through the strategic issues embedded in the strategic management model. The key is to focus on what's important—the set of managerial decisions and actions that determines the long-run performance of the company. The list of informal questions presented in **Table 13–1** may be more useful to a small entrepreneurial company than their more formal counterparts used by large, established corporations.

USEFULNESS OF THE STRATEGIC DECISION-MAKING PROCESS

As mentioned in **Chapter 1**, one way in which the strategic management model can be made action oriented is to follow the strategic decision-making model. The eight steps presented in that model are just as appropriate for small companies as they are for large corporations. Unfortunately, the process does not fit new entrepreneurial ventures. Such

TABLE 13–1	Formal	Informal
Informal Questions to Begin the Strategic Management Process in a Small Company or Entrepreneurial Venture	**Define mission**	What do we stand for?
	Set objectives	What are we trying to achieve?
	Formulate strategy	How are we going to get there? How can we beat the competition?
	Determine policies	What sort of ground rules should we all be following to get the job done right?
	Establish programs	How should we organize this operation to get what we want done as cheaply as possible with the highest quality possible?
	Prepare pro forma budgets	How much is it going to cost us and where can we get the cash?
	Specify procedures	In how much detail do we have to lay things out, so that everybody knows what to do?
	Determine performance measures	What are those few key things that will determine whether we can make it? How can we keep track of them?

a company must develop a new mission and new objectives, strategies, and policies out of a comparison of its external opportunities and threats to its potential strengths and weaknesses. Consequently, we propose in **Figure 13–1** a modified version of the strategic decision-making process; this version more closely suits a new entrepreneurial venture.

The proposed **strategic decision-making process for entrepreneurial ventures** is composed of the following eight interrelated steps:

1. **Develop the basic business idea—a product and/or service that has target customers and/or markets:** An **idea** is a concept for a product or service that currently doesn't exist or is not currently available in a market niche. It may be a brand-new concept (radical innovation) or an improvement to a current product or service (incremental innovation). The idea can be developed from a person's experience or generated in a moment of creative insight. For example, Vincent Norment conceived of a headband with a stay-on strap while attending a basketball game.

2. **Scan and assess the external environment to locate factors in the societal and task environments that pose opportunities and threats:** The scanning should focus particularly on market potential and resource accessibility.

3. **Scan and assess the internal factors relevant to the new business:** The entrepreneur should objectively consider personal assets, areas of expertise, abilities, and experience, all in terms of the organizational needs of the new venture.

4. **Analyze the strategic factors in light of the current situation, using SWOT:** The venture's potential strengths and weaknesses must be evaluated in light of opportunities and threats. This analysis can be done with an SFAS Matrix (see **Figure 6–1**) of the strategic factors.

5. **Decide go or no go:** If the basic business idea appears to be a feasible business opportunity, the process should be continued. An **opportunity** is an idea for a new product or service with a market that is willing to pay for that product or service so that it can form the basis of a profitable business. Otherwise, further development of the idea should be canceled unless the strategic factors change.

FIGURE 13–1 Strategic Decision-Making Process for New Ventures

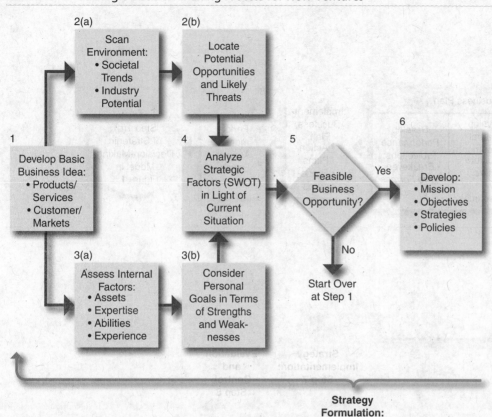

6. **Generate a business plan that specifies how the opportunity will be transformed into reality:** See **Table 13–2** for the suggested contents of a strategic **business plan**. The proposed venture's mission, objectives, strategies, and policies, as well as its likely board of directors (if a corporation) and key managers should be developed. Key internal factors should be specified and performance projections generated. The business plan serves as a vehicle through which financial support is obtained from potential investors and creditors. It increases a new venture's probability of survival and facilitates new product development.[20] Firms using business plans tend to have higher

TABLE 13–2

Contents of a Strategic Business Plan for an Entrepreneurial Venture

I. Table of Contents	X. Human Resources Plan
II. Executive Summary	XI. Ownership
III. Nature of the Business	XII. Risk Analysis
IV. Strategy Formulation	XIII. Timetables and Milestones
V. Market Analysis	XIV. Strategy Implementation—Action Plans
VI. Marketing Plan	XV. Evaluation and Control
VII. Operational Plans—Service/Product	XVI. Summary
VIII. Financial Plans	XVII. Appendixes
IX. Organization and Management	

NOTE: The Strategic Audit in Appendix 1.A can be used to develop a business plan. It provides detailed questions to serve as a checklist.

SOURCE: Thomas L. Wheelen, "Contents of a Strategic Business Plan for an Entrepreneurial Venture." Copyright © 1988 and 2005 by Thomas L. Wheelen. Reprinted by permission.

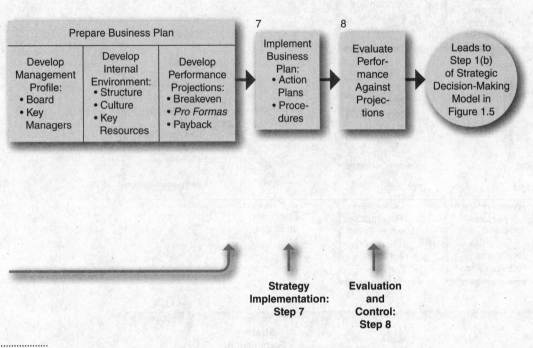

SOURCE: *T. L. Wheelen and C. E. Michaels, Jr., "Model for Strategic Decision-Making Process for New Ventures." Copyright © 1987 and 2005 by T. L. Wheelen. Reprinted by permission.*

revenue and sales growth than do those without them.[21] Starting a business without a business plan is the quickest way to kill a new venture.[22] For example, one study of 270 clothing retailers found that 80% of the successful stores had written business plans, whereas 65% of the failed businesses had not.[23]

A strategic audit (see **Appendix 1.A** at the end of **Chapter 1**) can be used to develop a formal business plan. The audit's sections and subsections, along with the questions within them, can be re-aligned to fit the model depicted in **Figure 13–1**. Instead of analyzing the historical events of an existing company, one can use the questions to project the proposed company's future. The questions can be reoriented to follow the outline in **Appendix 1.A**. A crucial building block of a sound business plan is the construction of realistic scenarios for the pro forma financials. The pro formas must reflect the impact of seasonality on the cash flows of the proposed new venture.

7. **Implement the business plan:** Do this through the use of action plans and procedures.

8. **Evaluate the implemented business plan through comparison of actual performance against projected performance results:** This step leads to step 1(b) of the strategic decision-making process shown in **Figure 1–5**. To the extent that actual results are less than or much greater than the anticipated results, the entrepreneur needs to reconsider the company's current mission, objectives, strategies, policies, and programs, and possibly make changes to the original business plan.

13.3 Issues in Corporate Governance

Corporate governance is much simpler in small entrepreneurial ventures than in large, established corporations. For one thing, the owners and the managers are usually the same people—the company founders (or their close relatives). If a venture is not incorporated, there is no need for a board of directors. It may be a sole proprietorship or a simple partnership. Those entrepreneurial ventures wishing to grow quickly or to limit the liability of the owners often incorporate the business. Once incorporated, the company can sell shares of stock to others (such as venture capitalists) to finance its growth. When the company is owned by shareholders (even if the shareholders are composed of only the founding owners who also manage the firm), the company must have a board of directors.

BOARDS OF DIRECTORS AND ADVISORY BOARDS

The boards of directors of entrepreneurial firms are likely to be either very passive or very active. Passive boards exist when the stock is closely held by the founding owners (and their immediate families) who manage the company on a day-to-day basis. As the only stockholders, they elect themselves to board offices and call meetings only when the law requires it—usually as a social occasion. There is no need for an active board since there are no other stockholders and thus no agency problems. The board typically has few or no external directors.[24] In most instances, the primary role of the board is simply to be a figurehead to satisfy the law. This place is on the far left end of the board of directors' continuum shown in Chapter 2's **Figure 2–1**.

Entrepreneurial ventures financed by venture capitalists typically have very active boards of directors. The venture capitalists expect to obtain seats on the board in exchange for their investment.[25] Once on the board, venture capitalists tend to be very powerful members of the board and are highly involved in strategic management.[26] The boards of directors of fast-growth entrepreneurial firms have around five directors, of whom about three are external. Almost 80% of them have written strategic plans with a time horizon of 12 to 24 months.[27] Venture capitalists usually require three years or more of pro forma financial statements broken out on a monthly cash flow basis for the first two years and on a quarterly basis thereafter.

Since closely held entrepreneurial ventures and small businesses tend to have relatively passive boards composed primarily of insiders, this type of business should use an advisory board to provide advice to the owner–managers. An **advisory board** is a group of external business people who voluntarily meet periodically with the owner–managers of the firm to discuss strategic and other issues. The members are usually invited to join the board by the president of the company. The advisory board has no official capacity but is expected to provide management with useful suggestions and act as a sounding board. Since the members typically receive no compensation for serving, quarterly business meetings are often followed by cocktails and dinner at a nearby country club, hotel, or prestigious restaurant. It is important to staff the advisory board with knowledgeable people who have significant business experience or skills who can complement the background and skills of the company's owner–managers. Using an advisory board is an easy way to obtain free professional consulting advice. Research indicates that advisory boards improve the performance of small businesses.[28]

IMPACT OF THE SARBANES-OXLEY ACT

Complying with the Sarbanes-Oxley Act is becoming a cost burden for small publicly held U.S. companies. Companies face higher audit and legal fees, new internal control systems, and higher directors' and officers' liability insurance premiums, among other expenses. Compliance costs are estimated at $500,000 for a small firm and in the millions for a large one.[29] As a result, 198 firms "went dark" in 2003 by delisting their stock from stock exchanges. By only trading via "pink sheets" in over-the-counter stocks, these firms do not have to comply with the act's minimum requirements, and they do not have to file with the Securities and Exchange Commission (SEC). Under SEC rules, a company may choose to terminate its registration if the corporation's securities have fewer than 300 holders of record or if there are fewer than 500 holders of record and the company's total assets don't exceed $10 million. A research study of firms going dark indicated that the firms delist their stock not only to avoid compliance costs but also to evade the outside monitoring and additional scrutiny required by Sarbanes-Oxley. According to Christian Leuz, co-author of the study: "We basically find that going dark can serve as a way to conserve cash, but it may also be exploited by insiders trying to avoid the scrutiny of the market. Whether insiders succeed, and whether the decision to go dark is a good or bad one therefore depends on the governance in place."[30]

13.4 Issues in Environmental Scanning and Strategy Formulation

Environmental scanning in small businesses is much less sophisticated than it is in large corporations. The business is usually too small to justify hiring someone to do only environmental scanning or strategic planning. Top managers, especially if they are the founders, tend to believe that they know the business and can follow it better than anyone else. A study of 220 small rapid-growth companies revealed that the majority of CEOs were actively and personally involved in all phases of the planning process, especially in the setting of objectives. Only 15% of the companies used a planning officer or formed a planning group to assist in the planning process. In the rest of the firms, operating managers who participated in strategic planning provided input only to the CEO, who then formulated the plan.[31] Unfortunately, the literature suggests that most small business owner–managers rely more on internal as opposed to external sources of information.[32] Conducting a periodic industry analysis using Porter's forces is just as important for a small business as for a large one. Nevertheless, few small businesses do much competitor analysis. If they do analyze competition, typical small business owners often only look locally, without considering competitors across town or in a nearby city.

A fundamental reason for differences in strategy formulation between large and small entrepreneurial companies lies in the relationship between owners and managers. The CEO of a large corporation has to consider and balance the varied needs of the corporation's many stakeholders. The CEO of a small business, however, is very likely also to be the owner—the company's primary stakeholder. Personal and family needs can thus strongly affect a small business's mission and objectives and can overrule other considerations.[33]

Size can affect the selection of an appropriate corporate strategy. Large corporations often choose growth strategies for their many side benefits for management as well as for shareholders. A small company may, however, choose a stability strategy because the entrepreneur is interested mostly in (1) generating employment for family members, (2) providing the family a "decent living," and (3) being the "boss" of a firm small enough that he or she can manage it comfortably. Some business owners don't pursue a growth strategy because they do not want the loss of control that results from bank debt or the sale of stock to outsiders. Some may even fear that growth will attract attention from larger competitors that might want to take over the company or drive it out of business.[34] Thus the goals of a small business are likely to be the same as the goals of the owner–manager.

Basic SWOT analysis is just as relevant to new entrepreneurial businesses as it is to established large ones. Both the greatest strength and the greatest weakness of a small firm, at least in the beginning, rest with the entrepreneur—the owner–manager of the business. The entrepreneur is the manager, the source of product/market strategy, and the dynamo who energizes the company. That is why the internal assessment of a new venture's strengths and weaknesses focuses in **Figure 13–1** on the founder's personal characteristics—his or her assets, expertise, abilities, and experience. Research reveals that founder competencies, motivations, and connections plus the firm's competitive strategies are direct predictors of new venture growth and success.[35] Intangible assets, such as leadership, strategy, and human and intellectual capital, were found to be more important than traditional financial measures for a venture's success in going public through an IPO.[36]

Just as an entrepreneur's strengths can be the key to company success, personal weaknesses can be a primary cause of failure. For example, the study of clothing retailers mentioned earlier showed that the owner–managers of 85% of the failed stores had no prior retailing experience.

SOURCES OF INNOVATION

Peter Drucker, in his book *Innovation and Entrepreneurship*, proposes seven sources for innovative opportunity that should be monitored by those interested in starting an entrepreneurial venture, either within an established company or as an independent small business.[37] The first four **sources of innovation** lie within the industry itself; the last three arise in the societal environment. These seven sources are:

1. **The Unexpected:** An unexpected success, an unexpected failure, or an unexpected outside event can be a symptom of a unique opportunity. When Don Cullen of Transmet Corporation spilled a box of very fine aluminum flakes onto his company's parking lot, he discovered that their presence in the asphalt prevented it from turning sticky in high temperatures. His company now produces aluminum chips for use in roofing. Sales have doubled every year since the product's introduction, and Cullen's company will soon dominate the business.

2. **The Incongruity:** A discrepancy between reality and what everyone assumes it to be, or between what is and what ought to be, can create an opportunity for innovation. For example, a side effect of retailing via the Internet is the increasing number of packages being delivered to homes. Since neither FedEx nor UPS can leave a package unless someone is home to sign for it, many deliveries are delayed. Tony Paikeday founded zBox Company to make and sell a hard plastic container that would receive deliveries from any delivery service and would be accessible only by the owner and the delivery services. "We're amazed that it doesn't exist yet," says Paikeday.[38]

3. **Innovation Based on Process Need:** When a weak link is evident in a particular process but people work around it instead of doing something about it, an opportunity is present for the person or company willing to forge a stronger one. Tired of having to strain to use a too-small keyboard on his personal computer, David Levy invented a keyboard with 64 normal-sized keys cleverly put into an area the size of a credit card.[39]

4. **Changes in Industry or Market Structure:** A business is ready for an innovative product, service, or approach to the business when the underlying foundation of the industry or market shifts. Black Entertainment Television, Inc. (BET), was born when Robert Johnson noticed that no television programmer was targeting the increasing number of black viewers. The BET brand has expanded into magazines and is now known by more than 90% of African-Americans.[40]

5. **Demographics:** Changes in the population's size, age structure, composition, employment, level of education, and income can create opportunities for innovation. For example, Pam Henderson started a company called Kids Kab to shuttle children and teenagers

to private schools, doctor and dentist appointments, lessons, and extracurricular activities. With the trend to dual careers, parents were no longer always available to provide personal transportation for their own children and needed such a service.

6. **Changes in Perception, Mood, and Meaning:** Opportunities for innovation can develop when a society's general assumptions, attitudes, and beliefs change. For example, the increasing dominance of a few national brewers have caused beer drinkers to look for alternatives to the same old national brands. By positioning Yuengling, a local Pennsylvania beer, as a full-flavored beer and providing it with an artsy, nostalgic-looking label, the small company was able to catch the fancy of young, trendy consumers who viewed it as Pennsylvania's version of Anchor Steam, the successful San Francisco beer.

7. **New Knowledge:** Advances in scientific and nonscientific knowledge can create new products and new markets. Advances in two different areas can sometimes be integrated to form the basis of a new product. For example, Medical Foods was formed to make foods that act like medicine to treat conditions from diabetes to arthritis. Its first product, NiteBite, is a chocolate-flavored snack bar designed to help diabetics manage nocturnal hypoglycemia, caused by low blood sugar. NiteBite gradually releases glucose into the bloodstream, where it lasts for six hours or more.[41]

FACTORS AFFECTING A NEW VENTURE'S SUCCESS

According to Hofer and Sandberg, three factors have a substantial impact on a new venture's performance. In order of importance, these **factors affecting new venture success** are (1) the structure of the industry entered, (2) the new venture's business strategy, and (3) behavioral characteristics of the entrepreneur.[42]

Industry Structure

Research shows that the chances for success are greater for entrepreneurial ventures that enter rapidly changing industries than for those that enter stable industries. In addition, prospects are better in industries that are in the early, high-growth stages of development.[43] Competition is often less intense. Fast market growth also allows new ventures to make some mistakes without serious penalty. New ventures also increase their chances of success when they enter markets in which they can erect entry barriers to keep out competitors.

Contrary to popular wisdom, however, patents may not always provide competitive advantage, especially for new ventures in a high-tech or hypercompetitive industry. A well-financed competitor could examine a newly filed application for a patent, work around the patent, and beat the pioneering firm to market with a similar product. In addition, the time and cost of filing and defending a patent may not be worth the effort. According to Connie Bagley, author of *The Entrepreneur's Guide to Business Law*:

> It might take 18 months to get a patent on a product that has a 12-month life cycle. By the time you finally get the damn thing litigated, it's meaningless. So people are focusing less on proprietary assurance and more on first-mover advantage. . . . The law is just too slow for this high-speed economy.[44]

Most new ventures enter industries that have a low degree of industry concentration (that is, no dominant competitors).[45] Industry concentration is not necessarily bad. It may create market niches being ignored by large firms.[46] Hofer and Sandberg found that a new venture is more likely to be successful entering an industry in which one dominant competitor has a 50% or more market share than entering an industry in which the largest competitor has less than a 25% market share. To explain this phenomenon, Hofer and Sandberg point out that when an industry has one dominant firm, the remaining competitors are relatively weak and are easy prey for an aggressive entrepreneur. To avoid direct competition with a major rival, the new venture can focus on a market segment that is being ignored.

Industry product characteristics also have a significant impact on a new venture's success. First, a new venture is more likely to be successful when it enters an industry with heterogeneous (different) products than when it enters one with homogeneous (similar) products. In a heterogeneous industry, a new venture can differentiate itself from competitors with a unique product; or, by focusing on the unique needs of a market segment, it can find a market niche. Second, a new venture is, according to research data, more likely to be successful if the product is relatively unimportant to the customer's total purchasing needs than if it is important. Customers are more likely to experiment with a new product if its cost is low and product failure will not create a problem.

Business Strategy

According to Hofer and Sandberg, the keys to success for most new ventures are (1) to differentiate the product from those of other competitors in the areas of quality and service and (2) to focus the product on customer needs in a segment of the market in order to achieve a dominant share of that part of the market. Adopting guerrilla-warfare tactics, these companies go after opportunities in market niches too small or too localized to justify retaliation from the market leaders.[47] It is crucial, however, that a new venture analyze its competitors to assess their likely response to the company's entry into the market.

To continue its growth once it has found a niche, an entrepreneurial firm can emphasize continued innovation and pursue natural growth in its current markets. The firm can also expand into related markets in which the company's core skills, resources, and facilities offer the keys to further success. It can leverage its resources by engaging in strategic alliances with other firms. Sixty-three percent of U.S. small business owners report that they are involved in strategic alliances, especially in marketing and distribution. Of those using strategic alliances, half maintain three or more.[48]

Some studies do indicate, however, that new ventures can also be successful following strategies other than going after an undefended niche with a focus strategy. A narrow-market approach may leave the new firm vulnerable and preordained to only limited sales. One possible approach would be to offer products that are substitutable to, but differentiated from, those offered by bigger firms.[49] For some practical suggestions for locating an opportunity and formulating a business strategy, see **Strategy Highlight 13.1**.

Entrepreneurial Characteristics

Four **entrepreneurial characteristics** are key to a new venture's success. Successful entrepreneurs have:

1. **The ability to identify potential venture opportunities better than most people:** Entrepreneurs focus on opportunities—not on problems—and try to learn from failure. Entrepreneurs are goal oriented and have a strong impact on the emerging culture of an organization. They are able to envision where the company is going and are thus able to provide a strong overall sense of strategic direction. As a result, their firms have a strong entrepreneurial orientation (EO)—that is, are innovative, proactive, and willing to take risks.[50]

2. **A sense of urgency that makes them action oriented:** They have a high need for achievement, which motivates them to put their ideas into action. They tend to have an internal locus of control that leads them to believe that they can determine their own fate through their own behavior. They also have a significantly greater capacity to tolerate ambiguity and stress than do many in established organizations.[51] They also have a strong need for

STRATEGY highlight 13.1

SUGGESTIONS FOR LOCATING AN OPPORTUNITY AND FORMULATING A BUSINESS STRATEGY

Given that differentiation and focus are the most popular and effective competitive strategies for a new venture, what are some of the ways to identify a new opportunity in which these strategies can be used? *Entrepreneur* magazine provides four interesting approaches:

1. **Tap the countertrend:** For every trend, there is likely to be a potentially lucrative countertrend waiting to be discovered. When a trend is hot, look for its opposite in a small but potentially growing market niche. Note how Hardee's successfully responded to the trend to low-fat and low-carb diets with it own monster-size bacon cheeseburger with more calories, carbs, and fat than its competitors. Because the idea was so outrageous, the Hardee's product received free coverage in newspapers and on television.

2. **Eat off the established company's plate:** Trend-watching.com coined the term "feeder business" for companies that feed off giants such as Amazon or eBay. When Eric Cohen and Joyce Shulman noticed that the typical blank pizza box was 16 inches of available advertising space, they decided to partner with the box makers to print paid advertisements on

them for pizzerias. They then branched out into coffee cups and ice bags.

3. **Switch the niche:** A company may be able to identify a successful product or service that caters to a particular market and tailor it to fit a different market niche. For example, when Una Cassidy encountered numerous women looking for beauty products for use during pregnancy, she founded Selph. Cassidy removed all the usual ingredients found in beauty products that would be harmful to a fetus during pregnancy and replaced them with superior products that were gentle on the skin.

4. **Borrow a business model:** Netflix developed a novel business model in which members are charged a set monthly fee to borrow an unlimited number of DVDs by mail. This model was picked up quickly by other entrepreneurs such as GameFly, which rents video games by mail, Booksfree.com, which rents paperbacks by mail, and Bag Borrow Or Steal, which rents designer purses by mail.

SOURCES: K. Axelton, "Fever Pitch," *Entrepreneur* (December 2004), p. 74; N. L. Torres, "Think Outside the Box," *Entrepreneur* (February 2004), pp. 108–111; A. Pennington, "Una Cassidy," *Entrepreneur* (November 2003), p. 24.

---

control and may even be viewed as "misfits who need to create their own environment." They tend to distrust others and often have a need "to show others that they amount to something, that they cannot be ignored."[52]

3. **A detailed knowledge of the keys to success in the industry and the physical stamina to make their work their lives:** Successful entrepreneurs have better-than-average education and significant work experience in the industry in which they start their businesses. They often work with partners to form a new venture. (Seventy percent of new high-tech ventures are started by more than one founder.[53]) More than half of all entrepreneurs work at least 60 hours per week in the startup year, according to a National Federation of Independent Business study.[54]

4. **Access to outside help to supplement their skills, knowledge, and abilities:** Over time, entrepreneurs develop a network of people who have key skills and knowledge, whom the entrepreneurs can call on for support. Through their enthusiasm, these entrepreneurs are able to attract key investors, partners, creditors, and employees. For example, the founders of eBay did not hesitate to bring in Meg Whitman as CEO because Whitman had the managerial skills that eBay needed to expand.

In summarizing their conclusions regarding factors affecting the success of entrepreneurial ventures, Hofer and Sandberg propose the guidelines presented in **Table 13–3.**

TABLE 13–3

Some
Guidelines for
New Venture
Success

■ Focus on industries facing substantial technological or regulatory changes, especially those with recent exits by established competitors.

■ Seek industries whose smaller firms have relatively weak competitive positions.

■ Seek industries that are in early, high-growth stages of evolution.

■ Seek industries in which it is possible to create high barriers to subsequent entry.

■ Seek industries with heterogeneous products that are relatively unimportant to the customer's overall success.

■ Seek to differentiate your products from those of your competitors in ways that are meaningful to your customers.

■ Focus such differentiation efforts on product quality, marketing approaches, and customer service—and charge enough to cover the costs of doing so.

■ Seek to dominate the market segments in which you compete. If necessary, either segment the market differently or change the nature and focus of your differentiation efforts to increase your domination of the segments you serve.

■ Stress innovation, especially new product innovation, that is built on existing organizational capabilities.

■ Seek natural, organic growth through flexibility and opportunism that builds on existing organizational strengths.

SOURCE: C. W. Hofer and W. R. Sandberg, "Improving New Venture Performance: Some Guidelines for Success," *American Journal of Small Business* (Summer 1987), pp. 17, 19. Copyright © 1987 by C. W. Hofer and W. R. Sandberg. Reprinted from *Entrepreneurship Theory & Practice* by permission of Baylor University. All rights reserved.

13.5 Issues in Strategy Implementation

Two key implementation issues in a small company are organizing and staffing the growing company and transferring ownership of the company to the next generation.

SUBSTAGES OF SMALL BUSINESS DEVELOPMENT

The implementation problems of a small business change as the company grows and develops over time. Just as the decision-making process for entrepreneurial ventures is different from that of established businesses, the managerial systems in small companies often vary from those of large corporations. Those variations are based on their stage of development. The stages of corporate growth and development discussed in **Chapter 9** suggest that all small businesses are either in Stage I or trying to move into Stage II. These models imply that all successful new ventures eventually become Stage II, functionally organized, companies. This is not always true, however. In attempting to show clearly how small businesses develop, Churchill and Lewis propose five **substages of small business development**: (a) existence, (b) survival, (c) success, (d) take-off, and (e) resource maturity.[55] A review of these small-business substages shows in more detail how a company can move through the entrepreneurial Stage I into a functionally oriented, professionally managed Stage II.

Stage A: Existence

At this point, an entrepreneurial venture faces the problems of obtaining customers and delivering the promised product or service. The organizational structure is simple. The entrepreneur does everything and directly supervises subordinates. Systems are minimal. The owner is the business.

Stage B: Survival

Those ventures able to satisfy a sufficient number of customers enter this stage; the rest close when their owners run out of startup capital. Those reaching the survival stage are concerned about generating the cash flow needed to repair and replace capital assets as they wear out and to finance the growth to continue satisfying the market segment they have found.

At this stage, the organizational structure is still simple, but it probably has a sales manager or general supervisor to carry out the owner's well-defined orders. A major problem of many small businesses at this stage is finding a person who is qualified to supervise the business when the owner can't be present but who is still willing to work for a very modest salary. An entrepreneur usually tries to use a family member rather than hire an outsider who lacks the entrepreneur's dedication to the business and (in the words of one owner–manager) "steals them blind." A company that remains in this stage for a long time is often called a "mom and pop" firm. It earns marginal returns on invested time and capital (with lots of psychic income!) and eventually goes out of business when "mom and pop" give up or retire. This type of small business is viewed more as a **lifestyle company** in which the firm is purely an extension of the owner's lifestyle. More than 94% of small private companies are in this category.[56]

Stage C: Success

By this point, the company's sales have reached a level where the firm is not only profitable but has sufficient cash flow to reinvest in itself. The key issue at this stage is whether the company should be used as a platform for growth or as a means of support for the owners as they completely or partially disengage from the company. The company is transforming into a functionally structured organization, but it still relies on the entrepreneur for all key decisions. The two options are disengagement and growth.

Stage C(1): Disengagement. The company can now successfully follow a stability strategy and remain at this stage almost indefinitely—provided that environmental change does not destroy its niche or poor management reduce its competitive abilities. By now functional managers have taken over some of the entrepreneur's duties. The company at this stage may be incorporated, but it is still primarily owned by the founder or the founder's family. Consequently, the board of directors is either a rubber stamp for the entrepreneur or a forum for family squabbles. Growth strategies are not pursued because either the market niche will not allow growth or the owner is content with the company at a size he or she can still manage comfortably. Strategic decisions make limited use of objective information and tend to be intuitive—based on personal desires and the founder's background.[57]

Stage C(2): Growth. The entrepreneur risks all available cash and the established borrowing power of the company in financing further growth. Strategic and operational planning are extensive and deeply involve the owner. Managers with an eye to the company's future rather than for its current situation are hired. This is an entrepreneurial high-growth firm aiming to be included in the *Inc. 500*. The emphasis now is on teamwork rather than on the entrepreneur's personal actions and energy. The personal values and philosophy of the founder are slowly transferred into a developing corporate culture.

Stage D: Take-Off

The key problems in this stage are how to grow rapidly and how to finance that growth. By now the firm is incorporated and has sold or is planning to sell stock in its company via an initial public offering (IPO) or via a direct public offering (DPO).[58] The entrepreneur must learn to delegate to specialized professional managers or to a team of managers who now form the top management of the company.[59] Delegation is a key issue for a company at this stage of development. A functional structure of the organization should now be solidly in place. Operational and strategic planning greatly involve the hired managers, but the company is still dominated by the entrepreneur's presence and stock control. Vertical and horizontal growth strategies are being seriously considered as the firm's management debates when and how to grow. The company is now included in the *Inc. 500* select group of firms.

At this point, the entrepreneur either is able to manage the transition from a small to a large company or recognizes personal limitations, sells his or her stock for a profit, and leaves the firm. The composition of the board of directors changes from dominance by friends and relatives of the owner to a large percentage of outsiders with managerial experience who can help the owner during the transition to a professionally managed company. The biggest danger facing the firm in this stage is the owner's desire to remain in total control (not willing to delegate) as if it were still a small entrepreneurial venture, even though he or she lacks the managerial skills necessary to run an established corporation. One study of small businesses found that fewer than one-third had written succession plans to replace the current owners.[60]

Stage E: Resource Maturity

It is at this point that the small company has adopted most of the characteristics of an established, large company. It may still be a small- or medium-sized company, but it is recognized as an important force in the industry and a possible candidate for the *Fortune 500* someday. The greatest concerns of a company at this stage are controlling the financial gains brought on by rapid growth and retaining its flexibility and entrepreneurial spirit. In terms of the stages of organizational growth and development discussed in **Chapter 9**, the company has become a full-fledged Stage II functional corporation.

TRANSFER OF POWER AND WEALTH IN FAMILY BUSINESSES

Small businesses are often **family businesses**. Within the United States, family businesses account for approximately 80% of the total 15 million businesses.[61] It is estimated that over one-third of the U.S. *Fortune 500* companies are either family owned or dominated. Of the world's largest firms, the proportion is over one-half.[62] Some of the world's largest family-owned or controlled firms are Wal-Mart, Ford Motor, Samsung, LG Group, Carrefour Group, Fiat Group, IFI, PSA Peugeot Citroen, Cargill, and BMW.[63] Interestingly, the 177 family companies in the 2003 *S&P 500* financially outperformed non-family companies over the previous 10 year period.[64]

Even though the founders of the companies are the primary forces in starting the entrepreneurial ventures, their needs for business support and financial assistance cause them to turn to family members, who can be trusted, over unknown outsiders of questionable integrity who may demand more salary than the enterprise can afford. Sooner or later, the founder's spouse and children are drafted into business operations either because the family standard of living is directly tied to the business or the entrepreneur desperately needs help just to staff the operation. The children are guaranteed summer jobs, and the business changes from dad's or mom's company to "our" company. The family members are extremely valuable assets to the entrepreneur because they are often also willing to put in long hours at low pay to help the business succeed. Even though the spouse and children might have no official stock in the company, they know that they will somehow share in its future and perhaps even inherit the business. The problem is that only 30% of family firms survive to the second generation, and just 15% survive to the third generation.[65] A common saying among European family businesses is: "The first generation creates, the second inherits, and the third destroys."[66] This saying is supported by research indicating that firm performance declines when descendents take over management of a firm.[67]

Phase 1	**Owner-Managed Business:** Phase 1 begins at startup and continues until the entrance of another family member into the business on a full-time basis. Family considerations influence but are not yet a directing part of the firm. At this point, the founder (entrepreneur) and the business are one.
Phase 2	**Training and Development of New Generation:** The children begin to learn the business at the dining room table during early childhood and then through part-time and vacation employment. The family and the business become one. Just as the entrepreneur identified with the business earlier, the family now begins to identify itself with the business.
Phase 3	**Partnership Between Generations:** At this point, a son or daughter of the founder has acquired sufficient business and managerial competence so that he or she can be involved in key decisions for at least a part of the company. The entrepreneur's offspring, however, has to first gain respect from the firm's employees and other managers and show that he or she can do the job right. Another issue is the lack of willingness of the founder to share authority with the son or daughter. Consequently, a common tactic taken by sons and daughters in family businesses is to take a job in a large, established corporation where they can gain valuable experience and respect for their skills.
Phase 4	**Transfer of Power:** Instead of being forced to sell the company when he or she can no longer manage the business, the founder has the option in a family business of turning it over to the next generation as part of their inheritance. Often the founder moves to the position of Chairman of the Board and promotes one of the children to the position of CEO. Unfortunately, some founders cannot resist meddling in operating affairs and unintentionally undermine the leadership position of the son or daughter. To avoid this problem, the founder should sell his or her stock (probably through a leveraged buyout to the children) and physically leave the company and allow the next generation the freedom it needs to adapt to changing conditions.

TABLE 13–4

Transfer of
Power in a
Family Business

SOURCE: N. C. Churchill and K. J. Hatten, "Non-Market-Based Transfer of Wealth and Power: A Research Framework for Family Businesses," *American Journal of Small Business* (Winter 1987), pp. 51–64. Reprinted from *Entrepreneurship Theory & Practice* by permission of Baylor University. All rights reserved.

Churchill and Hatten propose that family businesses go through four sequential phases from the time in which the venture is strictly managed by the founder to the time in which the next generation takes charge.[68] These phases are detailed in **Table 13–4**. Each of these phases must be well managed if the company is to survive past the third generation. Some of the reasons family businesses may fail to successfully transfer ownership to the next generation are (1) inherited wealth destroys entrepreneurial drive, (2) the entrepreneur doesn't allow for a changing firm, (3) emphasis on business means the family is neglected, (4) the business' financial growth can't keep up with rising family lifestyles, (5) family members are not prepared to run a business, and (6) the business becomes an arena for family conflicts.[69] In addition, succession planning may be ignored because of the founder's or family's refusal to think about the founder's death, the founder's unwillingness to let go of the firm, the fear of sibling rivalry, or intergenerational envy.

According to Joe Astachan of the Cox Family Enterprise Center at Kennesaw State University, families whose businesses survive over time tend to operate on a set of agreed principles that pass from one generation to another. These include the creation of an active board of directors, a process of strategic planning that allows everyone to debate and agree upon the company's direction, and two to four family meetings a year. The surviving businesses tend to have strong boards that usually include a significant proportion of outsiders.[70]

13.6 Issues in Evaluation and Control

As a means by which a corporation's implementation of strategy can be evaluated, the control systems of large corporations have evolved over a long period of time in response to pressures from the environment (particularly the government). Conversely, an entrepreneur creates what is needed as the business grows. Because of his or her personal involvement in decision making, the entrepreneur managing a small business has little need for a formal, detailed reporting system. Thus a founder who has little understanding of accounting and a shortage of cash might employ a bookkeeper instead of an accountant. A formal personnel function might never appear because the entrepreneur lumps it in with simple bookkeeping and uses a secretary to handle personnel files. As an entrepreneurial venture becomes more established, it develops more complex evaluation and control systems, but they are often not the kind used in large corporations and are probably used for different purposes.

Financial statements, in particular, tell only half the story in small, privately owned companies. The formality of the financial reporting system in such a company is usually a result of pressures from government tax agencies, not from management's desire for an objective evaluation and control system. For example, the absence of taxes in Bermuda has been given as the reason why business owners keep little documentation—thus finding it nearly impossible to keep track of inventory, monitor sales, or calculate how much they are owed.[71]

Because balance sheets and income statements do not always give an accurate picture, standard ratios such as return on assets and debt–equity are unreliable. Research reveals systematic differences among liquidity and solvency measures for small compared to large companies. The mean averages of both the current ratio and the debt ratio are systematically larger for the small companies.[72] Cash flow is widely regarded as more important for an entrepreneurial business than is the traditional balance sheet or income statement. Even though a small business may be profitable in the accounting sense, a negative cash flow could bankrupt the company. Levin and Travis provide five reasons why owners, operators, and outside observers should be wary of using standard financial methods to indicate the health of a small, privately owned company[73]:

- **The line between debt and equity is blurred:** In some instances, what appears as a loan is really an easy-to-retrieve equity investment. The entrepreneur in this instance doesn't want to lose his or her investment if the company fails. Another condition is that retained earnings seldom reflect the amount of internal financing needed for the company's growth. This account may merely be a place in which cash is left so that the owner can avoid double taxation. To avoid other taxes, owner–managers may own fixed assets that they lease to the corporation. The equity that was used to buy those assets is really the company's equity, but it doesn't appear on the books.

- **Lifestyle is a part of financial statements:** The lifestyle of the owner and the owner's family is often reflected in the balance sheet. The assets of some firms include beach cottages, mountain chalets, and automobiles. In others, plants and warehouses that are used for company operations are not shown because they are held separately by the family. Income statements may not reflect how well the company is operating. Profitability is not as important in decision making in small, private companies as it is in large, publicly held corporations. For example, spending for recreation or transportation and paying rents or salaries above market rates to relatives put artificially high costs on the books of small firms. The business might appear to be poorly managed to an outsider, but the owner is acting rationally. The owner–manager wants dependable income or its equivalent with the least painful tax consequences. Because the standard profitability measures such as ROI are not useful in the evaluation of such a firm, Levin and Travis recommend return on current assets as a better measure of corporate productivity.

Let's Summarize the Chapter with a Mind Map

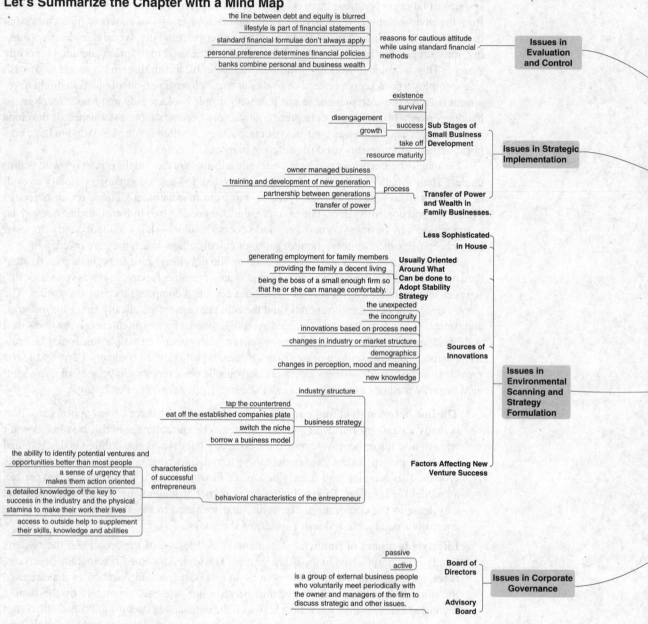

the line between debt and equity is blurred
lifestyle is part of financial statements
standard financial formulae don't always apply
personal preference determines financial policies
banks combine personal and business wealth

reasons for cautious attitude while using standard financial methods

Issues in Evaluation and Control

existence
survival
disengagement
growth
success
take off
resource maturity

Sub Stages of Small Business Development

Issues in Strategic Implementation

owner managed business
training and development of new generation
partnership between generations
transfer of power

process

Transfer of Power and Wealth in Family Businesses.

Less Sophisticated in House

generating employment for family members
providing the family a decent living
being the boss of a small enough firm so that he or she can manage comfortably.

Usually Oriented Around What Can be done to Adopt Stability Strategy

the unexpected
the incongruity
innovations based on process need
changes in industry or market structure
demographics
changes in perception, mood and meaning
new knowledge

Sources of Innovations

Issues in Environmental Scanning and Strategy Formulation

industry structure

tap the countertrend
eat off the established companies plate
switch the niche
borrow a business model

business strategy

the ability to identify potential ventures and opportunities better than most people
a sense of urgency that makes them action oriented
a detailed knowledge of the key to success in the industry and the physical stamina to make their work their lives
access to outside help to supplement their skills, knowledge and abilities

characteristics of successful entrepreneurs

behavioral characteristics of the entrepreneur

Factors Affecting New Venture Success

passive
active

Board of Directors

is a group of external business people who voluntarily meet periodically with the owner and managers of the firm to discuss strategic and other issues.

Advisory Board

Issues in Corporate Governance

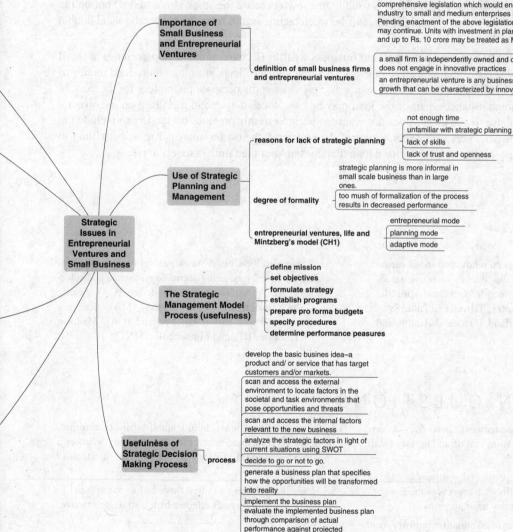

Strategic Issues in Entrepreneurial Ventures and Small Business

Importance of Small Business and Entrepreneurial Ventures

At present, a small scale industrial unit is an undertaking in which investment in plant and machinery, does not exceed Rs.1 crore, except in respect of certain specified items under hosiery, hand tools, drugs and pharmaceuticals, stationery items and sports goods, where this investment limit has been enhanced to Rs.5 crore. A comprehensive legislation which would enable the paradigm shift from small scale industry to small and medium enterprises is under consideration of Parliment. Pending enactment of the above legislation, current SSI/ tiny industries definition may continue. Units with investment in plant and machinery in excess of SSI limit and up to Rs. 10 crore may be treated as Medium Enterprises (ME).

definition of small business firms and entrepreneurial ventures

a small firm is independently owned and operated, not dominant in its field and does not engage in innovative practices

an entrepreneurial venture is any business whose primary goals are profitability and growth that can be characterized by innovative strategic practices

Use of Strategic Planning and Management

reasons for lack of strategic planning
- not enough time
- unfamiliar with strategic planning
- lack of skills
- lack of trust and openness

degree of formality
- strategic planning is more informal in small scale business than in large ones.
- too mush of formalization of the process results in decreased performance

entrepreneurial ventures, life and Mintzberg's model (CH1)
- entrepreneurial mode
- planning mode
- adaptive mode

The Strategic Management Model Process (usefulness)
- define mission
- set objectives
- formulate strategy
- establish programs
- prepare pro forma budgets
- specify procedures
- determine performance peasures

Usefulness of Strategic Decision Making Process — process
- develop the basic busines idea–a product and/ or service that has target customers and/or markets.
- scan and access the external environment to locate factors in the societal and task environments that pose opportunities and threats
- scan and access the internal factors relevant to the new business
- analyze the strategic factors in light of current situations using SWOT
- decide to go or not to go.
- generate a business plan that specifies how the opportunities will be transformed into reality
- implement the business plan
- evaluate the implemented business plan through comparison of actual performance against projected performance results.

- **Standard financial formulas don't always apply:** Following practices that are in contrast to standard financial recommendations, small companies often use short-term debt to finance fixed assets. The absence of well-organized capital markets for small businesses, along with the typical banker's resistance to making loans without personal guarantees, leaves the private owner little choice. Although a large amount of long-term debt is considered to be a good use of financial leverage by a large publicly held firm, it can drive a smaller firm into bankruptcy by raising its break-even point.

- **Personal preference determines financial policies:** Because the owner is often the manager of the small firm, dividend policy is largely irrelevant. Dividend decisions are based not on stock price (which is usually unknown because the stock is not traded) but on the owner's lifestyle and the tradeoff between taking wealth from the corporation and double taxation.

- **Banks combine personal and business wealth:** Because of the large percentage of small businesses that go bankrupt every year, bank loan officers are reluctant to lend money to a small business unless the owner also provides some personal guarantees for the loan. In some instances, part of the loan may be composed of a second mortgage on the owner's house. If the owner does not want to succumb to this pressure by lenders to include the owner's personal assets as part of the collateral, the owner–manager must be willing to pay high interest rates for a loan that does not put the family's assets at risk.

INFO-BITS

- Nations scoring highest on an innovation index measuring human resource skills, market incentive structures, and interaction between business and scientific sectors are the United States, Taiwan, Finland, Sweden, Japan, Israel, Switzerland, Canada, Australia, and Germany.[74]

- Regions in the United States scoring highest on a creativity index measuring technology, talent, and tolerance are Austin (TX), San Francisco (CA), Seattle (WA), Burlington (VT), Boston (MA), Raleigh-Durham-Chapel Hill (NC), Portland (OR), Madison (WI), Boise (ID), and Minneapolis (MN).[75]

DISCUSSION QUESTIONS

1. In terms of strategic management, how does a new venture's situation differ from that of an ongoing small company?

2. How should a small entrepreneurial company engage in environmental scanning? To what aspects of the environment should management pay most attention?

3. What are the characteristics of an attractive industry from an entrepreneur's point of view? What role does innovation play?

4. What considerations should small-business entrepreneurs keep in mind when they are deciding whether a company should follow a growth or a stability strategy?

5. How does being family owned (as compared to being publicly owned) affect a firm's strategic management?

STRATEGIC PRACTICE EXERCISE

Read **Strategy Highlight 13.1**, "Suggestions for Locating an Opportunity and Formulating a Business Strategy." Your strategy instructor may form multiple groups of five people each in your strategy class. Each group may be assigned one of the four approaches to identifying some ideas that could be opportunities for an entrepreneurial venture:

1. Tap the countertrend.
2. Eat off the established company's plate.
3. Switch the niche.
4. Borrow a business model.

When your group meets, discuss your assigned approach and identify one or more ideas that could be opportunities.

Remember that an idea is a concept for a product or service that doesn't exist or is not currently available in a market niche. An opportunity is an idea for a new product or service with a market that is willing to pay for that product or service so that it can form the basis of a profitable business. This means that the idea has to have the potential to be profitable. Bring your ideas to class and see what your instructor and others in the class think of your ideas. Once all the ideas have been presented, take a vote on which of the ideas have the most likelihood of being opportunities.

(If this concept is not used as a class exercise, you may choose to meet informally with several members of your class over coffee. See if you can come up with an idea for each of the four approaches. Are any of them opportunities?)

KEY TERMS

advisory board (p. 449)

business plan (p. 447)

entrepreneur (p. 444)

entrepreneurial characteristic (p. 453)

entrepreneurial venture (p. 443)

factor affecting new venture success (p. 452)

family business (p. 457)

idea (p. 446)

lifestyle company (p. 456)

opportunity (p.446)

small-business firm (p. 443)

source of innovation (p. 451)

strategic decision-making process for entrepreneurial venture (p. 446)

substage of small business development (p. 455)

NOTES

1. Summarized from N. L. Torres, "No Sweat," *Entrepreneur* (December 2004), p. 126.
2. "Small Business Resources for Faculty, Students, and Researchers: Answers to Frequently Asked Questions," *Small Business Advocate* (May 2004), p. 5.
3. W. J. Baumol, "Entrepreneurial Cultures and Countercultures," *Academy of Management Learning and Education* (September 2004), pp. 316–326; *The State of Small Business: A Report to the President* (Washington, DC: U.S. Government Printing Office, 1987), p. 117.
4. J. Castro, J. McDowell, and W. McWhirter, "Big vs. Small," *Time* (September 5, 1988), p. 49. This is supported by a 2003 study by the U.S. Small Business Administration which found that a small-firm patent is more likely than a large-firm patent to be among the top 1% of most frequently cited patents.
5. B. Headd, "Redefining Business Success: Distinguishing Between Closure and Failure," *Small Business Economics* (August 2003), as reported in "Frequency of Small Business Failure Reassessed by Advocacy Economist," *Small Business Advocate* (October 2003), p. 2.
6. M. J. Foster, "Scenario Planning for Small Businesses," *Long Range Planning* (February 1993), p. 123; M. S. S. El-Namacki, "Small Business—The Myth and the Reality," *Long Range Planning* (August 1990), p. 79.

7. J. Hopkins, "Study: New Company Failure Rate Not So High," *USA Today* (February 18, 2003), p. 1B. This article summarizes Brian Headd's 2003 study for the Small Business Administration. It revealed that after four years, the 50% that had closed included 33% that were considered unsuccessful. The remaining 17% were sold or closed but were considered successful by their founders. According to a study by Dun & Bradstreet of 800,000 small U.S. businesses started in 1985, 70% were still in business in March 1994. Contrary to other studies, this study counted firms as failures only if they owed money at the time of their demise. Also see J. Aley, "Debunking the Failure Fallacy," *Fortune* (September 6, 1993), p. 21.
8. R. N. Lussier, "Startup Business Advice from Business Owners to Would-Be Entrepreneurs," *SAM Advanced Management Journal* (Winter 1995), pp. 10–13.
9. J. W. Carland, F. Hoy, W. R. Boulton, and J. A. C. Carland, "Differentiating Entrepreneurs from Small Business Owners: A Conceptualization," *Academy of Management Review* (April 1984), p. 358; J. W. Carland, J. C. Carland, F. Hoy, and W. R. Boulton, "Distinctions Between Entrepreneurial and Small Business Ventures," *International Journal of Management* (March 1988), pp. 98–103.
10. S. P. Galante, "Counting on a Narrow Market Can Cloud Company's Future," *Wall Street Journal* (January 20, 1986), p. 17. Sexton's statement that entrepreneurial firms engage in more

sophisticated strategic planning than do small businesses is supported by C. H. Matthews and S. G. Scott, "Uncertainty and Planning in Small Entrepreneurial Firms: An Empirical Assessment," *Journal of Small Business Management* (October 1995), pp. 34–52. See also W. H. Stewart, Jr., W. E. Watson, J. C. Carland, and J. W. Carland, "A Proclivity for Entrepreneurship: A Comparison of Entrepreneurs, Small Business Owners, and Corporate Managers," *Journal of Business Venturing* (March 1999), pp. 189–214.

11. D. Fields, "Mrs. Fields' Weekends," *USA Weekend* (February 3–5, 1989), p. 16; M. Alpert, "In the Chips," *Fortune* (July 17, 1989), pp. 115–116.

12. J. S. Bracker, B. W. Keats, and J. N. Pearson, "Planning and Financial Performance Among Small Firms in a Growth Industry," *Strategic Management Journal* (November–December 1988), pp. 591–603; J. Kargar and J. A. Parnell, "Strategic Planning Emphasis and Planning Satisfaction in Small Firms: An Empirical Investigation," *Journal of Business Strategies* (Spring 1996), pp. 1–20; C. R. Schwenk and C. B. Shrader, "Effects of Formal Strategic Planning on Financial Performance in Small Firms: A Meta-Analysis," *Entrepreneurship Theory & Performance* (Spring 1993), pp. 53–64; L. W. Rue and N. A. Ibrahim, "The Relationship Between Planning Sophistication and Performance in Small Businesses," *Journal of Small Business Management* (October 1998), pp. 24–32.

13. W. H. Baker, H. Lon, and B. Davis, "Business Planning in Successful Small Firms," *Long Range Planning* (December 1993), pp. 82–88. Another study of 184 owner–managers of small businesses in the U.S. Midwest found that they were using strategic planning by formally documenting their mission (99%), objectives (95%), and strategies (93%). See D. F. Kuratko, J. C. Goodale, and J. S. Hornsby, "Quality Practices for a Competitive Advantage in Smaller Firms," *Journal of Small Business Management* (October 2001), pp. 293–311.

14. S. C. Perry, "The Relationship Between Written Business Plans and the Failure of Small Businesses in the U.S.," *Journal of Small Business Management* (July 2001), pp. 201–208.

15. D. B. Bradley III, "The Importance of Marketing Planning to Prevent Small Business Failure," paper presented to annual meeting of the Small Business Institute Directors Association (SBIDA) (San Diego, CA, February 7–9, 2002).

16. L. W. Rue and N. A. Ibrahim, "The Status of Planning in Smaller Family-Owned Businesses," *Family Business Review* (Spring 1996), pp. 29–43.

17. A. Thomas, "Less Is More: How Less Formal Planning Can Be Best," in *The Strategic Planning Management Reader*, edited by L. Fahey (Upper Saddle River, NJ: Prentice Hall, 1989), pp. 331–336; C. B. Shrader, C. L. Mulford, and V. L. Blackburn, "Strategic and Operational Planning, Uncertainty, and Performance in Small Firms," *Journal of Small Business Management* (October 1989), pp. 45–60.

18. R. B. Robinson, Jr., and J. A. Pearce II, "The Impact of Formalized Strategic Planning on Financial Performance in Small Organizations," *Strategic Management Journal* (July–September 1983), pp. 197–207; R. Ackelsberg and P. Arlow, "Small Businesses Do Plan and It Pays Off," *Long Range Planning* (October 1985), pp. 61–67.

19. M. Berry, "Strategic Planning in Small High-Tech Companies," *Long Range Planning* (June 1998), pp. 455–466.

20. F. Delmar and S. Shane, "Does Business Planning Facilitate the Development of New Ventures?" *Strategic Management Journal* (December 2003), pp. 1165–1185; S. Shane and F. Delmar, "Planning for the Market: Business Planning Before Marketing and the Continuation of Organizing Efforts," *Journal of Business Venturing* (November 2004), pp. 767–785.

21. *T. Mazzarol, "Do Formal Business Plans Really Matter? A Survey of Small Business Owners in Australia," paper presented to the 45th International Conference on Small Business (ICSB) World Conference 2000 (Brisbane, Australia, June 7–10, 2000).*

22. S. C. Perry, "The Relationship Between Written Business Plans and the Failure of Small Businesses in the U.S.," *Journal of Small Business Management* (July 2001), pp. 201–208.

23. V. Fowler, "Business Study Focuses on Failures," *Des Moines Register* (August 9, 1992), p. G1. For information on preparing a business plan, see R. Hisrich and M. Peters, *Entrepreneurship*, 6th ed. (New York: Irwin/McGraw-Hill, 2004).

24. M. K. Fiegener, B. M. Brown, D. R. Dreux IV, and W. J. Dennis, Jr., "CEO Stakes and Board Composition in Small Private Firms," *Entrepreneurship Theory & Practice* (Summer 2000), pp. 5–24.

25. L. W. Busenitz, D. D. Moesel, J. O. Fiet, and J. B. Barney, "The Framing of Perceptions of Fairness in the Relationship Between Venture Capitalists and New Venture Teams," *Entrepreneurship Theory & Practice* (Spring 1997), pp. 5–21.

26. V. H. Fried, G. D. Bruton, and R. D. Hisrich, "Strategy and the Board of Directors in Venture Capital–Backed Firms," *Journal of Business Venturing* (November 1999), pp. 493–503.

27. D. L. Sexton and F. I. Steele, *Leading Practices of Fast Growth Entrepreneurs* (Kansas City, MO: National Center for Entrepreneurship Research, 1997).

28. D. J. Garsombke and T. W. Garsombke, "An Empirical Investigation of the Utilization of External and Internal Boards of Directors and Management Advisory Assistance on the Performance of Small Businesses," *Journal of Business Strategies* (Fall 1996), pp. 167–184.

29. "Does Sarbanes-Oxley Hurt Shareholders and Hide Poor Management?" *Knowledge@Wharton* (November 17–30, 2004).

30. Ibid.

31. J. C. Shuman and J. A. Seeger, "The Theory and Practice of Strategic Management in Smaller Rapid Growth Firms," *American Journal of Small Business* (Summer 1986), p. 14.

32. R. C. Pineda, L. D. Lerner, M. C. Miller, and S. J. Phillips, "An Investigation of Factors Affecting the Information-Search Activities of Small Business Managers," *Journal of Small Business Management* (January 1998), pp. 60–71.

33. S. Birley and P. Westhead, "Growth and Performance Contrasts Between 'Types' of Small Firms," *Strategic Management Journal* (November–December 1990), pp. 535–557; J. L. Ward and C. E. Aronloff, "How Family Affects Strategy," *Small Business Forum* (Fall 1994), pp. 85–90.

34. P. Westhead, "Company Performance and Objectives Reported by First and Multi-Generation Family Companies: A Research Note," *Journal of Small Business and Enterprise Development*, Vol. 10, No. 1 (2003), pp. 93–105; J. Wiklund, P. Davidsson, and F. Delmar, "What Do They Think and Feel About Growth? An Expectancy-Value Approach to Small Business Managers' Attitudes Toward Growth," *Entrepreneurship Theory & Practice* (Spring 2003), pp. 247–270; A. Morrison, J. Breen, and S. Ali, "Small Business Growth: Intention, Ability, and Opportunity," *Journal of Small Business Management* (October 2003), pp. 417–425.

35. J. R. Baum, E. A. Locke, and K. G. Smith, "A Multidimensional Model of Venture Growth," *Academy of Management Journal* (April 2001), pp. 292–303; J. Florin, M. Lubatkin, and W. Schulze, "A Social Capital Model of High-Growth Ventures," *Academy of Management Journal* (June 2003), pp. 374–384.

36. J. Low and P. C. Kalafut, *Invisible Advantage: How Intangibles Are Driving Business Performance* (New York: Perseus Publishing, 2002), as reported in "Counting Intangible Assets," *Futurist* (September–October 2003), pp. 12–13.

37. P. F. Drucker, *Innovation and Entrepreneurship* (New York: HarperCollins, 1985), pp. 30–129.

38. F. Donnely, "Let zBox Accept Deliveries," *Des Moines Register* (October 31, 2000), p. TW1.

39. D. Stipp, "Inventor on the Verge of a Nervous Breakthrough," *Fortune* (March 29, 1999), pp. 104–117.

40. D. Whitford, "Taking BET Back from the Street," *Fortune* (November 9, 1998), pp. 167–170.

41. A. Bianchi, "Medical-Food Start-up Offers Tasty Treatments," *Inc.* (January 1997), p. 15.

42. C. W. Hofer and W. R. Sandberg, "Improving New Venture Performance: Some Guidelines for Success," *American Journal of Small Business* (Summer 1987), pp. 12–23. See also J. J. Chrisman and A. Bauerschmidt, "New Venture Performance: Some Critical Extensions to the Model," paper presented to the State-of-the-Art Symposium on Entrepreneurship (Ames: Iowa State University, April 12–14, 1992).

43. K. C. Robinson, "An Examination of the Influence of Industry Structure on Eight Alternative Measures of New Venture Performance for High Potential Independent New Ventures," *Journal of Business Venturing* (March 1999), pp. 165–187.

44. Interview with C. Bagley by J. Useem, "Forget Patents, Says Stanford Prof," *Inc.* (October 1996), p. 23.

45. K. C. Robinson, "An Examination of the Influence of Industry Structure on Eight Alternative Measures of New Venture Performance for High Potential Independent New Ventures," *Journal of Business Venturing* (March 1999), pp. 165–187.

46. J. Wade, "A Community-Level Analysis of Sources and Rates of Technological Variation in the Microprocessor Market," *Academy of Management Journal* (October 1996), pp. 1218–1244.

47. Supported by R. C. Shrader and M. Simon, "Corporate Versus Independent New Ventures: Resources, Strategy, and Performance Differences," *Journal of Business Venturing* (January 1997), pp. 47–66; R. Tonge, P. C. Larsen, and M. Ito, "Strategic Leadership in Super-Growth Companies—A Reappraisal," *Long Range Planning* (December 1998), pp. 838–847; G. Qian and L. Li, "Profitability of Small- and Medium-Sized Enterprises in High-Tech Industries: The Case of the Biotechnology Industry," *Strategic Management Journal* (September 2003), pp. 881–887.

48. K. M. Weaver and P. Dickson, "Strategic Alliances," *NFIB National Small Business Poll*, Vol. 4, Issue 4 (2004).

49. J. R. Baum, E. A. Locke, and K. G. Smith, "A Multidimensional Model of Venture Growth," *Academy of Management Journal* (April 2001), pp. 292–303; A. C. Cooper, G. E. Willard, and C. Y. Woo, "A Reexamination of the Niche Concept," in *The Strategy Process: Concepts, Contexts, and Cases*, 2nd ed., edited by H. Mintzberg and J. B. Quinn (Upper Saddle River, NJ: Prentice Hall, 1991), pp. 619–628; P. P. McDougall, J. G. Covin, R. B. Robinson, Jr., and L. Herron, "The Effects of Industry Growth and Strategic Breadth on New Venture Performance and Strategy Content," *Strategic Management Journal* (September 1994), pp. 537–554; C. E. Bamford, T. J. Dean, and P. P. McDougall, "Initial Strategies and New Venture Growth: An Examination of the Effectiveness of Broad vs. Narrow Breadth Strategies," in *Frontiers of Entrepreneurial Research*, edited by P. D. Reynolds, et al. (Babson Park, MA: Babson College, 1997), pp. 375–389; G. H. Lim, K. S. Lee, and S. J. Tan, "SMEs' Market Entry Strategy: Substitution

Instead of Niching," paper presented to the International Council for Small Business Conference (Naples, Italy, June 1999).

50. J. Wiklund and D. Shepherd, "Knowledge-Based Resources, Entrepreneurial Orientation, and the Performance of Small and Medium-Sized Businesses," *Strategic Management Journal* (December 2003), pp. 1307–1314; J. Kickul and L. K. Gundry, "Prospecting for Strategic Advantage: The Proactive Entrepreneurial Personality and Small Firm Innovation," *Journal of Small Business Management* (April 2002), pp. 85–97.

51. H. P. Welsch, "Entrepreneurs' Personal Characteristics: Causal Models," paper presented to the State-of-the-Art Symposium on Entrepreneurship (Ames: Iowa State University, April 12–14, 1992); A. Rahim, "Stress, Strain, and Their Moderators: An Empirical Comparison of Entrepreneurs and Managers," *Journal of Small Business Management* (January 1996), pp. 46–58; C. Korunka, H. Frank, M. Lueger, and J. Mugler, "The Entrepreneurial Personality in the Context of Resources, Environment, and the Startup Process—A Configurational Approach," *Entrepreneurship Theory & Practice* (Fall 2003), pp. 23–42.

52. M. Kets de Vries, "The Dark Side of Entrepreneurship," *Harvard Business Review* (November–December 1985), pp. 160–167.

53. A. C. Cooper, F. J. Gimeno-Gascon, and C. Y. Woo, "Initial Human and Financial Capital as Predictors of New Venture Performance," *Journal of Business Venturing* (Volume 9, 1994), pp. 371–395; H. R. Feeser and G. E. Willard, "Founding Strategies and Performance in High-Tech Firms," in *Handbook of Business Strategy, 1991/92 Yearbook*, edited by H. E. Glass and M. A. Hovde (Boston: Warren, Gorham & Lamont, 1991), pp. 2.1–2.18.

54. R. Ricklefs and U. Gupta, "Traumas of a New Entrepreneur," *Wall Street Journal* (May 10, 1989), p. B1.

55. N. C. Churchill and V. L. Lewis, "The Five Stages of Small Business Growth," *Harvard Business Review* (May–June 1983), pp. 30–50. The life cycle concept is supported by research by M. Beverland, "Organizational Life Cycles in Small Enterprises," paper presented to the 45th International Conference on Small Business (ICSB) World Conference (Brisbane, Australia, June 7–10, 2000).

56. J. W. Petty and W. D. Bygrave, "What Does Finance Have to Say to the Entrepreneur?" *Journal of Small Business Finance* (Spring 1993), pp. 125–137.

57. K. D. Brouthers, F. Andriessen, and J. Nicolaes, "Driving Blind: Strategic Decision-Making in Small Companies," *Long Range Planning* (February 1998), pp. 130–138.

58. See C. Farrell, K. Rebello, R. D. Hof, and M. Maremont, "The Boom in IPOs," *Business Week* (December 18, 1995), pp. 64–72, and S. Gruner, "When Mom & Pop Go Public," *Inc.* (December 1996), pp. 66–73.

59. A. Caruana, M. H. Morris, and A. J. Vella, "The Effect of Centralization and Formalization on Entrepreneurship in Export Firms," *Journal of Small Business Management* (January 1998), pp. 16–29.

60. F. David, D. Kelley, and F. David, "Small Business Owner Succession Planning: An Empirical Study," *Management in Practice*, Society for the Advancement of Management, No. 1 (2002), p. 3.

61. M. C. Sonfield, R. N. Lussier, S. Pfeifer, S. Manikutty, L. Maherault, and L. Verdier, "A Cross-National Investigation of First-Generation and Subsequent-Generation Family Members," paper presented to the Small Business Institute Conference (Clearwater, FL, February 12–14, 2004).

62. J. Magretta, "Governing the Family-Owned Enterprise: An Interview with Finland's Krister Ahlstrom," *Harvard Business Review* (January–February 1998), pp. 113–123.

63. "Passing on the Crown," *Economist* (November 6, 2004), pp. 69–71.

64. M. K. Allio, "Family Businesses: Their Virtues, Vices, and Strategic Path," *Strategy & Leadership*, Vol. 32, No. 4 (2004), pp. 24–33; J. Weber, L. Lavelle, T. Lowry, W. Zellner, and A. Barrett, "Family, Inc.," *Business Week* (November 10, 2003),pp. 100–114.

65. S. Birley, D. Ng, and A. Godfrey, "The Family and the Business," *Long Range Planning* (December 1999), pp. 598–608; "Passing on the Crown," *Economist* (November 6, 2004), pp. 69–71.

66. J. Magretta, "Governing the Family-Owned Enterprise: An Interview with Finland's Krister Ahlstrom," *Harvard Business Review* (January–February 1998), p. 119.

67. "Family Business: Why Firms Do Well When Founders Are at the Helm?" *Knowledge @ Wharton* (October 20–November 2, 2004).

68. N. C. Churchill and K. J. Hatten, "Non-Market-Based Transfers of Wealth and Power: A Research Framework for Family Businesses," *American Journal of Small Business* (Winter 1987), pp. 51–64.

69. J. L. Ward and C. E. Aronoff, "Shirt Sleeves to Shirt Sleeves," *Nation's Business* (September 1992), pp. 62–63.

70. "Passing on the Crown," *Economist* (November 6, 2004), pp. 69–71.

71. J. Applegate, "Business People in Bermuda Get Sloppy Without Taxes," *Des Moines Register* (July 6, 1992), p. 8B.

72. P. L. Huff, R. M. Harper, Jr., and A. E. Eikner, "Are There Differences in Liquidity and Solvency Measures Based on Company Size?" *American Business Review* (June 1999), pp. 96–106.

73. R. I. Levin and V. R. Travis, "Small Company Finance: What the Books Don't Say," *Harvard Business Review* (November–December 1987), pp. 30–32.

74. *Pocket World in Figures 2004* (London: Economist and Profile Books, 2003), p. 58.

75. R. Florida, "Breakthrough Ideas for 2004: No Monopoly on Creativity," *Harvard Business Review* (February 2004), pp. 14–15.

strategic issues in Not-for-Profit Organizations

Eight times a day, the Reverend Bernard McCoy solemnly chants prayer in Latin in the monastery chapel. He then goes back to his computer and telephone to manage LaserMonks. McCoy and four other monks at The Cistercian Abbey of Our Lady of Spring Bank in Sparta, Wisconsin, sell refilled inkjet and laser printer cartridges from their Internet site and telephone mail order center. LaserMonks offers the refills at prices 30% to 90% lower than offered at retail stores. Says McCoy, "You get quality products at great savings. We do good work with the extra income. Plus, the monks pray for you. I don't think Staples ever offered to do that."

Sales increased from $2,000 during their first year of business in 2002 to $500,000 in 2003, with a profit of $30,000. After expenses are paid for the business and the monastery, the money pays for everything from a defibrillator for the local fire department to providing free computer training for orphans in Vietnam. Worried about the monastery's not-for-profit status, LaserMonks was established as a profit-making corporation owned by the abbey. According to McCoy, "through charitable, legal means, we channel money to the abbey, which is how we don't jeopardize our tax-exempt status. . . We pay business taxes like everybody else." Responding to the concern that a monastery should not be involved in business activities, McCoy states, "We're not selling God; we're selling black dust and ink so we can give our profits away to good causes. But you do have to walk a fine line in your marketing and not be offensive to God, yourself, or any other groups that have various relations to divine things."[1]

LaserMonks is an example of *strategic piggybacking*, a not-for-profit strategy that is as old as Girl Scout cookies and museum gift shops. Today's not-for-profits are using profit-making ventures as a way to diversify their revenue streams in tight financial times.[2] Piggybacking is a way for not-for-profits to earn money in a secondary business activity to support their primary mission, which may be raising orphans or providing a free educational experience.

By the mid-1990s, most not-for-profit organizations were turning to strategic management and other concepts from business to ensure their survival. According to Cynthia Massarsky, Deputy Director of the Yale School of Management—The Goldman Sachs Foundation Partnership on Nonprofit Ventures, "Nonprofits are looking to be more efficient in the way they do

- Identify the types of not-for-profit organizations
- Explain how sources of revenue influence not-for-profit strategic decision making

- Compare and contrast the strategic management of profit-making with not-for-profit organizations
- Discuss popular strategies being used by not-for-profit organizations

things. By taking a few lessons from the business world, perhaps they've learned how to operate a little more efficiently."[3] This is a significant change from past attitudes because most not-for-profit managers have traditionally felt that business concepts were not relevant to their situation. According to Peter Drucker:

> *Twenty years ago, management was a dirty word for those involved in nonprofit organizations. It meant business, and nonprofits prided themselves on being free of the taint of commercialism and above such sordid considerations as the bottom line. Now most of them have learned that nonprofits need management even more than business does, precisely because they lack the discipline of the bottom line.*[4]

A knowledge of not-for-profit organizations is important if only because they account for an average of 1 in every 20 jobs in nations throughout the world. A study by the Johns Hopkins University Institute for Policy Studies found that in nine countries between 1990 and 1995, nonprofit jobs grew by 23% compared to 6.2% for the whole economy.[5] Not-for-profits employ over 25% of the U.S. workforce and own approximately 15% of the nation's private wealth.[6] In the United States alone, in addition to various federal, state, and local government agencies, there are about 10,000 not-for-profit hospitals and nursing homes (84% of all hospitals), 4,600 colleges and universities, more than 100,000 private and public elementary and secondary schools, and almost 350,000 churches and synagogues, plus many thousands of charities and service organizations.[7]

Typically, **not-for-profit organizations (NFP)** include **private nonprofit corporations** (such as hospitals, institutes, private colleges, and organized charities) as well as **public governmental units or agencies** (such as welfare departments, prisons, and state universities). Traditionally, studies in strategic management have dealt with profit-making firms to the exclusion of nonprofit or governmental organizations. This, however, is changing. Increasing numbers of not-for-profit organizations are adopting strategic management.

Scholars and practitioners are concluding that many strategic management concepts and techniques can be successfully adapted for not-for-profit organizations.[8] Although the evidence is not yet conclusive, there appears to be an association between strategic planning efforts and performance measures such as growth.[9] The purpose of this chapter is, therefore, to highlight briefly the major differences between profit-making and not-for-profit organizations, so that the effects of their differences on the strategic management process can be understood.

14.1 Why Not-for-Profit?

The not-for-profit sector of an economy is important for several reasons. First, society desires certain goods and services that profit-making firms cannot or will not provide. These are referred to as **public or collective goods** because people who might not have paid for the goods receive benefits from them. Paved roads, police protection, museums, and schools are examples of public goods. A person cannot use a private good unless he or she pays for it. Generally, once a public good is provided, however, anyone can use or enjoy it.

Certain aspects of life do not appear to be served appropriately by profit-making business firms yet are often crucial to the well-being of society. These aspects include areas in which society as a whole benefits from a particular service but in which a particular individual benefits only indirectly. It is in these areas that not-for-profit organizations have traditionally been most effective. Libraries and museums are examples. Although most people do not visit libraries or museums very often, they are usually willing to pay taxes and/or donate funds to support their existence. They do so because they believe that these organizations act to uplift the culture and quality of life of the region. To fulfill their mission, entrance fees (if any) must be set low enough to allow everyone admission. These fees, however, are not profitable—they rarely even cover the costs of the service. The same is true of animal shelters managed by the Humane Society. Although few people want abandoned pets running wild through city streets, fees charged for the adoption of these animals cannot alone pay the costs of finding and caring for them. Additional revenue is needed—in the form of either donations or public taxation. Such public or collective services cannot generate a profit, yet they are necessary for any successful civilization. Which aspects of society are most suited to being served by not-for-profit organizations rather than by profit-making business organizations? This is an issue that governments face when they privatize what has previously been provided by the state. See the **Global Issue** feature to learn more about this development.

A second reason why the not-for-profit sector is important is that a private nonprofit organization tends to receive benefits from society that a private profit-making firm cannot obtain. Preferred tax status to nonstock corporations is given in section 501(c)(3) of the U.S. Internal Revenue Service code in the form of exemptions from corporate income taxes. Private nonprofit firms also enjoy exemptions from various other state, local, and federal taxes. Under certain conditions, these firms also benefit from the tax deductibility of donors' contributions and membership dues. In addition, they qualify for special reduced-cost mailing privileges.[10] These benefits are allowed because private nonprofit organizations are typically service organizations, which are expected to use any excess of revenue over costs and expenses (a surplus rather than a profit) either to improve service or to reduce the price of their service. This service orientation is reflected in the fact that not-for-profit organizations do not use the term *customer* to refer to the recipient of the service. The recipient is typically referred to as a *patient, student, client, case*, or simply *the public*.

GLOBAL issue

WHICH IS BEST FOR SOCIETY: BUSINESS OR NOT-FOR-PROFIT?

Many nations throughout the world are attempting to privatize state-owned enterprises to balance their budgets. **Privatization** is (1) the selling of state-owned enterprises to private individuals or corporations or (2) the hiring of a private business to provide services previously offered by a state agency. The British government, for example, sold British Airways, its state-owned airline, to private investors. In the United States, many city governments now allow private companies to collect and dispose of trash—something that had previously been done by the city.

Problems can result, however, if privatization goes too far. For example, in converting from a communist-oriented, centrally managed economy to a more democratic, free-market economy, Eastern European countries are finding that profit-making business firms are unable to satisfy all of society's needs. What used to be provided by the state free of charge (but tax-supported) in Russia and other countries may now be provided only for the rich or not at all. The same problem is evident in the United States in the controversies over the provision of health care, retirement benefits, and private versus public education.

Some of the aspects of life that cannot easily be privatized and are often better managed by not-for-profit organizations are as follows:

- Religion
- Education
- Charities
- Clubs, interest groups, and unions
- Health care
- Government

The privatization of state-owned business enterprises is likely to continue globally because most of these enterprises must expand internationally in order to survive in the increasingly global environment. They cannot compete successfully if they are forced to follow inefficient, socially oriented policies and regulations (emphasizing employment over efficiency) rather than economically oriented, international practices (emphasizing efficiency over employment). The global trend toward privatization will probably continue until each country reaches the point where the efficiency of business is counterbalanced by the effectiveness of the not-for-profit sector of the economy. As political motives overcome economic ones, government will likely intervene in that decision.

14.2 Importance of Revenue Source

The feature that best differentiates not-for-profit organizations from each other as well as from profit-making corporations is their source of revenue.[11] A **profit-making firm** depends on revenues obtained from the sale of its goods and services to customers, who typically pay for the costs and expenses of providing the product or service plus a profit. A not-for-profit organization, in contrast, depends heavily on dues, assessments, or donations from its membership, or on funding from a sponsoring agency, such as the United Way or the federal government, to pay for much of its costs and expenses.

SOURCES OF NOT-FOR-PROFIT REVENUE

Revenue is generated from a variety of sources—not just from clients receiving the product or service from the not-for-profit. It can come from people who do not even receive the services they are subsidizing. One study of Minnesota nonprofits found that donations accounted for almost 40%, government grants for around 25%, and program service fees for about 35% of total revenues.[12] In other types of not-for-profit organizations—such as unions and voluntary medical plans—revenue comes mostly from the members, the people who receive the service. Nevertheless, the members typically pay dues in advance and must accept later whatever service is provided, whether they choose it or not and whether it is what they expected or not. The service is often received long after the dues are paid.

In profit-making corporations, there is typically a simple and direct connection between the customer or client and the organization. The organization tends to be totally dependent on sales of its products or services to the customer for revenue and is therefore extremely interested in pleasing the customer. As shown in **Figure 14–1**, a profit-making organization (*organization A*) tries to influence the customer (through advertising and promotion) to continue to buy and use its services. Either by buying or not buying the item offered, the customer, in turn, directly influences the organization's decision-making process. The business is thus market-oriented.

In the case of a typical not-for-profit organization, however, there is likely to be a very different sort of relationship between the organization providing and the person receiving the service. Because the recipient of the service typically does not pay the entire cost of the service, outside sponsors are required. In most instances, the sponsors receive none of the service but provide partial to total funding for the needed revenues. As indicated earlier, these sponsors can be

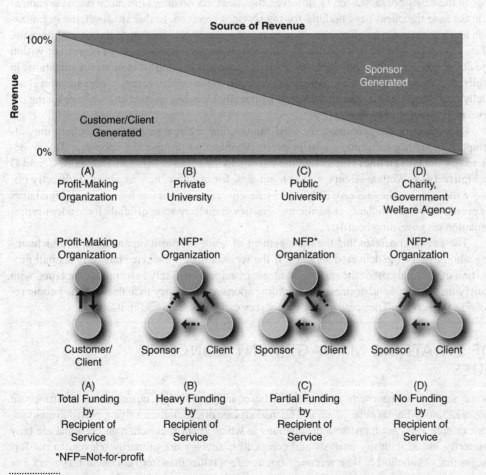

FIGURE 14–1 The Effects of Sources of Revenue on Patterns of Client–Organization Influence

the government (using taxpayers' money) or charitable organizations, such as the United Way (using voluntary donations). As shown in **Figure 14–1**, a not-for-profit organization can be partially dependent on sponsors for funding (*organizations B and C*) or totally dependent on the sponsors (*organization D*). The less money it receives from clients receiving the service or product, the less market-oriented is a not-for-profit organization.

PATTERNS OF INFLUENCE ON STRATEGIC DECISION MAKING

The **pattern of influence** on an organization's strategic decision making derives from its sources of revenue.[13] As shown in **Figure 14–1**, a private university (organization B) is heavily dependent on student tuition and other client-generated funds for about 70% of its revenue. Therefore, the students' desires are likely to have a stronger influence (as shown by an unbroken line) on the university's decision making than are the desires of the various sponsors such as alumni and private foundations. The sponsors' relatively marginal influence on the organization is reflected by a broken line. In contrast, a public university (organization C) is more heavily dependent on outside sponsors such as a state legislature for revenue funding. Student tuition and other client-generated funds form a small percentage (often less than 40%) of total revenue. Therefore, the university's decision making is heavily influenced by the sponsors (unbroken line) and only marginally influenced directly by the students (broken line).

In the case of organization D, however, the client has no direct influence on the organization because the client pays nothing for the services received. In this situation, the organization tends to measure its effectiveness in terms of sponsor satisfaction. It has no real measure of its efficiency other than its ability to carry out its mission and achieve its objectives within the dollar contributions it has received from its sponsors. In contrast to other organizations in which the client contributes a significant proportion of the needed revenue, organization D actually might be able to increase its revenue by heavily lobbying its sponsors while reducing the level of its service to its clients!

Regardless of the percentage of total funding that a client generates, the client may attempt to indirectly influence a not-for-profit organization through the sponsors. This is depicted by the broken lines connecting the client and the sponsor in organizations B, C, and D in **Figure 14–1**. Welfare clients or prison inmates, for example, may be able to indirectly improve the services they receive if they pressure government officials by writing to legislators or even by rioting. Students at public universities can lobby state officials for student representation on governing boards.

The key to understanding the management of a not-for-profit organization is thus learning who pays for the delivered services. If the recipients of the service pay only a small proportion of the total cost of the service, strategic managers are likely to be more concerned with satisfying the needs and desires of the funding sponsors or agency than those of the people receiving the service. The acquisition of resources can become an end in itself.

USEFULNESS OF STRATEGIC MANAGEMENT CONCEPTS AND TECHNIQUES

Some strategic management concepts can be equally applied to business and not-for-profit organizations, whereas others cannot. The marketplace orientation underlying portfolio analysis, for example, does not translate into situations in which client satisfaction and revenue are only indirectly linked. Industry analysis and competitive strategy are primarily relevant to not-for-profits that obtain most of their revenue from user fees rather than from donors or taxpayers. For example, as hospitals find themselves relying increasingly on patient fees for their revenue, they use competitive strategy to gain advantage versus other hospitals. Smaller not-for-profit hospitals stress the "high touch" of their staff over the "high tech" of competitors that have better diagnostic machinery. The concept of competitive advantage is less useful to a typical not-for-profit than the related concept of institutional advantage, which sets aside the profit-making objective of competitive advantage. A not-for-profit can be said to have **institutional advantage** when it performs its tasks more effectively than other comparable organizations.[14]

SWOT analysis, mission statements, stakeholder analysis, and corporate governance are, however, just as relevant to a not-for-profit as they are to a profit-making organization.[15] Portfolio analysis can be very helpful but is used very differently in not-for-profits than in business firms. (See the section on strategic piggybacking later in the chapter.) As with any corporation, nonprofits usually have boards of directors whose job is to ensure that the paid executive director and staff work to fulfill the organization's mission and objectives. Unlike the boards of most business firms, nonprofit boards are often required, however, to take primary responsibility for strategic planning and fund-raising. Many nonprofits find that a well-crafted mission statement not only helps in finding donors but also in attracting volunteers. Take the example of the mission statement of a local animal shelter:

> *To shelter and care for stray, lost, or abandoned animals and to responsibly place animals in new homes and enforce animal laws. We are also here to better educate people in ways to be solutions to animal problems, not causes.*[16]

Strategic management is difficult to apply when an organization's output is difficult to measure objectively, as is the case with most not-for-profit organizations. Thus it is very likely that many not-for-profit organizations have not used strategic management because its concepts, techniques, and prescriptions do not lend themselves to situations where sponsors, rather than the marketplace, determine revenue. The situation, however, is changing. The trend toward privatizing public organizations, such as converting subsidized community hospitals to independent (nonsubsidized) status, usually means that the clients/patients pay a larger percentage of the costs. As these not-for-profits become more market oriented (and thus client oriented), strategic management becomes more applicable and more increasingly used.[17] Nevertheless, various constraints on not-for-profits mean that strategic management concepts and techniques must be modified to be effective.

14.3 Impact of Constraints on Strategic Management

Several characteristics peculiar to a not-for-profit organization constrain its behavior and affect its strategic management. Newman and Wallender list the following five **constraints on strategic management**:

1. **Service is often intangible and hard to measure.** This difficulty is typically compounded by the existence of multiple service objectives developed to satisfy multiple sponsors.
2. **Client influence may be weak.** Often the organization has a local monopoly, and clients' payments may be a very small source of funds.
3. **Strong employee commitments to professions or to a cause may undermine allegiance** to the organization employing them.
4. **Resource contributors may intrude on the organization's internal management.** Such contributors include fund contributors and government.
5. **Restraints on the use of rewards and punishments** may result from constraints 1, 3, and 4.[18]

It is true that several of these characteristics can be found in profit-making as well as in not-for-profit organizations. Nevertheless, as Newman and Wallender state, the "frequency of strong impact is much higher in not-for-profit enterprises."[19]

IMPACT ON STRATEGY FORMULATION

The long-range planning and decision making affected by the listed constraints serve to add at least four **complications to strategy formulation**:

1. **Goal conflicts interfere with rational planning:** Because a not-for-profit organization typically lacks a single clear-cut performance criterion (such as profits), divergent goals and objectives are likely, especially with multiple sponsors. Differences in the concerns of various important sponsors can prevent management from stating the organization's mission in anything but very broad terms, if they fear that a sponsor who disagrees with a particular, narrow definition of mission might cancel its funding. For example, a study of 227 public Canadian hospitals found that more than half had very general, ambiguous, and unquantified objectives.[20] According to Heffron, an authority in public administration, "The greater openness within which they are compelled to operate—the fishbowl atmosphere—impedes thorough discussion of issues and discourages long-range plans that might alienate stakeholders."[21] In such organizations, it is the reduced influence of the clients that permits this diversity of values and goals to occur without a clear market check. For example, when a city council considers changing zoning to implement a strategic plan for the city, all sorts of people (including the press) will demand to be heard. A decision might be made based on pressure from a few stakeholders (who make significant contributions or who threaten to stir up trouble) to the detriment of the community as a whole.

2. **An integrated planning focus tends to shift from results to resources:** Because not-for-profit organizations tend to provide services that are hard to measure, they rarely have a net bottom line.[22] Planning, therefore, becomes more concerned with resource inputs, which can easily be measured, than with service, which cannot. Global displacement becomes even more likely than it is in business organizations.[23]

3. **Ambiguous operating objectives create opportunities for internal politics and goal displacement:** The combination of vague objectives and a heavy concern with resources allows managers considerable leeway in their activities. Such leeway makes possible political maneuvering for personal ends. In addition, because the effectiveness of a not-for-profit organization hinges on the satisfaction of the sponsoring group, management tends to ignore the needs of the client while focusing on the desires of a powerful sponsor. University administrators commonly say that people will donate money for a new building (which will carry the donor's name) but not for other more pressing needs, such as the maintenance of existing buildings. In this situation, powerful department heads might wine and dine the donor, hoping to get the money for their pet projects. This problem is compounded by the common practice of selecting people to boards of trustees/directors not on the basis of their managerial experience but on the basis of their ability to contribute money, raise funds, and work with politicians. (A major role of a not-for-profit board is to ensure adequate resources—usually translated to mean fund-raising.[24]) Directors usually receive no compensation for serving on the board. Their lack of interest in overseeing management is reflected in an overall not-for-profit board-meeting attendance rate of only 50%, compared with 90% for boards of directors of business corporations. This is one reason why boards of not-for-profits tend to be larger than are boards of business corporations. Eckerd College, for example, has a 52-member, extremely passive board of directors.[25] Board members of not-for-profit organizations tend to ignore the task of determining strategies and policies—often leaving that to the

paid (or sometimes unpaid) executive director. The larger the board, the less likely it is to exercise control over top management.[26]

4. **Professionalization simplifies detailed planning but adds rigidity:** In not-for-profit organizations in which professionals play important roles (as in hospitals or colleges), professional values and traditions can prevent the organization from changing its conventional behavior patterns to fit new service missions tuned to changing social needs. This rigidity, of course, can occur in any organization that hires professionals. The strong service orientation of most not-for-profit organizations, however, tends to encourage the development of static professional norms and attitudes. As not-for-profits attempt to become more business-like, this may be changing. One study of Minnesota nonprofits revealed that 29% of the program directors and 15% of the staff had degrees or experience in business administration.[27]

IMPACT ON STRATEGY IMPLEMENTATION

The five constraining characteristics also affect how a not-for-profit organization is organized in both its structure and job design. Three **complications to strategy implementation** in particular can be highlighted:

1. **Decentralization is complicated:** The difficulty of setting objectives for an intangible, hard-to-measure service mission complicates the delegation of decision-making authority. Because of the heavy dependence on sponsors for revenue support, the top management of a not-for-profit organization must be always alert to the sponsors' view of an organizational activity. This necessary caution leads to **defensive centralization**, in which top management retains all decision-making authority so that low-level managers cannot take any actions to which the sponsors may object.

2. **Linking pins for external–internal integration become important:** Because of the heavy dependence on outside sponsors, a special need arises for people in buffer roles to relate to both inside and outside groups. This role is especially necessary when the sponsors are diverse (revenue comes from donations, membership fees, and federal funds) and the service is intangible (for instance, a "good" education) with a broad mission and multiple shifting objectives. The job of a *Dean for External Affairs*, for example, consists primarily of working with the school's alumnae and raising funds.

3. **Job enlargement and executive development can be restrained by professionalism:** In organizations that employ a large number of professionals, managers must design jobs that appeal to prevailing professional norms. Professionals have rather clear ideas about which activities are, and which are not, within their province. Enriching a nurse's job by expanding his or her decision-making authority for drug dosage, for example, can cause conflict with medical doctors who believe that such authority is theirs alone. Because a professional often views managerial jobs as nonprofessional and merely supportive, promotion into a management position is not always viewed positively.

IMPACT ON EVALUATION AND CONTROL

Special **complications to evaluation and control** arising from the constraining characteristics also affect how behavior is motivated and performance is controlled. Two problems, in particular, are often noticed:

1. **Rewards and penalties have little or no relationship to performance:** When desired results are vague and the judgment of success is subjective, predictable and impersonal feedback cannot be established. Performance is judged either intuitively ("You don't seem

to be taking your job seriously") or on the basis of whatever small aspects of a job can be measured ("You were late to work twice last month").

2. **Inputs rather than outputs are heavily controlled:** Because its inputs can be measured much more easily than outputs, a not-for-profit organization tends to focus more on the resources going into performance than on the performance itself.[28] The emphasis is thus on setting maximum limits for costs and expenses. Because there is little to no reward for staying under these limits, people usually respond negatively to such controls.

Because of these and other complications, not-for-profits can waste money in many ways, especially on administrative costs and expenses. Because of this, it is becoming increasingly common to calculate ratios comparing total support and revenue with the amounts spent on specific service activities. For example, analysts become concerned when the total spent on the mission of the organization (e.g., community service) is less than 50% of total income received from sponsors and activities. Other rules of thumb are that a not-for-profit should not spend more than 35% on administrative expenses and that the costs of fund-raising should not account for more than 15% of total income.[29]

14.4 Not-for-Profit Strategies

One of the issues in the strategic management of not-for-profit organizations is the tendency of nonprofits to make program decisions based on a mission rather than on a strategy. Kasturi Rangan points out that many nonprofits don't have a strategy at all; instead, they rally under a particular cause, such as "Fight homelessness" or "Save the children."[30] Because that cause is so worthwhile, nonprofits tend to support any program that's even slightly related to the mission, so long as there is money available (at least in the beginning) to support the new program. Without a clear long-term strategy, this will eventually stretch the not-for-profit's core capabilities into unintended directions and create a budget with more expenses than revenues. The need to attract additional donors forces not-for-profits to go after grants or donations that fit within their broadly defined mission but only slightly fit their existing capabilities. The problem is that such a grant usually contains restrictions that the funding be spent on a particular program or initiative. Starved for money, not-for-profits accept these restrictions in order to obtain the funding. Because the funds barely cover the direct costs of the additional activity, unanticipated indirect costs force the not-for-profit to look for more funding, each time as a larger, less focused, and more cash-starved organization. The result is an organization with large bureaucratic overhead but not enough professionals to carry out all its programs effectively. This leads to increasing pressure to reduce costs and to use more volunteers—both of which may reduce the quality of service to clients. Professional employees become demoralized because of increasing service demands, less support, and marginal pay raises.

The organization's executive director is usually too busy administering a convoluted bureaucracy, dealing with bickering professional employees, and fund-raising to do any serious strategic planning. It is therefore usually left to the board of directors to call a stop to this *activity trap*. The board must define achievable objectives and propose a strategy to make them happen. It must decide not only what the organization will do but also what it will not do. Given that the primary mission is sacrosanct, the board should develop a narrow operational mission with measurable objectives and a strategy to go with them.[31] Once this is done, the organization is free to decide which programs to support and which to curtail.

If a not-for-profit organization has established an operational mission and measurable service objectives, it can consider various ways to support its priority programs without having to accept mission-extending donor requirements. Increasingly, not-for-profits are choosing the strategies of strategic piggybacking, mergers, and strategic alliances.

STRATEGIC PIGGYBACKING

Coined by Nielsen, the term **strategic piggybacking** refers to the development of a new activity for a not-for-profit organization that would generate the funds needed to make up the difference between revenues and expenses.[32] The new activity is typically related in some manner to the not-for-profit's mission, but its purpose is to help subsidize the primary service programs. It appears to be a form of concentric diversification, but it is engaged in not as part of the mission but only for its money-generating value. In an inverted use of portfolio analysis, the organization invests in new, safe cash cows to fund its current cash-hungry question marks and dogs. It is a type of **social entrepreneurship**, in which a not-for-profit organization starts a new venture to achieve social goals.

Although strategic piggybacking is not new, it has recently become very popular. As early as 1874, for example, the Metropolitan Museum of Art retained a professional to photograph its collections and to sell copies of the prints. Profits were used to defray the museum's operating costs. More recently, various income-generating ventures have appeared under various auspices, from the Girl Scouts to UNICEF, and in numerous forms, from cookies and small gift shops to vast real estate developments. A study by the U.S. General Accounting Office revealed that the amount of funds resulting from income-producing activities of not-for-profits has significantly increased since the 1970s. Hospitals are offering wellness programs, ranging from meditation classes to aerobics. Some 70% of colleges and universities now offer "auxiliary" services, such as bookstores, conference rooms, and computer centers, as sources of income.[33] The American Cancer Society earns millions annually by allowing its name to appear on products sold by private drug companies, such as GlaxoSmithKline's Nicorette chewing gum. The Metropolitan Museum of Art now has 16 stores outside the main museum and a fast-growing web site—all of which generate money. The Baptist Hospital of Nashville, Tennessee, built and operates a $15 million, 18-acre office and training-field complex, which it rents to Nashville's professional football team.

The U.S. Small Business Administration, however, views this money-making activity as "unfair competition." The U.S. Internal Revenue Service (IRS) advises that a not-for-profit that engages in a business "not substantially related" to the organization's exempt purposes may jeopardize its tax-exempt status, particularly if the income from the business exceeds approximately 20% of total organizational revenues. The IRS requires not-for-profits to pay an unrelated business income tax on commercial activities that don't relate to the organization's central mission. So far, not-for-profits are still considered tax exempt if their businesses are staffed by volunteers or if almost all their merchandise is donated. According to Marcus Owens, Director of Tax-Exempt Organizations for the IRS, "The ultimate question is should these institutions continue as tax-exempt entities. And it's being raised more than ever before."[34] This has caused many not-for-profits such as The Cistercian Abbey mentioned earlier to establish two separate entities. "Doing all the separate bookkeeping, accounting, and cost allocations can be a bit burdensome, time-consuming and distracting," says Jeffrey Tanenbaum, a lawyer specializing in representing nonprofits.[35]

Although strategic piggybacks can help not-for-profit organizations self-subsidize their primary missions and better use their resources, according to Nielsen, there are several potential drawbacks.[36] First, the revenue-generating venture could actually lose money, especially in the short run. Second, the venture could subvert, interfere with, or even take over the primary mission. Third, the public, as well as the sponsors, could reduce their contributions because of negative responses to such "money-grubbing activities" or because of a mistaken belief that the organization is becoming self-supporting. Fourth, the venture could interfere with the internal operations of the not-for-profit organization. To avoid these drawbacks, a not-for-profit should carefully evaluate its resources before choosing this strategy. See **Strategy Highlight 14.1** to see the resources needed for a piggyback.

STRATEGY highlight 14.1

RESOURCES NEEDED FOR SUCCESSFUL STRATEGIC PIGGYBACKING

Based on his experience as a consultant to not-for-profit organizations, Edward Skloot suggests that a not-for-profit should have five resources before engaging in strategic piggybacking:

1. **Something to sell:** The organization should assess its resources to see if people might be willing to pay for goods or services closely related to the organization's primary activity. Repackaging the Boston Symphony into the less formal Boston Pops Orchestra created a way to subsidize the deficit-creating symphony and provide year-round work for the musicians.

2. **Critical mass of management talent:** Enough people must be available to nurture and sustain an income venture over the long haul. This can be very difficult, given that the most competent not-for-profit professionals often don't want to be managers.

3. **Trustee support:** If the trustees have strong feelings against earned-income ventures, they could actively

or passively resist commercial involvement. When the Children's Television Workshop began licensing its Sesame Street characters to toy companies and theme parks, many people criticized it for joining business in selling more things to children.

4. **Entrepreneurial attitude:** Management must be able to combine an interest in innovative ideas with business-like practicality.

5. **Venture capital:** Because it often takes money to make money, engaging in a joint venture with a business corporation can provide the necessary startup funds as well as the marketing and management support. For example, Massachusetts General Hospital received $50 million from Hoechst, the German chemical company, for biological research in exchange for exclusive licenses to develop commercial products from particular research discoveries.

The U.S. National Association of College and University Business Officers predicts that within a few years, more than 90% of colleges and universities in the United States will be using strategic piggybacks.[37] A similar trend is expected for other not-for-profits that heavily rely on donations and taxpayer support for their revenue.

MERGERS

Dwindling resources are leading an increasing number of not-for-profits to consider mergers as a way of reducing costs through economies of scope and reducing program duplication and raising prices because of increased market power.[38] For example, the merger of Baptist Health Systems and Research Health Services created Health Midwest in Kansas City. The New York Hospital–Cornell Medical Center and Columbia–Presbyterian Medical Center combined to form the New York and Presbyterian Hospitals Health Care System. Since 1990, more than 45% of U.S. hospitals have been involved in mergers and acquisitions.[39]

STRATEGIC ALLIANCES

Strategic alliances involve developing cooperative ties with other organizations. Not-for-profit organizations often use alliances as a way to enhance their capacity to serve clients or to acquire resources while still enabling them to keep their identities.[40] Services can be purchased and provided more efficiently through cooperation with other organizations than if they were done alone. For example, four Ohio universities agreed to create and jointly operate a new school of international business. Alone, none of the business schools could afford the $30 million to build the school. The Collaborative Ventures Program of the Teagle Foundation has given more than $4 million in grants to help colleges set up money-saving collaborations. While only a handful of consortia existed in 1995, by 1998 there were at least 21, representing 125 colleges and universities.[41]

Strategic alliances and mergers are becoming commonplace among not-for-profit organizations. The next logical step is strategic alliances between business firms and not-for-profits. Already, business corporations are forming alliances with universities to fund university research in exchange for options on the results of that research. Business firms find it cheaper to pay universities to do basic research than to do it themselves. Universities are in need of research funds to attract top professors and to maintain expensive labs. Such alliances of convenience are being criticized, but they are likely to continue.

INFO-BITS

- Countries with the highest number of people in prison per 100,000 population are the United States (707), Russia (638), Belarus (554), Kazakhstan (522), Turkmenistan (489), Bermuda (447), Suriname (437), Bahamas (416), Ukraine (416), and South Africa (404).[42]

- Countries with the most hospital beds per 1,000 population are Japan (17.0), Norway (14.0), Russia (13.1), Moldova (12.9), Estonia (12.0), Belarus (11.8), the Netherlands (11.5), Martinique (10.7), Georgia (10.5), and Kirgizstan (10.4).[43]

DISCUSSION QUESTIONS

1. Are not-for-profit organizations less efficient than profit-making organizations? Why or why not?

2. How does the lack of a clear-cut performance measure, such as profits, affect the strategic management of a not-for-profit organization?

3. What are the pros and cons of strategic piggybacking? In what way is it "unfair competition" for not-for-profits to engage in revenue generating activity?

4. What are the pros and cons of mergers and strategic alliances? Should not-for-profits engage in alliances with business firms?

5. A number of not-for-profit organizations in the United States have been converting to profit making. Why would a not-for-profit organization want to change its status to profit making? What are the pros and cons of doing so?

STRATEGIC PRACTICE EXERCISES

1. Read the **Global Issue** feature in this chapter. It lists six aspects of society that it proposes are better managed by not-for-profit organizations than by profit-making organizations. Do you agree with this list? Should some aspects be deleted from the list? Should other aspects be added?

2. Examine a local college or university—perhaps the one you may be currently attending. What strategic issues is it facing? Develop a SFAS Matrix (see **Figure 6–1**) of strategic factors. Is it attempting to use any strategic management concepts? If so, which ones? What sorts of strategies should it consider for continued survival and future growth? Is it currently using strategic piggybacks to obtain additional funding? What sorts of additional piggybacks should it consider? Are strategic alliances with another college or university or business firm a possibility?

Let's Summarize the Chapter with a Mind Map

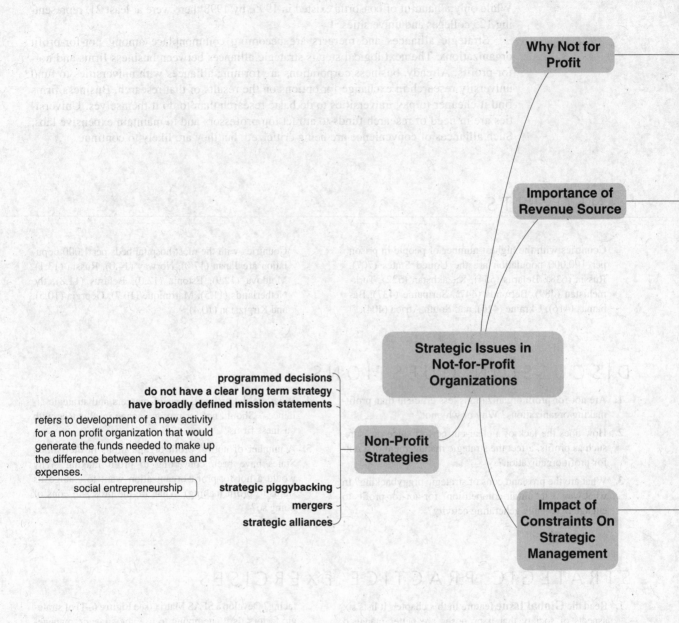

Why Not for Profit

Importance of Revenue Source

Strategic Issues in Not-for-Profit Organizations

Non-Profit Strategies

programmed decisions
do not have a clear long term strategy
have broadly defined mission statements

refers to development of a new activity for a non profit organization that would generate the funds needed to make up the difference between revenues and expenses.

social entrepreneurship

strategic piggybacking

mergers

strategic alliances

Impact of Constraints On Strategic Management

- society desires certain goods and services that profit making firms cannot and will not provide

- private non-profit organization tends to receive benefits from society that a private profit-making firm cannot obtain.

- differentiates not-for-profit organizations from each other as well as well as from profit making organizations
  - sale of goods and services to customers who pay for the cost and expenses of providing the product and services

- **source**
  - dues
  - assessments
  - donations
  - funding from an agency

- **five constraints**
  - service is often intangible and hard to measure
  - client influence might be weak
  - strong employee commitment to professions or to a cause may undermine allegiance
  - resource contributors may intrude on the organizations' internal management
  - restraints on the use of rewards and punishments

- **impact on strategy formulation**
  - four complications to strategic formulation
    - goal conflicts interfere with rational planning
    - an integrated planning focus tends to shift from results to resources
    - ambiguous operating objectives create opportunities for internal politics and goal displacement
    - professionalization simplifies detailed planning but adds rigidity

- **impact on strategic implementations**
  - complications to strategic implementation
    - decentralization is complicated
    - linking pins for external – internal integration become important
    - job enlargement and executive development can be restrained by professionalism

- **impact on evaluation and control**
  - complications to evaluation and control
    - rewards and penalties have little or no relationship to performance
    - inputs rather than outputs are heavily controlled

KEY TERMS

complication to evaluation and control (p. 475)

complication to strategy formulation (p. 474)

complication to strategy implementation (p. 475)

constraint on strategic management (p. 473)

defensive centralization (p. 475)

institutional advantage (p. 473)

not-for-profit organization (p. 468)

pattern of influence (p. 472)

private nonprofit corporation (p. 468)

privatization (p. 470)

profit-making firm (p. 470)

public governmental unit or agency (p. 468)

public or collective good (p. 469)

social entrepreneurship (p. 477)

strategic piggybacking (p. 477)

NOTES

1. R. Imrie, "Ink Venture Reaps Profits for High-Tech Monks," *Des Moines Register* (February 27, 2004), p. 3D; G. Williams, "Charity Begins at Work," *Entrepreneur* (December 2005), p. 40.

2. C. Penttila, "Heart of Gold," *Entrepreneur* (September 2004), pp. 19–22.

3. Ibid., p. 22.

4. P. F. Drucker, "What Business Can Learn from Nonprofits," *Harvard Business Review* (July–August 1989), p. 89.

5. "The Non-Profit Sector: Love or Money," *The Economist* (November 14, 1998), pp. 68–73.

6. G. Rudney, "The Scope and Dimensions of Nonprofit Activity," in *The Nonprofit Sector: A Research Handbook*, edited by W. W. Powell (New Haven, CT: Yale University Press, 1987), p. 56; C. P. McLaughlin, *The Management of Nonprofit Organizations* (New York: John Wiley & Sons, 1986), p. 4.

7. M. O'Neill, *The Third America* (San Francisco: Jossey-Bass, 1989).

8. K. Ascher and B. Nare, "Strategic Planning in the Public Sector," *International Review of Strategic Management*, Vol. 1, edited by D. E. Hussey (New York: John Wiley & Sons, 1990), pp. 297–315; I. Unterman and R. H. Davis, *Strategic Management of Not-for-Profit Organizations* (New York: Praeger Press, 1984), p. 2.

9. P. V. Jenster and G. A. Overstreet, "Planning for a Non-Profit Service: A Study of U.S. Credit Unions," *Long Range Planning* (April 1990), pp. 103–111; G. J. Medley, "Strategic Planning for the World Wildlife Fund," *Long Range Planning* (February 1988), pp. 46–54.

10. J. G. Simon, "The Tax Treatment of Nonprofit Organizations: A Review of Federal and State Policies," in *The Nonprofit Sector: A Research Handbook*, edited by W. W. Powell (New Haven, CT: Yale University Press, 1987), pp. 67–98.

11. B. P. Keating and M. O. Keating, *Not-for-Profit* (Glen Ridge, NJ: Thomas Horton & Daughters, 1980), p. 21.

12. K. A. Froelich, "Business Management in Nonprofit Organizations," paper presented to the Midwest Management Society (Chicago, 1995).

13. J. D. Hunger and T. L. Wheelen, "Is Strategic Management Appropriate for Not-for-Profit Organizations?" in *Handbook of Business Strategy, 1989/90 Yearbook*, edited by H. E. Glass (Boston: Warren, Gorham & Lamont, 1989), pp. 3.1–3.8. The contention that the pattern of environmental influence on the organization's strategic decision making derives from the organization's source(s) of income agrees with the authorities in the field. See R. E. Emerson, "Power-Dependence Relations," *American Sociological Review* (February 1962), pp. 31–41;

J. D. Thompson, *Organizations in Action* (New York: McGraw-Hill, 1967), pp. 30–31, and J. Pfeffer and G. R. Salancik, *The External Control of Organizations: A Resource Dependence Perspective* (New York: HarperCollins, 1978), p. 44.

14. M. Goold, "Institutional Advantage: A Way into Strategic Management in Not-for-Profit Organizations," *Long Range Planning* (April 1997), pp. 291–293.

15. K. Ascher and B. Nare, "Strategic Planning in the Public Sector," *International Review of Strategic Management*, Vol. 1, edited by D. E. Hussey (New York: John Wiley & Sons, 1990), pp. 297–315; R. McGill, "Planning for Strategic Performance in Local Government," *Long Range Planning* (October 1988), pp. 77–84.

16. Lorna Lavender, Supervisor of Ames (Iowa) Animal Shelter, quoted by K. Petty, "Animal Shelter Cares for Homeless," *ISU Daily* (July 25, 1996), p. 3.

17. E. Ferlie, "The Creation and Evolution of Quasi Markets in the Public Sector: A Problem for Strategic Management," *Strategic Management Journal* (Winter 1992), pp. 79–97. Research has found that profit-making hospitals have more mission statement components dealing with principal services, target customers, and geographic domain than do not-for-profit hospitals. See R. Subramanian, K. Kumar, and C. C. Yauger, "Mission Statements of Hospitals: An Empirical Analysis of Their Contents and Their Relationship to Organizational Factors," *Journal of Business Strategies* (Spring 1993), pp. 63–78.

18. W. H. Newman and H. W. Wallender III, "Managing Not-for-Profit Enterprises," *Academy of Management Review* (January 1978), p. 26.

19. Ibid., p. 27. The following discussion of the effects of these constraining characteristics is taken from pp. 27–31.

20. J. Denis, A. Langley, and D. Lozeau, "Formal Strategy in Public Hospitals," *Long Range Planning* (February 1991), pp. 71–82.

21. F. Heffron, *Organization Theory and Public Administration* (Upper Saddle River, NJ: Prentice Hall, 1989), p. 132.

22. V. K. Rangan, "Lofty Missions, Down-to-Earth Plans," *Harvard Business Review* (March 2004), pp. 112–119.

23. F. Heffron, *Organization Theory and Public Administration* (Upper Saddle River, NJ: Prentice Hall, 1989), pp. 103–115.

24. R. T. Ingram, *Ten Basic Responsibilities of Nonprofit Boards*, 2nd ed. (Washington, DC: National Center for Nonprofit Boards, 1997), pp. 9–10.

25. A. C. Smith, "Endowment Use Overlooked," *St. Petersburg Times* (June 23, 2000), p. 3B. Eckerd's board was strongly criticized because it had tolerated improper financial practices

on the part of the president and had allowed the college's endowment to dissipate.

26. I. Unterman and R. H. Davis, *Strategic Management of Not-for-Profit Organizations* (New York: Praeger Press, 1984), p. 174; J. A. Alexander, M. L. Fennell, and M. T. Halpern, "Leadership Instability in Hospitals: The Influence of Board–CEO Relations and Organizational Growth and Decline," *Administrative Science Quarterly* (March 1993), pp. 74–99.

27. K. A. Froelich, "Business Management in Nonprofit Organizations," paper presented to the Midwest Management Society (Chicago, 1995), p. 9.

28. R. M. Kanter and D. V. Summers, "Doing Well While Doing Good: Dilemmas of Performance Measurement in Nonprofit Organizations and the Need for a Multiple-Constituency Approach," in *The Nonprofit Sector: A Research Handbook*, edited by W. W. Powell (New Haven, CT: Yale University Press, 1987), p. 163.

29. J. P. Dalsimer, *Understanding Nonprofit Financial Statement: A Primer for Board Members*, 2nd ed. (Washington, DC: National Center for Nonprofit Boards, 1997), p. 17.

30. V. K. Rangan, "Loft Missions: Down-to-Earth Plans," *Harvard Business Review* (March 2004), pp. 112–119.

31. Ibid., p. 115.

32. R. P. Nielsen, "SMR Forum: Strategic Piggybacking—A Self-Subsidizing Strategy for Nonprofit Institutions," *Sloan Management Review* (Summer 1982), pp. 65–69; R. P. Nielsen, "Piggybacking for Business and Nonprofits: A Strategy for Hard Times," *Long Range Planning* (April 1984), pp. 96–102.

33. D. C. Bacon, "Nonprofit Groups: An Unfair Edge?" *Nation's Business* (April 1989), pp. 33–34; "Universities Push Auxiliary Services to Generate More Revenue," *Wall Street Journal* (April 27, 1995), p. A1.

34. M. Langley, "Nonprofit Hospitals Sometimes Are That in Little but Name," *Wall Street Journal* (July 14, 1997), p. A1. See also D. Brady, "When Nonprofits Go After Profits," *Business Week* (June 26, 2000), pp. 173–178; E. Skloot, "Should Not-for-Profits Go into Business?" *Harvard Business Review* (January–February 1983), p. 21; E. Felsenthal, "As Nonprofits Add Sidelines, IRS Takes Aim," *Wall Street Journal* (May 3, 1996), p. B1.

35. C. Penttila, "Heart of Gold," *Entrepreneur* (September 2004), p. 22.

36. R. P. Nielsen, "Piggybacking Strategies for Nonprofits: A Shared Costs Approach," *Strategic Management Journal* (May–June 1986), pp. 209–211.

37. "Universities Push Auxiliary Services to Generate More Revenue" (Business Bulletin), *Wall Street Journal* (April 27, 1995), p. A1.

38. R. A. Krishnan, S. Joshi, and H. Krishnan, "The Influence of Mergers on Firms' Product-Mix Strategies," *Strategic Management Journal* (June 2004), pp. 587–611.

39. Ibid.

40. K. G. Provan, "Interorganizational Cooperation and Decision Making Autonomy in a Consortium Multihospital System," *Academy of Management Review* (July 1984), pp. 494–504; R. D. Luke, J. W. Begun, and D. D. Pointer, "Quasi-Firms: Strategic Interorganizational Forms in the Health Care Industry," *Academy of Management Review* (January 1989), pp. 9–19.

41. "More Colleges Are Opting for Mergers," *The (Ames, IA) Daily Tribune* (August 12, 1998), p. B3.

42. *Pocket World in Figures 2004* (London: Economist and Profile Books, 2003), p. 95.

43. Ibid., p. 83.

PART 5

Introduction to Case Analysis

suggestions for
Case Analysis

Howard Schilit, founder of the Center for Financial Research & Analysis (CFRA), works with a staff of 15 analysts to screen financial databases and analyze public financial filings of 3,600 companies, looking for inconsistencies and aggressive accounting methods. Schilit calls this search for hidden weaknesses in a company's performance *forensic accounting*. "I'm like an investigative reporter," explains Schilit. "I'm interested in finding companies where the conventional wisdom is that they're very healthy, but if you dig a bit deeper, you find the emperor is not wearing the clothes you thought."[1] He advises anyone interested in analyzing a company to look deeply into its financial statements. For example, when the CFRA noticed that Kraft Foods made $122 million in acquisitions in 2002, but claimed $539 million as "goodwill" assets related to the purchases, it concluded that Kraft was padding its earnings with one-time gains. According to Schilit, unusually high goodwill gains related to recent acquisitions is a *red flag* that suggests an underlying problem.

Schilit proposes a short checklist of items to examine for red flags:

- **Cash flow from operations should exceed net income:** If cash flow from operations drops below net income, it could mean that the company is propping up its earnings by selling assets, borrowing cash, or shuffling numbers. Says Schilit, "You could have spotted the problems at Enron by just doing this."[2]

- **Accounts receivable should not grow faster than sales:** A firm facing slowing sales can make itself look better by inflating accounts receivable with expected future sales and by making sales to customers who are not credit worthy. "It's like mailing a contract to a dead person and then counting it as a sale," says Schilit.[3]

- **Gross margins should not fluctuate over time:** A change of more than 2% in either direction from year to year is worth a closer look. It could mean that the company is using other revenue, such as sales of assets or write-offs to boost profits. Sunbeam reported an increase of 10% in gross margins just before it was investigated by the SEC.

- **Examine carefully information about top management and the board:** When Schilit learned that the chairman of Checkers Restaurants had put his two young sons on the board, he warned investors of nepotism. Two years later, Checkers' huge debt caused its stock to fall 85% and all three family members were forced out of the company.

Learning Objectives

After reading this chapter, you should be able to:

- Research the case situation as needed
- Analyze financial statements by using ratios and common-size statements
- Use the strategic audit as a method of organizing and analyzing case information

- **Footnotes are important:** When companies change their accounting assumptions to make the statements more attractive, they often bury their rationale in the footnotes. Schilit dislikes companies that extend the depreciable life of their assets. "There's only one reason to do that—to add a penny or two to earnings—and it makes me very mistrustful of management."[4]

Schilit makes his living analyzing companies and selling his reports to investors. Annual reports and financial statements provide a lot of information about a company's health, but it's hard to find problem areas when management is massaging the numbers to make the company appear more attractive than it is. That's why Michelle Leder created her Web site, www.footnoted.org. She likes to highlight "the things that companies bury in their routine SEC filings."[5] This type of in-depth, investigative analysis is a key part of analyzing strategy cases. This chapter provides various analytical techniques and suggestions for conducting this kind of case analysis.

15.1 The Case Method

The analysis and discussion of case problems has been the most popular method of teaching strategy and policy for many years. The case method provides the opportunity to move from a narrow, specialized view that emphasizes functional techniques to a broader, less precise analysis of the overall corporation. Cases present actual business situations and enable you to examine both successful and unsuccessful corporations. In case analysis, you might be asked to critically analyze a situation in which a manager had to make a decision of long-term corporate importance. This approach gives you a feel for what it is like to face making and implementing strategic decisions.

15.2 Researching the Case Situation

You should not restrict yourself only to the information written in the case unless your instructor states otherwise. You should, if possible, undertake outside research about the environmental setting. Check the decision date of each case (typically the latest date mentioned in the case) to find out when the situation occurred and then screen the business periodicals for that time period. An understanding of the economy during that period will help you avoid making a serious error in your analysis, for example, suggesting a sale of stock when the stock market is at an all-time low or taking on more debt when the prime interest rate is over 15%. Information about the industry will provide insights into its competitive activities. *Important Note: Don't go beyond the decision date of the case in your research unless directed to do so by your instructor.*

Use computerized company and industry information services such as Compustat, Compact Disclosure, and CD/International, available on CD-ROM or online at the library. On the Internet, Hoover's OnLine Corporate Directory (www.hoovers.com) and the Security Exchange Commission's Edgar database (www.sec.gov) provide access to corporate annual reports and 10-K forms. This background will give you an appreciation for the situation as it was experienced by the participants in the case. Use a search engine such as Google to find additional information about the industry and the company.

A company's **annual report** and **SEC 10-K form** from the year of the case can be very helpful. According to the Yankelovich Partners survey firm, 8 out of 10 portfolio managers and 75% of security analysts use annual reports when making decisions.[6] They contain not only the usual income statements and balance sheets, but also cash flow statements and notes to the financial statements indicating why certain actions were taken. 10-K forms include detailed information not usually available in an annual report. **SEC 10-Q forms** include quarterly financial reports. **SEC 14-A forms** include detailed information on members of a company's board of directors and proxy statements for annual meetings. Some resources available for research into the economy and a corporation's industry are suggested in **Appendix 15.A**.

A caveat: Before obtaining additional information about the company profiled in a particular case, ask your instructor if doing so is appropriate for your class assignment. Your strategy instructor may want you to stay within the confines of the case information provided in the book. In this case, it is usually acceptable to at least learn more about the societal environment at the time of the case.

15.3 Financial Analysis: A Place to Begin

Once you have read a case, a good place to begin your analysis is with the financial statements. **Ratio analysis** is the calculation of ratios from data in these statements. It is done to identify possible financial strengths or weaknesses. Thus it is a valuable part of SWOT analysis. A review of key financial ratios can help you assess a company's overall situation and pinpoint some problem areas. Ratios are useful regardless of firm size and enable you to compare a company's ratios with industry averages. **Table 15-1** lists some of the most important financial ratios, which are (1) **liquidity ratios**, (2) **profitability ratios**, (3) **activity ratios**, and (4) **leverage ratios**.

TABLE 15–1	Financial Ratio Analysis		
	Formula	How Expressed	Meaning
1. Liquidity Ratios Current ratio	$$\frac{\text{Current assets}}{\text{Current liabilities}}$$	Decimal	A short-term indicator of the company's ability to pay its short-term liabilities from short-term assets; how much of current assets are available to cover each dollar of current liabilities.
Quick (acid test) ratio	$$\frac{\text{Current assets} - \text{Inventory}}{\text{Current liabilities}}$$	Decimal	Measures the company's ability to pay off its short-term obligations from current assets, excluding inventories.
Inventory to net working capital	$$\frac{\text{Inventory}}{\text{Current assets} - \text{Current liabilities}}$$	Decimal	A measure of inventory balance; measures the extent to which the cushion of excess current assets over current liabilities may be threatened by unfavorable changes in inventory.
Cash ratio	$$\frac{\text{Cash} + \text{Cash equivalents}}{\text{Current liabilities}}$$	Decimal	Measures the extent to which the company's capital is in cash or cash equivalents; shows how much of the current obligations can be paid from cash or near-cash assets.
2. Profitability Ratios Net profit margin	$$\frac{\text{Net profit after taxes}}{\text{Net sales}}$$	Percentage	Shows how much after-tax profits are generated by each dollar of sales.
Gross profit margin	$$\frac{\text{Sales} - \text{Cost of goods sold}}{\text{Net sales}}$$	Percentage	Indicates the total margin available to cover other expenses beyond cost of goods sold and still yield a profit.
Return on investment (ROI)	$$\frac{\text{Net profit after taxes}}{\text{Total assets}}$$	Percentage	Measures the rate of return on the total assets utilized in the company; a measure of management's efficiency, it shows the return on all the assets under its control, regardless of source of financing.
Return on equity (ROE)	$$\frac{\text{Net profit after taxes}}{\text{Shareholders' equity}}$$	Percentage	Measures the rate of return on the book value of shareholders' total investment in the company.
Earnings per share (EPS)	$$\frac{\text{Net profit after taxes} - \text{Preferred stock dividends}}{\text{Average number of common shares}}$$	Dollars per share	Shows the after-tax earnings generated for each share of common stock.
3. Activity Ratios Inventory turnover	$$\frac{\text{Net sales}}{\text{Inventory}}$$	Decimal	Measures the number of times that average inventory of finished goods was turned over or sold during a period of time, usually a year.
Days of inventory	$$\frac{\text{Inventory}}{\text{Cost of goods sold} \div 365}$$	Days	Measures the number of one day's worth of inventory that a company has on hand at any given time.

continued

TABLE 15-1 Financial Ratio Analysis, (continued)

	Formula	How Expressed	Meaning
Net working capital turnover	$\dfrac{\text{Net sales}}{\text{Net working capital}}$	Decimal	Measures how effectively the net working capital is used to generate sales.
Asset turnover	$\dfrac{\text{Sales}}{\text{Total assets}}$	Decimal	Measures the utilization of all the company's assets; measures how many sales are generated by each dollar of assets.
Fixed asset turnover	$\dfrac{\text{Sales}}{\text{Fixed assets}}$	Decimal	Measures the utilization of the company's fixed assets (i.e., plant and equipment); measures how many sales are generated by each dollar of fixed assets.
Average collection period	$\dfrac{\text{Accounts receivable}}{\text{Sales for year} \div 365}$	Days	Indicates the average length of time in days that a company must wait to collect a sale after making it; may be compared to the credit terms offered by the company to its customers.
Accounts receivable turnover	$\dfrac{\text{Annual credit sales}}{\text{Accounts receivable}}$	Decimal	Indicates the number of times that accounts receivable are cycled during the period (usually a year).
Accounts payable period	$\dfrac{\text{Accounts payable}}{\text{Purchases for year} \div 365}$	Days	Indicates the average length of time in days that the company takes to pay its credit purchases.
Days of cash	$\dfrac{\text{Cash}}{\text{Net sales for year} \div 365}$	Days	Indicates the number of days of cash on hand, at present sales levels.
4. Leverage Ratios Debt to asset ratio	$\dfrac{\text{Total debt}}{\text{Total assets}}$	Percentage	Measures the extent to which borrowed funds have been used to finance the company's assets.
Debt to equity ratio	$\dfrac{\text{Total debt}}{\text{Shareholders' equity}}$	Percentage	Measures the funds provided by creditors versus the funds provided by owners.
Long-term debt to capital structure	$\dfrac{\text{Long-term debt}}{\text{Shareholders' equity}}$	Percentage	Measures the long-term component of capital structure.
Times interest earned	$\dfrac{\text{Profit before taxes} + \text{Interest charges}}{\text{Interest charges}}$	Decimal	Indicates the ability of the company to meet its annual interest costs.
Coverage of fixed charges	$\dfrac{\text{Profit before taxes} + \text{Interest charges} + \text{Lease charges}}{\text{Interest charges} + \text{Lease obligations}}$	Decimal	A measure of the company's ability to meet all of its fixed-charge obligations.
Current liabilities to equity	$\dfrac{\text{Current liabilities}}{\text{Shareholders' equity}}$	Percentage	Measures the short-term financing portion versus that provided by owners.

TABLE 15–1	Financial Ratio Analysis, (continued)		
	Formula	How Expressed	Meaning
5. Other Ratios Price/earnings ratio	$$\frac{\text{Market price per share}}{\text{Earnings per share}}$$	Decimal	Shows the current market's evaluation of a stock, based on its earnings; shows how much the investor is willing to pay for each dollar of earnings.
Divided payout ratio	$$\frac{\text{Annual dividends per share}}{\text{Annual earnings per share}}$$	Percentage	Indicates the percentage of profit that is paid out as dividends.
Dividend yield on common stock	$$\frac{\text{Annual dividends per share}}{\text{Current market price per share}}$$	Percentage	Indicates the dividend rate of return to common shareholders at the current market price.

NOTE: In using ratios for analysis, calculate ratios for the corporation and compare them to the average and quartile ratios for the particular industry. Refer to Standard & Poor's and Robert Morris Associates for average industry data. Special thanks to Dr. Moustafa H. Abdelsamad, Dean, Business School, Texas A&M University—Corpus Christi, Corpus Christi, Texas, for his definitions of these ratios.

ANALYZING FINANCIAL STATEMENTS

In your analysis, do not simply make an exhibit that includes all the ratios (unless your instructor requires you to do so), but select and discuss only those ratios that have an impact on the company's problems. For instance, accounts receivable and inventory may provide a source of funds. If receivables and inventories are double the industry average, reducing them may provide needed cash. In this situation, the case report should include not only sources of funds but also the number of dollars freed for use. Compare these ratios with industry averages to discover whether the company is out of line with others in the industry. Annual and quarterly industry ratios can be found in the library or on the Internet. (See the resources for case research in **Appendix 15.A.**) In the years to come, expect to see financial entries for the trading of CERs (Certified Emissions Reductions). This is the amount of money a company earns from reducing carbon emissions and selling them on the open market. To learn how carbon trading is likely to affect corporations, see the **Environmental Sustainability Issue**.

A typical financial analysis of a firm would include a study of the operating statements for five or so years, including a trend analysis of sales, profits, earnings per share, debt-to-equity ratio, return on investment, and so on, plus a ratio study comparing the firm under study with industry standards. As a minimum, undertake the following five steps in basic financial analysis.

1. **Scrutinize historical income statements and balance sheets:** These two basic statements provide most of the data needed for analysis. Statements of cash flow may also be useful.

2. **Compare historical statements over time** if a series of statements is available.

3. **Calculate changes that occur in individual categories from year to year,** as well as the cumulative total change.

4. **Determine the change as a percentage** as well as an absolute amount.

5. **Adjust for inflation** if that was a significant factor.

Examination of this information may reveal developing trends. Compare trends in one category with trends in related categories. For example, an increase in sales of 15% over three years may appear to be satisfactory until you note an increase of 20% in the cost of goods sold during the same period. The outcome of this comparison might suggest that further investiga-

ENVIRONMENTAL sustainability issue

IMPACT OF CARBON TRADING

Do you know about carbon trading, emissions allowances, cap-and-trade, or CERs? These are terms you can expect to hear a lot more in the years to come. The concept of carbon trading is something that will soon be affecting the balance sheets and income statements of all corporations, especially those with international operations. It is one way to account for environmental sustainability initiatives.

The Kyoto Protocol established an emissions trading program that assigned annual limits on greenhouse gases emitted by facilities within each country's boundaries. The countries signing the pact, including Canada, Japan, and the European Union, were then able to trade emission surpluses and deficits with each other. In addition, individual countries or companies could invest in projects in developing nations that would reduce emissions and use those reductions to meet their own targets.

In 2005 the European Union initiated a trading system allowing individual facilities to sell credit allowances they had earned for reducing greenhouse gas emissions. It created a tradable commodity, the Certified Emissions Reduction (CER), which gave a facility the right to emit one metric ton of carbon dioxide annually. The CER was created by another facility that reduced its carbon dioxide emissions. (Reducing or trapping one metric ton of methane from entering the atmosphere was worth 21 CERs due to

methane's greater impact on global warming.) By 2006, a CER traded on the European market for around 25 euros with trading volume totaling one million CERs per day. Barclays, Citibank, Credit Suisse, HSBC, Lehman Brothers, and Morgan Stanley soon opened trading desks for CERs at London's Canary Wharf, the global center for carbon trading. By 2007, European and Asian traders bought and sold approximately $60 billion worth of emission CERs.

Carbon trading has created an opportunity for new and established companies. For example, Mission Point Capital Partners is one of more than 50 private equity and hedge funds specializing in carbon finance and clean energy. Mission Point created a joint venture in 2008 with GE and AES to develop large volumes of emissions credits. These would be sold to U.S. companies like Yahoo! and News Corp that wanted to become carbon neutral by offsetting their carbon emissions. Assuming that the U.S. federal government would soon establish a cap-and-trade market for emissions, the joint venture partners expected to produce 10 million tons of emission credits by 2010. According to Kevin Walsh, managing director of GE Energy Financial Services, "We think this is going to be an enormous market."

....
SOURCE: A. White, "Environment: The Greening of the Balance Sheet," *Harvard Business Review* (March 2006), pp. 27–28; M. Gunther, "Carbon Finance Comes of Age," *Fortune* (April 28, 2008), pp. 124–132.

tion into the manufacturing process is necessary. If a company is reporting strong net income growth but negative cash flow, this would suggest that the company is relying on something other than operations for earnings growth. Is it selling off assets or cutting R&D? If accounts receivable are growing faster than sales revenues, the company is not getting paid for the products or services it is counting as sold. Is the company dumping product on its distributors at the end of the year to boost its reported annual sales? If so, expect the distributors to return the unordered product the next month, thus drastically cutting the next year's reported sales.

Other "tricks of the trade" need to be examined. Until June 2000, firms growing through acquisition were allowed to account for the cost of the purchased company, through the pooling of both companies' stock. This approach was used in 40% of the value of mergers between 1997 and 1999. The pooling method enabled the acquiring company to disregard the premium it paid for the other firm (the amount above the fair market value of the purchased company often called "good will"). Thus, when PepsiCo agreed to purchase Quaker Oats for $13.4 billion in PepsiCo stock, the $13.4 billion was not found on PepsiCo's balance sheet. As of June 2000, merging firms must use the "purchase" accounting rules in which the true purchase price is reflected in the financial statements.[7]

The analysis of a multinational corporation's financial statements can get very complicated, especially if its headquarters is in another country that uses different accounting standards. See the **Global Issue** for why financial analysis can get tricky at times.

GLOBAL issue

FINANCIAL STATEMENTS OF MULTINATIONAL CORPORATIONS: NOT ALWAYS WHAT THEY SEEM

A multinational corporation follows the accounting rules for its home country. As a result, its financial statements may be somewhat difficult to understand or to use for comparisons with competitors from other countries. For example, British firms such as British Petroleum use the term *turnover* rather than *sales revenue*. In the case of AB Electrolux of Sweden, a footnote to an annual report indicates that the consolidated accounts have been prepared in accordance with Swedish accounting standards, which differ in certain significant respects from U.S. generally accepted accounting principles (U.S. GAAP). For one year, net income of 4,830m SEK (Swedish kronor) approximated 5,655m SEK according to U.S. GAAP. Total assets for the same period were 84,183m SEK according to Swedish principle, but 86,658m according to U.S. GAAP.

COMMON-SIZE STATEMENTS

Common-size statements are income statements and balance sheets in which the dollar figures have been converted into percentages. These statements are used to identify trends in each of the categories, such as cost of goods sold as a percentage of sales (sales is the denominator). For the income statement, net sales represent 100%: calculate the percentage for each category so that the categories sum to the net sales percentage (100%). For the balance sheet, give the total assets a value of 100% and calculate other asset and liability categories as percentages of the total assets with total assets as the denominator. (Individual asset and liability items, such as accounts receivable and accounts payable, can also be calculated as a percentage of net sales.)

When you convert statements to this form, it is relatively easy to note the percentage that each category represents of the total. Look for trends in specific items, such as cost of goods sold, when compared to the company's historical figures. To get a proper picture, however, you need to make comparisons with industry data, if available, to see whether fluctuations are merely reflecting industry-wide trends. If a firm's trends are generally in line with those of the rest of the industry, problems are less likely than if the firm's trends are worse than industry averages. If ratios are not available for the industry, calculate the ratios for the industry's best and worst firms and compare them to the firm you are analyzing. Common-size statements are especially helpful in developing scenarios and pro forma statements because they provide a series of historical relationships (for example, cost of goods sold to sales, interest to sales, and inventories as a percentage of assets) from which you can estimate the future with your scenario assumptions for each year.

Z-VALUE AND INDEX OF SUSTAINABLE GROWTH

If the corporation being studied appears to be in poor financial condition, use **Altman's Z-Value Bankruptcy Formula** to calculate its likelihood of going bankrupt. The *Z-value* formula combines five ratios by weighting them according to their importance to a corporation's financial strength. The formula is:

$$Z = 1.2x_1 + 1.4x_2 + 3.3x_3 + 0.6x_4 + 1.0x_5$$

where:

x_1 = Working capital/Total assets (%)

$$x_2 = \text{Retained earnings/Total assets (\%)}$$

$$x_3 = \text{Earnings before interest and taxes/Total assets (\%)}$$

$$x_4 = \text{Market value of equity/Total liabilities (\%)}$$

$$x_5 = \text{Sales/Total assets (number of times)}$$

A score below 1.81 indicates significant credit problems, whereas a score above 3.0 indicates a healthy firm. Scores between 1.81 and 3.0 indicate question marks.[8] The Altman Z model has achieved a remarkable 94% accuracy in predicting corporate bankruptcies. Its accuracy is excellent in the two years before financial distress, but diminishes as the lead time increases.[9]

The **index of sustainable growth** is useful to learn whether a company embarking on a growth strategy will need to take on debt to fund this growth. The index indicates how much of the growth rate of sales can be sustained by internally generated funds. The formula is:

$$g^* = \frac{[P(1 - D)(1 + L)]}{[T - P(1 - D)(1 + L)]}$$

where:

$$P = (\text{Net profit before tax/Net sales}) \times 100$$

$$D = \text{Target dividends/Profit after tax}$$

$$L = \text{Total liabilities/Net worth}$$

$$T = (\text{Total assets/Net sales}) \times 100$$

If the planned growth rate calls for a growth rate higher than its g*, external capital will be needed to fund the growth unless management is able to find efficiencies, decrease dividends, increase the debt-equity ratio, or reduce assets through renting or leasing arrangements.[10]

USEFUL ECONOMIC MEASURES

If you are analyzing a company over many years, you may want to adjust sales and net income for inflation to arrive at "true" financial performance in constant dollars. **Constant dollars** are dollars adjusted for inflation to make them comparable over various years. One way to adjust for inflation in the United States is to use the Consumer Price Index (CPI), as given in **Table 15–2.** Dividing sales and net income by the CPI factor for that year will change the figures to 1982–1984 U.S. constant dollars (when the CPI was 1.0). Adjusting for inflation is especially important for companies operating in the emerging economies, like China and Russia, where inflation in 2008 rose to 6.6%, the highest in 10 years. In that same year, Zimbabwe's inflation rate was the highest in the world at 2.2 million%![11]

Another helpful analytical aid provided in **Table 15–2** is the **prime interest rate**, the rate of interest banks charge on their lowest-risk loans. For better assessments of strategic decisions, it can be useful to note the level of the prime interest rate at the time of the case. A decision to borrow money to build a new plant would have been a good one in 2003 at 4.1% but less practical in 2007 when the average rate was 8.1%.

In preparing a scenario for your pro forma financial statements, you may want to use the **gross domestic product (GDP)** from **Table 15–2.** GDP is used worldwide and measures the total output of goods and services within a country's borders. The amount of change from one year to the next indicates how much that country's economy is growing. Remember that scenarios have to be adjusted for a country's specific conditions. For other economic information, see the resources for case research in **Appendix 15.A.**

TABLE 15–2	Year	GDP (in $ billions) Gross Domestic Product	CPI (for all items) Consumer Price Index	PIR (in %) Prime Interest Rate
U.S. Economic Indicators	1980	2,789.5	.824	15.27
	1985	4,220.3	1.076	9.93
	1990	5,803.1	1.307	10.01
	1995	7,397.7	1.524	8.83
	1996	7,816.9	1.569	8.27
	1997	8,304.3	1.605	8.44
	1998	8,747.0	1.630	8.35
	1999	9,268.4	1.666	7.99
	2000	9,817.0	1.722	9.23
	2001	10,128.0	1.771	6.92
	2002	10,469.6	1.799	4.68
	2003	10,960.8	1.840	4.12
	2004	11,685.9	1.889	4.29
	2005	12,421.9	1.953	6.10
	2006	13,178.4	2.016	7.94
	2007	13,807.5	2.073	8.08
	2008	14,280.7	2.153	5.21

NOTES: Gross Domestic Product (GDP) in Billions of Dollars; Consumer Price Index for All Items (CPI) (1982–84 = 1.0); Prime Interest Rate (PIR) in Percentages.

SOURCES: Gross Domestic Product (GDP) from U.S. Bureau of Economic Analysis, National Economic Accounts (www.bea.gov). Consumer Price Index (CPI) from U.S. Bureau of Labor Statistics (www.bls.gov). Prime Interest Rate (PIR) from www.moneycafe.com.

15.4 Format for Case Analysis: The Strategic Audit

There is no one best way to analyze or present a case report. Each instructor has personal preferences for format and approach. Nevertheless, in **Appendix 15.B** we suggest an approach for both written and oral reports that provides a systematic method for successfully attacking a case. This approach is based on the strategic audit, which is presented at the end of **Chapter 1** in **Appendix 1.A**). We find that this approach provides structure and is very helpful for the typical student who may be a relative novice in case analysis. Regardless of the format chosen, be careful to include a complete analysis of key environmental variables—especially of trends in the industry and of the competition. Look at international developments as well.

If you choose to use the strategic audit as a guide to the analysis of complex strategy cases, you may want to use the **strategic audit worksheet** in **Figure 15–1**. Print a copy of the worksheet to use to take notes as you analyze a case. See **Appendix 15.C** for an example of a completed student-written analysis of a 1993 Maytag Corporation case done in an outline form using the strategic audit format. This is one example of what a case analysis in outline form may look like.

Case discussion focuses on critical analysis and logical development of thought. A solution is satisfactory if it resolves important problems and is likely to be implemented successfully. How the corporation actually dealt with the case problems has no real bearing on the analysis because management might have analyzed its problems incorrectly or implemented a series of flawed solutions.

FIGURE 15–1
Strategic Audit
Worksheet

Strategic Audit Heading	Analysis		Comments
	(+) Factors	(−) Factors	
I. Current Situation			
A. Past Corporate Performance Indexes			
B. Strategic Posture: Current Mission Current Objectives Current Strategies Current Policies			
SWOT Analysis Begins:			
II. Corporate Governance			
A. Board of Directors			
B. Top Management			
III. External Environment (EFAS): **Opportunities and Threats (SWOT)**			
A. Natural Environment			
B. Societal Environment			
C. Task Environment (Industry Analysis)			
IV. Internal Environment (IFAS): **Strengths and Weaknesses (SWOT)**			
A. Corporate Structure			
B. Corporate Culture			
C. Corporate Resources			
1. Marketing			
2. Finance			
3. Research and Development			
4. Operations and Logistics			
5. Human Resources			
6. Information Technology			
V. Analysis of Strategic Factors (SFAS)			
A. Key Internal and External Strategic Factors (SWOT)			
B. Review of Mission and Objectives			
SWOT Analysis Ends. Recommendation Begins:			
VI. Alternatives and Recommendations			
A. Strategic Alternatives—pros and cons			
B. Recommended Strategy			
VII. Implementation			
VIII. Evaluation and Control			

NOTE: See the complete Strategic Audit on pages 34–41. It lists the pages in the book that discuss each of the eight headings.

SOURCE: T. L. Wheelen and J. D. Hunger, "Strategic Audit Worksheet." Copyright © 1985, 1986, 1987, 1988, 1989, 2005, and 2009 by T. L. Wheelen. Copyright © 1989, 2005, and 2009 by Wheelen and Hunger Associates. Revised 1991, 1994, and 1997. Reprinted by permission. Additional copies available for classroom use in Part D of *Case Instructors Manual* and on the Prentice Hall Web site (www.prenhall.com/wheelen).

ECO-BITS

- A 2007 McKinsey & Company survey of 7,751 people in eight countries found that 87% of consumers worry about the environment and the social impact of the products they buy.

- The same 2007 survey found that only 33% of the consumers said that they were ready to buy green products or had already done so.

- In a 2007 *Chain Store Age* survey of U.S. consumers, only 25% of them had bought any green products other than organic food or energy-efficient lighting.[12]

DISCUSSION QUESTIONS

1. Why should you begin a case analysis with a financial analysis? When are other approaches appropriate?

2. What are common-size financial statements? What is their value to case analysis? How are they calculated?

3. When should you gather information outside a case by going to the library or using the Internet? What should you look for?

4. When is inflation an important issue in conducting case analysis? Why bother?

5. How can you learn what date a case took place?

STRATEGIC PRACTICE EXERCISE

Convert the following two years of income statements from the Maytag Corporation into common-size statements. The dollar figures are in thousands. What does converting to a common size reveal?

Consolidated Statements of Income: Maytag Corporation

	1992	%	1991	%
Net sales	$3,041,223	100	$2,970,626	100
Cost of sales	2,339,406	—	2,254,221	—
Gross profits	701,817	—	716,405	—
Selling, general, & admin. expenses	528,250	—	524,898	—
Reorganization expenses	95,000	—	0	—
Operating income	78,567	—	191,507	—
Interest expense	(75,004)	—	(75,159)	—
Other—net	3,983	—	7,069	—
Income before taxes and accounting changes	7,546	—	123,417	—
Income taxes	(15,900)	—	(44,400)	—
Income before accounting changes	(8,354)	—	79,017	—
Effects of accounting changes for postretirement benefits	(307,000)	—	0	—
Net income (loss)	$(315,354)	—	$79,017	—

KEY TERMS

NOTES

1. M. Heimer, "Wall Street Sherlock," *Smart Money* (July 2003), pp. 103–107.

2. *Ibid.*, p. 105.

3. *Ibid.*, p. 105.

4. *Ibid.*, p. 105.

5. D. Stead, "The Secrets in SEC Filings," *Business Week* (September 1, 2008), p. 12.

6. M. Vanac, "What's a Novice Investor to Do?" *Des Moines Register* (November 30, 1997), p. 3G.

7. A. R. Sorking, "New Path on Mergers Could Contain Loopholes," *The* (Ames, IA) *Daily Tribune* (January 9, 2001), p. B7; "Firms Resist Effort to Unveil True Costs of Doing Business," *USA Today* (July 3, 2000), p. 10A.

8. M. S. Fridson, *Financial Statement Analysis* (New York: John Wiley & Sons, 1991), pp. 192–194.

9. E. I. Altman, "Predicting Financial Distress of Companies: Revisiting the Z-Score and Zeta Models," Working paper at http://pages.stern.nyu.edu/~ealtman/Zscores.pdf (July 2000).

10. D. H. Bangs, *Managing by the Numbers* (Dover, N.H.: Upstart Publications, 1992), pp. 106–107.

11. "Economic Focus: A Tale of Two Worlds," *The Economist* (May 10, 2008), p. 88; "Zimbabwe: A Worthless Currency," *The Economist* (July 19, 2008), pp. 56–57.

12. S. M. J. Bonini and J. M. Oppenheim, "Helping 'Green' Products Grow," *McKinsey Quarterly* (October 2008), pp. 1–8.

Resources
for Case Research

Company Information

1. Annual reports

2. Moody's *Manuals on Investment* (a listing of companies within certain industries that contains a brief history and a five-year financial statement of each company)

3. Securities and Exchange Commission Annual Report Form 10-K (annually) and 10-Q (quarterly)

4. Standard & Poor's *Register of Corporations, Directors, and Executives*

5. Value Line's *Investment Survey*

6. Findex's *Directory of Market Research Reports, Studies and Surveys* (a listing by Find/SVP of more than 11,000 studies conducted by leading research firms)

7. Compustat, Compact Disclosure, CD/International, and Hoover's Online Corporate Directory (computerized operating and financial information on thousands of publicly held corporations)

8. Shareholders meeting notices in SEC Form 14-A (proxy notices)

Economic Information

1. Regional statistics and local forecasts from large banks

2. *Business Cycle Development* (Department of Commerce)

3. Chase Econometric Associates' publications

4. U.S. Census Bureau publications on population, transportation, and housing

5. *Current Business Reports* (U.S. Department of Commerce)

6. *Economic Indicators* (U.S. Joint Economic Committee)

7. *Economic Report of the President to Congress*

8. *Long-Term Economic Growth* (U.S. Department of Commerce)

9. *Monthly Labor Review* (U.S. Department of Labor)

10. *Monthly Bulletin of Statistics* (United Nations)

11. *Statistical Abstract of the United States* (U.S. Department of Commerce)

12. *Statistical Yearbook* (United Nations)

13. *Survey of Current Business* (U.S. Department of Commerce)

14. *U.S. Industrial Outlook* (U.S. Department of Defense)

15. *World Trade Annual* (United Nations)

16. *Overseas Business Reports* (by country, published by the U.S. Department of Commerce)

Industry Information

1. Analyses of companies and industries by investment brokerage firms

2. *Business Week* (provides weekly economic and business information, as well as quarterly profit and sales rankings of corporations)

3. *Fortune* (each April publishes listings of financial information on corporations within certain industries)

4. *Industry Survey* (published quarterly by Standard & Poor's)

5. *Industry Week* (late March/early April issue provides information on 14 industry groups)

6. *Forbes* (mid-January issue provides performance data on firms in various industries)

7. *Inc*. (May and December issues give information on fast-growing entrepreneurial companies)

Directory and Index Information on Companies and Industries

1. *Business Periodical Index* (on computers in many libraries)

2. *Directory of National Trade Associations*

3. *Encyclopedia of Associations*

4. Funk and Scott's *Index of Corporations and Industries*

5. Thomas' *Register of American Manufacturers*

6. *Wall Street Journal Index*

Ratio Analysis Information

1. *Almanac of Business and Industrial Financial Ratios* (Prentice Hall)

2. *Annual Statement Studies* (Risk Management Associates; also Robert Morris Associates)

3. *Dun's Review* (Dun & Bradstreet; published annually in September–December issues)

4. *Industry Norms and Key Business Ratios* (Dun & Bradstreet)

Online Information

1. *Hoover's Online*—financial statements and profiles of public companies (www.hoovers.com)

2. U.S. Securities and Exchange Commission—official filings of public companies in Edgar database (www.sec.gov)

3. Fortune 500—statistics for largest U.S. corporations (www.fortune.com)

4. Dun & Bradstreet's Online—short reports on 10 million public and private U.S. companies (smallbusiness.dnb.com)

5. Ecola's 24-Hour Newsstand—links to Web sites of 2,000 newspapers, journals, and magazines (www.ecola.com)

6. Competitive Intelligence Guide—information on company resources (www.fuld.com)

7. Society of Competitive Intelligence Professionals (www.scip.org)

8. *The Economist*—provides international information and surveys (www.economist.com)

9. *CIA World Fact Book*—international information by country (http://www.cia.gov)

10. Bloomberg—information on interest rates, stock prices, currency conversion rates, and other general financial information (www.bloomberg.com)

11. The Scannery—information on international companies (www.thescannery.com)

12. CEOExpress—links to many valuable sources of business information (www.ceoexpress.com)

13. *Wall Street Journal*—business news (www.wsj.com)

14. Forbes—America's largest private companies (http://www.forbes.com/lists/)

15. CorporateInformation.com—subscription service for company profiles (www.corporateinformation.com)

16. Kompass International—industry information (www.kompass.com)

17. CorpTech—database of technology companies (www.corptech.com)

18. ADNet—information technology industry (www.companyfinder.com)

19. CNN company research—provides company information (http://money.cnn.com/news/crc/)

20. Paywatch—database of executive compensation (http://www.aflcio.org/corporatewatch/paywatch/)

21. Global Edge Global Resources—international resources (http://globaledge.msu.edu/resourceDesk/)

22. Google Finance—data on North American stocks (http://finance.google.com/finance)

23. World Federation of Exchanges—international stock exchanges (www.world-exchanges.org/)

24. SEC International Registry—data on international corporations (http://www.sec.gov/divisions/corpfin/internatl/companies.shtml)

25. Yahoo Finance—data on North American companies (http://finance.yahoo.com)

Suggested Case Analysis Methodology Using the Strategic Audit

1. READ CASE

First Reading of the Case

■ Develop a general overview of the company and its external environment.

■ Begin a list of the possible strategic factors facing the company at this time.

■ List the research information you may need on the economy, industry, and competitors.

2. READ THE CASE WITH THE STRATEGIC AUDIT

Second Reading of the Case

■ Read the case a second time, using the strategic audit as a framework for in-depth analysis. (See **Appendix 1.A** on pages 34–41.) You may want to make a copy of the strategic audit worksheet (**Figure 15–1**) to use to keep track of your comments as you read the case.

■ The questions in the strategic audit parallel the strategic decision-making process shown in **Figure 1–5** (pages 28–29).

■ The audit provides you with a conceptual framework to examine the company's mission, objectives, strategies, and policies as well as problems, symptoms, facts, opinions, and issues.

■ Perform a financial analysis of the company, using ratio analysis (see **Table 15–1**), and do the calculations necessary to convert key parts of the financial statements to a common-size basis.

3. DO OUTSIDE RESEARCH

Library and Online Computer Services

■ Each case has a decision date indicating when the case actually took place. Your research should be based on the time period for the case.

■ See **Appendix 15.A** for resources for case research. Your research should include information about the environment at the time of the case. Find average industry ratios. You may also want to obtain further information regarding competitors and the company itself (10-K forms and annual reports). This information should help you conduct an industry analysis. *Check with your instructor to see what kind of outside research is appropriate for your assignment.*

■ Don't try to learn what actually happened to the company discussed in the case. What management actually decided may not be the best solution. It will certainly bias your analysis and will probably cause your recommendation to lack proper justification.

4. BEGIN SWOT ANALYSIS

External Environmental Analysis: EFAS

- Analyze the natural and societal environments to see what general trends are likely to affect the industry(s) in which the company is operating.

- Conduct an industry analysis using Porter's competitive forces from **Chapter 4.** Develop an Industry Matrix (**Table 4–4** on page 119).

- Generate 8 to 10 external factors. These should be the *most important* opportunities and threats facing the company at the time of the case.

- Develop an EFAS Table, as shown in **Table 4–5** (page 126), for your list of external strategic factors.

- **Suggestion:** Rank the 8 to 10 factors from most to least important. Start by grouping the 3 top factors and then the 3 bottom factors.

Internal Organizational Analysis: IFAS

- Generate 8 to 10 internal factors. These should be the *most important* strengths and weaknesses of the company at the time of the case.

- Develop an IFAS Table, as shown in **Table 5–2** (page 164), for your list of internal strategic factors.

- **Suggestion:** Rank the 8 to 10 factors from most to least important. Start by grouping the 3 top factors and then the 3 bottom factors.

5. WRITE YOUR STRATEGIC AUDIT: PARTS I TO IV

First Draft of Your Strategic Audit

- Review the student-written audit of an old Maytag case in **Appendix 15.C** for an example.

- Write Parts I to IV of the strategic audit. Remember to include the factors from your EFAS and IFAS Tables in your audit.

6. WRITE YOUR STRATEGIC AUDIT: PART V

Strategic Factor Analysis Summary: SFAS

- **Condense the list of factors from the 16 to 20 identified in your EFAS and IFAS Tables to only the 8 to 10 most important factors.**

- Select the most important EFAS and IFAS factors. Recalculate the weights of each. The weights still need to add to 1.0.

- Develop a SFAS Matrix, as shown in **Figure 6–1** (page 178), for your final list of strategic factors. Although the weights (indicating the importance of each factor) will probably change from the EFAS and IFAS Tables, the numeric rating (1 to 5) of each factor should remain the same. These ratings are your assessment of management's performance on each factor.

- This is a good time to reexamine what you wrote earlier in Parts I to IV. You may want to add to or delete some of what you wrote. Ensure that each one of the strategic factors you have included in your SFAS Matrix is discussed in the appropriate place in Parts I to IV. Part V of the audit is *not* the place to mention a strategic factor for the first time.

- Write Part V of your strategic audit. This completes your SWOT analysis.

- This is the place to suggest a revised mission statement and a better set of objectives for the company. The SWOT analysis coupled with revised mission and objectives for the company set the stage for the generation of strategic alternatives.

7. WRITE YOUR STRATEGIC AUDIT: PART VI

Strategic Alternatives and Recommendation

A. Alternatives

▣ Develop around three mutually exclusive strategic alternatives. If appropriate to the case you are analyzing, you might propose one alternative for growth, one for stability, and one for retrenchment. Within each corporate strategy, you should probably propose an appropriate business/competitive strategy. You may also want to include some functional strategies where appropriate.

▣ Construct a corporate scenario for each alternative. Use the data from your outside research to project general societal trends (GDP, inflation, and etc.) and industry trends. Use these as the basis of your assumptions to write pro forma financial statements (particularly income statements) for each strategic alternative for the next five years.

▣ List pros and cons for each alternative based on your scenarios.

B. Recommendation

▣ Specify which one of your alternative strategies you recommend. Justify your choice in terms of dealing with the strategic factors you listed in Part V of the strategic audit.

▣ Develop policies to help implement your strategies.

8. WRITE YOUR STRATEGIC AUDIT: PART VII

Implementation

▣ Develop programs to implement your recommended strategy.

▣ Specify who is to be responsible for implementing each program and how long each program will take to complete.

▣ Refer to the pro forma financial statements you developed earlier for your recommended strategy. Use common-size historical income statements as the basis for the pro forma statement. Do the numbers still make sense? If not, this may be a good time to rethink the budget numbers to reflect your recommended programs.

9. WRITE YOUR STRATEGIC AUDIT: PART VIII

Evaluation and Control

▣ Specify the type of evaluation and controls that you need to ensure that your recommendation is carried out successfully. Specify who is responsible for monitoring these controls.

▣ Indicate whether sufficient information is available to monitor how the strategy is being implemented. If not, suggest a change to the information system.

10. PROOF AND FINE-TUNE YOUR AUDIT

Final Draft of Your Strategic Audit

▣ Check to ensure that your audit is within the page limits of your professor. You may need to cut some parts and expand others.

▣ Make sure that your recommendation clearly deals with the strategic factors.

▣ **Attach your EFAS and IFAS Tables, and SFAS Matrix,** plus your ratio analysis and pro forma statements. Label them as numbered exhibits and refer to each of them within the body of the audit.

▣ Proof your work for errors. If on a computer, use a spell checker.

SPECIAL NOTE: Depending on your assignment, it is relatively easy to use the strategic audit you have just developed to write a written case analysis in essay form or to make an oral presentation. The strategic audit is just a detailed case analysis in an outline form and can be used as the basic framework for any sort of case analysis and presentation.

Example of Student-Written Strategic Audit

(For the 1993 Maytag Corporation Case)

I. Current Situation

A. Current Performance

Poor financials, high debt load, first losses since 1920s, price/earnings ratio negative.

- First loss since 1920s.
- Laid off 4,500 employees at Magic Chef.
- Hoover Europe still showing losses.

B. Strategic Posture

1. **Mission**

   - Developed in 1989 for the Maytag Company: "To provide our customers with products of unsurpassed performance that last longer, need fewer repairs, and are produced at the lowest possible cost."
   - Updated in 1991: "Our collective mission is world class quality." Expands Maytag's belief in product quality to all aspects of operations.

2. **Objectives**

   - "To be profitability leader in industry for every product line Maytag manufactures." Selected profitability rather than market share.
   - "To be number one in total customer satisfaction." Doesn't say how to measure satisfaction.
   - "To grow the North American appliance business and become the third largest appliance manufacturer (in unit sales) in North America."
   - To increase profitable market share growth in North American appliance and floor care business, 6.5% return on sales, 10% return on assets, 20% return on equity, beat competition in satisfying customers, dealer, builder and endorser, move into third place in total units shipped per year. Nicely quantified objectives.

3. **Strategies**

   - Global growth through acquisition, and alliance with Bosch-Siemens.
   - Differentiate brand names for competitive advantage.
   - Create synergy between companies, product improvement, investment in plant and equipment.

4. **Policies**
  - Cost reduction is secondary to high quality.
  - Promotion from within.
  - Slow but sure R&D: Maytag slow to respond to changes in market.

II. Strategic Managers

A. Board of Directors

1. Fourteen members—eleven are outsiders.
2. Well-respected Americans, most on board since 1986 or earlier.
3. No international or marketing backgrounds.
4. Time for a change?

B. Top Management

1. Top management promoted from within Maytag Company. Too inbred?
2. Very experienced in the industry.
3. Responsible for current situation.
4. May be too parochial for global industry. May need new blood.

III. External Environment
(EFAS Table; see Exhibit 1)

A. Natural Environment

1. Growing water scarcity
2. Energy availability a growing problem

B. Societal Environment

1. **Economic**
   a. Unstable economy but recession ending, consumer confidence growing—could increase spending for big ticket items like houses, cars, and appliances. **(O)**
   b. Individual economies becoming interconnected into a world economy. **(O)**

2. **Technological**
   a. Fuzzy logic technology being applied to sense and measure activities. **(O)**
   b. Computers and information technology increasingly important. **(O)**

3. **Political–Legal**
   a. NAFTA, European Union, other regional trade pacts opening doors to markets in Europe, Asia, and Latin America that offer enormous potential. **(O)**
   b. Breakdown of communism means less chance of world war. **(O)**
   c. Environmentalism being reflected in laws on pollution and energy usage. **(T)**

4. **Sociocultural**
   a. Developing nations desire goods seen on TV. **(O)**
   b. Middle-aged baby boomers want attractive, high-quality products, like BMWs and Maytag. **(O)**
   c. Dual-career couples increases need for labor-saving appliances, second cars, and day care. **(O)**
   d. Divorce and career mobility means need for more houses and goods to fill them. **(O)**

C. Task Environment

1. North American market mature and extremely competitive—vigilant consumers demand high quality with low price in safe, environmentally sound products. **(T)**

2. Industry going global as North American and European firms expand internationally. **(T)**

3. European design popular and consumer desire for technologically advanced appliances. **(O)**

4. **Rivalry High**. Whirlpool, Electrolux, GE have enormous resources & developing global presence. **(T)**

5. **Buyers' Power Low**. Technology and materials can be sourced worldwide. **(O)**

6. **Power of Other Stakeholders Medium**. Quality, safety, environmental regulations increasing. **(T)**

7. **Distributors' Power High**. Super retailers more important: mom and pop dealers less. **(T)**

8. **Threat of Substitutes Low**. **(O)**

9. **Entry Barriers High**. New entrants unlikely except for large international firms. **(T)**

IV. Internal Environment
(IFAS Table; see Exhibit 2)

A. Corporate Structure

1. Divisional structure: appliance manufacturing and vending machines. Floor care managed separately. **(S)**

2. Centralized major decisions by Newton corporate staff, with a time line of about three years. **(S)**

B. Corporate Culture

1. Quality key ingredient—commitment to quality shared by executives and workers. **(S)**

2. Much of corporate culture is based on founder F. L. Maytag's personal philosophy, including concern for quality, employees, local community, innovation, and performance. **(S)**

3. Acquired companies, except for European, seem to accept dominance of Maytag culture. **(S)**

C. Corporate Resources

1. **Marketing**
   a. Maytag brand lonely repairman advertising successful but dated. **(W)**
   b. Efforts focus on distribution—combining three sales forces into two, concentrating on major retailers. (Cost $95 million for this restructuring.) **(S)**
   c. Hoover's well-publicized marketing fiasco involving airline tickets. **(W)**

2. **Finance** (see **Exhibits 4 and 5**)
   a. Revenues are up slightly, operating income is down significantly. **(W)**
   b. Some key ratios are troubling, such as a 57% debt/asset ratio, 132% long-term debt/equity ratio. No room for more debt to grow company. **(W)**
   c. Net income is 400% less than 1988, based on common-size income statements. **(W)**

3. **R&D**
   a. Process-oriented with focus on manufacturing process and durability. **(S)**
   b. Maytag becoming a technology follower, taking too long to get product innovations to market (competitors put out more in last 6 months than prior 2 years combined), lagging in fuzzy logic and other technological areas. **(W)**

4. **Operations**
   a. Maytag's core competence. Continual improvement process kept it dominant in the U.S. market for many years. **(S)**
   b. Plants aging and may be losing competitiveness as rivals upgrade facilities. Quality no longer distinctive competence? **(W)**

5. **Human Resources**
   a. Traditionally very good relations with unions and employees. **(S)**
   b. Labor relations increasingly strained, with two salary raise delays, and layoffs of 4,500 employees at Magic Chef. **(W)**
   c. Unions express concern at new, more distant tone from Maytag Corporation. **(W)**

6. **Information Systems**
   a. Not mentioned in case. Hoover fiasco in Europe suggests information systems need significant upgrading. **(W)**
   b. Critical area where Maytag may be unwilling or unable to commit resources needed to stay competitive. **(W)**

V. Analysis of Strategic Factors

A. Situational Analysis (SWOT) (SFAS Matrix; see Exhibit 3)

1. **Strengths**
   a. Quality Maytag culture.
   b. Maytag well-known and respected brand.
   c. Hoover's international orientation.
   d. Core competencies in process R&D and manufacturing.

2. **Weaknesses**
   a. Lacks financial resources of competitors.
   b. Poor global positioning. Hoover weak on European continent.
   c. Product R&D and customer service innovation areas of serious weakness.
   d. Dependent on small dealers.
   e. Marketing needs improvement.

3. **Opportunities**
   a. Economic integration of European Community.
   b. Demographics favor quality.
   c. Trend to superstores.

4. **Threats**
   a. Trend to superstores.
   b. Aggressive rivals—Whirlpool and Electrolux.
   c. Japanese appliance companies—new entrants?

B. Review of Current Mission and Objectives

1. Current mission appears appropriate.
2. Some of the objectives are really goals and need to be quantified and given time horizons.

VI. Strategic Alternatives and Recommended Strategy

A. Strategic Alternatives

1. *Growth through Concentric Diversification*: Acquire a company in a related industry such as commercial appliances.

    a. *[Pros]:* Product/market synergy created by acquisition of related company.

    b. *[Cons]:* Maytag does not have the financial resources to play this game.

2. *Pause Strategy*: Consolidate various acquisitions to find economies and to encourage innovation among the business units.

    a. *[Pros]:* Maytag needs to get its financial house in order and get administrative control over its recent acquisitions.

    b. *[Cons]:* Unless it can grow through a stronger alliance with Bosch-Siemens or some other backer, Maytag is a prime candidate for takeover because of its poor financial performance in recent years, and it is suffering from the initial reduction in efficiency inherent in acquisition strategy.

3. *Retrenchment*: Sell Hoover's foreign major home appliance businesses (Australia and UK) to emphasize increasing market share in North America.

    a. *[Pros]:* Divesting Hoover improves bottom line and enables Maytag Corp. to focus on North America while Whirlpool, Electrolux, and GE are battling elsewhere.

    b. *[Cons]:* Maytag may be giving up its only opportunity to become a player in the coming global appliance industry.

B. Recommended Strategy

1. Recommend pause strategy, at least for a year, so Maytag can get a grip on its European operation and consolidate its companies in a more synergistic way.

2. Maytag quality must be maintained, and continued shortage of operating capital will take its toll, so investment must be made in R&D.

3. Maytag may be able to make the Hoover UK investment work better since the recession is ending and the EU countries are closer to integrating than ever before.

4. Because it is only an average competitor, Maytag needs the Hoover link to Europe to provide a jumping off place for negotiations with Bosch-Siemens that could strengthen their alliance.

VII. Implementation

A. The only way to increase profitability in North America is to further involve Maytag with the superstore retailers; sure to anger the independent dealers, but necessary for Maytag to compete.

B. Board members with more global business experience should be recruited, with an eye toward the future, especially with expertise in Asia and Latin America.

C. R&D needs to be improved, as does marketing, to get new products online quickly.

VIII. Evaluation and Control

A. MIS needs to be developed for speedier evaluation and control. While the question of control vs. autonomy is "under review," another Hoover fiasco may be brewing.

B. The acquired companies do not all share the Midwestern work ethic or the Maytag Corporation culture, and Maytag's managers must inculcate these values into the employees of all acquired companies.

C. Systems should be developed to decide if the size and location of Maytag manufacturing plants is still correct and to plan for the future. Industry analysis indicates that smaller automated plants may be more efficient now than in the past.

EXHIBIT 1   EFAS Table for Maytag Corporation 1993

External Factors	Weight	Rating	Weighted Score	Comments
	1	2	3	4	5
Opportunities				
■ Economic integration of European Community	.20	4.1	.82	Acquisition of Hoover
■ Demographics favor quality appliances	.10	5.0	.50	Maytag quality
■ Economic development of Asia	.05	1.0	.05	Low Maytag presence
■ Opening of Eastern Europe	.05	2.0	.10	Will take time
■ Trend to "Super Stores"	.10	1.8	.18	Maytag weak in this channel
Threats				
■ Increasing government regulations	.10	4.3	.43	Well positioned
■ Strong U.S. competition	:10	4.0	.40	Well positioned
■ Whirlpool and Electrolux strong globally	.15	3.0	.45	Hoover weak globally
■ New product advances	.05	1.2	.06	Questionable
■ Japanese appliance companies	.10	1.6	.16	Only Asian presence in Australia
Total Scores	**1.00**		**3.15**	

EXHIBIT 2   IFAS Table for Maytag Corporation 1993

Internal Factors	Weight	Rating	Weighted Score	Comments
	1	2	3	4	5
Strengths				
■ Quality Maytag culture	.15	5.0	.75	Quality key to success
■ Experienced top management	.05	4.2	.21	Know appliances
■ Vertical integration	.10	3.9	.39	Dedicated factories
■ Employer relations	.05	3.0	.15	Good, but deteriorating
■ Hoover's international orientation	.15	2.8	.42	Hoover name in cleaners
Weaknesses				
■ Process-oriented R&D	.05	2.2	.11	Slow on new products
■ Distribution channels	.05	2.0	.10	Superstores replacing small dealers
■ Financial position	.15	2.0	.30	High debt load
■ Global positioning	.20	2.1	.42	Hoover weak outside the United Kingdom and Australia
■ Manufacturing facilities	.05	4.0	.20	Investing now
Total Scores	**1.00**		**3.05**	

EXHIBIT 3 SFAS Matrix for Maytag Corporation 1993

Strategic Factors (Select the most important opportunities/threats from EFAS, Table 4–5 and the most important strengths and weaknesses from IFAS, Table 5–2)	Weight	Rating	Weighted Score	SHORT	INTERMEDIATE	LONG	Comments
	1	2	3	4 Duration		5	6
▶S1 Quality Maytag culture (S)	.10	5.0	.50			X	Quality key to success
▶S5 Hoover's international orientation (S)	.10	2.8	.28	X	X		Name recognition
▶W3 Financial position (W)	.10	2.0	.20	X	X		High debt
▶W4 Global positioning (W)	.15	2.2	.33	X	X	X	Only in N.A., U.K., and Australia
▶O1 Economic integration of European Community (O)	.10	4.1	.41			X	Acquisition of Hoover
▶O2 Demographics favor quality (O)	.10	5.0	.50		X		Maytag quality
▶O5 Trend to super stores (O + T)	.10	1.8	.18	X			Weak in this channel
▶T3 Whirlpool and Electrolux (T)	.15	3.0	.45	X			Dominate industry
▶T5 Japanese appliance companies (T)	.10	1.6	.16			X	Asian presence
Total Scores	<u>1.00</u>		<u>3.01</u>				

EXHIBIT 4

Ratio Analysis for Maytag Corporation 1993

	1990	1991	1992	1993
1. LIQUIDITY RATIOS				
Current	2.1	1.9	1.8	1.6
Quick	1.1	1.0	1.1	1.0
2. LEVERAGE RATIOS				
Debt to Total Assets	61%	60%	76%	57%
Debt to Equity	155%	151%	317%	254%
3. ACTIVITY RATIOS				
Inventory turnover—sales	5.7	6.1	7.6	6.9
Inventory Turnover—cost of sales	4.3	4.6	5.8	6.5
Avg. Collection Period—days	57	55	56	0
Fixed Asset Turnover	3.9	3.6	3.6	3.6
Total Assets Turnover	1.2	1.2	1.2	1.1
4. PROFITABILITY RATIOS				
Gross Profit Margin	24%	24%	23%	5%
Net Operating Margin	8%	6%	3%	5%
Profit Margin on Sales	3%	3%	−0%	2%
Return on Total Assets	4%	3%		2%
Return on Equity	10%	8%	−1%	8%

EXHIBIT 5		1992	1991	1990
Common Size Income Statements for Maytag Corporation 1993	Net Sales	100.0%	100.0%	100.0%
	Cost of Sales	76.92	75.88	75.50
	Gross Profit	23.08	24.12	24.46
	Selling, general/admin. expenses	17.37	17.67	16.90
	Reorganization Expenses	.031	——	——
	Operating Income	.026	.064	.075
	Interest Expense	(.025)	(.025)	(0.26)
	Other-net	.001	.002	.009
	Income before accounting changes	.002	.042	.052
	Income taxes	.005	.015	.020
	Income before accounting changes	(.002)	.026	.032
	Effect of accounting changes for post-retirement benefits other than pensions and income taxes	(.101)	——	——
	Total Operating Costs and Expenses	74.9	76.0	76.3
	Net Income	**(.104)**	**.026**	**.032**

EXHIBIT 6	Implementation, Evaluation, & Control Plan for Maytag Corporation 1993					
Strategic Factor	**Action Plan**	**Priority System (1–5)**	**Who Will Implement**	**Who Will Review**	**How Often Review**	**Criteria Used**
Quality Maytag culture	Build quality in acquired units	1	Heads of acquired units	Manufacturing VP	Quarterly	Number defects & customer satisfaction
Hoover's international orientation	Identify ways to expand sales	2	Head of Hoover	Marketing VP	Quarterly	Feasible alternatives generated
Financial position	Pay down debt	1	CFO	CEO	Monthly	Leverage ratios
Global positioning	Find strategic alliance partners	2	VP of Business Development	COO	Quarterly	Feasible alternatives generated
EU economic integration	Grow sales throughout EU	3	Hoover UK Head	Marketing VP	Annually	Sales growth
Demographics favor quality	Simplify controls	3	Manufacturing VP	COO	Annually	Market research user satisfaction
Trend to super stores	Market through Sears	1	Marketing VP	CEO	Monthly	Sales growth
Whirlpool & Electrolux	Monitor competitor performance	1	Competition committee	COO	Quarterly	Competitor sales & new products
Japanese appliance companies	Monitor expansion	4	Head of Hoover Australia	Competition committee	Semi-annually	Sales growth outside Japan

Ending Case for Part Five

IN THE GARDEN

Walking with my watering can underneath the cherry tree, the apricot tree, the plum tree, and the nectarine tree, strawberry vines and raspberry canes at my feet, I gazed at my hedge and thought what would it take to avoid disease in the garden this year? I was amazed how this garden, so similar and different from previous seasons, had evolved from two saplings, purchased by chance, placed by happenstance, but planted with care. Now I wondered at the wild order.

....

This case was written by Mark Meckler, University of Portland and presented to the North American Case Research Association at its 2006 annual meeting. Copyright © 2006 by Mark Meckler. Edited for publication in *Strategic Management and Business Policy*, 12th edition and *Concepts in Strategic Management and Business Policy*, 12th edition. Reprinted by permission of Mark Meckler and the North American Case Research Association.

Was this the fruit I should be growing? How could I end up with the sweetest fruit, and what about the most fruit and the largest fruit? How would I set myself up for more success next year, and what of the years after that? And, I sadly thought, what shall I do with the wonderful apple tree I climbed as a child that now yielded so little fruit?

All these thoughts I had walking with my watering can under the cherry tree, the apricot tree, the plum tree, and the nectarine tree, strawberry vines and raspberry canes at my feet.

GLOSSARY

10-K form An SEC form containing income statements, balance sheets, cash flow statements, and information not usually available in an annual report.

10-Q form An SEC form containing quarterly financial reports.

14-A form An SEC form containing proxy statements and information on a company's board of directors.

360-degree performance appraisal An evaluation technique in which input is gathered from multiple sources.

80/20 rule A rule of thumb stating that one should monitor those 20% of the factors that determine 80% of the results.

Absorptive capacity A firm's ability to value, assimilate, and utilize new external knowledge.

Acquisition The purchase of a company that is completely absorbed by the acquiring corporation.

Action plan A plan that states what actions are going to be taken, by whom, during what time frame, and with what expected results.

Activity ratios Financial ratios that indicate how well a corporation is managing its operations.

Activity-based costing (ABC) An accounting method for allocating indirect and fixed costs to individual products or product lines based on the value-added activities going into that product.

Adaptive mode A decision-making mode characterized by reactive solutions to existing problems, rather than a proactive search for new opportunities.

Advisory board A group of external business people who voluntarily meet periodically with the owners/managers of the firm to discuss strategic and other issues.

Affiliated directors Directors who, though not really employed by the corporation, handle the legal or insurance work for the company or are important suppliers.

Agency theory A theory stating that problems arise in corporations because the agents (top management) are not willing to bear responsibility for their decisions unless they own a substantial amount of stock in the corporation.

Altman's Bankruptcy Formula A formula used to estimate how close a company is to declaring bankruptcy.

Analytical portfolio manager A type of general manager needed to execute a diversification strategy.

Andean Community A South American free-trade alliance composed of Columbia, Ecuador, Peru, Bolivia, and Chili.

Annual report A document published each year by a company to show its financial condition and products.

Assessment center An approach to evaluating the suitability of a person for a position by simulating key parts of the job.

Assimilation A strategy that involves the domination of one corporate culture over another.

Association of South East Asian Nations (ASEAN) A regional trade association composed of Asian countries of Brunei Darussalam, Cambodia, Indonesia, Laos, Malaysia, Myanmar, Philippines, Singapore, Thailand, and Vietnam. ASEA+3 includes China, Japan, and South Korea.

Autonomous (self-managing) work teams A group of people who work together without a supervisor to plan, coordinate, and evaluate their own work.

Backward integration Assuming a function previously provided by a supplier.

Balanced scorecard Combines financial measures with operational measures on customer satisfaction, internal processes, and the corporation's innovation and improvement activities.

Bankruptcy A retrenchment strategy that forfeits management of the firm to the courts in return for some settlement of the corporation's obligations.

Basic R&D Research and development that is conducted by scientists in well-equipped laboratories where the focus is on theoretical problem areas.

BCG (Boston Consulting Group) Growth-Share Matrix A simple way to portray a corporation's portfolio of products or divisions in terms of growth and cash flow.

Behavior control A control that specifies how something is to be done through policies, rules, standard operating procedures, and orders from a superior.

Behavior substitution A phenomenon that occurs when people substitute activities that do not lead to goal accomplishment for activities that do lead to goal accomplishment because the wrong activities are being rewarded.

Benchmarking The process of measuring products, services, and practices against those of competitors or companies recognized as industry leaders.

Best practice A procedure that is followed by successful companies.

Blind spot analysis An approach to analyzing a competitor by identifying its perceptual biases.

Board of director responsibilities Commonly agreed obligations of directors, which include: setting corporate strategy, overall direction, mission or vision; hiring and firing the CEO and top management; controlling, monitoring, or supervising top management; reviewing and approving the use of resources; and caring for shareholder interest.

Board of directors' continuum A range of the possible degree of involvement by the board of directors (from low to high) in the strategic management process.

BOT (build-operate-transfer) concept A type of international entry option for a company. After building a facility, the company operates the facility for a fixed period of time during which it earns back its investment, plus a profit.

Brainstorming The process of proposing ideas in a group without first mentally screening them.

Brand A name that identifies a particular company's product in the mind of the consumer.

Budget A statement of a corporation's programs in terms of money required.

Business model The mix of activities a company performs to earn a profit.

Business plan A written strategic plan for a new entrepreneurial venture.

Business policy A previous name for strategic management. It has a general management orientation and tends to look inward with primary concern for integrating the corporation's many functional activities.

Business strategy Competitive and cooperative strategies that emphasize improvement of the competitive position of a corporation's products or services in a specific industry or market segment.

Cannibalize To replace popular products before they reach the end of their life cycle.

Cap-and-trade A government-imposed ceiling (cap) on the amount of allowed greenhouse gas emissions combined with a system allowing a firm to sell (trade) its emission reductions to another firm whose emissions exceed the allowed cap.

Capability A corporation's ability to exploit its resources.

Capital budgeting The process of analyzing and ranking possible investments in terms of the additional outlays and additional receipts that will result from each investment.

Captive company strategy Dedicating a firm's productive capacity as primary supplier to another company in exchange for a long-term contract.

Carbon footprint The amount of greenhouse gases being created by an entity and released into the air.

Cash cow A product that brings in far more money than is needed to maintain its market share.

Categorical imperatives Kant's two principles to guide actions: A person's action is ethical only if that person is willing for that same action to be taken by everyone who is in a similar situation, and a person should never treat another human being simply as a means but always as an end.

Cautious profit planner The type of leader needed for a corporation choosing to follow a stability strategy.

Cellular/modular organization structure A structure composed of cells (self-managing teams, autonomous business units, etc.) that can operate alone but can interact with other cells to produce a more potent and competent business mechanism.

Center of excellence A designated area in which a company has a core or distinctive competence.

Center of gravity The part of the industry value chain that is most important to the company and the point where the company's greatest expertise and capabilities lay.

Central American Free Trade Agreement (CAFTA) A regional trade association composed of El Salvador, Guatemala, Nicaragua, Honduras, Costa Rica, the United States, and the Dominican Republic.

Clusters Geographic concentrations of interconnected companies and industries.

Code of ethics A code that specifies how an organization expects its employees to behave while on the job.

Codetermination The inclusion of a corporation's workers on its board of directors.

Collusion The active cooperation of firms within an industry to reduce output and raise prices in order to get around the normal economic law of supply and demand. This practice is usually illegal.

Commodity A product whose characteristics are the same regardless of who sells it.

Common-size statements Income statements and balance sheets in which the dollar figures have been converted into percentages.

Competency A cross-functional integration and coordination of capabilities.

Competitive intelligence A formal program of gathering information about a company's competitors.

Competitive scope The breadth of a company's or a business unit's target market.

Competitive strategy A strategy that states how a company or a business unit will compete in an industry.

Competitors The companies that offer the same products or services as the subject company.

Complementor A company or an industry whose product(s) works well with another industry's or firm's product and without which that product would lose much of its value.

Concentration A corporate growth strategy that concentrates a corporation's resources on competing in one industry.

Concentric diversification A diversification growth strategy in which a firm uses its current strengths to diversify into related products in another industry.

Concurrent engineering A process in which specialists from various functional areas work side by side rather than sequentially in an effort to design new products.

Conglomerate diversification A diversification growth strategy that involves a move into another industry to provide products unrelated to its current products.

Conglomerate structure An assemblage of legally independent firms (subsidiaries) operating under one corporate umbrella but controlled through the subsidiaries' boards of directors.

Connected line batch flow A part of a corporation's manufacturing strategy in which components are standardized and each machine functions like a job shop but is positioned in the same order as the parts are processed.

Consensus A situation in which all parties agree to one alternative.

Consolidated industry An industry in which a few large companies dominate.

Consolidation The second phase of a turnaround strategy that implements a program to stabilize the corporation.

Constant dollars Dollars adjusted for inflation.

Continuous improvement A system developed by Japanese firms in which teams strive constantly to improve manufacturing processes.

Continuous systems Production organized in lines on which products can be continuously assembled or processed.

Continuum of sustainability A representation that indicates how durable and imitable an organization's resources and capabilities are.

Contraction The first phase of a turnaround strategy that includes a general across-the-board cutback in size and costs.

Cooperative strategies Strategies that involve working with other firms to gain competitive advantage within an industry.

Co-opetition A term used to describe simultaneous competition and cooperation among firms.

Core competency A collection of corporate capabilities that cross divisional borders and are widespread within a corporation, and is something that a corporation can do exceedingly well.

Core rigidity/deficiency A core competency of a firm that over time matures and becomes a weakness.

Corporate brand A type of brand in which the company's name serves as the brand name.

Corporate capabilities See capability.

Corporate culture A collection of beliefs, expectations, and values learned and shared by a corporation's members and transmitted from one generation of employees to another.

Corporate culture pressure A force from existing corporate culture against the implementation of a new strategy.

Corporate entrepreneurship Also called intrapreneurship, the creation of a new business within an existing organization.

Corporate governance The relationship among the board of directors, top management, and shareholders in determining the direction and performance of a corporation.

Corporate parenting A corporate strategy that evaluates the corporation's business units in terms of resources and capabilities that can be used to build business unit value as well as generate synergies across business units.

Corporate reputation A widely held perception of a company by the general public.

Corporate scenario Pro forma balance sheets and income statements that forecast the effect that each alternative strategy will likely have on return on investment.

Corporate stakeholders Groups that affect or are affected by the achievement of a firm's objectives.

Corporate strategy A strategy that states a company's overall direction in terms of its general attitude toward growth and the management of its various business and product lines.

Corporation A mechanism legally established to allow different parties to contribute capital, expertise, and labor for their mutual benefit.

Cost focus A low-cost competitive strategy that concentrates on a particular buyer group or geographic market and attempts to serve only that niche.

Cost leadership A low-cost competitive strategy that aims at the broad mass market.

Cost proximity A process that involves keeping the higher price a company charges for higher quality close enough to that of the competition so that customers will see the extra quality as being worth the extra cost.

Crisis of autonomy A time when people managing diversified product lines need more decision-making freedom than top management is willing to delegate to them.

Crisis of control A time when business units act to optimize their own sales and profits without regard to the overall corporation. See also *suboptimization*.

Crisis of leadership A time when an entrepreneur is personally unable to manage a growing company.

Cross-functional work teams A work team composed of people from multiple functions.

Cultural integration The extent to which units throughout an organization share a common culture.

Cultural intensity The degree to which members of an organizational unit accept the norms, values, or other culture content associated with the unit.

Deculturation The disintegration of one company's culture resulting from unwanted and extreme pressure from another to impose its culture and practices.

Dedicated transfer line A highly automated assembly line making one mass-produced product using little human labor.

Defensive centralization A process in which top management of a not-for-profit retains all decision-making authority so that lower-level managers cannot take any actions to which the sponsors may object.

Defensive tactic A tactic in which a company defends its current market.

Delphi technique A forecasting technique in which experts independently assess the probabilities of specified events. These assessments are combined and sent back to each expert for fine-tuning until agreement is reached.

Devil's advocate An individual or a group assigned to identify the potential pitfalls and problems of a proposal.

Dialectical inquiry A decision-making technique that requires that two proposals using different assumptions be generated for consideration.

Differentiation A competitive strategy that is aimed at the broad mass market and that involves the creation of a product or service that is perceived throughout its industry as unique.

Differentiation focus A differentiation competitive strategy that concentrates on a particular buyer group, product line segment, or geographic market.

Differentiation strategy See differentiation.

Dimensions of national culture A set of five dimensions by which each nation's unique culture can be identified.

Directional strategy A plan that is composed of three general orientations: growth, stability, and retrenchment.

Distinctive competencies A firm's competencies that are superior to those of competitors.

Diversification A corporate growth strategy that expands product lines by moving into another industry.

Divestment A retrenchment strategy in which a division of a corporation with low growth potential is sold.

Divisional structure An organizational structure in which employees tend to be functional specialists organized according to product/market distinctions.

Downsizing Planned elimination of positions or jobs.

Due care The obligation of board members to closely monitor and evaluate top management.

Durability The rate at which a firm's underlying resources and capabilities depreciate or become obsolete.

Dynamic industry expert A leader with a great deal of experience in a particular industry appropriate for executing a concentration strategy.

Dynamic capabilities Capabilities that are continually being changed and reconfigured to make them more adaptive to an uncertain environment.

Dynamic pricing A marketing practice in which different customers pay different prices for the same product or service.

Earnings per share (EPS) A calculation that is determined by dividing net earnings by the number of shares of common stock issued.

Economic value added (EVA) A shareholder value method of measuring corporate and divisional performance. Measures after-tax operating income minus the total annual cost of capital.

Economies of scale A process in which unit costs are reduced by making large numbers of the same product.

Economies of scope A process in which unit costs are reduced when the value chains of two separate products or services share activities, such as the same marketing channels or manufacturing facilities.

EFAS (External Factor Analysis Summary) table A table that organizes external factors into opportunities and threats and how well management is responding to these specific factors.

Electronic commerce The use of the Internet to conduct business transactions.

Engineering (or process) R&D R&D concentrating on quality control and the development of design specifications and improved production equipment.

Enterprise resource planning (ERP) software Software that unites all of a company's major business activities, from order processing to production, within a single family of software modules.

Enterprise risk management (ERM) A corporatewide, integrated process to manage the uncertainties that could negatively or positively influence the achievement of the corporation's objectives.

Enterprise strategy A strategy that explicitly articulates a firm's ethical relationship with its stakeholders.

Entrepreneur A person who initiates and manages a business undertaking and who assumes risk for the sake of a profit.

Entrepreneurial characteristics Traits of an entrepreneur that lead to a new venture's success.

Entrepreneurial mode A strategy made by one powerful individual in which the focus is on opportunities, and problems are secondary.

Entrepreneurial venture Any new business whose primary goals are profitability and growth and that can be characterized by innovative strategic practices.

Entry barrier An obstruction that makes it difficult for a company to enter an industry.

Environmental scanning The monitoring, evaluation, and dissemination of information from the external and internal environments to key people within the corporation.

Environmental sustainability The use of business practices to reduce a company's impact upon the natural, physical environment.

Environmental uncertainty The degree of complexity plus the degree of change existing in an organization's external environment.

Ethics The consensually accepted standards of behavior for an occupation, trade, or profession.

European Union (EU) A regional trade association composed of 27 European countries.

Evaluation and control A process in which corporate activities and performance results are monitored so that actual performance can be compared with desired performance.

Executive leadership The directing of activities toward the accomplishment of corporate objectives.

Executive succession The process of grooming and replacing a key top manager.

Executive type An individual with a particular mix of skills and experiences.

Exit barrier An obstruction that keeps a company from leaving an industry.

Expense center A business unit that uses money but contributes to revenues only indirectly.

Experience curve A conceptual framework that states that unit production costs decline by some fixed percentage each time the total accumulated volume of production in units doubles.

Expert opinion A nonquantitative forecasting technique in which authorities in a particular area attempt to forecast likely developments.

Explicit knowledge Knowledge that can be easily articulated and communicated.

Exporting Shipping goods produced in a company's home country to other countries for marketing.

External environment Forces outside an organization that are not typically within the short-run control of top management.

External strategic factor Environmental trend with both high probability of occurrence and high probability of impact on the corporation.

Externality Costs of doing business that are not included in a firm's accounting system, but felt by others.

Extranet An information network within an organization that is available to key suppliers and customers.

Extrapolation A form of forecasting that extends present trends into the future.

Family business A company that is either owned or dominated by relatives.

Family directors Board members who are descendants of the founder and own significant blocks of stock.

Financial leverage The ratio of total debt to total assets.

Financial strategy A functional strategy to make the best use of corporate monetary assets.

First mover The first company to manufacture and sell a new product or service.

Flexible manufacturing A type of manufacturing that permits the low-volume output of custom-tailored products at relatively low unit costs through economies of scope.

Follow-the-sun-management A management technique in which modern communication enables project team members living in one country to pass their work to team members in another time zone so that the project is continually being advanced.

Forward integration Assuming a function previously provided by a distributor.

Four-corner exercise An approach to analyzing a competitor in terms of its future goals, current strategy, assumptions, and capabilities, in order to develop a competitor's response profile.

Fragmented industry An industry in which no firm has large market share and each firm serves only a small piece of the total market.

Franchising An international entry strategy in which a firm grants rights to another company/individual to open a retail store using the franchiser's name and operating system.

Free cash flow The amount of money a new owner can take out of a firm without harming the business.

Full vertical integration A growth strategy under which a firm makes 100% of its key supplies internally and completely controls its distributors.

Functional strategy An approach taken by a functional area to achieve corporate and business unit objectives and strategies by maximizing resource productivity.

Functional structure An organizational structure in which employees tend to be specialists in the business functions important to that industry, such as manufacturing, sales, or finance.

GE Business Screen A portfolio analysis matrix developed by General Electric, with the assistance of the McKinsey & Company consulting firm.

Geographic-area structure A structure that allows a multinational corporation to tailor products to regional differences and to achieve regional coordination.

Global industry An industry in which a company manufactures and sells the same products, with only minor adjustments for individual countries around the world.

Globalization The internationalization of markets and corporations.

Global warming A gradual increase in the Earth's temperature leading to changes in the planet's climate.

Goal displacement Confusion of means with ends, which occurs when activities originally intended to help managers attain corporate objectives become ends in themselves or are adapted to meet ends other than those for which they were intended.

Goal An open-ended statement of what one wants to accomplish, with no quantification of what is to be achieved and no time criteria for completion.

Good will An accounting term describing the premium paid by one company in its purchase of another company that is listed on the acquiring company's balance sheet.

Grand strategy Another name for directional strategy.

Green-field development An international entry option to build a company's manufacturing plant and distribution system in another country.

Greenwash A derogatory term referring to a company's promoting its environmental sustainability efforts with very little action toward improving its measurable environmental performance.

Gross domestic product (GDP) A measure of the total output of goods and services within a country's borders.

Growth strategies A directional strategy that expands a company's current activities.

Hierarchy of strategy A nesting of strategies by level from corporate to business to functional, so that they complement and support one another.

Horizontal growth A corporate growth concentration strategy that involves expanding the firm's products into other geographic locations and/or increasing the range of products and services offered to current markets.

Horizontal integration The degree to which a firm operates in multiple geographic locations at the same point in an industry's value chain.

Horizontal strategy A corporate parenting strategy that cuts across business unit boundaries to build synergy across business units and to improve the competitive position of one or more business units.

House of quality A method of managing new product development to help project teams make important design decisions by getting them to think about what users want and how to get it to them most effectively.

Human resource management (HRM) strategy A functional strategy that makes the best use of corporate human assets.

Human diversity A mix of people from different races, cultures, and backgrounds in the workplace.

Hypercompetition An industry situation in which the frequency, boldness, and aggressiveness of dynamic movement by the players accelerates to create a condition of constant disequilibrium and change.

Idea A concept that could be the foundation of an entrepreneurial venture if the concept is feasible.

IFAS (Internal Factor Analysis Summary) table A table that organizes internal factors into strengths and weaknesses and how well management is responding to these specific factors.

Imitability The rate at which a firm's underlying resources and capabilities can be duplicated by others.

Index of R&D effectiveness An index that is calculated by dividing the percentage of total revenue spent on research and development into new product profitability.

Index of sustainable growth A calculation that shows how much of the growth rate of sales can be sustained by internally generated funds.

Individual rights approach An ethics behavior guideline that proposes that human beings have certain fundamental rights that should be respected in all decisions.

Individualism-collectivism (IC) The extent to which a society values individual freedom and independence of action compared with a tight social framework and loyalty to the group.

Industry A group of firms producing a similar product or service.

Industry analysis An in-depth examination of key factors within a corporation's task environment.

Industry matrix A chart that summarizes the key success factors within a particular industry.

Industry scenario A forecasted description of an industry's likely future.

Information technology strategy A functional strategy that uses information systems technology to provide competitive advantage.

Input control A control that specifies resources, such as knowledge, skills, abilities, values, and motives of employees.

Inside director An officer or executive employed by a corporation who serves on that company's board of directors; also called management director.

Institution theory A concept of organizational adaptation that proposes that organizations can and do adapt to changing conditions by imitating other successful organizations.

Institutional advantage A competitive benefit for a not-for-profit organization when it performs its tasks more effectively than other comparable organizations.

Integration A process that involves a relatively balanced give-and-take of cultural and managerial practices between merger partners, with no strong imposition of cultural change on either company.

Integration manager A person in charge of taking an acquired company through the process of integrating its people and processes with those of the acquiring company.

Intellectual property Special knowledge used in a new product or process developed by a company for its own use and is usually protected by a patent, copyright, trademark, or trade secret.

Interlocking directorate A condition that occurs when two firms share a director or when an executive of one firm sits on the board of a second firm.

Intermittent system A method of manufacturing in which an item is normally processed sequentially, but the work and the sequence of the processes vary.

Internal environment Variables within the organization not usually within the short-run control of top management.

Internal strategic factors Strengths (core competencies) and weaknesses that are likely to determine whether a firm will be able take advantage of opportunities while avoiding threats.

International transfer pricing A method of minimizing taxes by declaring high profits in a subsidiary located in a country with a low tax rate and small profits in a subsidiary located in a country with a high tax rate.

Intranet An information network within an organization that also has access to the Internet.

Investment center A unit in which performance is measured in terms of the difference between the unit's resources and its services or products.

ISO 9000 Standards Series An internationally accepted way of objectively documenting a company's high level of quality operations.

ISO 14000 Standards Series An internationally accepted way to document a company's impact on the environment.

Issues priority matrix A chart that ranks the probability of occurrence versus the probable impact on the corporation of developments in the external environment.

Job characteristics model An approach to job design that is based on the belief that tasks can be described in terms of certain objective characteristics and that those characteristics affect employee motivation.

Job design The design of individual tasks in an attempt to make them more relevant to the company and more motivating to the employee.

Job enlargement Combining tasks to give a worker more of the same type of duties to perform.

Job enrichment Altering jobs by giving the worker more autonomy and control over activities.

Job rotation Moving workers through several jobs to increase variety.

Job shop One-of-a-kind production using skilled labor.

Joint venture An independent business entity created by two or more companies in a strategic alliance.

Justice approach An ethical approach that proposes that decision makers be equitable, fair, and impartial in the distribution of costs and benefits.

Just-In-Time A purchasing concept in which parts arrive at the plant just when they are needed rather than being kept in inventories.

Key performance measures Essential measures for achieving a desired strategic option—used in the balanced scorecard.

Key success factors Variables that significantly affect the overall competitive position of a company within a particular industry.

Late movers Companies that enter a new market only after other companies have done so.

Law A formal code that permits or forbids certain behaviors.

Lead director An outside director who calls meetings of the outside board members and coordinates the annual evaluation of the CEO.

Lead user A customer who is ahead of market trends and has needs that go beyond those of the average user.

Leading Providing direction to employees to use their abilities and skills most effectively and efficiently to achieve organizational objectives.

Lean Six Sigma A program incorporating the statistical approach of Six Sigma with the lean manufacturing program developed by Toyota.

Learning organization An organization that is skilled at creating, acquiring, and transferring knowledge and at modifying its behavior to reflect new knowledge and insights.

Levels of moral development Kohlberg proposed three levels of moral development: preconventional, conventional, and principled.

Leverage ratio An evaluation of how effectively a company utilizes its resources to generate revenues.

Leveraged buy-out An acquisition in which a company is acquired in a transaction financed largely by debt—usually obtained from a third party, such as an insurance company or an investment banker.

Licensing arrangement An agreement in which the licensing firm grants rights to another firm in another country or market to produce and/or sell a branded product.

Lifestyle company A small business in which the firm is purely an extension of the owner's lifestyle.

Line extension Using a successful brand name on additional products, such as Arm & Hammer brand first on baking soda, then on laundry detergents, toothpaste, and deodorants.

Linkage The connection between the way one value activity (for example, marketing) is performed and the cost of performance of another activity (for example, quality control).

Liquidation The termination of a firm in which all its assets are sold.

Liquidity ratio The percentage showing to what degree a company can cover its current liabilities with its current assets.

Logical incrementalism A decision-making mode that is a synthesis of the planning, adaptive, and entrepreneurial modes.

Logistics strategy A functional strategy that deals with the flow of products into and out of the manufacturing process.

Long-term contract Agreements between two separate firms to provide agreed-upon goods and services to each other for a specified period of time.

Long-term evaluation method A method in which managers are compensated for achieving objectives set over a multiyear period.

Long-term orientation (LT) The extent to which society is oriented toward the long term versus the short term.

Lower cost strategy A strategy in which a company or business unit designs, produces, and markets a comparable product more efficiently than its competitors.

Management audit A technique used to evaluate corporate activities.

Management By Objectives (MBO) An organization-wide approach ensuring purposeful action toward mutually agreed-upon objectives.

Management contract Agreements through which a corporation uses some of its personnel to assist a firm in another country for a specified fee and period of time.

Market development A marketing functional strategy in which a company or business unit captures a larger share of an existing market for current products through market penetration or develops new markets for current products.

Market location tactics Tactics that determine where a company or business unit will compete.

Market position Refers to the selection of specific areas for marketing concentration and can be expressed in terms of market, product, and geographical locations.

Market research A means of obtaining new product ideas by surveying current or potential users regarding what they would like in a new product.

Market segmentation The division of a market into segments to identify available niches.

Market value added (MVA) The difference between the market value of a corporation and the capital contributed by shareholders and lenders.

Marketing mix The particular combination of key variables (product, place, promotion, and price) that can be used to affect demand and to gain competitive advantage.

Marketing strategy A functional strategy that deals with pricing, selling, and distributing a product.

Masculinity-femininity (MF) The extent to which society is oriented toward money and things.

Mass customization The low-cost production of individually customized goods and services.

Mass production A system in which employees work on narrowly defined, repetitive tasks under close supervision in a bureaucratic and hierarchical structure to produce a large amount of low-cost, standard goods and services.

Matrix of change A chart that compares target practices (new programs) with existing practices (current activities).

Matrix structure A structure in which functional and product forms are combined simultaneously at the same level of the organization.

Mercosur/Mercosul South American free-trade area including Argentina, Brazil, Uruguay, and Paraguay.

Merger A transaction in which two or more corporations exchange stock, but from which only one corporation survives.

Mission The purpose or reason for an organization's existence.

Mission statement The definition of the fundamental, unique purpose that sets an organization apart from other firms of its type and identifies the scope or domain of the organization's operations in terms of products (including services) offered and markets served.

Modular manufacturing A system in which preassembled subassemblies are delivered as they are needed to a company's assembly-line workers who quickly piece the modules together into finished products.

Moore's law An observation of Gordon Moore, co-founder of Intel, that microprocessors double in complexity every 18 months.

Moral relativism A theory that proposes that morality is relative to some personal, social, or cultural standard, and that there is no method for deciding whether one decision is better than another.

Morality Precepts of personal behavior that are based on religious or philosophical grounds.

Most favored nation A policy of the World Trade Organization stating that a member country cannot grant one trading partner lower customs duties without granting them to all WTO member nations.

Multidomestic industry An industry in which companies tailor their products to the specific needs of consumers in a particular country.

Multinational corporation (MNC) A company that has significant assets and activities in multiple countries.

Multiple sourcing A purchasing strategy in which a company orders a particular part from several vendors.

Multipoint competition A rivalry in which a large multibusiness corporation competes against other large multibusiness firms in a number of markets.

Mutual service consortium A partnership of similar companies in similar industries that pool their resources to gain a benefit that is too expensive to develop alone.

Natural environment That part of the external environment that includes physical resources, wildlife, and climate that are an inherent part of existence on Earth.

Net present value (NPV) A calculation of the value of a project that is made by predicting the project's payouts, adjusting them for risk, and subtracting the amount invested.

Network structure An organization (virtual organization) that outsources most of its business functions.

New entrants Businesses entering an industry that typically bring new capacity to an industry, a desire to gain market share, and substantial resources.

New product experimentation A method of test marketing the potential of innovative ideas by developing products, probing potential markets with early versions of the products, learning from the probes, and probing again.

No-change strategy A decision to do nothing new; to continue current operations and policies for the foreseeable future.

North American Free Trade Agreement (NAFTA) Regional free trade agreement between Canada, the United States, and Mexico.

Not-for-profit organization Private nonprofit corporations and public governmental units or agencies.

Objectives The end result of planned activity stating what is to be accomplished by when, and quantified if possible.

Offensive tactic A tactic that calls for competing in an established competitor's current market location.

Offshoring The outsourcing of an activity or function to a provider in another country.

Open innovation A new approach to R&D in which a firm uses alliances and connections with corporate, government, and academic labs to learn about new developments.

Operating budget A budget for a business unit that is approved by top management during strategy formulation and implementation.

Operating cash flow The amount of money generated by a company before the costs of financing and taxes are figured.

Operating leverage The impact of a specific change in sales volume on net operating income.

Operations strategy A functional strategy that determines how and where a product or service is to be manufactured, the level of vertical integration in the production process, and the deployment of physical resources.

Opportunity A strategic factor considered when using the SWOT analysis.

Orchestrator A top manager who articulates the need for innovation, provides funding for innovating activities, creates incentives for middle managers to sponsor new ideas, and protects idea/product champions from suspicious or jealous executives.

Organization slack Unused resources within an organization.

Organizational analysis Internal scanning concerned with identifying an organization's strengths and weaknesses.

Organizational learning theory A theory proposing that an organization adjusts to changes in the environment through the learning of its employees.

Organizational life cycle How organizations grow, develop, and eventually decline.

Organizational structure The formal setup of a business corporation's value chain components in terms of work flow, communication channels, and hierarchy.

Output control A control that specifies what is to be accomplished by focusing on the end result of the behaviors through the use of objectives and performance targets.

Outside directors Members of a board of directors who are not employees of the board's corporation; also called non–management directors.

Outsourcing A process in which resources are purchased from others through long-term contracts instead of being made within the company.

Parallel sourcing A process in which two suppliers are the sole suppliers of two different parts, but they are also backup suppliers for each other's parts.

Pattern of influence A concept stating that influence in strategic management derives from a not-for-profit organization's sources of revenue.

Pause/proceed with caution strategy A corporate strategy in which nothing new is attempted; an opportunity to rest before continuing a growth or retrenchment strategy.

Penetration pricing A marketing pricing strategy to obtain dominant market share by using low price.

Performance The end result of activities, actual outcomes of a strategic management process.

Performance appraisal system A system to systematically evaluate employee performance and promotion potential.

Performance gap A performance gap exists when performance does not meet expectations.

Periodic statistical report Reports summarizing data on key factors such as the number of new customer contracts, volume of received orders, and productivity figures.

Phases of strategic management A set of four levels of development through which a firm generally evolves into strategic management.

Piracy The making and selling counterfeit copies of well-known name-brand products, especially software.

Planning mode A decision-making mode that involves the systematic gathering of appropriate information for situation analysis, the generation of feasible alternative strategies, and the rational selection of the most appropriate strategy.

Policy A broad guideline for decision making that links the formulation of strategy with its implementation.

Political strategy A strategy to influence a corporation's stakeholders.

Population ecology A theory that proposes that once an organization is successfully established in a particular environmental niche, it is unable to adapt to changing conditions.

Portfolio analysis An approach to corporate strategy in which top management views its product lines and business units as a series of investments from which it expects a profitable return.

Power distance (PD) The extent to which a society accepts an unequal distribution of influence in organizations.

Prediction markets A forecasting technique in which people make bets on the likelihood of a particular event taking place.

Pressure-cooker crisis A situation that exists when employees in collaborative organizations eventually grow emotionally and physically exhausted from the intensity of teamwork and the heavy pressure for innovative solutions.

Primary activity A manufacturing firm's corporate value chain, including inbound logistics, operations process, outbound logistics, marketing and sales, and service.

Primary stakeholders A high priority group that affects or is affected by the achievement of a firm's objectives.

Prime interest rate The rate of interest banks charge on their lowest-risk loans.

Private nonprofit corporation A nongovernmental not-for-profit organization.

Privatization The selling of state-owned enterprises to private individuals. Also the hiring of a private business to provide services previously offered by a state agency.

Procedures A list of sequential steps that describe in detail how a particular task or job is to be done.

Process innovation Improvement to the making and selling of current products.

Product champion A person who generates a new idea and supports it through many organizational obstacles.

Product development A marketing strategy in which a company or unit develops new products for existing markets or develops new products for new markets.

Product innovation The development of a new product or the improvement of an existing product's performance.

Product life cycle A graph showing time plotted against sales of a product as it moves from introduction through growth and maturity to decline.

Product R&D Research and development concerned with product or product-packaging improvements.

Product/market evolution matrix A chart depicting products in terms of their competitive positions and their stages of product/market evolution.

Product-group structure A structure of a multinational corporation that enables the company to introduce and manage a similar line of products around the world.

Production sharing The process of combining the higher labor skills and technology available in developed countries with the lower-cost labor available in developing countries.

Professional liquidator An individual called on by a bankruptcy court to close a firm and sell its assets.

Profit center A unit's performance, measured in terms of the difference between revenues and expenditures.

Profit strategy A strategy that artificially supports profits by reducing investment and short-term discretionary expenditures.

Profitability ratios Ratios evaluating a company's ability to make money over a period of time.

Profit-making firm A firm depending on revenues obtained from the sale of its goods and services to customers, who typically pay for the costs and expenses of providing the product or service plus a profit.

Program A statement of the activities or steps needed to accomplish a single-use plan in strategy implementation.

Propitious niche A portion of a market that is so well suited to a firm's internal and external environment that other corporations are not likely to challenge or dislodge it.

Public governmental unit or agency A kind of not-for-profit organization that is established by government or governmental agencies (such as welfare departments, prisons, and state universities).

Public or collective good Goods that are freely available to all in a society.

Pull strategy A marketing strategy in which advertising pulls the products through the distribution channels.

Punctuated equilibrium A point at which a corporation makes a major change in its strategy after evolving slowly through a long period of stability.

Purchasing power parity (PPP) A measure of the cost, in dollars, of the U.S.-produced equivalent volume of goods that another nation's economy produces.

Purchasing strategy A functional strategy that deals with obtaining the raw materials, parts, and supplies needed to perform the operations functions.

Push strategy A marketing strategy in which a large amount of money is spent on trade promotion in order to gain or hold shelf space in retail outlets.

Quality of work life A concept that emphasizes improving the human dimension of work to improve employee satisfaction and union relations.

Quasi-integration A type of vertical growth/integration in which a company does not make any of its key supplies but purchases most of its requirements from outside suppliers that are under its partial control.

Question marks New products that have potential for success and need a lot of cash for development.

RFID A technology in which radio frequency identification tags containing product information is used to track goods through inventory and distribution channels.

R&D intensity A company's spending on research and development as a percentage of sales revenue.

R&D mix The balance of basic, product, and process research and development.

R&D strategy A functional strategy that deals with product and process innovation.

Ratio analysis The calculation of ratios from data in financial statements to identify possible strengths or weaknesses.

Real options approach An approach to new project investment when the future is highly uncertain.

Red flag An indication of a serious underlying problem.

Red tape crisis A crisis that occurs when a corporation has grown too large and complex to be managed through formal programs.

Reengineering The radical redesign of business processes to achieve major gains in cost, service, or time.

Regional industry An industry in which multinational corporations primarily coordinate their activities within specific geographic areas of the world.

Relationship-based governance A government system perceived to be less transparent and have a higher degree of corruption.

Repatriation of profits The transfer of profits from a foreign subsidiary to a corporation's headquarters.

Replicability The ability of competitors to duplicate resources and imitate another firm's success.

Resources A company's physical, human, and organizational assets that serve as the building blocks of a corporation.

Responsibility center A unit that is isolated so that it can be evaluated separately from the rest of the corporation.

Retired executive directors Past leaders of a company kept on the board of directors after leaving the company.

Retrenchment strategy Corporate strategies to reduce a company's level of activities and to return it to profitability.

Return on equity (ROE) A measure of performance that is calculated by dividing net income by total equity.

Return on investment (ROI) A measure of performance that is calculated by dividing net income before taxes by total assets.

Revenue center A responsibility center in which production, usually in terms of unit or dollar sales, is measured without consideration of resource costs.

Reverse engineering Taking apart a competitor's product in order to find out how it works.

Reverse stock split A stock split in which an investor's shares are reduced for the same total amount of money.

Risk A measure of the probability that one strategy will be effective, the amount of assets the corporation must allocate to that strategy, and the length of time the assets will be unavailable.

Rule-based governance A governance system based on clearly stated rules and procedures.

Rules of thumb Approximations based not on research, but on years of practical experience.

Sarbanes-Oxley Act Legislation passed by the U.S. Congress in 2002 to promote and formalize greater board independence and oversight.

Scenario box A tool for developing corporate scenarios in which historical data are used to make projections for generating pro forma financial statements.

Scenario writing A forecasting technique in which focused descriptions of different likely futures are presented in a narrative fashion.

Secondary stakeholders Lower-priority groups that affect or are affected by the achievement of a firm's objectives.

Sell-out strategy A retrenchment option used when a company has a weak competitive position resulting in poor performance.

Separation A method of managing the culture of an acquired firm in which the two companies are structurally divided, without cultural exchange.

SFAS (Strategic Factors Analysis Summary) matrix A chart that summarizes an organization's strategic factors by combining the external factors from an EFAS table with the internal factors from an IFAS table.

Shareholder value The present value of the anticipated future stream of cash flows from a business plus the value of the company if it were liquidated.

Short-term orientation The tendency of managers to consider only current tactical or operational issues and ignore strategic ones.

Simple structure A structure for new entrepreneurial firms in which the employees tend to be generalists and jacks-of-all-trades.

Six Sigma A statistically-based program developed to identify and improve a poorly performing process.

Skim pricing A marketing strategy in which a company charges a high price while a product is novel and competitors are few.

Small-business firm An independently owned and operated business that is not dominant in its field and that does not engage in innovative practices.

SO, ST, WO, WT strategies A series of possible business approaches based on combinations of opportunities, threats, strengths, and weaknesses.

Social capital The goodwill of key stakeholders, which can be used for competitive advantage.

Social entrepreneurship A business in which a not-for-profit organization starts a new venture to achieve social goals.

Social responsibility The ethical and discretionary responsibilities a corporation owes its stakeholders.

Societal environment Economic, technological, political-legal, and sociocultural environmental forces that do not directly touch on the short-run activities of an organization but influence its long-run decisions.

Sole sourcing Relying on only one supplier for a particular part.

Sources of innovation Drucker's proposed seven sources of new ideas that should be monitored by those interested in starting entrepreneurial ventures.

Sponsor A department manager who recognizes the value of a new idea, helps obtain funding to develop the innovation, and facilitates the implementation of the innovation.

Stability strategy Corporate strategies to make no change to the company's current direction or activities.

Staffing Human resource management priorities and use of personnel.

Stages of corporate development A pattern of structural development that corporations follow as they grow and expand.

Stages of international development The stages through which international corporations evolve in their relationships with widely dispersed geographic markets and the manner in which they structure their operations and programs.

Stages of new product development The stages of getting a new innovation into the marketplace.

Stage-gate process A method of managing new product development to increase the likelihood of launching new products quickly and successfully. The process is a series of steps to move products through the six stages of new product development.

Staggered board A board on which directors serve terms of more than one year so that only a portion of the board of directors stands for election each year.

Stakeholder analysis The identification and evaluation of corporate stakeholders.

Stakeholder measure A method of keeping track of stakeholder concerns.

Stakeholder priority matrix A chart that categorizes stakeholders in terms of their interest in a corporation's activities and their relative power to influence the corporation's activities.

Stall point A point at which a company's growth in sales and profits suddenly stops and becomes negative.

Standard cost center A responsibility center that is primarily used to evaluate the performance of manufacturing facilities.

Standard operating procedures Plans that detail the various activities that must be carried out to complete a corporation's programs.

Star Market leader that is able to generate enough cash to maintain its high market share.

Statistical modeling A quantitative technique that attempts to discover causal or explanatory factors that link two or more time series together.

STEEP analysis An approach to scanning the societal environment that examines sociocultural, technological, economic, ecological, and political-legal forces. Also called PESTEL analysis.

Steering control Measures of variables that influence future profitability.

Stewardship theory A theory proposing that executives tend to be more motivated to act in the best interests of the corporation than in their own self-interests.

Strategic alliance A partnership of two or more corporations or business units to achieve strategically significant objectives that are mutually beneficial.

Strategic audit A checklist of questions by area or issue that enables a systematic analysis of various corporate functions and activities. It's a type a management audit.

Strategic audit worksheet A tool used to analyze a case.

Strategic business unit (SBU) A division or group of divisions composed of independent product-market segments that are given primary authority for the management of their own functions.

Strategic choice The evaluation of strategies and selection of the best alternative.

Strategic choice perspective A theory that proposes that organizations adapt to a changing environment and have the opportunity and power to reshape their environment.

Strategic decision-making process An eight-step process that improves strategic decision making.

Strategic decisions Decisions that deal with the long-run future of an entire organization and are rare, consequential, and directive.

Strategic factors External and internal factors that determine the future of a corporation.

Strategic flexibility The ability to shift from one dominant strategy to another.

Strategic group A set of business units or firms that pursue similar strategies and have similar resources.

Strategic inflection point The period in an organization's life in which a major change takes place in its environment and creates a new basis for competitive advantage.

Strategic management A set of managerial decisions and actions that determine the long-run performance of a corporation.

Strategic management model A rational, prescriptive planning model of the strategic management process including environmental scanning, strategy formulation, strategy implementation, and evaluation and control.

Strategic myopia The willingness to reject unfamiliar as well as negative information.

Strategic piggybacking The development of a new activity for a not-for-profit organization that would generate the funds needed to make up the difference between revenues and expenses.

Strategic planning staff A group of people charged with supporting both top management and business units in the strategic planning process.

Strategic R&D alliance A coalition through which a firm coordinates its research and development with another firm(s) to offset the huge costs of developing new technology.

Strategic rollup A means of consolidating a fragmented industry in which an entrepreneur acquires hundreds of owner-operated small businesses resulting in a large firm with economies of scale.

Strategic sweet spot A market niche in which a company is able to satisfy customers' needs in a way that competitors cannot.

Strategic type A category of firms based on a common strategic orientation and a combination of structure, culture, and processes that are consistent with that strategy.

Strategic vision A description of what the company is capable of becoming.

Strategic window A unique market opportunity that is available only for a particular time.

Strategic-funds method An evaluation method that encourages executives to look at development expenses as being different from expenses required for current operations.

Strategies to avoid Strategies sometimes followed by managers who have made a poor analysis or lack creativity.

Strategy A comprehensive plan that states how a corporation will achieve its mission and objectives.

Strategy formulation Development of long-range plans for the effective management of environmental opportunities and threats in light of corporate strengths and weaknesses.

Strategy implementation A process by which strategies and policies are put into action through the development of programs, budgets, and procedures.

Strategy-culture compatibility The match between existing corporate culture and a new strategy to be implemented.

Structure follows strategy The process through which changes in corporate strategy normally lead to changes in organizational structure.

Stuck in the middle A situation in which a company or business unit has not achieved a generic competitive strategy and has no competitive advantage.

Suboptimization A phenomenon in which a unit optimizes its goal accomplishment to the detriment of the organization as a whole.

Substages of small business development A set of five levels through which new ventures often develop.

Substitute products Products that appear to be different but can satisfy the same need as other products.

Supply-chain management The formation of networks for sourcing raw materials, manufacturing products or creating services, storing and distributing goods, and delivering goods or services to customers and consumers.

Support activity An activity that ensures that primary value-chain activities operate effectively and efficiently.

SWOT analysis Identification of strengths, weaknesses, opportunities, and threats that may be strategic factors for a specific company.

Synergy A concept that states that the whole is greater than the sum of its parts; that two units will achieve more together than they could separately.

Tacit knowledge Knowledge that is not easily communicated because it is deeply rooted in employee experience or in a corporation's culture.

Tactic A short-term operating plan detailing how a strategy is to be implemented.

Takeover A hostile acquisition in which one firm purchases a majority interest in another firm's stock.

Taper integration A type of vertical integration in which a firm internally produces less than half of its own requirements and buys the rest from outside suppliers.

Task environment The part of the business environment that includes the elements or groups that directly affect the corporation and, in turn, are affected by it.

Technological competence A corporation's proficiency in managing research personnel and integrating their innovations into its day-to-day operations.

Technological discontinuity The displacement of one technology by another.

Technological follower A company that imitates the products of competitors.

Technological leader A company that pioneers an innovation.

Technology sourcing A make-or-buy decision that can be important in a firm's R&D strategy.

Technology transfer The process of taking a new technology from the laboratory to the marketplace.

Time to market The time from inception to profitability of a new product.

Timing tactics Tactics that determines when a business will enter a market with a new product.

Tipping point The point at which a slowly changing situation goes through a massive, rapid change.

Top management responsibilities Leadership tasks that involve getting things accomplished through and with others in order to meet the corporate objectives.

Total Quality Management (TQM) An operational philosophy that is committed to customer satisfaction and continuous improvement.

TOWS matrix A matrix that illustrates how external opportunities and threats facing a particular company can be matched with that company's internal strengths and weaknesses to result in four sets of strategic alternatives.

Transaction cost economics A theory that proposes that vertical integration is more efficient than contracting for goods and services in the marketplace when the transaction costs of buying goods on the open market become too great.

Transfer price A practice in which one unit can charge a transfer price for each product it sells to a different unit within a company.

Transferability The ability of competitors to gather the resources and capabilities necessary to support a competitive challenge.

Transformational leader A leader who causes change and movement in an organization by providing a strategic vision.

Transparent The speed with which other firms can understand the relationship of resources and capabilities supporting a successful firm's strategy.

Trends in governance Current developments in corporate governance.

Trigger point The point at which a country has developed economically so that demand for a particular product or service is increasing rapidly.

Triggering event Something that acts as a stimulus for a change in strategy.

Turnaround specialist A manager who is brought into a weak company to salvage that company in a relatively attractive industry.

Turnaround strategy A plan that emphasizes the improvement of operational efficiency when a corporation's problems are pervasive but not yet critical.

Turnkey operation Contracts for the construction of operating facilities in exchange for a fee.

Turnover A term used by European firms to refer to sales revenue. It also refers to the amount of time needed to sell inventory.

Uncertainty avoidance (UA) The extent to which a society feels threatened by uncertain and ambiguous situations.

Union of South American Nations An organization formed in 2008 to unite Mercosur and the Andean Community.

Utilitarian approach A theory that proposes that actions and plans should be judged by their consequences.

Value chain A linked set of value-creating activities that begins with basic raw materials coming from suppliers and ends with distributors getting the final goods into the hands of the ultimate consumer.

Value-chain partnership A strategic alliance in which one company or unit forms a long-term arrangement with a key supplier or distributor for mutual advantage.

Value disciplines An approach to evaluating a competitor in terms of product leadership, operational excellence, and customer intimacy.

Vertical growth A corporate growth strategy in which a firm takes over a function previously provided by a supplier or distributor.

Vertical integration The degree to which a firm operates in multiple locations on an industry's value chain from extracting raw materials to retailing.

Virtual organization An organizational structure that is composed of a series of project groups or collaborations linked by changing nonhierarchical, cobweb-like networks.

Virtual team A group of geographically and/or organizationally dispersed coworkers that are assembled using a combination of telecommunications and information technologies to accomplish an organizational task.

Vision A view of what management thinks an organization should become.

VRIO framework Barney's proposed analysis to evaluate a firm's key resources in terms of value, rareness, imitability, and organization.

Web 2.0 A term used to describe the evolution of the Internet into wikis, blogs, RSS, social networks, podcasts, and mash-ups.

Weighted-factor method A method that is appropriate for measuring and rewarding the performance of top SBU managers and group-level executives when performance factors and their importance vary from one SBU to another.

Whistle-blower An individual who reports to authorities incidents of questionable organizational practices.

World Trade Organization A forum for governments to negotiate trade agreements and settle trade disputes.

Z-value A formula that combines five ratios by weighting them according to their importance to a corporation's financial strength to predict the likelihood of bankruptcy.

NOTE: This glossary contains terms used in the twelve chapters of this textbook plus the three additional chapters provided on the publisher's Web site to buyers of this book.

NAME INDEX

SUBJECT INDEX